Martin Heidegger's Changing Destinies

Martin Heidegger's Changing Destinies

Catholicism, Revolution, Nazism

Guillaume Payen

Translated from the French by
Jane Marie Todd and Steven Rendall

Yale UNIVERSITY PRESS NEW HAVEN AND LONDON

Published with support from the Fund established in memory of Oliver Baty Cunningham, a distinguished graduate of the Class of 1917, Yale College, Captain, 15th United States Field Artillery, born in Chicago September 17, 1894, and killed while on active duty near Thiaucourt, France, September 17, 1918, the twenty-fourth anniversary of his birth.

Originally published in France as *Martin Heidegger: Catholicisme, révolution, nazisme*.

Set in Scala type by IDS Infotech Ltd.
Printed in the United States of America.

Library of Congress Control Number: 2021952942
ISBN 978-0-300-22832-8 (hardcover : alk. paper)

A catalogue record for this book is available from the British Library.

This paper meets the requirements of ANSI/NISO Z39.48-1992 (Permanence of Paper).

10 9 8 7 6 5 4 3 2 1

This American edition
in memoriam
Jane Marie Todd

Uxori filiisque dulcissimis

Contents

A Note on the Translation

A translator, according to the etymology of the word, is one who carries over; she bundles up what is expressed in one language and escorts it across the "language barrier." Translators know that this barrier is not a wall to be scaled, disembodied meanings in tow, but rather an infinite number of fissures between and even within words. Sometimes we are given the opportunity to explore minutely these cracks and crevices. In *Martin Heidegger's Changing Destinies,* at least three languages are in play: the German in which Heidegger wrote his texts and the ambient language he absorbed over a lifetime, including the discourse of Nazism; French, the language of Guillaume Payen's biography; and the translators' own English—with occasional excursions into ancient Greek and Latin.

What became evident as we were preparing this translation is that a number of terms that slip seamlessly from Heidegger's German into Payen's French pose challenges when the attempt is made to translate them into English. Nowhere is this clearer than with the adjective *geistig,* which Payen most often renders as *spirituel.* The German noun *Geist,* like the French *esprit,* means both "spirit" and "mind"; the adjective can thus signify "spiritual" and also "intellectual." It is important to realize that these are not two separate meanings: in French, the *spirituel* stands in opposition to the *matériel,* the material, and thus encompasses both things of the mind and things divine. In English, however, we use two different words for these two aspects of the *spirituel.* In short, "spiritual" occupies a narrower semantic field than either *geistig* or *spirituel.*

The *spirituel* is one of the through-lines of the three destinies (Catholicism, revolution, and Nazism) that Payen traces in Heidegger's life. As a young

Catholic and aspiring priest, Martin Heidegger focused his attention on the divine. When he lost his faith and turned to secular philosophy, his interest turned to the intellectual. And when he embraced Nazism, he did so as an oracle for the spirit, the *Geist,* of the German people, who, he believed, had a special role to play in the unfolding of history and philosophy—of the history of philosophy as history in general. The various inflections of *Geist* and the *geistig* were not merely consecutive in Heidegger's life: they also overlapped. Even as a priest in training, he was interested in the destiny of his people; and his religious background and training informed his notion of himself and his philosophy even after he had lost his faith.

As translators, we believed it was important to capture that continuity, even at the cost of stretching the usual sense of "spiritual" and "spirit." We use these terms whenever possible, even when the more obvious renderings would be "intellectual" and "mind." For example, in a letter of 8 September 1920, Heidegger writes to his wife that "sometimes one could really almost become a *geistiger Antisemit.*" We retain the choice made by R. D. V. Glasgow, the translator of these letters into English, of "spiritual anti-Semite," even though the French translation that Payen cites, and subsequently adopts in his discussion, renders the expression as *antisémite de l'intelligence* (we do note parenthetically the alternative sense of "intellectual"), a strange expression that Payen goes on to gloss. In this way, we allow the term "spiritual" to resonate with its earlier meanings—associated with Heidegger's religious childhood and his dialogue with Thomas Aquinas and Augustine—and with those it later takes on in the Nazi period.

A number of other terms also occupy semantic fields that correspond in German and French but not in English.

Kampf (*combat* in French) we translate variously as "battle," "combat," and "struggle" (in the context of Heidegger's discussion of the Heraclitean term *polemos*). For English-language speakers, the best-known and most notorious use of this term is in the title of Adolf Hitler's *Mein Kampf,* which the French know as *Mon combat. Kampf* becomes an important philosophical term in Heidegger's *Being and Time* (1927). Payen traces the notion back to the philosopher's experience as a young man working at a meteorological station during the First World War, hence to the specific context of battle or combat. In Heidegger's philosophy, *Kampf* comes to designate a more general attitude, *Dasein*'s relation to freedom, time, and death. Payen's interest in the interactions between the biographical, the more broadly historical, and the philosophical is encapsulated in this tracing of the term *Kampf/combat* in

Heidegger's philosophical texts and in German culture generally. Readers should therefore be alert to the German term lurking behind the various English words.

Boden (*sol* in French) we render as "ground" or "soil." The term can signify a philosophical ground or foundation, but it also designates the native soil, as in the Nazi ideology of *Blut und Boden,* "blood and soil." It appears in the compounds *Bodenlosenkeit* (*absence du sol,* "groundlessness") and *Bodenständigkeit* (*assise sur un sol véritable,* "groundedness" or "ground to stand on"). A *bodenständige Kultur* is "a culture rooted in the soil." Payen explores the intertwined meanings of *Boden/sol,* which, once again, the English language separates into two words.

The term *Boden* is associated with the *Heimat* ("native region," "little homeland," or simply "home") and with two other Heideggerian expressions: *Verwurzelung* (*enracinement,* "rootedness") and *Entwurzelung* (*déracinement*). We usually translate *déracinement* as "uprootedness," though it should be kept in mind that, in the context of anti-Semitism, the more common usage in English is "rootlessness," as in "rootless cosmopolitans." When the English-language translations of Heidegger use different terms for these notions, we only infrequently modify them.

The German term *Art,* which Payen sometimes translates as *race,* also raises special problems in English. Although racially inflected, *Art* does not signify "race" in its English meaning, which is narrower than that of the French cognate. The French *race* can refer to any human group with shared characteristics. For example, it is not uncommon to find references to the *race paysanne,* "the peasant race," which would make little sense in English. The German *Art* is closer to this meaning: it can designate an ethnic group or an animal species and has the more general sense of "sort" or "kind." Its connotations during the Nazi period in particular were anti-Semitic, with the exclusive and exclusionary sense found in the English expressions "they're not our kind" and "we don't associate with that sort." We translate it with different terms (including "folk"), depending on the context, and usually give the German term in parentheses.

More generally, we often revert to Heidegger's German terminology rather than translating the French word into English, and we provide translators' endnotes for particularly thorny terms.

Finally, there is the term *l'homme.* In the laudable pursuit of gender-neutral language, authors and editors and translators have tended to substitute "the human being" or "human beings" in places where earlier generations wrote "man." We believe that this practice is anachronistic. In the philosophy of history, as in other realms, man is "the Subject, he is the Absolute," while woman is "the Other" (Simone de Beauvoir, *The Second Sex,* ed. and trans. H. M. Parshley, New York: Random House, 1974, p. xix). That is, man is the hero of philosophy. It is true that *der Mensch* in German means "human being," as distinguished from *der Mann,* a person of the male sex, and that Heidegger's preferred term, *Dasein,* is neuter and thus requires the pronoun "it" and the possessive adjective "its," rather than "he," "him," and "his." But that does not mean that his use of the terms is gender-neutral or gender-inclusive in practice. The relation between *Dasein* and women is not a given: it is a complex question still in need of serious consideration.

In contemporary contexts, we strive to be inclusive in our translation, though the practice in French is still to adhere to the generic "he." When Payen refers to his *lecteur,* for example, we may designate that reader as "she" or "her"; when he writes of *l'historien [. . .] il,* to refer to himself and his professional colleagues, both men and women, we may translate the terms as "historians [. . .] we." But with few exceptions—places where Heidegger specifically raises the question of gender—when Payen translates *Mensch* and *Dasein* as *homme,* we render it as "man," which best captures the peculiarity de Beauvoir points out, namely, that "the relation of the two sexes is not quite like that of two electrical poles, for man represents both the positive and the neutral" (ibid., p. xviii).

The linguistic ground we stand on is fissured, and our translation attests to that instability.

J.M.T.
Portland, Oregon
May 2020

Preface

All authors write to be read, during their lifetime or after their death. Being published is a stroke of good luck; being translated is a privilege. Writing about a subject as rich, difficult, and evolving as Martin Heidegger is a long test that the uninitiated can hardly imagine. Two years after putting the final touches on this book, I am about to do the same with its second edition, corrected and updated, on the happy occasion of its publication in English, German, Russian, and Japanese. I have been able to improve certain passages, and write others that publishing deadlines had prevented me from composing earlier; I have taken advantage of exchanges with my readers and of Heidegger's correspondence with his brother, Fritz, which has recently been published and usefully complements the picture I painted.

Some critics have blamed me for not having condemned Heidegger, for not having sought to inspire in them the reassuring indignation that allows us to know who is bad and what evil is; but authors who are eager for knowledge serve their audience only if they are able to resist commonplace inclinations toward prejudicial emotion in the analysis of their subject. Of course, some of Heidegger's texts shock us: for example, in 1946, when he denies the Holocaust in his secret "black notebooks," writing that "the failure to recognize" Germany's "destiny" would be a crime incomparably greater than "the horror of the 'gas chambers.' "[1] Can historians remain impassive when confronted with such a sentence? Obviously not. Do we have to set ourselves up as judges? We do not. When history becomes a courtroom, it risks losing its scholarly rigor. If we were to establish a court of justice in the shadowy theater of our imaginations, we would abandon the questions and sources that guide us in establishing the facts. To properly carry out our task, we must strive to avoid being swayed by our feelings, though without becoming numb to them; what we lose in force of expression, we regain in accuracy and nuance, making truthfully present what was lost in a past dissimilar to our own time. Historians are modest, leaving it to philosophers to reflect on the good; to legislators to embody it in law; to defense lawyers, prosecutors, and judges to debate it in court. Like Spinoza, we also try to understand people's actions, rather than mocking, lamenting, or execrating them.[2] Faced with Heidegger's exorbitant radicalism, I had to pluck up my courage to overcome my disgust or my indignation: that was the only way to establish the human, if not humanistic, element in his action and thought. I am aware that sensational books sell better; I console myself by reflecting that it is silly to pursue a scholarly career in the hope of making money, because other professions guarantee incomparably greater profits. As for glory, what honest scholar wants it if it comes at the cost of a travesty of our subject?

Some philosophers are astonished that I set forth Heidegger's thought without disputing it. Although certain philosophical interpretations draw their sparkle from ideas, my muse, far from this ideal splendor, operates in the penumbra of the human cave, prosaic and changing—a penumbra which it seeks to enlighten by means of the questioning and methods peculiar to historians, regarding modernity and the reactions it elicits: social and political identities, politically engaged intellectuals, the violence of war, the discourses and practices of hatred, revolutionary systems, their component of secularized faith and their propensity for terror and crime, the history of the media and of public opinion—all subjects that minds averse to the empirical regard as dull. So I should not be reproached for being insufficiently philosophical: my aim is elsewhere. Let philosophers who read me prepare to enter foreign territory; they will recognize many objects and many persons in many places, illuminated by a disturbing, barbarous light; sometimes disappointed, sometimes disconcerted, they will harvest a few savory and unusual fruits that they can taste, and a few evergreen, nourishing plants that they can acclimatize. Let them recognize my sole claim in their domain: to demonstrate through facts, as Diogenes the Cynic demonstrated through motion,[3] that philosophers, even when they are conversing in ethereal regions, remain more or less in a time that is also that of their society, and that their human condition cannot be neglected without running the risk of misinterpreting, sometimes seriously, their ideas. And, finally, let the commentators who pride themselves on appealing to history do so with the awareness that history cannot be reduced to a succession of facts, philosophy reserving for itself the task of interpreting them: history also has its methods, its established facts, its controversies, and mastering them requires more than a playful attention.

Criticizing a character, vilifying an author: that is not the task of a biographer; that is not the duty of a historian. Recounting a life, understanding a time: that is what I have sought to do. I do not forbid those who read me to give their wrath free rein, or to accept or reject what they wish in Heidegger's philosophy. A book, once completed and published, seems self-contained; but though its author is not beside each reader to discuss it with her, the reader, if she has read and liked it, continues it, changes it, and enriches it through her thoughts or her writings, a fate I can only wish the present volume to have.

Paris, 30 August 2017

Acknowledgments

Because only a single author's name appears on the cover of a book, it might appear that he acted alone. But one can do little or nothing by oneself. I would therefore like to thank those dear to me who provided their support: in addition to my families, Carole Avignon, Emmanuel de la Chapelle, Lise Denis, Joëlle Hecker, Bernard Klein, Charles-François Mathis, Jean-Pierre Minaudier, Emmanuel Plat, Marie Sirinelli, and Jean-Pierre Tronche. All of them knew that, when they asked how I was doing, they were also asking about Heidegger, and they often took time to read over what I was working on. Among the colleagues who guided me in various capacities and to various degrees, I would like to thank Jeffrey Barash, Rainer Hudemann, Olivier Lazzarotti, and Jean-François Sirinelli, whose advice was always invaluable to me. I feel particular gratitude toward Jérôme Grondeux, who was the first to convey to me the advantage of combining two proclivities, historical and philosophical, and who gave me an outstanding model for a historiography of intellectuals that does not disdain their ideas; toward Jean-Paul Bled, who trusted me from the start, allowed my research to flourish thanks to his great kindness, and was good enough to grace the original edition of this book with a preface; toward Hugo Ott, whose level-headed judgments, tenacious investigations in hostile and still largely unexplored territory, and consistent graciousness served as an example and sustained my work.

I would be ungrateful if I did not mention the students whose writings on Nazi Germany I have directed: to teach is to learn; being listened to can sometimes result in self-understanding. Thanks to them, I was able to find the proper tone for speaking and arguing as a historian about that criminal regime. In addition to the cat wandering among the books, I must make special mention of my wife, who has selflessly assisted me since the beginning of this undertaking; and my two sons, Alexandre and Jules, who tolerated it, even though it often stole their father away from them, and who even helped it along through the daily joy with which they have filled our home. If the liberal arts are those worthy of a free man, they can be practiced only by the grace of a private income or funding from an institution, which both the Université Paris-Sorbonne and the Fondation pour la Mémoire de la Shoah generously granted me. My thanks again to that foundation, for the richness and fruitfulness of its seminar directed by Dominique Trimbur. Finally, this superb American edition fills me with gratitude when I consider the outstanding work made by Jane Marie Todd and Steven Rendall: if being translated is a privilege, it becomes an honor when it is done by such brilliant translators. A last word of acknowledgment for my German translator, Herr Walther Fekl, who helped us decisively find the German references that were still lacking and without which this book wouldn't be complete.

Martin Heidegger's Changing Destinies

Introduction

Boredom, dustiness, jargon, served up in drab prose, seem to many people the necessary garments of knowledge; in my view, a text is to be judged by the liveliness, the accuracy, and the precision of its content. I shall certainly not make Martin Heidegger return from the dead, the power of writing cannot go that far; but, rejecting the empty vestments of an austere science, I want to leave the impression that he did actually live, feel, think, and take part in the fracas of history, where he was comparable to other people. Although my imagination will not run free on the path blazed by historical reason, I shall not disdain the painter's brush, especially since, no matter how historical it may be, a biography is always a portrait of a human being.

A portrait that is mobile both physically and intellectually: Heidegger grew up without growing tall, whereas his girth slowly expanded as years went by; he acquired the delicate oval of his mother's face and its rather long nose, adding to them eyes that were sometimes piercing, sometimes evasive; and he cultivated a mustache, which he reduced to a square under his nose when the Führer made that fashionable. A portrait at times contradictory, because of the changing times and the multiplicity of the person himself: imbued with Catholic truth, which he believed he possessed, he gradually became the enemy of Rome; a friend and lover of Jews, he wanted to battle the "jewification" of Germany. A portrait that is sometimes touching, as when the sexton's two sons ring their native town's bells. A portrait that is often ambiguous: an attentive reader and a skilled speaker capable of persuading his interlocutors of the interest, admiration, friendship, or even love he felt for them, Heidegger could also be at times scornful, mendacious, and egocentric. His readings and personal relations were countless, his activities few: he spent most of his time talking or writing, delivering lectures, and composing various philosophical texts as well as numerous letters; skiing, rowing, or hiking. According only limited time to his sons, he cultivated an immense love of women, which exasperated his wife. Hegel believed that biography has the historical world as its background, that the individual is interwoven with that world, and that biography's purely sentimental aspect has a ground and an interest different from those of history.[1] However, it is difficult if not impossible to find the sentimental in a pure state; every feeling acquires its meaning in a mental construct issuing from a time, a social milieu, and the more or less singular consciousness of an individual, and this will prove true even in Heidegger's relation to sexuality. In this way, biography brings us back to history, in an interlacing that we must follow, and not cut through.

History is not written anywhere before it is written by historians: we ask our questions, prepare our sources, apply our methods, and, drawing on a reliable body of literature, imprison our imaginations within the walls of what was and what the vestiges of the past allow us to write. If we imagine what might have been, it is only to better understand what actually happened; every new document enlarges the limited space within which we move; every original questioning opens an unsuspected perspective on what we see. Depending on raw materials that we cannot invent, working on them with the tools that are those of our own period, we historians have to resign ourselves to seeing our work as one moment, more or less ephemeral, in an ongoing effort constantly renewed by a myriad of authors seeking to depict humanity's past as another present whose future is uncertain even if it is already past. Writing about Martin Heidegger requires even more modesty because of the difficulty of his language and the number of his published texts, which, growing ever more numerous, repeatedly lift the veils that covered his thought, his action, and his personality; for instance, his *Black Notebooks,* philosophical diaries whose publication has created so much commotion in recent days. The brilliant penumbra in which the philosopher wanted to remain, the better to control his work's reception, has gradually diminished; it will subsist only so long as the actors directly involved in maintaining it are still alive. Soon, a new generation of his heirs may have the courage to open to all scholars the holdings of the Marbach archives, where items considered compromising still remain hidden away.

A book often appears more coherent than it is. Once it is printed, a manuscript that was covered with additions and erasures, denatured, seems to have been conceived as a whole, written in a single draft, and that appearance is even less true of this one than of others. This palimpsest, ordered, recast, and corrected, brings together my investigations into the philosopher from Baden over the past twelve years; and with them, the images of him that changed during the progress of the whole work. In the beginning, there was my astonishment that in the philosophy courses I took at Versailles and even more in those I took at the Sorbonne, which adopted Martin Heidegger's nationalist view of history, assigning to his people, "the metaphysical people,"[2] "the people of the poem and of thought,"[3] the mission of resuscitating Greek philosophy after a Latin Middle Ages, this idea was never resituated in the ultranationalist context to which it belongs: the Third Reich, whose leader himself spoke of the Germans as a "people of singers, poets, and thinkers."[4] Although it seemed to me doubtful that Heidegger's conception of history was a simple, straightforward expression of the Nazi regime, I doubted still more that it had no connection with it; and this connection, which would be interesting and delicate to establish, had to be the object of an investigation that was both historical and philosophical. The question of Heidegger's national and patriotic allegiance interested me all the more because in my view it appeared against the background of a need for a broader understanding linked to our time and to the history of my own family. Whereas today, in France and in Western Europe, patriotic consciousness has ceased to be taken for granted by everyone, I had to see how, earlier in the twentieth century, it had been able to awaken the heroism of ordinary people like my grandfather, who was an adolescent at the time of the German occupation. He joined the Resistance, later explaining this serious decision in a few words of enigmatic simplicity: "The Germans had invaded my France, I had to do something." Studying the patriotism of a philosopher like Heidegger had the advantage of offering a plethora of sources and of allowing the stubborn or rash historian to hope that the results of his labors might be more solid than they would have been had he chosen an ordinary man who left few writings behind him.

My ideas were refined in the course of my research. Very quickly, it appeared to me that political commitment went hand-in-hand with patriotism and nationalism; a paradoxical commitment, since apart from the short period when he was rector of the University of Freiburg, Heidegger's relation to politics—distant and scornful—was that of a German professor who thought he was in possession of a political truth that was superior and more essential than the one at work in the everyday functioning of a modern state, a truth that he wanted to make active through his words and writings. I brought these three relationships to the political together by considering them from the point of view of biography; and, inspired by my subject himself, I decided to call what I was trying to understand and trace in Heidegger "political existence": the way—conscious and unconscious, rational and yet laden with affects, life, and images, in short, existential—he had of living, acting, and representing for himself his *polis,* that is, his state, his people, his territory, and the place of each person within the political community, as well as his view regarding what exceeds that framework, other states, Europe, the world—and all that in a period turned upside down by modernity. "Roots and struggle," a synthetic expression emerging from recurrent metaphors in Heidegger's texts, finally came to express for the reader what seemed to me a leitmotif that was as constant in its importance as it was changing in the meaning it took on during the eighty-seven years of the philosopher's political existence. In addition, Germany, as Heidegger experienced and imagined it in his political existence, seemed to be capable of being depicted and understood through Marcel Proust's idea of *côtés* (ways).

In Proust's *In Search of Lost Time,* the country around the family home in Combray is divided into two very distinct and contrasting "ways": one, the Guermantes way, is "typical of river scenery"[5] but nevertheless full of dreams; it is where the Duke and Duchess of Guermantes are said to live; the narrator has never seen the Guermantes, but he imagines them as coming straight out of the Middle Ages. The other way is toward Méséglise, which has "the finest view of a plain,"[6] over which the wind, "the tutelary genius of Combray,"[7] never failed to blow and give the narrator the impression that he was coming closer to Gilberte Swann, who lived there in the distance. This personal geography of Proust's book fuses subject and object, exteriority and interiority; it displays the diverse setting in which the character developed, as well as his affective, imaginary, and intellectual interiority, which merged with these external places to the point that the latter crystallized not only themselves, but also the feelings, imagination, and thoughts that imbued them. The two physically dissimilar *côtés,* the Guermantes way and the Méséglise way, become even more distinct because of the subjective life that gives them aspect and soul, to the point that they constitute "two entities" whose "cohesion" and "unity" belong only to "the figments of the mind."[8] Their reciprocal distance becomes radical, so that "the mere distance in miles" was "one of those distances of the mind which not only keep things apart, but cut them off from one another and put them on different planes."[9]

Like Proust's narrator, who contrasts two places in Combray that are separate in almost every respect, both physically and within himself, I discerned a similar opposition in Heidegger's personal geography, which characterized his relationship to Germany, and whose evolution expressed his inner development. Two "ways" initially emerged: the first, the Meßkirch way, gave concrete form to the intense relationship that bound Heidegger to his *Heimatstadt,* from his birth to his death, and beyond that home town, to a profoundly religious ideal of life that was rooted in an age-old local, rural tradition; the second, the Berlin way, condensed in the extreme the metropolis and modernity, the heart of the crisis of the modern world, which is rootless, without relation to the soil, even "jewified," but also the site of all the opportunities for a great career and the center of the German nation's political destiny. To these two primordial ways, a third must be added, Todtnauberg, in the Black Forest. In 1922 Heidegger had a cabin constructed in Todtnauberg, and it was there that he did a considerable part of his writing, to the point that he came to identify his work with these mountains in Baden. Todtnauberg was a kind of quintessence of the rural and Alemannic, Swabian aspect of Meßkirch; to go to Todtnauberg, one had first to go toward Meßkirch, and then continue on until the city disappeared altogether and gave way to a hamlet scattered over a medium-sized wooded hillside. In this simple, remote place, dominating the vast Germany caught up in the course of history, the philosopher returned to the principles of existence and "Beyng." The mountain of philosophy, Todtnauberg rose up beyond the opposition between the Meßkirch and the Berlin ways, establishing itself as a possible link and at the same time as the Meßkirch way's intellectual extremity. Thus three ways appeared, corresponding to the same number of personal itineraries for Heidegger and for his view of his homeland and the world: complex and contrastive, composed of conflicts in which he had a prominent role to play, indicating the place where the destiny of Germany and of Being was to be played out.

The study of the philosopher's imagination and his thought presupposed unmediated access to the texts, without the sometimes-questionable interpretations that presided over their translation into French. Resituating Heidegger in an ideological context likewise required that I be able to trust ancillary texts such as those that constitute the Nazi canon, first of all *Mein Kampf* and Alfred Rosenberg's *Myth of the Twentieth Century.* However, the French translations of these works cannot be used for scholarly research: in the French version of Hitler's emblematic book the untranslatable term *völkisch* is rendered as *raciste,* which omits the other denotations of the German word, such as "national," "ethnic," and "popular," and leads to confusion with the word *rassistisch,* which designates solely the belief that the human races are unequal in value.

I have therefore checked the original texts and retranslated them when it seemed to me necessary to do so, giving priority to accuracy and avoiding embellishments and overinterpretations of the text.

After studying Heidegger's political existence, I chose, for this book, to emphasize the philosopher's changing destinies, in order to describe the role of social determinations and his own belief in a providence governing the course of the world, combined with the destinies he set for himself throughout his life. Binding, because they were both external and internal, these destinies were also changing: life is linear only in retrospect, when a rapid overview erases the effect of chance and of the battle of contrary forces. In Heidegger's life, there were three such destinies, which succeeded and conflicted with one another: Catholicism, coinciding with the philosopher's youth up to the end of the First World War; revolution, which was his political and intellectual aspiration from that point up to 1936; and Nazism, in which he saw, from 1930 on, the path that Germany had to follow to carry out this philosophical revolution. After the Nazi regime fell, he suffered in large part the fate he had chosen for himself, and even now, his reception remains difficult to dissociate from his political orientation. Was Heidegger the prophet of the thinking about Being or the brown-shirted rector? Was he a friend of Jews or a ferocious anti-Semite?

Initially, I had chosen to avoid focusing my research on Nazism, concluding my doctoral thesis with the year 1933; the task I assigned myself at that time was already sufficiently ample, and it seemed to me more opportune to contribute something new on a subject that had been less exhaustively studied. But the project of writing a biography of Heidegger up to and after his death required me to give the topic of his Nazism considerable attention, with a conviction that I retain today: almost no one doubts that the philosopher was a Nazi, for even François Fédier, the leader of French orthodox Heideggerians, concedes that his teacher adhered intellectually to a "national socialism"[10]—which, however, he hastens to distinguish from ordinary Nazism. One point on which the discussion crystallizes in particular is how long the Nazi phase persisted: was it limited to the period when he was rector, summarily presented as only a few months,[11] or did it, on the contrary, last the rest of his life? And what significance should be accorded to his resignation as rector?

From the beginning of my research, the main historiographic question has seemed to me to be less whether Heidegger was a Nazi than what this philosopher's Nazism allows us to understand about Nazism in general. Heidegger is particularly interesting for the study of the NSDAP's power to attract support and what lay behind it: why was such a subtle and demanding philosopher enthralled by a populist, anti-intellectual movement that was not addressed to his peers but rather to the intellectual rabble? The socioeconomic explanation, pointing to the destabilizing effects that the financial crisis of 1929 had on Germany, seems to have little relevance for a philosopher who was often not very attentive to the details of his contemporaries' lives. He was focused instead on principles, while his enviable position as a university professor sheltered him from the poverty, despair, or rage that some of his less privileged contemporaries experienced.

Therefore the explanation must be sought in the area of culture, which was the only one that really concerned Heidegger: he was not the target at which Nazi propaganda was aimed but exactly the opposite. Hitler said it clearly and repeatedly in *Mein Kampf*: propaganda "must be addressed always and exclusively to the masses" and not to "the scientifically trained intelligentsia";[12] based essentially on the living word, its success was to be judged "not by the impression" made on "a university professor," but by its effect "on the people";[13] convinced that "the broad mass of a nation does not consist of diplomats, or even professors"[14] any more than it does of "philosophers,"[15] the Führer took into account the fact that the "abstract knowledge" of the great masses was "limited," and that therefore it was necessary to play on their emotions, which were responsible for their "negative or positive attitude."[16] In addition, since their "receptivity" was "very limited," their "intelligence" small, and "their power of forgetting" "enormous," it was important to limit propaganda "to a very few points" and to "harp on these in slogans until the last member of the public understands what you want him to understand by your slogan."[17]

In Nazism, Heidegger saw an instrument for his own revolution: making a tabula rasa of earlier culture so that he could give the new regime a philosophical content. However, his support for Nazism was broader, as can be seen when we examine not only the core of his discourse—his intentions and self-representations—but also more marginal elements that pop up here and there, whose interest emerges when they are compared with the cultural historiographies of the rise of Nazism. A crucial question I have tried to answer is to what extent we can explain Heidegger's path toward support for Nazism by the theory of the greater "brutalization" of German political life after the First World War that George Lachmann Mosse saw as a consequence of the development of the "Myth of the War Experience,"[18] and to what extent we must also take into account a "quasi-apocalyptic anxiety"[19] promoted by the serious threats immediately after the war that caused people to fear that Germany would be destroyed by France, the Jews, or communism, a threat, it was believed, that required a response commensurate with the danger. This question has been studied by Christian Ingrao, Michael Wildt,[20] and Thomas Weber,[21] each in his own way.

The advent of the Third Reich does not explain away the cultural and political reasons for Heidegger's support; but it does add others, which, because they are more diverse, deserve attention. Once it had established its first foundations, the new regime aroused Heidegger's desire to get involved: did he illustrate at that time a kind of freedom left to the base to co-invent Nazi policies and ideology? How much did he know about the regime's criminal policies, which were carried out largely in secret? Can it be said that the fall of the regime led him to dissociate himself from Nazism, or even that he ever really broke with it? The question of Heidegger's Nazism involves that of his relationship to "Jews," those whose parents or grandparents adhered to Judaism, whether or not they themselves practiced it, and whom Nazism considered to be Asiatic elements foreign to the German people. How much of that ambient hostility did the philosopher adopt?

Whatever questions I asked of the past, one principle remained inviolable in my mind: I had to force myself to abide by the rigor of historical reasoning in assessing the reliability of sources, in examining the diverse or contradictory factors within the multiple temporalities of the individual and the period, and in reflecting on any ruptures or continuities that might exist within an existence that was rich and caught up in the convulsions of the twentieth century; but I also had to abide by the impartiality that historians must show in dealing with their subjects. We like to talk about objectivity, even though the study of human beings and societies of the past requires us to lend them our own humanity in order to give them new life. "Without anger and zeal,"[22] as Tacitus has it; the goal of historians is not to take sides; on the contrary, we must vigorously submit feelings, both positive and negative, that might hold sway over us to a faculty of reason seeking to determine the past in and of itself. Historians, challenging the tribunal where efforts are made to force us to testify against those who have had the misfortune to displease our contemporaries, consider nothing human foreign to us, not even pride, blindness, mendacity, or violence, all malign dispositions from which we know we are not by nature exempt. Only by postulating the common humanity we share with the strangers lost in time whose history we are writing, only by accepting the disagreeable idea that, had we been molded by and placed in the same conditions, we might have acted or thought in the same way as those whom our modern perspective stigmatizes—only in that way can we achieve the goal of our investigation: to spread the enlightenment of culture, of historical doubt and argument, hoping in that way to serve, not only the pleasure and instruction of our readers, but also the cause of humanity, which demands more peace and reason.

In addition to this intellectual ethics that provides the basis of historical rigor, neither my temperament nor my own past induced me to pillory Heidegger. I have the soul neither of a polemicist nor of a disciple; and whereas the scandal that some people cultivate is as unnatural to me as the apologetics in which others indulge, I prefer to distribute praise rather than blame. As a former student of the orthodox Heideggerian Gérard Guest, I was prepared to allow myself to be seduced by the fable according to which the man who was the rector and the *Führer* of the University of Freiburg was subsequently transformed into a member of the resistance. Research is an adventure that may begin under sunny skies and end up in a storm: that was my experience with Martin Heidegger's changing destinies, the outcome of which forced me to struggle with great energy against an anger and revulsion that almost won out. It was easy to work on the Freiburg master when he was only a Catholic philosopher, and then a revolutionary, even if I certainly did not forget that he had been a Nazi; but from that point on, when I made my own estimate of how much his radicalism had espoused that of Nazism, I was inclined to condemn him, at least morally, to the flames. Did we ultimately have to burn Heidegger, or at least pull all his works from the libraries of philosophy? Once again, history came to my rescue, reminding me that one mustn't hand scourges to one's neighbor when one might need to do penance oneself. A German and a Nazi, Heidegger is even less than others an exception to a troubling fact: having appeared in a European context,[23] Nazism remained European by its politics as well as by its ideology,[24] finding its singularity above all in its extreme radicalism. As much as he is a German, Heidegger, who claimed to be occidental, is a European historical figure, as we can see if we consider the Catholicism of his youth, the culture that he later developed, the subjects that interested him, his relationships, his reception, and everything that, in one way or another, shaped his life. Like many other right-wing intellectuals in Germany and elsewhere in Europe, he wanted a revolution,[25] including it in a vast movement of opposition to liberalism and ambivalence with regard to modernity that began at the end of the nineteenth century at the latest,[26] in a period of profound political, economic, social, and cultural upheavals.[27]

Instead of using the expression "Conservative Revolution"[28] to describe Heidegger's view, I prefer to use the term "revolutionary right," which is equally autochthonous[29] but more neutral and clearer, and has the advantage of simplicity thanks to its conceptual opposition to the moderate and conservative right.

Martin Heidegger, a philosopher of worldwide importance, deserves to be studied as much as for what he allows us to understand about his time as for his thought. I will follow Jérome Grondeux, who is convinced that "history must also take an interest in what is said, in the sources of a way of thought, in its main themes, its degree of originality, and the manner in which it is connected with practice."[30] I will also endorse Johann Chapoutot's watchword: just as we must "take seriously" the Nazis' ideas,[31] we must also take seriously Heidegger's political ideas, which assumes that we do the same with all the sources rejected by so many prudish or disembodied interpreters: when the philosopher writes a letter or an occasional piece, it is not someone else who is thinking; and what he writes expresses, to varying degrees, his underlying ideas. In this respect Heidegger often evades philosophers because of their disdain for a supposedly "private" and "nonphilosophical" man, but he seems to evade history as well, despite the praiseworthy studies of my predecessors Bernd Martin,[32] Domenico Losurdo,[33] and especially Hugo Ott.[34] If this book succeeds in entertaining its audience and definitively annexes Heidegger to historiography, I shall not have wasted my time. So now we are going to see how a Catholic destiny came to be transformed into a revolutionary and then a National Socialist destiny.

I

A Catholic Destiny

(1889–1918)

1 • A Catholic Childhood in a Town in Southwestern Germany

(1889–1903)

The Happy Childhood of a Petty Bourgeois Country Boy

The story begins at the end of the nineteenth century, on the eastern limits of the Grand Duchy of Baden, in southwestern Germany, a frontier zone detached from the massive kingdom of Württemberg, which was dotted with enclaves belonging to the little principality of Hohenzollern. This small region, which extends from Lake Constance in the south to the eroded mountains of the Swabian Jura in the northwest, offers a rural landscape crisscrossed by valleys and punctuated by groves, irrigated by the humble Ablach River. Atop a steep hill is the little town of Meßkirch, recognizable by St. Martin's Church, which towers over it and whose copper dome attracts the traveler's eye from a distance. The view might have seemed atemporal had modernity not already powerfully cast over it the threads—a highway, a railroad, and telegraph lines—that stitched the region together and linked it to the outside world.

Founded in the Middle Ages, this little city, which had lost its walls, retained in its heart a dense maze of streets with irregular, half-timbered buildings, stuccoed or painted in bright colors and topped by tall gables that looked down on passersby; below them, the many little windows that pierced the walls often provided only dim illumination because they were surrounded by narrow streets that blocked the sunlight. Meßkirch opened up only here and there: around the church on the town's heights, in the marketplace below the town, and on the Adlerplatz, which, being more recent and larger, was on the edge of the old town.

In this "parsimonious country"[1] located about 600 meters above sea level and subject to the broad variations in temperature typical of a continental climate, the inhabitants made a living essentially from a diversified agricultural activity in which sheep and cattle raising played a very large part. Far from simply following Germany's overall economic growth, Meßkirch was in its van: a major brewery, Stärk, sold its products over a wide area[2] and thus contributed to the wealth and pride of all; livestock raising in particular was cutting-edge. During the first half of 1890 alone, Upper Baden exported 5,590 animals, half of which came from the canton of Meßkirch, for a value of approximately 1.5 million marks. Notables flaunted their success with top hats and cigars, while their wives and daughters followed the fashions of the big cities with lavish corseted dresses; they all lived in large houses and engaged in the urban ritual of the promenade on the grounds of the castle. At the leading edge of modernity, nights in Meßkirch were illuminated by electric lights spread out like so many artificial stars, suspended in this municipal microcosm lost in the midst of a vast, dark countryside; and this rarity, this modern magic that illuminated Meßkirch's streets at night, was admired by many of its residents: "Yesterday, it was so very delightful to see the electric lights shining for many hours in broad daylight. The reason was that the batteries' regulation of the current was being inspected. Connections to public lighting are increasing from day to day, and we hear truly laudatory comments on this beautiful, regular, and silent illumination when it is on. Since yesterday evening the Kunz brush factory has been provided with electric lighting."[3] Meßkirch was very rural. The surrounding lands and forests were cultivated by many inhabitants, and oxcarts crisscrossed the town amid hens cackling in its streets. It was a true small city, and it had its attractions, such as a railway station, steeples, schools, a city hall, and its burghers. In this simultaneously modern and traditional milieu, Martin Heidegger was born on 26 November 1889, the first son of Friedrich (1851–1924) and Johanna Heidegger, née Kempf (1858–1927), who were rural, petty bourgeois Catholics. Friedrich was a cooper and a sexton; Johanna was a homemaker. Little Martin soon had a sister, Marie (1891–1956), and then a brother, Friedrich (1894–1980), nicknamed Fritz, and they filled the church square with their shouts and play. For most of these years, the Heideggers lived in the house reserved for the sexton, which, like so many other buildings in the center of Meßkirch, consisted of two stories with a gable roof joined to a modest mezzanine with four small windows, narrow and close together, that looked out on this Catholic, historic town center.

The father, Friedrich Heidegger, was a taciturn man;[4] his son, and then his daughter and younger son, maintained relations with him that were largely silent, full of respect and unspoken affection: "As a little boy well provided with my mother's recommendations and pulling behind me my little blue cart, I went to see my fascinating father in his workshop. At that time, this workshop, which had a flat dirt floor, was set up in the left wing of the temporary church building. The thought of the path to my father's workshop still moves me today."[5] A mysterious and emotive presence, Heidegger's father was the kind of person one went to see, about whom one thought, and around whom one played without saying many words. Having no lack of orders to fill, Friedrich Heidegger was kept busy in his workshop ten hours a day, except Sundays, fashioning "chopping blocks, vats, pails, and large manure barrels, as well as tuns made of sparkling, golden yellow oak for cider and wine."[6] The young Martin, who often worked with the hammer and plane, "helped his father with the cooperage & forced the hoops into place around the barrels, the hammer-blows resounding through the small, winding alleys."[7] The wood scraps were particularly well suited to childhood games, and the Heideggers' elder son spent a great deal of time "puttering"[8] with his young brother, making from the oak bark "their boats, which, fitted with a rower's bench and a rudder, floated on the Mette River or the school pond."[9]

With the birth of Fritz, Martin had gained a playmate. Despite the five years that separated them, the two Heidegger boys enjoyed an evident closeness; as is usual when there is such a considerable difference in age between children, the predominant role fell to Martin, the elder. Their games and physical exercises were the ones allowed by their modest, rural milieu: they played largely outdoors, with simple toys such as balls and ice skates, depending on the season. On the occasion of his brother's eightieth birthday, Fritz Heidegger wrote: "Between spring and autumn, there were, at the heart of our free time, alongside bowling games played on the market square, games of tag and ball games of all kinds, which were usually played on the great square between the church and the castle," on the latter's grounds, and "near the former school [. . .] beyond, toward the Mette River."[10] As they grew older and more self-assured, the boys began to engage in sports: Fritz reminded him that "the pleasure taken in sports characterized your youth."[11] Martin showed both a taste and an aptitude for various disciplines; he became "an agile gymnast on the fixed bar and the parallel bars, a good swimmer in the summer and a graceful skater on the frozen pond below the Hegele mill."[12]

For a long time, the children's mother kept watch over their games, within a space that "went no further than her eyes and hand could reach." "It was as if her discreet solicitude protected everyone": Johanna Heidegger, lovable and loving, appears in Heidegger's essay "The Fieldpath" as a guardian angel under whose wing her children's lives flowed peacefully, dreaming of the "playful crossings" of these little wooden boats that "at that time knew nothing about expeditions in the course of which every shore lies far behind."[13] This closed and limited life was carefree, enlivened and supervised by the mother, and sheltered within a relatively narrow horizon around the parental home.

Although in a portrait of her and her husband, Johanna Heidegger might seem solemn, the industrious pride that dwelled in her did not rule out a profound gaiety that often declared that "life is so well made that there's always something to be happy about." "Sociable," as Fritz describes her, loving "serious conversations as well as pleasantries," and not disdaining "chattering with her fellows," Heidegger's mother provided an affable counterpoint to her husband.

With a cooper and a sexton at its head, the family was socially modest, but protected from financial problems throughout the time when Martin remained in Meßkirch. As Fritz wrote later on, "from the financial point of view, our parents were neither poor nor rich; they enjoyed a petty bourgeois affluence; it was neither poverty nor opulence." Because of their limited income and their solid bourgeois mentality, the Heideggers formed a thrifty milieu, where living meant counting pennies, both to avoid money problems and to provide a more secure life for their family and themselves, and in this way to gain the satisfaction of a well-ordered household produced by a good paterfamilias's management: "The fashionable word 'save' was written in capital letters: having one's own money, which was as rare as real pearls, was for many people 'the heart of everything.' "[14] The portrait of Johanna and Friedrich Heidegger illustrates their son's remarks: dressed in their finest clothes, as people did at a time when photography was not yet fully democratized and had only recently been substituted for painting, which was even more expensive, Heidegger's parents struck a pose simultaneously dignified, severe, and even rigid, in keeping with their petty bourgeois clothing. The father's black suit and bow tie, like the full, dark-colored dress of the mother, who for the occasion has taken off the apron she always wore, were intended to be sober, far removed from any luxury, while at the same time showing that they belonged to the respectable fringe of society constituted by the bourgeoisie. Black, especially for men, was at that time the bourgeois color—or noncolor—par excellence, symbolizing rigor and respectability. By contrast, women, if their husbands possessed significant financial means, often had great freedom in choosing colors, forms, and patterns, provided they could seem suitable. This austere portrait of the Heideggers shows how important the values of parsimony and a fierce desire for profit, the guarantees of a well-kept household, and gradual social ascent were for them—in contrast to a wealthier and more extravagant bourgeoisie. In that very way the Heideggers were in accord with the whole hard-working European bourgeoisie that could be recognized in Adolphe Thiers's remark: "The father was a peasant, a factory worker, a sailor on a ship. The son, if the father has worked hard and been thrifty, will be a farmer, a manufacturer, or the captain of a ship. The grandson will be a banker, notary, doctor, lawyer, perhaps a head of state. Thus the generations rise one above the other."[15]

Social differences were "astonishingly great in Meßkirch," Fritz Heidegger recalled. His petty bourgeois family did not belong to the upper classes, at least in their financial wealth, which determined, then as now, a large part of the sense one had of the social standing of a person, a family, or a milieu. These differences were reflected in the ways space was used and favored a de facto segregation. For that reason the Lion Inn was closed to Friedrich Heidegger and his sons by a sort of invisible wall that rose in front of them: despite the central position that his office as sexton gave his family in the local Catholic community, which included most of the residents of Meßkirch, Martin and Fritz's father was not for all that a "Herr," because he was neither a "property owner," nor a "graduate," nor "anything at all."[16]

In school, despite obvious social distinctions, the little Heideggers were ordinary children, because many of their classmates came from families of craftsmen with comparable incomes. An 1896 study on craftsmen—and more particularly blacksmiths, cartwrights, and saddlers, lines of work close to that of coopers—conducted by the Association for Social Policy (Verein für Socialpolitik)[17] shows that among the 130 independent craftsmen surveyed, the majority (eighty-three) fell into the modest bracket, with 500–2,000 marks of taxable revenues. The Heideggers, whose income in 1903 was 960 marks, fell into this same group. Friedrich received 500 marks a year for his work as sexton,[18] and owned real estate worth 2,000 marks.[19]

Culture was of little importance in Martin Heidegger's childhood, a sign of the humbleness of his milieu. For example, he seems not to have played a musical instrument. In contrast, bourgeois culture, which was largely secular, accorded an important place to secular music, the art of sociability par excellence: thus private parties and receptions might either be lulled by the sublime plenitude of the solo piano, or enjoy the convivial warmth of chamber music that brought family and guests together in a cordial harmony in which the piano was often joined by voices or strings. Pianos and the lessons to learn to play them were expensive, which probably explains why neither this instrument nor any other was played in the Heideggers' home. This was probably also a matter of culture: as a choirboy and the son of the sexton, young Martin was obliged to sing during the service. This very Catholic culture distinguished his family from many more bourgeois families, even in Meßkirch, where the notables, who were often not very religious, had, moreover, developed their musical tastes: three teachers, Müller, Tschmugel, and Reiser, made up a string trio; and a male chorus directed by Reiser included big businessmen, industrialists, and town councilors.[20]

The same difference applied to reading: although they both showed real aptitude in school, the Heidegger boys were far from being "child prodigies"[21] who devoted themselves entirely to the intellect and spent all their time reading and thinking about their books. Heidegger's only explicit mention of the latter concerns the volumes stored in the church's attic: he "rummaged about in the dusty old books in the church loft & felt like a king among the piles of books which he did not understand but every one of which he knew & reverentially loved."[22] These books seem to have been theological or scholarly works, some of them probably in Latin, and thus beyond the reach of the child that the future philosopher was then, even if they were among future seeds to grow later. Outside the church, at a time when they were still relatively rare and expensive, Meßkirch had other ways of gaining cheap access to books, notably the two reading societies, the Kasinogesellschaft and the Bürgermuseumgesellschaft, which allowed members to borrow their books.

Book learning was not foreign to the little Heideggers, even outside the schoolhouse: they sometimes pretended to be Indians in a game "freely inspired by Karl May" (1842–1912).[23] These games indicated a genuine interest in the exotic that transported them far beyond the valleys of their native Heuberg—north of Meßkirch, near Stetten am kalten Markt—into the middle of the American Great Plains, on the borders of civilization. Following Old Shatterhand—a young German, the first-person narrator, and the author's stand-in—from the first page of the book, the young readers left their native Germany behind and explored the distant Wild West. The magic of reading and of all the popular culture conveyed by peddled newspapers and books thus allowed rural children, who had very few opportunities to meet people who had traveled so far, to explore a part of the world occupied by wild horses, buffalos, and bears, whose inhabitants were often either ignorant, crude white men, or Indians who, while they differed in the color of their skin, their language, and their customs, remained fully human. An encounter with them could be as attractive as it was dangerous.

On a daily basis, Meßkirch's openness to the world took place largely through the reading of newspapers: the nationalist-liberal *Oberbadischer Grenzbote,* founded in 1872, and the Catholic *Heuberger Volksblatt,* founded in 1898. They were relatively inexpensive; the former cost one mark for three months, the latter 1.15 marks if it was purchased in Meßkirch, which made them affordable for many craftsmen's families. Thus these newspapers influenced almost all the residents, whether the readers bought them themselves or borrowed them from acquaintances, as was often done at the time. Heidegger's father, Friedrich, who had installed his cooperage in a building adjacent to the *Heuberger Volksblatt,* to which he also had an affinity by virtue of his militant Catholicism, must have had particularly easy access to the information it provided. Relying on news agency dispatches and articles published in the major newspapers, the *Heuberger Volksblatt* and the *Oberbadischer Grenzbote* devoted up to a third of their space to foreign news, as much as that devoted to news of the empire and their region.

Despite these newspapers, the Heideggers' physical and intellectual horizon was limited chiefly to their town and its surroundings. The parents, who had not attended secondary schools, had little general culture and spoke no foreign languages. They did not go on long trips, ordinarily moved about on foot, and did not hesitate to walk for hours to get where they were going. This is confirmed by a letter written by the philosopher, who was at that time giving lectures at the training camp in Heuberg: his mother and his sister, Marie, walked for four and a half hours to see him, or for a total of nine hours including the return trip, which they made the same day.[24] With the exception of walking—whose cost was small, since it consisted mainly of wear and tear on shoes—the Heideggers had neither the means nor, it seems, the idea of traveling far away; indeed, that idea would have seemed to them contrary to good household management, an extravagant expense that could only reduce the family's assets and was thus contrary to the principle of prudent saving to which they were so attached. The Heideggers' horizon was all the more limited because they were not among the local notables, contact with whom might have led them to take advantage of the latters' greater cultural or economic openness.

The young Martin Heidegger's daily life was rural, taking place in a town and a countryside whose limited scope was taken for granted by the people who lived there. The familiarity Meßkirch could inspire at this time was the result of its small population, some 2,000 residents in 1895,[25] and, in equal measure, of the great homogeneity of its inhabitants, most of whom had lived in the region from time immemorial. Those who came from other parts of Germany consisted solely of a handful of Jews and a small minority of Protestants, and many of them must have come, as was the case in other areas in Baden with Catholic majorities, from poor, rural areas in eastern Germany. Thus it was almost universally assumed that everyone belonged to the community and the region.

This familiarity with the small, self-enclosed world in which Heidegger grew up was reinforced by his family's memory, which was rooted in long family lines nourished by the native land. Genealogical research[26] has proved that his paternal ancestors settled near Leibertingen in the seventeenth century. At that time, the family acquired a sheepfold located on the banks of a bend in the Danube, whose high valley, steep-sided and winding, with lofty ledges of white stone surrounded by dark firs, was surmounted by the Castle of Wildenstein, built in clumsy imitation of the Renaissance style. In this sheepfold, which was handed down from generation to generation, the future philosopher's grandfather, Martin Heidegger, was born in 1803; when he grew up, he set up shop as a cobbler in Meßkirch, about fifteen kilometers away. The philosopher later remembered him doing his work in the already distant time of his childhood, when he saw the "glass globe by the light of which his grandfather sat on a three-legged stool and hammered nails into shoes."[27]

The local roots of the paternal side of the family were similar to those on the maternal side. This family of peasants that had settled in Göggingen, a village eight kilometers from Meßkirch, had made a slow social ascent connected with the land and as a result had a deep attachment to it. Johanna Kempf, Heidegger's mother, grew up on the "farm in the hole," to which she always remained attached, even when her marriage required her to move to Meßkirch on 9 April 1887. Her son Martin often accompanied her to this house so freighted with ancestral memories, and all the more willingly because he had a playmate there, his cousin Gustav Kempf, who was about the same age: as Heidegger noted when his cousin died in 1972, they had led a "carefree life"[28] there.

Heidegger was also marked by his mother's native village through its elementary school, where his uncle Jakob Vetter (d. 1919), the husband of his aunt Gertrud Kempf (1856–1937), taught. In 1936, on the occasion of the latter's eightieth birthday, the philosopher mentioned this rural school as an ideal past, consisting of the happy dream of a childhood imbued with the spirit of the place and of things: "This primary school, with its garden—only the eyes and the heart of childhood are able to feel all its magic: the hidden paths between the heavily laden gooseberry bushes, the beds of colorful flowers, the fertile kitchen garden, the fountains behind them with the bucket, where there was enough water to play with and still more to splash about, close to the little house with the bread oven, around which the smell of fresh bread filled the air."[29] In this school where all the windows were "decorated with bright flowers," the teacher, "sitting at his desk," underlined in red the errors in his pupils' workbooks,[30] while the "careful, light sound of the goose quill scraping over the pages made itself heard."[31] For his part, little Martin found it "remarkable" that the window that looked out on the village allowed him to see only its "high flowers" and the sky, which he barely glimpsed.[32] The philosopher concluded that his "stays in this community schoolhouse" were among the most precious of his childhood.[33]

The son of loving and attentive parents, sheltered from poverty, Martin Heidegger spent a modest, simple childhood, of which he wanted to retain the comforting memory of a carefree existence. Over the years, his few public references to his childhood are unequivocal in a way as confounding as it is unreal: whether they concern the family farm, the primary school and its garden in Göggingen, or the bell tower[34] and the little boats[35] in Meßkirch, the key words that constantly recur are "insouciance," "dream," and "magic," qualifying without any reservations these early times, a past paradise whose still-present effects are made perceptible again by the emotiveness of the memory.

Although retrospective emotion is natural, and although happiness and insouciance are frequent at that age, they are never so absolute that they dominate completely the beginnings of a life that includes, like every life, instances of fear, shame, conflict, humiliation, frustration, and more broadly all the experiences and feelings whose bitterness is inextricably mixed with the fullest happiness. It is only in fairy tales that happiness can be depicted as unmixed, no matter how much we may desire it to be the only master of our destiny. In contrast to spoken or published statements referring unambiguously to the "dream," "magic," and "insouciance" of his childhood, in the letters written to his wife during the 1920s, Heidegger sharply criticized the narrowness of his childhood milieu, which had prevented him from "assimilating" certain matters, "however valuable"[36] the things his parents had provided him. He thought that they had "grown up into a distorted form of life from which no one can extricate them."[37] Although he was aware of the potential moral consequences of the weakness of their culture, in his judgment the family's narrow-mindedness was connected above all with its Catholicism, which was responsible for the family's "inner lack of freedom," and with the "pious-acting despotism of conscience."[38] After he became hostile to the Church, Heidegger blamed these character traits less on the narrowness of his parents' milieu in a small town subject to the strong social constraints inherent in tightly knit communities than on the Church, whose influence on this family "so much a part of the parish house"[39] was extremely powerful.

A Childhood between Church and School

As a rural small town, Meßkirch was huddled around St. Martin's Church, which towered over its center; more than the castle, which was across from it, it was the symbol of the town. Typical of Baroque architecture in Upper Swabia, its octagonal bell tower, topped by a small, gray-green copper onion dome with a spire, brought to mind its kinship to so many other bell towers in the region, such as that of Saint Martin's Church in Biberach. A sentinel of visible time that could be seen from afar, it told the passerby the time with the hands of its clock, visible over the rooftops from a street corner or a square; even as, like costly works of art paid for by the piety of the faithful, its bells made the common faith resound from the heights of Meßkirch to all the surrounding areas, which they filled with a singular religious atmosphere, marking the time of day and of the year and reaching even the ears of the peasants working in their fields.

Far from being merely a visual or sonorous reference point, the parish church was the site of the great moments of communal life that were then celebrated there, shared to the sound of bells, prayers, and sermons: Easter, Christmas, Corpus Christi—all these special occasions brought the faithful together in a procession whose itinerary, before ending up in the parish church, passed by the main sites of Meßkirch, symbolically marking the town's adherence to its religion. Many secular celebrations also had a religious element, and a mass was said for the emperor's birthday. The Church counted in families' lives; it was the place for each individual's rites of passage, the great ceremonies, simultaneously religious and social, that punctuated the life of each person from birth to death: baptism sealed the acceptance of the newborn; first communion and then confirmation marked the transition to adolescence; marriage consecrated the union of two spouses and the advent of adulthood; and funerals were everyone's farewell to the deceased.

Assisting the priest and his vicar, the sexton Heidegger was responsible for ringing the bells. Far from fulfilling this task like a cold automaton, he rang the bells with feeling. Though he was taciturn, as a sign of the renewed feeling that this responsibility elicited in him, he passionately recited at least eight times between 1904 and 1911[40] Schiller's long poem "The Song of the Bell"

(Das Lied von der Glocke, 1800), which is at once a narrative of the casting of this instrument that connects earth and heaven, men and God, and a description of human life, which, for the individual as for the community, is expressed in the sounds made by the bronze. So many words coming out of this normally silent mouth did not fail to surprise, so rarely did it happen. Such was the power of faith and the sounds of the bell over Meßkirch's sexton that it conferred the ability to speak on someone almost completely deprived of it.

As the sexton's son, Martin Heidegger thus spent his childhood among "modest, pious people in the country."[41] When he was baptized in 1889, he was given his grandfather's first name, which was also that of the saint to whom the parish church had been consecrated.[42] Through his family, he was in contact not only with the parish priest and the vicar, but also with the Benedictine monks who had been established since 1863 in Beuron, a locality situated some ten kilometers from Meßkirch in neighboring Hollenzollern. This was an important intellectual and artistic center that made its close proximity felt all around; young Martin often went there with his mother, following the former pilgrimage route that led to the abbey,[43] near which the ancestral sheepfold was located. The church was like a large household in which each of the Heideggers took part in the common tasks: whereas their mother and their sister, Marie, decorated the church for the high holy days, Martin and his brother, Fritz, who had become choirboys, gathered candle stubs for their own altar in the sacristy, where they celebrated the mass;[44] above all, they helped prepare for the service, picked flowers to decorate the church, ran errands for the priest, and rang the bells.

The bell tower rose like the "center of the framework" of their youth. Ringing the bells every day was for them "half duty, half play."[45] When he was alone up there, the contemplative little Martin "savored all the wonderful poetry open to a sexton's son,"[46] often "lay for hours up in the church tower & gazed after the swifts," his mind wandering through the countryside, dreaming "his way over the dark pine forests."[47] When the time came, the two boys interrupted their play and, sometimes accompanied by little friends, went to scorch their hands by pulling on the ropes to make "the clapper, whose amusing and somber silhouette"[48] no one forgot, strike the smallest bell.

"On the Secret of the Bell Tower," a three-page text written by Heidegger in 1954, recalls the name, the sound, and the time peculiar to each of the bells. The carillon rang the hours, the midday bell marked the end of the morning, and the "alarm bell" was rung at four p.m. to waken people who were still napping; the "children's bell" called them to catechism and rosary worship; more exceptionally, the death knell announced every tragic event, and the large bell was rung on the eve and the morning of the high holy days. Between Maundy Thursday and Holy Saturday, the bells were silent; then they pealed continually.

The bells were connected with special moments in Martin's family life. During the Christmas holidays, the young bell ringers came to the sexton's house toward half-past three in the morning. Martin's mother had laid the table with cakes and milky coffee. Lanterns were lit, and they climbed the stairs to the dark, cold bell tower, where the ropes were frozen and the clappers covered with ice.[49] Fifty years later, Heidegger remembered, in addition to the happiness of these moments, the spiritual value of the sounds that came from the bronze when it was struck by the clapper: "The mysterious fugue in which the church feasts, the days of vigil, and the passage of the seasons and the morning, midday, and evening hours of each day fitted into each other, so that a continual ringing went through the young hearts, dreams, prayers, and games—it is this, probably, that conceals one of the most magical, most complete, and most lasting secrets of the tower."[50]

The bells and their sounds constituted a kind of initiatory experience, one of those rare experiences which, whether isolated or repeated, in any case shape a deep sensibility. The importance of this pertains not only to Heidegger's late writings, such as "On the Secret of the Bell Tower" and "The Fieldpath" (1949), both of which appeared after the war, but also to early texts such as "All Souls' Moods" (1909),[51] "We Want to Wait" (1911),[52] and "Abraham a Sancta Clara" (1910), in which bells and the bell tower are key elements.

Martin Heidegger was not the only one who was fascinated by the church's bell tower; his brother was also, as were many children of their age. Fritz described the bells in emotional terms in a long letter addressed to Conrad Gröber (1872–1948), the archbishop of Freiburg and a native of Meßkirch like himself: "Perhaps—the greatest happiness of a child in Meßkirch—you were a bell ringer, and knew all the bells," their times, their forms, the difficulties peculiar to each of them, such as "the midday bell, the proud one, cast right when America was being discovered, with its high-placed yoke; it could be rung only by a strong and experienced ringer."[53] Conrad Gröber, in his diary written in Rome between 1893 and 1898, long remembered the parish church with its bells: "It dominates royally. It rises up toward the east, solid and defying time, its square tower with white clock faces bordering it on the sides. A gray-green copper onion dome covers the tower with a fine boldness of line."[54] Then he recalls the sounds that came out of the bell tower: "A superbly deep sound, among the most ancient and the greatest of all. Then, to let the melodious sound enter like a perfume, a window is suddenly thrown open in many of the little town's houses and also in my father's workshop."[55]

Climbing into the bell tower, playing tag,[56] and ringing the bells were among the greatest pleasures enjoyed by the children of the town. Martin Heidegger, who was responsible for the keys that his father had entrusted to him, granted the privilege of climbing with him to anyone he pleased, which gave him considerable power over the children of his age: lord of the bell tower, he "had a certain prestige" and "was always the leader in all the raids and games of soldiers, the only one allowed to carry the *iron* saber."[57]

Martin Heidegger began elementary school (Volksschule) at the age of six, and the worldview shaped by his family and the milieu of Meßkirch's intransigent Catholics was complemented and challenged by the one that the Grand Duchy of Baden and the German Empire wanted him to have.

Around 1900, the schools had an eminently political function: on their benches, in front of the blackboard and surrounded by wall maps, reading various texts or listening to the teacher's accounts and explanations, children received a whole worldview, simultaneously abstract and laden with emotions and images. Once they had reached adulthood, they were expected, having learned the three R's and mastered their trades, to be citizens full of civic feeling, loyalty to their leaders, and the ideal, collective ardor that is love of country and the nation.

The liberals of Baden had worked to bring together on the same school benches all the Grand Duchy's children, regardless of their religious denomination, with the goal of educating citizens of Baden and of Germany, not Catholics or Protestants. Since 1876, therefore, the schools had served both denominations, a measure of limited import in Meßkirch, where, as was usual in rural areas in the Grand Duchy, Catholic children were far more numerous.

Although it was partially secularized, the school was not atheistic: children received four hours of instruction in the religion of their denomination. The priest taught the catechism, which clarified the principles that were to regulate their lives: "We are on Earth to recognize God, to love Him, serve Him, and in that way to earn Heaven." To that end, they were to "1) believe everything God has revealed, 2) observe the commandments that God has ordered us to observe, 3) make use of the means of Grace, which God has ordered for our salvation."[58] Revelation was made by the patriarchs, the prophets, and then by God's son Jesus Christ and the apostles, and reached modern peoples either "through writing, with the Holy Scriptures or the Bible," or "orally, through transmission, or inherited doctrine (tradition)."[59]

This historical process of revelation was based on the eternal and changeless truth of God, who guaranteed its value, for He is "eternal and immutable, omnipresent, omniscient, perfectly wise, all-powerful; He is infinitely holy and just, good and merciful, truthful and loyal."[60] Since He is truthful, "He reveals only the truth, for He can neither deceive nor lie"; since He is loyal, "He keeps His promises and acts on His threats."[61] The faith of the pupils, as young Catholics, had to "be 1) general, 2) solid, 3) lasting, and 4) living."[62] It was supposed to elevate them to God, who is three persons in a single God: the father, the son, and the Holy Spirit; Jesus is God come to be incarnated among men. He "wished to suffer and die to put an end to our sins, to obtain once again for us the Grace we have lost and in that way to redeem us and make us blessed."[63] It fell to the pope, Peter's successor as bishop of Rome, to direct the Church, leading the faithful to salvation while awaiting the return of Christ, who is supposed to come again "at the end of the world, all-powerful and sovereign, to judge all people, the good and the evil"; the former will go to Paradise, the latter to Hell.[64] This medieval belief remained alive in the 1920s, and troubled the old age of Martin Heidegger's parents.[65] His mother also believed in Purgatory, and used it to threaten her children when they were tempted to be naughty.[66]

The intransigent Catholicism of this milieu may have favored anti-Semitism. Hostility toward the Jews for being Christ killers, an ancient element of Catholicism, had arrived in Europe at the end of the nineteenth century: in France, the Catholic and anti-Semitic publishing house La Bonne Presse had been repeating since the 1880s that the "Jewish problem" had its origin in the "question of Christ," and the conclusion drawn was clear and implacable: "They are damned and we are Christians."[67] Although anti-Semitism was not completely absent from the programs of Zentrum, the German lay Catholic political party,[68] Catholic voters remained relatively unresponsive to it.

Catholicism in Baden had a tradition emerging from the Enlightenment. The catechism allotted the Jews a small role in the history of the Church: disposing of the question of the Philistines' and merchants' possible responsibility for Jesus's crucifixion, the manual preferred to focus soberly on the person who had sentenced him, "the proconsul Pontius Pilate."[69] The level-headedness of the catechism that Martin Heidegger was taught did not mean that anti-Semitism was completely absent from Meßkirch, where, as a widely shared prejudice, it could serve as the backdrop for apparently anodyne statements. For example, in 1914 the *Heuberger Volksblatt* urged Catholics to develop the interpersonal skills of the Jews, who were so well connected to the authorities in Berlin, to ensure that the Catholic faith would inspire greater respect for its rights and that the Jesuit order would be authorized once again.[70] This discourse of a minority that felt oppressed at the same time expressed a hostility rather widespread among German Catholics with regard to another minority that was seen as more favored by the Reich.

In the classes that brought together all the children of his age in Meßkirch, regardless of their denomination, Heidegger received, under the direction of the government of Baden, an initiation to the adult life he was called upon to lead. In addition to the first rudiments of education, he was given numerous lessons seeking to develop love for his little region, his homeland, and his nation.

The schoolteachers in Meßkirch were ardent patriots and played a major role in the choir that was part of every patriotic event: Herr Hauptlehrer Müller, the president and leader of the choir, Herr Hauptlehrer Futterknecht, the treasurer, and Herr Hauptlehrer Tschugmel, an active member, celebrated with their voices and their authority as teachers such lofty political events as the emperor's birthday, the death of Chancellor Bismarck, and the fiftieth anniversary of the death of the city's favorite son par excellence, the composer Conradin Kreutzer.[71]

The political zeal that drew solemn songs from them was also expressed in their teaching, in accord with the goals of public education at that time. Thus geography, a spatial discipline, was given the assignment of teaching love of country as one of its highest tasks; the work of Julius Gischendorf, intended to help Volkschule teachers prepare their lessons on German geography, was driven as much by pedagogical concerns as by the sense of nation and homeland: "The teaching of geography [. . .] must be based upon the teacher's national feeling and awaken, maintain, and strengthen the student's national feeling. [. . .] We want, in the cares and sufferings of everyday life, in one's work and trade, pleasure and success, in one's standing and political party, not to forget the unique, great thing: we have a great and magnificent land, a land that we must at all times hold to be lofty and holy, loftier and holier than anything else that glows and shines in everyday life."[72] Referring to maps so that the relief, waterways, cities, and borders might be learned by heart, and to which were added images, drawings, and even slides that made it possible to appreciate the beauties of their native region, teachers and pupils studied successively the homeland's various scales: in conformity with the principles of the pedagogy of the time, the teacher started from the limited circle of the *Heimat,* the little homeland that the pupils knew through an experience at once concrete and sensory, and then began gradually, as the years went by, to teach more abstract and general material related to the homeland, the state, and finally the *Reich*—a pedagogical model that had influenced republican France, a country with a reputation for Jacobin centrism and hostility to local forms of patriotism, and which in fact favored the small regions the better to make people love the greater nation.[73]

The cult of the local and of popular traditions was a primordial element of the national identity, on which German patriotism was largely based. The turn of the century marked an apogee of the cult of the *Heimat* in Germany, and modernity, combining technological progress, higher incomes, and the spread of literacy, proved to be a powerful factor in the diffusion of this traditional culture. Literature, scholarly journals, and newspapers, in which this culture figured as a major theme, underwent a vigorous development thanks to advances in paper and printing. In the same way, popular images of varying qualities and types—watercolors, drawings, engravings, lithographs, photographs,[74] postcards—enjoyed an undeniable success with a large and varied audience that liked these representations of typical farms, traditional rural clothing, and old city buildings, in which science and aesthetics mingled with the clear sentimentality of an idyllic *Heimat.*

In addition to these factors that the young Heidegger shared with his fellow citizens, who saw in their distinctive local traits the surest sign of their Germanness, there was the value accorded to traditions peculiar to Catholicism. Traditionalism is a dogmatic principle essential to Roman Catholicism: dogma is the historical development of an eternal, universal truth whose gradual understanding is reflected in the coherent accumulation of dogmas by ecclesiastical tradition. This traditionalism was found more broadly in a hostility to schisms of any kind—political, but also social or cultural—that led to the celebration of popular traditions preserved in the countryside, especially in the age of industrial and urban revolution that followed the wave of political revolutions. Catholic traditionalism was thus fully aligned with the growing regionalism that was developing in Germany. The regionalist culture of the *Heimat* flourished in Meßkirch, and particularly in the Catholic *Heuberger Volksblatt,* which regularly published learned articles and covered every initiative that might be related to the *Heimat* and its cult, reporting on numerous and varied regionalist projects. In this way it announced the first issue of the review edited by the monks of Beuron, *Gottesminne;* these monks, who were so important for the young Heidegger and his family, wrote in 1903 a vibrant manifesto in favor of a popular art—that is, an art embedded in the tradition of rural and regional culture, based on faith in the close bond linking Catholicism and regionalism, religion and *Heimat:*

> Today's art has lost contact with the people. That is the main reason why we no longer have any genuine religious poetry. What does it mean to cultivate religious art? Nothing other or better than: plunging to the very bottom of the people's fountain of youth, seeking the path toward the people's soul, and clinging to what we find there with every fiber of our soul. [. . .] The people is the source of all genuine art and culture. Moderns have all the same lost this origin; only here and there, now and then, does a nature full of power succeed in striking a chord on the delicate strings of the people's soul. It is time to move beyond the yawning abyss. Popular art, that is the watchword.[75]

Far from the folkloric naïveté of backward peasants, the celebration of popular art, which proceeded from the rural areas of the *Heimat,* took place in connection with respectable scholarship. Consider, for instance, the title that the monks of Beuron, under the leadership of Ansgar Pöllmann (1871–1933), chose for their review: *Gottesminne* is a reference to courtly poetry (*Minne*), one of the brilliant expressions of medieval culture in which Swabia had distinguished itself, notably in the person of the poet Walter von der Vogelweide (1170–1228). In alluding to the spiritual filiation with this prestigious regional heritage, the monks of Beuron claimed to be celebrating the love of God (*Gottes-minne*). Martin Heidegger, who through his family maintained close relations with the monks of Beuron, had been brought up since early childhood in the heart of this holy chorus that sang of the *Heimat* and its rural traditions.

The Catholicism of Heidegger's family was itself conservative, hostile to an atheistic modernity. Tradition, humility, and submission to the Creator were the watchwords, as is shown by "God, Man, and Nature," a poem by Valerian Kempf (1841–1918), Heidegger's maternal uncle and a sometime poet as well as the mayor of Göggingen:

> [. . .] Oh, let time's flow whirl and boil
> Here below in this cold world.
> One day you'll precede us all as servant
> To the sunny vault of heaven.[76]

Prizing local traditions, the Catholicism in which the future philosopher grew up also tended to forge a Catholic identity for him which, if not fully universal or even cosmopolitan, was marked first of all by a growing interest in Rome: in Heuberg around 1900, the influence of the papacy on fervent Catholics like the Heidegger family was very strong, stronger than it had been a century earlier. The nineteenth century had seen the Holy See's hold on the national churches growing stronger, especially starting in the 1840s; the city of the pope became increasingly the living heart of Catholicism, even for ordinary believers.

Over time, Rome came to count even more for the Heidegger family's eldest son. The parish priest, Camillo Brandhuber, had noticed how promising this young man was, and wanted him to go to the seminary and become a priest, which would fulfill his family's expectations. But first he had to learn Latin,[77] the language of the Church and the language of European culture, despite the competition that modern languages such as French or English might offer. The young vicar gave Martin lessons that were not easily absorbed: "When that boy came home from Latin at the young vicar's and often brought mistakes with him, he would cry his heart out on his good mother's shoulder, though she herself could not give him any help."[78]

Catholicism thus tended to offer little Martin Heidegger a broader European horizon, especially since the attention paid to Rome by fervent believers like his family was accompanied by a growing interest in other great centers of Catholicism both inside and outside their own region. As a result of the surge of miracles and especially of the publicity about them, great pilgrimage sites, such as Lourdes in France, gained a European or even global dimension that was clear to more and more Catholics.

The Boiling Cauldron of a Century of Conflicts

Like adult activities, children's games are imbued with obvious facts regarding the world that surrounds them; and for some people, these facts are already political, even if they remain embryonic. As a young boy in Meßkirch, Martin Heidegger already had a clear sense of belonging to his native town. Playing soldiers with his neighborhood pals, he showed a masculine fearlessness on the grounds of Fürstenberg Castle: as the captain of the little soldiers of Meßkirch, he proudly wore at his side an iron saber borrowed from the father of his friend Karl Fischer. Thus equipped, he led his troops through the fields of Igelwies and Menningen to meet enemies from Göggingen, his mother's native village, where he knew all the children. His adversaries were waiting for him, under the proud supervision of their captain. But the boys from Göggingen had only wooden sabers. When a wooden saber faced an iron saber, the conflict was over before it had started. The victory—symbolic, as those of children playing at war usually are—was obtained for Meßkirch's little army thanks to the prestige of their general, Heidegger.[79] Beyond the anecdotal, this kind of play was based on an evident and friendly childhood pride, with each side defending its own locality, Meßkirch versus Göggingen. As such, it was part of a diffuse but perceptible climate of vigorous community patriotism that united Meßkirch's residents. Spurred by the liveliness of young boys' imagination, the war games played by Martin Heidegger and his little friends against the children of Göggingen also reflected a time grounded in part in war and violence.

War games are common among young boys, but Fritz Heidegger explained that they were "very much in fashion"[80] in a period that was particularly bellicose. The discipline of two groups armed with wooden swords, each commanded by a captain—one of them, Martin Heidegger, even having a genuine iron saber—goes well beyond the simple aggressiveness natural to human beings (man is wolf to man, according to the proverb), who from their earliest childhood take pleasure in the harm they can do their fellows. It was a genuine warlike culture that was being expressed—still children, already soldiers. And thanks to the discretionary power given him by the keys to the bell tower, Heidegger "was always the leader in all the raids and games of soldiers,"[81] and that increased his pugnacity at the head of his troops.

The military excitement evinced during Martin Heidegger's childhood went back to a certain state of mind that ruled at the highest levels of the state: the kaiser, who led the German Empire, was the king of Prussia, in the line of sovereigns descended from Frederick William I, "the Soldier King" (1713–1740), whose indefatigable zeal had established, despite the mediocre size and wealth of his kingdom, the fourth-largest army in Europe,[82] and perhaps the most disciplined and best trained. From that time onward, the army, along with the great landowners and the high administration, counted among the natural supporters of the emperor, and imbued a large part of society with its prestige, because its resounding victories over adversaries as formidable as Austria in 1866 and France in 1870–1871 had given it an unprecedented aura of glory. Germans were all the prouder of this because they were subject to general conscription. Even the way German was spoken was affected, at least as Friedrich Nietzsche heard it, by the prestige of the military: "Something scornful, cold, indifferent, and careless in one's voice—that is what the Germans now consider elegant. I hear the good will to achieve such elegance in the voices of young officials, teachers, women, merchants; even little girls are beginning to imitate this officers' German." Nietzsche concludes: "Could the Germans really be a musical people? Unquestionably, the Germans are becoming militarized in the sound of their language. Probably, once they are accustomed to speaking in a military tone, they will eventually also write that way."[83]

The army, which had constituted the strength and then the glory of Prussia, did the same for this Reich that was so Prussian, where nationalistic, patriotic enthusiasm made itself felt even in the Catholic countryside, which was at first not very favorable to Prussia. Such was the case for the Heuberg area, which had provided its contingent of soldiers to fight France in 1870. Valerian Kempf, Heidegger's maternal uncle, was one of them: the composer of soldiers' songs such as the "German Song" of 1870,[84] he expressed his patriotic, nationalist, and military joy at German unity and the victory over France, despite the "numerous German brothers" who had died "on the long, broad battlefield."[85] The "hereditary enemy," having "fallen at the feet of Germany," had been forced to allow Alsace to return to the German Empire. Unlike Bismarck, the architect of this national unity achieved at the cost of great pain and suffering, who believed its meaning was primarily military, in that it created a neutral zone between France and Germany, Heidegger's uncle celebrated the incorporation into the German homeland of blood brothers, Germans in spite of themselves, whom he exhorted to become, in all fraternity, "truly Germans."[86] Valerian Kempf was thus in agreement with the liberal notables of Meßkirch who, on the occasion of the anniversary celebration of the German victory at the Battle of Sedan in 1877, drank a toast to their "heroic Emperor William" (*Heldenkaiser*), as well as to the German army and its leaders.[87]

Patriotic, nationalist, and military references abounded in the everyday life of schoolchildren in Meßkirch, even in physical education. Martin Heidegger, who was very athletic, was in particular "an agile gymnast on the horizontal bar and the parallel bars."[88] Gymnastics was the only sport taught in the school, two hours a week; similarly, since 1862 there had been a gymnastics club (*Turnverein*) in Meßkirch.[89] This sport, which was part of the athletic tradition of ancient Greece, was at that time intended not only to develop graceful bodies but also to prepare students for combat. That was particularly the case in Germany, where Friedrich Ludwig Jahn (1778–1852), the "father of gymnastics" (*Turnvater*), at least in its modern German form, had rooted his thought and practice entirely in the Napoleonic occupation of his time, when the values of national liberty and sovereignty were being trampled upon by those who had brandished them as their flag. Jahn, calling like Fichte for an uprising of the German nation[90] to establish "the freedom and unity of the German homeland,"[91] wanted gymnastics to forge bodies and hearts to oppose the invader. Gymnasts wore uniforms, originally made of rough gray cloth and considered the ancient German manner of dress, one that erased the singularity of individuals in order to develop the feeling of equality and esprit de corps[92] indispensable for the troops to operate smoothly. Singing,[93] they engaged in games to elicit joy and camaraderie and exercises to develop emulation among equals that would lead to greater agility, energy, and will.[94] That is the reason for the preponderant role played by gymnastics equipment such as bars, rings, and the pommel horse, which required courage and self-mastery to face the void and the danger of falling.

If the young Heidegger's performances suggested how receptive he was to this teaching under the aegis of Bellona, goddess of war, the son of Meßkirch's sexton also received instruction in intellectual subjects permeated with the nationalist and military spirit. This is clearly shown, for example, by Julius Gischendorf's work on geography:

> Ever since the interests of our people—a people of sixty-five million individuals—have become global interests, we need, more than before, a national geography that seeks to strengthen national consciousness, the kind of national consciousness that is expressed so openly among other peoples, such as the French and the English, but is still very underdeveloped among us Germans. [. . .] In the heyday of our homeland, our fathers fought for it, thousands of them fell on foreign soil and took all their wishes and hopes with them into the darkness of the tomb: should we become unfaithful to them, if something in life does not correspond to our little wishes and interests?[95]

The German fatherland, the land of the German people who developed it and defended it over so many centuries of wars, had to fill the minds and hearts of the young schoolchildren, who would be called upon, once they were adults, to follow in the footsteps of their ancestors. This conception linking homeland and war was exceedingly common at the time. The French historian Ernest Lavisse used similar terms when he told instructors how to teach history: "Moral and patriotic history: that should be the aim of teaching history in the schools." If the pupil "has not learned how much blood and effort it has cost to create the unity of our country [. . .], if he does not become a citizen imbued with his duties and a soldier who loves his rifle, the instructor will have wasted his time."[96]

Permeated by the militarism of the period, the conflictual atmosphere in which Heidegger grew up was also fed by the intransigent Catholicism of his milieu, which was similar to the Catholicism that had been establishing itself in Europe since the 1840s. The general rejection of modernity within the papacy was summed up in a striking manner in the eightieth "error" listed in the *Syllabus of Errors* issued in 1864, under Pope Pius IX: "The Roman Pontiff can, and ought to, reconcile himself to, and come to terms with, progress, liberalism, and modern civilization."[97] The rejection of the ascendancy of the earthly world was explained in particular by the claim made by the popes, as spiritual sovereigns directly descended from Gregory the Great (1073–1085), to govern people's conduct even in the life of their states; the latter had to obey the pope and conform to the Church's precepts. Admitting the separation of Church and state was out of the question; a denomination other than Catholicism could no longer legitimately be a state religion.

Catholicism's multiform hostility to modernity coincided with a hostility to technology from which Heidegger's family was not free. In a poem entitled "Change of Period," Martin's maternal uncle Valerian Kempf offered an acute and amusing criticism of the automobile, which had recently appeared in the peaceful valleys of the Heuberg:

> In the town and in the castle,
> In the countryside in every village,
> Automobiles are already well known.
> Everybody thinks the auto can
> Foul the air and pollute it. [. . .]
> Thus a motorist is also
> A boor for the town, the village, the air
> And with his rubber wheels
> He's also a grave-digger.[98]

The clergy was often more intransigent, especially in southern Germany and in Austria, where antimodernism and hostility to modernity along the lines of the *Syllabus of Errors* were strong.[99] The monks of Beuron, who were close to the Heideggers, published *Gottesminne,* a review of religious poetry that was often violently opposed to modernity. Taking pleasure in the return of a certain number of believers to Catholicism, as had been the case in Meßkirch at the end of the preceding century, the editorial in the review's first issue set out to settle scores with secular modernity, which it called "materialism" and accused of being sterile:

> Through modern humanity there passes a profound aspiration to a reign that is not that of this world. Among many people, materialism burned like a fire, and they exulted in the happiness of having found the flaming birthplace of an immortal phoenix. Where is that miraculous bird now, the flaming wing of a new culture? Nowhere in the wake of the modern messiah of a new life [. . .]. See here the great discourse of materialism, the death of all true art and culture, the hereditary enemy of everything that delights the heart of man.[100]

The intransigence of Heidegger's Catholic milieu had been sharpened by the conflictual spirit that reigned in Meßkirch. Having won out over Baden's conservatives in 1860, the liberals ended up allying themselves with the latter to carry out their program inspired by *Kulturkampf.* The "battle for culture" is a polemical expression coined by the Prussian liberal politician Rudolf Virchow in 1873, whose aim was to demolish the influence of Roman Catholicism, which he considered obscurantist, a mixture of miracles and dogmas that the positivists sought to destroy because it deprived the people of their freedom through the schools, over which it had substantial control, and through its monarchical organization, which gave sovereignty to a single man, the pope, a foreign sovereign who exercised power over national believers to the point of competing with the legitimate authority issuing from the nation. The "New Era" (1860–1866) in Baden brought about many reforms intended to sap the Church's power, such as the introduction of mixed-denomination schools, civil marriage, and an examination on general culture for clerics.

The conflict inflamed the whole community in the 1870s, and died down only slowly during Heidegger's youth. In addition to the politics of *Kulturkampf* pursued by the government of Baden, there was also the politics of the Reich reshaped by Bismarck in 1871, which became violently anti-Catholic. As the liberal politician Johannes Miquel put it, "Today's Germany came into being *against* you. You have sought to prevent it by all means. Today you are the vanquished."[101] German Catholics were thus *Reichsfeinde,* enemies of the empire that had supported Catholic Austria against Protestant Prussia, a grievance added to the Church's alleged obscurantism and to the still greater submission to a foreign sovereign since the proclamation of pontifical infallibility in 1870.

This violent anti-Catholicism was accompanied by a schism within the Roman Church that was particularly notable among the liberal Catholics in Baden: the First Vatican Council's proclamation in 1870 of the dogma of papal infallibility favored the break with the Church by a movement that called itself "Old Catholic," and rejected the innovations introduced by the council. However, despite its apparent attachment to a tradition that had been challenged, that movement expressed still more a desire for modernity, for a certain freedom in matters of religion, practiced in a national framework, and in particular for local management of parishes, the election of priests, the abolition of the requirement of celibacy, and stricter limits on the worship of saints. During these years, Meßkirch, which was a veritable bastion of Old Catholicism, because almost half its male population adhered to it, was divided into two communities violently opposed to one another, socially, religiously, and politically. Despite their numerical inferiority—the Old Catholics never constituted more than a third of the total population—they dominated the town, in both the city hall and the schools. Conrad Gröber, the archbishop of Freiburg, who was born in Meßkirch, testified to this fact: "Young people were deprived of happiness in the hard years during which the rich children of the Old Catholics rejected the poor children of Catholics, giving them and their priests mocking nicknames, beating them, and plunging their heads in troughs to rebaptize them. We know this because, sadly, we were the objects of this treatment. Experience taught us that Old Catholic teachers themselves designated the scapegoats, giving Catholic pupils the affectionate nickname of 'sickly blacks,'[102] and making them feel in their bones that the roads to Rome could not be taken with impunity."[103]

The use of churches and ecclesiastical goods was a major issue, both symbolic and material, in the *Kulturkampf* in Meßkirch. Officially recognized by the Grand Duchy's government, the Old Catholic community received part of the benefices that came from Rome, and especially the right to use, without exclusivity, Saint Martin's Church; the Roman Catholics made a sharp rejoinder to this announcement by the Grand Duchy, but got nowhere; on 10 February 1875, the first Old Catholic mass was celebrated in Saint Martin's Church. Considering it profaned, the Catholics abandoned it. Their defeat was complete, because in the same year they lost 1,328 marks per year in revenue, as well as the house of the sexton Heidegger, the future father of the philosopher. With the help of the monks of Beuron, they then transformed an old fruit warehouse into a temporary church, which, in a clear sign of ultramontane piety, was consecrated to the Sacred Heart. The sexton Heidegger's family and his cooper's workshop were moved into this building, and it was there that his son Martin was baptized.

The Roman Catholics' victory over the Old Catholics was slow in coming, and proceeded from the steep decline of the schismatic Church, which lost a considerable number of parishioners during the 1890s, because so few of them attended services. In 1895, the town had about 2,000 residents, but only 391 of them were Old Catholics.[104] In addition, *Kulturkampf*, both in the Reich and in Baden, had died down. Thus in 1893 the Old Catholics lost, along with their arrogance, Saint Martin's, the parish church in which an Old Catholic priest officiated and which was by then almost empty.

When on 1 December 1895 a ceremonial mass made the Catholics' victory official, little Martin, who was six years old and the son of one of the first "resistors," had a prominent role in the triumphal restoration of Catholicism: since the Old Catholic sexton, Bosch, could not bring himself to hand the key over to his Roman Catholic adversary, he gave it to Martin, who was playing on the square.[105] The following year, the Heideggers moved to Schloßstsraße 12, a house on the square in front of the church that was allocated to the sexton, and the family subsequently remained there.

Although the years between 1896 and 1903 were marked by relative tranquility regarding religion, they gave way to political fighting—the Catholic Zentrum party wanted to gain through elections an influence equivalent to that enjoyed by the Church among Meßkirch's believers, while the Katholische Volkspartei, a party defining Catholic interests founded in 1869 that had become the Badische Zentrumspartei in 1888, was an extremely pugnacious political group. Its leader, Theodor Wacker, nicknamed the "lion of Zähringen," undertook a systematic battle against the liberals, in the Landtag as well as in the Reichstag, with the slogan "not a single vote for a national-liberal." Heidegger's family remained actively involved in the Catholic cause.[106]

As we have seen, the Heideggers were fervent Catholics; the father was the sexton, Martin and his brother were choirboys, and his mother and his sister were also active in the Church. They were ensconced in the Roman Church's political institution: having at that time only a few lay managers, the priests, such as Camillo Brandhuber, who was in charge of the parish from 1898 on, were the party's spearheads. Born in 1860 in the neighboring city of Sigmaringen, Brandhuber was a man of character whose oratorical ardor allowed him, after he left in 1906 to take up a curacy in Hechningen, to become a representative of the Hohenzollern in the Prussian Landtag from 1908 to 1918. After the revolution of November 1918, he was a representative in the

Hohenzollerns' Kommunallandtag, over which he presided until 1922.[107] In this respect, Brandhuber was in fact in the vanguard of Zentrum in Meßkirch, responding to the wish of Theodor Wacker, who was himself a curate and the leader of Zentrum in Baden, that priests get involved in the political struggle. Brandhuber, by word and by example, was the model whose clarity influenced this choirboy and sexton's son: political engagement was the natural consequence of being a priest. Ordination, which consecrated the priest and entrusted him with the task of leading his parishioners to the Most High, called him here below to spread the Good News and to defend the Roman Church against the world's attacks by taking part in secular battles.

The virulence of the confrontation between Catholics and liberals gives an invaluable explanation of the weakness of anti-Semitism in Martin Heidegger's milieu, which sheltered him from the anti-Semitic fever that was establishing itself elsewhere in Germany and in Europe, notably in Vienna. This was probably a result of the *Kulturkampf* of which Catholics were the victims, particularly in Meßkirch. While at the same time the local economy was flourishing, Roman Catholics were already busy with the liberals, and therefore had no need for any other outlet.

2 • From the Future Priest to the Young Antimodern Philosopher

(1903–1913)

I am entirely a child of the forests. [. . .] One had to know many things in the forest: birds' flight and the paths taken by animals. The language of all things that spoke of danger . . . that is, the language of birds, of spiders, of plants, of pinecones, of clouds, of winds. But later I had to become a child of the cities, of concepts, of sciences, of dogmas, of civilization. I bore my cross like everyone else.

Ernst Wiechert, "Heimat und Herkunft," Sämtliche Werke, *vol. 10, p. 713ff.*

Fourteen years old, of modest origin but talented, "the little brooder"[1] left Meßkirch to attend a Gymnasium and a minor seminary (that is, a preparatory seminary for adolescents). The son of the cooper and sexton set out to seek knowledge and ordination, which promised him an exceptional position within the Catholic community of his native countryside, a vocation that could fill a pious family with pride. It was his mother's dearest wish; the father went along with silent approval; and the son saw it as his future.

From Konstanz to Freiburg, or Six Years of Secondary School and Minor Seminary

Heidegger's departure for Konstanz was desired by his family but not inevitable. There was a Gymnasium very close to Meßkirch, in Sigmaringen, in neighboring Hohenzollern. Above all, the Gymnasium in Konstanz, formerly run by the Jesuits, was a state school, to be sure, but at a time when education, which was very expensive, was becoming almost prohibitively so for anyone who was not a member of the wealthy bourgeoisie: tuition was as high as 150 marks per year, to which had to be added 150 marks more to cover the costs of room and board at the minor seminary.[2] Thus the total amount to be paid was considerable for the Heidegger family, representing almost a third of its taxable income in 1903. The modest origin of the son of Meßkirch's cooper would usually have led him to rapidly learn a trade and become a craftsman like his father or a clerk, as his brother, Fritz, did a few years later.

Noting Martin's intellectual inclinations and piety, Meßkirch's parish priest, Camillo Brandhuber, had proposed to his family that he be sent to Konstanz to attend Gymnasium and minor seminary. To that end, for the previous three years Brandhuber had had his young vicar give the boy lessons in Latin. This inclination and application to his studies were confirmed at the end of the year of *tertia,* when Martin was awarded a first prize by the primary school, an honor that earned him and a few of his schoolmates a notice in the local newspaper.[3]

The financial means to pay for the expensive secondary school training for this very promising young mind still had to be found. Conrad Gröber, who was then the rector of the minor seminary in Konstanz, asked the archbishopric of Freiburg, which ran the Saint Conrad minor seminary, the Konradihaus,[4] to exempt the young man from his hometown from paying room and board, but he obtained only a reduction to 100 marks a year. Brandhuber had greater success, obtaining, from a foundation in Meßkirch, 100 marks a year to pay Martin's tuition and fees; this "Weiß" scholarship was awarded during Martin's three years of study in Konstanz (1903–1906), but it left fifty marks that had to be paid by the Heidegger family, in addition to room and board. The scholarship was ultimately raised to 300 marks, covering all the expenses of maintaining the minor seminarian.[5]

Although the Gymnasium in Konstanz accepted not only children from wealthy families but also those of more modest origins, like Heidegger, these children often owed their good fortune to the Roman Church; they were lodged in the Konradihaus, where they also received instruction in religion. In the Catholic countryside of Europe, the Church was the way out for poor but gifted students, who were often made priests; the young minds that bloomed among the fields, meadows, and woods returned to feed the fervor of the village communities by serving as their parish priests. At that time, the networks of Catholic solidarity were rapidly expanding throughout Europe: Catholic foundations, associations, and federations had been increasing in number since the late nineteenth century. The Volksverein für das katholische Deutschland, intended to supervise the whole of society and especially the working classes, was founded in 1890: it brought together twenty-seven associations and 6,000 members, before reaching 1,041 associations and 114,422 members in 1914.[6]

Raised in the fervent heart of Catholicism in Meßkirch, Heidegger, a promising student, was supposed to become a priest, and that was why he went to Konstanz rather than to Sigmaringen, which had no minor seminary. When he left his native town, where he could have attended secondary school, he began to follow the Catholic path indicated by his gifts, a path which, to reach the priesthood, led as far as Freiburg, where there was a university and a seminary. This path had been taken by Conrad Gröber, the rector of the Konradihaus and the future archbishop of Freiburg, who was also a native of Meßkirch: the modest son of a craftsman, he had been able to study in these places before joining the Collegium Germanicum et Hungaricum in Rome, which destined him for the highest ecclesiastical offices. This path was also the one taken by Heidegger's cousin, Gustav Kempf,[7] a year later, and the one that Heidegger's younger brother, Fritz, began to follow not long afterward, but had to give up because he stammered[8] and hence could not pursue the classics program, in which the art of eloquence was a crucial element.

When he first went there, Martin Heidegger knew Konstanz only by name. It was very different from what this fourteen-year-old adolescent had experienced in his native town. The rather large railroad station, surmounted by a neo-Gothic steeple vaguely inspired by that of the Palazzo Vecchio in Florence, was the destination of many travelers from the surrounding area, from Germany like little Martin and from all over Europe, including tourists who wanted to enjoy the attractions offered by the lakeside city. Konstanz stretched out peacefully along the shores of the lake. And this site, which was so different from the damp and rustic countryside of Heidegger's Heuberg, made the most of its low altitude and the protection of the Swabian Jura Mountains to portray itself as a German equivalent of the South of France, with a temperate climate well suited to holiday resorts. Far away from the range of hills where Meßkirch's Simmental cattle grazed, Lake Constance was covered with boats, especially in summer, because in addition to the local fisherman in traditional dress there were the vacationers dressed in city clothes who took advantage of the clement weather to go for walks or boating excursions, or even to take a dip in the lake, an activity in which women were then engaging for the first time. Sometimes a regatta even included vessels of various kinds—steamers, sailboats, rowboats—giving the water, usually so calm, the liveliness of sporting activities. The lake testified to the considerable boom in tourism that occurred once Konstanz was connected to the railway system in 1863, as much by the flood of people savoring its charms as by the development of its shores, the municipal park with promenades shaded by palm trees, private villas, and new establishments varying in luxury along its shores, such as the Baths Hotel, the Lake Hotel, and the Island Hotel.

With its many public structures, schools, and hospital, all marked on their own scale by this megalomania of stone, Konstanz deliberately gave itself the appearance of a great city of the early twentieth century. This impression was corroborated by the multiplicity of new apartment buildings, both in the suburbs and in the old city center, which was regularly torn up and rebuilt. These homes were modern, not only in appearance but also in the utilities provided: gas, running water, and sewers. A few privileged customers, both individuals and businesses, had telephones; the Riedmatter Hotel even showed the latest moving pictures.[9] As for the city's shops, they had become large enough in some cases to resemble, with their big display windows, increasingly gaudy signs, and fashionable goods, the department stores in Paris, Berlin, or Vienna, a similarity enhanced by street lighting with gas and electricity.

A genuine city, whereas Meßkirch was more a bridge between rurality and urbanity, Konstanz marked a deep break with the past for this adolescent who was leaving his family and found himself lost in a great city unlike anything he had seen before, constrained by the narrow limits of a secondary school[10] and a minor seminary, alone among other young strangers. At first, Martin experienced a violent wrenching feeling.[11]

At first foreign and strange, Konstanz gradually came to be more pleasant and familiar. As time passes, the feelings that things inspire in us change. The mildness of the climate allowed often-luxuriant vegetation, as in the vineyards of Meersburg, or on Mainau, the island of flowers that had been bought in 1853 by Frederick I, who was at that time regent of Baden, but became grand duke in 1856. To make Mainau his summer residence, Frederick had an extensive, sumptuous, and complex garden of flowers and Mediterranean or exotic trees planted on it. In addition, the millennial history of this area favorable to human life had left charming medieval cities and splendid monuments, such as Meersburg, Überlingen, and Reichenau. Competing with its surroundings for the favors of its residents, the city of Konstanz itself had an appeal that increased that of the islands and the lake: "On the whole," Günther Dehn wrote, "a very agreeable atmosphere reigned in Konstanz. One could easily take pleasure in this friendly little city. [. . .] The people were agreeable, spirited, and jovial. They lived and let live there."[12]

Heidegger could hardly have enjoyed the amusing atmosphere that prevailed outside the walls of the Gymnasium and the minor seminary: not only were his financial means very limited, but above all, the minor seminary's rigorous discipline left him no more than an hour of free time per day.[13] The minor seminary, more than the Gymnasium, made Martin feel at home in Konstanz. The teaching at the Konradihaus was religious, absolutely congruent with the Catholic climate into which he had been born in Meßkirch; and a year later, he was joined there by his cousin and playmate from Göggingen, Gustav Kempf,[14] whose familiar face reminded him of his carefree youth in his *Heimat*. Although the living conditions were less easy than those of the secular Gymnasium students, Heidegger's stay at the Konradihaus was happy; as he wrote in a letter of 30 May 1928 to Matthäus Lang, his former ecclesiastical prefect, who was in charge of the younger students and who congratulated him on his appointment to Husserl's chair at the University of Freiburg: "I think back with pleasure and gratitude to the beginnings of my student career at the Konradihaus."[15]

Heidegger might have spent in Konstanz the six years of secondary school necessary to take the *Abitur* (the German terminal exam); instead, in 1906 he went to Freiburg. In Konstanz, he was about forty kilometers from Meßkirch, and still relatively close to his family home; Freiburg was much farther away, some eighty kilometers from Meßkirch by the train that crossed the Black Forest.

Alfred Denker thinks this departure was a reaction to an unforeseen situation. Heidegger supposedly had a romantic relationship with one of his rare comrades, Hilma von Kahlden-Senn, a baron's daughter and one of the pioneering young women pursuing a secondary education in Germany. For a candidate for the priesthood like Heidegger, this relationship would have been inopportune, and inopportune as well for a baron's daughter, whose relationship with a rustic petty bourgeois could have only raised the prospect of a disastrous misalliance. For Martin's parents, as for his mentor Conrad Gröber, this embarrassing situation would have required a quick and radical response to what threatened to be the probable ruin of the young man's career in the priesthood. Thus, according to Denker, Heidegger left for Freiburg, his heart heavy with a love so soon sacrificed on the altar of his priesthood; but despite this departure, the philosopher is said never "to have forgotten his Hilma."[16]

This thesis is as seductive as it is fragile; the romanticism of the situation described strongly resembles a novel and is set forth in a way pleasant to read in a biography; but its foundations are slim and corrupted by anachronism, since it is based on a single, late source that does not deal with this episode, a passage from a letter of 7 February 1947 addressed to Heidegger's former schoolmate in Konstanz, Paul Motz, in which he writes, regarding a future reunion of former students, "I replied to Hilma that I would gladly come to the reunion on 12 June. I imagine the meeting will be very delightful."[17]

Hugo Ott suggests more prosaically that the departure was a matter of money, drawing on the *exeat* written in 1909 by Leonhard Schanzenbach, the rector of the minor seminary in Freiburg: "Martin Heidegger [. . .] left the grammar school and seminary in Constance and entered the 'Obersekunda' at this school, being obliged to change schools in order to qualify for receipt of an Eliner studentship."[18] Ott argues that "what prompted the move to Freiburg was the material and financial situation of Heidegger's parents."[19] His key argument rests on the amount of the scholarship Heidegger could receive by going to Freiburg: 400 marks, that is, a third more than he was receiving in Konstanz.

The move to Freiburg once again put the minor seminarian in a large, beautiful city. "I could write a whole book about Freiburg, it is the city of cities, all the old things preserved in such a pretty way, with so much love, a superb site, a crystalline brook, an old fountain in every little lane, [. . .] vines everywhere: all the walls of the city, its ancient fortifications, are planted with grape vines."[20] Freiburg had changed a little from the flattering description Sulpiz Boisserée gave to Goethe; but like Konstanz, it remained a pleasant city that attracted many tourists and appealed to Heidegger. His discovery of Freiburg in 1906 did not provoke the same feeling of being uprooted that he had experienced three years earlier upon arriving in Konstanz.[21] To be sure, he must have felt a real disorientation that had to do with the broadening of his horizon: with a population of 80,000 in 1906,[22] Freiburg was a middle-sized city that must have seemed to him quite large—four times larger than Konstanz, and forty times larger than his native Meßkirch; its dialect was more remote from that of Meßkirch, when compared to the Konstanz dialect; and the many tourist attractions that supported both Konstanz and Freiburg brought in vacationers from Germany and abroad.

It is easy to understand why Heidegger did not have the same sense of being uprooted that he had felt upon arriving in Konstanz: the disorientation that had at that point marked the fourteen-year-old adolescent who had never left the little area around Meßkirch could not have been replicated exactly in a city that retained a genuine similarity to Konstanz: being part, as it was, of southwestern Germany, its old as well as its modern buildings resembled what Heidegger knew already. Moreover, the minor seminary's austere structures were located near the cathedral, in the heart of the old city, far from the modern suburbs that the railroad passed through.

Freiburg was beautiful; it had avoided many of the hideous features that industry was then inflicting on numerous German cities; but although it had retained its concentric network of streets crisscrossed with small canals, decorated with fountains and climbing vines, it had been profoundly modernized like Konstanz, with comfortable apartment buildings, and tramways and automobiles on its streets. A modern large city, Freiburg also evoked the Middle Ages and the countryside: some ancient buildings, such as Saint Martin's Gate, had been reconstructed in a neo-Gothic style similar to that of Louis II of Bavaria's Neuschwanstein Castle—a sublime pasteboard movie set, because modernity wished so much to be medieval that it rebuilt its old monuments to make them correspond better to its romantic dream.

If not when he first arrived in Freiburg, at least over time, Heidegger seems to have become sensitive, less to the details that strike the tourist wandering through its streets, than to the overall impression the city produced, especially when viewed from the belvedere of the Schlossberg, where it is possible to look out over the western side of the city, Breisgau, and the Rhine Valley, as far as the Vosges Mountains, which had in 1871 become the new border with France. In a letter of 21 July 1918, Heidegger opined that the view of "Freibg. & its Minster & and the outlines of the Black Forest Mountains" was "simply Great and *Divine*":[23] the city is set at the foot of the Black Forest, at the conjunction of the valleys of the Rhine and of the Hölle; the houses, and the concentric lanes and streets, lose their individuality and huddle like sheep around the cathedral that dominates them with the majesty of its dark ochre steeple; on the surrounding hillsides, grape vines loaded with fruit in the autumn take on the warm and melancholy colors of the season, while the rounded summits of the Black Forest are covered by firs.

"The entire period of my schooling was nothing other than a constant and wearisome boredom, accompanied year after year by an increased impatience to escape from this treadmill. [. . .] For us school was compulsion, ennui, dreariness, a place where we had to assimilate the 'science of the not-worth-knowing' in exactly measured portions—scholastic or scholastically manufactured material which we felt could have no relation to reality or to our personal interests."[24] The austere buildings, the programs provided, the book learning committed to memory, the subordination of students to teachers in a forced and distant obedience: it is easy to stress, as Stefan Zweig does, how little European secondary schools of that time sought to further the self-fulfillment of their students. Nonetheless, this coherent program of instruction, which was reserved for a narrow elite and opened broad intellectual horizons, was a stroke of luck for Martin Heidegger, and he knew how to judge it at its true value, all the more easily because his teachers were often important figures who elicited the enthusiasm of young people curious about intellectual matters.

Heidegger remembered that in Freiburg as in Konstanz, "excellent teachers" conveyed a "fertile teaching,"[25] particularly in Greek, Latin, and German. Even more than the modern secondary school (Realgymnasium), the classical secondary school (Gymnasium) put heavy emphasis on ancient literature—this was the rule in Europe, where the cult of antiquity was part of the common culture. For example, in 1901 the Prussian programs specified that the last six levels of the Gymnasium, which Heidegger completed, had to include seven or eight hours of Latin and six hours of Greek (amounting to between thirteen and fourteen hours per week), which constituted the heart of the thirty hours of instruction. These were to be accompanied by three hours of history-geography, German and French in equal measure, four hours of mathematics, two hours of natural sciences, and two hours of religion.[26]

The spirit of teaching in the classical Gymnasium led the Catholic Church to prefer it to the modern Gymnasium, so that though the Catholics of Baden came from humbler backgrounds, and hence fewer of them pursued secondary studies, they were far more likely to go to the classical schools.[27] The latter offered a program that was naturally more in harmony with Catholic traditionalism and with the importance of erudition and ancient languages in the culture of the clerics that candidates for the priesthood were to assimilate.

In the proud but cramped seventeenth-century building in Konstanz, there reigned a "clearly humanistic" "spirit"[28] inspired by a "congenial" director, Matthy,[29] whose teaching of Greek was "captivating": Heidegger's Greek instructor was probably Schott, who taught the intermediary levels in the Gymnasium (*Untertertia, Obertertia,* and *Untersekunda*), that is, precisely the ones in which the son of Meßkirch was placed in Konstanz. A colorful figure, extremely ill-dressed, addressing every student in the third person rather than the second, and thus saying, "I beg Mr. Heidegger to come to the blackboard and recite his lesson," he began his classes with a dictation of Greek expressions that he had taken from the text for that day, along with five verses from the *Odyssey* that had to be learned by heart for each new session.[30]

In the last year (*Oberprima*) at the Berthold Gymnasium in Freiburg, Professor Widder used Plato to introduce his pupils "to philosophical problems, very deliberately, though without theoretical rigor."[31] In addition to the role philosophy played in Heidegger's life, Widder's importance can be seen in the fact that he is the only teacher at the Gymnasium mentioned in his 1915 *Lebenslauf,* which also notes that this teacher on the path of thought had died a few years earlier.

This program in which classical humanities had such a large place often had a major effect on students, whether by inspiring a profound boredom when presented without enthusiasm, or on the contrary by shaping, at least temporarily, their language, their references, and even their worldview. Bloch, the friend of the narrator of Proust's *In Search of Lost Time,* is exemplary in this regard, dotting his remarks with Homeric epithets. For example, he introduces his sisters to the Marquis of Saint-Loup, a young aristocrat embarking upon a military career, in the following terms: " 'Whelps, [. . .] I present to you the cavalier Saint-Loup, hurler of javelins, who is come for a few days from Doncières to the dwellings of polished stone, fruitful in horses.' " And he borrows almost literally from Homer phrases such as "the first flush of Eos, the rosy-fingered."[32] These epithets and borrowings come accompanied by much more modern references, which did not always avoid affectation at a time when, discovering in large measure the world of the intellect, the young man's desire to shine can be just as great as his presumption. The narrator having alluded to a journey to Venice, Bloch replies: "Yes, of course, to sip iced drinks with the pretty ladies, while pretending to read the *Stones of Venighce* [*sic*] by Lord John Ruskin, a dreary bore, in fact one of the most tedious old prosers you could find." "Thus Bloch evidently thought that in England not only were all the inhabitants of the male sex called 'Lord,' but the letter 'i' was invariably pronounced 'igh' "[33] (as in "nigh").

Following the example of Belle-Époque France, the role of the classical humanities was beginning to shrink, and instruction became increasingly nationalist and patriotic: "We must bring up young Germans in the national spirit, not as young Greeks or Romans,"[34] Wilhelm II proclaimed in 1890. The teaching of history was emblematic in this respect. Bismarck had sought to institute "two history courses [. . .] one to disseminate general culture, the other (perhaps taking priority over the former, which was to start with recent Prussian history) would deliver, to pupils, including elementary pupils, a political and monarchical catechism in plain language, which, on the model of the Christian catechism, they would learn by heart as a scientific certainty."[35]

Martin Mertens's textbook of German history, published by Herder in Freiburg, provides a clear view of this Prussian and monarchical way of looking at German history even in the Grand Duchy of Baden. It consists of three parts, the first going from the origins to the end of the Middle Ages, the second from the beginnings of modernity with Luther, and the third tracing the rise of Prussia in Germany starting with the elevation of Frederick II of Prussia (1712–1786), known as Frederick the Great. Each part has approximately the same number of pages, but there is a clear imbalance in the length of time dealt with, and this has as much to do with the political necessity of writing the "political-monarchical catechism" Bismarck wanted as it does with the disproportion in the sources and knowledge. This was a nationalist history, because it was an ethnic history of the German people from its disunion and its rediscovered union around the purest German state;[36] it was a dynastic history, because it proclaimed the almost providential role of the Hohenzollern, who reestablished around themselves the unity of their people, which was so inclined to division; and it was a political history very much in accord with Bismarck's wishes, intended less to forge a critical spirit by providing landmarks and historical distance than to inculcate as a truth established by science a catechism that was intended to consolidate a German, imperial, and militaristic credo. A veritable modern mythology, the history taught in schools was, far more than it is today, a way of looking at the past that was supposed to strengthen the loyalty of the kaiser's subjects.

Of all the subjects that interested Heidegger within the vast intellectual horizon that then opened up to him, it seems that German literature was the domain to which he gave the most attention, if we believe the certificate written by Leonhard Schanzenbach, the rector of the minor seminary: "He is gifted, diligent and of good moral character. He had already attained a certain maturity when he came to us, and he was used to studying on his own initiative; indeed, his studies in German literature, an area in which he proved to be extremely well read, were sometimes pursued at the expense of his other subjects."[37] This pronounced taste for literature is found in the speech Heidegger gave before the Heidelberg Academy of Sciences, in which he mentions, for this period, his readings of Stifter and Hölderlin, both of whom were "destined to become immortal." It is noteworthy that these two authors who so strongly marked Heidegger did not write avant-garde literature by any means, even though the latter often interested the elite young minds of his fellow secondary school students.

Heidegger retained ties with the Gymnasium in Konstanz and was invited to reunions of former students,[38] even after the war,[39] but nothing suggests that he formed strong friendships at the minor seminary. It may even be doubted that he entertained good relations with a majority of his classmates at that time. As Günther Dehn wrote, whatever their personal qualities, the students in the Konstanz minor seminary were often shunned, promptly scorned, emasculated, and accused of being "capons": "We always looked on the capons with a certain condescension. They were badly dressed and, we thought, not always well washed. We considered ourselves superior. But that did not prevent us from exploiting them ruthlessly. They were forced to do their exercises very conscientiously. During recess, they had to read us their translations, and they never balked."[40] Even setting aside a social inferiority complex, we can infer that in Konstanz, at least, Heidegger experienced the conflictual relationship between Catholics and liberal or Protestant notables that he had already known in Meßkirch. In addition, there was his own character: taciturn like his father, he was not prompt to join in the collective enthusiasms that can seize young people; this is confirmed by his reference to his "isolated development."[41]

Heidegger was not attracted to novelty in itself; he maintained a relationship of confidence, esteem, and interest with his teachers in both the Gymnasium and the minor seminary. They strongly stimulated his intellectual orientation, which was, moreover, endowed with a genuinely autonomous vitality. This character trait can be observed in his relationship to mathematics and the natural sciences, to which he was at that time particularly attracted: "When, in the upper second year (*Obersekunda*), lessons in mathematics departed from simple problem-solving to pursue more theoretical avenues, what had been a simple predilection for this discipline became a true objective interest that also extended to physics."[42]

During the three years that Heidegger spent at the Berthold Gymnasium, the courses on religion were taught by the rector of the minor seminary, Leonhard Schanzenbach, who also taught Hebrew. Astonishingly, these courses, which one might have expected to be based on Scholastic science, were on the contrary open to modern developments in the sciences. In 1915, Heidegger referred to "the stimulation of the courses on religion, which led me to undertake many readings on the theory of biological evolution."[43] Through the work of the Frenchman Jean-Baptiste Lamarck (1744–1829), the Englishman Charles Darwin (1809–1882), and the German Ernst Haeckel (1834–1919), a consensus had gradually been established that placed man within an evolution of species and of living beings in general; the discussion had shifted to focus on the modalities of this evolution, whereas its reality was accepted. The courses on religion that Heidegger took led him to open himself up to the challenges made by science and to inquire into theories that put in question a literal reading of Genesis's account of man created by God all at once on the sixth day. Obviously, he did this from an apologetic point of view: the question was which Catholic mode of argument to adopt when confronted by the challenges of modern science.

Among the authors Heidegger read were the "excellent modern theologians"[44] Paul von Schanz (1841–1905) and Herman Schell (1850–1906), both of whom were Christian apologists from the University of Tübingen. They were involved in a vigorous debate with modern natural science and did not hesitate to make use of an intimate knowledge of the latter to oppose what they saw as irreligious positivist tendencies. Schell, whose apologetic importance Heidegger stressed again in 1915,[45] was a reformer motivated by the conviction that Catholicism was a "principle of progress."[46] Confronted by "the new age," "the old faith" had to be reformed;[47] it was imperative that Catholicism, to make up for its cultural deficit, open itself to science and modern culture, respect freedom of thought, introduce German into teaching and the liturgy, and accord believers a greater place within the Church. These theses were judged to be subversive and were put on the Index in 1898.

It is unlikely that Rector Schanzenbach assigned these forbidden works to his students;[48] by contrast, Schell had written on the theory of evolution, on Haeckel (*Haeckel's Monism and Christian Belief in God and in the Holy Spirit,* 1901),[49] and more broadly on the relation between biology and religion (*Faith in God and Knowing the World through the Natural Sciences,* 1904),[50] works that Heidegger probably read, because they opposed atheistic evolutionism. *Haeckel's Monism and Christian Belief in God and in the Holy Spirit* was based on the idea of a direct battle against Haeckel's monism, "a great spiritual force that has to be confronted publicly and radically." One of the means Schell employed was to draw attention to the inexactitude and lack of rigor that characterize these worldviews, which, like Haeckel's, were presented as complete explanations of the world and "a perfect substitute for religious faith."[51]

Schell was thus a model of Catholic combativeness; far from taking refuge in traditional apologetics, he tried to descend into the arena of modernity to vanquish Catholicism's enemies with the weapons provided by a renewed way of thinking, clear and purely rational argumentation, without theological or scriptural references. Inspired by the Cartesian *cogito,* he criticized Haeckel's materialism, accusing him of not taking into account the fact that "the primary reality of experience, the first and unique immediate certainty is not the corporeal external world and the reign of matter, but rather sensation and consciousness itself! For critical thought, matter and corporeality have to be proved to be external realities, but the soul and the interiority of consciousness do not!"[52] The primacy of the soul's certainty over matter undermined Haeckel's materialist monism. As for the question of evolution, Schell maintained that it was not incompatible with the divine creation of the world. On the contrary: adapting to the context of scientific debate the traditional cosmological proof of God's existence, which argues from the beauty and order of the world to infer a providential Creator, he posited that "creation and evolution are not contraries; indeed, as a principle of explanation, evolution from the inferior to the superior in accord with laws requires a creative wisdom."[53]

The works Heidegger read on his own were closely connected with his training and his religious belief as a minor seminary student. Following the model of his mentor Conrad Gröber, he chose books oriented toward scientific modernity with the intention of defending Catholic belief, and paid little attention to modern literature.

At various points in his life, Heidegger said how much Conrad Gröber, his "paternal friend,"[54] mentor, and fellow resident of Meßkirch, meant to him. In his 1915 curriculum vitae, written when he was twenty-six, he noted that Gröber had had "a decisive spiritual influence" on him.[55] In his last text, written a few days before his own death in 1976, Heidegger noted: "today renewed our memory of the archbishop, Dr. Conrad Gröber, who was also born in our native village. At different times and in different ways, he was crucial for both of us [Heidegger and the Catholic philosopher Bernhard Welte]."[56] The strong tie between Heidegger and Gröber can be truly understood only if one considers how much a great professor shapes his students by what he is, even more than by the content of what he says. In the modern context of the minor seminary and the bond between Gröber and Heidegger, the teacher's influence was all the more important because it was exerted during the pupil's adolescence, a decisive point in a person's development when the mind is already less malleable but more alive than before and capable of grasping more rapid and subtle ideas. Even though it is becoming set, the adolescent mind receives intellectual impressions that are all the more profound because they are fresh and correspond to the virtualities peculiar to a developing character. This holds particularly true when the influence continues over time; far from being limited to the years they spent together at the Konradihaus, the relationship between the two men remained close even after Gröber took over Trinity parish in Konstanz in 1905, and after Heidegger left to go to the seminary and the

Berthold Gymnasium in Freiburg in 1906. Meßkirch, their native city, was a place where they would meet up again.

Gröber was an intransigent but open-minded person. The trust he accorded the young people in his care and their freedom to embrace the rigor of Catholicism by themselves, was in no way the effect of a religion corrupted by the secular world. He remained traumatized by the assaults of an aggressive anti-Catholicism; in 1912, he wrote a history of the Old Catholic controversy in Meßkirch, a sign of how much these events that had wounded his youth remained present during the period when Heidegger was so much under his influence. He looked on modern culture with suspicion, though he did not reject it altogether.

Gröber's attachment to the Church's dogmas went hand in hand with an intellectual combativity; confronted by the positivist and atheistic challenge of the secular world, Catholicism was forced to question itself in order to recover the creativity it still had in the Romantic period.[57] It was necessary, not to return to a mythical past, but to modernize without altering a Catholic culture that had eternal truth on its side. Thus, in the 1920s Gröber was a pioneer in the use of radio, broadcasting sermons that were later issued as a book,[58] whereas many ecclesiastics were still hostile to this modern medium. At the turn of the century, the modernity he accepted to serve the eternal Catholic truth led Gröber to express a deep admiration for Leo XIII, a pope who wanted to "Christianize modernity and modernize Christianity," to precisely the same end: without in any way renouncing Catholicism, to adapt it to the modern world and thus to recover the promised dominion over the secular world. Gröber praised the boldness and self-assurance the pope had shown with regard to science when in 1881 he opened the Vatican archives to historical research: "He knows full well that a severe and deserved condemnation weighs on the history of his predecessors, but he is equally convinced that the light proceeding from the Vatican's immense treasures is spreading over science, clearing away the shadows inherited from dark centuries, or will be eclipsed by the unique grandeur of many of Saint Peter's successors. [. . .] Only great men and great institutions do not deny or dissimulate their weaknesses and their dark periods."[59] Contrary to Matthäus Lang, who was so attached to the Church's authority that it seemed to him to be the ultimate answer, Gröber was critical in a very intelligent way, driven by a genuine inner freedom from which Heidegger benefited.

An important moment in their relationship, and more generally in Heidegger's life, came in 1907, when Gröber gave him one of the books that was destined to determine his thought: Franz Brentano's doctoral dissertation, "On the Several Senses of Being in Aristotle."[60] A Catholic priest and university professor, Brentano (1838–1917) belonged to the tradition of the Scholastic interpretation of Aristotle and medieval Aristotelianism; in this respect his work was compatible with the effort to rehabilitate Thomism in accord with the encyclical *Aeterni Patris* of 1879, as a means of inspiration for both research and teaching. Gröber had discovered neo-Thomism in Rome, where he was impressed by the French theologian Louis Billot, an ardent promoter of neo-Thomism. Thus Gröber's choice of this book as a gift for his young protégé was in accord with his aspiration for a renewal of Catholic culture on its own terms. Although Brentano was of course traditional, he was nonetheless modern; he put at the center of his thought the notion of intentionality, which was drawn from his interpretation of Thomas Aquinas, and was essential in the genesis of Husserlian phenomenology. Fully a Catholic and an innovator, Brentano was thus a perfect author to introduce to a young, promising Catholic student like Heidegger. Once again, Gröber showed his intelligence—or his ignorance—by following Brentano's evolution after he wrote his dissertation, when he opposed the pontifical infallibility proclaimed in 1870 and ended up leaving the Church, marrying, and being forced to give up his chair in Vienna.

At that time, Heidegger was not impressed by the notion of intentionality: in his 1957 speech at the Heidelberg Academy of Sciences, he implied that Brentano provided the first, intermediary access to Aristotle's writings by way of the "numerous Greek quotations, most of them long," which "took the place of the book [. . .] which I still lacked, and which, taken out of the school library, was to be in my desk only a year later."[61] Above all, as he emphasized twelve years later in "My Way to Phenomenology," this book was "the rod and staff [*Stab und Stecken*] guiding my first, awkward efforts to enter philosophy."[62] It was a disorienting introduction to the question of being: "Rather vague, this reflection troubled me: if being is predicated in manifold meanings, then what fundamental signification is dominant? What is called being?"[63] Retrospectively, this initiation into ontology seemed to him decisive, having marked out the path that led to the masterpiece he would later write: "The question of the simplicity of the diversity of being which, at the time, was being raised, obscure and undecided and awkward, remained, through many changes in opinion, errors, and confusions, the constant foundation of the treatise that appeared two decades later, *Being and Time*."[64] In reading Brentano, Heidegger was exposed to philosophy and ontology for the first time, and this experience was reinforced when he read a work by Carl Braig, *On Being: An Introduction to Ontology* (1896); later on, in the Catholic seminary in Freiburg, he even attended Braig's classes.[65] Through the person of Gröber, Heidegger's *Heimatstadt* of Meßkirch, and more broadly his native region, showed him the path that he was to follow during his life, despite the distance that he later took from the Church. In any case, that is what Heidegger subsequently thought.

Gröber's influence was not solely theoretical: "So far as a sense of home and love of country go, we Catholics are not about to take lessons from anyone."[66] Gröber was an ardent patriot; the peace that Leo XIII managed to make with the empire at the time of the *Kulturkampf* allowed Gröber to recover his internal peace after being torn between Catholicism and patriotism. Loving his greater homeland, though not blindly, he also had a strong sense of his native region, which expressed itself in a taste for its history and art. He wrote a long history of the Jesuit grammar school and Gymnasium in Konstanz,[67] which was published in 1904, and followed it a few years later with a history and description of the cathedral (1914),[68] as well as two volumes on the art of Reichenau, which appeared in the *Badische Heimat* yearbook (1922 and 1924).[69] This love of popular arts and traditions was common among the clergy; in addition to following the example of Heidegger's mentor by doing scholarly research, some clerics even ran associations devoted to the study and defense of the *Heimat*. The seeds of love for the region planted in the minor seminary first blossomed when Heidegger reviewed the 1913 Catholic Yearbook for the city of Konstanz:[70] "The yearbook can rightly be recommended as an example for imitation and study. [. . .] Anyone who likes Konstanz will certainly take an interest in this yearbook and make it part of his library."[71] In addition, Heidegger had retained close ties with the monastery of Beuron. In one of his very first publications, while he was still at the seminary, he emphasized the quality of its "first-rate" periodical in his review of it for the Catholic newspaper of Meßkirch: " 'Minne' ["Courtly Love of God," the title the monks gave their yearbook] belongs on the desk of every cleric. It will become a cherished friend of the house in all cultivated families."[72] Like Gröber, the monks of Beuron prized popular traditions and promoted the necessary renewal of Catholic culture as a means to stand up to the secular world.

Heidegger returned to Meßkirch during vacations. He was not only the sexton's son who was studying for the priesthood, but also a local celebrity thanks to his academic successes that were praised in the newspapers: when the hometown boy was granted the *Abitur* with honors, the *Heuberger Volksblatt* published an enthusiastic little article on 21 July 1909: "Mr. Martin Heidegger, a student in *Oberprima,* has passed the *Abitur* examination in Freiburg with the greatest success. This extremely assiduous and talented young man intends to devote himself to the study of theology."[73] A few years later, Heidegger himself expressed his pride by recounting how, "when he brought home nothing less than a 'Schiller' as first prize, he was even in the local paper."[74]

However, this success, which strengthened Heidegger's feeling that he was being directed by a destiny, did not transform the athletic young man full of energy that he had been before his departure for the Gymnasium and the minor seminary: as his brother, Fritz, told it later, "until the *Abitur,* during long vacations the students in the general and technical secondary schools formed an amateur soccer club. Even today I see how, attacking as the left wing, you often remained tense for a moment after a powerful shot until the ball had flown precisely into the goal."[75]

Endowed with special status even in his hometown, thanks to the life that he was leading outside it, Heidegger deepened the book learning that had been alien to him and that was making him increasingly remote from his own origins. According to his brother, before going to Konstanz Martin was certainly intellectually gifted, but primarily interested in sports; now he had become a great reader. "The Fieldpath" describes this period of his youth in Meßkirch, during which Heidegger read some of his first philosophical texts, which were as memorable as they were difficult for an adolescent. This dialogue situates these early readings in the context of a country path that leaves the castle and its garden: "Sometimes there lay on the bench one or another of the works of the great thinkers, which an awkward youth was trying to decipher. When the enigmas became urgent and no way out appeared, the fieldpath was of great help, for it quietly led our steps along its winding way across the expanse of this austere country."[76] In 1947, after the war and the fall of Nazism, the mature Heidegger depicted himself as a youngster and even an adolescent grappling with the difficult discovery of the great authors of philosophy; his "awkward youth," his clumsy inexperience, found help in the countryside that he was crossing on the fieldpath. Delightful for the fifty-eight-year-old Heidegger's retrospective image of himself as a son of his native region, this repetitive and mythical scene is only partly true. To be sure, starting when he was at the Gymnasium, Heidegger began to read, and to read extensively, even during his vacations at home in Meßkirch: "From then on, as people still say today, he was never again seen in the holidays without a book";[77]

but as another letter makes clear, he discovered the walk through the beautiful countryside of his little homeland only later on, accompanied by Elfride, the woman he had chosen as his wife: "Formerly, as a student indeed I had no 'time' for it."[78]

The Heartbreaking Wanderings of a Catholic Destiny

Heidegger's brilliant success on his *Abitur* examination naturally opened to him the way to higher education as well as to the seminary. In September 1909, his project was no longer simply the one his native region had laid out for him: his family, in particular his mother, along with Camillo Brandhuber, the Meßkirch priest, and his mentor, the former rector of the minor seminary in Konstanz, Conrad Gröber, all expected him to become a priest. In addition, the Eliner scholarship he had received meant that he was expected to enroll to study theology at the University of Freiburg. But on 30 September 1909, Heidegger became a novice in the Society of Jesus, at Tisis, near Feldkirch, in the Vorarlberg, a region in western Austria near Lake Constance. His choice of Austria was not accidental: the Jesuits had been expelled from Germany in 1872 as a result of the *Kulturkampf.* The only way for him to join the Society of Jesus was to leave the German Empire; and Austria was the obvious choice because of its spatial and cultural proximity. Heidegger was deviating from the path that had been laid out for him. As his teacher Leonard Schanzenbach noted: "He is quite sure he wishes to pursue a theological career and favors the life of a religious order."[79] This inclination resulted from the life that he had been leading for six years in the minor seminary, which was in some respects already monastic, and from the influence of the way of life of the monks of Beuron, whose library he assiduously frequented during vacations and which offered him the image of a religious community devoted to the service of God through prayer and the life of the mind. Heidegger could have asked to be admitted as a novice at Beuron, but he preferred the Jesuits, elite soldiers of Christ who defended the Roman Catholic faith in speech and writing.

Admitted as a novice on 30 September by the Provincial P. Thill, Heidegger left the Society of Jesus on 13 October. After the two regulation weeks of probation, during which he did not take the cloth and participated only partly in the community's life, he was deemed unsuited; a hike through the mountains near Feldkirch had made Heidegger's heart problems obvious. Heidegger was thus prevented from following the spiritual itinerary that seemed to him more desirable than the priesthood. His heart did in fact bother him, but the problem seems to have been psychosomatic; these cardiac problems "of a nervous origin" manifested themselves particularly at key moments in his youth, as when he joined the Jesuit order.

Heidegger's profound desire was to become a scholar and not a priest;[80] the Society of Jesus offered the advantage of making knowledge the primary focus of his calling, but it required him to take vows. Deviating from the career foreseen by his mother and his milieu, enjoined to make a definitive commitment to a way of life that he was probably not sure he really wanted to embrace, his nervous agitation manifested itself through his heart, which struggled to make the intense effort required by a hike through the mountains. Although this agitation bore on the delicate question of taking vows, if he resumed the path to the priesthood, it could only lead to a dead end; and yet that is what Heidegger did, returning to Freiburg to enroll in theology at the university and at the same time in the Charles Borromeo Seminary. The modesty of his financial means and the Church's support in the form of the Eliner scholarship required that he enroll in the seminary to pursue advanced studies; by doing so he also pleased his teachers, the parishioners in Meßkirch, and his parents, especially his mother.

The return to Freiburg put Heidegger back on familiar ground. Freiburg is a tourist destination, but it is just as much a university town, indeed a town-university that clearly bears the stamp of the institution with which Heidegger was to be associated, first as a student and then as a professor, until 1947.[81] In Heidegger's time, the University of Freiburg, which had been founded in 1457 by the archduke of Austria, Albrecht VI,[82] was the Habsburgs' second most important possession, after Vienna. It had the four major Faculties: Arts,[83] Law, Medicine, and Theology; having come under the control of Baden, in 1820 it received from Grand Duke Ludwig of Baden an endowment intended to ensure its permanence. Thereupon it took the name "Albert-Ludwigs University" to honor these two founding figures, while retaining its location in the heart of the city in buildings that had hardly changed since the very end of the Middle Ages—its enrollment did not exceed 500 students. The university that Heidegger entered in 1909 came about as a result of the abrupt transformation of an institution that had changed little over more than four centuries. An institute of the natural and clinical sciences was created north of the city, and in the 1880s the number of students exploded, reaching 2,000 (including thirty-three women) in 1904 and 3,000 in 1911,[84] housed in new, imposing buildings built between 1896 and 1911 around the old city center. Dominating the tall windows on the west façade of lecture building no. 1 is a symbol of this triumphant university: the gilt letters of its motto taken from the Gospel according to John: "The truth shall set you free" (*Die Wahrheit wird euch frei machen*).[85] The University of Freiburg was only one example among others of the spectacular growth of German higher education around the turn of the century: the number of Reich students attending a university rose from 14,000 in 1869 to 60,000 in 1914;[86] thus in 1913, 72 percent of them were taking a path that their fathers had not.[87] This was the case for Martin Heidegger, the son of a sexton who had not even completed secondary school; and for Martin's cousin Gustav Kempf as well, who once again joined him a year later.[88]

A new departure, the beginning of his studies in theology also sealed the end of Heidegger's prehistory, a period for which there are few autograph sources, a scarcity that makes it extremely difficult to reconstitute his emotional and intellectual private life; his ancient history begins with the first texts written in his own hand at that time, along with a certain number of later writings that sometimes contradict them.

The courses for which Heidegger enrolled during these four semesters of theology covered the history of the Church, exegesis, canon law, logic, metaphysics, art history, the history of the Middle Ages and the Renaissance, and the history of law to the contemporary period, in addition to theology proper. These semester-long courses[89] made for a full schedule: twenty-one hours a week in the first semester, twenty-two in the second, twenty-three in the third, but only thirteen in the fourth, most of which Heidegger missed for reasons of ill health. Some of his professors, such as Below and Finke, were not members of the Faculty of Theology. Of these eleven teachers, one was already known to Heidegger: Carl Braig, a professor of dogmatics whose treatise on ontology he had already read during his last year at the Gymnasium.[90] Braig's influence subsequently increased; with an open, brilliant mind, he was a model for the young student of theology and remained so, even though he had left the path toward ordination. Receptive to "the penetrating mode of thought that [Braig] made present in every hour of lecturing," Heidegger received from him "the vocation—decisive and hence ineffable—for his own later university teaching."[91] Braig planted the initial seed of an academic vocation that was to establish itself permanently.

In terms of German Catholicism, one of Braig's distinctive characteristics was that as a theologian he abandoned to some extent the "doctrinal system of Scholasticism" and centered his thought on the philosophical and Protestant tradition of the University of Tübingen and two of the most illustrious representatives of German Idealism, Schelling and Hegel. Reinterpreting

Braig's intellectual legacy from the point of view of his reflection on the "onto-theological structure of metaphysics," the mature Heidegger drew the conclusion that "the tensions between ontology and speculative theology entered into the horizon of his [Braig's] research as the constitutive structure of metaphysics." As a student in theology, and then in philosophy, Heidegger had not yet gone that far—above all, he saw opening before him a broader, stimulating philosophical horizon that included modern non-Catholic authors. Finally, if ontology was an essential theme for Braig, as it was to become for Heidegger, the same was true of logic, on which the theologian had also written a treatise, *On Thought: A Handbook of Logic,*[92] which may have interested Heidegger more than Braig's treatise on ontology because of the young Heidegger's predominant interest in logic.

Thanks to Braig,[93] Heidegger—and this is a clear sign of his philosophical modernity—made the crucial discovery of Husserl, whose *Logical Investigations* was "decisive for the path taken by his scientific development," whereas "the earlier work by the same author, the *Philosophy of Arithmetic* [. . .] shed an entirely new light on mathematics."[94] Abandoning problem solving to go back to the principles of these disciplines, this great contemporary philosophy responded to the young Heidegger's speculative interest in logic and mathematics, which seemed to him to be the branches of human knowledge closest to the eternity of divine truth. At first, Heidegger read "freely, without good guidance."[95] Retrospectively, this seemed to him a genuine initiation into phenomenology, which nonetheless retained its mysteries for lack of adequate guidance: "From the first semester on, the two volumes of Husserl's *Logical Investigations* were in my desk at the seminary. They belonged to the university's library. The loan could always be easily extended. The work was clearly not in much demand from the students. [. . .] I remained so affected by Husserl's work that in the following years I plunged back into it without discerning satisfactorily what was impeding me. The magic the work emanated reached as far as the cover and the title."[96]

This first, essential name of Braig, which was already known to Heidegger, was joined by those of two other authors who still counted after these early years: the historian Heinrich Finke (1855–1938) and the art historian Josef Sauer (1872–1949). They were to watch over his philosophical début, the latter with his courses on Rhenish mysticism, which acquainted Heidegger with Meister Eckhart, who remained the philosopher's intellectual companion even in his old age.[97] For the Rhenish mystic, God, because he is being (*Sein*) itself, is nothing; he is not *a* being (*Seiende*), a thing;[98] he is known only negatively, in an absolute break with what is visible to humans. Thus in 1948 Heidegger wrote that "God is truly God" only "in what [the] language [of things] does not say."[99] Meister Eckhart's mysticism was a seed from which one of the major postulates of his philosophy would grow, the ontological difference between being (*Sein*) and beings (*Seiende*): there are no beings without being, but being is not *a* being; being does not become really accessible in a predicative judgment, but through questioning, in a quest that, positing at the outset the emptiness of the question, allows the least inadequate access to what is neither this nor that.

In addition to discovering Husserl and Meister Eckhart, Heidegger turned toward what constituted the heart of the Church's philosophical tradition, namely Scholasticism, using handbooks that responded only rather poorly to his philosophical inquiries: "They procured for me a certain instruction in formal logic, but did not give me what, from a philosophical point of view, I was looking for."[100] Formal logic, initially conceived by Aristotle as a simple *organon* of thought, an instrument, did not respond to the more theoretical inquiries that were troubling this young seminarian who was so philosophical. Already in the Gymnasium, mathematics, which was related precisely to logic through their common instrumental nature, had awakened Heidegger's particular interest when the instruction shifted from simple problem solving to more theoretical perspectives, a shift that the formal logic dispensed in these Scholastic manuals did not make. More than from the latter, Heidegger drew his Scholastic spiritual nourishment from the great classics of medieval philosophy: "Thomas Aquinas's Shorter Summa" and "scattered works by Bonaventure,"[101] to which his 1922 *Vita* added Aristotle, read from a Thomist point of view, and Augustine, thus completing the pantheon of thinkers as it was redefined by the encyclical *Aeterni Patris* issued in 1879. Alongside these canonical readings, Heidegger did not disdain modern Catholic scholarship, particularly in the apologetic domain, with the works of Schell and Schanz,[102] which were in the van of Catholic modernity, and were not looked upon with favor when the pontificate of Pius X (1903–1914) took a harder line on doctrine. Heidegger may also have read Maurice Blondel, if we believe the late, oral testimony he gave to Henry Duméry.[103]

Heidegger's remarks about the instruction in philosophy that he received in the Faculty of Theology were not very positive: "The lectures on philosophy prescribed at that time hardly satisfied me";[104] he was referring to the courses given by Johann Übinger, a rather taciturn academic who had defended his thesis on Nicholas of Cusa in Würzburg in 1880, and who taught Heidegger logic four hours a week during the winter semester of 1909–1910 and metaphysics for four hours a week during the summer semester of 1910. After his break with Catholicism, Heidegger constantly denigrated his years at the seminary; if he is not entirely fair to those who were his first teachers (the Catholics Gröber, Schanzenbach, Braig, and Sauer, who sought to modernize Catholicism while at the same time safeguarding its doctrinal orthodoxy), he does make it clear that for him, the university was a broader, more open, freer world, even if he initially studied in the Faculty of Theology. In addition, Heidegger made a few friends in the seminary, for instance Friedrich Helm, "a very cultivated but shy young man, who later became court chaplain and private secretary to two archbishops of Freiburg, Thomas Nörber (deceased 1921) and Carl Fritz (deceased 1931)."[105] At the university, he met Ernst Laslowski, a student in history who came from Kreuzburg in Upper Silesia,[106] and with whom he formed a genuine friendship that was stimulating on the level of scholarship as well as on that of religion, and whose beginnings Heidegger recalled in a letter written for his friend's sixtieth birthday:

> I still clearly remember the first time I visited you in your room in Hildastraße in the summer of 1910—so clearly that I still smell the odor drifting through in the room. This setting is so closely linked to your first stories about your Silesian homeland and your family over there, linked to a free possibility of existence, and to the fine intellectual goods to be possessed and appropriated. Coming from the narrowness of the minor and the major seminary, I found this free and yet self-assured way of dealing with spirituality and the sciences a new experience. In the same way, there was also a growing and expanding agreement between us, dwelling in everything essential and worthy of being thought at that time.[107]

During this period at the seminary, between the summer of 1909 and that of 1911, Heidegger tried to attack the erring ways of the time, the lack of religious belief in the big cities, the egotism of modern culture, and, even within Catholicism, the attempts to carry out a historical revision of Bible interpretation, the condemnation of which put an end to what has been called "the modernist crisis" (1902–1907).

At the beginning of September 1909, Heidegger presided over the festival given in Hausen im Tal on the occasion of the bicentenary of the death of Abraham a Sancta Clara (1644–1709), who was born in the nearby village of Kreenheinstetten, and whom Emperor Leopold I had appointed court preacher. In this way he had held concurrently several high ecclesiastical offices and produced a brilliant body of literature. Despising the appetite for pleasure and the corruption in the cities, and assailing the impious intellect that no longer submitted to the Church's revealed truth, Abraham a Sancta Clara had become a local icon. As the *Heuberger Volksblatt* put it, the goal of the festival given in his honor in September 1909, over which Heidegger presided, was to remind people of the work done by this local luminary, so that it might inspire everyone's life.[108] This celebration was part of the commemorative cycle that had begun in February 1909 with the opening of a subscription for the erection of a monument to Abraham,[109] and was to end with the inauguration of this monument on 15 August 1910, in Kreenheinstetten.

The *Heuberger Volksblatt* lavished praise on the young seminarian who, despite being a country boy, displayed "a great deal of mastery and a keen intelligence" as well as a German style that was ornate ("he opened the festival with poetic expressions") and polished ("a truly classical language"[110]), far from the rustic parlance in which he had grown up. In 1909, his language was certainly that of a cleric, religious and erudite, but it was especially that of a well-educated citizen, remote from the peasant dialect to which he alluded in "Abraham a Sancta Clara" in August 1910, where the local accent serves to sketch a picturesque tableau addressed to urban readers: "The naturalness and freshness of this accent, which is sometimes rather thick, are the specific mark of this event."[111]

Presiding over the festival, Heidegger was able to express his convictions regarding contemporary Catholicism, which were clearly in favor of a vigorous antimodernism. He participated in the lively controversy pursued from 1904 to 1909 between the two German-language Catholic literary reviews, the *Gral* of Richard von Kralik (1852–1934)[112] and the *Hochland* of Karl Muth (1867–1944).[113] The point was to determine whether Catholic culture ought to embrace modern national-Protestant literature within the *Kleindeutschland* (Lesser Germany) dominated by Prussia or, instead, work to restore Catholic culture in the spirit of the Counter-Reformation, in conformity with the spirit of *Großdeutschland* (Greater Germany) that was dominant in Vienna and clearly conservative. Kralik's *Gral* adopted the latter position, while *Hochland* defended the former, denouncing the spirit of the *Kulturkampf* and the prudery and narrow-mindedness that its editor in chief, Karl Muth, saw in contemporary Catholic culture. He wanted to give that culture new life by favoring a high-quality literature of entertainment that was open to modernity. The young Heidegger recognized Muth's good intentions, but condemned "the immoderate criticism of Catholic authors" that "simply demolished what its editor Karl Muth wanted to build."

More partisan than sectarian, Heidegger accused Muth of attacking the wrong enemy, even though he suspected him of relations with "the modernist current" in which he "was still sailing." This suspicion seems to have been nourished by his reading of the encyclical *Pascendi Dominici Gregis* (Feeding the Lord's Flock) of 8 September 1907, in which Pius X had condemned as a "modernist" error the separation of Church and state, not to mention the subordination of the former to the latter. The resolute acceptance of Protestant and Prussian Germany as a legitimate state, the view that religion was a private and not a public matter, and the citizen's unconditional obedience to the empire all represented an attack on the absolute authority of the Church, which had been instituted by God. Opposed to *Hochland*'s modernism, the young seminarian called upon his "audience, in particular secondary school students, to subscribe to *Gral* and to join its youth group."[114] As early as 1909, Heidegger showed his conception of his role: a mastery of speech and writing that was destined to guide the masses, but especially cultivated young people, toward what seemed to him to be right; he did not hesitate to get involved in collective organizations such as the *Gral* youth group, to which he belonged and which took its inspiration from Richard von Kralik.

In the same year, 1909, Kralik had published a synthesis of his ideas under the title "A Program for Catholic Culture," a clerical program that was indissolubly religious and political. Kralik undertook to lead his readers toward a Catholic Germany that would restore, together with Austria, the former Holy Roman Empire of the German Nation, in which the true faith, Roman and eternal, was to triumph over the modern deviancies of a secular world led into atheistic error. A Romantic utopia issuing directly from a memory of the Middle Ages, his Holy Roman Empire of the German Nation was to bring all Germans together around the pope,[115] without giving any consideration to the powerful nationalism that had succeeded in unifying Italians around a king.

For Heidegger, the question of the Church's influence on the state or the latter's secular nature was as significant in his time as the "social question." From this he derived the idea of a fight to the death between the Church and nonclerical doctrines,[116] in particular social democracy, whose "cynicism was well known": "[Social democracy] presents religious faith scornfully, as a private matter, but in truth it fights against it, because it allegedly prevents man from seeking his good on earth, postponing it until heaven."[117]

Similarly, Kralik opposed the "intellectualism" inspired by the Enlightenment, not only because this positivism tended to oppose the Church by refusing to recognize the truth of its faith,[118] but also because it proposed an ideal of social progress to be achieved by spreading knowledge and promoting higher education. Since not everyone could become an intellectual, the number of university graduates had to be limited and a good social harmony maintained to avoid encouraging revolutionary intrigues in which future dangers loomed: "There can be no doubt that our age suffers from this disproportion, that we are raising an educated proletariat for which we cannot provide satisfactory trades, and consequently we are raising a reserve army for the Revolution. According to statistics, this disproportion is especially unhealthy among the Jews. Our first task is to try to determine—and this is a difficult calculation—whether this proportion is proper among Protestants and Catholics, before we advise Catholic peasants and workers to send their sons to secondary schools and universities in greater numbers."[119] A conservative, Kralik was also an anti-Semite who thought that too many Jews had university degrees; this fear of the Jewish revolutionary was among those that, only a few years later, in the face of the large number of socialist or communist Jewish intellectuals, would nourish the still greater fear of the "Red peril" and Judeo-Bolshevism.

Kralik's inclination toward anti-Semitism is not surprising; he was from Vienna, where anti-Semitism was strong, especially since it was encouraged by its populist mayor, Karl Lueger (1844–1910). Lueger had made a strong impression on the young Adolf Hitler, who was living in Vienna precisely at this time (between 1908 and 1913) and later complained in *Mein Kampf* about all the Jewish names that were prominently displayed on advertisements for cultural events in Vienna.[120] It is not clear that the young Heidegger shared this anti-Semitism: in the review of the festivities connected with the inauguration of the monument to Abraham a Sancta Clara (15 August 1910), which he wrote for the conservative periodical *Allegemein Rundschau,* he did mention the "unforgettable Lueger," who had died a few months earlier, on 10 March 1910. The use of the adjective "unforgettable," in itself neutral, to describe Lueger can be explained by the common feeling shared at the festivities, which united Vienna and Kreenheinstetten; conversely, Heidegger also considered Lueger, like Abraham a Sancta Clara and Hofbauer, to be a "visionary" for "a city that is prey to disturbances,"[121] thus perhaps showing an anti-Semitism in tune with the ambient anti-Semitism in Vienna's Catholic circles. The sources are too sparse to authorize more than suppositions in this regard.

Above all, the young Heidegger wanted to assert the value of his native region, of its authentic people and its traditions, in contrast to the decadence of cities in the grip of a decadent "epoch of superficial culture and agitation,"[122] corrupted by the spirit of pleasure, money, and atheistic materialism. In an article entitled "All Souls' Moods," he depicts city people whose physical weakness is merely the expression of a moral and spiritual weakness: "Bundled up, people go along shivering and pale. Without joy, without will, blasé, their colorless, lifeless eyes are unsettled in the blurring, biting November fog. The All Souls' bells ring—they ring in the mournful morning. People in a metropolis do not hear them. They detest their sound, they are looking for the sun and wander through the dark, the dark night that torments them."[123] The irreligious metropolis has no name. It could be Berlin, but in Heidegger's mind it must have been Freiburg. It was also, however, an atopic commonplace of reactionary culture. Both a physical place and an imaginary place, the metropolis is a strong polarity in Heidegger's imagination that we will encounter later: it is a genuine Berlin "way" in Proust's sense, a diseased, disbelieving way opposed to the healthy, pious Meßkirch way, of which the vigorous people of the Heuberg are one of the incarnations—with the sole reservation that Heidegger's personal geography is not strictly local like Proust's, where it is limited to the countryside around Combray; here it is expanded to the scale of Germany as a whole.

In accord with the monks of Beuron and their periodical *Gottesminne,* Heidegger thought the sole source of all genuine art was the people, which had remained faithful to its traditions, as is shown by his review of a travel narrative by the Danish poet Johannes Jørgensen (1866–1956), a convert to Catholicism: "the desire for one's native country" and its traditions, "plenitude" and "the search for God," which are closely linked, were for Heidegger the brilliant inspiration that drove Jørgensen's writings, the "powerful ferment of his art."[124] Similarly, in his positive assessment of Cüpper's *Sealed Lips,* a "narrative taken from the life of the Irish people of the nineteenth century," the young seminarian concluded that "impervious to fashion, [the author] pursues the tranquil path of his healthy art, which has risen up from the people and is instructive."[125]

The perverted spirit of modernity was distinguished by its egotism and rejection of traditions. "In our time [. . .] the artist's person is emphasized. Thus we hear much talk about interesting men, O. Wilde, the dandy; P. Verlaine, 'the brilliant drunkard'; M. Gorki, the great vagabond; the superman Nietzsche: interesting men." Condemning the exaltation of the originality of the great men of letters of the period, Heidegger bases himself on the example of Jørgensen's conversion in 1896, which participated in the fin de siècle movement that led so many intellectuals to convert or return to Catholicism, a movement that was particularly spectacular in France, with Huysmans,

Claudel, Péguy, and so many others. Disappointed by the religions that their time offered them, they turned toward the mysteries and promises of salvation afforded by Roman Catholicism. In Heidegger's view, Jørgensen, who had been "an atheist at the age of eighteen" and was immersed in modern Danish literary trends, in which "the spirit of Nietzsche and Zola was becoming omnipotent," converted to Catholicism, not as a result of a cult of the self eager for new ways of dramatizing itself, but as a personal itinerary like that of Augustine, a private and solemn effect of the Holy Spirit that grants its Grace to a person who was formerly so far away: "And if you want to live by the spirit, earn your salvation, then die, annihilate the unworthiness in you, act with supernatural grace and you will be reborn. Thus the philosopher-poet, fortified by will, reassured by hope, now reposes in the shadow of the Cross: a modern Saint Augustine."[126]

Imbued with Augustinism, from this time onward Heidegger thought more as a philosopher than as a believer, even if he was engaged in defending the self-evidence of religion. Philosophy had to be "the bulwark of faith and the strong defense of religion."[127] His conception of philosophy was in perfect harmony with Rome's: if Grace is granted by God, philosophy, as the servant of the faith and of theology, must serve the latter as "the firm rampart of religion"[128] against the attacks of the secular world. It was up to philosophy to dissipate the false enlightenment of a sophistical reason by means of a logic centered on the principle of noncontradiction, in harmony with a conception of a truth that was revealed by natural and supernatural enlightenment, in history, to be sure, but that was in itself not subject to evolution. Heidegger's philosophy was conservative and fundamentally ahistorical: "in truth a mirror of the eternal,"[129] a *philosophia perennis* valid in all times because it is absolutely true de jure if not de facto, it condenses people's continual efforts, past and present, to understand Creation and the Creator into a rational totality seen *sub specie aeternitatis,* that is, from the point of view of eternity and of God.

A "mirror of the eternal," philosophy is constituted within a tradition that continues but does not challenge the obvious truth of what the Church has recognized all through the centuries as its "eternal treasure of truth,"[130] adding to the Church Fathers the Scholastics, as *Aeterni Patris* puts it: "the doctors of the Middle Ages, who are called Scholastics, addressed themselves to a great work—that of diligently collecting, and sifting, and storing up, as it were, in one place, for the use and convenience of posterity, the rich and fertile harvests of Christian learning scattered abroad in the voluminous works of the holy Fathers."[131] If it is to evolve, Catholic thought must set its sights on a greater precision, not a revolution; an eternal and rational portrait of Creation and the Creator, philosophy can only be refined and not reconsidered.

All modern doctrines in contradiction with Scholasticism are in error. The mutual contradictions of new philosophic trends demonstrate in and of themselves their manifest error: "The flagrant contradictions of our time, here the mad fanaticism of the reality of the naturalist-socialist order of life, there the new imaginary worlds and values of existence that construct the philosophy of immanence, are the result of an unrestrained autonomism."[132] For the young Heidegger, this absence of logic, this debauchery of subjectivity, is only the result of the lack of virtue of the modern spirit, which is at once too weak and too lazy to meet the demands of logic: "A rigorous, glacially cold logic is repugnant to the delicacy of the modern soul. 'Thought' can no longer allow itself to be confined within the immutable limits and eternal principles of logic. [. . .] Rigorous logical thought that is hermetically sealed off from any affective influence proceeding from the heart, and scientific work that is truly without assumptions, are based on an ethical power, the art of distancing oneself and alienating oneself from oneself."[133] Rigorous thought is thus a kind of asceticism, a mortification of the self in order to receive—if not Grace and rebirth as a Christian (*per mortem ad vitam*, "through death toward life," as Heidegger entitled his first article on Jørgensen)—at least the rational truth that can only fall into line with the great ideas of the past, that is, the Church Fathers and the Scholastics. Without that, the mind can only invent an eclectic worldview and fall into the multiple and contradictory errors of the time, which include Nietzsche's superman, Darwinism and its monistic avatars (Haeckel), and Zola's "natural socialism."

His conviction that Catholic truth was eternal led Heidegger to adopt an antimodernist position concerning exegesis, in conformity with that of *Der Akademiker*,[134] for which he wrote, and which adopted the position taken by F. W. Förster in his *Authority and Freedom:* "And the Church will, if it is to remain true to its eternal treasure of truth, justifiably counteract the destructive influences of modernism, which is not conscious of the most acute contradictions in which its modern views of life stand in relation to the ancient wisdom of the Christian tradition."[135] Heidegger refers to the Church's "eternal treasure of truth" in the context of the modernist crisis: with his encyclical *Pascendi Dominici Gregis*, Pius X had condemned a disparate collection of theses which, within the Church itself, sought to renovate it by taking advantage of the modern development of the sciences, notably historiography.[136] The Bible was subjected to a critical reading (Moses, for example, was no longer the indisputable author of the Pentateuch), and Jesus, the dogmas, and the Church were resituated in a human history. Particularly targeted was Alfred Loisy, who had been excommunicated in 1908. Heidegger seems not to have had a precise knowledge of this question; modernism as he conceived it involved a critique of subjectivism, of inner feeling as a source of knowledge flowing from pride and a cult of the self in revolt against the Church's authority. The encyclical had condemned the same flaws in the modernists.[137] But Heidegger's remarks were directed more against the Church's external enemies than against the enemies within that the pope had designated. He assailed primarily modernity's aberrations, in line with Catholic criticism since the *Syllabus,* and especially with that of his teacher Braig.

In "What Should an Educated Man Know about Modernism?,"[138] which purports to be a commentary on *Pascendi Dominici Gregis,* Braig noted that the word "modernism" was not used to target modern science in general, but only a "nest of errors"[139] whose "root" is a "false philosophy," "agnosticism":[140] "The modernist is agnostic, asserting that man can know nothing about God and the divine, and hence he makes fun of those who are, on the contrary, convinced of the possibility and certainty of a rational knowledge of God."[141] Proceeding from this point of departure in line with the encyclical, the theologian shifted his target away from the Catholic Church and toward Protestant theology and Kantian and neo-Kantian philosophy: "The modernists are the (French, Italian, British) students of the Kants, Schleiermachers, Ritschls, and Harnacks, with a rationalistic, theologically liberal philosophical discourse emerging from German Protestantism."[142] For Braig, modernism was merely an immoderate assertion of the religious feeling of a self that resisted anything outside itself, and first of all the Church's authority, tradition, and historical truth. In his view, "historical truth, like all truth—the most triumphant brilliance here is mathematical truth, the most rigorous form of eternal truth—is anterior to the subjective self and exists without it. I cannot write its history, but only understand it [. . .]. No Kant, no Kantian, no effort to place things vis-à-vis the autonomous self can change the law that holds that the human self is oriented in relation to things."[143] The injustice toward Alfred Loisy's rigorous thinking is patent, but that was not what was at stake: Braig was defending the Church's tradition, supporting the pope and his encyclical, and to do so, half philosophically, half sophistically, he set forth the principles of his conception of knowledge, implicitly postulating that his adversaries were violating them.

Following Braig, Heidegger believed that the issue was the opposition between an "unlimited autonomization [of the self]" and a glacially rigorous logic that demanded obedience to the Church's authority and to its eternal treasure of truth. The details of the criticism of the Bible, of the story of Christ, and of Church history mattered less to him than this death of the self, which alone made it possible to be born into true life, in and through the religion of the Church. This led Heidegger to be extremely intransigent: of course he found genuine virtues in Förster's work and recommended it to others; but he thought it was lukewarm because, "along with the interspersed glosses providing a deeper understanding of Nietzsche, the remarks on biblical criticism, the Christ myth,[144] and so on, one occasionally finds, precisely at the end of the book where the author deals with modernism, passages which call for a critique, or at least a sharper distinction."[145]

In everything he wrote during this period, Heidegger played the role of an apologist: he sought to use philosophy to defend the Church's treasure of truth, to dismantle modern quibbles, and to guide minds toward the right path.[146] He had occasion to do so especially in Meßkirch, which was disrupted in the spring of 1911 by another episode of *Kulturkampf* triggered by a demand that Pius X had included in his *Sacrorum Antistitum*,[147] issued on 1 September 1910: before being ordained, priests were required to take an antimodernist oath, and this decree allowed liberals not only to return to the well-worn theme of Catholicism's hostility to science but also to point to a Jesuit conspiracy against the intellect.[148] In keeping with the denunciation of the Catholic Church's obscurantism, an article of 5 April 1911 mocked the works on Hell written by the theologian Josef Bautz and expressed deep concern regarding their possible effects on the teaching of geology in secondary schools, precisely because of the antimodernist oath:

> Let us imagine a case in which a teacher who is an ordained priest finds himself obliged to talk, in *Prima* or *Obertertia*, about the interior of the Earth. Having set forth the well-supported theory of magma, as a man of honor he would have to go on: "That is the conception of so-called free science, or rather pseudo-science. The conception approved by the Catholic Church is the following." Then he would teach the view proposed by Bautz, a specialist on Hell who lives in Münster, Germany—pointing out that Bautz's doctrine should be seen as completely reliable and theological in general.[149]

This classic *Kulturkampf* discourse, simply adapted to the quarrel over the modernist oath, was countered by an equally classic Catholic defense denouncing the liberals' relentlessness and ultimate intolerance, the contradiction between their acts and the principles of freedom they professed.[150] For his part, Heidegger forwent political controversy and situated his reply within scientific and religious polemics. Not without scorn, piling up references to Jesuit works recognized outside the Church for their intrinsic value, he tried to crush his opponent under the weight and the solidity of his argumentation: "If the author knows and has studied even one of these works, how does he arrive at these assertions that don't hold water? If he doesn't know them, and hasn't studied hem, how can he allow himself, as the author of a 'scientific' article, to disregard the first commandment of any learned work: 'Never talk or write about what you do not understand'? I would like to give the author a piece of advice, sincerely and with good will: he should keep quiet about philosophical questions, otherwise he might once again fall into an awkward situation he doesn't understand."[151] In addition to these accumulated arguments from authority, and beyond the contempt he showed, Heidegger sought to refute the idea that the antimodernist oath would oblige priests teaching in secondary schools to teach Josef Bautz's ideas about Hell. He resituated Bautz's opinions within the framework of the levels of truth recognized by the Church and the limits it imposed on research, limits he regarded as purely negative, defining what cannot be accepted rather than what must be accepted: "The Church does not prescribe positively to the researcher the result at which he must arrive; more than that, it provides only a negative norm."[152]

Moving beyond simple defense, Heidegger attacked the errors of modern science, whose dogmatism he denounced by challenging the justification of human evolution supported by the discovery of human remains from earlier stages of development. Fossils were not in themselves proof for the young Heidegger,[153] who probably thought he was defending in this way the Church's traditional position that man was created by God in his own image, and was not the result of a millennia-long evolution from animals. This critical posture with regard to modern science and what he considered to be its errors led Heidegger to make an apologetic use of logic, in line, moreover, with the Christian view of logic according to Raymond Lull (1235–1315): this Catalan Franciscan's magnum opus, the *Ars Magna,* determined the set of combinations of all possible propositions, in order to refute definitively the arguments advanced by "infidels" and lead them to convert. As much as he could, Heidegger introduced logical subtleties (the simple difference in degree of knowledge and not in its substance between *demonstrari* and *cognosci,* between the possibility that God's existence can be demonstrated on the basis of knowledge of the Creation and the fact that it can simply be known). He did not hesitate to tell his opponent that his "logic had feet of clay" and that one of his arguments was not only not pertinent to the question (the reference to the Cartesian *cogito, ergo sum*, "I think, therefore I am," in the dispute over the antimodernist oath), but also logically weak in itself: "What the developments on Descartes are doing here seems to me unclear. That his proposition, like his whole rationalist method in metaphysics, is untenable has long since been shown by rigorous logic."[154] With a certain smugness in his judgment of Descartes, not entirely unjustified with regard to his opponent, Heidegger expresses himself in a tone that testifies to a scorn and an anger far removed from the distancing of self that he thought a glacially rigorous logic required.

In any case, Heidegger showed that he had learned the lesson of Husserlian logic, using in this way the modern distinction between content and logical act, which he put in the service of the antimodernist oath: "However, the author wants to alert me, with commonplace evidence, that each act of knowledge is a psychological process of the knowing subject, and hence subjective. The psychological act is subjective, but not the logical content; and that is precisely what is at issue in this case."[155] A logical operation requires a subject to perform it, and he does so at a specific moment, but that cannot in any way challenge as such the eternity and universality of the content itself. In this case, the intervention of a knowing subject is certainly necessary to arrive at the knowledge that God created the world, based on the observation of its order, but that intervention does not logically taint with subjectivity the knowledge thereby obtained. As interpreted by Heidegger, this was the position of the Vatican Council on which the antimodernist oath was based.

As for the content itself, Heidegger did not consider the oath very scandalous: in addition to the fact that it added nothing new to Catholic doctrine,[156] it seemed to him normal that the Church should require absolute obedience on the essential points of dogma. What was at stake was the battle against modernism, rather than the oath itself. Above all, for Heidegger the seminarian, the antimodernist oath was a matter for specialists: just as the anti-Dreyfusards believed that intellectuals had no more right to have an opinion regarding military justice than a soldier an opinion on a question of prosody, as a student in theology, Heidegger thought that only experts, theologians, and philosophers specializing in the question could offer judgments on the oath. In that regard, Heidegger was able to make his scholarly and moral legitimacy accepted in his hometown, which, under the influence of the

Heuberger Volksblatt,[157] recognized his knowledge and his eloquence as well as his authority as an apologist.

A Promising Catholic Philosopher (1912–1914)

The seminarian entered all the more vigorously into this controversy in his native region because in the spring of 1911, he was idle in Meßkirch. He had, at first temporarily, then definitively, abandoned his theological studies. He went no further than the fourth semester, and then enrolled in the Faculty of Mathematics, a break that he explained in his 1922 *Vita* by tracing its origin back to his beginning at the seminary: "In the course of the first semester my program in philosophy and theology had taken a direction such that at the beginning of 1911 I stopped studying theology because I could not take the [anti] modernist oath that was then expressly demanded."[158] When he was thirty-three years old and applying for a chair in philosophy at the—Protestant—University of Göttingen, he explained his break with Catholicism both by his modern philosophical orientation (Lotze, Husserl) and by his Protestant and liberal readings in the history of religion; having become a modernist, he could not have taken the oath that the Church would have required of him for his ordination. It was therefore logical, natural, and desirable that he declare his opposition to the unacceptable and leave a degree program leading to ordination as a Catholic priest.

The pains Heidegger took to disguise his Nazi past—which, as Hugo Ott has demonstrated, involved transforming an authentic, revolutionary enthusiasm for National Socialism into an effort to safeguard the university against Nazism—were not unprecedented. The 1922 *Vita* is a striking example of how much Heidegger rewrote his life when his self-interest was at stake. In 1911, the young theologian had no objections to the antimodernist oath; on the contrary, he publicly defended it, writing and speaking to demonstrate its legitimacy, and violently attacking modernism, which he conceived much more broadly than did the encyclical *Pascendi Dominici Gregis* of 1907, without his will to do battle with modernism relenting as a result. One couldn't be too rigorous in fighting modernism.

The reason he ended his studies in theology lay elsewhere than in his alleged opposition to the oath required by the pope. As with the Jesuit novitiate, so too with the seminary: his heart problems led his superiors to order him to give up the path to the priesthood. On 16 February, because of these problems "of an asthmatic nature," Dr. Heinrich Gassert, the Freiburg seminary's physician, suggested that Heidegger should return to Meßkirch for a few weeks of "complete rest."[159] Dr. Bilz, the seminary's rector, thus wrote a note dated 2 April 1911: "Martin Heidegger (second course) had to interrupt his work in mid-February, following further cardiac problems of a nervous nature. He has gone home with our permission. It has been recommended that he suspend all work until he completely recovers."[160] In his 1915 curriculum vitae, Heidegger explained these troubles in terms of both overwork and a physical weakness due to excessive athletic activity: "Busying myself increasingly with philosophical problems, alongside duties imposed by my professional studies, I suffered, after three semesters, from severe overwork. My cardiac disease, which was due to an excess of athletic activity in the past, manifested itself so strongly that later employment in the service of the Church was presented to me as being out of the question."[161] It seems that, when his condition did not improve, the seminary removed Martin Heidegger from its rolls.

Heidegger's cardiac troubles were not manifesting themselves for the first time, and they continued, more or less, from then on. They were psychosomatic, reflecting both a physical fragility and an unbearable internal tension in which overwork might have played a role, but not exclusively. The Jesuit novitiate had confronted him with obedience to irrevocable vows, at least one of which, chastity, seemed absolutely incompatible with what he later showed himself to be: a philosopher who moved with agility in the heaven of ideas, but a being in the flesh for more than one woman. Perhaps still more important was the growing desire, inspired by his model Carl Braig, for an academic career rather than ordination.[162] These moments of doubt shed a different light on Heidegger's engagement in his hometown during the spring of 1911: having time to work on behalf of the Church, he must have found at least the comfort of doing what seemed to him right, even if he probably would have preferred to pursue his studies in Freiburg. The bitter scorn and anger he showed during the modernist quarrel in Meßkirch expressed in part his discontent at this time.

Since Heidegger's condition was not improving significantly, the seminary discouraged him altogether from following the path to the priesthood.[163] Thereupon, he enrolled in Freiburg's Faculty of Mathematics for the winter semester of 1911–1912, to study mathematics, physics, chemistry, and botany before taking the state examination to teach in a Gymnasium. At first glance, this choice might seem surprising, but it was deeply anchored in the utility that Heidegger recognized in the mathematical and natural sciences, all "objective" sciences that made it possible to approach God's truth, and familiarity with which would also enable him to combat the agnostic or irreligious temptations at work within an increasingly secular society. He resumed the path of another of his models, the Christian apologist Paul von Schanz, who had initially taught mathematical and natural sciences for six years at the Gymnasium in Rottweil before taking a chair in Tübingen, at first in exegesis, and then in dogmatics and apologetics.

Heidegger followed that path for three semesters. He received instruction in various subjects—analytical geometry, algebraic analysis, integral calculus, advanced algebra, differential calculus, theory of differential equations, experimental and theoretical physics, inorganic experimental chemistry, botany, and zoology—which did not diminish "[his] philosophical interest, [. . .] on the contrary."[164] He studied with Arthur Schneider (1876–1945) and Heinrich Rickert (1863–1936). These courses, in which a large role was given to the philosophy of the sciences, complemented the science classes Heidegger had taken and his inclination for logic, which was further strengthened by the discovery, in Rickert's seminar, of the writings of one of Rickert's former students, Emil Lask (1875–1915), *The Logic of Philosophy and the Doctrine of Categories* (1911) and *The Doctrine of Judgment* (1912),[165] which were also inspired by Husserl. Similarly, he read more broadly in authors who were not very Catholic, like Bergson, Spinoza (a Jew by descent whose philosophical deism had become for many people synonymous with atheism), and Kant (a rationalist Protestant attacked by Heidegger's Catholic teacher Carl Braig). Subsequently, Arthur Schneider directed Heidegger's doctoral thesis, and Heinrich Rickert his habilitation thesis. The latter, which allowed Heidegger to hope that he might be authorized to teach at a university, explains in part why, in the 1915 curriculum vitae, he discussed at length the importance of Rickert and his school, whereas he said almost nothing about Schneider. Thanks to Rickert's school, Heidegger learned "above all to see philosophical problems as problems" and received "an overview of the essence of logic, the philosophical discipline" that interested him most, "yesterday and today," without this altering his "fundamental philosophical convictions," which "remained those of Aristotelian and Scholastic philosophy."[166]

Their published correspondence shows that Rickert really counted for Heidegger. Along with Windelband and Lask, Rickert was the last of the three representatives of the Southwest German School, or Baden School, one of the two essential movements in neo-Kantianism that had developed in Germany starting in the 1870s, with the goal of moving beyond the Hegelianism that was then dominant. The other neo-Kantian school was that of Marburg, represented by Cohen, Natorp, and Cassirer, to whom we shall return later. Rickert was well aware of his pupil's Scholastic convictions, which Heidegger himself mentions in his curriculum vitae; they were more an enrichment of than an obstacle to their exchanges, as is apparent in the long and interesting letter that Heidegger sent Rickert from Meßkirch on 12 October 1913: "Unfortunately, it is only today that I am able to express to you my warmest thanks for the lively stimulation and philosophical training that I was able to derive from your lectures and especially from the seminar. It is true that my fundamental philosophical intuitions are very different; nonetheless, I would be the last to adhere to that famous and pitiful method that consists in seeing in modern philosophy nothing more than a 'series of errors,' the result of 'atheism' and things of that kind."[167] Rickert opened his young student's mind, making him aware of a modern mode of thought that was non-Catholic but nonetheless valuable, and that did not fall under the jurisdiction of logic, as Husserl's philosophy did.

Moreover, between 1910 and 1914 Heidegger is supposed to have read many and diverse works that helped him acquire a knowledge of history and fashionable authors—not only Nietzsche's *Will to Power,* but also Kierkegaard and Dostoevsky, Rilke's and Trakl's poetry, and the complete works of Dilthey.[168] Heidegger probably discovered the latter during Rickert's seminar in the winter semester of 1913–1914, which included exercises on "the philosophy of history (methodology of the sciences of culture)." His readings of Dilthey went hand in hand with an awakening of his interest in history elicited by Rickert's lectures on the history of philosophy from Kant to Nietzsche, Finke's lectures on the Renaissance, and then on the origins of the Reformation, and still more by Wilhelm Vöge (1868–1952), about whom he later said that he received from him, as much as from Carl Braig, "the vocation that was decisive, and which therefore could not be expressed in words, for [his] own later university teaching."[169] A historian of art and Erwin Panofsky's teacher, Vöge was the author of *The French Plastic Art;*[170] in the winter semester of 1913–1914 he gave a course of lectures, which Heidegger attended, titled "Albert Dürer and German Painting in the Fifteenth and Sixteenth Centuries."

No one knows what guided the choice of these two courses by Finke and Vöge, which were very coherent with one another: both covered the period of the Reformation in Germany and its beginnings, a theme Heidegger had encountered in the history of the Church while he was at the seminary, though the approach to it was entirely different, because it was Catholic and thus focused on the Counter-Reformation. Finke opened up a completely different perspective on the same theme, seen from the point of view of the Protestant reformers, whereas Vöge completed the picture of this period by studying a major German painter and his relationship to the national painting of the time. As a result, Heidegger's intellectual and even religious horizons became even broader.

This new course of study, these new readings, and the intellectual development that resulted from them did little to calm the deep uneasiness that troubled Martin Heidegger and continued to foster his poor health, his overwork, and his insomnia, as a result of which the doctor had "forbidden any intellectual effort for a more extended period."[171]

His insomnia, which was sometimes absolute, attested to the psychosomatic nature of the disorders that had prevented him from completing the novitiate with the Jesuits, and then barred the path to the priesthood. Giving up his destiny as a priest was hard for him, and his mother did not understand this change. "He delved & sought & became quieter and quieter & already he had a vague ideal—the scholar—in his mind—though his pious, simple mother hoped for a 'priest'—and it was a struggle for him to win the right to live purely on knowledge."[172] The conflict with his mother's imperious desire that he become a priest, his deep wish to become a scholar, and his difficulty in explaining to her what philosophy was and its role in the salvation of human beings (their "eternal happiness"): all that is obviously true. But of course with distance, Heidegger simplified his itinerary: he knew that there was no incompatibility between becoming a Jesuit and becoming a philosopher, as can be seen in what he wrote about the Meßkirch controversy during the spring of 1911. Ultimately, there was no real incompatibility, either, between becoming a priest and pursuing a course of theological study that could put philosophy at the center of scientific interest—Carl Braig was a clear example of this for the former seminarian. Heidegger's presentation of this conflict with his mother enabled him modestly to conceal his failures, which would not help him win the heart of a Protestant girl like Elfride Petri. Similarly, it illustrated the state of his relationship to a career in the priesthood: kicked out of the theology program, he had fully appropriated the path of philosophy, which gradually took root after the interlude in mathematics. There remained a violent sense of guilt and an equally violent conflict with his mother: aspiring to be a philosopher, Heidegger strayed from the path that his family had laid out for him.

Along with his sense of guilt, the lack of money ate away at him. Ott has shown that starting in the summer semester of 1912, the University of Freiburg gave Heidegger a scholarship of 400 marks, but this did not suffice, nor did the money he earned by tutoring; his friend Laslowski tried to get him a loan, which he finally succeeded in obtaining, at the end of 1912 or the beginning of 1913, from a former member of his confraternity of Catholic students, Unitas of Breslau.[173] This material support, meager but vital, was granted Heidegger because through his philosophical production he had come to be seen as a young and brilliant hope for Catholic thought. He began to take the exhilarating and disturbing paths of autonomous, responsible thinking. He succeeded in publishing an article entitled "The Problem of Reality in Modern Philosophy" in the *Philosophisches Jahrbuch*, edited by Clemens Baeumker, a professor of philosophy at the University of Strasburg and president of the Görres Gesellschaft, which wanted to encourage new generations of Catholic philosophers. Similarly, in 1912 Heidegger published, in three parts, his "New Investigations in Logic" in the review *Literarische Rundschau*, edited by Joseph Sauer, who had been his teacher at the seminary.

Sauer was a Catholic reformer close to Hermann Schell, Albert Ehrard, and Martin Spahn.[174] His research on the history of art and Christian archeology sought to revitalize Catholic thought by means of these positive disciplines. The spirit of the articles by Heidegger that Sauer published was in complete accord with this aspiration to an orthodox renewal of Catholicism in opposition to the modern world's challenges to the Church and its doctrine. Heidegger wanted to contribute to the "religious and cultural development of our Church"; instead of adopting a strategy of introversion, Catholicism had to resolutely stand up to science, as Heidegger said well in a letter to Sauer written in March 1912[175]—not reject it as a whole, but develop it philosophically in accord with Catholicism, and with complete intellectual rigor. Heidegger distanced himself from the view of philosophy as a bulwark of religious faith: he wanted to go beyond "a sterile exercise in faultfinding" and a Scholastic "exposure of contradictions," that is, beyond the purely defensive use of philosophy around a fixed faith and worldview driven into a corner by the evolution of the secular world. Logic must not be merely negative; external reality had to be conceived in an objective and constructive way in conjunction with mathematics, through the articulation of the abstract but universal conception of the object by means of logic and mathematics with space and time, with due attention to the revolution to which Albert Einstein had subjected physics with his special theory of relativity, as formulated in his article "On the Electrodynamics of Moving Bodies" (1905).

These works, and his "New Investigations in Logic" in particular, put Heidegger in the van of a Catholic revival in Baden; his friend Laslowski, who was studying in Rome in 1912, was able to inform Heidegger of the success of this article, telling him, on 20 January 1913, that the loan they had hoped to obtain was going to be granted. Laslowski enthusiastically expressed his admiration of his friend: "My dear fellow, I have the feeling that you are destined to become one of the truly great, and the universities will be falling over each other to get you. Anything less would be inadmissible."[176] Before that could happen, however, Heidegger still had to earn a doctorate; he therefore set out on that path, giving up mathematics and the natural sciences.

Martin Heidegger defended his thesis, "The Theory of Judgment in Psychologism,"[177] on 26 July 1913. Directed by Arthur Schneider, a professor of Christian philosophy, it was a complete success: the jury awarded the degree *summa cum laude*.[178] Like his letter to Josef Sauer, his starting point was classically Catholic and Scholastic, but he reshaped this intellectual tradition, as he noted in his 1915 curriculum vitae: "However, my fundamental philosophical convictions remained those of Aristotelian Scholasticism. Over time, I recognized that the intellectual heritage of which it is the depository allowed and required a much broader exploitation and use. That is why I tried, in my thesis 'The Theory of Judgment in Psychologism,' to shed light on a central problem in logic and in the theory of knowledge, basing myself on both modern logic and the fundamental judgments of Aristotelian Scholasticism; these analyses were supposed to provide the foundation for further research."[179] Attacking proponents of psychologism like Theodor Lipps and Wilhelm Wundt, who wanted to subordinate logic to psychology, Heidegger drew notably on one of Husserl's ideas that we have already seen him expound: the distinction between a logical operation, which requires a subject embedded in a particular time, and a logical content, which on the contrary belongs to the domain of the eternal and universal. True to his first ideas when he was at the seminary, Heidegger sought to confine the self to its proper place, subordinate to an objective reality which, whether internal or external, reflected God.

At least for a time, the glory conferred by the doctorate erased the torments of having to give up his studies in theology. In Germany, the doctorate was the intellectual title of nobility par excellence; as elsewhere in Europe, it made its holder a notable of the respectable bourgeoisie. For example, in Austria, "only 'academic' training, which opened the gates to the university, conferred all its value on a young man in these times of 'enlightened liberalism.' That is why every 'good' family's ambition was that at least one of its sons could add some kind of doctoral title to his name."[180] The holder of a doctorate in Germany used the title "doctor" even if he was not a physician. This was not the case in France: in his novel *A Sentimental Education,* Flaubert mocks with mordant humor Deslauriers, the friend of the indecisive antihero Frédéric Moreau, a lawyer who sees to it that he is introduced as "Dr. Deslauriers" to Mme. Arnoux, who replies that she has not asked for a physician.[181]

The portrait done of Heidegger in his office after he received his doctorate depicted this new position: with a sober hairstyle and a carefully trimmed mustache on his upper lip, the twenty-four-year-old philosopher is trying to look calm, his left hand tucked into his jacket, his right arm resting on the desk, and dressed in an appropriate suit and tie, with his books in the background. Less ill at ease than his father is in the portrait of his parents that has come down to us, the doctor of philosophy is still dressed in black, which was for men the color or noncolor emblematic of bourgeois respectability. The books arranged behind him and piled up in disorder in front of him were the tangible sign of his new social position, based on knowledge and incomparably higher than that of his parents. In fact, his doctorate surrounded him in a cloud of glory not only in Freiburg, but also in Meßkirch, even in the milieu of liberal notables who despised the Catholic petty bourgeois tradesmen and farmers from whom Heidegger was descended; in that respect, he had forged a kind of social revenge for himself. The sexton's son had become a gentleman.

Heidegger began to earn back his family's unconditional pride, despite the fact that his friends and family had little familiarity with these bourgeois and academic heights. "His father [. . .] was proud & is so to this day, however strange and incomprehensible all his son's work might be to him."[182] This was also an opportunity to reshape the family mythologies, as when the old godmother complacently claimed: "I always knew it, his great-grandfather was just the same, always busy with books; in the Danube Valley where his estate lay among the towering castles of the von Zimmern, he would sit on Sundays with the books he had picked up at the market in Ulm."[183] Heidegger was a celebrity in his hometown. As he later recalled, "it was in the local paper."[184] In fact, the *Heuberger Volksblatt*—always ready to celebrate the successes of native sons, a group in which Heidegger held a prominent place—continued to maintain this ink-and-newsprint link by warmly congratulating the sexton's son who had become a doctor: "On Saturday, we had very delightful news from Freiburg. Mr. Martin Heidegger, a student who is the son of Heidegger, the local sexton, has completed his doctorate in philosophy and mathematics and, indeed, with honors (*summa cum laude*). We heartily congratulate Dr. Heidegger and his rejoicing friends and family! According to our information, Mr. Heidegger will soon undertake a greater intellectual project. We wish him the best of luck!"[185]

The celebration of this veritable collective glory made this "a fete for the little town such as had never been seen before." To be sure, Heidegger was not the first son of Meßkirch to become a doctor—if only because Conrad Gröber, his paternal friend, had been a doctor before him; conversely, he may have been the first to be rewarded with a fete in honor of this great success. At the center of his Catholic community, the sexton's son still figured prominently in local life when he returned to his region, and his doctorate was in itself an event for the Catholics of Meßkirch.

The attention the Catholics from Heidegger's hometown accorded him also resulted from his activities in his hometown, where he continued to give lectures—seven of them between 1912 and 1913, usually delivered in a tavern (Straub's "Bear Inn") on Sundays or Mondays, all sponsored by Catholic organizations, the Central Men's Association (Männerverein Zentrum), or the Catholic Youth Association (Katholische Gesellen- und Jünglingsverein), founded in 1909. His audiences were sometimes large; for example, on 21 October 1912 he spoke before ninety members of the Men's Association.[186] The reviews in the *Heuberger Volksblatt* reflect a growing warmth and esteem for the young Heidegger, who is described on 14 March 1913 as "an old acquaintance and a very popular speaker."[187] His themes were diverse: in early 1912, they tended mainly toward the natural sciences (earthquakes, the animal origin of the human species, spiritualism), and later toward philosophy and politics (Nietzsche, support for the Görres Society, socialism from the standpoint of science), in harmony with the philosopher's evolution at this time in his life.

Contrary to the high esteem in which Heidegger later held Nietzsche, at this time he considered the latter an atheistic thinker, a veritable "poison for youth," whose thought was characteristic of the "metropolis"[188] and of madness, as well as the source of free-thinking. Jointly condemned for the aberrations of an atheistic age despite their opposite positions, Nietzsche and socialism were united in their hostility to God. The laudatory commentary in the *Heuberger Volksblatt*[189] gives little precise information regarding the content of the twenty-four-year-old Heidegger's speech on socialism. By contrast, it allows us to understand clearly on what level he sought to approach politics: not on the superficial and trivial level accessible to the common man, but instead on the profound scientific and philosophical level, where the true nature of things becomes comprehensible to a few rare minds capable of delving so deeply. Here we find again the position Heidegger formulated regarding the antimodernist oath: this is a matter for specialists, and others would do well to avoid making judgments about it. Perhaps Heidegger's proclivity for acting as a guide derived from his status as a leader among the children of Meßkirch that was once conferred on him by his possession of the key to the bell tower, or simply from the example of active involvement set by the parish priest, Brandhuber.

It was imperative that the people support Catholic knowledge and its pastors, whether ordained or lay. The article of 25 October 1912 reports the review that Heidegger wrote about a general assembly of the Görres Society held in Freiburg the same year, an opportunity for the young student subsidized by the Society to advertise it and try to persuade the Central Men's Association to support it by becoming a member.[190] Heidegger had certainly understood that the organization of the faithful, a growing tendency within the Church, was an extremely powerful grassroots movement at work in the society of his time; however, the magic of his words did not suffice to give the fervent Catholics of Meßkirch the collective resources necessary to satisfy him without an intolerable financial sacrifice—money being, even in the pious (but parsimonious) country of the Swabian Jura, something that was particularly painful to give up.

These four years were decisive: having left in 1909 to enter the Jesuit order, the young Heidegger emerged in 1913 with a doctorate in philosophy from the University of Freiburg, having been forced to abandon the novitiate, and then the seminary, because of his psychosomatic cardiac problems. Although he now preferred a career as a scholar to a career in the priesthood, he wanted to be in the van of Catholic knowledge, battling against impious modernity, using the weapons of a renewed philosophy and logic. A Catholic reformer in this respect, Heidegger was also an anti-modernist out of loyalty to the Church's "treasure of truth" and a concern for coherence with the priceless legacy of both the Catholic and the popular traditions; he was all the more attentive to defending the Church and the *Heimat* against an impious secular world that was deaf to the legacy of the past because he was a fierce adversary of the revision of the religious sciences. He situated himself resolutely in the opposition between two "ways": that of Meßkirch, of the Catholic countryside faithful to itself and to Rome, and that of Berlin, which wanted to do away with the Church and replace the Roman Catholic faith with some kind of liberal scientism.

3 • A Philosopher in the Great War

(1914–1918)

> War, however, is only our wretched expedient of asserting a right by force, an expedient adopted in the state of nature, where no court of justice exists which could settle the matter in dispute. In circumstances like these, neither of the two parties can be called an unjust enemy, because this form of speech presupposes a legal decision: the issue of the conflict—just as in the case of the so-called judgments of God—decides on which side right is. Between states, however, no punitive war (*bellum punitivum*) is thinkable, because between them a relation of superior and inferior does not exist. Whence it follows that a war of extermination, where the process of annihilation would strike both parties at once and all right as well, would bring about perpetual peace [*Friede*] only in the great graveyard [*Friedhof*] of the human race.
>
> *Immanuel Kant,* Perpetual Peace: A Philosophical Essay, *trans. M. Campbell-Smith, 1, 6*

2 August 1914, the bloody dawn of a century of steel and death: the artillery barrages on the Somme or at Verdun, like the gas attacks at Ypres and Caporetto, were the ancestors of the gas chambers and carpet bombing of the Second World War. Sabers, bayonets, rifles, machine guns, cannons, tanks, planes, bullets, shells, and gas: what Western peoples had industrialized to remake the Earth in the image of their desires, they turned around en masse, to destroy one another and to reveal to the whole world the mysteries of the industrial death that put its stamp on the twentieth century. Strangely, given its extremely serious consequences, the Great War had its immediate origin in the assassination, perpetrated on 28 June 1914 by Serbian independence

fighters, of Archduke Franz Ferdinand of Austria—an event in itself minor and far from being able to explain by itself this war, whose length, intensity, and consequences were then unimaginable.

Martin Heidegger was in Meßkirch,[1] as he usually was during vacations, when the pleasant summer of 1914 witnessed the blossoming of a sinister harvest. The philosopher volunteered on 1 August,[2] when the general mobilization was decreed, but was declared unfit for service; he made a further attempt to enlist the same month, with the same result: "Before a week had passed, I had to be demobilized again, because the lesion of the heart valves from which I suffer manifested itself too intensely, and I was no longer able to take part in the marches."[3]

War or Career? (1914–1917)

Widespread in Germany as in belligerent Europe, military enthusiasm affected even university professors, who made it a point of honor not to dissociate themselves from Prussian militarism. In their declaration of 16 October 1914, 3,016 of them protested "with indignation" against "the enemies of Germany, with England at their head," seeking to "establish an opposition—allegedly in our favor—between the spirit of German science and what they call Prussian militarism."[4] Every winter, the University of Freiburg organized a series of lectures for which it charged admission, the proceeds going to the German Red Cross. These lectures were initially given at the university on Saturday evenings, from eight to nine o'clock, and then also in the cities of Baden and Alsace; they were supposed to "be academic in character but conceived for the general public, and to address in one way or another the current situation."[5] Heidegger volunteered for this, too, offering to deal with the subject "culture, national consciousness, and war,"[6] but the subject chosen was different: "national culture and individual personality."[7] He proposed to deliver his lecture in Konstanz, a site outside Freiburg where he could probably count on being lodged by his cousin Vetter.[8] In the end, Heidegger did not give these lectures; he was prevented from doing so, it seems, by his military service, which involved censoring mail. However, the titles of the lectures, at least, diverged sharply from the young philosopher's prewar preoccupations. This was especially true of the first one, whereas the second introduced the theme of "individual personality," reflecting the Youth Movement's ideals of authenticity and responsibility.

Despite his efforts to get involved, the young philosopher expressed himself little during this period. He signed with the title of doctor an article published on

13 January 1915 in the *Heuberger Volksblatt,* "The *Triduum* of War in Meßkirch," an article worth reading to gain an understanding of his ideas five months after the fighting began. He sketched a picture of the spiritual situation of the German people, drawing attention to the fact that the "great majority of the troops returning from the battlefield are asking for three books: the New Testament, Goethe's *Faust,* and Nietzsche's *Zarathustra.*"[9] These three works call for meditation, each in its own way, but taken together they express the spiritual confusion of the time, which considered modern horrors and mistakes as valuable as the immortal masterpieces of the past—with the result that, in the realm of painting, cubism and futurism were prized as highly as Michelangelo's Sistine Chapel.

These judgments Heidegger made regarding modern culture reflected his traditionalism, which led him to condemn modern movements that broke with tradition (cubism by erasing perspective and juxtaposing different planes of a single subject, futurism by glorifying modernism itself), just as much as those which, belonging to civilizations foreign to Europe, had no part in it—for instance, Buddhism or ancient Persia's sun worship; in addition, there were works and tendencies he considered vulgar, such as German literature of the Renaissance or contemporary French "divorce novels," which Heidegger might have conflated with naturalism. At the end of his article, Heidegger stated the conclusion to be drawn from his diagnosis:

> We moderns have often lost our respect for the simple; anything complicated or questionable annoys us; whence the terrified fear of *principles,* which are, as such, always what is simplest, whence the complete unavailability for the grandiose simplicity and the serene grandeur of the Christian worldview and the Catholic faith. If we don't want to be defeated by victory in the future, then *we must in principle leave behind this absence of principles in life's most elementary questions.*[10]

The spiritual and intellectual turmoil of the prewar period was partly dissipated when the fighting began, radically changing the face of Germany; the challenge was then to transform this turnaround into a genuine and lasting conversion, and the *triduum* of war, the three days and one evening of meditation preceding Easter, provided an opportunity to do so. Heidegger wanted to take part in this work of conversion to a genuine cultural profundity that could only be Catholic; his philosophical apologetics was based on a true meditation on what meditation means.

Starting from the analysis of the etymology of the word *Besinnung,* translated here as "meditation," Heidegger showed that this was a rigorous quest for meaning (*Sinn*) that puts the thinking self fundamentally in question, tracing it back not only to what it is, but also to what it must do, calling upon it to do what must be done and to acquire the means to do it; then the aimless wandering of one who is afraid to meditate disappears and he follows the inclinations of the moment. The individual is no longer dominated by his life, but instead dominates it, thanks to his own submission to the duty that his conscience has revealed to him. Probably drawing on his reading of Dilthey's *The Human World*,[11] Heidegger henceforth found grace in the self and in life, leaving behind the glacial chill of logic: "My *life* is *my* life."[12] A meditation on life is real only insofar as it returns me to myself and shows me what I am and what I must do. In light of this imperative of meditation, which was supposed to lead to Catholic truth, the patriotic emergency and concern about people exposed to the life-threatening dangers of war seemed very secondary; the battle against Germany's enemies counted less than the battle against the Church's enemies, persons less than ideas. Politics was secondary to the spiritual; Heidegger continued his simultaneously religious and intellectual battle as if the war had changed nothing essential.

This war, which did not change the priorities Heidegger assigned to the Germany of his time, upset neither his daily life nor his pursuit of a career. Having earned a doctorate and becoming increasingly prominent, he was one of the rising figures in Catholicism. He therefore hastened to complete his habilitation thesis, which would allow him to teach at a university. Unlike his earlier writings, this thesis, "The Doctrine of Categories and Meaning in Duns Scotus," bears on a topic in medieval Scholasticism and deals in fact with one of Duns Scotus's pupils, Thomas of Erfurt. This new delight taken in the history of philosophy, this veritable intellectual conversion that shifted his focus from the eternity of numbers and from mathematical and logical reasoning to an understanding of a singular mode of thought situated in a past time probably resulted from the courses he attended (taught by the historian Finke) and his readings (of the philosophers Fichte, Hegel, Rickert, and Dilthey), which completely destroyed his "aversion to history, an aversion fed by [his] predilection for mathematics."[13]

This conversion to history remained limited: neglecting the overall historical context, ignoring "the historical relations between the different thinkers" that were usually discussed in the history of philosophy, in his study of pseudo–Duns Scotus Heidegger sought instead "to understand and interpret the theoretical content of their philosophy, using the means of modern philosophy."[14]

Noncontextual, this conception of philosophy was fully coherent with the profound conviction Heidegger had stated a few years earlier: philosophy is a mirror of eternity; a medieval thinker remains potentially of the greatest relevance to the present thanks to an interpretation capable of resituating old ideas in a contemporary debate.

The choice of pseudo–Duns Scotus was not unrelated to career considerations. In 1913 Finke, who had been Heidegger's protector since his thesis director, Arthur Schneider, had left to take a chair in Strasburg, urged him to work on the history of philosophy. Scholasticism was in fashion: thanks to his subject, on 20 August 1913 Heidegger was able to ask the bishopric of Freiburg to grant him a Schätzler scholarship (created in 1901–1902 by a couple who were descended from a line of industrialists and bankers in Augsburg, Bavaria, who had converted to Catholicism and wanted to encourage Thomist studies). Heidegger received 1,000 marks per annum for three years, until the summer of 1916. Money was henceforth no longer a problem; the young philosopher's practical life became easier, and thanks to the success of his thesis, it was easy for him to find support. But he still had to move in the direction that was dominant within the Church, which was putting increasing emphasis on Scholasticism and neo-Thomism. The letter Heidegger wrote on 13 December 1915 to request support for the third year perfectly expresses his awareness of both his own Catholic convictions and the Church's philosophical expectations: "The obedient undersigned ventures to think that he can show something at least of his lasting gratitude for the valued trust placed in him by the Reverend Cathedral Chapter by dedicating his scholarly lifework to the task of harnessing the intellectual and spiritual potential of scholasticism in the future struggle for the Christian-Catholic ideal."[15]

Heidegger had a philosophical freedom, inventiveness, and ambition that went far beyond the simple presentation of a spiritual and intellectual legacy from the past. Although he considered fidelity to tradition essential, atheistic modernity and its errors required him to undertake an audacious offensive that would drive it into a corner, and not to remain, as the time inclined him to do, in the shelter of the venerable bulwarks that had been built by Scholasticism centuries earlier. The "the coming intellectual battle for the Catholic-Christian ideal of life" demanded nothing less, but the young Catholic philosopher could hardly make the archiepiscopal chapter understand that.

The habilitation thesis was as well received as his doctoral thesis. Rickert, under whom Heidegger prepared for his habilitation, asked Krebs to read the text, assigning him the task of preparing a report on it. The thesis was finally approved by Rickert, and Heidegger had to deliver a lecture on 17 July 1915 whose subject was "the concept of time in historical science"; he had to demonstrate not only his intellectual abilities but also his skill as a professor by showing the mastery of spoken language without which one cannot be a consummate teacher. Like his thesis, this lecture was approved, and Heidegger was authorized to give lectures at the university. He became a *Privatdozent*, an adjunct lecturer who was paid by his students. Thus he became part of the intellectual proletariat that taught at the university, holding a position as precarious as it was prestigious, which was supposed to be the prelude to a regular position. The son of Meßkirch's sexton earned his living by training Germany's future elite. This enviable beginning of a career, following a brilliant course of university studies, did not escape the attention of his little hometown of Meßkirch, whose Catholic newspaper published an item regarding one of its most promising sons: "The decision made by the Faculty of Philosophy of the University of Freiburg im Breisgau to grant Doctor Martin Heidegger, who comes from this city, the right to give lectures, has received the approval of the grand duchy's ministry."[16]

Authorized to teach, Heidegger saw his ideal of becoming a scholar and not a priest turning into a reality. He nonetheless remained aware that he came from a modest sociocultural background, and that this would normally have prevented him from going to study at the university: "How it came about that he might write [his thesis] & rose further & gained access to the university, without having all the wealth & abundance of a refined spiritual education, without the so powerful & much-used expedient of patronage, how it came about—it is a wonder to himself & a reason for deep gratitude & childlike humility."[17] The "miracle" can be understood in two ways. Statistically, the son of Meßkirch's sexton and cooper had very little chance of reaching the summit of the German educational system, of successfully defending his thesis and managing to be authorized to teach—though this was not, for all that, as rare as a miracle, since Heidegger's generation benefited from the massive expansion of secondary and higher education in Germany. Subjectively, it was for this sincere Catholic a sign of divine election, a sanction of his exceptional destiny, which resided in a career as a scholar and not as a priest, as he and his family had previously believed. Knowing his origins were modest to such a degree, the young Heidegger attributed to them his superior humility; for the same reason, he grasped, better than others, the deep meaning of what, beyond an enviable position among the elite of the educated bourgeoisie, amounted to a veritable calling. A "distant ideal," "a priesthood, something to which only the 'ordained' may gain entry," an "ordination," a "mission": Heidegger conceived of his career in terms so religious that one might think he was talking about the priesthood.

Grounds for pride, but also for the feeling of how far this course of studies and this beginning of a career were from depending on his own strengths alone; the discovery in the university library of the works of the theologian Johannes Henricus Heideggerus (1633–1698) led him to see the latter as an ancestor, and his own path as a new version of a Catholic academic vocation within a Swabian-Alemannic *Heimat* that encompassed southwestern Germany and German-speaking Switzerland, in which he reinscribed the history of his family: "You ask how they came to the Danube Valley and the von Zimbern [Zimmern]? The trail leads to South Tyrol, where my ancestors in Switzerland came from—which included a theologian famous at the time [. . .] whose many books are catalogued even today in the Freiburg University Library & right below them is his descendant's clumsy dissertation."[18] Faced with the miracle of his career resituated in what he considered the family destiny, Heidegger seemed not to acknowledge, or not to want to acknowledge, the role played successively by several people without whom his advance would have been blocked, from his departure for the Gymnasium thanks to Brandhuber and Gröber to his habilitation funded thanks first to Schneider's protection and then to Finke's.

Apart from his battle for science, apart from social and academic glory, Heidegger does not appear to have been very happy. Being still conflicted about the priestly vocation that his mother was trying to impose on him, he was far from having found the bliss that, according to what he wrote, the happy certainty of his destiny as a thinker was supposed to confer on him. And then there was the troubled relationship with a young woman, Marguerite Weninger,[19] the daughter of a customs officer in Strasburg whom he had probably met in that city, where Arthur Schneider, his thesis director, had accepted a chair. Marguerite suffered from a serious pulmonary disease that led her to seek treatment in Davos. Secretly engaged to her since December 1913,[20] Heidegger was probably racked by guilt for keeping the news from his parents, but this lie by omission must have seemed to him the only possible attitude in view of the rejection he would have faced from his mother—a striking example among others of how prompt he was to dissimulate when it was convenient for him to do so. In November 1915, Heidegger broke off the relationship, and Laslowski rejoiced in his letter of the 21st of that month. Heidegger's work required this sacrifice; the glacial heights of science could be attained only by ridding the heart of the warmth of love.[21]

Working intensely, his vocation undergoing a painful transformation, his heart torn between love, guilt, and ambition, Heidegger found himself in poor moral and physical condition. That was also the view taken by the military's medical authorities, who deemed him still not fit for combat. Although at first rejected, he was called up again on 18 August 1915:[22] the war, which everyone had thought would be short, was on the contrary going on and on, an insatiable Moloch demanding more and more young people to satisfy its need for fire and blood. Because of his condition, the philosopher was obliged to stay in the military hospital of Mülheim-Baden from 13 September to 16 October, probably for observation; finally, a diagnosis of neurasthenia and cardiac problems provided grounds for not sending him to the front.

Nevertheless, since the army managed to use as fully as it could all men of fighting age, it classified Heidegger "fit for work"[23] and put him in the reserves (*Landsturm*), ordering him to censor mail in Freiburg, where, starting on 2 November 1915, he joined "a very mixed bunch of Freiburg tradesmen, women conscripted for labor, men pronounced unfit for garrison service."[24] They were to open suspect letters from the armies, and especially those being sent to neutral countries, because it was feared that they might contain strategic information that could fall into the hands of the enemy. Of little interest in itself, this military sinecure allowed Heidegger not only to remain in Freiburg, but also to pursue his academic career until the end of 1917 without firing a shot.

Toward the Break with Catholicism (1914–1917)

The war period witnessed Heidegger's gradual break with Catholicism. The philosopher had always wanted to be in the vanguard of orthodoxy, which, as such, neither could nor should remain static. But with the pontifical *motu proprio* of 29 June 1914, Pius X established Thomas Aquinas's *Summa theologica* as the sole norm of truth in Catholic teaching. This letter on teaching, whose canonical authority was limited to Italy and the surrounding islands, was the unacceptable symbol of a negation of Catholic thinkers' intellectual freedom. Heidegger had defended the antimodernist oath, but this interpretation of the relationship between the papacy and science was no longer tenable; this was a positive norm, that is, it indicated precisely what science had to be followed. Henceforth, it was a mold to which one had to conform. Heidegger attached great importance to the alienation of self in science, but with the idea that this alienation consisted of the egotism that a good scientist achieved through the healthy, coldly logical use of reason. From then on, whereas all the modern riches of philosophy increasingly seemed to him weapons he could put to use in fighting for the ideal of a Catholic-Christian life, Heidegger found himself completely on the margins of official Roman Catholic science. The Catholic vanguard had become a dangerous periphery abandoned by the ebb tide of the Catholic norm of science.

In reaction to what he experienced as an implicit, violent disavowal of his scientific activity, Heidegger was mordantly ironic in a letter written to Engelbert Krebs on 19 July 1914, in which he also expressed the spiritual brotherhood uniting the two young Catholic thinkers:

> The *motu proprio* on philosophy was all we needed. Perhaps you, as an "academic," could propose a better procedure, whereby anyone who feels like having an independent thought would have his brain taken out and replaced with Italian salad.
>
> And for philosophical requisites they could set up vending machines in the railway stations (free of charge for those who don't have any money). I have received dispensation for the duration of my studies.[25]

This hardening of the neo-Thomist line was not in itself a complete discovery for Heidegger. The Schätzler scholarship that funded him at that time presupposed that he would remain "faithful to the spirit of Thomist philosophy," but nonetheless, for any independent thinker, the space between the spirit and the letter is so large that he can see a whole cosmos contained within it. Reduced to its letter alone, neo-Thomism would have crammed the young Heidegger's fertile mind into a cage where he could no longer move. His view of the Church then changed completely. As a doctrinal institution, it gradually became the "system of Catholicism," very different from the spiritual purity and fervor that he had experienced in Meßkirch and that had sustained him up to that point; a system of imperious domination over minds, it increasingly resembled the black legend that a number of Protestants and liberals were writing about it.

The personal relationships Heidegger formed during these years also give us a glimpse of the critique that was growing in his heart, even as it remained loyal to his original faith. In this respect, Engelbert Krebs, a Catholic priest and young academic for whom Heidegger had genuine esteem, played a role that must not be underestimated. Discussing their courses intensely, forming an intellectual bond, the two young thinkers went for frequent walks together. For Heidegger, Krebs's disapproval of the antimodernist oath he had been compelled to take was obviously a reason for concluding that one might be a sincere Catholic and a rigorous thinker and, at the same time, disavow the Catholic hierarchy, even including the pope. Thus Krebs declared: "I regard the oath against modernism as an unmerited vote of no confidence by Pius X, which simply represents a formal tightening-up of the existing constraints imposed by dogma."[26] A level-headed criticism, and all the more powerful for it.

Another major disappointment for Heidegger, which this time came from the University of Freiburg's Catholicism: Heinrich Finke, the dean of the Faculty of Philosophy at Freiburg, had hinted to Heidegger that there was a chance he might be named to the vacant chair of Catholic philosophy. Engelbert Krebs was there and would take over in the interim, until Heidegger had completed his habilitation. But things did not go that way. Krebs, despite the friendship and esteem he felt for Heidegger, was sick of being used and decided that the temporary position in Catholic philosophy that he had held since the winter semester of 1913–1914 had lasted long enough. On 12 March 1915, he therefore wrote to the ministry in Karlsruhe, declaring that in the following semester he would no longer serve in that capacity and that an appointment should be made.[27] Not having been nominated as one of the potential candidates, Heidegger was deeply annoyed and told Laslowski that "time teaches one [. . .] to see all kinds of people for what they really are."[28] However, Krebs, having been appointed to a chair of theology, quickly withdrew from the competition to succeed Schneider, which took place during the summer semester of 1916.

The job description was favorable to Heidegger, stipulating instruction in philosophy "with special emphasis on the history of medieval philosophy."[29] This corresponded not only to Heidegger's habilitation thesis on pseudo–Duns Scotus, but also to the course on the "principles of ancient and scholastic philosophy" that he gave for two hours a week during the winter semester of 1915–1916. But on 23 June 1916,[30] after numerous meetings, the committee chose Josef Geyser, born in 1869, a full professor in Münster. He was twenty years older than Heidegger, who had not yet turned twenty-seven. The latter's youth must have counted against him: he had taught little, written little. Above all, the dominant view at the time, which was exclusively that of neo-Scholasticism, disqualified Heidegger, who was opposed to it as an orthodox but modern Catholic. In fact, the committee's judgment was an insult to Heidegger, to whom the post had been promised: it specified that no candidate other than Geyser had "academic abilities in research and teaching" that were "beyond question,"[31] to the point that no position as a paid lecturer (*extraordinarius*) was foreseen in the event that Geyser ended up not accepting the chair that was to be offered him. Heidegger was mentioned only as a *Privatdozent* who could offer a substitute course in case Geyser did not come. Despite Finke's consolatory words reminding Heidegger that he was still young,[32] he felt that the Catholic Church, which had forbidden him to enter the Jesuit order and then the priesthood, was now opposing his career in philosophy as well.

Geyser's arrival in Freiburg accentuated the bitterness of the young philosopher, who had little esteem for his rival: "looks like a Chinaman, inordinately conceited, implacably one-sided, thinks Windelb.[and] & Richert are nonsense, Husserl absolutely unoriginal—value philosophy—in short a narrow-minded pedant who goes around peddling his second-hand, cramped textbook philosophy & almost makes me feel sorry for him."[33] Heidegger, who had so resolutely taken the path of a renewal of Catholic thought in keeping with its tradition while at the same time going beyond the repetition of a worn-out philosophy taught in the schools, saw himself rejected in favor of a weak, narrow-minded conformist, a pale representative of the textbook philosophy who was ignorant of the stakes involved in modern philosophy and of its risks, but especially of the opportunities for Catholicism offered by non-Catholic thinkers like Windelband, Rickert, and Husserl. Heidegger found himself between a rock and a hard place: suspect in the eyes of Catholic academics, who were waiting to see him develop before making up their minds regarding his orientation; and again disqualified because many other academics, Protestant or atheist, including Husserl, saw him as a Catholic.

That same year, Edmund Husserl, recognized as "the most outstanding scholar and teacher,"[34] was appointed to the chair in Freiburg vacated by Rickert, who had left for Heidelberg.[35] The phenomenologist succeeded the neo-Kantian in the summer semester of 1916. To judge by the 1922 *Vita,* Heidegger was enthusiastic from the outset; the influence that Husserl exerted on him did not prevent him from showing a kind of arrogance that led him to tell his friend Laslowski in January 1916: "He lacks the necessary breadth of vision"[36]—a statement whose self-importance was fueled by the conviction that logic alone was not sufficient in philosophy, because life could by no means be contained by it. His intellectual itinerary as well as his academic career led him to move closer to the phenomenologist, with whom he was in contact beginning in 1914 at the latest.[37] Husserl showed only a polite interest in him; a Jew who had converted to Protestantism, he naturally felt the young Catholic philosopher was of little concern to him. This is indicated by a letter he wrote in October, responding to Paul Natorp of Marburg, who had inquired into Heidegger's qualifications for a post as a lecturer in the history of medieval philosophy: even if he had moved closer to phenomenology, Heidegger had "confessional allegiances" "since he was 'under the protection,' so to speak," of Husserl's colleague Finke, their "resident Catholic historian," who considered Heidegger "an eminently suitable candidate on confessional grounds"; still young, Heidegger had taught little because of the war and his service as a postal censor, giving lectures that were "systematic rather than historical," about which he had heard "very good" but also sometimes "unfavorable" judgments, a consequence of Heidegger's efforts to "make his name in systematic philosophy."[38]

Husserl was not the only one whose assessment of Heidegger's lectures was mixed. Taking over for Krebs to cover the chair of Catholic philosophy while waiting for Geyser to begin, Heidegger taught, during the winter semester of 1916–1917, "Basic Problems in Logic," and, as Krebs noted in his diary, a large audience came from the lay faculties but few from the Faculty of Theology, which Krebs explained this way: "He uses a difficult terminology and expresses himself in a way that is too complicated for beginners!"[39] As for Heidegger himself, he explained in his 1922 *Vita* that "his course was barred to theologians,"[40] which seems unlikely. The context of the war played an important role, because most of the young men of an age to attend the university had left for the front, causing enrollments in Freiburg to plummet, despite the increasing numbers of young women at the university. Moreover, the Faculty of Theology, which was oriented toward the priesthood, was all the more affected by the war because it was chiefly for young men, who were being torn away from it by sabers, trumpets, and flags.

If he did not please everyone, if he upset more than one person, Heidegger aroused enthusiasm in some students. From the outset, he felt that he had achieved a clear success with his first course of lectures on ancient and Scholastic philosophy.[41] This success was not solely intellectual; in the research on Kant's *Prolegomena* that he directed during the same semester, he won over Elfride Petri (1893–1992), a Protestant student from Saxony who was destined to deeply change her young professor.

In the autumn of 1915, Heidegger was twenty-six years old, and Elfride twenty-two. She had to give a report; at the end of a lecture delivered at the beginning of December 1915, she went to see Heidegger, who offered to help her, inviting her to come for that purpose to no. 1, Hohenzollernstraße, where he lived with an aunt.[42] Heidegger's letters do not allow us to reconstitute with precision how teaching gave way to love; at least we can say that neither of them was without its attractions.

The photograph that Heidegger sent Elfride on 10 December 1915, at the very beginning of their relationship, was intended to please his young conquest. The picture is carefully posed, the light that enters the room from the left delicately sculpts the young philosopher, small and slender, his arms crossed behind his back, leaning against a wall that helped him remain motionless during the long exposure time that the camera, which was not very sensitive, required in this rather dimly lit room. His gray suit alludes to his bourgeois status, but nonetheless allows glimpses of his modest origins: wrinkled, ill-fitting, its pockets stretched out of shape, the jacket balloons out in front, too big for his puny body; a fashionable small shirt collar gives a glimpse of a dark tie, which circles his neck before disappearing into his jacket. The awkwardness of his dress does not prevent Heidegger from radiating a certain charm: despite having to hold a long pose, he looks relaxed; he has lost the stubbornness that hardened his adolescent face; and despite a rather inelegant nose, the dainty features he owed to his mother are more noticeable, with the hint of a smile below his shaved upper lip. In the lecture hall, eager to win students and driven by the energy that he put into his spiritual battle, he must have been much more impressive than one might guess from this delicate portrait of his private self.

The day after Heidegger sent Elfride this photograph, she sent him one of herself, also intended to attract him; taller than he, her hair held back by a headband and then bound up in a bun to show her neck, she stands in a garden, wearing a long, elegant, flowing dress that left her arms bare. Turned toward a hedge where sunflowers are growing, she pretends to be picking one to give to her lover, illustrating in this way the title she had given the picture: "Dearest soul—looking for sunflowers to bring them to you."[43] And in her note, she adopted the nickname that Heidegger had given her, referring to the heroine of a best-selling novel,[44] *The Saint and Her Fool*.[45] Elfride looks more natural in another picture taken earlier (in 1912), a sign that this technology was becoming commonplace in well-off circles. She is dressed in a white blouse with a round collar and a long, dark skirt, equally severe, with no jewelry except on her fingers and in her hands. She is neither beautiful nor ugly, her round eyes, nose, face, and figure all expressing the slight plumpness that was a sign of good health and comfortable affluence expected of women at the time. Heidegger was particularly taken by Elfride's "dear mountain-lake eyes" that lit up;[46] though the photograph provides only an unsatisfactory hint of this, it presents the vivacity of expression of which Elfride was capable, allowing us to glimpse her open, enterprising spirit, which was assuredly more seductive than her slightly overweight body.

Born in Leisnig, Saxony, in 1893,[47] from 1905 on Elfride grew up in Chemnitz and then in Wiesbaden in Hesse. These were all cities in central Germany, which was provincial and Protestant, contrasting strongly with the Catholic southern Germany exemplified by Freiburg, capital of the Black Forest. Elfride was the daughter of a colonel, Richard Petri. On the inactive list, he had inherited half the shares of a canvas factory, which he managed, in the small town of Alfeld, in Lower Saxony. His wife Martha took care of the household. This privileged social and cultural status had allowed Elfride to pursue secondary school studies, which was rare in German society, especially for girls: in that respect, she was a pioneer. Although she did not pass the *Abitur* examination the first time, she received a teacher's certificate in 1913, which was crowned in 1914 by her success as a student teacher, which authorized her to enter the profession.

An ambitious young woman, in the summer semester of 1914 she enrolled at the University of Kiel, in the large military port city of northern Germany, in a program that would allow her to teach "at the women's school" that stood in for a Gymnasium, at a time when women had little opportunity to pursue secondary education. Despite an interlude caused by the war—during which she contributed, first in Berlin and then in Wiesbaden, to setting up, in the context of the National Women's Service (NFD), a childcare center[48] made necessary by the work done by women replacing their husbands who had left for the front—Elfride took the *Abitur* examination in 1915, as an extramural student in a modern Gymnasium (*Realgymnasium*) in Kassel. University study was completely open to her; in the winter semester of 1915–1916, she went to Freiburg to study political economy. She was interested in social questions, and particularly the role of women.

This course of study, which was exceptional for a woman at that time, had been pursued with a geographical mobility that had no parallel in Heidegger's life. He had remained in southwestern Germany, moving from Meßkirch to Konstanz and then Freiburg; Elfride knew cities as dissimilar as Leisnig, Chemnitz, Wiesbaden, Kiel, Berlin, Kassel, and Freiburg, the north as well as the south of Germany. In addition to this itinerary through the empire, which was connected to her studies, there were also her personal travels: she stayed for a time in Nice, studying French while her father spent the winter of 1907–1908 there because of his ill health; in the summer of 1908, she went to

London, where she attended courses to improve her English before touring England and Wales. This openness to the world did not conflict with a powerful nationalism that tended toward racism and led her to prefer tall, blond, athletic men, who best embodied the bright-eyed Nordic heroes. Heidegger, who was short and dark-haired, and whose skin quickly tanned in the sun, corresponded only minimally to this *völkisch* image. She consoled herself by nicknaming him "Little Blackamoor":[49] perhaps she was thinking of the theory of the best-selling essayist Houston Stewart Chamberlin, according to whom "the noble Moor of Spain is nothing less than a pure Arab of the desert, he is half Berber (from the Aryan family), and has so much Gothic blood in his veins that even today some aristocrats living in Morocco can still trace their genealogy back to Germanic ancestors."[50]

It was into the hands of this intelligent young woman, strong-willed and ultranationalist, that Heidegger placed his sacred academic mission, suggesting to her that they sow and cultivate happiness on the cold summits of pure knowledge;[51] in the same way that he saw philosophy's function as sacred, he viewed this new love as the result of providence and its impenetrable paths that were guiding them.[52] Corresponding to the task that he assigned to Elfride, that of providing the conditions for their happiness, he assigned to himself the role of being a protector assuring that his protégée was "in totally safe hands,"[53] "quite free from brooding torment,"[54] and promised her "quite complete trust,"[55] a task to which he added that of a spiritual guide showing the way to the eternal, immutable truth, truer and deeper than the affective life of the soul. The latter, while no longer considering itself necessarily doomed to alienation, as in Heidegger's earliest writings, found its true legitimacy only in the rigorous framework of a philosophical asceticism that revealed to the young couple their own meaning in the light of eternity, which was that of God. Heidegger's conception of the couple when he was twenty-seven was perfectly inegalitarian and traditional, repeating tired stereotypes regarding the distinction between man and woman: the woman, a fragile, sentimental being, was passive, and had to accept without question what the active man gave her in abundance—reason and truth.

In the name of this calling of philosophical reason, Heidegger vigorously imposed a spiritualized version of human sexuality: "If it were not something infinitely higher, deeper, altogether heavenly that makes our heart quiver in the most blissful embrace rather than the animal's rut—then I'd rather be swallowed up by nothingness today—It does not bear thinking about—we are guided by, and within us lives, our ownmost *consciousness,* which finds expression in veneration & devotion; these are experiences that give man his unique position among everything else that is real."[56] The philosopher saw or wanted to see the carnal act as a mutual gift of self, a moral act that created an immortal bond and could be enjoyed by the whole body.

Beyond the adoption of philosophical concepts ("consciousness," "innermost experience," "good in itself"), we can only be struck by the character of this letter, which is more rhetorical than philosophical, with rhetorical questions, parataxis, and hyperbole. These long developments on the relationship between sex and God are akin to sublimation, an effect of the probable guilt that Heidegger—whom his mother destined to priestly chastity, but who was anything but chaste, being voluptuously sensual in his relations with his student—felt about sexuality in a prudish age (the nineteenth and the early twentieth century were the period of "the great repression"). *A contrario,* Elfride, a young woman from the upper bourgeoisie, displayed a striking sexual freedom, engaging in sex before they were married and in erotic play shortly after her relationship with Heidegger began, though he conceived of it as a "holy sacrifice" on her part that made him so "small & poor," acquainting him with a "new wellspring of experience" whose "holy thirst" he would never be able to quench. He turned lyrical when he watched his lover putting her clothes back on.

This sensual and sublimated romantic relationship between Heidegger and Elfride brought a happiness that he had never known and that, despite the certainty that he initially showed, constantly disconcerted him with its novelty, for which he was not prepared: "I've never felt so restlessly, vibrantly, glowingly, and blissfully the absence of antagonisms, the attainment of peace of mind—the capacity for complete and utter rest."[57]

This happiness, despite its plenitude, did not eradicate the tragic bitterness of Heidegger's character, which led him to see pain and suffering as the conditions of a great and creative life.[58] These utterly Nietzschean overtones reflected, in addition to his reading of *The Will to Power* a few years earlier, the harshness with which he experienced his own life: a battle to assert his identity as a scholar in his family, to overcome the obstacles to his academic career, to vanquish errors and the enemies of the truth that he was seeking in a ferocious struggle against the mysteries of existence. Filled with the emotional assurance provided by the happiness of a love finally possessed, and with the intellectual assurance that his repeated success as a teacher brought, Heidegger revised his conception of his philosophical battle in the direction of a "philosophy of vibrant life" at war with rationalism, a battle he wanted to wage "to the bitter end—without falling victim to the anathema of unscientific thought."[59]

This increase of laborious and belligerent energy came to him from the presence of Elfride, who was transformed into his muse.[60] In April 1916, far away from her because he was staying in Meßkirch with his parents, he lamented her absence and its effects on his weakened philosophical intuition, against which his beloved could do nothing: "My beginning is titanic & it ends in concepts—the world falls from my trembling hands, cold, unexpressive, unimpressive, a piece of lava growing cold, & within me I feel the bubbling & welling up of the fiery, surging energies—you artist of my self, dispelling homesickness—I am straining my powers of imagination to have your image alive before me—it is just an 'image,' remains just an image."[61] A muse, she was also a "resting place" when he returned "tired from the distant land of the great questions."[62] She played the protective role of a mother, while he often signed his letters "your Boy," or, later on, "your little Blackamoor": the philosopher saw her as vested with a "motherly mission" within their "metaphysical destiny,"[63] a "mission" that even included discussing his courses and his writings, as well as doing the long work of correcting the proofs of his habilitation thesis, which were coming from the printer in September 1916.[64] A protective mother, Elfride also seemed to him a child. Heidegger frequently called her a child in his letters, marking his own role as her spiritual protector, calming her fears, showing her the path to philosophical truth. She was also a playmate: during a snowfall in January 1916 that reminded him, like Proust's madeleine, of the happiness of a past moment, he relived "all the pleasures of young days"[65] spent in his native Meßkirch in the winter, with which he associated the desire for a snowball fight with his beloved; then, anticipating further, he imagined their common future in the comforting guise of a warm family home, while the cold was spreading white outside, while the son they hoped for played in the enclosure of a garden at the foot of the mountains.

As early as December 1915,[66] their intense relationship led Martin Heidegger and Elfride Petri to consider starting a family, which presupposed that they would have a religiously mixed marriage. While Elfride's parents were not particularly opposed to this idea,[67] his parents did not understand how he could marry a Protestant. Visiting them in Meßkirch in April 1916, he wrote to Elfride: "I now also realize the reason for my parents' silence—they still haven't got over the fact that we're of different denominations."[68] In the snug nest of his work and his romantic happiness with a Protestant student, Heidegger had become remote from the world of his origins, to the point that he had not anticipated the negative reaction of his parents, though they were profoundly Catholic. This proposed mixed marriage aroused the same negative reaction in Ernst Laslowski, Heidegger's friend who was so close to him during his moments of doubt before he met Elfride. The latter having written him a letter in early 1917 mentioning their coming marriage, Laslowski sent his friend a worried letter, exhorting him to be patient and prudent.[69]

In addition to the hesitations of his friends and family, there were also Heidegger's own fears regarding his career as a Catholic philosopher in Freiburg. At the beginning of their love affair, he and Elfride saw each other relatively little. Heidegger's intensive preparation for his courses certainly occupied most of the time that his work for the postal service left free, but his career worries also kept him from advertising a relationship with a Protestant student, and marriage would only accentuate the problem.

So many impediments arising from his Catholic milieu, in both Meßkirch and Freiburg, prevented Heidegger from granting Elfride the prompt wedding she ardently desired.[70] After asking for Elfride's hand in a letter he sent her father on 6 March 1916, he was invited by his future in-laws to spend Easter 1916 with them in Wiesbaden,[71] but in the end he did not go. Annoyed, Richard and Martha Petri forbade their daughter to continue seeing this indecisive and uncivil young man, but she did not comply with their demand.[72] The situation eventually calmed; Heidegger sent an offprint of his thesis to his future father-in-law, who wrote him a thank-you note accompanied by the first portrait of him that Elfride had drawn.[73] On leave from 7 to 10 October 1916, Heidegger went to Wiesbaden. He did not meet Elfride's father, who was busy in Borna, near Leipzig, but he was pampered by Elfride and her mother.[74]

Postponed because of Heidegger's uncertain position at the university and the appointment of Geyser, which made the possibility of setting up a bourgeois household[75] suddenly seem less feasible financially, the wedding finally took place in March 1917. There was, in fact, not one but three weddings: on 20 March 1917, the civil marriage; on 21 March, the Catholic ceremony; and on 25 March, the Protestant union.[76] The Catholic ceremony was held in the magnificent Freiburg Cathedral, in the university chapel, rich with its brilliant past, among the marvelous works of art that adorned it and the inspiring presence of the professors who had been buried there earlier, including Christoph Eliner, Heidegger's distant compatriot from Meßkirch who had become a professor of theology and rector at the University of Freiburg, and in whose name a scholarship had been created at his death in 1574—a scholarship that funded the young man's studies in the minor seminary and at the Faculty of Philosophy in Freiburg.[77]

More than the setting, the modalities of the ceremony were of great importance. Celebrated at 10 a.m. on 21 March by his friend Krebs, it was a particularly sober and discreet wartime wedding, for which Krebs had been delegated by the military chaplain, Monsignor Wächter: "Wartime marriage service without organ, bridal dress, wreaths or veils, coaches and horses, wedding breakfast or guests; conducted with the blessing of both sets of parents (conveyed by letter), but in their absence,"[78] as Krebs noted in his diary. Apart from the absence of decorum that might have identified the couple as two believers attending a private mass said by a priest in the university chapel, the wedding was even more discreet because it took place in wartime and therefore did not have to be included in the marriage register of the parish where it occurred, but could be recorded instead in the autonomous register kept by the military chaplains. That is what happened. Similarly, wartime marriages did not require the posting of banns, which were in fact not published in this case;[79] Krebs himself had been informed at the last minute, or rather, the same month, and the Catholic wedding was de facto a kind of clandestine wedding, kept secret not from the families but from the local Catholic community and its hierarchy—here we find once again the dissimulation Heidegger used when he thought it served his interests.

The real wedding, public and festive, took place four days later, at the home of Elfride's parents in Wiesbaden; it was celebrated in observance of the Lutheran rite by Pastor Lieber,[80] the father of Friedel, Elfride's best friend, and her brother Karl. This minister was a person of great importance for the bride: he had prepared her to take the Latin test for the extramural *Abitur* in Kassel, and she admired his culture and visited him frequently in his presbytery when she went to Wiesbaden.[81] Six-year-old Elfridchen, Elfride's goddaughter, the daughter of her half-sister Else, showered the couple with flower petals. Heidegger wore a Territorial Army uniform, while his bride was dressed in virginal white, with a veil. The Protestant wedding was followed by a reception organized by Elfride's mother, her father being unable to leave Borna.[82] Heidegger's marriage to the daughter of a Prussian colonel and the half-owner of a canvas factory allied him with the Prussian bourgeoisie, crowning a social ascension that would have made his ancestors buried in Heuberg exultant with pride, if only the bride had not been a Protestant.

Heidegger was not impervious to the bourgeois comfort he shared with Elfride; staying at his parents' home in April 1916, he longed for the time spent with his lover, referring not only to the sweet words he was unable to say to her because she was far away, but also to "such little lovely things as a supper with you, by candlelight, with flowers, you in your smart dress, happiness in our eyes, full of delightful joy, the restrained glow of our souls, pulsating with the expectantly glowing timidity of beauty, the completion of life."[83] The home into which they moved after their wedding was not very comfortable: a two-room apartment on Karlstraße.[84] In the autumn they moved to another that was calmer, sunnier, and more agreeable, located on the top floor of a building at no. 8, Lerchenstraße, which they set up using family furniture and the money from Elfride's dowry.[85] Though they both ate every day at the Kolpinghaus, a kind of German youth hostel,[86] they soon had a maid, Fräulein Giesert.

More than this comfort, Heidegger derived from his union with Elfride a greater assurance, a feeling of complete mastery over his moral and intellectual faculties; and this assurance, connected with Elfride, made him see his future in a new light: that of an exemplary household, not only for the children who would be born into it but also for the students at the university. Even as he attacked the idea of both "mysticism" and "secret societies," Heidegger wanted to be at the heart of the "intellectual community" peculiar to the "invisible Church"[87] as conceived by Rudolf Sohm (1841–1917), a Lutheran jurist specializing in Roman law.

Heidegger's frames of reference were less and less Catholic, and in that respect his philosophical commitment was at the crossroads between theology and politics, in the indissociable union of his private and his public lives. This was Elfride's doing; and just as "Greece in its capture then captured its rough-mannered conqueror, thereby / Bringing the arts into countrified Latium,"[88] this young woman in Heidegger's thrall led him to an affective, political, and religious revolution, upsetting, with her bourgeois, Protestant, and urban culture, the mental frameworks of a man who—though increasingly open to the rest of his time's culture, and even though his convictions were shaken by the recent evolution of the Church, which was tending to reject him once again—still remained in many respects a sincere Catholic from the countryside, still a prisoner of his family's milieu.

Like many young people in her milieu, Elfride was marked by the Youth Movement (Jugendbewegung). In early August 1917, she went with her friend Friedel Lieber to the Lorelei, on the banks of the Rhine, to attend a meeting of the Freideutscher Bund, which, having emerged from the Freideutsche Jugend, was part of the *Wandervogel*.[89] Similarly, as soon as she arrived in Freiburg in 1915, she became a member of the Freiburg Students' Association and the Hüttenzunft, the Cabin Guild founded by female students in 1910;[90] she went to the Black Forest regularly, to the guild's cabin, an hour's hike from the train station at Hinterzarten at an altitude of more than 1,000 meters, on the summit of the Silberberg. There she rejoiced in finding herself back in nature, so much so that their maid, "their house philosopher," drew a parallel that her husband reported to her in a letter: "Isn't it right, Dr. Heidegger, you're happy when you can work all on your own for days on end & that's part of your nature just the way Frau Heidegger beams at the very thought of getting out into nature to be with the flowers."[91] Elfride had been not only an enthusiastic hiker but also a skier ever since 1913, when her parents had given her a pair of Norwegian skis.

Hiking and skiing were activities that put Germans in close contact with nature, which tore city-dwellers away from urban society, where they denature themselves—so that they could better rediscover, in a spirit of freedom and responsibility, their true nature, which is healthy and authentically German. In the spirit of the Youth Movement, this was a genuine regeneration of the German people through a return to a way of life that was natural because healthy (Elfride asked Heidegger, in order to tend to his fragile health, not only not to stay up late working but also to abstain from drinking and smoking,[92] hygienic principles that were typical of the Youth Movement) and imbued with natural landscapes, conceived as so many untouched beauties of the German fatherland.

This valorization of natural beauty and the health of country people was in full harmony with Heidegger's conservative Catholic convictions, as we have already encountered them. The practice of hiking in the context of youth movements had also found Catholic imitators and an equivalent had emerged among them in Meßkirch: the Quickborntag, which met for the first time in 1914, in the Black Forest.[93] German Catholic traditionalism valorized the countryside and local traditions, which, for Heidegger, had remained in the sphere of words: regionalist erudition and literature, traditionalist discourses. When Elfride initiated him into the Youth Movement, he would encounter nature in its wild state, especially in the mountains, through skiing and hiking, urban dwellers' practices taking place in nature. As Heidegger noted, for Elfride there was "something ultimate" about "the experience of nature"—a notion he challenged at the time,[94] showing himself at first impervious to the moral, spiritual, and political value of this experience.

This gradually changed. In contact with Elfride, who often came to spend vacations in her student guild's cabin, he came to love in his imagination these mountains his beloved visited: he imagined hiking "through the mountains to the cabin" and kissing her forehead at her bedside, wiping away the "severity" around her mouth, so that "a blissfully happy smile" would light up her face "like the little candle on the tree."[95] A month later, he felt the desire to hide in a cabin in these mountains, where he could devote himself completely to this sacred experience of tender, carnal love that his relationship with Elfride had revealed to him and that he conceived in mystical terms.[96] A month after that, Heidegger wrote to Elfride, telling her how much he himself had experienced a form of illumination during the hike they had taken together in the Black Forest, and saying that he owed this experience to her and to Friedel Lieber, her closest friend[97] and a pastor's daughter, who was deeply imbued with the ideals of the Youth Movement (Heidegger even liked to imagine her with the symbolic guitar of the Jugendbewegung),[98] and who regularly stayed with Elfride in the Silberberg cabin as a guest, until Friedel herself became a member of the Hüttenzunft.[99] "Life had come to me—& being allowed to accompany you two fresh-sunny creatures on your climbing expedition lit up this life for me—there was a chiming & singing in me, all the hidden sources of delightful experience burst open—all because I bear the semester within me—thus was it possible for your end of semester to become a silent joy for me." This illumination, which clearly changed the direction of his philosophy, filled him with a silent joy that brought him back to the carefree days of his childhood and to the tales and legends that populated the collective childhood imagination: "Now I take this little joy around with me like a little boy with his new picture book: dwarves and elves, Snow White & Mrs. Holle & [the gnome] Rübezahl & all the delights of sunny childhood, but I take deep pleasure when I see before me that I have a living philosophy to be lived—& it is no coincidence that yesterday I worked out & wrote down my theory of consciousness so felicitously, purely intuitively."[100]

Philosophy, which can seem a cold edifice built on general principles from which, by means of a set of distinctions and combinations, one draws analyses and abstract conclusions marked with the seal of pure reason, is nourished above all by an intimate experience and intuition which the reflection and writing that follow them can sometimes entirely mask behind a structure as impressive as it is fallacious, because it is a result and not a point of departure. In that respect, this passage from the letter to Elfride shows how everything mingles together in an intellectually fertile life: to arrive at his course on consciousness, Heidegger's sensible experience of a hike in the mountains joined with the ideals of the Youth Movement underlying it. This was a world straight out of the collective childhood imagination and yet profoundly rooted in his own childhood in his native region because of the very personal happiness it brought back to him.

Heidegger finally went to the Silberberg cabin, where he spent the day of 7 July 1917;[101] with Elfride, he discovered the Black Forest within the aura of the fullness of love and life, and then rediscovered Lake Constance with the same power of inspiration that she was able to exert on him. In the summer of 1916, accompanied by her friend Gertrud Mondorf, she took advantage of Heidegger's leave to go spend a few days with him in this place of his early adolescence. On seeing this lakeside landscape again, Heidegger wrote a poem, "Evening Walk on Reichenau," an expression, in a flat and meditative Romantic style, of the emotion he felt when confronted by this splendor: the water, the gardens, the old buildings on the lake:

> Seawards flows a silver radiance
> to distant dark shores,
> and like a muted word of love
> night falls in the summer-weary gardens
> damp with evening.
> And one last birdcall from the old tower roof is caught
> among moon-white gables—and what the bright summer's day
> brought me lies heavy with fruit—
> ever a transcendent freight—
> in the grey desert of a great simplicity.[102]

Reichenau Island, the jewel of Lake Constance, already very much a tourist site in Heidegger's time, accommodated, in the verdant setting of gardens that took advantage of the mild climate conducive to farming, the superb religious buildings connected with the first Benedictine abbey in Germany—founded in 724 by Saint Pirmin—whose artistic and intellectual activity had a major influence in Europe.

Rather than this Catholic heritage that had interested his mentor Conrad Gröber, Heidegger in love remembered the overall ambiance of the island, the "pediments," the "gardens," the lake, an idyllic setting in which they walked, read Meister Eckhart,[103] waded in a creek, and got engaged to be married.[104] They both put on gold wedding rings that Elfride had been given by her mother, who had received them from her own parents; but Elfride's slipped into the water while they were canoeing, and a new one had to be bought, on which was engraved "Dearest Soul 1915 Lake Constance 1916."[105] This moment became mythical: when Heidegger went back to Konstanz in 1919 with his friend Theophil Rees, he made a kind of pilgrimage to Reichenau in search of these instants.

The rediscovery of Lake Constance thanks to Elfride was followed in August 1917 by that of Meßkirch and its region. Friedrich and Johanna Heidegger having accepted their son's mixed marriage, Elfride was introduced to the two branches of the family, which gave her an opportunity to roam the surrounding area[106] and to "suddenly" open her husband's mind to the beauty of his native country.[107] When three years later Heidegger averred simply that, as a university student, he had "had no 'time' for it," he seemed not to see how urban and bourgeois a practice walking was. It was certainly followed in Meßkirch—for example, on Sundays on the castle grounds—but the long, athletic hikes covering kilometers of the countryside were completely unknown to him before Elfride—in that respect, the Protestant, urban Germany symbolized by Berlin revealed to him his native, Catholic, rural Meßkirch.

Elfride broadened the philosopher's horizon, getting him to engage in tourism even in the heart of his little region; this discovery of Germany's beauties was accompanied by a moral initiation into the ideal of the Youth Movement, whose motto had been formulated on the Hohe Meißner in 1913: "Free German youth wants to take responsibility for determining on its own the form it will give to its life, faithful to its inner truth." Heidegger was particularly sensitive to the importance of individual responsibility, of each person's authenticity, his engagement in the deepest part of himself with his own life, for which he is responsible. In March 1917, almost on the eve of his wedding, he conceived this in terms that were simultaneously epistolary, theological, and romantic: "To me your letters are always a symbol of our real life in our own house—that life-long togetherness freely and actively shaped from the ultimate depths of our ownmost personal being. [. . .] May the Lord protect us, i.e., preserve us in this vocation—in faithfulness to ourselves—the pledge of our strong, ardent love and cheerful joy."[108]

Elfride and her family brought Heidegger into contact with a large part of what Berlin symbolized in his childhood: a Prussian, Protestant, and urban milieu opposed point for point to his Swabian, Catholic, and rural Meßkirch, though the Petris' provincial origin somewhat attenuated this opposition. Wiesbaden was a large city, but still not the metropolis of Berlin. His wife and her family and friends confronted him with a different political culture, imperial conservatism, nationalist and militarist, as it existed among many Protestants in the Kingdom of Prussia, notably in the army. Constituting 65 percent of the German population, in 1913 Protestants provided no less than 81 percent of the German army's officers;[109] their cardinal values were respect for the ruler's authority and for the inequalities instituted by God, the exaltation of the glory of the emperor, the army, and the nation, particularly in this period when an already harsh war was becoming harsher and the military's grip on the state was growing stronger, in the name of total war.

These nationalist, authoritarian, and militaristic values that Heidegger encountered among his in-laws were not as such foreign to his conservative Catholicism. These Prussians differed from what he knew mainly by a certain hostility to the Catholic faith, which seemed to them opposed to the Reich, alien to the German people, and by the fact that they obeyed the emperor and king of Prussia, considering him also their *summus episcopus,* the head of their church—which assuredly must have had particular importance for the Lieber family, Elfride's closest friends, the father being a pastor. Heidegger's Catholic conservatism and his wife's Protestant conservatism had points in common: the rejection of parliamentary democracy, hostility to socialism, and a tendency toward anti-Semitism.

In contact with Elfride, Heidegger started thinking about the young soldiers at the front, which he did in a manner more philosophical than religious, attesting to his spiritual evolution: "We must not give our young heroes stones instead of bread when they come back hungry from the battlefield, not unreal & dead categories, not shadowy forms & bloodless compartments in which to keep a life ground down by rationalism neat and tidy, and let it molder away."[110] If this greater sensitivity to the war might also have come from his service at the postal censorship office and the experience of the battles that were making themselves increasingly felt (starting in the autumn of 1916, there was air combat over Freiburg),[111] Heidegger, a philosopher behind the front lines, was nonetheless becoming aware of his duty with regard to the young people who were heroically risking their lives and who had to receive, not only the fruits of the earth—such as those that Elfride was sending to her friends who had gone to fight[112]—but also the spiritual fruits promised by the philosophy of life, the "bread" of the spirit. Rationalism offered only "stones." Through this philosophical appropriation of the spiritual destiny of these "young heroes," Heidegger marked more than ever the real, not metaphorical, convergence between philosophy as combat and the armed nation fighting a very real war of steel and blood.

Heidegger became an anti-Semite at least partly through his association with Elfride, who was anti-Semitic and remained so throughout her life. And though up to this point we have found no source indisputably showing that the philosopher shared this rejection or hatred of Jews, the letter he sent to Elfride on 18 October 1916 marked a turning point: "The jewification [*Verjudung*] of our culture & universities is certainly horrifying & I think the German race [*Rasse*] really should summon up the inner strength to find its feet again. The question of capital though!"[113] The crucial importance that Heidegger attached to culture and the university is here somewhat along the lines of Kralik's anti-Semitism. The young philosopher was judging culture and the German universities, which he saw as endangered by the growing part played in them by Jews, who remained parasites on the German race even if they had citizenship and spoke the language. The theme of an inner power, present in Heidegger's work from the outset, is here used not in reference to an individual but to a human group, an ethnicity closed in on itself, competing with others for domination. The key to this passage is given by the last sentence: "The question of capital though!," an ironic denunciation of the socialism that saw capital and capitalism as obstacles to the achievement of human happiness through the equality of all. Like the fear of the place occupied by Jews in the culture of the time, this antisocialism went back to political ideas developed by the intransigent Catholic milieu in which Heidegger was brought up. For the Heidegger of 1916, German culture and universities were being "jewified," perhaps because more Jews were active in them; in any case, and certainly in his eyes, because socialism was developing there, a Jewish, non-German political doctrine, a veritable opium for many German intellectuals, whom it numbed as they attempted to rise toward domination. Whereas it seems that his antisocialism had not earlier been linked to anti-Semitism, though it could be read between the lines in Kralik, at this point Heidegger established a connection that his wife must have woven at least in part.

This political rapprochement with Elfride was strengthened by an intellectual and religious rapprochement that led Heidegger to refer to their "spiritual [*geistig*] closeness."[114] When he conceived of his philosophical work as a climb toward the heights of pure knowledge, he included Elfride, who gave him strength that allowed him to make the ascent, and to whom he brought back the treasures from his "wanderings, enriching the spiritual life of his lover and making her *more assured*."[115] Moreover, Elfride, seeking spiritual enlightenment, was drawn to mysticism, as was Heidegger, with the difference that the latter felt primarily drawn to reason and only secondarily to the mystical.[116] Furthermore, his wife even went so far as to envisage converting to Catholicism: sincerely or not, that is what she told Krebs during the preparations for the marriage. Krebs cautiously advised her to wait until after the wedding and to take her time making a decision on a subject that would involve a total commitment.[117] As for Heidegger, he considered their religious differences "secondary";[118] for him, they did not constitute a serious obstacle to the fusion of their souls.

This was all the truer because he was moving in the direction of Protestantism: the preeminence of the Lutheran wedding ceremony over the Catholic ceremony, and even the fact that the former took place at all, proves that Heidegger had moved far away from the religion of his youth. The authors he was reading provide another clue: in the course of the summer of 1917 he studied the second of Schleiermacher's speeches in *On Religion,* and as his friend Heinrich Ochsner wrote, "To raise the tone and say a rather special thank-you for our friendship, Heidegger delivered some observations on the problem of religion in Schleiermacher,"[119] adding in a later letter that he had remained obsessed all week by Heidegger's talk. The relationships he maintained apart from Elfride, and increasingly through her, also tended in the direction of this distancing with regard to his original faith: the people they counted as belonging to their "small circle" were either Protestants, like Friedel, her brother Karl, and his wife, Gertrud Lieber, or Catholics who had moved away from the Church, like Ochsner, a witness to their marriage who was studying philosophy after studying Catholic theology. Heidegger formed cordial relationships—with friends or mere acquaintances—which he moreover liked to denigrate, emphasizing that "all the connections that come with this little club are such that I could jettison them at any moment without feeling deprived in the innermost life of my soul."[120]

What was essential for him was philosophy, which tended to absorb the world as a whole, with the exception of his lover, who remained like a bridge between him and the outside: "It's perhaps my bane that I have a philosophical gift which when activated makes everything else sink away & I neglect my personal concerns, treat them as irrelevant. I must not saddle myself so much with relations to all sorts of people—these days I've often unconsciously dreamt of our little house, where I shall produce my life's work within your great understanding."[121] Heidegger had a high opinion of his philosophical activity, which was in fact the center of his life, and whose productive shelter would be the household run by Elfride. He was also aware of a clear disparity between his conceptual thought and his relations with other people: "In a metaphysical sense I suppose I may have a maturity & assurance, whereas I completely lack this in natural life precisely on account of my highly speculative attitude—perhaps because I've never lived, associated, exchanged ideas with people a great deal."[122] We see this awkwardness in his relations with other people later on as well, and first of all in political and academic matters. Nevertheless, he exaggerated his solitude, his independence with regard to other people: his lack of a need or an appetite for human relationships concerned primarily common, ordinary people, those who were not, as he was, touched by the grace of philosophy; conversely, his colleagues, and even more his teachers, who were central to the activity in which his whole mind was engaged, were far more likely to have a great influence on him—first of all Heinrich Rickert, and soon Edmund Husserl. They were all Protestants, as was usual outside the Faculty of Theology.[123]

The Faculty of Philosophy, through its teachers, the women it allowed Heidegger to meet there, and to a lesser degree the student friendships he made there, constituted a milieu that encouraged a decisive distancing from the Meßkirch way from which he had come and which had led him to consider a large city like Freiburg a place of perdition. Heidegger's horizon opened up toward an urban and Protestant, militarist and anti-Semitic Germany. The Berlin way was beginning to take over.

The Inner Experience of the War (1918)

The beginning of 1918 marked for Heidegger the real beginning of the war. The ongoing conflict required more men, even more than the latest group of recruits provided. The army had to bring together all the men who could go to the front, no matter what their military value, because the supreme command of the German armies wanted to take advantage of the collapse of Russia (which the armistice signed on 15 December 1917 had just sanctioned), in order to win a quick and decisive victory on the Eastern Front before American troops landed en masse and were added to the Triple Entente's increasing number of tanks. A major offensive was therefore planned for the spring.

On 17 January 1918,[124] Heidegger was sent to the Karlskaserne barracks in Freiburg.[125] As Heinrich Ochsner noted on 24 January 1918, Heidegger's health appeared "to be suffering greatly under the stress of his new duties";[126] however, a medical examination declared him fit for active service[127] and on 28 February 1918 he was added to the Fourth Company of the 113th Reserve Battalion.[128] He had to complete his military training at the Heuberg training camp and in the countryside around Meßkirch, where Baden could find room for its military activities—this space, moreover, was strictly limited by the urbanization and small size of its territory, squeezed between the Rhine and the Black Forest.

Heidegger spent two periods of two weeks, between 11 and 22 March and then between 5 and 17 May,[129] in the open air of his native region, learning in the field how to be a soldier fighting for the grand duchy and the empire. His first stay there pleased him, and he saw it as an adventure. Physically, his health was excellent, "splendid" despite a "bit of a cold" that was "already passing," and that he must have contracted the day before during the battalion's night exercise in the snow. He found the exercise itself "interesting"; they returned to the sound of music: "How it entered our tired bones, a positively blissful feeling." He enjoyed greatly this cold, snowy winter weather, which reminded him of his childhood in his native country: "Today [the snow is] quite hard, deep blue sky, glorious sunshine & the air, quite wonderful." In addition, he was "already" serving as a "squad leader"—"i.e., as corporal," he explained to his wife, the result of his holding a doctorate and being a lecturer at the university. Because he was a prominent person, the officers, and even the battalion's commander, Baron von Villiez, treated him "extremely kindly," and the latter had talked to him "for quite a long time," telling him that it was "very much to his credit that he was joining in with army service in these surroundings and finding his feet there."[130]

But everything in the army did not in fact please Heidegger, starting with the lack of privacy.[131] The mail, which was "dreadfully sluggish," also annoyed him by depriving him, at first, of news from his wife. He was comforted in Elfride's absence by the snowdrop she had given him, which he carried in his cartridge bag and which beamed "a cheerful greeting" to him everywhere he was on duty—"lying in the woods as a gunner or going along a bright country road between the brown fields singing the stirring marching songs" with his comrades. Another comfort was a visit from his mother and his sister, who "marveled at their strapping soldier," to whom they brought food, "butter, bacon, egg dainties." In a sign that she was getting used to the idea of this mixed marriage, Johanna Heidegger asked her son, "the way she does," whether her daughter-in-law's stay with them in Meßkirch had really pleased her, whether Elfride "wanted to come again & if the bed had been alright as well." His mother brought more good news: Fritz, who was also in the army, was doing "very well," stationed with his regiment "at a quiet spot" for the time being. As for their father, he was delighted by the prospect of a chair for his son in Berlin or in Marburg. "It's moving how pleased the man is," Heidegger concluded, "& I'm relieved to be able to ease some of the worries my parents had on my account during my student days." The Landsturm soldier on maneuvers in Heuberg signed this letter to his wife "Your radiant Boy."[132]

Heidegger returned to the training camp between 5 and 17 May. The novelty had worn off, he missed Elfride more, and he also missed their "spiritual communion" and "heart-to-heart talks," thanks to which everything became "utterly clear." He dreamed of their destiny guided by God, who had brought them together, of their common aspiration to theology and the "elemental religious life" he would succeed in building, a life imbued with the ideals of the Youth Movement, "which radiates its power of influence over all personal work" and over their "circles of friends & fellow human beings."[133] On 12 May, there was a clear change in the way the philosopher saw the army: "Inwardly I'm suffering so dreadfully on account of my surroundings—the worthlessness that erupts here can hardly even be put into words & the worst thing is one cannot escape—& one's there in the middle of it & has to go along with it as a mere number—you can hardly imagine what a letter from you means to me then."[134]

The source of these remarks, as bitter as they are vague, seems to lie in his being treated with less respect by his superiors: whereas during his first stay he had been asked to assume the functions of a squad leader, he was now treated like a number, according to rank alone, and not as a unique person. Heidegger's pride was wounded, whereas he had at first been flattered. The philosopher drew conclusions both harsh and general regarding the state: "What the state in its present form & its lack of ethical-metaphysical orientation has already curbed, poisoned, inhibited & destroyed in the way of the inner wealth & potential of personality cannot be calculated in terms of the national debt—nor can it be measured using the prevailing yardsticks—& perhaps we acquire our worth precisely by renouncing any original valuation on the part of the state anyway."[135] The German Empire, before and during the war, seemed to him organized in denial of each individual's personality, in a mechanical system where what counted above all were appearances as empty as a service number. Each individual was accorded value to the degree that he abdicated his authenticity in order to mold himself to perform a function that the state designated without consideration for his person. For Heidegger, the result was a national debt toward every citizen, one that could not be calculated in keeping with its values because, without an ethical and metaphysical orientation, the state lacked the appropriate frames of reference.

Heidegger's diatribe, which starts with the army and then attacks the state, subsequently arrives at the living principle of the ethical and metaphysical foundation of any commonwealth: the university—in this case, the university as Heidegger knew it, namely the University of Freiburg, which he criticizes with the greatest violence. Elfride seems to have attended an official lecture on the philosopher Schlegel given by the historian Finke, in his capacity as a vice rector.[136] For Heidegger, this lecture was "a deadly sin among scholars given his complete lack of understanding of the modern history of ideas, one for which he can be forgiven all the less as he committed it in his office as pro-vice chancellor." Despite Finke's strong interest in Schlegel (he edited Schlegel's correspondence and the same year wrote a book on his relationship with his wife, Dorothea), as Heidegger saw it, the historian did not have the right to talk about this philosopher from a historical as opposed to a speculative point of view, and the young academic denounced the culture of appearances, seductive but lethal for the mind, that was rampant in Freiburg, and from which he himself had difficulty escaping. He concluded: "Our university in Fr.[eiburg] must be left to its own devices—we have to gain the necessary distance from it—a lack of concern with its proceedings, which are mainly the work of people who don't have the least awareness of its limits." Drawing the logical consequence of the idea that they had to leave Freiburg and its dramas, Heidegger concluded his diatribe by asserting confidently: "We must definitely go to Göttingen or Berlin *together* after the war."[137]

The war led Heidegger to find some cultural value in the capital city, which for him had previously symbolized modern decadence as a whole; and this criticism that he formulated against the university was not simply a fit of bad temper. The university had to regenerate the spirit of the German people, with the little circle formed around Heidegger and his wife at its center, radiating outward. He would be its heart and spirit, from whom word and example would proceed. This theme also appears in the letters to Elisabeth Blochmann (1892–1972), who was at first Elfride's friend, then the couple's, and who was later one of the first women to become a professor at the university and one of the important specialists on pedagogy: "Your close association with our circle of relations must strengthen your conviction that you are right in the midst of a movement of peaceful spiritual life that is still just beginning—you also have to draw from it the will to explain yourself in depth, setting aside any conventional barrier and any embarrassment."[138]

Beyond communication without "embarrassment" between "kindred souls" flouting conventional barriers established by an inauthentic bourgeois order, Heidegger positioned himself as a spiritual advisor: "Be assured of my full and complete participation in your personal and spiritual life and destiny—for me, this companionship in the dangerous flow of life is a precious opportunity to give *and to receive*." A spiritual advisor for a faith and a philosophy of authenticity which, despite his professed horror at the "noisy proclamations of plans that are going to fix everything," he saw as called upon to direct the life of the university as well as that of each individual: "Spiritual life must once again become a truly effective life for us—it must be ballasted by a personal weight that can operate a 'reversal' in order to compel us to get back on our feet for good, and this weight proves to be authentic only in a stripped-down simplicity, not in what is blasé, decadent, forced."[139]

Having returned to Freiburg on 17 May,[140] Heidegger was ordered to go on 5 July to Meteorological Station 414 on the front, a Württemberg unit stationed in Berlin-Charlottenburg, to receive training there. The development of meteorological services was supposed to improve the effectiveness of poison gas; it was hoped that by predicting wind patterns, they could prevent poison gases from being blown toward friendly lines. Even though it was clear to everyone that the war was coming to an end, though the outcome was not yet clear, more than ever all resources had to be used as effectively as possible. German science could help win the war; that is why on 25 August 1918 an order from the War Ministry defined in detail the role of the meteorological services.[141]

Heidegger accordingly left for Berlin along with twenty university and secondary school instructors;[142] at the outset, he showed how green a soldier he was by forgetting his gas mask at home. This trip was an opportunity to get to know regions of Germany that were unfamiliar to him, the northern part of Hesse, with Kassel, the March (*Mark*), and then the Harz mountains; his way of seeing them was almost caricaturally rustic: Kassel, the big city, was "dreadful," whereas the Mark was "wonderful—the endless ripening cornfields with their sleepy windmills in the evening sun—the birch forests & lakes—I've never taken such great pleasure in a new landscape." On 7 July, he reached Charlottenburg, a large city west of Berlin that housed the Heimat-Wetter-Warten command,[143] which Heidegger was to join. That evening, he and his comrades slept in the uncomfortable storehouse of the command building, but they were informed that they would henceforth arrange their everyday lives on their own and find room and board.

So the following day, he wrote: "from 9 in the morning till 8 in the evening up & down stairs, dead tired & not eaten anything decent as we didn't yet have any vouchers." Heidegger, who liked comfort, found more than decent lodging, "a very clean room at a Frau Wolff's," who had a son in the navy, with a good bed, a bathroom, and a view of a courtyard with flowers, all for 45 marks, though the municipal authorities paid only 24; he could have taken a room for 30 marks, but on the fifth floor and "unclean," "the people less pleasant." He justified this personal expense, high in wartime when their household was not well-off, by the fact that his comrades, themselves bourgeois, were "for the most part paying the same rent or more" and were already complaining about bedbugs, whereas his room was "meticulously clean & nice."

Although his lodgings were pleasant, the food was bad: 2.3 kilos of bread to last a whole week cost two marks, and to round out his diet, a field kitchen for ninety pfennigs, where he found much of the food "revolting." Since in wartime people live and eat far less well in the cities than in the countryside, he planned to send the following day a telegram "home"—that is, to his parents, to ask them for something to eat, dreaming in particular of potatoes and bread; through their friends the Reeses, Elfride could get jam for him; and especially he hoped to be able to rely on her for money, so that, like the others, he could "eat a little better," because "otherwise one gets to the front fatigued."[144] Like a good wife, Elfride did her best to improve her husband's everyday life by sending clothing and food, and their parents did the same. Nonetheless, she was very worried about the precarious state of their finances, whereas he spent freely on books and food.[145]

Heidegger was assigned to the corps that worked with weather balloons[146] and was trained as a meteorological observer; as he explained to his wife, "the set-up is probably only a month old—before that there were just isolated stations near the actual airships—now the observations of temp., barometer, wind, etc. are to be expertly & systematically provided for the artillery & air force by us. One station is usually under a ltnt. or staff sergeant & 5 more men—one of them, with scientif. training & previous experience, is the assistant (actual) observer."[147] His training was supposed to last eight weeks, "milit.[ary] activity" that Heidegger considered "very nice & decent"; afterward, he would be sent, along with his comrades, "to the weather stations at the headquarters—life there interesting—not dangerous—pleasant."[148] The training courses were intensive and interesting: after a week, Heidegger could already write that he had "learnt many new things" and "took more pleasure in it each day." He added: "With this terrific heat everything is very strenuous & I wasn't so used to sitting on school benches anymore either—I need the time in the evenings for work as well (consolidation, expansion, specialization)."[149] The pleasure he took in the courses was accompanied by agreeable relationships. When he first arrived, he met "an old acquaintance" from his youth, with whom he had been at the Gymnasium in Freiburg[150] and who had also been assigned to the weather balloon specialists. In addition, Heidegger made a new friend—this was rare for him—whose background was as rural as his own: he came from Oberkirch in the Black Forest and had "been studying mathemat. & chemistry for just 2 semesters in Heidelberg—very clever, unspoilt—awkward—but very receptive in matters of the spirit."[151]

Up to that point, despite his Catholic conservative prejudices against big cities, Heidegger had looked with favor on Berlin. The food shortage was on display in the streets and aroused his admiration for these Berliners; he saluted "how they accept and understand that they must go *hungry.*"[152] Then homesickness and Elfride's absence filled him with a melancholy that soon shrouded in gray and black the metropolis surrounding him, made worse by the rain that was falling on the "lonely Sunday afternoon" when he wrote her, more than two weeks after leaving Freiburg: "I've only ever been as homesick as this when I first went to grammar school in Constance as a little boy." Without Elfride, in this rainy weather, ruminating on memories that made him homesick, Heidegger was not in the best mood to appreciate Berlin, all the less so because to amuse himself, he had gone to explore the busy city center with his comrade from Oberkirch.

The two wide-eyed country boys walked down Friedrichstraße, but without venturing into a café, because they "didn't have the courage." They remained outside, watching what was going on, before leaving at half-past eleven, both of them "disgusted to the marrow": "I presume we only saw the surface—but it is wilder than I could have ever imagined; I'd never have believed such an atmosphere of artificially cultivated, most vulgar & sophisticated sexuality was possible."[153] Reading this passage in Heidegger, one might imagine that he had inadvertently found himself in a street full of loose women, prostitutes and actresses kept by young or old bourgeois men—mainly old in this period when most of the young men were at the front. Yet Friedrichstraße, though certainly open to pleasures with its cafés, theaters, cabarets, and hotels, was at the same time an opulent street where a large part of the capital's luxury was concentrated, and it retained the appearance of decency.

Heidegger and his comrade thought they were looking at a new Babylon, a whore-city, even though Friedrichstraße was a condensed version of metropolitan life, its anonymity and its superficial hustle and bustle. A confirmation of this is provided by the comparison he made when he went to see the University of Berlin and its library, from which he returned horrified. The shock of discovering the metropolis lent a new gleam to Freiburg: "Now I do understand Berlin better—the character of Friedrichstrasse has rubbed off on the whole city—& in such a milieu there can be no true intellectual culture [. . .]—& even if every perfect remedy were to hand—it lacks what is simply Grand and *Divine*. When I think of Freibg. & its Minster & the outlines of the Black Forest Mountains—!"

Berlin, henceforth seen as a site of decadence, of the denial of personality and an authentic spirituality, was completely in line with the ideas he had had as a young Catholic conservative. Heidegger, horrified, called for a reconquest of this Babylon of inauthenticity that could be carried out only from places that were still best suited for professing authenticity and living authentically—the provincial universities, from which "a culture rooted in the soil [*bodenständige Kultur*] should emanate" (translation modified). As a sign of radicalization, he managed to find a spiritual interest in the war, which he hoped might purify the society of his time: "The war hasn't yet become frightful enough for us."[154]

Heidegger remained in Berlin another month before being sent to the Western Front. But although "during the last days of freedom" that he had enjoyed after his training, he had "still worked very well in the Royal Library" and thought that "there still remained a great deal of work" for him to do in the capital, that did not prevent him from being "happy to leave." He was beginning to "grow weaker due to the shortage of food" and had not "succeeded in meditating inwardly"[155] under this reign of superficiality.

Having left with its instruments on 23 August[156] for a five-day trip in a goods convoy,[157] front Meteorological Station 414 arrived in Lorraine, near the Belgian border, half-way between Sedan and Verdun, to set up in the village of Nouillonpont, which was near Vauban's citadel of Montmédy. Although connected with the Third Army's meteorological service, it was stationed in the First Army's theater of operations; in the Battle of the Marne, which had begun on 15 July 1918, its mission was to cover the First Army's left wing, which was supposed to advance toward Reims.[158]

Heidegger considered the trip "very interesting"[159] and even "prodigious":[160] Longwy, Luxembourg, Longuyon ("in a wonderful location—but badly shot up"), then a stop in Montmédy for two days, long enough to receive "further information from the army weather station." There he also met "people from the 28th res. div. (Baden reg.)," that is, from home.[161] Then they were set up outside the village of Nouillonpont ("350 inhabitants, 80 are still there") on a "lovely plateau with woodland & lovely meadows—a clear air health resort" that inspired in Heidegger a feeling of happiness, gravity, and longing combined.

Alongside more theoretical or political developments, Heidegger's letters to his wife are a space of nostalgic reverie that gives free rein to love: "Knowledge of one's innermost & absolute belonging with the most beloved person among the living—above all, the absolute, simple pleasure in this possession in the midst of the destruction, primitiveness, harshness, & impoverished meaning of one's surroundings, has a deeply invigorating effect, & latently so."[162]

Heidegger was surrounded by agreeable people, prominent men like himself: two secondary school teachers, one from Mannheim, the other from the

Rhineland, with a corporal who was a "nice" Berlin merchant; they lived and worked in a "nice little hut built for that purpose and which is fitted out very prettily." Topped with an observation platform, the hut had an office and a telephone booth on the left: the meteorologists slept on the right, where they looked out on Fort Douaumont, which was "clearly visible."[163] The beds were crude, like everything else: the mattress was only a "sack filled with wood chips on wire mesh" (translation modified); the sleepers covered themselves with tent canvas and woolen blankets. Heidegger had a little bookshelf over his bed where he put his books and displayed a few images: small reproductions of "Dutch masters from the Kaiser Friedr. Museum"[164] and two photographs of Elfride, including the one with the sunflower that she had sent him in December 1915 in response to the portrait of himself he had sent to her. Only rats under their hut and fleas in the wood chips of their mattresses diminished their comfort, but they were going "to put things in order."[165]

Their laundry was done in the village,[166] but the task of chopping firewood fell to them, which greatly pleased the philosopher.[167] The food he ate varied: when he arrived, he wrote: "Fried potatoes are being prepared right now! the fare doesn't seem to be bad."[168] However, two days later he declared that he was finding it rather difficult "to get used to the food," which caused "all kinds of indisposition": "We get soup once at midday (with pearl barley & meat in it), in the evening coffee with butter or jam or sausage—I'll just see how it all works out—whether we get by—I think so, if we sleep a lot & there's time for that all right."[169] The army often provided them with jam, 150 grams a day, for which Heidegger asked Elfride to send him a little pot, and another for the butter;[170] he also asked for cookies, sugar, and Hoffmann's Drops;[171, 172] he also received pâté and bread rolls.[173] These packages improved his day-to-day life, whereas he did the same for his wife by sending her cocoa and soap.[174]

Heidegger remained in the combat zone for two months, until the armistice. He took advantage of these living conditions, which were very agreeable for a soldier at the front in that period; his position was calm, far from what he suggested in his 1934 curriculum vitae, in which he says that he was "outside Verdun."[175] To be sure, when he arrived there Heidegger mentioned "an air-raid in Montmédy—I saw the military hospital—which is situated right next to the station—i.e., irresponsibly & ineptly." At the camp itself there was "hardly any danger" for them: "Not even from planes, as we're quite off the beaten track." This allowed him to write that "there is something strangely serious—& yet peaceful—open—trusting—about existence in the field."[176]

In the hut, he had "a lot of telephone duty,"[177] transmitting great quantities of numbers over a vast network, which amused him very much and left him a great deal of time for sleeping and taking "rest-cures"; he was off duty every four days, which allowed him to read and work on his philosophy, which he could do even when he was on call, because his duty was "not that strict." His lieutenant, a reserve officer who was a geologist, had defended his thesis in Tübingen that spring, and was thinking about doing his habilitation: for that reason, he showed Heidegger particular good will and assured him he would make sure Heidegger could work well.[178]

For all the soldiers, the war was full of slack periods that books could pleasurably fill. Ernst Jünger, assigned on 20 May 1917 to a reserve company in the Siegfried Position near Saint-Quentin, was able to read "with extreme pleasure all of Ariosto."[179] Similarly, Heidegger had plenty of time to read Dostoevsky's *Brothers Karamazov*[180] as well as Friedrich Hölderlin, whose poem "Socrates and Alcibiades" he quoted ("He who has thought what is deepest, loves what is most alive"), and which seemed to him "a new experience," as if he were "approaching him wholly primordially for the first time." In addition to these readings, Heidegger felt "a great need to do some writing,"[181] which led him to write many letters to his wife and, less regularly, to acquaintances like Elisabeth Blochmann and Edmund Husserl.

Heidegger was still developing as a philosopher and gradually moved closer to Husserl, even if in May 1917 he still saw himself as Rickert's student, and still more as having been spawned by his own works. He participated in the seminar that Husserl ran in the winter semester of 1917–1918, on the relations between "logic and the general theory of knowledge," accompanied by his friend Heinrich Ochsner, who sensed in the seminar the "proximity to the divine."[182] He therefore set about seriously studying phenomenology, which Husserl "made much easier" for him through their conversations. The young philosopher thereby came to "experience the fact that one becomes truly involved only in living relationships."[183]

Husserl had become a genuine mentor for him. The phenomenologist's letters went from being courteous to being warm in January 1918, and subsequently adopted a paternal tone: "Oh, your youth! How happy it makes me and warms my heart that you let me share in it through your letters."[184] The relationship of constructive philosophical dialogue, or *symfilosofein* (*συμφιλοσοφειν*), of which Husserl was so fond, was accompanied by a more simply human interest in a young soldier who reminded him of his two sons who had gone to war. One of them, Wolfgang, a lieutenant, had been killed in 1916,[185] and the serious wound that their son Gerhart had suffered filled the Husserls with concern; Heidegger, who was then at the front, not far away, immediately went to Sedan to visit the wounded man at the hospital, but in vain, because he had already been sent home.[186]

The conditions under which Heidegger and his comrades lived and fought were incomparably more secure and comfortable than those of most soldiers at the front, particularly those who were on the front lines at that time. Heidegger faced little more danger than a stray artillery shell hitting his meteorological observation hut; above all, he was exposed to the idea of the actual possibility of his own death. Finally, the danger increased, came closer.

The last major German offensive in the summer of 1918 fizzled out. The end of the season of good weather led to the gradual retreat of the empire's troops, in anticipation of defeat, though neither the soldiers nor the populations behind the lines had been clearly informed about it. Heidegger, who remained stationed in Nouillonpont almost to the end, saw the combat zone coming nearer, making more obviously present the front lines, their dangers, and the risks that weighed on everyone even in the rear, whereas in Freiburg there were rumors of an impending aerial attack or a French invasion.[187] On 13 September, the philosopher testified to this military activity that was intensifying in a worrying manner around him. He himself was more active: "It's still very early in the morning, you'll still be pleasantly 'nodding'—& the little Blackamoor's long since awake—sitting at the telephone & passing huge quantities of numbers on to the artillery, airshipmen, gas officers, etc. & as he does so the heavy artillery rumbles & the bombs thunder, making everything in the hut shake—it'll probably get livelier yet—."[188]

Heidegger was right: the artillery bombardments subsequently increased, by day and by night, as he could see looking toward Fort Douaumont, of which his hut had a good view: "At night from the tower we can watch the muzzle flashes & even more the impact of the bombs—which makes everything in the hut shake—but you get used to it, and even keep on sleeping."[189] Despite this disturbing environment, and despite the apparently unfavorable development of the war, Heidegger remained confident about his fate and that of his country. "You don't need to worry about me—we already have the truck for retreat too—but I don't think we'll need it as there are good people stationed there."

The lack of awareness of the actual military situation, which now doomed Germany to a certain defeat that only the high staff knew about, was accompanied by a strange euphoria, the joy of curiosity and the discovery of a world of danger, adventure, and heroism in which he was more than anything a spectator: "I'm very well—taking pleasure in the new things I see—your inquisitive Blackamoor is getting his money's worth now—in the village the convoys go close behind one another in threes—assault battalions march through, young, rather pale, sharp faces—resolute looks in their eyes [. . .] but quite unflagging strength [. . .] the men are all silent, lost in thought, a few kilometers & they're in Hell."[190]

Heidegger had a front-row seat, not to see the fighting, but to see the soldiers leaving and their resoluteness in facing death, which they were going to defy in those storms of steel that Jünger described so well. Except in his imagination, he knew nothing of the heroic marches toward glory and death made by the shock troops' commando squads, which, far more than life in his meteorological observation hut, exposed the soldier to death and the thought of his own probable end. Nonetheless, this idea marked him, and he felt moved to make choices for himself in view of his own death, which, it seemed to him, could come at almost any time.

This subject arose in September 1918 with the expected arrival of a child, whose name, Jörg, had already been chosen. As a father-to-be, Heidegger often let his imagination run wild about the anticipated child, about the happiness that would come along with him, his soul infused with "life's clarity" and a "genuine religiousness,"[191] which required a decision that could change a believer: the choice of the denomination in which the child would be raised. In canon law, there was no question about it: the Catholic Church insisted that the offspring of a mixed marriage had to be baptized and educated in the Roman Catholic faith. The Heidegger couple had expressly committed themselves to do so when they got married. This was no longer Elfride's view, and she was followed in this by her husband in a long letter on the subject: "Many thanks for your 3 letters—I was prepared for what they contain in the way of decisive matters—and for me too the decision has already been taken—& from the bottom of my heart at that."[192]

The decision to raise Jörg as a Protestant meant that they would "lead & guide the newly glowing young soul of our child & provide him with *the* most valuable of life's opportunities ordained by God in such a way that the life that grows forth from ours & carries it on is one inhabited at root by an orientation toward God together with a powerful will to action within the frame of influence of meaningful human existence [*Dasein*]."[193] This authentic decision was made in his inner depths in conformity with his inner voice, from among all the possibilities without exception that might have presented themselves to his free will; it was not a decision made superficially with regard to what was expected of him. In that respect, the decision was completely in harmony with the concern for authenticity and responsibility conveyed by the Youth Movement with which Elfride had acquainted him, in a conversion that shook the foundations of his Catholicism.

For his parents, Heidegger had had each time only one choice, the right one, which corresponded to what he was obligated to do: become a priest, pursue his studies in theology, and, if all else failed, marry a Catholic and bring forth children raised in the Roman Catholic faith. This decision regarding Jörg's upbringing was of major consequence: it implied a painful rupture with his family, which already had hardly understood his choice of a Protestant wife; it was a rebellion without any way of compromising with "the pious-acting despotism of conscience" that was expressed by his parents, and especially by his mother. He knew how great their incomprehension and anger would be, concluding that "all argument, therefore, is utterly futile, & would be so even if my parents had a higher level of education—you see, they've grown up into a distorted form of life from which no one can extricate them. If I ask them for their trust in my serious will & resolve, they won't even be able to take that fully seriously & will accordingly judge me to be thoughtless, weak, ungrateful, & disobedient. [. . .] They regard any deviation from their own will (itself unfree) as disobedience. And at the same time this is then the measure of my ingratitude & neglect of duty." He had to either displease his parents and cause them pain or abdicate his own will and that of his future child: faced with this Cornelian dilemma, confronted by "what is tragic about the whole thing," Heidegger saw "no way out & no mitigation either."

The magnitude of the stakes, namely, "the truthfulness & inherent value of one's own decision," a decision that they had made themselves and that bore within it "all the benefits of spiritual emancipation, of shared vitality, of rich opportunities for shaping our future family life," to which was added the "intrinsic value" of having been made "in the face of the system imposed & passed on" by tradition, meant that it was irremediably necessary to go through "this tragedy."[194] Heidegger had distanced himself so much from Catholicism that he had come to see it as an enemy, an oppressive "system" from which he had to liberate himself; tradition, in which he earlier saw only something excellent, had become the secret force of a past imposed without proper reflection, even the henchman of inauthenticity. His family, "so much a part of the parish house," was the victim of the "Catholic system's inner lack of freedom." The decision to raise Jörg as a Protestant was therefore the desire to raise him free, and was in no way turned against Heidegger's parents, against whom he made no reproach.

Heidegger drew important conclusions about himself: "All my earlier insecurity, untruthfulness, & casuistry are the simple consequence of an ultra-Catholic education, which on the other hand I always sought to break out of with inadequate means."[195] Before he went to the front, he was grateful to Elfride for her salutary influence. He knew that he owed his "sincerity" to her "sweet presence," her "immediate being," and asked her to give him time to "cast off completely everything that counts as false for our innermost being, everything that represents an inner restraint" on his work itself.[196] In short, the presence of his own death, associated with Elfride's insistence, had forced Heidegger to make a decision and led him to oppose his parents directly on a particularly difficult point, the choice of his son's religion.

The war had thus played a major role in this break with Catholicism. Before Heidegger left for the front, the discussion regarding the religion in which Jörg would be raised had led to discord, because Heidegger had remained faithful to his parents' religion, which he did not want to betray. Now he saw it in these terms: "Perhaps when we've spoken about it we've lacked the necessary seriousness & failed to appreciate the magnitude of what was called for." In his view, this shift proceeded from what he experienced at the front: "Today and in the last few weeks, seeing oneself reduced to one's simplest & most elemental existence [*Existenz*], petty standards & anxious considerations have all ceased to apply—in the primitiveness of existence [*Dasein*] issues of ultimate significance approach one another with due immediacy, strength, & clarity."[197] Probable death drives man back to himself: tearing away the veil of superficiality with which he likes to cover his face, it confronts him radically with his possibilities, enjoining him to resolutely make a determination on the basis of the situation and himself.

Accordingly, at the front, far from one's wife, "in the midst of a sphere of existence [*Dasein*] where life is no longer worth anything, where every man's face bears one particular feature, a characteristic look of having settled the score & being ready, where comforts have ceased to exist," the view of existence is purified, and the true value of each thing appears, "great gratitude bursts forth for each flower & each ray of sunshine, each moment of harmless laughter & each comradely favor," and "one first fully feels the blissful happiness that is encapsulated within the thought of one's dearest and most beloved one." Each individual's personality is then revealed and indicates his duty to him: "The most painstaking discharge of duties & sense of responsibility are the prevailing content of day & night" and "one first experiences what 'home' [*Heimat*] means."[198]

In this proximity to death that contributed to making everything simple, blissful, the score settled, the philosopher's insouciance, indeed this sort of exaltation that took hold of him, hardly slackened: in October, he again let his friend Elisabeth Blochmann know that, to be sure, he was "outside Verdun, in a not very reassuring spot" where the life led was "primitive," but that nonetheless he was "doing well," "was succeeding in setting to work," and down deep felt "remarkably fresh and vigorous."[199] This insouciance receded only at the extreme end of the conflict. On 6 November, five days before the armistice, Heidegger was on the move, because of the retreat of the German forces, and if Germany's situation now seemed to him hopeless, he comforted himself by embracing the ideal of the authentic spirit: "Each day brings its share of vicissitudes—along with uncertain tomorrows—but I firmly believe in the spirit and in its power, whoever lives in it and for it never wages a hopeless battle."[200] On 10 November, as the German army was collapsing, Heidegger, caught up in talk about the suspension of mail delivery and the "wildest" rumors about the signing of an armistice, which "one after another [. . .] prove to be false," was scandalized that the "gunfire goes on the same as ever—pointless sacrifice of human lives."[201] Insouciance disappeared, replaced by waves of anger that grew ever stronger the longer he stayed at the front.

Since his earliest writings, Heidegger had cultivated a virulent critique of the society of his time and its superficiality, a critique that his relationship with Elfride had transformed into a denunciation of inauthenticity inspired by the Youth Movement and made fiercer by his departure for the war and his experience in Berlin. In the time the philosopher spent at the front, this critique acquired an intensity that was previously unequaled and that continually grew until the signing of the armistice. In October, Heidegger vigorously reformulated his diagnosis: "We're bogged down in a horribly deformed culture with a spurious appearance of life—in most people all root connections with the fundamental sources of true life have withered away—superficial existence prevails everywhere, but is all the more brazen, insistent, demanding—we lack the great enthusiasm of the soul and spirit for the true life & experience of valuable worlds." This state of affairs seemed to him an ancient, profound evil, attributable to a narrow, wild materialism that concealed man's humanity, in oneself and in the other: "In recent decades or even during the whole of the last century we've not taken enough care—if any at all—of the inner human being in ourselves *& in others*. Values such as soul & spirit have been lacking, their meaning could no longer be experienced—or at most as a perfect object of destruction for exact scientific (both natural sci. & 'histor.') analyses."[202] This superficiality was found in the press, which was "governed by spiritual adolescents"[203] and fueled a bitter discourse on philosophy in the name of a "more outwardly oriented, seemingly 'active' lifestyle—and would reproach philosophy for being out of touch with & turning away from life," an unjust and symptomatic critique of the exteriority into which time vanishes: on the contrary, the sole valid "criterion" for judging must be formed "from the innermost unfolding of the spirit itself"[204]—in a word, from a personal, inner, and authentic practice of philosophy.

This general withering of the "root connections with the fundamental sources of true life" reached the very foundations of prewar political life, because "this whole aimlessness & hollowness & alienation from values have dominated political life & the concepn. of the state in general." But on the eve of the defeat this withering was experienced even more cruelly among the soldiers at the front, who, after "the sufferings of 4 years," lacked "any truly rousing sense of purpose." They were "systematically nauseated by pan-German pipe dreams," and all the more disoriented because the disastrous outcome of the war no longer fostered the dream of German supremacy over Eastern Europe, which had been encouraged by the Treaty of Brest-Litovsk imposed on defeated Russia on 3 March 1918. As a result, soldiers faced "a hollow-eyed aimlessness." Radically criticizing pan-Germanism as one of the forms of the time's superficiality and spiritual withering, Heidegger was not for all that without nationalism, at least understood as a conscious love of one's own nation accompanied by love of self and of the other. For that reason, he regretted that these soldiers were laboring "under a sense not of national belonging based on true love & helpfulness—but of being deceived & abused for the selfish purposes of spiritually misguided or indeed completely unspiritual, backward power groups."[205]

An escape from this spiritual "hardship" could come only with "new human beings who harbor an elemental affinity with spirit & its demands," new human beings who would have to be "leaders" (*Führer*), because "only the individual is creative even in leadership, the masses never." As one might expect, it had been Elfride in the first place who had asserted this idea of the "necessity" of a *Führer* (*die Notwendigkeit der Führer*) forcefully called for by Heidegger. The philosopher adds: "I myself recognize ever more urgently the necessity for leaders [*Führer*]."[206] His wife tended to see them as political leaders, as Prince Max of Baden might turn out to be. The heir to the Grand Duchy of Baden, appointed on 3 October 1918 as chancellor of the empire and minister-president of Prussia, a liberal—marking a sharp difference from the conservative empire without being a dangerous social democrat—Max of Baden seemed "undoubtedly one of the new people,"[207] as Heidegger recognized shortly afterward. For him, the essential point lay elsewhere: "truly spiritual men" were needed, men who would not "flinch precisely now, but on the contrary [. . .] resolutely assume the role of guides and educate the people to be sincere and make an authentic evaluation of the authentic values of existence."[208]

The idea of being able to remedy the German people's spiritual poverty, which was so much greater than its material poverty, filled Heidegger with joy as the military defeat became increasingly clear: "However gloomy & threatened by fate things are around us, I hold out joyful hope for the assured creative reawakening of our entire existence. [. . .] it's a joy to be alive, because we're facing completely new horizons & discover new territory."[209] That was why he considered the German defeat not only inevitable, given the military situation, but desirable because of the country's political and spiritual condition over the past century: "This end [. . .] had to come and [. . .] it is our only salvation."[210] The Great War led Heidegger to a radicalism in spiritual combat that was even more pronounced than the Catholicism of his early youth; in addition, this idea that the defeat was a "necessary" end, and that it was urgent to take the people in hand, is typical of the feelings of Conservative Revolutionaries at the end of the war. As Ernst von Salomon wrote in *The Outlaws,* "in 1918, the men who returned from the trenches had felt that we had to lose the war in order to win the nation. They had felt a great upheaval in themselves, and they had seen that nothing new had been built and that everything was possible."[211] The idea that the revolution that befell imperial Germany and the defeat that it marked were useful was also expressed by Arthur Moeller van den Bruck in 1923: "What is revolutionary today will be conservative tomorrow. That is how disorder is repaired, how what has been dislocated is 'reset.' We do not want to continue the revolution but to pursue the realization of its ideas. [. . .] We want to connect these revolutionary ideas with conservative ideas, we want to create a kind of conservative-revolutionary alloy. [. . .] We want to win the Revolution! [. . .] What does that mean? It has put an end to the war through our collapse. We want it to appear, just like the war, to be a detour useful for our history."[212]

Heidegger also saw the necessity of a radically revolutionary commitment, because although it was "only in such periods that hours of the birth of the spirit awakened," the situation was far from being sufficient in itself: "Hardship must at most be an external cause & stimulus but never a reason & motive for a change in direction of spirit & soul—for this an original turning inwards is required, which we are still very far from grasping."[213] In this "disaster" for the nation, Heidegger thought that "only through this quite radical purification will there be anything to hope for—& only through radicalism—complete commitment of the human being as a whole—will we ourselves advance as real revolutionaries of the spirit."[214]

The university and the combination of research, teaching, and education[215] were thus of crucial importance for the future spiritual revolution: "Only the young will save us now—& creatively allow a New Spirit to be made flesh in the world."[216] Heidegger was in fact convinced that "spirit finds whomsoever it is meant to find, & from those found one wave after another sweeps forth, rousing, agitating & keeping in agitation, into the many who are lethargic & massive in quality & number. [. . .] Once we have regained full trust in spirit, we'll reach a position to allow unreflective creative culture to rise up again & continue to exert an influence."[217]

For that to happen, "young lecturers" still had to be up to the task, "capable of forming a genuine association animated by new convictions & gaining acceptance." Heidegger was "pessimistic" about this, and preferred to pin all his hopes on the students themselves[218]—which amounted to saying that he pinned the hope of a spiritual revolution that would spread to the whole German people on his own teaching, through the intermediary of his students. With this goal in mind, he formulated the wish that, "especially in the first decade straight after the war & probably for good," he could "give a course of one-hour lectures on the essence of university & academic study"; full of faith and optimism, he had "an inner conviction that it would help make young people inwardly awake & strong & they will go out as a 'leaven' into the future life of the state and the people."

However, their authenticity had to be nurtured, they had to be persuaded to cast off "everything merely short-lived & determined by the milieu" and foster instead "the great *critique* of principles." To that end, he thought that "all the material from the Academic Volunteer Corps [*akademische Freischar*] & the Free Germans in general would be extremely useful." A very robust philosopher, Heidegger nonetheless subscribed fully to the spiritual movement to which he had converted: he saw his "calling"[219] as that of a "truly spiritual" man, a new man, a guide because he was a researcher and an educator, whose role was primarily cultural but had political repercussions both mediated and fundamental; his political engagement was and thus had to be that of a teacher, and for that he needed the materials from the Youth Movement, which had probably contributed to his own conversion. Henceforth, one had "to expect a few external privations and renunciations—but only inwardly poor aesthetes and men who, claiming to count among the best 'spirits,' have up to now only played with spirit, as others play with money or pleasure, will now collapse and sink, distraught, into despair—help and valuable directives are hardly to be expected from them."[220]

To pave the way for the coming spiritual revolution, Heidegger preached to his comrades, who proved to be not very receptive to his doctrine of salvation through authenticity: "I've approached my comrades a little & tried to suggest quite crudely & unphilosophically what the new demands of the spirit will be—I met with alarming standards—a bourgeois mediocrity & an attitude to life I really wasn't prepared for." Undaunted, he drew the conclusion that his efforts and those of his students "will at first be limited to just small circles, & there [they] will continue to grow of [their] own accord; quantity isn't what counts at all in the early days anyway, but rather the force & devotion with which it asserts itself."[221] Quality was far more important than quantity, reinforcing his conviction that "never will cultural artillery, however far it is taken, bring us one step closer to immediate life & experience," whereas the "innate vehemence of spirit renders superfluous everything which as a practical philosophy of life abuses the term 'philosophy.' "[222] As the leader of the little group formed around his wife and himself, Heidegger thus tried to work to build powerful and loyal groups of students around him, as storm troopers, elite spiritual commando squads that would win the war for German spiritual revolution.

Despite the feeling that the army's disorganization was increasing, the last days of the war differed little from what Heidegger had known up to that point. On 5 November, he was promoted to lance-corporal, then discharged on 16 November by the 10th Air Reserve Battalion.[223] He was delighted to be demobilized in Freiburg, without passing again through Berlin.[224] The armistice was signed on the 11th, making Germany's military collapse official. In the end, the Great War had forced Heidegger to spend no more than five months outside his native region, from July to November 1918. But despite its brevity, his military service profoundly changed Heidegger, leading him to discover Germany as far as Berlin and cross the borders of the empire to be stationed in Lorraine. The time he spent at the front made him a revolutionary, which he had not been previously, which reinforced a pugnacity in him that was struggling to find expression. Despite his view of society and the state at this time of defeat, the philosopher was ultimately not much dislodged from his preoccupations, which were primarily spiritual and academic, even if they then acquired a radicalism and a vehemence that they had not previously had, and which resolutely connected Heidegger with the Conservative Revolutionaries, who believed the old order was doomed to disappear, though it ought not to be replaced by a socialist state. If a revolution was desirable, it had to be conservative, as Moeller said, in order to ensure "that everything in Germany that deserves to be protected, will be protected."[225]

II

A Revolutionary Philosopher (1919–1933)

4 • The Memory of Meßkirch Fades Away

(1919–1923)

"We civilized peoples now know that we are mortal." Each of the victorious and vanquished countries that took part in the Great War in Europe experienced profound economic, spiritual, and political challenges, of which Paul Valéry provided a radical formulation. As a whole, Europe had experienced its mortality; through the "accident"[1] of a war, it was able to join forever the bygone past of history. Germans experienced these painful convulsions of the immediate postwar period more than other European peoples did. And while the defeat shook the nation's foundations, Martin Heidegger thought that it was time for a philosophical revolution. Despite his emotion upon returning to his hometown, this revolution that shook him caused him increasingly to forget the region of his birth, its religion, and its values. The Meßkirch way was fading away without his realizing it.

Indifference toward Germany's Defeat?

Germany's defeat, and the signing of the armistice that made it official, shocked the people, who had until very recently been expecting the impending victory that had been promised by the High Command, which, moreover, refused to take responsibility for the defeat. Confronted by the prospect of a final battle to save the navy's honor, the sailors in Kiel mutinied; councils of workers and soldiers inspired by the Russian example were set up, and on 9 November the Republic was proclaimed in Berlin by the Social Democratic Party (SPD) politician Philipp Scheidemann. A revolution broke out that called for peace and subsequently nourished the reconstructed illusion of a "stab in the back" (*Dolchstoß*) perpetrated by socialists and Jews against a Germany that was still bravely fighting its enemies abroad, and which for that reason had not lost the war militarily. This idea—which was false, because Germany had been finally defeated, suffocated by the economic blockade, submerged by the influx of American soldiers, and crushed by the effectiveness of tanks in which it had not believed—constituted a consensus that was widely shared on both the right and the left. Even President Friedrich Ebert and his chancellor, Philipp Scheidemann, insisted that Germany had not been defeated militarily, since the Allied troops had not invaded the territory of the Reich.

Although the reaction of Germans in general is well known, we have only fragmentary information regarding Heidegger's reaction. He seems not to have taken an interest in the details of these events; in addition, Freiburg did not experience much in the way of revolutionary convulsions, and neither did its councils of workers and soldiers.[2] By contrast, Heidegger was unsettled by the Spartacists' attempted coup d'état in early 1919, which further fed the antisocialism that he had been showing since his youth in Meßkirch, though he did not draw any general political conclusions from it: "I hope," he wrote to Blochmann, "that the mad situation of our dear homeland is not depriving you of serenity and confidence in the spirit."[3]

The peace treaty signed at Versailles on 28 June 1919—the *diktat* imposed on Germany, first by France, which wanted to deprive it as much as possible of all the instruments of power that might enable it to become a danger again—seems not to have attracted his attention either, no matter how hard the conditions promulgated might have been. Acknowledged to be responsible for the war, Germany had to pay, for forty-two years, reparations in the exorbitant amount of 132 billion gold marks;[4] it lost one-seventh of its prewar territory plus its colonies in Africa, and was not allowed to keep the considerable territories it had gained in the east at Russia's expense. Unable to wage another war, the army was reduced to a minimum to keep watch over the country and its coasts. Although Chancellor Scheidemann, to whom these conditions had been dictated, chose to resign rather than approve them, the Republic bore the weight of the defeat, which for many Germans had taken place not so much in the bloody trenches of the battlefields as in the hushed rooms of diplomacy, where the nation had been betrayed by its Social Democratic government after being stabbed in the back by the Red revolution. The electoral consequences were clear: the three parties of the Weimar coalition, the DDP (German Democratic Party), Zentrum (Center Party), and the SPD (Social Democratic Party), which had won 76 percent of the votes in the constitutional elections held on 19 January 1919,[5] taken all together won only 43.6 percent of the votes in the

Reichstag elections on 6 June 1920; the rest went to the revolutionary left and the ultranationalist right.

Heidegger's reaction was similarly unpoliticized when France occupied the Ruhr in 1923, in reprisal for Germany's repeated failures to deliver the goods required as part of the reparations. Although he was suffering from the housing shortage in the city of Marburg, where he set up his household at that time, he did not point out that this situation proceeded in part from the French occupation that had caused refugees to flood in. He merely noted, when he moved to the university, the terrible inflation; it had been considerable since late 1922, and was now accelerating so fast that the currency was collapsing; inflation seemed to him a natural hazard, like bad weather that would go away the following week.[6] His lack of economic and political knowledge was manifest, as was, more broadly, his lack of understanding of the concrete life of a state and international relations.

Heidegger was uneducated in politics. He had been born at a time when the culture of suffrage, of citizens' partisan participation in politics, had not spread throughout Germany, and in a state, the Second Reich (1870–1919), which had undergone only a relative democratization. The Catholic Church had given him the model of a hierarchical political community that was infallible on the essential points, commanded obedience, and accorded little importance to discussion and debate; his discovery of the Jugendbewegung and the time he spent in the army had revived this idea in him, giving it a turn that was more secular and more in contact with nature, but not more liberal. Hans Jonas, one of his students, reported one of their conversations in 1929: he had just come back from Basel, where he had attended the sixteenth Zionist Congress: Heidegger put him up for the night, which allowed them to talk more freely, less academically. He asked Jonas to explain what Zionism was; he knew nothing about it. "Zionist congress—what goes on there? I suppose the whole thing takes place in a big tent?" he asked, probably thinking of the Youth Movement's meetings, out in nature, like that of the oath taken on the Hohe Meißner in the autumn of 1913. "No," Jonas replied, "there's a conference center where the participants stay, a hotel." As Jonas noted, on this subject Heidegger "had very primitive notions, picturing a Zionist conference as some kind of campout. He had no idea what such a political gathering was like! Yet in addition to the Zionist congress, there were also socialist congresses and all sorts of other political conventions. But Heidegger was oblivious to such things."[7]

Apolitical because he lacked knowledge of and esteem for concrete politics, Heidegger accorded much less attention to current events and to his contemporaries than to philosophy and to authors of the past, which he knew something about.[8] Despite his strong propensity for abstraction and his lack of interest in the details of political life, Heidegger absorbed the atmosphere of the time, particularly from his wife. The abstract ideas he expressed sometimes amplified the views around him, and, no doubt unconsciously, he was influenced by Germany's violent rejection of the Treaty of Versailles. Particularly on the right, there was a widespread belief that the defeat had not taken place on the battlefield but under the crystal chandeliers of Louis XIV's palace, and soon the myth of the *Dolchstoß*, according to which the German army had been stabbed in the back by the Revolution of 9 November, was also in circulation. This myth, popularized by Hindenburg, was adopted massively by the right wing for the Reichstag elections of June 1920,[9] and often the right discerned behind the SPD the specter of a Jewish conspiracy.[10] The year 1920 witnessed for the first time the entrance of polemology in Heidegger's teaching: his course titled "Phenomenology of Religion" introduced the conception of philosophy as a battle or struggle (*Kampf*), in this case against common sense ("sound human understanding").[11] Above all, his lectures included no fewer than thirty-two occurrences of the word *Kampf* and repeatedly referred to the Apostle Paul's battle against the "Jews" and "Jewish Christians."[12] Although these formulations were neutral, they took on their full meaning in light of the philosopher's anti-Semitism: it was during this same summer of 1920 that two new occurrences of anti-Semitism appeared in his correspondence.

The first of these dates from late August, in Meßkirch, when food shortages (particularly shortages of wheat and meat) were threatening, making Heidegger wonder whether he should take the opportunity to stock up on provisions: "Here there's a lot of talk about how many cattle now get bought up from the villages by the Jews & how that'll then be the end of buying meat in winter. [. . .] the farmers are gradually getting insolent up here too & everything's swamped with Jews and black marketeers [*Schieber*]."[13] In the context of this disorganization of the economy, which was connected with the conversion back to peacetime production and with the inflation that followed the unprecedented expansion of the monetary supply (too much currency had been issued and too many loans taken out to pay for the war), shortages and price increases were quickly understood to be the result of speculation (which they might also have been). The guilty party was as quickly found as it was obvious: the Jews, unscrupulous speculators whose virulent vice was contaminating even the peasants and merchants, transformed into "black marketeers."

The second occurrence of anti-Semitism came only a few weeks later: "Manesse [?]—Hölderlin is so grotesque one can only laugh—one wonders whether from this contamination we'll ever get back to the primordial freshness & rootedness of life again—sometimes one could really almost become a spiritual anti-Semite."[14] The expression "spiritual anti-Semite" seems curious at first: doesn't being an anti-Semite mean hating the Jewish people and its culture? Then why add "spiritual"? The problem evaporates when one tries to understand who this "Manasse [?]" was (it seems that the name is difficult to decipher in the manuscript): Heidegger is referring to Georg Mönius (Manesse, Mönius), a Catholic priest who had published, precisely in 1920, his doctoral thesis entitled "Hölderlin as a Philosopher."[15] A pacifist and a Europeanist critical of German nationalism and Prussian militarism,[16] Mönius's sensibility was in the minority in German Catholicism at the time: this Catholic priest, spiritually (that is, intellectually) a Jew, was so because, as a European and a universalist, he was becoming rootless and anti-German. However, these political positions did not appear so clearly in his thesis, where traces of Hölderlin's cosmopolitan humanism appear almost by accident. That may not be the only cause, or even a principal one, of Heidegger's very clear-cut opinion. Mönius's thesis on Hölderlin, short and printed in large letters, was bad and resembled a biographical sketch followed by a schoolboy compilation of themes without any genuine vision, without a "problematic," or without "primordial freshness" or "rootedness of life" in Heideggerian terms. Mönius had composed a term paper pretending to be philosophical without asking the slightest question that would root it in his own existence, without anything that was authentically alive or original. "Spiritual anti-Semitism" thus may have referred to the priest's cosmopolitanism; and surely, in any case, to the lack of intellectual weight of his thesis, far removed from an original rootedness in actual life. In this case, anti-Semitism was a hostility not to Jews, but rather to what Heidegger considered to be the Jewish spirit, without the latter necessarily referring to Israelites. It was a vague generality, a kind of metaphor common at the time, just like the identification of the spirit of usury and speculation with "Jewry." This anti-Semitism, which was real, in no case made Heidegger a fanatic; some of his friends and acquaintances were Jewish, at least by background (though it is impossible to determine exactly how aware he was of that fact): his friend the philosopher Silhelm Szilasi, his student Karl Löwith, his teacher Edmund Husserl. In addition, as Heidegger saw it, the true political stakes were the philosophical revolution that would refound the German people's spiritual life; but he still had to have a post at the university, which he owed to the protection of Husserl, whose assistant he became, first de facto and then de jure.

Assistant and Revolutionary

On 7 January 1919, Husserl had asked the ministry in Karlsruhe to name Heidegger an assistant in the first philosophy seminar, with a fixed annual salary. At that time, such positions existed only in medicine, where they were still rare; in Heidegger's case, the appointment came through only more than a year later. In the interim, the Heideggers were left in a state of profound precariousness and worry, because the financial assistance provided by Elfride's family ended[17] as a result of the economic crisis of the immediate postwar period. Moreover, Elfride was pregnant with another child, Hermann, who was born on 20 August; the family's financial situation then became so difficult that Heidegger even considered entering the civil service. The philosopher's activity was impeded, and his wife no longer came out of her "shell."[18] The position was finally approved in the summer of 1920. Heidegger was greatly relieved. It is not possible to say how inwardly grateful he was to Husserl, despite the words of gratitude that he must have addressed to him; he was grateful to Elfride, who had supported him during this difficult time and had not forced him to take a government job that would have better ensured their household's bourgeois comfort.[19] In any case, he felt that this privilege that had been accorded him made him beholden in other people's eyes, "for the ones who were 'passed over' " were going to be watching him closely.[20]

Heidegger had grown closer to Husserl, becoming his main disciple. He shared with Husserl his own ideal of authenticity and the hatred of idle talk that he had inherited from his father, and declared himself against the "university & the philosophical business of the Schools, of discussions & chatter."[21] As for his students, "there are only very few who can keep up & feel their way into the real intentions—many of them get absorbed by the words & sentences."[22] Heidegger found similar dispositions in Husserl, as we are told by Karl Löwith, who was moving completely in this direction: a student of the phenomenologist after leaving Munich in the spring of 1919, he praised Husserl not only for training his students "through his magisterial phenomenological analysis, the sober clarity of his presentations, and the humane rigor of his scientific teaching," but also for the work in the seminar's exercises, in which Husserl "forced [. . .] them to avoid big words, to compare each term with the intuition of phenomena, and to give him in response to his questions not big bills but 'small change.' "[23]

Thus it was only at this time that Heidegger truly became a phenomenologist. His motto was now "back to the things themselves," to "the origin," to "the concrete problems" in which he had learned to "immerse" himself only in the course of the semester of 1919. Because Heidegger was moving closer to Husserl intellectually, he was taking his distance from Rickert, his earlier teacher. Reading Rickert's *Object of Cognition* now inspired in him "an inner hostility toward this unparalleled style of constructive & yet unmethodical thought."[24] In 1919, in addition to the genuine intellectual affinities between the two men, Husserl still had the advantage of functioning as a "counterbalance" for Heidegger because, as he told his wife with a certain lucidity, "even at the age of 30 one isn't yet fully fledged & still enjoys kicking over the traces, even if only in private—here H.[usserl] is a good counterbalance in spite of the unmistakable signs of age." Moreover, he went on, Husserl "does not exactly come bothering me with every new issue & disturbing my independence."[25]

Heidegger wanted to be an original and radical philosopher. A revolutionary of the spirit, he wrote in 1920 to his student Karl Löwith: "Living in the current situation of a de facto revolution [*Umsturz*], I am pursuing what I feel to be 'necessary' without worrying about whether a 'culture' will emerge from it or whether my research will lead to ruin."[26] This revolution had been made necessary by the madness of the time: "What will be the joke next week? I believe that a madhouse seen from the inside looks clearer and more reasonable than this period does."[27] Postulating "the negation in principle of everything that existed, as well as all programs for reform," Heidegger, as Löwith saw him, sought first of all a destruction, an undermining, of the existent: "Heidegger also warned us against a false interpretation and overestimation of his own works, as if he might himself have something 'positive' to say or 'new results' to show."[28] Rejecting a verbose, juvenile philosophy, a scientistic phenomenology and worldviews that are visionary but also without theoretical foundations and spiritual consequences, Heidegger's destructive action, if it did not produce anything, at least went somewhere: he wanted to be radical, going to the ground [*Grund*] of questions, appropriating for his own ends Husserl's return to things themselves. For that, it was necessary "simply to take everything that is given [. . .] originally in 'intuition' as what it is given to be,"[29] making a tabula rasa of everything that has been said or thought in the scholarly tradition; in his view, this way of proceeding presupposed digging deeper than the foundations of science to which his teacher tended to limit himself in order to reach actual life: "Life in its elemental power is deeper & fuller than cognition, & all our philosophy indeed suffers from the fact that it allows its further problems to be predetermined by what is already cognized [*Erkanntheiten*]—with the *result* that they are disfigured & afflicted with paradoxes from the outset." For him, "everything great is rooted in radicalism alone."[30] As he summed up his project in a letter to Rickert, "whereas Husserl essentially takes the mathematical science of nature as a model, and on that basis not only gives himself the problems in advance, but also allows them to determine his procedure in a way that is probably justified," Heidegger tried "to reach living, historical life itself, that is, the actual experience of the surrounding world [*Umwelt*]." To do that, he made the concept of the "interpretation of meaning" central, because "phenomenological intuition does not consist in fixing experiences as things," but rather as meaning, requiring a "comprehensive, hermeneutic intuition."[31] To attain its goal of returning to things themselves, it was therefore imperative that phenomenology return to the experience of the real life of things and interpret their meaning within a factual (*faktisch*)[32] life, which explained why Heidegger resorted to the term "hermeneutic" (art of interpretation) borrowed from Schleiermacher.

In his 1919 course on "the philosophical idea of philosophy and the problem of worldviews," Heidegger pointed to the inadequacies of the conceptual pairs of self and world, subject and object, which are incapable of grasping this "original attitude of living." What was at stake in these reflections was crucial for the young phenomenologist: "We are at a crossroads of methodological paths, where the life or death of philosophy is decided, on the edge of an abyss: either we take the path of nothingness, in other words of absolute objectivity, or we succeed in making the leap into another world, or, more precisely, the leap that makes us enter the world for the first time."[33] The better to show his students what was at stake, he led them to experience in their minds the discovery of the lectern: a return to things themselves, a return to life, thus a return to an object characteristic of scholarly life as teachers and students cognize it and commonly miscognize it. First, students had to put themselves in a situation in order to see and experience: how did they come to experience the lectern from which Heidegger was giving his lecture? To begin with, from a point of view, that of a student or professor who constitutes himself in a given situation occurring in everyday life: "You arrive as usual in this lecture hall at the habitual time and you are going to sit down in your usual seat. Remember this experience of the 'sight of your seat,' or reconstitute my own case: entering the lecture hall, I see the lectern." Next arises the question of what "see" means. Does seeing the lectern amount to having a mathematical, geometrical view of it, "brown surfaces that intersect at right angles"? No, because materially, the lectern appears as a whole, "a box, a rather large box, surmounted by another, smaller one," but this view, still very geometrical and too objective, makes us miss the originary phenomenon of seeing the lectern: when Heidegger saw the lectern, he saw it as an object, to be sure, but an object in a close relationship with him, because it was from it that he "was to speak," just as his students saw it above all as the position from which their professors—including Heidegger—spoke. The original phenomenon of the lectern is consequently not the objective lectern, but the lectern as it is experienced, the lectern from which professors speak and the students hear them.

Subject and object, self and world mingle in a reality more originary than these concepts: *qua* an experienced phenomenon, the lectern does not allow its objective materiality to be dissociated from the subjective relationship that students and professors have with it, just as one cannot dissociate its reality, as a lectern serving to facilitate professors speaking and students listening to them, from its material reality as a wooden box, because, as Heidegger shows, everything comes at the same time—we don't see it broken down into "brown surfaces that intersect," then as a "box," next as a "lectern," and finally as a "university lectern": one sees it "all at once," and we are immediately in relation to it, like Heidegger who, on arriving, "sees the lectern and [sees] that it is too high for him," and that, moreover, there is a book on it and it immediately appears to him "as a disturbing object."

As a totality of meaning including both object and subject, the lectern as a lived experience is itself caught up in a world from which the self cannot be dissociated: the book on the lectern, which is disturbing, is accompanied by the lighting, the background, the angle from which one sees the lectern within a world that surrounds the self that sees it and experiences it as a lectern. Heidegger's conclusion: "When I see this view of the lectern, each thing gives itself to me from my immediate environment. What surrounds me [. . .] is not things without a certain character of meaning, objects grasped as such and meaning this and that," but rather a totality meaningful for me: "Living in an environment, this has a meaning for me, everywhere and always, everything is of the world, it worlds [*sic*]."[34] The lectern is an element of its world, from which it is indissociable; it therefore refers as much to Heidegger as to what surrounds him, elements that are themselves indissociable in their lived experience from this lectern that is found in them. The philosopher arrives at the surprising expression "it worlds," in the same way that "it rains," because each element of an environment refers to the world from which it is indissociable and makes it present in the same way as the rain, which brings with it in its falling a whole rainy world.

Heidegger's phenomenological radicalism, applied to the study of the "original attitude of living," thus led him to invent new words, to manhandle language to make it say what had never been said: the break with tradition, its problems and its superimposed ideas, also presupposed a break with the inherited language and an act of violence against it. The period was ripe for a cultural revolution that would be at once philosophical, artistic, literary, and linguistic; Martin Buber and Franz Rosenzweig gave an example of this linguistic revolution with the translation, or rather "Germanization" (*Verdeutschung*), of the Old Testament they undertook starting in 1925, reinventing words and grammar rules to bend them poetically to the original text. Similarly, for Heidegger the point was not linguistic re-creation alone; it was, just as much, an effort to revitalize ontology and the history of philosophy. In his letter to Jaspers on 27 June 1922, he stated that "the old ontology (and the structures of categories that have grown out of it) must be rebuilt from the ground up," starting with "the old ontological separation between *what* something is, and *that* something is [*die alte ontologische Scheidung von Was- und Daßsein*]," in other words, between essence and existence, which had to be reduced to "an experience of the being of life (in short, the *historical*)" available to us, and "its sense of being," which meant "grasping and directing one's own present life in its basic intentions."[35]

In what is only an apparent paradox, this innovative approach, targeting man's modern existence, had to take a detour through history because it required a "critique of all ontology hitherto, with its roots in Greek philosophy, especially in Aristotle," a radical critique which, to be radical, entailed giving new life to the history of philosophy, and first of all to Greek philosophy, by acting in such a way as to understand "the thematic problems of the Greeks from the motives and the attitude of their way of access to the world, from their ways of addressing objects, and their ways, in so doing, of carrying out the formation of concepts." The history of philosophy had to serve the philosophy of the present, in a dense and critical interpretive dialogue; it had to "livingly pursue this in respect to the question of the explication of the meaning of the being of life, as *the* object that we *are*."[36] The Heidegger of 1922 found another historical impulse similar to the Heidegger of 1915, when he was working on pseudo–Duns Scotus; through this historical concern applied to ontology, he accordingly moved away from Husserl's ahistorical perspective.

He no longer confined himself to simply going back to the things themselves; his philosophical radicalism now entailed a return to the historical roots of philosophy, Greek ontology, which would allow him to lay the foundations for the true renewal that modernity called for. Heidegger was becoming even more of a conservative revolutionary: the present, discredited, had to be swept away, in favor of a modern body of work that found its origin in what in the past deserved to be retained, or even, as in the case of Greek ontology, brought back to the life of the present.

This bygone past was a weapon against the flatness and decadence of the present, which Heidegger quickly came to experience as "bourgeois." At the end of his service at the front, he had expressed to Elfride his scorn for the bourgeoisie and its conventions, after trying to convert his comrades to the ideals of the Youth Movement and encountering "a bourgeois mediocrity & an attitude to life" for which he was not prepared.[37] In 1917 and then again in 1919, he also expressed his scorn for "bourgeois" marriage.[38] His radicalism, this hostility to the bourgeoisie, corresponded to the difference in generations that separated him from Husserl: the latter, of Jewish and Austrian descent, was the product of the "period of security" that Zweig described, which was oriented entirely toward stability, comfort, and bourgeois status; Heidegger and Jaspers belonged to the generation of young people who wanted to challenge these established certainties and rely resolutely on destiny and action—even if that action was purely a philosophical discourse. Heidegger noted in 1925: "If from time to time I now compare Husserl & Jaspers—looking at their philosophical *existence*—then it's like night & day: on the one hand—to exaggerate—interest in the school—acknowledgment of the master—lack of understanding for destiny & decisions; on the other hand—sovereignty—modesty—personal commitment & a real sense of a man who takes action."[39]

This contempt for the bourgeoisie, this rejection of tradition and the authority of earlier generations, were typical of these avant-garde intellectuals of the 1920s, revolutionaries on both left and right. The postwar period was a time for overthrowing all established values, intellectual, moral, or aesthetic: for instance, the French visual artist Marcel Duchamp (1887–1968), who was close to Dadaism and who had emigrated to the United States, invented the "readymade," a work already in existence even before the artist conceived of it. The readymade was often mass-produced, like Duchamp's *Fountain* of 1917, an upside-down urinal, signed and placed in an art gallery, which acquired the status of an artwork by means of an artistic provocation that changed the perception of this trivial object, thanks to the aesthetic shock of its new presentation. In this way, the new art was no longer defined as the virtuoso realization of an exceptional aesthetic work, but as a singular, disturbing in-between space, somewhere between an initially banal object and a way of seeing that unveiled it as a work of art thanks to the artist's mediation.

If this rejection of bourgeois conventions placed Heidegger within the European avant-garde, his praise of heroic action placed him among the intellectuals of the revolutionary right. As a state of exception, the war led such thinkers as Carl Schmitt and Karl Jaspers to believe that "limit situations" (as discussed below) reveal the true essence of things, sovereignty for the jurist and political theorist, existence for the psychologist and philosopher. Even though Carl Schmitt lived far from the front, the war's impact on him was clear; what he learned from it was that "sovereign is he who decides on the exception"; in his view, this was the only definition that captured sovereignty as a "borderline concept."[40] The borderline concept has the virtue of providing access to the very essence of its object as it persists on every occasion, including, therefore, in a state of exception, like a state of emergency or a state of siege, which are characteristic of the circumstances during a crisis or war. Far from being merely exceptions or aberrations with regard to a normal state, that of the legal norm, these states reveal the substance constituting a legal notion and which normality covers over. Consequently, "the exception is to be understood to refer to a general concept in the theory of the state, and not merely to a construct applied to any emergency decree or state of siege."[41] From this, Schmitt arrived at his definition of "sovereign" as "he who decides on the exception": the sovereign is both the person who decides that a situation is in fact exceptional by its urgency and, at the same time, the person who decides what measures are to be taken to cope with it; legal norms, valid in normal situations, are therefore only customs, which are binding on the sovereign only as promises to be kept in the usual order of things, and can be suspended in the event of a crisis. The jurist, inspired by his reading of Ancien Régime law, had also learned the lesson of the development of the German state in the course of the war, as it moved, under the aegis of Hindenburg and Ludendorff, toward a suspension of a number of freedoms granted by the emperor in peacetime.

With this meditation on the "state of exception," Schmitt's heroic rejection of legal conventions as the foundation of law took place on a ground similar to the limit situations (*Grenzsituationen*) described by Jaspers, whose *Psychology of Worldviews* was the object of a long and inspired commentary by Heidegger.[42] Jaspers's limit situations were "certain decisive, essential situations that are connected to man's being as such, which are inevitably given along with finite existence [*Dasein*]."[43] Where man reaches his limit, there his being is found, which is to be finite, and which he experiences in four situations he cannot transcend: combat, death, chance, guilt. Contrary to a traditional characterization of man as being endowed with reason, the use of which allows him both to live in society and to increasingly dominate nature through technology, Jaspers found man's being in these other states of exception, where man reveals himself better than elsewhere, in that he identifies with his untranscendable finitude. There too, war, by placing man in the throes of a battle that must be fought and that the enemy wages against him, and in the throes of the death he must inflict and may also suffer, could make him experience, even at a distance, what these limit situations might be, far from the world of security, established certainties, and bourgeois conventions.

In accord with these intellectuals whose thought had been radicalized by the Great War, Heidegger nonetheless found himself in a relationship to Husserl that consisted of an ironic paradox: while consigning his teacher to a past doomed to disappear, that of a sclerotic bourgeois thought, the young philosopher built his radicalism on the same ground that his teacher had cleared—the idea of a rupture with tradition, of a liberation of the gaze from prejudices and readymade philosophical concepts, in order to go back to "the things themselves." He merely broadened and radicalized his reflection by placing it on the terrain of an ontology of lived existence, enriched by history and hermeneutics. The long, powerful deflagration of the Great War—whose blast, as destructive as it was novel, finally suffused the philosopher—was frequently just one element in the radicalization of prewar European avant-garde thinkers, who had often already been radical before the war. Heidegger's ontological phenomenology cannot be understood without Husserlian phenomenology, which was itself contemporary with radical challenges to the European tradition, such as Picasso's cubism (the *Demoiselles d'Avignon* of 1907 mounted an assault on perspective as it had been understood since the Renaissance), Schoenberg's atonal music (in particular, his *Pierrot lunaire* of 1912, which suspended tonality in a way that foreshadowed his later development of twelve-tone composition), and Apollinaire's poetic revolution with the *vers libre* (*Alcools*, 1913) and calligrams (written between 1913 and 1916, published in 1918). Heidegger's break with tradition was ultimately closely connected with the one carried out in architecture by the Bauhaus, which Walter Gropius founded in Weimar in 1919. The Bauhaus certainly marked the beginnings of modern architecture through its use of an uncluttered geometry oriented toward the building's use, but it was nonetheless directly indebted to the industrial aesthetics of the Deutscher Werkbund, founded in Munich in 1907, which facilitated the break with ornamental architecture and its pastiches of the styles of earlier periods, from antiquity to the Renaissance.

This affiliation weighed more and more heavily on Heidegger, who rejected it in private with a virulence and scorn that reached their apex with the appointment of Husserl in Berlin in 1923:

> You already know that Husserl has been offered an appointment in Berlin. He behaves worse than a *Privatdozent* who mistakes the *Ordinariat* for eternal bliss. What is happening is shrouded in darkness. To begin with, he sees himself as *Praeceptor Germaniae*. Husserl is completely falling to pieces—if the pieces were ever together in the first place, which has lately become more and more questionable to me. He swings back and forth and talks trivialities, so that it would move one to pity. He lives with the mission of being the *founder of phenomenology*. No one knows what that is. Whoever is here for a semester knows what is wrong. He begins to perceive that people are no longer going along with him. He believes, naturally, that it is too difficult; naturally no one understands the *mathematics of the ethical* (the latest!), even when he has advanced further than Heidegger, about whom he now says: Of course he must immediately give lectures himself and can't visit mine; otherwise, he would have advanced further. *This* is now supposed to redeem the world in Berlin.[44]

When he wrote this, Heidegger knew that Husserl had made up his mind not to go to Berlin, but didn't want the fact known so that he could more easily renegotiate his salary with the ministry in Karlsruhe.[45] Heidegger took every opportunity to mock his teacher; the renegade disciple was becoming addicted to this virulent pleasure and never tired of it.

The distance he took from Husserl, even his rift with him, were not without practical consequences. Thus in a letter to Elfride in 1920, Heidegger wrote that at present, to support the two of them financially, he had to "find the possibilities for going along with [Husserl] without violent conflict or emphasis upon such conflict."[46] His relationship with his teacher was in fact partly self-interested, consisting of "practical reasons": "Appearing on the same title page as H. might well mean something—in the smaller circle of Frbg. Univ. but also in the acad. literature in general."[47] Husserl's great kindness did in fact lead him to encourage his protégé's publications. As Heidegger reported:

"Husserl also told me I needn't worry about opportunities for publication, the Jahrbuch will be open to me automatically & with 'carte blanche.' " The young philosopher did not immediately take advantage of this opportunity to be published in the *Jahrbuch für Philosophie und phänomenologische Forschung,* the journal Husserl had founded; his great philosophical ambition prevented him from rushing because he wanted to provide "something decisive, well rounded, & distinctive."[48]

Busy writing his lectures, maturing philosophically, and resisting the temptation to publish too quickly, he thereby created a major obstacle to the advancement of his career.

Since the war, Heidegger had found himself alone in his enterprise of philosophical revolution. Husserl seemed to him insufficiently radical, and the break with Catholicism had cut him off from his religious friends, especially Engelbert Krebs, with whom he had worked closely when he began as a lecturer. Despite his arrogance, Heidegger regretted this solitude, as he wrote to his wife in 1920: "Perhaps I might also have the good luck some time to find an eminent academic person of my age as a friend, who is not exactly in the same field—but moves within the same spiritual orientation."[49] He gradually found this friend in Karl Jaspers.

Before they met, Jaspers had roused Heidegger's esteem and hostility. Jaspers's book, *The Psychology of Worldviews,* had, in his view, "to be opposed in a much more clear-cut way, precisely because it offers many things, because it has taken knowledge from everywhere, and because it espouses a characteristic feature of our period."[50] Its failure lay less in its somewhat unfavorable reception than in its lack of theoretical foundations: "It fails completely in what is fundamental. Jaspers is not aware of the magnitude of the task, which requires a radical foundation for his own way of seeing and interpreting."[51]

Heidegger and Jaspers met two months later, in Freiburg, on the occasion of Edmund Husserl's birthday on 8 April 1920.[52] Sitting in a large circle around a table, the guests drank coffee and talked. Malvine Husserl, the master's wife, introduced Heidegger as the "child of phenomenology."[53] Jaspers was sorry that Afra Geiger, one of his students who wanted to attend Husserl's seminar, had not been admitted, and therefore expressed his regret that "academic formalities had prevented Husserl from seeing the person herself" and thus caused both of them "to miss a good opportunity."[54] This concern about respect for the person, this sharp rejection of administrative blindness, could not fail to please Heidegger, not only because these ideas were in accord with the ideology of the Youth Movement, but also because they revived, in the depths of his memory, the still painful recollection of his second period at the training camp, during which, in the same way, his own person had not been taken into consideration, only his rank:[55] thus he approved of Jaspers "vehemently."[56] The two men found common ground in the personalist cult of youth: "There was a kind of solidarity of young people opposed to the authority of abstract orders."[57] Both of them rejected the starchiness of the bourgeois spirit: "I seemed to feel something petty bourgeois, narrow, there was a lack of free, face-to-face encounters, the spiritual spark."[58] Standing out from all the other guests, Heidegger seemed different to Jaspers, who subsequently visited him: "I sat down with him in his little cell, I saw him studying Luther, saw the intensity of his work; his way of speaking, penetrating and concise, was pleasing to me."[59] The discovery was mutual: Heidegger, who spent an evening with Jaspers and his wife at their home in Heidelberg, returned convinced that they were working "at revitalizing philosophy from the same fundamental situation."[60] This feeling of having a common goal, that of giving new life to their discipline, was essential for Heidegger insofar as it was precisely his project, simultaneously intellectual and moral, and, in its consequences for the people and the state, political.

Over the following years there was an intense exchange about the critique of *The Psychology of Worldviews* and about the commentary on it that Heidegger composed, with many deletions and modifications. This demanding dialogue brought the two men much closer together, causing Jaspers to declare that, "in my opinion, your review is, of all of those I have read, the one that digs the deepest to the roots of the ideas. It has, therefore, really touched me from within. [. . .] I found several judgments to be in error. Nonetheless, I will postpone all of this until we speak in person. I grasp more in question and answer than in lecturing, but no one among the younger *philosophers* interests me more than you. Your critique can do me some good. It has already done me some good, because it makes me really think and allows no rest."[61]

Heidegger urged Jaspers to give his philosophy of psychology a new foundation in ontology. In trying, "in a positive way, to understand psychical causality in the old sense, from within the world of the humanities [*Geisteswissenschaften*]," Heidegger argued, Jaspers was asking questions "in the old way," neither phenomenological nor ontological, as when Jaspers wondered: "How can these *spheres* (e.g., of the schizophrenic) be *fit into* a permeation of life that is unifying in principle and conceptually categorical, according to the meaning of its being and objectivity?"[62] Going back to the very being of human existence, an approach more radical, therefore, than a mere examination of the mind of the schizophrenic, Heidegger argued that "the psychical is not something that the human *has* consciously or unconsciously, but something that he *is* and that lives in him. That means principally: there are objects that we do not *have* but that *are*."[63] The tendency of science and philosophy to distinguish between subject and object is not only erroneous, insofar as the two belong to each other in a manner that makes opposition false and artificial; these disciplines also tend, in their study of man, to classify him among objects, occulting in this way his being itself: schizophrenia, as an affliction of the human mind or spirit, is something that man can have; to go no further than this first observation, though it is correct, leads to error, for the schizophrenic not only *has* schizophrenia, but *is* it, because he experiences it in his being itself, in his existence from which it is inseparable.

Heidegger had thus formed a friendship of the kind he mentioned in his letter to Elfride, with "an eminent academic person" his own age.[64] In their common battle to revitalize philosophy, which presupposed being resolved to place themselves and their writings "in this struggle at knifepoint on the basis of a discussion of principles," Jaspers seemed to Heidegger to be working from psychology to attempt to reach "the original categorical structure of the object *life*." This constituted, according to Heidegger, "the principal meaning of the investigations" in which Jaspers wanted "to fit the schizophrenic and the like into the meaning of the being of life." Heidegger therefore arrived at the observation that they were united in a "rare and independent comradeship in arms," one that, "even today," he found nowhere else.[65] The week Heidegger spent at his friend's home in September 1922, in the absence of Jaspers's wife, each man working and exchanging ideas freely in the relative comfort of the apartment in Heidelberg (Heidegger slept on the couch in the library), further strengthened this feeling they shared: "The eight days spent with you are continually with me. The suddenness of these days, which were externally uneventful, the sureness of *style* in which each day unaffectedly grew into the next, the unsentimental, austere step with which friendship came upon us, the growing certainty from both *sides* of a mutually secure comradeship-in-arms—all of that is uncanny for me in the same sense as the world and life are uncanny for the philosopher."[66]

Bound together by their battle for a philosophical revolution, they nonetheless diverged in the way they waged it: Jaspers proposed an ambitious project to found a journal, which did not rouse Heidegger's enthusiasm; he was convinced that "the fundamental reconstruction of philosophizing in the universities [. . .] will never be achieved by merely writing books. [. . .] The more organically and concretely and inconspicuously the downfall occurs, the more persistent and certain [it] becomes." For that, an "invisible *community*"[67] was necessary. Writing was therefore not enough, not even if done together in a journal; the very life of the university had to be transformed, which required a revolution of the spirit and its institutions. They would be undermined not by overt action like that of a political party or a labor union, but rather in the manner of a secret society of conspirators acting in the shadows. Heidegger's taste for dissimulation thus found expression even in his plans for a philosophical revolution. But they still lacked the *kairos,* the favorable opportunity without which any takeover is doomed to fail.

The growing importance of polemology in Heidegger's reflections was another mark of the postwar period. A revolutionary philosopher, he was more than ever filled with a rhetoric of combat that was very typical of this era of "brutalization."[68] Whereas many young people joined the Marxist militias and attempted, in 1919, a second revolution in Berlin and then in Munich, others joined the Freikorps, fighting to reestablish order in opposition to the Bolshevik menace. In March 1920 they attempted a putsch led by Wolfgang Kapp in Berlin and by Gustav von Kahr in Munich, then followed Hitler in his attempted Beer Hall Putsch in 1923, opposed the Lithuanian annexation of Memel and the French occupation of the Ruhr, and even responded to the calls for murder from a prominent member of the German National People's Party, Karl Helfferich, directed at Germany's alleged internal enemies. In particular, Scheidemann survived an attack with prussic acid,[69] and Erzberger[70] and Rathenau[71] were both assassinated. Although in 1933 Heidegger celebrated Albert Leo Schlageter, a Freikorps leader who was shot by the French and became a German martyr and a Nazi hero,[72] for his part he experienced this battle within philosophy: he had to "struggle at knifepoint" with his writings, and he was planning a philosophical revolution with Karl Jaspers, whom he saw as joining him in a "rare and independent comradeship in arms,"[73] with a "growing certainty from both *sides,*"[74] a comradeship radically opposed to the dusty, humdrum university that had long since lost the difficult courage that science demanded.

Heidegger's polemology was merely a sign of how this belligerent period was consuming itself; another was the reactivation of racist prejudices, the first concerning "Senegalese Negroes," an expression that was in itself without racism, despite its historical connotations. During the war German newspapers had thundered against the French, who were putting in their trenches these black men so close to apes, to fight against white, blond, dolichocephalic Germans. In 1919, Heidegger used the expression in a lecture[75] to illustrate the idea that the world is for us intrinsically meaningful, even when it seems meaningless; he asked his students to imagine a "Senegalese Negro" who had wandered into the lecture hall and saw the lectern from which he (Heidegger) was delivering his lecture. Wouldn't this black man find himself confronted with something stripped bare of meaning, because incomprehensible to him? Even in this case, meaning exists, indissolubly linked to the thing: in the case of the Negro, it would simply be "I don't understand." Beyond his black skin, the Senegalese Negro occurred to Heidegger as a caricatural example of primitive humanity, whose limited world, poor in meaning, would not include a lectern, the object par excellence of the portion of humanity that had developed a particularly rich and intellectual understanding of the world.

Although it was based on a stereotype, the idea of cultural primitiveness, adopted by Heidegger regarding the "Senegalese Negro," could have been neutral, not implying a value judgment radically opposing whites and blacks as two human races, irreconcilable because substantially different, had not Heidegger made another, undoubtedly racist reference in 1922. Because they were particularly primitive men, blacks tended to form representations of the human being that were so aberrant that only the philosophical elucubrations about a consciousness separate from the body could be more erroneous. Maintaining that the thesis of "an isolated, free-floating [. . .] consciousness," distinct from the body, consists of "impossibilities," Heidegger concluded that "we cannot *post festum* introduce *evil* reality and stick spiritual acts onto a body (even the Negroes do not have such representations of *Dasein* as those that circulate in today's scientific philosophy)."[76] He adopted the commonplace racist classification that arranges skin colors in a hierarchy, with the white race at the top and the black race at the bottom, only slightly tempering the hierarchy by suggesting that in their misguided ways, certain European philosophers might have sunk lower than blacks in their representation of human beings.

Very optimistic during the war as to the possibility of a spiritual revolution in Germany by virtue of his teaching at the university, hardly more than two years later Heidegger nonetheless proved reserved: "I have lost all of my optimism about today's students, both male and female," he wrote in January 1921. Having already encountered a narrow-minded response to his ideas among his comrades in arms, the philosopher now found a great mediocrity among most of his students, far from the authenticity and rigor without which thinking could never be more than idle talk, learned but inconsequential, even among the best students. They were, in his view, "either religious enthusiasts (theosophists who have also established themselves in protestant theology, followers of George and the like), or they fall into an unhealthy eclecticism, where they know nothing about everything and everything about nothing." The latter spread themselves too thin and ultimately got nowhere, while the former had the advantage of going in only one direction and keeping to it even if it was intrinsically bad. In this case, these students became followers of the nationalist and mystical poet Stefan George, who was then enjoying a great success among young, educated Catholics. They all lacked "a genuine understanding of scholarly work and a real power of perseverance, of sacrifice, of true initiative,"[77] and were thus unable to follow the example of their professor, coming to seek the questions and the answers in themselves, pursuing them with an authenticity, rigor, and radicalism far removed from a mere classroom exercise.

The magic of his philosophical word did not, of course, transform as if by grace all the students who, having come to hear Heidegger, were touched by it: but he was not always so negative. At the end of the summer semester of 1920, he pointed out to Elfride the positive effects of his lectures on the very substance of his thought, to whose rigor and breadth his students contributed through their questions and their exchanges, which made his semester resemble "an assault." He then added: "One needs this discipline of lectures & the corrective of an advanced audience until one finally has oneself safe in hand."[78] The philosopher's investment in his teaching was so complete that in January 1922, his body overcome by a bout of flu that had already struck Elfride, he worried about how little energy he would have for writing his lectures: "When I now think it through objectively, it's actually much too much that I'm offering in my lectures."[79]

This feeling that he was providing something essential, that each of his lectures was itself an event, borne aloft by the enthusiastic word of a professor in the grip of philosophical inspiration that swept away "the philosophical business of the Schools, of discussions & chatter,"[80] was of a nature to attract to Heidegger many loyal students, among them Franz-Josef Brecht, who went on vacation with him in the winter of 1920;[81] Romano Guardini;[82] Karl Löwith, his student since the summer semester of 1920, who did his habilitation in Marburg in 1928, under Heidegger's direction;[83] Helene Weiss, Hans Jonas, and Hans-Georg Gadamer, who took his courses starting in the summer semester of 1923.[84] Gadamer was impressed by Heidegger's charisma: "At that time an incomparable aura already radiated from him."[85] His audience was jolted as if "by an electric shock";[86] his lectures caused a "complete upheaval of all excessively premature self-confidence."[87] For his part, Löwith recounted his early days with Heidegger: "The fascination he exerted is explained in part by the opacity of his nature: no one really understood him, and both his personality and his lectures were the object of lively controversies for years. Like Fichte, he was only half a man of science; he was besides, and perhaps especially, someone who loved to resist and a preacher who knew how to seduce by provoking, and who was driven by a hostile attitude toward the period and himself."[88] Löwith added: "For his students, the essential element of his actions was not the expectation of a new system, but on the contrary the indetermination of the content and the pure call of his philosophical teaching [. . .]. One day a student came up with a very significant joke: 'I am resolute, it's just that I don't know about what.' "[89]

Hans Jonas met Heidegger for the first time at a seminar on Aristotle's *De anima*. The *Privatdozent* began by asking him if he knew Greek. When Jonas said that he did, Heidegger replied, "That's fine, then." For Jonas, this was a "sort of rendezvous with destiny," because even if he didn't understand much of Heidegger's obscure remarks, being only in his first semester at the university, Heidegger knew how to involve his students by making them read a sentence in the text and then asking: "How do you interpret this? What's Aristotle saying here? What does this word mean?" In addition, he knew how to draw the students out,[90] which promoted greater involvement on their part. For his lecture on Augustine's *Confessions*, Heidegger arrived in the lecture hall carrying an enormous folio edition, probably the massive edition produced by the Benedictines of St. Maur, which he mentioned later[91] and whose Latin text he kept before his eyes. Jonas understood only a little, but he nonetheless had the feeling that here was philosophy in the making, even if he, Jonas, didn't understand it. This impression was not so disagreeable; on the contrary, he felt he was "up against a mystery," "convinced it was worth the trouble to become an initiate. In that instinctive feeling I wasn't alone; the other students likewise fell under the spell of his suggestive language, though I'm sure they understood much more than I. But in those days the impression was becoming widespread that this was of great moment. Even before *Being and Time* Heidegger had acquired a sort of crypto-fame, and among those in the know word had got around that here a philosopher was striking out in a new direction: 'This is where you have to come to learn philosophy!' "[92]

In these early years, with these lectures to which he devoted almost all his energy, Heidegger succeeded in uniting around him students who were often brilliant, and he formed them into a philosophical sect with its own language as well as a master, whom some of them tried to imitate. Löwith, who was a little older than the others, was particularly good at this. These successes that Heidegger enjoyed with the students encouraged a growing confidence in himself that soared to lofty heights, leading him to affirm in 1922 his belief that he was an independent philosopher who had exhausted what his contemporaries could offer him: "I've gained such great assurance that in fact I can learn nothing more from contemporary philosophers & to pursue my own enquiries just have to battle my way through enquiries into what for me are the decisive philosophers in history."[93]

The Break with His Childhood Faith and the Discovery of Rootedness

As a revolutionary, Heidegger had broken with the Meßkirch way, whose religious and political culture, received during his childhood, was inseparable from its bell tower, its streets, and the surrounding fields. The philosopher's time at the front had brought him face to face with himself, facilitating a break with his moral and intellectual heritage that had already been approaching for a few years, and which his relationship with Elfride and the coming birth of their son Jörg hastened. The official request that Husserl filed on 7 January 1919, that Heidegger be appointed as a paid assistant, allowed Heidegger to break with Catholicism, which he no longer needed for his career. This break, vehemently set forth in the letters to his wife, was expressed with great respect and courtesy in a letter of 9 January 1919 to Engelbert Krebs, his Catholic friend and a professor of dogmatics in Freiburg, who had performed his wedding ceremony and whose Catholicism, as sincere as it was critical of the harder line taken by the papacy, had been a first and forceful catalyst for Heidegger.

The philosopher conceived this break not in terms of faith (he remained a believer) but in terms of philosophy and connected it with the evolution he had undergone over the two preceding years. He drew one unambiguous conclusion: "had I been constrained by extraphilosophical allegiances"—that is, by obedience to the dogmas defined by the Church—"I could not have guaranteed the necessary independence of conviction and doctrine."[94] For the young Heidegger this seemed to be liberty itself: the act of conforming, despite its difficulty, to Truth, which was in its entirety only the truth recognized by the Roman Catholic Church, now seemed to him an arbitrary attachment, a restriction essentially contrary to philosophy's freedom, which implied the ability to approve or disapprove a thesis in good conscience, and also a restriction on teaching, which had to follow the professor's scientific and pedagogical conscience alone, and not an external authority. Referring to phenomenology in a letter to his former teacher Rickert in 1920, he wrote straightforwardly: "Here, too, there must be no pope, and although many people think there should be, for my part I do not want, from this point of view, to be subject to any ultramontane authority."[95]

In his letter to Krebs, Heidegger attributed this fundamental change in the conception of the philosopher's freedom solely to his intellectual development, leaving aside his connections to Protestantism, which had nevertheless been crucial—first and foremost through Elfride, and secondarily through Husserl, who, a Protestant and a philosopher intransigent on the subject of the independence of science, looked with regret on conversions to Catholicism as a "sure sign of people's spiritual poverty."[96] In Heidegger's view, moreover, a decisive factor was his encounter with "epistemological insights applied to the theory of historical knowledge" that for him "made the *system* of Catholicism problematic and unacceptable."[97] Put more clearly, his reading of Dilthey, and the latter's conception of the role of subjectivity in the *Geisteswissenschaften* in general, had made Heidegger understand the full value of subjectivity. According to Dilthey, one can have access to the meaning of phenomena only through subjectivity, so that mental realities assume their meaning, their nature, and their force through the work of a mind caught up in history, and this work restores their life to them in a process that is not the application of an objective, mathematical, disembodied, and timeless logic, but its opposite. As a result, it was no longer a question of giving up subjectivity, making it fit the straitjacket of a cold, external truth. On the contrary, subjectivity had to be allowed to blossom authentically with its own life.

In addition to Dilthey, Heidegger was reading Schleiermacher, which led him to grant more importance to feeling and inner experience in cognition. Heidegger had been impressed by Schleiermacher's second speech on religion, even writing to Elisabeth Blochmann that only a woman, by nature more sensitive, could fully understand the philosopher and Protestant theologian[98]—a sign of how much he now valorized subjectivity and feeling. The influence of the founder of hermeneutics, the art of interpretation (of texts primarily), did not diminish subsequently: Heidegger gave a course in the summer semester of 1923 on the hermeneutics of facticity (*Hermeneutik der Faktizität*),[99] in which he focused on the inner interpretation of the facticity of human existence.

For all that, Heidegger's break with the "system of Catholicism" was not a repudiation of Catholic culture. Although he was an apostate, during these years he drew a great deal of sustenance from reading Aristotle, Augustine, and the medieval mystics. He did not break with metaphysics, though it was now taken in a new sense. The philosophical tradition after Plato and Aristotle, revived by the Scholastics, questioned the principles of all things: metaphysics was thus becoming a fully autonomous activity rather than a bulwark or a spearhead of the Roman Catholic faith. Although that philosophical activity sustained faith, the latter could no longer dictate anything to it; the servant had become the master. Heidegger's hostility was directed at the Church, but not at Catholic culture: he wanted to be a Christian and a free philosopher, while retaining Catholic foundations, which could be undermined only with difficulty.

Heidegger's spiritual and intellectual evolution was subsequently determined by the interplay of Catholicism, Protestantism, and philosophy. The philosopher found in Martin Luther another precious ally for freeing himself from the grasp of Catholicism, calming his doubts, and feeding his thought: "Since I read Luther's Commentary on Romans, much that before was troubling & dark to me has become bright & liberating." In this case, he was thinking about the moments when he felt abandoned in existence, far from God, "times of abandonment [*Ver-lassenheit*]," which, he said, were now "experienced in an authentic way" (translation modified), only "if they are times of trusting composure [*Gelassenheit*]" and trust in God. Another positive effect of his reading Luther was that he had "quite [a] new understanding of the Middle Ages & the development of Christn. religiousness," and "wholly new perspectives on the problems of the philos. of religion" had opened to him.[100] In 1920, Heidegger could still assert with full enthusiasm: "I'm right in my element. The Luther edition has already become indispensable to me."[101]

In January 1919, this Lutheranism, combined with his Augustinianism, led him to discredit the legitimacy of a truth instituted by an external authority: declaring that he wanted to do everything in his power "to further the spiritual life of man—that and *only* that,"[102] he clearly ruled out serving the Church. Increasingly a philosopher and a Protestant, Heidegger saw his mission, assigned by God, as an inner quest for both God and the truth that was later to be transmitted by word, pen, and example, first of all to his students, a difficult and painful path, despite its grandeur and nobility, which distinguished him from the foot soldiers of knowledge.

In the immediate postwar period, years of a break with the spiritual and political heritage of Meßkirch, the theme of rootedness in Heidegger's native region began to appear as such for the first time, though this theme had exogenous origins. Heidegger's ties with his family, his parents, his brother, and his sister were enriched by Jörg's birth on 21 January 1919; as a birthday gift and a sign of family love, the grandfather, a cooper and sexton, made a bassinet for his little grandson,[103] who nevertheless had to wait for more than a year before getting to know the countryside, one of his "little homelands." Although Heidegger went to spend two weeks in Meßkirch in September 1919, his hometown was no longer the natural setting of his earlier vacations; it had been transformed into a holiday resort similar to others. In 1919 he stayed longer in Konstanz, trying to comfort his friend Theophil Rees, who was mourning the death of his wife, Marta. She had been pregnant when she succumbed to the terrible Spanish flu epidemic that killed 180,000 people in Germany and reached Freiburg in the autumn of 1918.[104] He also took advantage of this vacation to visit the Vetter family,[105] cousins he was close to and among the first people he had informed of Jörg's birth.[106]

Heidegger did not arrive in Meßkirch until 12 September 1919, where he remained for two weeks. There he encountered his parents' incomprehension regarding his break with the Catholic Church,[107] a situation that changed little with time. His father and mother feared Hell, for themselves and for their children; they could not look on with indifference as their son left the true faith and carelessly headed toward obvious eternal damnation, where he was leading his own son, who was soon baptized a Lutheran. An advantage of Heidegger's stay in his native region was the calm he enjoyed far from Freiburg, the university, and his own household, "at home" in his little room.[108] Although these conditions were favorable for his work, which made everything else acceptable, Heidegger's relation to his hometown and his family had radically changed in 1919; he was exiled far from his life and his spouse, in a land that had lost its familiarity over time. The sole moment of living happiness it contained was a memory of Elfride, though she was, quite foreign to it, so urban, Prussian, and Protestant in this Catholic countryside in Baden.

The Freiburg philosopher returned to Meßkirch in the summer of 1920, this time for a longer period and accompanied by his son. Elfride was pregnant again and was expected to deliver soon; she was, of course, surrounded by women friends who helped her, but her husband had to relieve her of Jörg's care. Meßkirch was the right place because another mother would take over: Heidegger's own. During this time he would rest and work. In Meßkirch, the grandparents were impatiently awaiting them: "They were both standing & waiting up on the hill—[Jörg] made friends at once." That evening, Jörg was "ceremonially" put to bed "by the whole family" in a "very sweet little bed"; and "early in the morning when he was awake, his grandfather came to his little bed & looked at him in silence."[109]

The son's days filled his father with joy: Jörg emptied his aunt's wardrobe; he had a rocking horse of which he was still afraid; very happy, he sang and played with blocks,[110] and in the living room he was "really engrossed" in a "wonderful" big stove with doors. But, said Heidegger, "it is even better when I hide *behind* the stove & can play peekaboo."[111] "It's delightful to see how Putz now pays attention to everything—he loves listening to the dicky-bird in the Hofgarten park," where his father had so often played.[112] Because caring for her three children and her grandson was too much for Johanna Heidegger, Jörg's Aunt Marie frequently watched him. Marie was conscientious and followed Elfride's instructions scrupulously, but she treated her nephew with a touching modesty, which her younger brother gently mocked. As Martin reported, "[Fritz] cracked a good joke this morning: Marie was just washing the little lad's nether regions & I said she shouldn't beat about the bush but do it properly; and he said she wouldn't do that, otherwise she'd have to go to confession!"[113]

Heidegger wanted to rest, the better to go back to work. Meßkirch was an ideal place for that, since it freed him of the burden of caring for his son and provided a change of scenery: "Here I really am quite free & far away from any surroundings that remind me of university & the philosophical business of the Schools, of discussions & chatter. I'm gradually beginning to feel physically fresh again too."[114] As soon as he arrived in Meßkirch, he told Elfride how happy he was to see his homeland, "the meadows & fields":[115] "It's so wonderfully peaceful & fresh up here."[116] And so, he said, "I go along the pathway at half past 6 in the early autumn, which I love so much." Accompanied in his imagination by Elfride, whom he always saw at his side, Heidegger usually met no one other than his former teacher from the first year of primary school (*Volksschule*). This teacher, who was well known in Meßkirch and was one of the gentlemen who had obviously been superior to the Heideggers by virtue of his university degree and his position when he was the future philosopher's teacher, was acutely aware of the social distance that now separated him from the man who had received a doctorate and now taught in a German university, and, as such, was a notable in a large city like Freiburg. This social reversal was completely normal, but it did not fail to disturb Heidegger: "I find the respect with which he greets me puts me to shame." His reaction was not astonishing: the deference, obedience, and even admiration we have been taught to show during childhood for adults who have direct authority over us do not always dissipate as quickly as time passes, so that the honorable *Privatdozent* Heidegger still felt like the schoolboy he had been and sensed the distance that separated him from his teacher.

Walking through the surrounding countryside was a pleasure he had discovered with Elfride, who opened his mind to the beauty of his home region; he had never done this when he was a student because he felt he "had no 'time' for it." Now he felt good only when he had "been outside either just before the meal or in the evening" and took "new delight" each day.[117]

By walking, Heidegger was in fact observing a specifically bourgeois rite that in Meßkirch took place on the grounds of the castle. He was somewhat original in the itinerary he followed, which was rural insofar as it left from the former residence of the counts of Zimmern and then took him down the field-path and through the forest; it was rural, then, but also urban in spirit because imbued with the ideas of the Youth Movement, which was specifically urban and bourgeois.

Paradoxically, it was through that same urban and even cosmopolitan culture that Heidegger began to feel explicitly rooted in a region. On arriving in his homeland, he wrote to his wife: "Gradually I feel what it means to have one's roots in the soil [*Heimat*]—in fact this only fully struck me through Dostoyevski." And he added: "If you have time, do try to read Dost[oyevs]ki's political writings, they'll make a big impression on you—I meant to tell you before we left."[118] In a final expression of this awareness of rootedness, he added: "I love the country so much & am noticing this time more than ever how deeply rooted I am after all in the soil & the local folk [*Art*]."[119] Today, Dostoevsky is better known for his novels than for his political writings, which, precisely, valorize rootedness in a way that was fully in accord with the *Blut und Boden* sensibility that had characterized the German right wing since before the war. The same sensibility is found in Heidegger's writings during this summer, especially in his use of the term *Art* (kind, sort, species). This word does not express the idea that he belonged to the human race of white-skinned Indo-Europeans; it refers rather to the Swabian ethnic group from which he felt he was descended and with which he identified on witnessing the rural manners and customs that had remained alive in the land of his ancestors.

The paradox was that, through his reading of Dostoevsky, this regionalist culture acquired for Heidegger an authentically cosmopolitan dimension, in a strong tension between the erasure of boundaries between the peoples who had created that culture and the local focus of its content. A foreign author who promoted *völkisch* political culture, and who was "popular" in the sense of "authentically national," Dostoevsky became known to German readers through Arthur Moeller van den Bruck, who had himself discovered him through the Russian poet Dimitri Merezhkovsky (1866–1941). Over a period of ten years (1905–1915), Moeller van den Bruck had translated Dostoevsky's complete works with the help of a young Latvian woman, Less Kaerrick. Sales were as high as the translation was difficult: 135,000 copies were sold in 1920, 84,000 in 1921, and no fewer than 179,000 in 1922.[120] In addition—and this is not widely known today—Dostoevsky was an anti-Semite. Does not the immense novel *Crime and Punishment* develop the theme of whether it is possible to kill someone whose death would be in the public interest, the vilest possible person, an old Jewish woman who is a usurer? Heidegger may have been receptive to this attitude: the first two occurrences postwar of anti-Semitism in Heidegger's writings came not only with the spread of the *Dolchstoß* legend, but also after he had read Dostoevsky.

In his native Heuberg, along with the "fieldpath," Heidegger was particularly fond of Beuron. He felt at home there. Jörg having to some extent gotten his bearings, his father left him on 1 August 1920 to go visit the abbey with his friend Theophil, who had come from Konstanz.[121] His return to this place of spiritual retreat must have seemed ideal for his work; since Marie and his mother were "very careful" with Jörg, he thought there was "no harm in [. . .] going away for a few days" and said he would "keep informed." Thus he returned to Beuron a few days later and remained there from 6 August[122] to 11 August[123] to immerse himself in his work behind the walls forming a serene bulwark against the secular world and its everyday preoccupations: "I'm hard at work once again—in the mornings the new lectures—in the afternoons the reworking of the old lectures & toward evening dictating."[124] When he returned, Jörg was well; very proudly, Heidegger noted that he was "very lively & rather unruly—everyone thinks he's 3"; he was even "turning into a proper little chubby chops," to the point that his father wondered if he was being "overfed" and disapproved of his family's tendency to feed him to the point of satiation. Heidegger could have told his mother or his sister that it was not good for him to eat so much; instead, he relied on Elfride, asking: "How about sending further 'instructions'—or is it all right as it is?"[125] As a father, the philosopher had only a rather limited influence on his son's practical education: such was the rigid division of labor between husband and wife, man and woman, at the time, and such was the character of Heidegger, who had a hard time making his choices known in the family and concentrated on his work, which was for him a passion and a refuge. Moreover, in Meßkirch, his work was favored even by Fritz, who took an interest in his brother's philosophy and typed up his manuscripts.[126]

Meanwhile, Elfride gave birth to Hermann on 20 August, but she remained in the hospital for a long time, and she was still there when her husband and their elder son returned on 30 August.[127] Heidegger did not stay long at home; taking advantage of the fact that Hilde, one of Elfride's friends, was helping her at this difficult time, a week later he returned to his parents' home to work in peace. This second stay in Meßkirch was particularly productive, and Heidegger expressed his pleasure in working: "I'm working so well *and steadily* [. . .] with the enthusiasm of moving 'forwards' and 'through.' " Leisure was the indispensable complement to this studious fervor, and in the evening, tired out by the day's labors, Heidegger loved to play " '66' with Father & Fritz," which distracted him before he went to bed: "Otherwise I'm too deeply preoccupied by philos."[128] To be sure, he missed Elfride, but this time away from her was not unbearable for him.[129] Thus he returned from his hometown only at the beginning of the semester, despite the illness that struck his wife and forced her mother to come from Wiesbaden to help her.[130]

Heidegger did not completely idealize Meßkirch, despite the comfort of his stay there. Shortly after he arrived in late July, he had written to his wife: "I don't know whether I could work here—in the long run it'd be too quiet. It's too small for our Fritz [i.e., Jörg] as well."[131] In early September, this criticism bore on inauthenticity and once again he gave Elfride all the credit for the change in him: "And how much I'm discarding in the way of what is inauthentic or determined by my limited origins & isolated develpmt I notice with each year that passes & owe it to no one but you."[132] This denunciation of "inauthenticity" and his "limited origins" was becoming a regular theme; it first appeared while he was at the front, and continued to appear until the end of the 1920s.[133] Heidegger's stays in Meßkirch brought him closer to his "ultra-Catholic" origins, and his break with the Church and Jörg's baptism as a Protestant were subjects of conflict. But his stays with his parents did not consist of constant fighting: his taciturn father must have usually kept quiet about his grievances, while his mother, though authoritarian, was also kind, and took care to envelop her children in love. These personality traits of his parents must explain in part why his letters to Elfride contain only occasional, though sharp, resurgences of criticism of his family's narrow-minded Catholicism and its dictatorial nature.

Heidegger subsequently made only short visits to Meßkirch, a sign both of his estrangement and of the degree to which this summer of 1920 spent in his hometown is to be explained by Elfride's new pregnancy and the need for tranquility that he and his wife both felt. Although they visited the town together in August 1921,[134] they certainly did not do so in 1922, when the philosopher had to stay in Freiburg because he was hoping to be appointed to a chair in Göttingen or Marburg, and this required three weeks of intensive work[135] on his *Phenomenological Interpretations of Aristotle*. The only remaining link was related to food, the question of sending potatoes expressing Johanna Heidegger's concern about her son and his family.[136]

Heidegger was moving away from Meßkirch in large part because of the powerful attraction of Elfride and the home she had been able to build. Despite his career worries, the philosopher had been happy since their marriage: his cardiac problems and his insomnia, which were psychosomatic, disappeared in 1918, during his active service in the army,[137] and did not reappear; Heidegger was much less rooted in Meßkirch than he was attached to the home that his wife was creating around him. He was aware of the importance of these surroundings even in his own philosophical activity, which certainly required him to return to his existential solitude to think authentically—that is, for himself and not for others—but at the same time could be carried out only in a human environment that was anything but contingent.[138] Even if the boys' games and shouts might distract him, Elfride and their two sons favored his thinking by their very existence and the familial happiness they produced. Referring to Jörg, their "little man,"[139] their "little country-boy,"[140] their "Putz,"[141] Heidegger said that when he was away he felt "homesick for him & his calming presence."[142] He was aware of how much the boy had strengthened their household: "His inner cheer & little life has already had a really deep influence on us, hasn't it, & we always leave his basket with a joyful ringing in our hearts—[. . .] The solitude that is fertile ground for research work doesn't consist in merely being undisturbed outwardly—but in fact in coming out from & being able to go back into a rich 'environment.' "[143]

Elfride provided not just a favorable but an external environment vis-à-vis his philosophical activity; she lent him a great self-assurance and seemed to him to be at the root of his own radicalism.[144] She was also a genuine interlocutor, endowed with phenomenological intuition, far from the idle chatter in which the students took pleasure: "I can still remember very well our last phenomenological talk—as well as my astonishment—which has been on my mind again & again."[145] She influenced him considerably, having led him to Protestantism and still more to the ideals of the Youth Movement, in whose light he henceforth saw their partnership,[146] his work, and himself through this value of authenticity, in powerful counterpoint to his tendency to mendacity and dissimulation: "This sincerity of being is something I owe to your sweet presence, your immediate being." He asked his wife to give him time "to cast off completely everything that counts as false for our innermost being," everything that represented an inner restraint on his work itself.[147]

The sweetness of his home inclined Heidegger to be indulgent toward his wife when she told him about the affair she'd had with Friedel Caesar, a childhood friend who was in fact Hermann's biological father—which Heidegger knew and accepted, though he felt scorn for Friedel. Elfride felt an "inner conflict"[148] and considered leaving her husband. This was a difficult moment amid the happiness he was enjoying. Although he struggled to understand Elfride and her doubts,[149] at least he retained what he saw as essential: his wife and their household. In the end, through Heidegger's deeply rooted desire to live with Elfride, the birth of Hermann on 20 August 1920[150] brought them together as Jörg's had previously done—giving him occasion to meditate on authentic love as opposed to "bourgeois" marriage,[151] on "a giving that is not a giving-away," and that allows one to become oneself. He concluded: "I often find myself thinking how pale, untrue, & sentimental everything is that is usually said about marriage. And whether we aren't giving shape to a new form of it in our life—without a program or intention—but just letting authenticity come through everywhere."[152]

5 • Rootedness on the Mountain Heights of Todtnauberg?

(1923–1933)

From Exile in Marburg to the Outpost in Freiburg

The chair that Heidegger held in Marburg from 1923 to 1928, long in coming, was the happy news that followed so many disappointed hopes: Freiburg and Tübingen in 1916; Heidelberg in 1917;[1] Marburg in 1917–1918,[2] then again in 1920;[3] Heidelberg in 1921; Göttingen and Marburg in 1922; Königsberg in 1923.[4] This situation had been hard for everyone: Heidegger himself, his parents,[5] and his wife. Useful for the household's financial security, a chair was to give him greater serenity of mind, what he needed to be "very glad" in his work, which would thereby be "more *free* and *uninhibited*."[6] The chair in Marburg allowed him finally to enjoy a stable position, at the age of almost thirty-four, and to leave career worries behind without having to give up his proud originality. He owed this relief to the tireless support of Husserl, whose previously fruitless efforts succeeded this time, though not without difficulty.

Paul Natorp (1854–1924), a full professor in Marburg, was retiring and looking for a successor. In late January 1922, Husserl informed him that Heidegger could be a candidate, even though his publications to date were few, old, and not concerned with phenomenology. Husserl emphasized his student's success with students and the originality of his project of a phenomenology of religion, which he saw as centered on Luther and thus in a hostile environment in Catholic Freiburg, whereas Protestant Marburg would be a favorable terrain that he would enrich by giving new life to the Faculty of Theology.

Although Heidegger did not get the job, which was offered to Nicolai Hartmann, an associate professor at Marburg, this setback at the beginning of 1922 laid the foundations for the success that followed when the question of

Hartmann's own succession came up: academic appointments often resembled a game of musical chairs in which a post that became available to one candidate freed up the post that the latter had previously occupied. Thus on 26 September 1922 Heidegger received a sibylline card from Husserl: "Please come"—the telephone system being still largely undeveloped, mail remained the normal way of communicating across distances. When he arrived at Husserl's home, the mistress of the household read him a long letter from Natorp, which Heidegger summed up for his wife with great enthusiasm: "They're *determined* to have me; Natorp mentions Ha[rt]mann, who is fully informed of my effectiveness [. . .]—and further that he's recently heard the very best things from Marburg students (Ph.D. students who have been with me here in the last two semesters)[7]—in Marbg. they want a phe[nomeno]logist—& also someone with a critical command of the Middle Ages (those theologians)!)."[8]

A university finally recognized the originality of Heidegger's line of thought, which had moved from Scholasticism to phenomenology, while he devoted almost all his energy to training his students through his lectures. He was in a good position to get the job, but the chair was not offered to him immediately, and he had to write a report presenting his research. This took three weeks of intense work that prevented him from going to Meßkirch, as he was supposed to do in October. He chose excerpts from his course on "phenomenological interpretations of Aristotle," preceded by an introduction, then dictated the resulting sixty pages to Malvine Husserl, who had agreed to retranscribe them. Heidegger then "had Husserl send a copy each to Marburg and Göttingen."

At Göttingen, Heidegger's candidacy was only a succès d'estime: he was included on the list of candidates, but nowhere near the top. At Marburg the outcome looked more promising, though Heidegger, who was used to failure, was pessimistic, convinced he would not get the job, despite his qualifications. He imagined that Richard Kroner, who was "*the older one*" and above all had "a lot of paper,"[9] would win out because of his age and the number of his publications. His wounded pride saw what a "*disgrace*" "such a ranking" would be for him, giving precedence to an insignificant philosopher. Above all, he was weary: he wanted finally to be at peace, because "this being led on with half-prospects, bungling with recommendations, etc., brings you into a terrible state, even when you make up your mind not to get caught up in it."[10] Heidegger's despair misled him; Hartmann and Natorp had, on the contrary, been won over[11] and, following their recommendations, the Faculty of Philosophy put Heidegger at the top of the list.[12]

Nevertheless, this was only a first step; the ultimate choice had to be made by the ministry in Berlin, and it was delayed. The decision caused a stir; pressures were exerted on every side against the Marburg list. Heidegger, worried and resentful, suspected that Scheler, the phenomenologist in Munich, was behind it; he sought to temper Elfride's optimism, emphasizing that the forthcoming publication of his *Aristotle* would be an additional obstacle, because "they'll take care not to set a fox to catch a thief."[13] He heard rumors that Geyser was to be made a full professor (*Ordinarius*) in Marburg, that it would not be desirable to have two professors from Freiburg. He wondered how great the theologians' demands were on the teaching program and, concerned that he might suffer the consequences of his growing hostility to Catholicism, was very afraid that the government "wouldn't dare" appoint him "for fear of the fuss of the Zentrum [Party]."[14] Finally, on 18 June he received the news of his appointment in Marburg "for the *Extraordinariat* with the position and privileges of an *Ordinarius*."[15]

Soon afterward, Heidegger learned why his appointment had been delayed: Richard Kroner, his unsuccessful competitor, having been ranked third among the candidates, had traveled to Berlin in January and "whined all over the place." Subsequently, he "even presented himself in person in Marburg," going so far as to promise that if he were appointed, he would attend Hartmann's courses as a student. Finally learning about that, Heidegger exploded, displaying a scorn equal to the torments he had suffered for such a long time and to Kroner's lack of dignity: "I have never seen such wretchedness in a human being—now he allows himself to be pitied like an old woman—the only favor one could do for him now would be to take away his *venia legendi* [authorization to teach]." Although it was not in Heidegger's power to prevent Kroner from continuing to teach, he vowed to make a violent impression on him with his group of students: "I will in the manner of my presence—make Hell hot for him. A shock troop of sixteen persons is coming with me. Many are the inevitable fellow travelers, but some are entirely serious and capable."[16]

Heidegger's appointment put an end to his agony and provided him with the relatively modest remuneration of an *Extraordinarius,* with the dignity, freedom, and responsibility of an *Ordinarius*—which was the most important thing. The years in Marburg promised to be happy and serene, propitious for a permanent transplantation: "I look forward to the peaceful little town and the undisturbed work."[17]

On 12 October 1923, Heidegger moved into lodgings in Marburg, initially under precarious conditions, subletting a two-room apartment,[18] and then changing rooms[19] several times because of the housing shortage and the influx of refugees from the Ruhr, which the French had occupied. Nonetheless, the philosopher liked the city very much; he felt he had a perfect osmosis with this new place: "The little town is quite delightful—it's just right for me—Yesterday afternoon the sun came out & I strolled through the bumpy streets with their pretty little houses—each one looks different & they're all huddled together like the Hessian girls going shopping in their finery. The Lahn has plenty of water & flows through between great willow trees—from one bridge there's a view like in Heidelberg up the Neckar. I have the feeling that everything will be all right with my work here."[20] His only regret was temporary: the absence of Elfride, to whom he hoped to be able to show the city.

The housing shortage did not prevent Heidegger from finding a house for his family at no. 21, Schwanallee. Having examined it, he could not contain his joy: "It'll be a very nice place for us—a lovely garden—No doubt you'll get around to cultivating it too—The wood very near—nice high ceilings." He was delighted that he could obtain milk from a neighbor who had a cow, and also "whenever we like from the nearby village of Ockershausen." Elfride's diligence got them the house, which filled her husband with enthusiasm.[21] In this way, the Heideggers realized their suburban dream in a German provincial city that gave them the impression they were living in the countryside and could undertake there what had not been possible in Freiburg.

The university, warmly welcoming him, also won Heidegger's approval: he found the Hartmanns "charming" and thought he would get along well with his colleague; he went for walks with Natorp, whose wife was "rather loud & effusive—but nice even so"; he visited the Gadamer family: Hans-Georg had been one of his best students and, having come from Marburg to Freiburg, had followed Heidegger to the university in Hesse and helped him find lodgings.[22] Spending an afternoon with the Gadamers, Heidegger found the "old gentleman" "very nice" and made the acquaintance of the new rector and Professor Busch, a specialist in modern history who had been in Freiburg in the 1890s. All these people seemed to him "very warm." And he added: "The registrar explicitly assured me that the university is very much awaiting me, especially the Theolog. Faculty."[23]

Later, Heidegger was more negative. Although he liked the weather during the summer,[24] as a southern German he suffered from Marburg's climate, which tended toward the misty, making him feel like he was living in a "foggy nest."[25] Of the air in Marburg, he could not help noting that "this weak, light stuff down here ruins you over time."[26] Moreover, their beautiful house with the magnificent garden was in fact "unhealthy," and they left it in late July 1926;[27] at the end of the winter semester of 1926–1927 they moved into a new apartment closer to the city center, located at no. 15, Barfüßertor. It was "much healthier and nicer,"[28] even "magnificent,"[29] with a no less beautiful garden.[30] Heidegger hoped that as a result his stay in Marburg would be "substantially easier."[31] That was the case, as he enthusiastically told Blochmann, mentioning his "marvelous" study "on the left, a view of the castle, on the right a view of the Frauenberg," so that during the first two weeks "I haven't poked my nose outside."[32] What Heidegger told Jaspers about the university was more critical, as in a letter written in 1928:[33] "I cannot cite to you anything that speaks for Marburg. I haven't felt at ease here for a single hour. The faculty here is the same as anywhere else—the student body heavily oriented toward exams or completely given over to fraternities. The only thing: the theologians—but this is a patchy matter."[34]

Heidegger really did not feel so bad in Marburg. After many hesitations, he decided to stay there instead of accepting a superb opportunity in Japan, where he would have gone to teach for three years. On 17 June 1924, the Japanese count Kuki Shūzō (1888–1941), to whom he had given private lessons in Freiburg during the summer of 1923,[35] had come, "officially commissioned," to offer him a teaching position in "an institute [. . .] for the study of European culture, with special consideration for the human sciences." The conditions were tempting: in addition to the opportunity to teach at the University of Tokyo as well—where Heidegger could hope to be appointed to the vacant chair in the history of philosophy, ultimately establishing himself definitively in Japan—the financial advantages offered by this institute, founded "by Japanese nobility and high finance" and subsidized by the government, were considerable: "free relocation with family" and an annual salary of 10,000 yen (17,000 marks), a sum that corresponded to the salary of a German university professor and that would have allowed him to build himself a house in the area. Elfride was enthusiastic and wanted to give it a try;[36] but another voice spoke out against this Japanese option: Natorp said he would be "very sorry" if Heidegger "were to abandon Marburg."[37] As for Heidegger himself, he hesitated to say no, even though he was strongly inclined to do so, pointing out that he was "not certain" whether he needed such an "excursion" or whether he should undertake it.

To be sure, Heidegger clearly lacked the adventurous spirit of his wife, who was always full of enthusiasm. Nonetheless, Marburg was not a default choice: a biographer has to treat with particular circumspection the critical judgments

Heidegger expressed to his friend Jaspers. As was often the case in the letters he sent to Jaspers, Heidegger was adopting a pose, exaggerating, denigrating his city, his students, and his colleagues, only one of whom found favor in his eyes: the theologian Rudolf Bultmann, with whom he got together every week, and who was "not at all stuffy."[38] We can gauge the exaggeration in these remarks by comparing them with the letters to Elfride, in which he sometimes showed esteem for a few other colleagues, such as Natorp, whose death on 17 August 1924 devastated him. He remembered the impromptu visit of the older man, who had "sat in the leather armchair for a long time—& [. . .] spoke of his plans—his kind, animated eyes were hoping and searching for friendship"; his death left Heidegger seemingly without anyone at the university to whom he could look up with admiration.[39] His esteem and respect proceeded not only from the fact that Natorp had been the first person besides Husserl who had found sufficient value in Heidegger's work to want to see him appointed to a chair and had later sought out his friendship. He grew significantly closer to Natorp because of the special value that the latter attributed to Greek philosophy and the sympathy he had shown for the Youth Movement during the meeting on the Hohe Meißner in the autumn of 1913.[40]

Natorp's death isolated Heidegger somewhat in the Faculty of Philosophy, where he was "surrounded by squabbling conniving professors."[41] This was an occasion for Heidegger to express his anti-Semitism once again, in a letter to his wife in which he reported a conversation he'd had with his Jewish colleague Jacobsthal. Jacobsthal was paid at the highest level, even though he had received no outside job offer, an occasion for renegotiating one's salary; and his assistant, also without an opportunity to leave Marburg, had succeeded, thanks to his protector's intrigues, in negotiating a comfortable salary that was equivalent to that of Heidegger—who, however, held a higher rank. Heidegger understood all this in terms of anti-Semitic stereotypes ("These Jews!")[42]—by nature, Jews were greedy and cunning; they knew how to use their craftiness to get what they wanted.

These negative stereotypes were commonplaces in German universities—even in Marburg. Heidegger presented the situation this way within the committee of specialists in the Faculty of Philosophy, to which he now belonged: "One part of the faculty has a single principle: no Jews and, if at all possible, a German national: the other part (Jaensch and his followers), only something mediocre and nothing dangerous."[43] On one side, then, an anti-Semitic and ultranationalist fringe, monarchists hostile to the Weimar Republic and sympathizing with the Nazi Party (NSDAP), to the point of denying that the Jews had merit and giving precedence to a political criterion in appointing a peer; on the other side, a clan grouped around the psychologist Erich Rudolf Jaensch (1883–1940) that rejected any original, charismatic person who might overshadow him in one way or another. Heidegger disliked this colleague's pronounced taste for academic intrigues.

Disappointed by the Faculty of Philosophy, Heidegger found comfort in the Faculty of Theology, which included Rudolf Bultmann, who soon became his friend. In December 1923, Bultmann already had an excellent opinion of Heidegger, a connoisseur of classical theology, Scholasticism, and Luther, and also of modern theology, Friedrich Gogarten, and Karl Barth.[44] Thus in the winter semester of 1923–1924 he participated in Heidegger's seminar on Saint Paul's ethics, first on 10 January, for a discussion of Romans 6 and life in the faith, and then on 14 and 21 February, for a report on the problem of sin in Luther. Their exchanges were so rich that for Heidegger, Bultmann was the only one of his acquaintances in Marburg who could equal Jaspers.[45]

Heidegger's friendship with Bultmann tended to bring their two families together: thus Jörg spent the afternoon of 30 June 1925 at the Bultmanns' home, where his father was invited to dine that evening. Both of the Bultmanns wanted to give him "a special treat";[46] after dinner, Frau Bultmann sang excerpts from Gluck, while her husband accompanied her on the piano. Heidegger had come to greatly appreciate secular music, a bourgeois practice lacking in his childhood; he and his wife now had a piano, which they could afford because of the higher remuneration associated with this chair as an *Extraordinarius*. Although Heidegger seems not to have known how to play the piano, he liked to listen to music, even while he was working.[47] The close association with Bultmann was thus nourished by spiritual conversations, friendly visits, and music given and received, so that, at a time when human relationships remained particularly formal, as early as October 1928 Heidegger and Bultmann addressed each other using the informal *du*,[48] a sign of their close friendship that was all the clearer because the philosopher never used this mark of intimacy with Jaspers, the special respect he had for him keeping Heidegger at a distance.[49]

Heidegger's years in Marburg acquainted him with intense exchanges with Protestant theologians, who granted him brilliant recognition: for example, his 25 July 1924 lecture on the concept of time "went down well," according to Bultmann and von Rohden—even and especially among those whose interests had been remote from his up to that point. For his part, Heidegger proudly announced: "The theology lecturers are very excited & that is good."[50]

This intellectual stimulation through his colleagues was accompanied by that coming from his students. Heidegger sometimes admitted the pleasure he took in teaching—to his wife in January 1928, for example: "My seminar on Schelling is very gratifying—the papers & reports get better & better. In the lecture I have the audience right in the palm of my hand, though the material is now becoming more difficult every day for them."[51] Despite the exaggerated complaints he formulated for Jaspers, he was surrounded by a small number of first-rate students. In addition to the "shock troop" that had followed him to Marburg[52]—as Hans Jonas told it, in what was perhaps an overstatement, "all his students had migrated with him"[53]—there were new students who were not without merit, such as Günther Stern,[54] Leo Strauss, Gerhard Nebel, Gerhard Krüger, and Hermann Mörchen (whose thesis Heidegger considered "quite excellent,"[55] like that of Hans Jonas), as well as Hannah Arendt, who like others had traveled from far away to hear Heidegger—she came from Königsberg in East Prussia.

The praise he gave his students could sometimes be long in coming: Jonas wrote that, having submitted his thesis in the autumn of 1928, he rather quickly received a negative opinion from "a sort of glorified high-school teacher"[56] who was serving as a second reader—probably Franz-Josef Brecht, one of Heidegger's former students, who had particular esteem for him. Heidegger took months to render his judgment, leaving Jonas to suffer the torments of uncertainty. In the winter, the answer came incidentally:

> One evening I went to a concert, and was already in my seat when Heidegger showed up and had to squeeze past me to reach his seat in the same row. As he did so, he remarked, "Your dissertation is excellent." And continued down the row. So that was how he treated a candidate in suspense, and I think it didn't trouble him in the slightest that a student had been waiting in fear and trembling to hear how something he'd spent years working on would be received.[57]

This hardness, this insensitivity in his relations with his students, was also displayed in the lecture hall: "We saw him working, just for himself," Löwith wrote, "without paying the slightest attention to his audience, which he shook up more than instructed. He remained standing, very aware of his isolation on his podium, and presented his lecture, turning the pages with a self-assurance that was almost routine."[58] For the last lecture he gave in Marburg, his students had placed a bouquet of white roses on his lectern in the large lecture hall. When he arrived, "looking down at the floor, as usual," he showed "an extreme repugnance" for these flowers, which seemed to him "out of place,"[59] and which he ignored until the end of his lecture.

The master's coldness did not prevent his students from showing an ardor that often rose to the level of devotion. Hans Jonas, who had made the move from Freiburg to Marburg after a short delay, was shocked by the increasingly cultish relationship that united the philosopher with his disciples. Although he "had no trouble joining the discussion under way," he found "the Heidegger cult among the philosophy students [. . .] hard to take. Its chief characteristic was a kind of bigoted arrogance, with members of the group almost going so far as to claim a monopoly on divine truth. This wasn't philosophy; it was more like a sect, almost a new religion," and Jonas found it "profoundly repellent."[60] Since many of these students were Jewish, this atmosphere, which "wasn't healthy," seemed to Jonas to resemble the relation that believers maintained with the "Lubavitcher rebbe," as if Heidegger were "a zaddik, a miracle rabbi, or a guru."[61] The master for his part understood this quasireligious relationship in terms of his model of life and thought, which had first been shaped by the Catholic Church; his philosopher persona was ultimately only a secularization of the priest's, as he had experienced and imagined it, so that he lectured with the same penetration, the same gravity, as that of a pastor preaching from the pulpit or elevating the Eucharist. Like Stefan George,[62] and then later like Hitler,[63] Heidegger had succeeded in establishing a "charismatic authority"[64] over a number of his students, who were transformed into disciples and who nicknamed him "the little magician from Meßkirch."[65] Heidegger established himself as a kind of Messiah or prophet of the spirit, as much by his enthusiasm and radicalism as by the hermetic quality of his discourse. He astonished his audience "by causing to disappear" "what he had just shown them. The technique of his presentations consisted in building the structure of an idea that he subsequently demolished himself, placing his listeners before an enigma and then abandoning them in the void."[66]

His students—through their religious background, their penchant for George in some cases, their youth, their ignorance, and their own radicalism in this postwar period, when everything could be called into question—were predisposed to being subjugated by an orator whose personal authority was further increased by the academic position he held, though not all of them bowed down and worshipped him. Although fascinated, Walter Bröcker, Jonas, and Arendt seem to have been among those who retained some measure of free will and independence of mind, enough "to find all the veneration unpleasant" and to remain resistant to "this arrogant, exclusive adulation of

Heidegger."[67] These reservations did not prevent them from having esteem for the master, and in fact contributed to it: Jonas remembered the favor that Bröcker enjoyed, though he could not read Greek; and it was with Hannah Arendt that Heidegger formed the most important extramarital and intellectual relationship of his life.

This relationship is easily romanticized. It began in mid-February 1925. Arendt was only eighteen, Heidegger twice her age. Lively and reserved, she housed a fine mind in the slender body of a well-behaved young woman; the first time she crossed the threshold of Heidegger's office, she was "in a raincoat, her hat low over her quiet, large eyes."[68] She had not planned to throw herself into the arms of her professor, whom she had gone to see to discuss her studies. Although it was twilight, Heidegger had not turned on the lights, leaving the room in semidarkness. "Softly and shyly," she gave "a brief answer to each question,"[69] gradually revealing to him the "deep joy"[70] within her. When their discussion was over, she rose and he walked her to the door. Then, "suddenly he went down on his knees before me," she told Jonas, who was her close friend. "And I bent down, and from below he reached up his arms toward me, and I took his head in my hands, and he kissed me, and I kissed him."[71]

According to Jonas, Heidegger "took an interest in a woman student from time to time" already in this period; and apparently none of them ever resisted him. The relationship with Arendt nonetheless went far beyond sex. Divided between what he called "our storm"[72] and a demanding intellectual dialogue, a bond of love both physical and intellectual formed, a bond that resembled the one between Phaedrus and his teacher Socrates. The flames of Heidegger's letters often ignited intimate feelings and philosophical conceptions, expressed, for example, in this passage from a letter of 8 May 1925, which implicitly developed the theory of the *Mitwelt,* the "common world," in the context of the turmoil at the beginning of their affair. In the surrounding world (*Umwelt*), others are inseparable from us and color the world as it is experienced, a fortiori in the framework of a passion in which everything refers to the beloved other: "And still one would like to 'say' something and to offer oneself to the other, but we could only say that the world is now no longer mine and yours—but *ours*—only that what we do and achieve belongs not to you *and* me but to *us*. Only that gable and paths and May morning and scent of flowers—are ours."[73]

Although their relationship was interrupted from time to time, it contributed to the pleasure that the philosopher took in his everyday life in Marburg, even if he was careful not to say a word about it to Jaspers, preferring to write that the students were "simple-minded, without any particular motivation,"[74] and were helping him deepen the existential experience of negativity and nothingness. Unlike ennui, which renders everything tasteless, passion made Heidegger lyrical. He described springtime in Marburg in the sensual colors of the ideal: "When the new semester comes it will be May. Lilac will leap over the old walls and tree blossoms will well up in the secret gardens—and you will enter the old gate in a light summer dress. Summer evenings will come into your room and toll the quiet serenity of our life into your young soul. Soon they will awaken—the flowers your dear hands will pick, and the moss on the forest floor that you will walk on in your blissful dreams."[75]

As Arendt told him three years later, despite the solitude of the mistress forced to keep silent about her love, and despite difficulties and interruptions, her passion remained ardent: "I love you as I did on the first day—you know that, and I have always known it, even before this reunion. The path you showed me is longer and more difficult than I thought. It requires a long life in its entirety. The solitude of this path is self-chosen and is the only way of living given me."[76] For his part, Heidegger pulled back, so that the following year, Arendt was ardently trying to revive his interest: "I am turning to you with the same security and with the same request: do not forget me, and do not forget how much and how deeply I know that our love has become the blessing of my life."[77] This letter might have come from a faithful, lonely lover; in fact it came from a soulmate informing the object of her passion that she is going to marry another, in this case Günther Stern, one of Heidegger's former students, whom he didn't much like. Before bidding him farewell and closing her letter with "I kiss your brow and eyes," she wrote, "I would indeed so like to know—almost tormentingly so—how you are doing, what you are working on, and how Freiburg is treating you."[78]

Although Heidegger went back to Freiburg in 1928, the return to the foot of the Black Forest was not a matter of course, though the prospect had been very present in the minds of Husserl and Heidegger. When his student left for Marburg, Husserl had told him he wanted to make Heidegger his successor: "The motto is—'*he will go.*'"[79] This promise made in July 1923 was not a prophecy: the time Heidegger spent in Marburg was happier than he sometimes wanted to admit, and he might have stayed there more willingly had the ministry in Berlin not been so narrow-minded. In 1924, after hesitating, he decided not to go to Japan; the same year, an attempt to open Geyser's chair to members of other faiths, in order to bring Heidegger back to Freiburg, fizzled out.[80] The Faculty of Philosophy had certainly told him, through its dean, that it would like to have him, but, he wrote, "I wouldn't accept the offer anyway—unless I were quite independent of the Catholics."[81] Since this was not the case, he remained in Marburg.

The position in Freiburg after Husserl's retirement was a very different matter. As Karl Löwith tells it, after 1916 Husserl had become "the main philosophical attraction not only of the University of Freiburg, but of German philosophy in general," emphasizing that "many foreigners also attend his lectures."[82] In addition to the glory of taking the chair of such a master,[83] even one held in contempt, there were the conditions of this succession, which marked a brilliant recognition of Heidegger's philosophical career: Husserl wanted him to be nominated *unico loco,* that is, as the only name on the list proposed by the university, an exclusive preference that nevertheless added a certain risk, to the point that Heidegger asked his former teacher "to consider this plan carefully though, as such proposals can often prove damaging."[84] His fears were unjustified: "One citadel after another" was being taken:[85] on 21 January 1928 the committee assigned to draw up the list adopted Husserl's view;[86] on 7 February,[87] the committee's decision was ratified "*unanimously* by the Faculty";[88] and the ministry in Karlsruhe followed suit on 25 February.[89]

But for all that, Heidegger did not necessarily have the chair: he had to negotiate with Victor Schwoerer at the ministry and make sure the conditions being offered were satisfactory. In the capital of Baden, the negotiations were short; Schwoerer was "extremely friendly and fraternal," asking Heidegger "rather directly" about his salary in Marburg and noting down his requests. He had the ministry's proposals sent to the philosopher on 6 March:

1. Beginning of service on October 1.
2. Basic salary according to the fourth level of salary group A1 with 11,600 marks. Housing bonus 1,728. Children bonus.
3. Instructional fee guarantee, 3,000 marks.
4. Reimbursement of moving expenses.
5. Years of service calculated from the time of habilitation (re: retirement).
6. Housing construction bonus—will be reviewed with good will.

Regarding his wishes, Heidegger noted that "number 3" was "reduced" and "number 6 very uncertain,"[90] but he had reason to hope that an agreement would be found; in Jaspers's opinion, these conditions were "not bad," even if he regretted that, "almost without exception, reductions are made in the attempt to reach agreement!"[91] Subsequent negotiations led to the withdrawal of these unpleasant reductions, and on 25 March Heidegger was able to write that "what was previously stricken has been directly agreed to by Schw.[oerer]." That was, however, still not the final word: on 28 March, a telegram from Richter summoned Heidegger to Berlin[92]—the Prussian ministry probably wanted to make a better offer to keep Heidegger in Marburg. Alas! It offered him the same thing that he was receiving in Baden.[93] Heidegger therefore gave his definitive answer to Karlsruhe on 30 March:[94] it was positive, and Husserl's efforts to bring his student back to Freiburg had finally succeeded.

Martin Heidegger's prestigious appointment to be Edmund Husserl's successor *unico loco* at the University of Freiburg had been made possible by the master's diligence, certainly, but also by the publication of a book that would remain the disciple's masterpiece: *Being and Time*.

Heidegger, hesitating because of his tremendous ambition and rigor, had for a long time put off publishing a book. In his Todtnauberg cabin on 8 April 1926, as he was happy to note in his epigraph, he had been able to bring a new work to its conclusion. But, pressured by the demands of his career and the opportunity that Husserl offered him to publish in his teacher's journal, Heidegger had written in haste a book unlikely to appeal to a wide audience and which bore the marks of the conditions of its composition. All its flaws—its ungainly Scholasticism, its redundancies, the hurriedly written passages, the mangling of language, and even the incompleteness of the book as a whole (he never wrote part 2 and did not get beyond the first two thirds of part 1)—would have condemned the book to anonymity were it not for its originality and richness, its forcefulness and the way it resonated with the age. In its simplicity, its title had a clarity that immediately spoke to the intellect; in its abstraction, it raised hopes of an absolute radicalism that would lead back to the twin roots of the real, being and time.

Being (*Sein*), without being one thing or another, this or that, is at the root of everything—the object, the idea, the event; everything from the little blue wagon pulled by a child, to the ball struck by an adolescent, to Einstein's special theory of relativity, which the young student of mathematics had studied, and the spiritual revolution to which the phenomenologist aspired. Despite their diversity, these are all just beings (*Seienden*). Although essential, ontology, the science of being (*Sein*) as being, or of *a* being (*Seiende*) as a being, has been forgotten by modern science, which is divided into disciplines. Having laid their foundations, scientists in these disciplines confine themselves to accumulating positive data about beings without ever seeing the unity of knowledge or challenging their own basic concepts.[95] Science is uprooted, weakened by its lack of ground, because of the influence of three particularly damaging prejudices:[96] first, that being is the most general concept; second, that being is impossible to define, because it cannot be linked to a higher class or genus in relation to which its specificity could be shown;[97] and third, that the concept of being is self-evident and therefore does not require examination.

In his aim to revolutionize science through ontology, Heidegger did not want to be the successor pure and simple of the Scholastics, who had opened his eyes to metaphysics when he was a young man. Motivated by Husserl's preoccupation with going back to the things themselves, without concern in the first place for what the tradition had said about them, Heidegger believed that Scholastic ontology, in explaining being with reference to the supreme being (*Seiende*), namely, God, rested on shaky foundations. Man, who inquires into being, cannot disassociate himself from his experience of it, especially since, for him, questioning is a "mode of *Being*."[98] Still embracing the hermeneutic preoccupation with the interpretation of meaning, which he had taken from Schleiermacher, Heidegger maintained that this new ontology ought to inquire into the "meaning of Being"; to do so, it ought to take as its starting point man himself, by considering, precisely, his being (*Sein*).[99] This task is all the more essential and existential in that man, whether he refuses or agrees to take on that task, must determine himself in light of what is. *Dasein* (being-there), which replaces the concept of man in Heidegger's texts, is distinguished from every other being (*Seiende*) by the fact that, "in its very Being, [. . .] Being is an issue for it. [. . .] *Understanding of Being is itself a definite characteristic of* Dasein's *Being*."[100] The term *Dasein* has remained something like the emblematic, frightening, incomprehensible word in Heidegger's philosophy, a change of terminology that is not neutral. Because of it, his ontological refoundation can conceive of man from the angle of being. To that end, *Dasein,* a common German term synonymous with "existence," gradually acquires in Heidegger's writings a meaning far removed from the usual understanding of the word: man is not there, he is "the there"; he is not posited and defined as a thing, an object, he is that through which everything that is can take place.

As with this revitalization of the term *Dasein* or the neologism "being-in-the-world," the book as a whole was filled with obscure terms. And if the term itself was not obscure, its usage was. Heidegger was not afraid to manhandle the language, and he explained the "harshness" or ugliness of his mode of expression in the following terms:

> It is one thing to give a report in which we tell about beings, but another to grasp *beings* in their *Being*. [. . .] We may compare the ontological sections of Plato's *Parmenides* or the fourth chapter of the seventh book of Aristotle's *Metaphysics* with a narrative section from Thucydides; we can then see the altogether unprecedented character of those formulations which were imposed upon the Greeks by their philosophers. And where our powers are essentially weaker, and where moreover the area of Being to be disclosed is ontologically far more difficult than that which was presented to the Greeks, the harshness of our expression will be enhanced.[101]

Placed under the aegis of Plato and Aristotle, *Being and Time* could thus speak of being on the basis of the being-there. In his book Heidegger was able to indicate that, from this standpoint, being is not so much space as time.

Time is what gives meaning to the being of man, whether understood as an individual or as the human group to which he belongs. Heidegger made good use of his Catholic heritage, reappropriating Saint Augustine's philosophy, according to which, for man, the reality of time is a threefold present: the presence of the past, or memory (*memoria*); the presence of the present, or attention (*contuitus*); and the presence of the future, or anticipation (*expectatio*).[102] Heidegger, for his part, saw the future as a project, a projection of self into the future carried out in the present, a projection that conditions man's very being through his way of relating to or evading the end of his existence in the future. The individual is finite: death, his own death, comes to delimit his being—not like an ocean that peacefully interrupts the serene course of the river flowing into it, but like a waterfall whose inevitability controls all navigation upstream. Future but certain, this dispossession of self summons man to choose, to define his being (*Sein*) for himself, to make one choice amid an infinite number of possibilities. The result is anxiety or angst, an idea borrowed from Kierkegaard's *Concept of Anxiety*. Unlike fear, anxiety has no object; it is man's vertigo in the face of his freedom and responsibility, when he is exposed to the possibility of making a mistake and losing his way.

Men habitually dodge as much as they can that injunction of being, that existential angst, and distract themselves in a thousand ways. Without saying so, Heidegger was taking on the inflections of Pascal, with whom he was very familiar. Although Heidegger rejected Pascal's position on being,[103] he kept a portrait of the French writer on his desk, next to one of Dostoevsky.[104] Nonetheless, he gave little thought to the two infinities, the infinitely small and the infinitely large, between which man finds himself, and which the invention of the microscope and the telescope had disclosed to humanity in the seventeenth century. No, Heidegger was thinking primarily of death, the idea of his own end, and the anxiety resulting from his freedom to choose what he wanted to become. Furthermore, in place of the elegant prose of the French master of the *pensée* and of the written form, the German philosopher preferred a Scholastic ungainliness as the means to reflect on *das Man* (the "they" or the "one"),[105] by which *Dasein* falls out of its own existence. Like Martin Buber, whose masterpiece, *Ich und Du* (1923), took the "I" and the "thou" as its subject, Heidegger conducted a meditation on a pronoun. He distinguished six modes of *das Man:* (1) "distantiality," which consists of the many ways of being concerned with distance from others, whether in the desire to establish it or to abolish it; (2) "averageness," which corresponds to the mediocre, even timeworn norm prescribed by *das Man;* (3) "leveling down," by means of which all the possibilities of the being of *das Man* tend to become equivalent or even alike; (4) "publicness," because *das Man* claims that everything is obviously known to everyone and "everything gets obscured, and what has thus been covered up gets passed off as something familiar and accessible to everyone"; (5) the absence of "answerability," by which man in everyday life hides behind *das Man,* which "presents every judgment and decision as its own" and exempts man from deciding for himself; and (6) "disburdening" or accommodation, which prevents man from making every effort to leave *das Man* behind, so that *das Man* "retains and enhances its stubborn dominion."[106] Beyond the multiplicity of its modes, *das Man* is in its essence a diversion that turns *Dasein* away from the choice it must make of its being (*Sein*) in view of its coming death.

Heidegger had had the experience of thinking about death during the war. There, exposed to the risk of a stray shell or the aerial bombardment of his meteorological observation hut, he had discovered what in *Being and Time* he called "Being-toward-death," an essential structure by which man essentially determines his being in the face of the possibility of his no longer being: "Only by the anticipation [*Vorlaufen*] of death is every accidental and 'provisional' [*vorläufige*] possibility driven out. Only Being free *for* death gives *Dasein* its goal outright and pushes existence into its finitude. Once one has grasped the finitude of one's existence, it snatches one back from the endless multiplicity of possibilities which offer themselves as closest to one—those of comfortableness, shirking, and taking things lightly—and brings *Dasein* into the simplicity of its *fate* [*Schicksals*]."[107] Thinking intimately and resolutely about one's own death, as the soldier does, and bravely accepting one's civic, social, and familial responsibilities, lead to such a complete reduction of the possibilities offered man that he then finds himself confronting his destiny, a life plan entirely imposed on him, which fully determines the course of the time he must follow.[108] With that theory of the relation to death arising from his own experience, Heidegger was in tune with his generation of First World War combatants. He borrowed the concept of generation from Dilthey. According to that notion, individuals of the same age encountered the meaning of their being partly as a group, as had been the case for the young men called up together to go to war. Although every individual defines himself authentically, the being of *Dasein* is neither individual nor atemporal. It is rooted in a community that is caught within time and that is composed of a tradition and a culture, on the basis of which all understanding comes about and all decisions are made in the present with the future in view: being is time, because human existence is characterized essentially by its historicality.

The introduction to *Being and Time* also evoked a second aspect of the time of being: its inscription in a philosophical history, composed of the superimposition of interpretations that conceal being to an ever greater degree. The philosopher wanted to look critically at the past in order to deconstruct it, "disobstruct" it, and thus disengage being. Heidegger did not pursue that objective, he only announced it. *Being and Time,* as it was published, barely went beyond an existential and ontological anthropology characterized by its insistence on time. Concerned with arriving at being by examining being-there, *Dasein,* Heidegger spoke primarily of man. That anthropology remained partial, because man's body and heart, constitutive of his existence, were, if not forgotten, then at least minimized. With the theory of *Stimmung* (mood, attunement, emotional tenor, disposition), which is indissociable from human existence, inasmuch as man is always "disposed" one way or another, there was the potential for a phenomenology of the body, of love, and of sexuality, but it was not expressed in the book in a manner commensurate with the importance of these subjects. Paradoxically, Heidegger was without peer when it came to the cult of Eros. This god, absent from his magnum opus, does appear in his correspondence, in which he once again turned to Augustine, practicing the ontology of *Dasein* in a different way. At the time, he would write in letters to his mistresses: *volo ut sis,* "I want you to be." Had he not been so antagonistic toward the French Enlightenment, Heidegger might have found food for thought in the Marquis de Sade's "Philosopher Teacher." In a tone somewhere between seriousness and blasphemy, Sade conceived of the relationship between unity and multiplicity in terms of sexual activity and its ultimate expression in coitus, when two become one while remaining two or even three, with

Sade's amusing exemplification of the Trinity.[109] Can this lacuna in *Being and Time* be ascribed merely to a lack of time? No, it was rather a form of prudery, a repression of embodiment in keeping with the moral inheritance Heidegger had received from his family, an inheritance still present in the 1920s, at a time when the loosening of moral strictures in society was apparent, but only on a small scale. Despite the timidly rising hemlines in the big cities, flesh in that era was still concealed behind fabric or silence.

Despite its limits, its lacunae, and its incompleteness, *Being and Time* left its mark on the history of twentieth-century philosophy, by virtue of its reception well beyond the borders of Germany. Heidegger himself had written in the book: "Publicness [*Öffentlichkeit*] proximally controls every way in which the world and *Dasein* get interpreted, and it is always right."[110] The world received the book so positively that Heidegger's life was altered. Granted, in spring 1927 he was not a complete unknown. He had been the subject of thirteen miscellaneous writings,[111] primarily reviews of his habilitation thesis, two of them as early as 1925: one in a German review of Kantian studies,[112] the other in an Italian Franciscan review.[113] The same year, he was honored with an article in the major Spanish-language encyclopedia, the *Enciclopedia Espasa-Calpe*.[114] During the 1920s he had made something of a name for himself among students in Germany, benefiting from his teacher's celebrity: people came to listen to Husserl and discovered Heidegger. Some of the students were foreigners, such as the Japanese Tanabe Hajime, Miki Kiyoshi,[115] and Kuki Shūzō. Representatives of the Kyoto School,[116] founded by Nishida Kitarō (1870–1945) as the intellectual expression of the Meiji era, they had traveled to Europe, particularly Germany and France, to be trained in Western philosophy, both classic (Pascal) and modern (Bergson, Rickert, Husserl). Heidegger had even been offered a position in Japan, which he turned down.

Audible even before the publication of his magnum opus, the trumpet of renown now sounded incomparably louder for Heidegger, and the fanfare traveled incomparably farther. Hans-Georg Gadamer, exaggerating slightly, wrote: "All of a sudden, there was worldwide fame."[117] It is true that interest in Gadamer's teacher grew spectacularly: Heidegger was the subject of twelve articles in 1928, twenty-four in 1929, and fifty-two in 1930. The educated English public could discover Heidegger's work in Gilbert Ryle's 1929 review of *Being and Time*.[118] Heidegger's audience extended far beyond his students: the Japanese Watsuji Tetsurō read the book while in Berlin in 1927 and, upon his return to Japan the following year, undertook a dialogue with Heidegger's philosophy from his lectern in Kyoto.[119] Emmanuel Levinas, a Frenchman of

Lithuanian ancestry, discovered *Being and Time* in Strasbourg, at the recommendation of the Protestant minister Jean Hering, a former student of Husserl's, who had taken an interest in the disciple's work.[120] The bilingual border region of Alsace facilitated exchanges between France and Germany. Levinas enrolled at the University of Freiburg in 1928–1929, to take classes from Husserl and Heidegger. He was so dazzled by Heidegger that, three years later, he began an article with these words:

> The prestige of Martin Heidegger and the influence of his thought on German philosophy is a new phase—and one of the apogees—of the phenomenological movement. Older scholars, surprised, clarify their attitude toward the new doctrine. It exerts a fascination on the young. And in extending beyond the limits of the permissible, it is already making inroads in the salons. As chance would have it, Glory has not erred and, despite all her habits, she did not arrive late. Whoever has practiced philosophy cannot keep from observing, in the presence of Heidegger's works, that the originality and force of his efforts, which are the product of genius, are combined with a conscientious, meticulous, and robust elaboration, the work of a patient laborer, the pride of the phenomenologists.[121]

Being and Time attracted other students to Heidegger: Germans such as Herbert Marcuse and foreigners such as the Italian Ernesto Grassi, Heidegger's first supporter in Italy, and the Japanese Seinosuke Yuasa, who in 1930 translated the German philosopher's lecture "What Is Metaphysics?"[122] And *Being and Time* changed the way people saw Heidegger: a professor of philosophy who has published little or nothing is primarily a teacher, whereas an ambitious and voluminous book, by its physical and intellectual weight, turns its author into a full-fledged philosopher. Henceforth, dropping the nickname "little magician of Meßkirch," students called him the "sage of time."[123] Students both old and new played a role in the dissemination of his thought, writing review articles alongside his theologian friend Bultmann and his former teacher Rickert. Although Heidegger was piquing the curiosity of another Protestant theologian, Heinrich Barth,[124] Catholics were less enthusiastic, pretending to be afraid that Heidegger's scholarly contribution "would serve only to inject a sort of tragic heroism into Dilthey's 'historicity.' "[125]

Heidegger was on the cutting edge of philosophy. Although he was in conversation with such classical authors as Plato, Aristotle, and Augustine and carried on the Scholastic ontological tradition, he also contributed toward challenging scientistic positivism in Europe, alongside such figures as Husserl,

Dilthey, Bergson, Gentile, and Croce, who since the 1880s had been revalorizing, in one way or another, subjectivity in philosophy.[126] That taste for a less coldly rational intellect spread among German youth, attracting greater attention to the works of contemporary authors—the essayist Oswald Spengler and the theologian Karl Barth, for example—and bringing posthumous fame to Kierkegaard, Nietzsche, and Dostoevsky. Heidegger issued an anxious challenge to bourgeois scientism, by forcefully inserting himself into movements such as existentialism, the reason behind Kierkegaard's popularity, and the Youth Movement, whose demand for authenticity and heroic responsibility Heidegger made his own. In that way, he was fulfilling the expectations of a young educated public, as Herbert Marcuse noted. Discovering Heidegger at the time, Marcuse had the sense he had found what other contemporary authors were not offering: something concrete.[127] "We experienced his book (and his courses, for which we had notes) as being, ultimately, a *concrete* philosophy; it had to do with existence, our existence, angst and care and tedium, etc."[128]

The global reception of *Being and Time* was all the more extraordinary in view of how belatedly the translations appeared. The first translations into Romance languages were not published until the 1950s: the Spanish in 1951[129] and the Italian in 1953.[130] The book did not come out in English until 1962, in the translation of John Macquarrie and Edward Robinson,[131] which illustrated the difficulty peculiar to that language of distinguishing between *Sein* and *Seiende*. Hence the title chosen, *Being and Time*, can mean either *Sein und Zeit* or *Seiende und Zeit*. The first complete editions in French date to the 1980s: the official translation, by François Vezin,[132] was decried for its bias; the second—not for public sale because done without authorization—was by Emmanuel Martineau.[133] Granted, partial French translations had come out before that time:[134] by 1938 the general public had access to excerpts collected by Henry Corbin in *Qu'est-ce que la métaphysique?*,[135] a collection decisive for the dissemination of Heidegger's thought in France. It served as an entry point for Sartre: it was thanks to Corbin[136] that he published his own *Being and Nothingness* in 1943, its title loudly proclaiming its Heideggerian inspiration. Despite their undeniable importance, the translations played only a belated role in the tremendous reception Heidegger met with. His continued efforts to diffuse and revise his thinking contributed a great deal to his renown. In 1929 he published a second book, *Kant and the Problem of Metaphysics*, which grew out of the aborted plan for part 2 of *Being and Time* and was itself reviewed many times. Likewise, his new fame allowed him to deliver more lectures, which in turn made him better known, especially since some of them—"What Is Metaphysics?," for example—were published and even translated into other languages.

By first obtaining a position for him as an assistant, then by publishing his work in his journal, and finally by clearly designating him as his successor, Edmund Husserl had done a great deal for Heidegger, whose appointment in Freiburg crowned his teacher's efforts. But he was not to enjoy this success for long. So long as his career had not yet been fully established, Heidegger had to keep himself in Husserl's good graces, hold onto his esteem and affection. After a stay at the Husserls' home in October 1927 (Heidegger was still living in Marburg), he wrote an almost filial letter to his teacher that began, "Dear, paternal friend," and thanked him for receiving him as if he were a son.[137] And in fact Husserl did promote his former disciple's career in a paternal way. Everything changed once Heidegger had succeeded him: "After he had succeeded me, our relationship lasted about two months, then it was over, without conflict," Husserl wrote in a letter of 1931; "in the simplest way in the world [Heidegger] withdrew from any possibility of scientific discussion, something that was clearly pointless, undesirable, and disagreeable for him. I saw him once every other month, more rarely than other colleagues."[138] Jaspers wrote many years later that Heidegger "seemed like a friend who betrayed you while you were away," but who was sometimes "unforgettably close."[139] This profound duplicity, this astonishing warmth combined with an acute sense of calculation and dissimulation, was suddenly revealed to Husserl: Heidegger's fierce pride suffered from his outward submissiveness to a master; his own thought was moving ever further away from Husserl's efforts to constitute a "scientific phenomenology," and Heidegger was now able to cut the ties that for the past ten years had bound them so closely together, heart and soul. The "dear paternal friend" was no more.[140]

Husserl was filled with great bitterness when he realized that their relationship had been based on his own blindness. This was confirmed when he carefully reread *Being and Time* and then read Heidegger's subsequent texts: "I came to the distressing conclusion that on the philosophical level I can do nothing with this Heideggerian profundity, with this ingenious, nonscientific way of thinking; that Heidegger's overt and dissimulated criticism is based on a crude misunderstanding; that he is caught up in the elaboration of a philosophical system of the kind that I have constantly sought, in my teaching, to make forever impossible. Everyone else saw that long ago. I have not hidden my conclusion from Heidegger."[141] This conclusion was painful for the old philosopher: "This reversal of my scientific assessment and of my relationship to this person was one of the hardest trials of my life."[142]

Thanks to his former teacher, the ungrateful student found himself in an eminent academic position that ensured him genuine daily comfort in this southern part of Germany, sunny and close to his mountain of Todtnauberg. On 16 April, the Heideggers bought a lot at no. 47, Rötebuckstraße,[143] in Zähringen, a somewhat higher neighborhood on the outskirts of Freiburg. Elfride had always wanted to "create an exemplary house for the young people in particular,"[144] as much by its walls as by its occupants; she now had a perfect opportunity to do that. The house she designed was in a hybrid style, bourgeois in its architecture, alpine in its wood paneling and the shingles that covered the outer walls and roof, as in a Black Forest chalet; she chose furniture based on the existing pieces and above all took care to provide a vast study for her husband, so vast that it was the largest room in the house. The dwelling was constructed rapidly, so that they were able to move in on 20 October 1928, only six months after they purchased the land. Heidegger's new colleagues remarked ironically that "the Heidegger family's moving into the country."[145]

Despite the comfort of his house and the prestige of his chair, the pleasure Heidegger took in Freiburg was not unmixed. Beyond his students, and the numerous curiosity seekers and "spies" he thought he saw slipping in among "the traveling public" the first week, his overall view was negative: "The philosophy faculty has gotten essentially worse."[146] This judgment was premature: some of his students were outstanding, such as Herbert Marcuse and Emmanuel Levinas, and some were Catholics: Max Müller, Eugen Fink, and Ernesto Grassi. Heidegger liked to complain and vituperate in the letters he wrote to Jaspers: writing ironically, he attributed this deterioration to the "incredible *progress*" made by Catholics at the University of Freiburg: he saw "young *Catholic Privatdozents* sitting everywhere," who would one day succeed there "out of necessity."[147] Having become irreligious, he now considered those of his own background, those in his former camp, to be the enemy; Catholicism's continual advances deprived him of any hope of changing the spirit prevailing at the university, which he expressed in the polemical terms to which he had become accustomed: "I surely knew that I was taking up this outpost—though it is a *lost* one in my deepest conviction."[148] In the same way, recalling in a letter to Rickert the defense of his habilitation thesis in 1915, he opined that the University of Freiburg was "hardly recognizable when compared to its glory days in 1913," and that, like his former teacher, he "would not retreat" "to avoid a battle" that was perhaps even harder now than it had been in Rickert's time.[149] However, there was something positive in this outpost where he found himself: "The only thing new is that I am *no longer hiding* in my philosophizing. Somewhere it has pulled together."[150]

Todtnauberg, or the Mountain of Philosophy

Neither Marburg nor Freiburg fully satisfied Heidegger. When they moved to Marburg, the Heideggers already had a secondary residence at Todtnauberg, in the Black Forest, a cabin with which Heidegger wanted to identify his thinking. In the beginning, there were the Szilasis. Wilhelm Szilasi (1889–1966) was a Hungarian philosopher, a friend of Emil Lask and Georg Lukács and the son of the Jewish linguist Moritz Szilasi (1845–1905); he had married Elisabeth Rosenberg,[151] wealthy heir to the industrialist Herman Rosenberg. Szilasi had just left Hungary after the fall of Béla Kun's dictatorship in the Hungarian Soviet Republic, in which he had played a small part. In the fall of 1919, he moved to Freiburg; he attended Husserl's lectures and became part of his entourage, where he met Heidegger.[152] It was this couple, resolutely urban, rich, and cosmopolitan, in no wise peasants rooted in the Black Forest, who revealed to Elfride what gradually became the symbol of Heidegger's rootedness in his *Heimat*.

In early January 1920, the Szilasis invited Heidegger to stay with Karl and Gertrud Lieber at Sankt Märgen in the Black Forest, to ski and work.[153] Heidegger's financial situation was still precarious, and this offer of a friendly visit was welcome, especially when it was extended for the whole month of February.[154] The philosopher spent the month there, with the exception of one week when he remained in Freiburg to help Elfride with their house.[155] Far away from the worries and commotion of the household, in a closed and agreeable place, he could work with greater concentration. A break in the daily routine makes it possible to distance oneself and see things in a detached or even new way, an experience Heidegger had in Sankt Märgen: "Up here—along with the spatial distance, I've also acquired an inner distance in considering my situation."[156]

In February of the following year, the Szilasis decided to go to the small Austrian ski resort of Mittelberg, in the upper Walstertal, a charming alpine valley surrounded by summits as high as 2,500 meters, and which was accessible only by the road through Bavaria. Once again, they invited Heidegger, who liked the place very much: "It's quite magnificent up here—skiing, eating

& sleeping, one after the other." The only genuine reservation he expressed regarding his stay in Austria concerned the absence of Jörg, who was only one year old, and of Elfride: "We must definitely come up here some time—when we can."[157] A wish that was never fulfilled; Heidegger's enthusiasm for Mittelberg did not take him back there.

In January 1922, the Szilasis opted for the Black Forest: they went to Todtnauberg, an out-of-the way resort that the philosopher, using new skis, was barely able to reach. He was alone, because although Jörg was now old enough for high altitudes, the boy's mother, who often fell ill, was sick in bed in their Lerchenstraße apartment.[158] In February, once she had recovered from her illness, she was able to get to know Todtnauberg during a weekend trip there; she was enthusiastic about the place, enjoying there the alpine pleasures she had first known at the cabin in Silberberg with her student friends from the *Hüttenzunft*. Todtnauberg, she believed, would allow her to realize her ideals inspired by the Youth Movement: a healthy, authentic life in harmony with nature and the local German traditions. She therefore decided to buy a field in upper Todtnauberg and have a ski cabin built on it like the one in Silberberg, but adapted to the size of one family.

The Heideggers had no money; Elfride asked for an advance on her inheritance of 60,000 marks, which enabled her to pay the carpenter Schweizer in kind (leather or flour)—the runaway inflation Germany was facing after the difficult reconversion of the postwar German economy had led to a partial return to barter. The carpenter found land for her, a pasture that had a spring and belonged to a peasant named Pius Brender, called "Black Pius," and then quickly began building, using wood he had in stock.[159] On 9 August 1922, the Heideggers moved into their brand-new cabin, though it was unfinished, still lacking the outbuildings, the toilet, and the plumbing leading from the spring; they set up housekeeping there in haste, because starting on 1 August, the apartment in Lerchenstraße was to be sublet to Americans who paid in dollars,[160] which were welcome at this time when the German currency was collapsing.

From then on, in this Black Forest that was the usual vacation spot for many academics from Freiburg, and the preserve of the *Heimat*'s folklore par excellence, the Heidegger family had a secondary residence, a place where they could rest and work that corresponded to the description of it given by Heidegger in "Why Do I Stay in the Provinces?":

> On the steep slope of a wide mountain valley in the southern Black Forest, at an elevation of 1,150 meters, there stands a small ski hut. The floor

> plan measures six meters by seven. The low-hanging roof covers three rooms: the kitchen, which is also the living room, a bedroom, and a study. Scattered at wide intervals throughout the narrow base of the valley, and on the equally steep slope opposite, lie the farmhouses with their large overhanging roofs. Higher up the slope the meadows and pasture lands lead to the woods with its dark fir trees, old and towering. Over everything there stands a clear summer sky, and in its radiant expanse two hawks glide around in wide circles.[161]

Heidegger gradually appropriated the place. When he could, he stayed at Todtnauberg during the breaks between semesters, from March to April and from August to early October, as well as during Christmas vacation, often for several weeks; there he got the rest he needed before being able to fully concentrate on his work, which was made easier by the departure of Elfride and the children. However, the cabin was intended first of all for everyone's recreation and only secondarily for the philosopher's work. In the autumn of 1922, upon his return from a visit to Jaspers in Heidelberg, Heidegger stayed in Freiburg to enjoy the peace and quiet while his wife and children were at the cabin;[162] in 1926, he set up his office in the Brenders' neighboring farmhouse,[163] where he found more calm, though the tranquility was not complete. At Christmas the same year, he accordingly remained in Freiburg to pursue his work on the proofs of *Being and Time*.[164] Conversely, in the late 1920s he resided more than ever at Todtnauberg, sometimes for months, as in the autumn of 1932, when his sabbatical leave allowed him to remain at the cabin from August to 22 October.[165]

With his family, or with students like Gadamer, or friends like Elisabeth Blochmann or the Szilasis,[166] Todtnauberg was a place of entertainment. In the summer, the Heideggers played prison dodgeball "by the rules" or left from the cabin for hikes to Todtnau, the Feldsee, the Herzogenhorn,[167] Belchen,[168] or the Feldberg, a "wonderful" climb to the highest summit, 1,493 meters, in the Black Forest; and when the "outsiders" left, it was "so wonderfully isolated now" and nature felt "so very close."[169] In winter, there were the pleasures of skiing, the sun, and powdery snow, which were just so many "seductions"[170] that frequently distracted him from his work. In this place so distant from his everyday life at the university, even the chopping of wood was less a constraint than a leisure activity that made him return to his body and gather new strength; and he went back to his writing all the better for it.[171]

With Elfride, Heidegger's home had given rise to a pleasant secondary residence in the Black Forest, Todtnauberg. However, it did not have absolute dominion over the space opening in the philosopher's imagination. In Marburg, Heidegger was already so fond of his study at no. 15, Barfüssertor that he sometimes went two weeks almost without emerging from it;[172] with the construction of a house at no. 47, Rötebuckstraße, the cabin acquired a worthy lowland adversary in Freiburg-Zähringen, which was still not very built-up. Whereas Todtnauberg was above all a marvelous pied à terre for alpine pleasures, teaching took place on the plain, where it benefited from the "solid and gay anchorage"[173] provided by the house, so that, partly thanks to it, Freiburg became the center of his *Heimat*, as we can see in the letter he wrote to Viktor Schwoerer on 2 October 1929: "We are presently spending the finest days of autumn in our new house and every day I rejoice that in my work I am united with my native country."[174]

Each place, the mountain cabin and the house in the lowlands, had its own role in the gestation of his thought: the former was the space of inspiration and rough drafts, the latter of the finished work. "Everything sprouts and grows up there, whereas the fruit falls here." After a long, inspiring stay at Todtnauberg the preceding autumn, his time there after Christmas 1932 was cut short; the philosopher returned to Freiburg in mid-January 1933 because, in addition to the fact that there was "still very little snow," he missed "the *complete* workshop, with its various ancient manuscripts—so that [he] preferred to stay down below. The room where [he] worked, the whole household, and the tranquility that prevailed there, also had *their* own strengths." Once his current work was finished, in March he returned to the cabin, because he "had a great need again for seed and germination"; and for that, he relied on "March's sun and its storms. It's strange waiting for it, without forcing anything. And that is the true great benefit derived from these months: the space freed up for a laborious *far niente* that allows things to come to one."[175]

Heidegger was particularly sensitive to the variations of the Todtnauberg landscape, both large and tiny, which he took pleasure in describing at length in his letters. The philosopher liked, of course, summer and the brilliance of its clear sky;[176] he loved autumn even more, with its flamboyant colors that heralded winter and the snow that would soon come to these heights. The first snow fell in mid-October, and Heidegger, alone in the cabin with his son, wrote on 17 October 1928: "You should have seen the impatience with which the little fellow opened the shutter this morning! Where from the bedroom we usually saw the steep hillside covered by the dark stand of firs, there was nothing but white merging with the sky, so that one caught oneself thinking for a moment that the cabin was surrounded by a dense fog." He went on to emphasize the difference between snow in the mountains and snow in cities: "Up there, the snow is very different from what it is in the city, where it is only an inconvenient kind of filth and merely increases the wretchedness and bewilderment where nature is conspicuous for its absence."

Autumn, a transitional period, is enriched as much by the two extremes it unites as by its own life and colors: "During the day, the scarlet, golden yellow, and green foliage of the maples stretches out in the sun against the snow-covered mountain slope, and between the two, snowless areas stand out; to the west, the shingled roofs of the farmhouses are a somber black, while in the distance one can make out in the background the wooded outlines of the mountains with a light dusting of snow. It's cold, to be sure, when the northwest wind from the Stübenwasen comes to howl around the cabin, but in the daytime the sun often treats us to a summery warmth."[177] With autumn and the winter following it, he wrote, "cabin existence [*Dasein*] has found its proper form" among the pastures, the fields, and the woods white with frost in the "hard" air, where the sun struggles to break through because "the thin, smoky mist settles in front of its rays," while inside "the smell of the potato fires pervades the air"[178] before a storm comes with the night. On the day before they left to celebrate Christmas 1931 as a family in the cabin, the philosopher thus rejoiced in advance of his stay there: "There will be the snowstorm once again, and the howling of the foxes in the snow-covered woods, and the high night sky, and the solitary excursions in the quiet, high valleys."[179]

Heidegger had a Romantic predilection for mistiness and storms in the mountains, which seemed to him most closely connected with his thought. With mist, nature makes a radical break with the world: "This morning a snake of grey mist lay over Rütte & crept its way as far as the pass—; now there's a thick blanket & the bells of the herd are ringing through the mist. I've got well into my work & live with the woods & mountains, the meadows & brooks—which give me what I need. Quite away from all contingency—in profound indifference to the non-necessary."[180] Storms, which prevented him from sleeping, at the same time favored his philosophy: "To the accompaniment of the storm this week I've made very good progress with my work." "The last few days the weather's been wild up here. Yesterday afternoon the storm got worse from one hour to the next—it was at its wildest at 10 o'clock—the Cabin was creaking at the joints—I sat in the study & worked—sleeping was out of the question—as on the previous nights too. Suddenly at half past 10 there was deathly silence and then came the snow—it's good to be close to nature like this. This morning everything was covered in snow."[181]

Storms did more than transport the philosopher "quite away from all contingency"; like Jaspers's limit situations, they placed him radically face-to-face with existence: "It is already deep in the night. A storm sweeps over the mountains; the beams creak in the cabin; life lies before the soul: pure, simple, and great. [. . .] Sometimes I no longer comprehend how we can play such strange roles down below."[182] With storms, man's petty existence is erased when confronted by "life" and "nature," which cause the philosopher to experience the feeling of the sublime as Kant conceived it and as it inspired the Romantics: man, who is finite, is lost in nature, which is infinitely great, and consequently feels a dizziness that makes him lose his everyday individuality, and he finds himself indissolubly merged with a whole that absolutely transcends him and causes him to break every human attachment. Heidegger's distance from the university and the pettiness of his colleagues' scheming only became the greater: "Professors & everything that goes with them—have come to seem so remote from me—& I don't feel the slightest need of their worries and machinations."[183]

His descriptions of Todtnauberg were influenced by Hölderlin's *Hyperion*, which Hannah Arendt had given him and which he kept "among the few books" sitting on his writing desk.[184] Written during Hölderlin's youth, it is an epistolary novel that assembles the letters of the Titan Hyperion's modern namesake, an account of his gradual decision to withdraw to an island in the Aegean, there to live a hermit's life. The beginning is exemplary of the Romantic relationship to nature, presenting the narrator alone, far away from humans and their malice, who, in a prophetic pantheism, blends into the spectacle of the surrounding nature:

> My whole being falls silent and hearkens when the tender surge of the air plays about my breast. Often, lost in the wide blue, I look up at the ether and into the holy sea, and I feel as if a kindred spirit opened its arms to me, as if the pain of solitude dissolved into the life of the divinity.
>
> To be one with the all—that is the life of the divinity, that is the heaven of man.
>
> To be one with all that lives, to return in blessed self-oblivion into the All of nature, that is the summit of thoughts and joys, that is the holy mountain height, the place of eternal repose, where the midday loses its swelter and the thunder its voice and the boiling sea resembles the billowing field of grain.[185]

Heidegger's writings often allow a peek at the lectures he was giving at the time; and just as in the summer of 1920 he discovered rootedness and favored expressions of anti-Semitism thanks to Dostoevsky, the summer of 1925 marked the beginning of Heidegger's prophetic lyricism at Todtnauberg, after he had read *Hyperion*. On 23 August, in his first letter mentioning Hölderlin's novel, he wrote:

> Here I am once more with nature and native soil [*Heimat*], and I seem to feel even the ideas growing, as it were. Roaming amid the firs is wonderful meditation. Very rarely, I meet someone chopping wood—there are no spa guests and the like here. I know every firebreak or little spring, or deer run—or grouse site. In such an environment, the work has a different texture than when one is surrounded by squabbling, conniving professors.[186]

The union of the thinker and the Black Forest depicted in "Why Do I Stay in the Provinces?" was thus formulated as early as 1925. Even though the Heideggerian *Heimat* par excellence was still associated with Meßkirch,[187] he identified Todtnauberg more broadly with the soil of his "homeland" expanded to include southwestern Germany; in 1928, he mentioned the "Alemannic air,"[188] including Jacob Burckhardt's Swiss Basel. The same year, he expressed his sense that there was a borderline south of Heidelberg, an area that, though certainly in Baden, was Protestant, and where a dialect of Middle German (*Mitteldeutsch*) was spoken: "For my part, I was in a hurry to get back to the Black Forest, and I was happy to find myself, after a long trip, south of Heidelberg, back home, which has appeared to me this time again as it did the first time."[189] Tourists, who stayed for a shorter time, seemed to him to be "foreigners,"[190] whereas he felt, with his wife, at home "up here."[191]

Because of this rural sensibility he was cultivating, he liked books that were not local but had the same sense of place; in addition to Adalbert Stifter, whom he read as a boy and returned to in the 1920s, and Hölderlin, whom he rediscovered in 1925, he also felt that way about the Norwegian Nobel Prize–winner Knut Hamsun (1859–1952), whose *Wayfarers* inspired strong praise: "Hamsun is a philosopher, but in such a way that his art is unburdened. And the glorious closeness to the earth, to landscape, to instincts, to the elemental—the unbroken wholeness of life that is always present in his work even after three sentences."[192] Along with Dostoevsky and his political writings, Hamsun and his *Wayfarers* were an indication of the degree to which Heidegger's *Heimat* culture was no longer simply national, but European or even cosmopolitan. In Todtnauberg, the philosopher lived in a world of books almost more than in the places surrounding him.

Starting in 1923, inspired by the return to the *Heimat* encouraged by the Youth Movement, which remained important for the Heideggers until at least 1928,[193] they liked to wear clothing with a folklore theme: photographs immortalized Jörg and Hermann wearing lederhosen, and Elfride in a simple peasant's dress; as for her husband, he wore what his students in Marburg called, with gentle irony, an "existential costume":[194] over stockings and cloth breeches, a checkered jacket, lined and sewn with a double row of buttons like the jackets worn in the Black Forest. In addition, in a shop in Munich he bought a pair of Haferls, traditional shoes from the Allgäu in Upper Swabia that he considered "very nice & solid,"[195] and which were about to become luxury products for wealthy connoisseurs; and Heidegger rejoiced in having bought them for 58,000 marks rather than 78,000, as in other shops.

For the philosopher, life in Todtnauberg favored an identification with the peasants who surrounded him. A significant anecdote: in 1926 he sent Blochmann a postcard depicting a farmhouse in Todtnauberg.[196] In that year[197] he had made friends with peasants with whom he entertained neighborly relations. The Brenders and the Schneiders came regularly to celebrate his birthday on 26 December;[198] he worked at the Brender home in his "peasant room"[199] when his family was at the cabin. These rather easy and agreeable relationships, where little was at stake other than sociability, contrasted with those that the philosopher maintained with some of his colleagues: "I have no desire for the company of professors; the peasants are much more pleasing and even more interesting."[200] He became even closer to his neighbors in the late 1920s. "Today on the way from the village," he wrote Elfride, "I met Old Brender tending his herd at the Hasenloch & invited him to share some of the bottle still remaining. Black Pius was constantly lurking around the cabin with his two cows & with the cold wind blowing I ended up serving him a kirsch. He then told me—clearly using hunters' jargon—some yarns about how many grouse he'd shot in the old days."[201] In 1928, Heidegger offered to give a little speech for the Schneiders' thirtieth wedding anniversary.[202] Meals with them sometimes proved to be a trial, which he faced on two occasions in the autumn of 1932 during the slaughter celebration: "A good job that afterwards there was beerenauslese [wine] & I helped it down with kirsch as well & came through it all fine; it worked out quite well that I didn't have to go into the village in the awful weather."[203] Even his son Jörg came to like this alpine life; Heidegger was proud of this, considering him "a true little peasant so far as placidity is concerned. When the weather was dismal and rainy in the morning, he declared it 'lousy weather,' turned over, and went back to sleep without another word."[204]

First imagined by Elfride, the cabin at Todtnauberg was the realization of a *völkisch* dream, the wood-and-stone concretization of an ideology of *Blut und Boden,* "blood and soil," as some of Heidegger's students were able to see at the housewarming to which he had invited them. Günther Stern described this event as follows:

> Among the amusements that we accorded ourselves that night (or which he accorded us), there was a rather singular contest to see which of us could stand on our heads the longest. I was very good at this game, I could easily remain in that position for a good five minutes, which flabbergasted Heidegger. More precisely, he seemed to be positively offended by it, because it contradicted the negative image he had of me, the image of a literary hack. That someone like me could stand on his head, and do it longer than his pet students, who were all tall and blond, ran counter to his prejudices, which were not very remote from *Blubo* [*Blut und Boden*]. The next morning, full of energy, we all walked back down to Freiburg, or more precisely, we ran down; I was running—I'll never forget this, because it was the proof of the National Socialists' incredible lack of instinct—hand in hand with Frau Heidegger, who then looked like the girls in the youth movements, of which she was probably a member. Since she had absolutely no idea of what a Jew might look like (and I couldn't really hide what I was), she began, as we were racing down the hill, to talk about National Socialism, asking me if I didn't want to join the movement, too. "Look at me!" I said to her, "and you'll see that I'm one of those you want to exclude." I just said "exclude" because of course, one could not yet say "vilify," not to mention "liquidate."[205]

Although no other source attests to such a precocious Nazi sensibility in Elfride, as early as 1923 Max Müller's testimony confirms the perception that students may have had of her husband's *völkisch* ideology: during excursions to Todtnauberg, on skis or on foot, that the master took with his disciples, Heidegger expressed the connection he naturally made with "the ethnic group [*Volkstum*], nature, and also the Youth Movement," explaining that the word *völkisch*—a term that is difficult to translate because it is saturated with connotations, simultaneously popular, national, ethnic, and even racist—was "very familiar"[206] to him (*Das Wort "völkisch" stand ihm sehr nahe*).

This identification with the peasants of the Black Forest was a fiction insofar as Heidegger, a professor at a German university, was a bourgeois, a notable of the city who was no more like his neighbors in the Black Forest than he was like his own peasant ancestors in the Swabian Alps: the mountains were for him a place of rest and leisure, which his financial resources made more agreeable—thus the new skis that the philosopher was able to buy for himself in 1927, "real Norwegian skis, admirably shaped,"[207] had no parallel among his peasant neighbors, but were instead akin to the ones that Elfride received from her parents in 1913.[208] As for the work—the intellectual work—that he did on this remote mountain, and the students he sometimes invited to come with him, they were ultimately only relocated from his urban activity as an academic philosopher, which allowed him to live comfortably. This obvious social difference meant that the Heideggers could take their maid with them to relieve Elfride of housework,[209] or that the philosopher could stay alone with the children at the cabin during the summer of 1928 while his wife oversaw the construction of the house in Freiburg.[210]

Heidegger's identification with Todtnauberg was all the easier and all the less alpine because mountains had long been associated with philosophy, as an image and as a space, as is shown by the example of Nietzsche writing his last books in the Engadin, at Sils-Maria; he even said that his own philosophy was a "philosophy of the heights": "Philosophy, as I have so far understood and lived it, means living voluntarily among ice and high mountains."[211] And when Heidegger gradually came to identify his work with the Black Forest, one model forced itself on him with a dazzling clarity: his teacher Edmund Husserl, who regularly walked on the hill in Freiburg known as the Loretto[212] and liked to retire to the mountains for long periods during vacations, to Bernau in the Black Forest or to Silvaplana in the Engadin, where he sought, just as his student would later on, a "time of calm contemplation"[213] that contrasted with his everyday life in Freiburg, where he was constantly being disturbed. Heidegger was thus far off the mark in 1933 when he asserted: "The inner relationship of my own work to the Black Forest and its people comes from a centuries-long and irreplaceable rootedness in the Alemannian-Swabian soil."[214] On the contrary, this osmosis that he felt between his work and his favorite landscape proceeded from a cultural construct that went hand in glove with the city—whether it took the form of the Youth Movement, Hölderlin, Stifter, Hamsun, or the history of philosophy to the time of his teacher Husserl.

A place more propitious for thought than any other, Todtnauberg was the mountain of philosophy looking down on the modern world that was struggling on the plain below, the way of the Heideggerian world that was henceforth to be opposed with the utmost clarity to the Berlin way. A place for vacations that tended to make him denigrate his place of work, his mountain cabin was in fact only the rebellious son of Marburg, which had engendered it, a fictive place, a place of the false but plausible invention of a German university professor living like a peasant in a secondary residence overlooking a winter sports resort. Connected to the imaginary of a culture marked by soil and rootedness, the Todtnauberg way was important in that it was dreamed up both as a place for rest and work and as a self-portrait of this supposed son of the *Heimat,* this philosopher possessing a soil into which he could sink the roots of his thought.

The theme of soil or ground (*Boden*), linked to that of rootedness in Heidegger's thought, is of a complexity that prevents us from reducing it to a banal *Blut und Boden* conception, even if it is connected with race. In the lectures on Plato's *Sophist* that he gave in Marburg in 1924–1925, the term *Boden* has a purely intellectual meaning of "theme, background, which serves as a basis for reflection." One example among many others: Heidegger notes that when Aristotle states that "the philosopher's pure consideration in fact contributes to something [. . .] by the simple fact of being possessed and accomplished," he "proposes a comparison which can be understood only if the ground [*Boden*] of the comparison is first assured,"[215] namely, the analogy between the health of the body and the health of the soul. In the physical sense, *Boden* is a kind of environment (*Umwelt*)[216] that corresponds in the best of cases to the *Heimat,* as Todtnauberg did, whereas Berlin, the symbol of the great metropolis, suffered from a "dreadful" "groundlessness."[217] Between these two meanings, spatial and intellectual, exterior and interior, the link is not necessarily metaphorical, as we see for example when Count Yorck calls Dilthey's attention to the "psychic and physical" *Boden.*[218] For Heidegger, the solitude of Todtnauberg, especially when the last city-dwellers had left, was an ideal place where students' visits, meetings with colleagues, and "bureaucratic nonsense"[219] would not disturb him; a *Boden,* that is, where it was easy for him to be *bodenständig,* to keep himself intellectually grounded, because the calm and the environment in which he found himself, the physical ground, favored introspection and philosophical meditation, guaranteeing him fertile intellectual soil.

A place with excellent soil and offering human existence remarkable grounding in a familiar environment, Todtnauberg allowed Heidegger to be as close as possible to what he saw as the "formal existential expression for the

Being of Dasein": being-in-the-world (*In-der-Welt-sein*). Drawing on etymology, Heidegger posits that being-in-the-world, "existential" reality based on the "I am," the *ich bin,* signifies " 'I reside' or 'dwell alongside' the world, as that which is familiar to me in such and such a way."[220] If the profound sense of being in the world is the experienced fact of living in a familiar world, whereas the city is the constantly changing place where man is exposed at every instant to the risk of being wrenched from that familiarity, the *Heimat,* the countryside, the familiar and unchanging place where one was born, is the *Umwelt* par excellence, in harmony with this profound sense of being-in-the-world. Even if he does not mention it, Heidegger is in full agreement with Hölderlin's *Hyperion,* which he was "slowly beginning to understand":[221] "the felicity of forgetting the self," a constricted self, the fusion with the "whole of nature," the full experience, unaltered from the being-in-the-world that dwelling in a solitary and alpine *Heimat* offers, makes it possible to attain "the ultimate summit of ideas and joys, the sacred crest, the place of eternal quietude."[222] The passage in Arendt's letter of 23 August 1925 thereby acquires its philosophical foundation: Todtnauberg's familiarity was not only pleasing, since Heidegger, in contact "with nature and native soil," the soil of his *Heimat,* and feeling most intensely the familiarly-dwelling-in-the-world that was for him the deep sense of the formal existential expression of *Dasein,* could state that he felt, "so to speak, how thoughts come to grow from it."[223]

Farewell to Meßkirch

Heidegger's rooted philosophy did not emerge merely from fusion with a bucolic mountain landscape; as it turns out, it was fed directly by a personal and collective history, the history of a bloodline or a race, on a soil he identified with the town of Meßkirch, at the very moment when he was breaking with his childhood home.

For Heidegger, man is his past, a past inextricable from that of his "generation."[224] Whatever he does, he defines himself based on an "explicating" of existence (*Dasein*) "carried through" to him, which he "has grown up into" and which proposes to him an understanding of the world and a future to pursue: "In terms of this, *Dasein* understands itself proximally and, within a certain range, constantly."[225] This past is, notably, that of the upbringing a child receives from his family (rural for Heidegger) or at school (at the Konradihaus in Konstanz, among others), on the basis of which man chooses his future. Hence *Being and Time* was a treatise of phenomenological ontology, which continued to make present Franz Brentano's views in his thesis "On the Several Senses of Being in Aristotle,"[226] which Heidegger had received from Conrad Gröber, and those in Carl Braig's treatise *On Being: An Outline of Ontology.*[227] The past, important as it is, is not the totality of human existence. Man is just as much the choice he makes in the present for his future, whether he takes responsibility for that choice or not.[228] He may be a traditional, inauthentic repetition of what he has received, that which cuts him off from himself; or he may be an elective, authentic repetition of the past that formed him and which he is, chosen or rejected in light of his own death, that which roots man in his own being. To be sure, Heidegger placed himself within the tradition of ontology, both Greek and Scholastic, and within that of phenomenology. But, having left the Church, and believing that a hermeneutics of the lifeworld made it possible not to consider the self a mere correlate of scientific knowledge[229] and thereby to avoid "theory's destructive infection of the surrounding world,"[230] he did not fashion a work of Catholic philosophy or simply continue Husserl's scientistic project.

Rooted in his own existence, Heidegger reappropriated the history of his family, which since time immemorial had had its roots in Meßkirch. In his letter to Matthäus Lang, the philosopher linked *Being and Time* to his *Heimat,* in whose soil, he said, "all my efforts [. . .] are deeply rooted."[231] And, a year earlier, after visiting his parents when *Being and Time* was about to be published, he wrote to his wife: "What I received from my paternal home & my hometown has passed into my work."[232] That feeling of being rooted in a landscape and a people or lineage was linked to the very conception of his philosophical activity, to the idea of a spiritual inheritance of peasants rooted in their native region, which Heidegger had held onto but which modern city-dwellers had lost.[233] Consistent with his letter of 1920, in which he said: "I am noticing [. . .] how deeply rooted I am after all in the soil & local folk [*Art*],"[234] the philosopher thus still had a *Blut und Boden* notion of his identity, proceeding not from biological inheritance but from the tradition of a way of life in an environment conducive to thinking and in the rootedness of the existence he had adopted directly from his rural ancestors.

Being and Time thus turned out to be an upscale *Blut und Boden* work. Heidegger had in fact used his memories of Meßkirch, of his family, and of his *Heimat* to write the book. This can be seen clearly in his analysis of the world (*Welt*) and the notions of *Umwelt* and *Mitwelt*. Most of the examples chosen in his masterpiece hearken back to the countryside where he spent his childhood, with, in particular, analyses of the workshop, the cooper, and especially the cobbler. The shoe, therefore, gives rise to a whole complex world, composed of a system of interconnections, stamped, notably, with the mark of utility. The shoe is connected to the one who will wear it, by virtue of its size and the purpose for which it was produced. That system of interconnections also functions from "within," because "in the work there is also a reference or assignment to 'materials': the work is dependent on [. . .] leather, thread, needles, and the like. Leather, moreover, is produced from hides. These are taken from animals, which someone else has raised. Animals also occur within the world without having been raised at all; and, in a way, these beings still produce themselves even when they have been raised."[235]

The *Umwelt,* through that system of interconnections, which thus includes nature itself, is not limited to utility. It is always linked to a human society and thus inserted in a shared world, a "with-world" (*Mitwelt*), where the presence, at least implicit, of other men is always evident. The shoe is connected all at once to the cobbler who made it, to the wearer for whom it was made, and to the tanner who prepared the leather. And, like the circumscribed society of Meßkirch, where anonymity was rare, the world that comes to Heidegger's mind is a familiar world, where everything and its owner are easily recognizable: "When, for example, we walk along the edge of a field but 'outside it,' the field shows itself as belonging to such and such a person, and decently kept up by him; the book we have used was bought at So-and-so's shop and given by such and such a person, and so forth."[236] In the *Mitwelt,* the known is the rule. The world Heidegger describes, that of the familiarity of men and things, inspired by his native Meßkirch—so like Proust's Combray, where only Sunday strollers were really known to no one[237]—is at the opposite extreme of the big cities, where anonymity reigns.

The world in Heidegger's philosophy is truly rooted in his native region, his home, but its scope is not limited to that region. The same is true for the many reflections the philosopher makes about man himself, which originated in his parents' house in Meßkirch. Although I will not claim that this is the only source for Heidegger's arguments about excessive care of the other, a care that tends to disburden man completely of the care of self, while imperceptibly imposing on him the other's "dominion,"[238] these arguments did come from his experience with his mother. As he later notes, that intrusive care for the happiness of the other is, in "everydayness," naturally directed toward practical things, such as food, clothing, health, and, in general, everything having to do with the practicalities of existence and the imperatives they dictate. But it could also be directed toward more profound subjects, such as salvation. Such was the case for his mother, worried for the salvation of her son, who had taken his distance from the Church and was not raising his children in the Catholic faith.[239]

Another example: idle talk (*das Gerede*) and silence. Heidegger, in denouncing idle talk—which his mother, affable by nature, was never short on—and valuing meaningful talk (*die Rede*)—which one holds back when talking is unnecessary, as his father, a taciturn man, tended to do—Heidegger used his perception of his parents as a couple to feed his philosophical reflections: "The person who keeps silent can 'make one understand' (that is, he can develop an understanding), and he can do so more authentically than the person who is never short of words. Speaking at length [*Viel-sprechen*] about something does not offer the slightest guarantee that thereby understanding is advanced. On the contrary, talking extensively about something covers it up and brings what is understood to a sham clarity—the unintelligibility of the trivial."[240] Consciously or not, Heidegger was alluding to his perception of his father and of himself: in the self-portrait he sent to Elfride in a letter, he evokes "his father, whose brooding taciturnity" the son had "inherited."[241]

Being and Time was often a self-portrait between the lines of Heidegger and of his identity, rooted much more in Meßkirch than in Todtnauberg. But his *Bodenständgikeit,* his "groundedness," was not confined to the immemorial rural roots that nourished him. It resulted from the "radicalism"[242] he demonstrated in his approach to philosophical problems.

Although he claimed to be a rooted philosopher, at the same time Heidegger's actual relationships with his hometown were distended to the point of nearing a de facto break. In 1923, he spent a week there with Jörg on the occasion of the birth of his sister's daughter, named Clothilde, on 5 April;[243] then a few days in early October, still with his son, but under less happy circumstances—his father was ill. "His eyesight has suddenly declined so much that he can no longer go out alone. I suppose it'll be a gradual death over the winter."[244] He died on 2 May 1924. The philosopher hurried to Meßkirch, where he described his deceased father: "Father is lying at rest & looks very peaceful among lots of wreaths," "holding a lovely posy of wild flowers & a simple 'funeral cross' among them."[245] Having suffered a stroke[246] two days before, Friedrich Heidegger had subsequently "slept calmly for another hour," and then his heart had started to beat frenetically again; he had been able to get up in the afternoon, ate "with the best of appetites," and "smoked two more cigars." His agony was "dreadful," though his features, calmed by death, did not betray that:

it lasted "from 1 o'clock at night until the following lunchtime at half past 12. Haematoma the cause." During this time he remained unconscious; "half an hour before the end he then went all quiet. Fritz held Father's hand & could feel his pulse stop beating. It was lucky for Father that he was unconscious when he died—he's said to have been terribly afraid of Hell." The burial was to take place at 2:30 the following afternoon, in the cemetery above Meßkirch. The ringing of the bells in honor of the dead sexton was to be "an especially good performance."[247]

Heidegger returned to Meßkirch in October 1925, first to see his mother, and then on the occasion of his brother's wedding on the 15th to Elisabeth Walter, nicknamed "Liesel."[248] In the speech he gave at his brother's wedding in Meßkirch, he said how happy he was that Fritz and Liesel were from the same town, and added that the value of this union could be gauged only if one thought how much modern life pushed people toward the great metropolises, where people were rootless. He hoped the young couple would be able to lead this life with exemplary simplicity, rooted in the native soil, but his remarks went further: "The groundlessness of modern life is the root of the growing decadence [*Verfall*]. And all the reforms and innovations remain hopeless if they do not succeed in bringing back the guiding and fertile forces that issue from the native soil [*aus heimatlichem Boden*]."[249] In fact, Heidegger was alluding to his philosophical project of revitalizing the German people's spiritual existence, which would owe its strength and success to its own rootedness in a *Heimat*.

Heidegger was reinventing the Meßkirch way. The postcard he wrote to Bultmann on the occasion of this wedding summed up his new view of his native town: on the back of a photograph of Wildenstein Castle, overlooking the majestic valley of the Upper Danube, he sent his friend a "cordial greeting from his native country," adding: "Above the castle, about which the Zimmern Chronicle was written, stands the Heideggers' farm. The monastery of Beuron is half an hour away."[250] Meßkirch disappeared behind its countryside and this beautiful valley where the Heideggers' sheepfold was located, of the two familial "places of memory" the one that better lent itself to the thinker's Romantic portrait of himself rooted in the sublime of the landscape. Heidegger mentioned a few tourist attractions: Wildenstein Castle, whose lofty site and massive sixteenth-century style made it vaguely resemble Neuschwanstein; the Zimmern Chronicle, which related the history of these lords of Meßkirch and had become a place of memory for the community, but which Heidegger nonetheless attributed exclusively to Wildenstein Castle, also constructed by the Zimmern; and the Beuron monastery, in the same valley, where he had so often studied as an adolescent during vacations, before spending several days of intense work there in August 1920. The native town was eclipsed by this Romantic tableau composed of nearby elements from which it was nevertheless excluded.

Although the year 1926 was taken up by intensive work on *Being and Time,* which kept Heidegger cloistered in Todtnauberg during his vacations, in 1927 he returned to Meßkirch several times. Johanna Heidegger was seriously ill with intestinal cancer, for which she was to undergo an operation. In early February, her son came to her bedside. Since her operation, Johanna had been unable to get up, lying there without hope of improvement, and tortured by the question of her son's salvation and her own. Over time, the philosopher's hostility to Catholicism had grown; he saw Catholic doctrine as a kind of "uprootedness" insofar as it was based on tradition. "When tradition [. . .] becomes master, it does so in such a way that what it 'transmits' is made so inaccessible, proximally and for the most part, that it rather becomes concealed."[251] It transmits the past's legacy as if it were self-evident, and "blocks our access to those primordial 'sources' from which the categories and concepts handed down to us have been in part quite genuinely drawn."[252] Catholic tradition, within which "Aristotle has been interpreted on the basis of Thomas Aquinas," was the unconscious legacy of an intellectual error: the Aristotle of Thomas, and then the Aristotle of Thomism and Neo-Thomism, was not the living Aristotle who thought and wrote in Greek on a ground that had nothing to do with Christianity. Since tradition does not follow the historical method, of which "elaborating the ground" is a "basic part,"[253] it corrupts the philosophical knowledge it transmits, because it loses its life along with the ground in which it has taken root. As a result, "*Dasein* has had its historicality so thoroughly uprooted by tradition that it confines its interest to the multiformity of possible types, directions, and standpoints of philosophical activity in the most exotic and alien of cultures; and by this very interest it seeks to veil the fact that it has no ground of its own to stand on."[254] Whether Catholic or Neo-Kantian (in this last passage, Heidegger was thinking especially of Cassirer's *Mythical Thought*), tradition thus leads to an uprooted philosophy, lacking both an intellectual foundation and intellectual vitality. Catholicism was no longer the people's religion, healthy and rooted in a soil, but a moribund system of thought that cut people off from the roots of their existence.

Raising his sons as Protestants, and more and more distant from Catholicism or even hostile to it, the philosopher was "of course a great worry to the poor thing," his mother, who still believed she was "responsible" for him; and despite his efforts to reassure her, she remained tormented. Feeling her demise approaching, Johanna Heidegger no longer had the strength to hide her concern behind a mask of maternal sweetness: "Mother was very serious, almost hard even—as though her true nature were concealed. 'I can no longer pray for you,' she said, 'for I have enough to do for myself.' I must bear this, & indeed my philosophy shouldn't only exist on paper."[255] These last hours with his mother were "a piece of *practical philosophy*" that he said would remain with him, concluding more generally: "I believe that for most *philosophers* the question of theology and philosophy—or, better, belief and philosophy—is purely for the writing desk."[256] The confrontation with his dying mother afflicted Heidegger profoundly and made patent what she had usually kept to herself. His feeling of a profound break with his origins grew: "I now feel even more strongly than ever that nothing ties me directly to the world here anymore; what I received from my parental home & my hometown has passed into my work."[257] The only surviving part of this world of his childhood was the one that memory offered the philosopher, who wanted to stand on the ground of his experiences in his native region. Since these experiences could hardly be repeated, *Being and Time* was the swan song of the Meßkirch way insofar as it was fertile for thought.

Two months later, the philosopher returned to his mother's bedside, where he saw her for the last time, briefly. Very weakened and usually "dozing," she no longer took anything but wine and water, and after a few hours she was gripped by violent spells of vomiting: "It's a pitiful sight & Mother herself wants it all to end."[258] Deliverance was granted her two weeks later, on 3 May. Her son had been obliged to return to Freiburg, where the publication of his masterwork was imminent; nevertheless, he said, "I was able to take my leave from Mother without being troubled, but this abundance of goodness at first made the separation most difficult."[259]

The death of Heidegger's father, and then of his mother, struck two heavy blows to Heidegger's rootedness in Meßkirch. Returning in October 1927 to meditate in the cemetery, he found his mother's tomb "very nicely adorned" and located in "a nice spot." One of his mother's childhood friends gave Heidegger a portrait so that he could have it reproduced; and he finally went to visit "old cousin Karl," who had been "very lonely" since Johanna's death. In addition, the family sheepfold, located between Hausen im Tal and Beuron, and which the paternal side of the family had owned since the end of the seventeenth century, was sold in 1925 by Thomas Heidegger (1856–1931), a cousin of the philosopher (he was his grandfather Martin's nephew). Increasingly tenuous, the ties between the philosopher and his hometown were based on his growing love for Lake Constance: on the way to his mother's grave, he noted that his journey to Meßkirch "through autumn on the Baar plateau & in the Hegau & along Lake Constance was quite wonderful. I've never enjoyed the landscape so much."[260]

Moreover, his hometown was seriously rivaled as a vacation spot by Todtnauberg, as well as by all the lakes and rivers on which he liked to go sailing; the ease of pleasure boating won out over rootedness in Meßkirch. The Heidegger family made a brief visit to Meßkirch in the summer of 1929, following happy vacations in Feldafing, on Lake Starnberg, and then on Lake Constance: "The days spent at Lake Starnberg were very fine, and allowed everyone to recover their strength. Elfride was finally freed of all the worries she has 'at home,' we all liked that very much. Jörg learned to swim, and as for myself, I was often on board a sailboat and I rediscovered the exciting and reinvigorating joys of that sport. Then we spent two splendid days on the shores of Lake Constance, and finally went to Meßkirch. We all came back to Freiburg fresh and full of good cheer. On 22 August we left for the cabin."[261] Similarly, on 2 August 1930, Heidegger and Elfride, along with two colleagues from the Faculty of Medicine, traveled by train through the valleys of the Hölle and the Danube, as far as Ulm, with collapsible canoes: "The next day we put the canoes together and, after an initial, difficult passage under the bridge in Ulm, we floated through a superb landscape, heading on the first day for Donauwörth, the next for Ingolstadt, then Ratisbonne, and finally Straubing."[262] The philosopher returned briefly to Meßkirch on 14 October 1930 for the wedding anniversary of his brother, Fritz, who now had three sons;[263] then he went to stay at Beuron, as he also did the following year, from 9 to 25 October, after spending part of his vacation sailing on Lake Constance with Herr Magirus, the husband of Heidegger's former fiancée, Marguerite Weninger.[264] Although he sometimes saw his brother in Freiburg[265] and received visitors from Meßkirch there,[266] Beuron was now the living root that still deeply attached him to his native region.

Heidegger had reconnected with Beuron during a visit in the summer of 1929, accompanied by Elisabeth Blochmann. As he had done in 1920, in 1930 and 1931 he spent a few weeks meditating in the same cell, enjoying both the large library and the countryside, which could be experienced even inside the monastery, with its barns and stables.[267] He liked the magnificent autumn landscape outdoors: "the peaceful valley" "resplendent with all the golden tones of autumn" and "the rocks jutting up in the luminous brightness of the blue sky."[268] "Each day now is more magnificent than the one before, the gold of the autumn leaves glows along the Jura cliffs between the stretches of pine forest. And below, the silent river winds its way through the meadows."[269] In this idyllic setting, Heidegger fully abided by "the monks' strict and cloistered habits,"[270] a "demanding" way of life that alternated work and periods of recreation when the monks were allowed to speak, and which were punctuated by the offices: "We get up shortly before 4 o'clock & then there's almost two hours' divine office in church"; high mass was celebrated at 9 a.m., followed by vespers at 2:30 p.m. Finally, at 8 p.m., came compline: "at half past 8 everything is quiet; one can go on working in one's cell, but the first few days I've been too tired & probably will be in the next few days as well."[271] He "would have even preferred to wear a monk's habit": he would then no longer have been seen as an outsider in the community, and even his clothes would have blended in; he felt the "incongruity of walking about the abbey in 'civilian' clothes."[272]

Of course, clothes don't make the man, or the monk, but Heidegger had the feeling that he now benefited a great deal from the example set by these monks and their way of life, which usually allowed him to spend "a very quiet time"[273]: "Only now am I capable of letting the full richness of the wisdom of this monastic existence take effect. [. . .] Even though I cannot go along with the way of faith actually called for, it does all help me to reflect & find inner strength." His stay in Beuron caused the painful question of Heidegger's break with Catholicism to rise up again, but he seemed to find a certain peace: "This time it's a settling of accounts with everything from before & a new awakening into the future."[274] Heidegger had broken with the "system," understood both as an organization (the Church and its hierarchy) and as a total, closed body of thought (dogma and the official philosophy of the time, Neo-Thomism), more than with Catholic culture. In this respect, his purchase at this time of recordings of Gregorian chant made by the monks of Beuron—who thus often sang in the philosopher's living room in Freiburg, thanks to modern technology—was symbolic.[275]

Heidegger felt an affinity for this life turned toward meditation, all the more so because the monks, whether old or new acquaintances, gave him a warm welcome: "Of the older monks I know, only the Dutchman [painter-monk] Verkade is there & he has a serious heart condition. The archabbot is away too (in Palestine)." He remained a close friend of Father Anselm Manser (1876–1951) until the latter's death. Manser had worked at Beuron until 1906, and then again starting in 1925; Heidegger probably met him when he came to study in the abbey's library during the vacations he spent in Meßkirch as an adolescent, and he met him again in 1929, establishing a new, adult relationship with him. As he wrote, "Father Anselm is touchingly concerned; he'd already put all sorts of philosophical books in my cell to welcome me; [some] Mörike as well—I've gained a lot from contact with him & have come to trust him."[276] Their friendship was built on books; Father Anselm brought him "all the treasures of the library—unless I went to dig around in it myself."[277] It was composed just as much of good-natured intellectual exchanges regarding lectures that Heidegger gave to thank the monks for their hospitality: in 1930, one entitled "On the Essence of Truth," and another on time in Book 11 of Augustine's *Confessions;* in 1931, one on the Platonic theory of truth. The monk's personality seemed to calm the philosopher, who praised his "beautiful equanimity" and "his way of seeing everything," which "shines with peaceful delight."[278] Conversely, Heidegger found a sharp contrast between Father Anselm and the young Benedictine monks suffering from uprootedness: "In the autumn I spent ten days at Beuron, speaking with Father Anselm every day. [. . .] The firmness that he showed in all the areas we took up is equaled only by his openness and his indulgence, and the clear view that he—and perhaps he alone—has that the uprooting and standardization of our way of being today already threatens young monks and undermines the Benedictine spirit."[279]

The close relations between Heidegger and Beuron went beyond the anecdotal and became part of the weave of his thought. The excursion to Beuron he made with Elisabeth Blochmann in the summer of 1929 to attend compline, which conflates darkness with the evil that befalls the world, found expression in the course he gave the following semester, "The Fundamental Concepts of Metaphysics: World—Finitude—Solitude." Despite his "execration" of Catholicism, to which he now added Protestantism, he stated in his letter of 12 September that the experience of the office he shared with Blochmann in the monastery "will develop like the seed of something essential," from the inner conviction that "the original mythic and metaphysical power of Darkness can still be felt in compline, so that we must ceaselessly try to break through the darkness in order to truly exist. For Good is good only when it has prevailed over Evil." Heidegger returned to the themes of the *das Man* and of busyness, as he had developed them in *Being and Time,* and of going astray as in "On the Essence of Truth," using the metaphor of darkness inspired by the office:

> The fact that every day human beings are gradually sinking into darkness is, for man today, at best a commonplace. For from darkness he usually makes light, in the way he understands light, as a busying of himself, a giddiness. Men today make use of great resourcefulness in the meticulous organization of all things, but they are no longer capable of a contemplation that welcomes Darkness. We give the appearance of being substantial and successful when we are caught up in the "movement" of everything that "moves"—but let repose and leisure come, and we no longer know what to do.

The Catholic liturgy and metaphysics join together in the native region to get to the root of the essential, namely, the full presence of nothingness and the distress essential to human existence. Whence the professorial maxim that Heidegger drew from it, "that we need to teach and educate [our students] concretely" that "this negative element is decisive in its immemorial power: nothing to place across the path that leads to the depth of *Dasein*." Whence, in the same way, the hope that this darkness might be the source of a spiritual revolution: "It is only in this way that we will produce a turning point in the age, starting with its most profound mainspring."[280]

The course titled "The Fundamental Concepts of Metaphysics" that Heidegger gave after returning to Freiburg took into account the lesson he had learned from the darkness of compline at Beuron, as well as the political, economic, and social crises that began to shake Germany during this winter semester of 1929–1930. In paragraph 38 of the published lecture, Heidegger highlights the different "crises" that his period was experiencing, even as he insists on the fact that the problem lay deeper and went back further: "Everywhere there are disruptions, crises, catastrophes, distress [*Nöte*]: the contemporary social misery, political confusion, the powerlessness of science, the erosion of art, the groundlessness [*Bodenlosigkeit*] of philosophy, the impotence of religion."[281] Furthermore, he emphasized that these various particular crises and the measures one might want to take to resolve them concealed their common origin: "This bustling self-defense against this distress *precisely does not allow any distress to emerge as a whole*."[282] Heidegger had arrived at a heroic and critical discourse valorizing inner strength, the acceptance of danger, and the rejection of bourgeois comfort, in opposition to modern society, in which "a universal smug contentment in not being endangered" prevails, so that we come to believe "that we no longer need to be strong in the ground of our essence": "Strength and power [*Kraft und Macht*] [. . .] can never be replaced by the accumulation of learned competencies."[283]

Heidegger's critique of happiness developed a theme that was central for the Conservative Revolutionaries, the critique of the pursuit of happiness and security. In 1918, in his *Reflections of a Nonpolitical Man,* Thomas Mann had decried "the utilitarianism of the Enlightenment and the philanthropy of happiness," the promise of the "greatest possible happiness for the greatest possible number,"[284] an element of *Zivilisation,* a decadence that stood opposed to true culture. Ernst Jünger, writing in *The Worker* (1932), considered the "big cities that appeared at the turn of the twentieth century" to be "ideal citadels of security," adding that "any victory of technology is in reality a victory of comfort" in a materialist world determined by "the economy."[285] As for Oswald Spengler, in 1933 he denounced, in *The Hour of Decision,* "the life of happiness and quietude to which people so aspire these days, life without danger, in dull contentment [*breites Behagen*]," which he saw as "tiresome and demented" as well as "conceivable, but impossible."[286]

Far from being new, the idea of the importance of distress for creativeness and thought was also central in Nietzsche,[287] who, long before Heidegger, denounced "the so-called 'social crises' of all classes." Crisis, external distress, was necessary for people of the time, who thus found a "monster" they could fight, the better to distract themselves from the ennui of their existence: "If these people who crave distress felt the strength inside themselves to benefit themselves and to do something for themselves internally, then they would also know how to create for themselves, internally, their very own authentic distress. Then their inventions might be more refined and their satisfactions might sound like good music, while at present they fill the world with their clamor about distress and all too often introduce into it the *feeling of distress.*"[288] Distress was thus a fashionable theme, and the experience of compline at Beuron introduced only a variation on it—Darkness—and Heidegger was not the only one to do so. *Journey to the End of the Night,* Céline's famous novel, which Heidegger probably did not know, made use of this nocturnal metaphor to depict a journey within the distress and darkness of the world. Converging with his readings and a spirit of the time shared by the European revolutionary right, the native region fed Heidegger's inner experiences without leading him to discover anything at all that was not shared by his time.

Heidegger's close relations with the monks of Beuron may seem astonishing: the successive deaths of his father and then his mother allowed him to move toward a growing irreligion. Once he was a professor in Freiburg, just as he no long hid the inner distance separating him from Husserl, he no longer dissimulated his intransigence with regard to the obstacles that religious faith might place in the path of philosophical freedom, and increasingly criticized religion for its false assurances concerning existence, and for the illusory happiness it promised. In 1929, in his introductory course on academic studies, he outlined his conception of religion and science with his interpretation of Plato's allegory of the cave, which appears at the beginning of Book 7 of the *Republic.*

In this text, Socrates seeks to paint a picture for Glaucon of "our nature in respect of education and its lack." He asks Glaucon to imagine people living in a cave since their childhood, chained up and unable to move or turn their heads; the only thing they can see are the shadows that a fire burning higher up projects against the back of the cave; the shadows are those of "objects of all kinds" and "human images and shapes of animals"[289] manipulated by puppet-masters, some of whom talk to us, while others keep quiet. Then Socrates asks Glaucon to imagine himself taking one of these prisoners, who are "like to us,"[290] freeing him from his fetters and forcing him to turn around and lift up his eyes to the light and the puppet-masters, before climbing for the first time the path that leads outside the cave, where the sun shines brightly. Constantly incommoded, dazzled, blinded, the liberated man must be forced to follow this painful path that leads him to the outside world and the intelligible truth of ideas. Finally, his eyes having become used to so much light, he now sees everything for what it is, and the cave as the prison of ignorance dominated by the sophists and their false knowledge. He now has no more inclination to return to the cave than he earlier had to emerge from it.

Heidegger reinterpreted this allegory of philosophy and its liberating movement toward the Ideas and truth, asserting that "we can also describe the stage of *Dasein* in the cave as [that of] religion. Religion is not a feeling, an experience, but rather a fundamental disposition of *Dasein* determined in relation to all beings [*Seienden*]." Just like science and philosophy, religion is therefore a relationship to the world and to truth. However, avoiding the question concerning the essence of religion, the philosopher explained that it is "very difficult" to determine today, because religion, a fundamental disposition that is impure, mixed, "comes to us [. . .] as a religion of culture, that is, permeated by a determinate historical interpretation as well as by science." What particularly interested Heidegger was "religion as *Dasein*'s security," which he considered "a fundamental disposition that does not totally dominate *Dasein* the whole time that it exists"; this desire for security, the desire for salvation, the desire for a truth founded in God for all eternity, through which man finds reassurance in religion, leads him not to acknowledge the finitude of his existence and his essential distress. Thus for Heidegger, religion was "a basic stage" (*Grundstadium*) in the relationship to science, an expression that for him entailed no value judgment. He himself came to science through religion, before moving away from the latter; for him, it was a common, normal, obvious point of departure that philosophy led him to leave behind; over and over, he encountered the question of the relation between the Catholic faith and the freedom of science, from his earliest writings at the time of the modernist crisis to his break with his childhood religion; but, he was eager to explain in his lecture, "that does not concern here the petty bourgeois question of the relation between religion and free science, but rather the history of man's being. Religion is a basic stage of *Dasein* in the face of science. *Dasein* can exist without knowing anything about leaving the cave, that is, it can remain at the basic stage indefinitely."[291]

A Catholic apostate expressing his views at a university where there were many Catholics, Heidegger did not want to launch an attack that would denounce, in a spirit of hackneyed *Kulturkampf,* Catholic obscurantism and its radical opposition to the freedom of science. Wishing to think beyond denominational differences, he maintained that religion imprisons man in a determinate interpretation of the world and of beings, an interpretation that is simply received, revealed. Through it man reassures himself, and he uses it as the backdrop for his thinking, without rising to the sun of being and *Dasein,* to which he prefers the illusory and less dazzling fire of the cave of religion. Hence, for Heidegger this was far less a matter of value judgment than of the being of man and his history, which he may know or not know, depending on whether he has been freed from this basic stage and succeeded in facing the blinding brilliance of the truth of *Dasein*. As he explained, "In liberation, [. . .] an essential metamorphosis takes place, of truth itself and of *Dasein* itself. *Dasein* no longer has truth as security in what is [*Seiende*], but as the insecurity of beings themselves, and that is why liberation is accompanied by suffering, and there is an ardent desire to return to the state of security."[292]

Heidegger's hostility to his childhood religion was very real, but he wanted to be subtle, philosophical, attacking his target much more radically than did the assailants he himself had fought in his youth. The absence of a radical questioning was displayed in an exemplary way by metaphysics, as Heidegger explained in his inaugural lecture "What Is Metaphysics?" To conceive the origin of what is, "Christian dogma denies the truth of the proposition *ex nihilo nihil fit* [from nothing, nothing comes to be] and thereby bestows on the nothing [. . .] the sense of the complete absence of beings apart from God: *ex nihilo fit—ens creatum* [from nothing comes—created being." As a result, "the nothing becomes the counterconcept to being proper, the *summum ens,* God as *ens increatum,*" the uncreated being; and yet "the questions of Being and of the nothing as such are not posed. Therefore no one is bothered by the difficulty that if God creates out of nothingness, He must be able to relate Himself to nothingness."[293]

For Heidegger, the crucial issue in this battle around being lay in the determination of truth and freedom. Whereas Christianity was based on the idea displayed in gold letters on a pediment at the University of Freiburg, "The Truth Shall Set You Free,"[294] the apostate Heidegger would turn the passage from the Gospel of John on its head by positing that, more profoundly, freedom is the essence of truth.[295] That is the gist of his lecture "The Essence of Truth," first given in Bremen in 1930. To determine the essence of truth, Heidegger started from the ordinary concept: what is true is what is actual, as opposed to what is merely appearance, in the same way that gold is opposed to gilt copper, gold plate, or brass, which are not "genuine" gold. But since gold and gilt copper are both actual, being actual is not a sufficient criterion of truth; hence "the true, whether it be a matter or a proposition, is what accords, the accordant [*das Stimmende*]. Being true and truth here signify accord, and that in a double sense: on the one hand, the consonance [*Einstimmigkeit*] of a thing with what is supposed in advance regarding it and, on the other hand, the accordance of what is meant in the statement with the thing."[296]

Heidegger then arrived at the traditional Scholastic conception of the essence of truth as *adaequatio rei et intellectus,* the "adequation of intellect to thing," which he considered the forgotten origin of our ordinary conception of truth. Truth as adequation associates the truth of the thing with the truth of judgment without conceiving them in the same manner: "*Veritas* as *adaequatio rei ad intellectum* [. . .] implies the Christian theological belief that, with respect to what it is and whether it is, a thing, as created (*ens creatum*), is only insofar as it corresponds to the idea preconceived in the *intellectus divinus,* i.e., in the mind of God."[297] In this context, where everything refers back to a creating mind and where everything is only a thing created by God, the human mind introduces a particularly complex adequation: when the mind makes a true judgment, that judgment is in adequation with the truth of the thing, which is itself in adequation with the divine mind. In that way, it finds itself in adequation with the idea that God conceived of the human mind and its faculty of cognition, so that "if all beings are 'created,' the possibility of the truth of human knowledge is grounded in the fact that the thing and the proposition measure up to the idea in the same way and therefore are fitted to each other on the basis of the unity of the divine plan of creation." The modern conception of scientific truth has developed on this theological ground. Without even necessarily presupposing a creator-God, it posits that the world has a universally intelligible order that man can know through the mind. This is a postulate and a false axiom: "Even where the effort is made—with a conspicuous lack of success—to explain how correctness is to occur, it is already presupposed as being the essence of truth."[298]

Heidegger sought to highlight truth as *aletheia* (*ἀλήθεια*), unveiling or, better, revelation, which he saw as older than the Scholastic concept of truth as adequation, and as the forgotten foundation of the ordinary concept of truth. His reflection on the Greek concept of truth came to him first through Bultmann, whose article on *aletheia*[299] Heidegger had judged far better than the lecture on truth given by Hans von Soden:[300] ironically, his criticism of the theological conception of truth thus originated in works by theologians reflecting on truth and Revelation. Their argument was as follows: "That which is revealed, that to which a presentative statement as correct corresponds, are beings opened up in an open comportment." This revelation presupposes human freedom, which is neither political nor moral, but rather ontological: the freedom through which man makes himself free, open, available. "Freedom [. . .] lets beings be the beings they are."[301] Thus Heidegger posited that "the essence of truth is freedom."[302] Freedom brings beings out of their original forgetfulness (*λήθή, lethe*), before they are revealed, opened up, and enter the realm of truth. Forgetfulness has its own force: the "errancy" that results from forgetting this forgetfulness means that "man takes his bearings [*verhält sich*] constantly in his comportment toward beings; but for the most part he acquiesces in this or that being and its particular revealed character." Consequently, "man clings to what is readily available and controllable even where ultimate matters are concerned. And if he sets out to extend, change, newly assimilate, or secure the revealed character of the beings pertaining to the most various domains of his activity and interest, [. . .] he still takes his directives from the sphere of readily available intentions and needs."[303] The forgetfulness that forms the backdrop for revelation presupposes that it be taken seriously as a forgetfulness essential to being, which arouses *Dasein*'s anxiety, because beings become uncertain in their essence and deprived of the fallacious axioms of everyday life. Religion participates in the forgetting of this forgetfulness, a false reassurance: we are in Plato's cave.

This forgetfulness is not synonymous with happiness; on the contrary, this aversion to mystery leads man to "turn toward the most readily available beings." "Man's flight from the mystery toward what is readily available, onward from one current thing to the next, passing the mystery by—this is *erring* [*Irren*]," which is both the essential error in which man finds himself and the restlessness that leads him from one being (*Seiende*) to another.[304] Man's philosophical liberation takes place against the backdrop of his essential distress: "Man is [. . .] subjected to the rule of the mystery and the oppression of errancy. [. . .] The full essence of truth, including its most proper nonessence, keeps *Dasein* in distress by this perpetual turning to and fro."[305] Thanks to philosophy, this distress, which *Being and Time,* following Kierkegaard, conceived as anxiety or angst (an anxiety about the withdrawal of beings), can, once it is resolutely accepted, open a path to beings conceived as such, and finally, to the question of being, to metaphysics.[306]

Heidegger, who had started out as an aspiring priest, had thus become a determined adversary, not only of Catholicism but also of religion as such. What he had written to Krebs in 1919 nonetheless remained true in the early 1930s: "In modifying my fundamental position I have not allowed myself to sacrifice objectivity of judgment, or the high regard in which I hold the Catholic tradition, to the peevish and intemperate diatribes of an apostate."[307] Nobly, radically, he opposed religion and anything else that falsely reassured man and surrounded him in a nimbus of certainties; the insistence on revelation, on truth as adequation, on the supreme being (*Seiende*) and creator, seemed to him comforting masks illusorily hiding the originary phenomena of being, nothingness, forgetfulness, and distress. Truth, freedom, and philosophy could be found only against this backdrop, recognized and accepted as a burden and as angst in the face of existence. For Heidegger, God could no longer be the center of Revelation because he saw God as the foundation of the Undisclosedness of Christianity. God vanished in the face of the mystery of Being, even though Being was neither something nor someone. To a large extent, this hostility had its source in what Heidegger had received from his childhood religion: ontology, metaphysics, negative theology, and Rhineland mysticism, which insisted on the mystery constitutive of human existence and the inaccessibility of the Creator to creatures, who could approach the Creator only through the negation of everything they knew; his interpretation of Bultmann's *aletheia,* combined with Kierkegaard's notion of angst, both pious references that ought to have pushed him toward religion, instead pushed him away, just as an invitingly peaceful harbor reminds the sailor of the urgency of getting back to sea.

How are we to understand that, with such a radically critical view of religion, Heidegger was able to reestablish close ties with the monks at Beuron after 1929? Although he was an apostate who had left the Church, he did not reject Catholic culture or its believers: in Freiburg, he was still friends with Heinrich Finke,[308] his former professor of history and the dean of the Faculty of Philosophy who had protected him long ago. It was with the same friendliness that he replied to Matthäus Lang, his rector at the minor seminary in Konstanz, who, on learning of Heidegger's new notoriety with the publication of *Being and Time,* had written him a cordial letter redolent of his native region: "Since then I have inquired frequently about you, your work, and life at the school. Now I should have more opportunities of visiting you and looking back at the world in which I started out as a young 'Untertertianer.' "[309] Neither did the philosopher necessarily despise his Catholic students, some of whom were brilliant and receptive to his thought, such as Eugen Fink and Max Müller, with whom he pursued relationships that lasted long after their years at the university. Heidegger treated Catholics the same way he treated Jews: if they liked him, and if in addition they had ideas similar to his, or even some relation to his native region, the philosopher was inclined to welcome them as friends, as he had Father Anselm at Beuron.

Almost ideal, Heidegger's relationship to the monks of Beuron was nonetheless seriously disrupted, even broken off: after his stay with them in the fall of 1931, the monks were reprimanded by the archbishop of Freiburg[310] for inviting Heidegger, who was increasingly taking positions that were irreligious and hostile to Zentrum. Even though he did not respond, telling Elisabeth Blochmann he did not want to interrupt his work and the perfect solitude at his cabin at Todtnauberg,[311] Heidegger was mortified by this reprimand and did not return to the abbey until November 1949.

Heidegger was aware that he had distanced himself from his native region, though he did not reject the importance of a local patriotism. In his course "The Fundamental Concepts of Metaphysics," he went so far as to make homesickness (*Heimweh*) the fundamental tonality, the spiritual disposition that forms the backdrop of the philosopher's thought. Citing the Romantic poet Novalis, who wrote that "philosophy is really homesickness, an urge to be at home everywhere," Heidegger initially made this comment: "A strange definition, Romantic of course. Homesickness—does such a thing still exist today at all? Has it not become an incomprehensible word, even in everyday life? Has not contemporary city man, the ape of civilization, long since eradicated homesickness? What is all this talk about philosophy as homesickness?"[312] He began his interpretation of Novalis from the commonplace that civilization is an ineluctable cultural decadence, a notion Spengler had popularized. For Heidegger, this era of global cities explained why people no longer understood what philosophy is and its close relationship to homesickness, a relationship that he saw in the triad of notions forming the subtitle of his course: world, finitude, solitude.

> This demand to be at home *everywhere,* which means to exist among beings *as a whole,* is nothing other than a peculiar questioning about the meaning of this "as a whole," which we call *world.* What happens here in this questioning and searching, in this back and forth, is the *finitude* of man. What occurs in such becoming finite is an ultimate *solitariness* of man, in which everyone stands for him- or herself as someone unique in the face of the whole. [. . .] This questioning by way of conceptual comprehension is ultimately grounded in a *being gripped.* [. . .] All being gripped is rooted in an attunement [*alle Ergriffenheit wurzelt in einer Stimmung*]. What Novalis names *homesickness* is ultimately the *fundamental attunement of philosophizing.*[313]

Man, who is finite, having returned to his existential solitude by thinking about his own death, inquires into the meaning of the world in which he feels estranged; then, feeling homesick, he finally tries to feel at home everywhere, by means of the inner philosophical knowledge he has wrested from his distress at being finite. Heidegger thus conceived the relationship between the *Heimat* and philosophy in a way that is both more essential, because it establishes a necessary link between the two, and more abstract, because the native region and its rurality are not developed, even though, implicitly, in this era of total uprootedness, only a peasant could feel what the native region is and the suffering that stems from being far from home. Here we have a reiteration of the remark that the philosopher made in a letter to his wife sent from Davos: "I also think that the young people sense that the roots of my work are to be found somewhere that today's city-dweller no longer has—indeed no longer even understands."[314] In the end, the native region is thus both an origin that allows one to philosophize through the homesickness one feels facing the world alone, and a program, the desirable and abstract outcome of this quest for the meaning of the world made possible by philosophy. Developing his reflection on the connection between philosophy and the *Heimat,* Heidegger continued the line of thought pursued in *Being and Time,* insofar as the philosopher, whose activity is a quest for familiarity with the foundations of his existence, which are at first surrounded by mystery, moves closer to the feeling of being at home in the world, with the elucidation of the fundamental constitution of *Dasein,* whose deep meaning seemed to him to be precisely familiarly-dwelling-in-the-world, which is forgotten by contemporaries far more than by peasants still rooted in their own existence.

At the same time, this stronger tie between philosophy and the *Heimat* was accompanied by a strengthening of the affinities between philosophy and struggle (*Kampf*). The thinker is not the person who launches the attack on the concept but the one who receives it: "In the philosophical concept [*Begriff*], man, and indeed man as a whole, is in the *grip of an attack* [*Angriff*]—driven out of everydayness and driven back into the ground of things." The concept is guided not by man, but by his being-there, his *Dasein: "in philosophizing the* Da-sein *in man launches the attack upon man."* The philosopher must therefore show courage in this struggle that his questioning *Dasein* imposes on him, because this questioning is a challenge to the very ground of his own existence: "Man is [. . .] someone in the grip of an attack, attacked by the fact 'that he is what he is,' and already caught up in all comprehending questioning. Yet being comprehensively included in this way is not some blissful awe, but the struggle [*Kampf*]."[315] The philosopher's courage is manifested by the actual will to continue fighting and not to run away and hide: "This is precisely what is difficult: to really stay with what is being asked about here, and not to steal away on detours. This staying is what is particularly difficult, especially because as soon as we seriously inquire about philosophy, philosophy withdraws from us into a peculiar obscurity of its own where it properly resides as human activity in the ground of the essence of human *Dasein.*"[316] Whether there was a fortuitous affinity to Nietzsche or an actual influence, Heidegger returned to the Nietzschean view of the philosopher, namely, that he exposes himself to thought with greater or lesser courage and strength:[317] "How much truth does a spirit *endure,* how much truth does it *dare?* More and more that became for me the real measure of value. Error (faith in the ideal) is not blindness, error is *cowardice.* Every attainment, every step forward in knowledge, *follows* from courage, from hardness against oneself, from cleanliness in relation to oneself."[318]

The *Heimat* still inspired Heidegger's philosophy, but its influence significantly decreased, to the advantage of his dialogue with the Greeks and Germans, thinkers as well as poets. He was imbued with the spirit of the time, which brought him closer to the Conservative Revolutionaries and their Nietzschean inspiration. Moreover, around 1929–1930 he reached what he called the *Kehre,* the turning point, shifting the center of his meditation from *Dasein* to *Sein,* from being-there to being. Less anthropological, his thought accorded, de facto, less space to arguments inspired by human experience. This shift was, among other things, a sign that the native region's inspiration had run dry for him, resulting in a break with the Meßkirch way, the countryside, and his parents' house—a break he had already sensed in 1927.[319]

His family, his religion, his native region: Martin Heidegger's origins did lie in Meßkirch. The internal evolution that he followed during and after the war led him to tear himself away voluntarily: he broke openly with Catholicism, his ties to his family grew more tenuous. He returned to his region less and less often, so that by 1933 it was no longer anything but the place where he was born, and his political culture became the exact opposite of the one he had inherited in his hometown. Like a sun gradually receding into the distance before flaming out altogether, the Meßkirch way gradually faded away during these years, when Heidegger did not bid farewell but actually took his leave.

6 • The Wind Blowing from Berlin

(1927–1933)

Berlin as Seen from Todtnauberg

Martin Heidegger was becoming cut off from his roots. From his hometown the philosopher retained only an intellectual fidelity to the countryside, which made him vehemently opposed to the rootless big city. A tough battle against Berlin was taking shape, so great was the work of uprooting during that era. The big city's dominion over the spiritual life of the German people was increasing, as Heidegger observed via the different manifestations of uprootedness.

One of its first manifestations is *das Man*. A well-known theme in *Being and Time, das Man* is everything by which *Dasein* loses its way because, "as everyday Being-with-one-another, it stands in subjection [*Botmässigkeit*] to Others." *Das Man* is no one in particular, it is everyone, inasmuch as everyone bears within himself the indeterminate gaze of the Others, which constrains him in his everyday being, so that *das Man* decrees what he must wear, think, and do. It is thus an internalized conformism, the fashion to be followed, a way of acting and living, as much as a social constraint and a morality imposed from the outside: "We take pleasure and enjoy ourselves as *they* [*man*] take pleasure; we read, see, and judge about literature and art as *they* see and judge; likewise, we shrink back from the 'great mass' as *they* shrink back; we find 'shocking' what *they* find shocking."[1] Modern urban societies are the quintessential place of *das Man,* because they concentrate the Others in the form of a crowd of anonymous people: "In utilizing public means of transport and in making use of information services such as the newspaper, every Other is like the next."[2]

In 1927 Heidegger, finishing *Being and Time,* adopted a tone similar to the one he had assumed in 1918, when, from Berlin, he denounced the tendency of the big cities and the modern media to cast man down into absolute inauthenticity and uniformization.[3] Curiously, in his critique of urban culture, the philosopher seems to have been blind to cinema and deaf to the music hall and radio, three mass media whose development in the 1920s gave increasing power to the superficial "instant culture" he denounced, which was quick to spread fashions of all sorts and thus reinforce the dominion of *das Man.* As a result, in the city even more than in the countryside, everyone is uniform, anonymous, without a personality of his own.

Criticism of the modern media was a commonplace of the European revolutionary right, which saw it as a troubling symptom of the spirit of the times. For Drieu la Rochelle, writing in *The Young European* (1927), the music hall, with its large auditoriums where everyone was isolated from everyone else—trapped in a crowd of spectators—reflected the decadence at work in contemporary times. Social life, marked by the age of the masses, was suffering because "everywhere, increasing numbers make everything abstract, dismantle all relationships based on the measure of our senses: the soldier no longer sees his general, the citizen does not know the minister. We are entering an age when life is merely a collective dream. Men pursue parallel destinies; everyone thinks only of his individual person, but he does not find anything to nourish that individual except a coarse bread soup, an increasingly thin broth."[4] Cinema (still silent at the time) was for Drieu the latest expression of the loss of substance of contemporary society, which was more individualistic but, paradoxically, more than ever trapped in collective senselessness: "Peer into a movie theater at that crowd swimming in a uniform darkness. As in an aquarium, that fish knocks up against the luminous wall of the screen, the only outlet for all those submerged, smothered egos. The exasperated, exhausted individual is going to die and from him will be born a fluid, inevitable communism. That frightens me. What twisty evolution is humanity following? For the moment, that is where we are, at that monotonous alignment of signs without any personal value any longer, increasingly disembodied."[5]

In that troubling spiritual situation, increasingly disembodied for Drieu, increasingly uprooted for Heidegger, the countryside was for the German philosopher no longer the haven of authenticity. It was only loss of self to a less pronounced degree, because Heidegger's break with Catholicism had led him to criticize "inauthenticity" and the reflexes determined by his "limited origins & isolated developmt."[6] "Decline" or "decadence" (*Verfall*), the generalized fall into the inauthenticity of *das Man,* though emblematic of the spirit of the cities—whose influence was increasingly felt—was not one state of affairs among others. It proceeded from the very being of man in his everyday relationship with being.[7] *Dasein* was caught in a "downward plunge into and within the groundlessness [*Bodenlosigkeit*]" of its inauthentic being, a motion that "constantly tears the understanding away from the projecting of authentic possibilities, and [leads it to] [. . .] the tranquillized supposition that it possesses everything, or that everything is within its reach."[8]

Das Man brings about an uprooting, therefore, in the countryside but even more in the city, which supplies ample means and media to wrest man away from his own understanding of his existence. "What is said-in-the talk" (*das Geredete*), which is *das Man* inasmuch as it makes reference to the usual usages of talk (*die Rede*) and the received opinions they convey, was all the more powerful as a result. What is specific to *das Geredete* is that it allows for a conversation in which we talk without really knowing what we are talking about. The repetition of conventional expressions allows us to believe superficially that we understand what we are talking about, but in fact we understand only the words, which form a screen, and not what they refer to.[9] In confining itself to *das Geredete, Dasein,* "as Being-in-the-world," is "cut off from its primary and primordially genuine relationships-of-Being toward the world, toward Dasein-with, and toward its very Being-in."[10] But the result is also a cause, because *das Geredete* originates in man's ontological uprootedness: it "is the kind of Being which belongs to Dasein's understanding when that understanding has been uprooted." Its understanding is thereby "uprooted existentially, and this uprooting is constant."[11]

This theory of a modern rootless culture had already surfaced in a letter to Elfride of October 1918,[12] and it now took an original form in Heidegger's phenomenological ontology. The theory nevertheless repeated a conservative commonplace: there was a great continuity between it and the views of the young, intransigent Catholic Heidegger. With one exception, however: the countryside was now simply less inauthentic than the big city. That theorization of uprootedness was a theme in vogue among intellectuals on the right, because of the upheavals Europe had experienced since the nineteenth century. In Germany, this idea was accompanied by the notion of Westernization, a uniformization on the model of England, the United States, and France, which was making Germany lose its national character. For Oswald Spengler, that growing uprootedness of the West brought about the transition from culture to civilization, loss of life, and decadence, of which Western democracies, more than other societies, displayed the dangerous but ineluctable symptoms.

For Spengler, uprootedness took the form, in space, of the decline of provincial life in favor of life in the metropolises, the growing prominence of the "world city," and the decay of the *Heimat*.[13] Like Heidegger, he saw it as a global phenomenon, geographical, moral, cultural, scientific, and political all at once. What these diverse aspects had in common was their affirmation of the universality of reason and of the individual. Cosmopolitan universalism replaced love of one's native region; calculating self-interest prevented a quasi-religious repetition of the past; science, which no longer recognized faith, was becoming purely rational; the political bond was weakening within a society so individualistic that men were no longer anything but atoms, with nothing keeping them on course, while the laws on which their organization rested were those that reason recognized in man, by virtue of his universal nature, and not those history had granted and guaranteed.

In his critique of uprootedness, Spengler thus put the emphasis on politics, denouncing the loss of life he saw in the transformation of traditional European societies, religious and rural, into states founded on rationality and the universality of human rights, a movement that had finally reached Germany with the Weimar Republic. Heidegger, for his part, did not give priority to political reflections; in an approach that sought to return to being, they could only be secondary. His political philosophy is expressed in few words, primarily in paragraph 74 of *Being and Time,* which summed up what the book had established. It is nonetheless of major importance and, in its ambition to outline what could form the authentic bond uniting men into a people, it proves to be a radical critique of parliamentary democracy, a thread that once again linked Heidegger to the intellectuals of the revolutionary right.

For Heidegger, the people, essentially a community of fighters free in their confrontation with death, could not be separated from the idea of destiny, the acceptance of a common mission, within a tradition that everyone repeats by following heroes he chooses, but without mimicking them.

Destiny is "Dasein's primordial adventure [*Geschehen*],[14] which lies in authentic resoluteness and in which Dasein *hands* itself *down* [*überliefert*] to itself, free for death, in a possibility which it has inherited and yet has chosen."[15] The inherited possibility comes from the past, from a familial or collective history. The authentic choice of that possibility is made in the present, as a creative adaptation and not a mechanical repetition. The resolute man's individual decision does not cut him off from the Others; it even brings him to them: "But if fateful Dasein, as Being-in-the-world, exists essentially in Being-with-Others, its adventure is a collective adventure [*Mitgeschehen*] and is determinative for it as *destiny* [*Geschick*]. This is how we designate the adventure of the community, of a people."[16] Consciously or not, Heidegger adopted the communitarian political ideology of the Youth Movement, whose nationalism required from each of its young members an authenticity and a responsibility expressed as an availability for service. That availability had taken on a clear military coloring with the First World War and the immediate postwar period. With the common destiny, being "free for death" was all the more necessary, in that it could easily lead man to encounter his death in the manner of soldiers who, exposed to bombs, shrapnel, grenades, and trench knives, could actually see their own deaths approaching through the spectacle of the deaths of others. For Heidegger, that idea came to the fore during his own experience of combat. Perhaps it was also a reminiscence of Hegel meditating on the struggle against Napoleonic France. According to Hegel, the acceptance of death in combat, the death one causes and the death to which one exposes oneself, sublates into freedom and morality the contingency that necessarily determines every human life: "The transience of the finite now becomes a willed evanescence, and the negativity which underlies it becomes the substantial individuality proper to the ethical being."[17]

That narrow conception of destiny, in which man was at one with his people in a communion both metaphysical and political, meant that this destiny could not be arbitrary, nor could it be determined in several different ways, in accordance with the individual's free will. According to Heidegger, within a community where authentic membership demanded solidarity, demanded that one not split oneself off as an autonomous, even volatile part—as a liberal notion positing the primacy of the individual would have required—the common destiny was seized, deliberately taken on, but not created: "Our fates have already been guided in advance, in our Being-with-one-another [*Miteinandersein*] in the same world and in our resoluteness for definite possibilities."[18] The direction destiny would take was set out by the history of the people, which required that each of its members follow the general movement and indicated the same direction for them all, provided they were free for their own deaths and took full responsibility for their existence. Man's participation in the life of the people, through the acceptance of destiny, was not the alienation of a private, individual life. On the contrary, it was the most perfect realization of his being: "Dasein's fateful destiny [*schicksalhafte Geschick*] in and with its 'generation' goes to make up the full authentic adventure of Dasein."[19] As Heidegger imagined it in retrospect, in knowing how to embrace resolutely his common destiny, he had been led to experience the "full authentic adventure" of his existence, like all the young Germans of the same age who had volunteered at the start of the First World War.

Understood in this way, the nation is not founded on natural laws such as human rights but on the full acceptance of everyone's involvement in a collective history. The meaning of this resoluteness is indicated by that history itself, repeated and metamorphosed in the instantaneous "rejoinder." In a flash of authenticity, it is only in that rejoinder that Dasein "has its own history made manifest" for the first time.[20] Contrary to progressive ideologies such as communism, which posits the future as criterion, and contrary to reactionary ideologies such as the nostalgic conservatism of the Second Reich, which saw a bygone past as the touchstone for the action to be taken, in Heidegger's eyes "repetition does not abandon itself to that which is past, nor does it aim at progress. In the moment of vision authentic existence is indifferent to both these alternatives."[21]

That relationship to time, which grounds the future in a reactivated past that becomes both destiny and mission, was a commonplace of the Conservative Revolution. Moeller van den Bruck affirmed the need to retain from the inheritance of the past only what deserved to be retained and to carry it resolutely toward the future, but without aspiring to be "progressive": "At present, that will is not called conservative. It is called nationalist. It desires the safeguarding in Germany of everything that deserves to be safeguarded. [. . .] Nationalism is turned exclusively toward the future. It is conservative because it knows there is no future that is not rooted in the past." "The conservatism of a nation strives to safeguard these values, by conserving traditional values insofar as they are still vital and in assimilating new values insofar as they contribute toward promoting the nation's vitality."[22]

In grounding the nation not in natural laws but in a living tradition revived in the present, Heidegger also resembled the intellectuals of the Italian revolutionary right, particularly Giovanni Gentile, who had inspired the "Manifesto of the Fascist Intellectuals" (1925). For Gentile, fascism, in opposing the materialistic individualism embodied in social democracy, presented the fatherland as "an idea, one which would provide the individual with his reason for being, his freedom, and all his rights," "an ideal that is a continuous and inexhaustible process of historical actualization, [. . .] a distinct and singular embodiment of a civilization's traditions which, far from withering as a dead memory of the past, assumes the form of a personality focused on the end toward which it strives. The fatherland is, thus, a mission."[23]

Consonant with Gentile's idea of a shared, vital, and disinterested tradition, Heidegger maintains that heroes are at the heart of this tradition that discovers a destiny: "The authentic repetition of a possibility of existence that has been—the possibility that Dasein may choose its hero—is grounded existentially in anticipatory resoluteness; for it is in resoluteness that one first chooses the choice which makes one free for the struggle of loyally following in the footsteps of that which can be repeated."[24] The heroism with which Heidegger was imbued originated in the classics. Borrowed from Goethe's *Iphigenia in Tauris*,[25] the expression "choose its hero" is spoken by Pylades, who is trying to spur on his cousin Orestes while they are being held in a Tauris prison: "Everyone must choose his hero, whose paths he follows even to the summit of Mount Olympus."[26] The model for that tragedy might have been the intrepid Achilles; it was instead Odysseus, a courageous but cautious and cunning warrior. Both were emblematic heroes from antiquity, and in particular from the world of Homer, for whom, as Moses Finley pointed out, "everything pivoted on a single element of honor and virtue."[27] The bellicosity so important to German culture in the 1920s would not have disavowed that courage in combat.

The heroism of Heideggerian resoluteness, which placed a high value on camaraderie on the front lines, a camaraderie that prompted soldiers to relieve those already there, must also be understood in terms of the many postwar publications, in Germany and elsewhere in Europe, which for Heidegger's generation made military heroism as much a fashion as a decisive experience. *Being and Time* took its place within a series of texts that included Ernst Jünger's *Storm of Steel* (1920), *Battle as Inner Experience* (1922), *Assault* (1923), *Copse 125*, and *Fire and Blood* (1925), which are the literary quintessence of such heroism. In that respect, this German literature contrasted sharply with the French literature of the same era. Whereas the humanistic, pacifist tone of Erich Maria Remarque's *All Quiet on the Western Front* was an exception in Germany, postwar military literature in France—for example, Roland Dorgeles's *Wooden Crosses* (1919) and the first chapter of Céline's *Journey to the End of the Night* (1932)—clearly leaned toward pacifism. France, the victor, wrote about the "war to end all wars," while Germany, feeling humiliated, dreamt of heroism and sometimes of revenge. Italy as well, exposed to the communist menace, burning with resentment at the stolen victory, provided fertile ground for the development of fascism.

Outside literature, it was the age of militarism, which invaded civilian life. The streets were regularly filled with members of veterans' leagues in uniform, who paraded waving flags; with political party militias, such as the Nazi Party's Sturmabteilung (SA) or the KPD's Roter Frontkämpferbund (RFB; Red League of Front-Line Combatants); with far-right paramilitary groups (for example, the 50,000 men in the Jungdeutscher Orden, the Young German Order);[28] and with youth organizations such as the Bündische Jugend, successor to the Youth Movement, the Scouts, and the *Wandervogel.* All adopted military uniforms, a military organization, and the military ethos, which they cultivated through exercises, parades, camps, and marches.

That glorification of combat was not necessarily aggressive or military. In his *Decline of the West,* Spengler (like Heidegger) conceived of it in peaceful terms, distinguishing the different forms it took. He maintained that "to the Culture belong gymnastics, the agon, and to the Civilization belongs sports."[29] Whereas a people on the decline practices sports, a degraded form of peaceful combat, at the height of its vitality it devotes itself to gymnastics (as Jahn had advocated), to tournaments like medieval knights, or to the agon (*ἀγών*) like the Greeks. Although Spengler did not rule out military combat, he remained within the tradition of Fichte, who condemned imperialism, associated with French expansionism. Spengler nonetheless believed it inevitable, like the transition from culture to civilization: "Imperialism is Civilization unadulterated. In this phenomenal form the destiny of the West is now irrevocably set. The energy of culture-man is directed inwards, that of civilization-man outwards."[30]

That ambivalence about struggle could also be found in Heidegger. In 1925 he made it central to the view of love he described to Hannah Arendt: "The joyful struggle—and the definitive commitment to something chosen—are ours.—Ours. That can never be lost—but can only become richer, clearer—more certain, so as to develop into a great passion for existence."[31] Although the heroes man can choose from the past are primarily warriors, whom man can replace in combat, resoluteness and combat are overarching concepts relevant to all areas of his existence, including love. These heroes from the past can thus also be other figures of humankind, foremost among them philosophers.

Both the soldier and the philosopher require courage, a resoluteness when confronting the ultimate possibilities of their existence. In his 1925 course "History of the Concept of Time: Prolegomena," Heidegger publicly adopted the theme of combat to characterize the difficult initiative undertaken by the phenomenologists: "To abide by what we see without asking [. . .] in the face of the most obvious of matters [. . .] is the most difficult thing we may hope to attain, because man's element is the artificial and mendacious, where he is always already engaged in idle talk."[32] As a result, "it is erroneous to think that phenomenologists are models of excellence; rather, they stand in their resoluteness to wage an all-out war with this element, in their positive will-to-disclose and nothing else."[33] Socrates, combining military and philosophical courage, an upright citizen who battled courageously for his city in Potidaea, Delium, and Amphipolis, and who showed the same courage in the philosophical education of his people to the bitter end, with his resolute acceptance of the unjust death sentence handed down by the court of Athens, was thus the hero par excellence, whom man could take as his model from the past—more so than Albert Leo Schlageter, whose praises Heidegger sang in 1933.[34]

The two possible dimensions of authentic combat, military and philosophical, allow us to understand the position Heidegger tried to defend in Marburg regarding physical exercise, which he favored. It was an urgent debate at the time: the Treaty of Versailles had limited ground forces in Germany to 100,000 men, and the promotion of gymnastics was a way to circumvent these restrictions, just as Jahn had wanted to prepare a large number of Prussians for combat by that means, despite the reduced contingent of soldiers Napoleon had imposed. Given these constraints, a militarily satisfying response to the question of how to replace military service needed to be found. In a long meeting on the matter in January 1928, with in attendance "the ministerial undersecretary—the registrar—the rector & many others," Heidegger set out his position: "I spoke [. . .] in very fundamental terms & above all addressing the undersecretary—University, Youth Movement, Physical Culture." Having embraced the Youth Movement's ideals of authenticity, a movement that had taken on a military tone with the war, the philosopher believed that physical exercise was indispensable, but only if rigorously complemented by a spiritual education that valued " 'culture,' aristocracy of spirit, & rank." "For only when one has this in a genuine way & from primordial [?] sources can one then incorporate physical culture into life—whereas otherwise the latter becomes a surrogate for everything under the most disparate interpretations." Thus combining the activities of the body and those of the mind or spirit, Heidegger's educational program adopted both dimensions of authentic combat, military and philosophical. "The penny dropped," he noted, "although in practice nothing can be expected." As he explained to Elfride, "the ministry is infested with fundamentally wishy-washy educational ideals" and "is under pressure from the professional interests of gym teachers in the schools," which he saw primarily as "the outburst of the masses against 'culture,' aristocracy of spirit, & rank."[35]

In placing philosophy at the foundation of the authentic national community, Heidegger, however, granted no place to political speech or dialogue. All that mattered was resoluteness, which shows man (be he statesman or citizen, general or soldier), in the light of his own death, what he seizes as destiny. "A rejoinder [. . .] *in a moment of vision,*" resoluteness does not result from a dialogue, either within oneself or on the public square. Even less is it the result of a compromise. Without being explicit, Heidegger's denunciation of parliamentary democracy, which he associates with *das Man,* is thus clear and radical. When power is collective and decisions are made in common, they are not rooted in anyone's existence. In the end, parliamentary debates are only the idle talk of irresolute bourgeois fleeing their own death. That type of critique, typical of the rightist opposition to Weimar, could also be found in Carl Schmitt's *Political Theology,* with its key concept of "decision." Turning to his own account the Spanish counterrevolutionary Juan Donoso Cortés (1809–1853) and the question of "the bloody decisive battle" waged in the nineteenth century "between Catholicism and atheist socialism," Schmitt maintained that "it was characteristic of bourgeois liberalism not to decide in this battle but instead to begin a discussion." He concluded: "A class that shifts all political activity onto the plane of conversation in the press and in parliament is no match for social conflict."[36]

That animosity toward public speech also appears in Thomas Mann's *Reflections of a Nonpolitical Man,* in which the author takes direct aim at lawyers and at the *Zivilisationsliterat,* the "civilized literary man," whom he also calls the "radical literary man." Lurking behind these words is a critique of the intellectual (on the left, *à la française*), who is "the representative of the literarized, politicized, in short, of the democratized spirit, a child of the French Revolution, spiritually at home in its sphere, in its country."[37] For Mann, the democratization of Germany would be a scandalous "de-Germanization,"[38] expressed as the rise of "the eloquent citizen, the literary lawyer of the Third Estate, as I have said, the representative of its spiritual as well as, not to forget, of its material interests." "Its champions are the lawyer and the literary man, the spokesmen of the 'Third Estate,' and of its emancipation, the spokesmen of the Enlightenment, of reason, of progress, of 'the philosophy,' against the *seigneurs,* against authority, tradition, history, 'power,' kingdom and church—the spokesmen of the spirit that they consider to be the unconditional, sole, and dazzlingly true one, spirit itself, spirit in itself, while it is really just the political spirit of the middle-class revolution that they mean and understand."[39]

A philosopher ill at ease among his peers, to whom he preferred the solitary company of the mountain of Todtnauberg, Heidegger nonetheless found, in an original form, his place among the Conservative Revolutionaries, who were in fact hostile to parliamentary democracy and human rights, emphasizing rootedness, tradition, and combat, authentically uniting the German people as a community of fighters resolutely taking up its destiny once again in the face of death. In the same way, he moved closer to right-wing revolutionaries in Europe such as Drieu la Rochelle and Giovanni Gentile. Although Berlin was the symbol of a Germany constantly uprooting itself, it preserved around it all the strength of its future destiny as a German people that had courageously returned to its rootedness, to its tradition, to its authenticity. Engaging in dialogue with his era in his philosophical writings, Heidegger still hoped to realize this destiny that remained for the moment on hold.

Having lost his Christian faith, like many Conservative Revolutionaries Heidegger believed in a form of silent providence whose signs could be interpreted and which was at the heart of a de-Christianized, secularized religion that he held on to and which served as a point of view from which he gazed at himself: "I now have an increasingly strong sense of a gradual transformation, which extends even into my way of working, of asking and saying. Even though I can only advance slowly & don't want to fool myself, in everything that happens I sense a great providence, which gives me faith & trust."[40]

A few years earlier, Thomas Mann had seen his country's entry into the war as a response to destiny: Germany had shown an "authentically Germanic obedience to its destiny" by taking part in a struggle that was "terrible, bold, and irrational in the most grandiose sense of the term, against the worldwide Entente of civilization."[41] In 1923 Moeller van den Bruck thought that Germans needed "leaders who feel that they are one with the nation; who connect the nation's destiny with their own fate, for the sake of which they call for subversion; and who, whether today they descend from the old dominant stratum or are gradually forming a new one, are determined, for Germany, to bear the future of the nation with their will, their resolution, and indeed their ambition."[42]

The resoluteness in the face of existence that the Germans had to show was the condition for the fulfillment of their destiny, for bringing about the philosophical revolution that Heidegger glimpsed. It was up to them to repeat the earliest beginnings of Western philosophy among the Greeks, from the pre-Socratics to Plato and Aristotle. As he wrote to Blochmann, it seemed to Heidegger "increasingly clear that the beginning of our Western philosophy must return again to the present for us, so that in the presence of such a model we can truly begin by learning that not everyone has the right or the requisite qualifications to accomplish anything at all, just as not everyone is qualified for everything, and that a being *is* not unless it has *its* own law, *its* own ground, *its* own origin, and its own *rank*."[43] In this extremely aristocratic view of knowledge, the greatness of Greek philosophy's early days, up to Plato and Aristotle, had to be taken as the measure of any speech and any silence: "We have to learn again to be quiet and observe a long silence to recover the strength and the vigor of language and the criteria for what it is licit and imperative to say." In the Greek manner, "the essence of the human being" would be "achieved after a hard struggle" by salvaging "the elementary ballast of the original questions."[44]

The continuation of present debates would not put an end to idle talk: "I do not believe that we can find our bearings so long as we are hitched to 'the current situation' instead of turning our backs to it, relying on the knowledge that, for our own virtualities in the realm of existence, our being can only begin to be deployed on the scale of a history from the wellspring of the discourse of antiquity."[45] Thus Heidegger still had a conception characteristic of the spirit of the Conservative Revolution: in view of the decadence of the time, a revolution had to come to overturn the present and retain only what deserved to be retained—the peasant rootedness in existence and the return to Greek philosophy's original questioning. In addition, in his very Romantic devotion to the ancient Greeks, he delighted in the mutilations of this heritage, which were significant in Plato and Aristotle's works, and major in the works of the pre-Socratics, of which only fragments remained: "The ruins of the Greek temples and the statues of gods are like the bits and pieces of the ancient pronouncements of their philosophers. What would it be like if we had all that intact and without any mutilation whatever? Routine and emptiness would have overcome them long ago. Things being what they are, or what remains of them, a struggle must necessarily begin to appropriate them, and it is this beginning—surrounded by obscurity and questions—that we have to bear with us and carry forward, in all its grandeur, for this is our burden."[46]

Heidegger's philosophical revolution was not without nationalism: it had to come from Germans, the people which, alone among all others, was "capable of rivaling"[47] the Greeks. This philosophical nationalism came, according to him, from Nietzsche—probably from *The Birth of Tragedy*, an early work that saw the German people as the hope for a Dionysian renewal of Europe in the wake of Wagner's music. In that respect, Heidegger forgot or did not know how critical Nietzsche later became of his people, writing that "it is part of my ambition to be considered a despiser of the Germans *par excellence*."[48] In *Ecce Homo,* Nietzsche correctly judged them to be ultranationalists: "The Germans have no idea how vulgar they are; but that is the superlative of vulgarity—they are not even *ashamed* of being merely Germans."[49] Nietzsche even went so far as to think that Germany's climate was bad for intellectual activity.[50]

The close connection between Greece and Germany had been a commonplace in the latter country since the Romantic period. Beyond the fascination with Greece that runs through Hölderlin's *Hyperion,* Hegel, for example, wrote: "The name of Greece strikes home to the hearts of men of education in Europe, and more particularly is this so with us Germans."[51] This identification with Greece had its distant origin in the Reformation and Luther's assimilation of Rome to the papacy, both of them considered the negation of the national principle in Germany. This anti-Roman nationalism was confirmed by the quest for a national antiquity in Tacitus's *Germania,* which was read as an apologia for the German barbarians. This German identity constructed against Rome and the Latin spirit remained alive even in Thomas Mann's *Reflections of a Nonpolitical Man,* in which civilization stood opposed to the German spirit:

> Literary humanism, the legacy of Rome, the classical spirit, classical reason, the generous language accompanied by a generous act, the exhilarating phrase worthy of man, celebrating the beauty and dignity of the human being, the academic rhetoric in honor of the human race—in the Latin West all that makes life worthy of being lived and makes man a man. [. . .] What we call "civilization" [. . .] is nothing but the [. . .] spread of the bourgeois spirit that has become political and literary, its colonization of the inhabited land. *The imperialism of civilization* is the last form of the idea of Roman union, against which Germany "protests."[52]

Contrary to imperialist Rome, which was oppressive and decadent, and had passed the baton to France and Britain, since the end of the eighteenth century Greece had been seen as an ideal of freedom and culture, which Wilhelm von Humboldt had made a model for the classical Gymnasium and whose legacy the Germans claimed.

Positing that the German people were alone capable of rivaling the Greeks, Heidegger seems to have ultimately been inspired much less by Nietzsche than by Fichte, whom he read in his youth and had recently rediscovered in connection with a course[53] in which Heidegger situated Fichte with respect to Hegel and Schelling in German Idealism.[54] Fichte saw the identity and superiority of the German people in their rootedness: Germans "have remained in the original living space of their ancestors, whereas other peoples have emigrated elsewhere."[55] This rootedness had virtues: "The Germans, who have remained in the mother country, possess all the virtues that grew on their soil long ago: loyalty, honesty, a sense of honor, simplicity."[56] The retention of their original language, which they have "preserved and cultivated," was nonetheless a greater cause of superiority, because although men construct their living space, they "are shaped by language, more than language is shaped by men." Other peoples, like the French, had "adopted a foreign language that they gradually modified":[57] "The neo-Latin languages are naturally and by their very origin unintelligible. There is no remedy for that, since the peoples that speak neo-Latin have no living language with whose help they could correct the dead language." Inversely, "the German continues to speak a living language, still drawing strength from the original source."[58] The Germans, as the only ones who still speak an original language, are thus the only people who can be compared with the ancient Greeks, who also spoke an original language whose vitality was intact.

Conceived as an essential link with the Greeks, of whom the Germans were the only genuine heirs, Heidegger's philosophical nationalism was part of a Western—that is, European—history within a Europe determined without too great a geographical fetishism. The expression "the West" and the conception underlying it had been made fashionable by Spengler in his *Decline of the West*, which made this choice explicit in a note on the "landscape of Western Europe":

> Here the historian is gravely influenced by preconceptions derived from geography, which assumes a Continent of Europe, and feels himself compelled to draw an ideal frontier corresponding to the physical frontier between "Europe" and "Asia." The word "Europe" ought to be struck out of history. There is historically no "European" type, and it is sheer delusion to speak of the Hellenes as "European Antiquity" (were Homer and Heraclitus and Pythagoras, then, Asiatic?) and to enlarge upon their "mission" as such.[59]

With the term "Europe" and its spatial definition—which had become canonical—as a continent stretching from the Atlantic to the Urals, bordered to the south by Africa and, especially, to the east by Asia, Spengler was challenging a narrow geographical conception based on a bookish cartography. Just as the contours of modern Europe do not respect the "natural" borders traditionally assigned to it (it includes in its margins even the state of Israel, which participates in the Eurovision Song Contest and the European soccer championship), to Spengler it seemed that though the coasts and nearby islands of Asia Minor—which were populated by Hellenic peoples from antiquity until the period after the First World War—were, if not fully "European" in the usual sense of the word, at least Western. Thus Homer, Heraclitus, and Pythagoras, paragons of European culture (the first two were born in Asia Minor, the third on the island of Samos, not far from the Ionian coast), had to be designated by a term that was no longer opposed to "Asia" and that made them the unadulterated origin of modernity. Heidegger proceeded in the same way when he meditated on Western philosophy: the autochthonous nature of Greek thought owed nothing to Asia; and that was also true of the Germans, the Greeks' heirs.

Despite Heidegger's philosophical and ontological perspective, in his work this way of making German philosophy European in fact reproduced the structure of allegiances he had received from Meßkirch: a vigorous nationalism and patriotism included more broadly within a Europe assimilated to Christianity as it was to be ruled spiritually by the pope. And in the works of Richard von Kralik, who influenced Heidegger during his youth, the German people was united within a German Holy Roman Empire that was supposed to be reconstituted with no consideration for the wishes of nonnative peoples such as the Italians.

Vigorously identifying himself with Germany, and secondarily with Europe, Heidegger nonetheless had an original and critical view of political identities. In his course titled "The Fundamental Concepts of Metaphysics," he asked: "Who are we now? How do we understand ourselves now when we say 'we'? [. . .] This history of the spirit—is it uniquely German, Western and indeed European? Or should we draw the circle in which we stand even wider?"[60] The answer was still more general as well as much closer: "We must situate ourselves, so as to connect ourselves with our 'being-there' in such a way that this 'being-there' is the only thing that unites us."[61] This rejection of an incorporation into a German, Western, or European history was only apparent, because this history was reintroduced by the reference to ontology and *Dasein:* the philosopher was in fact repeating his view of an authentic community as he outlined it in paragraph 74 of *Being and Time,* a community of fighters united by the determination of each member, each *Dasein,* to acknowledge that they belong to a people, if necessary at the cost of their lives and their own passing into nothingness. Rooted in the ground of the "essential distress of *Dasein,*" the individuals belonging to a people are then united in a community held together by "the unity endowed with the roots of an essential action,"[62] and this "essential action" was necessarily a creative repetition of the common history, through which "destiny" is revealed.[63]

Around 1930, when Heidegger considered Germans the vanguard of the history of the Western spirit, his objective was not to glorify his people; rather, he thought he recognized a mission that came from the ground of being and its history, a mission his people had to take on. This idea that Germany had a European destiny was also found in the work of his "comrade in arms," Karl Jaspers. In a reply to Hannah Arendt, who had written to say that she felt German only by language and culture, he wrote: "When you speak of native language, philosophy, and literary creation, you have only to add historical and political destiny, and then there is no longer any difference. Today, this destiny is the fact that Germany can exist only in a united Europe, that the recovery of its former splendor can be achieved only by the unification of Europe, that the devil is the French petty bourgeois fear with which it will inevitably be necessary to come to terms. The empire of the Germans, which should extend from Holland to Austria, and from Scandinavia to Switzerland, is impossible and would still be too small for the present age."[64]

Europe, and beyond it, a global consciousness, was in fashion among intellectuals around 1930, on both the left and the right. A nationalist recognizing the value he saw in his people within European history and, more profoundly, within the history of being, Heidegger was similar to Conservative Revolutionaries like Spengler, with his idea, in *The Decline of the West,* of an inevitable Faustian, global imperialism, and Jünger, with his notion in *The Worker* (1932) of the world order of technology. Both writers situated their political views within an ineluctable global context; for them, nationalism was ultimately a "provincial ideology."[65] This view was not limited to these German right-wing revolutionaries: for example, Drieu la Rochelle expressed similar ideas in *The Young European,* where, convinced of "the decadence of Europe, Asia, America, the planet,"[66] he asserted that "the instinct of self-preservation" that made him write was connected with "something more and more general. It was no longer a matter of preserving the Frenchman, or even the European, but the human. Preserving the human, acting so that for a long time still there might be a human expression of the world in songs, dances, and monuments."[67]

Despite his desire for a renewal of the West's spirit and culture, Heidegger would probably have disapproved of Drieu's profession of faith, which would have been too humanistic for him. Placing the touchstone for all value in being, and thus at a more profound level than Drieu's humanity, his horizon of belonging was consequently more restricted. For Heidegger, the collective reality of *Dasein* was anti-universalist: it was the people, a soil and a blood caught up in the history of a civilization, that had to find its way back to its *Heimat*. The way was not so easy to take, because Heidegger himself was attracted to the metropolis.

The Appeal of the Metropolis

In January 1928, when the appointment in Freiburg was becoming a possibility, Heidegger considered moving to Berlin—an idea that originated not only in his ambition to set the tone for German universities and for the German people but also, in the first place, in his desire to see Elisabeth Blochmann. She lived in Berlin and had become his mistress: "In my soul and conscience, I am allowed to be the servant of the vast domains of your heart. *Volo ut sis,* I want you to be—that's how Augustine came to define love. And in doing so he recognized it as the innermost freedom of one person with regard to the other. Okay for Berlin, let that decision free up all the forces that exist in you and make your heart worthy of living a life of great inner richness."[68] It seems that this plan came from Blochmann alone; the university did not officially solicit Heidegger in any way. He discussed with Elfride and Husserl the possibility of moving to Berlin, but both of them were against it: "Husserl had a nice talk with me & above all—like you—advised me against going to Berlin for now or in the next ten years." Heidegger seemed to have decided they were right: "And this is quite right—for I'm just beginning now & all I need is concentration & passion for work, which is there but simply gets shoved to one side by the bureaucratic professor in me."[69] The return to the familiar theme of tranquility for his work makes this reply credible, but its date disqualifies it, because it was on the very next day that he wrote to Blochmann: "Okay for Berlin"[70]—only one more example of Heidegger's duplicity. When he was actually appointed in Freiburg, this Berlin plan, which hadn't a shred of reality, became less pressing: although he may have spoken about it in Berlin on 28 March, it is certain that nothing interesting came of it; finally, he wrote to tell Blochmann that she had to leave Berlin if she didn't want to burn out in her best years, for lack of the tranquility necessary to regenerate and enrich herself.[71]

His desire to be in a large city, where his influence would be greater, or where, ideally, he might finally be reunited with Jaspers, enables us to understand his attempts to move to Frankfurt in 1929. Jaspers had suggested the idea in his letter of 12 November 1928: invited to the city to participate in appointments to several chairs, he imagined that Heidegger and he ought to "have the philosophical positions and that Wertheimer should have the one in psychology," and he "flirted a little with the thought, even though it appeared impossible," because, he believed, his friend "would hardly go to Frankfurt," and in any case he himself would do so "only very reluctantly."[72] Frankfurt would have allowed them to realize their old dream of teaching at the same university, but Heidegger took it further, considering that eventuality, whereas Jaspers seemed resolved to remain in Heidelberg after he had renegotiated his salary.[73] On 24 January, on the occasion of a lecture titled "The Philosophical and Metaphysical Anthropology of *Dasein*" at the Kant Society in Frankfurt, Heidegger made the acquaintance of Kurt Riezler, registrar at the university, whom he met again at Davos[74] in March, and with whom he henceforth remained in close contact. In March, Riezler told him that he now truly hoped that Heidegger would be appointed in Frankfurt—but "it just takes time."[75] In early August, he informed Heidegger that "the ministry was under pressure from all sides to open a chair of pedagogy in Frankfurt. The prospects would be very meager in view of its demands." Heidegger rejoiced and made a vow: "Would to God it should fall to me!"[76]

The Frankfurt plan had not yet come through when, on 28 March 1930,[77] Heidegger was offered a position in Berlin. This was an offer not to be refused: a prestigious chair (he would have succeeded Ernst Troeltsch)[78] at the university that had been, since the beginning of the nineteenth century, a model for Germany and for Europe. Having learned the news in the following day's paper, Jaspers wrote to Heidegger to congratulate him: "To you has not only fallen the greatest honor granted to a university philosopher; you will take up the most visible post and, in so doing, will experience and assimilate impulses of your philosophizing that are hitherto unknown."[79] Heidegger was overjoyed, but restrained himself for fear of seeming vain, because Jaspers himself had earlier hoped to be offered the same position: "Yesterday afternoon I received, out of the blue, a telegraphed offer of appointment to Berlin. I am asked to go there on April 7 for negotiations. I would be very grateful to you if before my trip, which will probably take place on April 5, I could thoroughly discuss this with you."[80]

Heidegger's visit to Berlin was pleasant. Blochmann met him and they walked with friends, the Bauers, on the shores of Lake Wannsee. Then they went to Potsdam, a Prussian "place of memory"; Heidegger found "splendid" the Neues Palais built by Frederick the Great, adding: "All in all I have a real impression this time—; it was worth living in the vicinity of Old Fritz."[81] The terms of appointment offered by the university were advantageous, and Walter Bauer thought Heidegger could "demand to take sabbaticals at least every 3 semesters or at will, & suchlike."[82]

The circumstances of the job offer were, however, enough to temper his desire to take the chair being offered him. The faculty had initially voted to name Cassirer *unico loco;* it had only expressed a negative opinion regarding Heidegger and Hartmann, his predecessor in Marburg; hence he had been named by the ministry to join a faculty that was a priori hostile to him. Heidegger, like Jaspers, was aware that this offer was the result of a generational change at work in Germany: "That my appointment coincides with the rise of the young generation of Brüning, Treviranus & even Grimme too—in its general spiritual direction—is no accident."[83] Everywhere, men of his age were coming to power: Heinrich Brüning (1885–1970), a conservative and member of Zentrum who had been called to the chancellery by President Hindenburg, thanks in particular to Gottfried Treviranus (1891–1971) of the DNVP,[84] who became a minister; old Marshal Hindenburg, along with his entourage, wanted to put an end to Hermann Müller's Social Democratic cabinet by drawing on the extraordinary powers conferred on him by Article 48 of the Weimar constitution. Heidegger was right: "Our epoch is bringing about this very change,"[85] because with Müller's resignation on 27 March the great political crisis had just begun—a crisis which, combined with the economic and social crisis, would finally destroy the Republic. In his own way, and despite being religious and a Social Democrat, Adolf Grimme (1880–1963), the brand-new minister of education and culture for Prussia, was part of the profound challenge to the established order in Germany. A former student of Husserl's in Göttingen, he also wanted a profound spiritual change inspired by phenomenological radicalism,[86] and that was why he had decided to impose Heidegger on the University of Berlin.

Heidegger was aware that the times were favorable for him politically, and that Berlin would be his for the taking. Nevertheless, he felt that politics and "the history of spirit" were not perfectly synchronic: "how & whether the two can be separated in this way, or how this is to be given the right new form, is unclear to me, because neither of them are fixed quantities, but change."[87] All the same, he still had the firm conviction he had had in 1918,[88] that Berlin "must be *conquered from the outside.*"[89]

He therefore turned down the appointment, though his reason for doing so was not obvious. Should we believe his remarks on the uprootedness of this place? That was the justification he gave on 17 August to Julius Stenzel, a Hellenist in Kiel, writing that "the essence of the metropolis elicits only incitation and excitation: the illusion of a state of awakening. The best will in the world is stifled in sensation and representation—the anti-essence of all philosophy." Thus he feared that "the meager forces of an isolated individual" were wasted in an "unnatural monster"[90] like the University of Berlin. It is true that uprootedness, groundlessness, the monstrosity of big cities in general and of Berlin in particular, were for him more than empty words.[91] This monstrosity was certainly obvious to him, but it does not by itself explain the rejection of a chair in Berlin that was otherwise so desirable in what it allowed.[92] Heidegger was actually very sensitive to the way he felt in a place. This time, even though he was very unfamiliar with the metropolis, in fact he felt almost comfortable there: "The sheer groundlessness of the place is dreadful & yet it is *still* no genuine abyss for philosophy after all."[93]

Heidegger's remarks to Elisabeth Blochmann in December 1927 were even less stereotypical: comparing Pragerstrasse, where Blochmann lived, with the Black Forest, he understood "the importance of a few days spent in the cabin" in Todtnauberg, and, immediately correcting himself, he added: "There is, in truth, a factor I have set aside at present: modern life, the fact of being plunged into the vortex of history. This appeared to me clearly in Berlin as well as in Köln and Bonn. The working conditions there are easier in many ways, even if in the last analysis one must count only on oneself."[94] The metropolis, a dreadfully groundless place, was not such a "genuine abyss for philosophy" and could even facilitate it by immersing the philosopher "in the vortex of history" and "modern life."[95] What comes through in this letter is the uneasiness Heidegger felt among other people, an uneasiness accentuated by the metropolis, where they were so numerous—even at the university. In Köln and Bonn, where he met with "a fine and real success," he had even experienced a genuine human environment favorable to him; the organizers and the audience gave him a warm welcome, and he felt so good there that he spoke "with full freedom, and for that reason with greater ease and in a more relaxed way than usual."[96] In his rehabilitation of the metropolis, Heidegger was still far from Ernst Jünger's radical acceptance. In *The Worker,* Jünger wrote that the universal grip of technology had changed the city and the countryside, the mechanical and the organic worlds, to the point that "the celebrated difference between city and countryside survives today only in the Romantic imagination; it is just as untenable as the difference between the organic and the mechanical world." For Jünger, efforts to remedy the situation—as Heidegger did in drawing his strength in Todtnauberg from "nature reserves"[97] created in the midst of modernity—were no more than a Romantic dream of utopia with no future.

Heidegger was hinting at the idea that the time for the metropolis had come; it was not merely a negative for thought. Why then, in 1930, did he refuse the appointment that was not to be refused, that of a chair in philosophy at the University of Berlin? Not mincing words, he wrote to Minister Grimme, who wanted to hire him against the faculty's wishes: "Today, when I have already arrived at the beginning of a secure position in philosophy, I feel insufficiently prepared to occupy the chair in Berlin in the way I must demand of myself or of anyone else. Only a philosophy that is truly a philosophy of its time—in other words, that is master of its time [*ihrer Zeit mächtig*]—can become a really lasting philosophy [*Wirklich bleibende Philosophie*]."[98] Heidegger did not yet feel sure enough of his strengths in the colossal enterprise to which he aspired and which he thought any Berlin philosopher had to undertake: namely, to embody a "lasting" philosophy that was truly of its time and thus made itself "master of its time," that set the tone for the whole culture of the era, as he thought Plato, Aristotle, and Descartes had done for their eras.

This problem continued to absorb him later on, a sign that it was in large part the true cause of his hesitation and finally of his refusal: "Not accepting this offer did not put an end to the time of reflection it required; on the contrary, that reflection has only just begun. As for the work that awaits me and how to set about it, as for how to adopt an eminently personal position, and in what form, in the face of everything that drapes itself in the name of philosophy, even in its organized exploitation, in the face of the encirclement in which you find yourself under pressure from all sides, in the face of that whole body of literature that pushes you to speak up and tugs at your sleeve to make your inner confidence and composure falter—to what safe place can you entrust the ultimate power of questioning?"[99] In Berlin, Heidegger would have wanted to be able to change the course of history through the power of thought and his teaching, even though the capital was the beating heart of modern culture. He did not yet feel strong enough for that. So he remained in Freiburg, not having yet grasped how he could make himself philosophically the master of Berlin and his time.

As the months passed, he even seems to have lost hope of ever being able to do so. He was upset by his powerlessness: "To be sure, these worries constantly accompany any life worthy of the name, but you cannot imagine how much they affect my work."[100] Increasingly famous because of the resounding success of *Being and Time,* he was discouraged about his project and his powers: "For a long time now—already before the Berlin episode—I have been shocked over my dubious success, and I have known ever since that I have dared to go too far beyond my own existential power and without clearly seeing the confines of what is materially in question for me."[101] Having turned forty, referring to a kind of maturity that in southern Germany is called "the Swabian age" (*Schwabenalter*), he wanted to abandon the project of writing a work of his own and take refuge in reading and teaching the pages of philosophy's great past, to which he wanted to give new life. This led him to compare himself modestly to a guard in a museum: "Since then, I exist in the role of an overseer in a gallery, who, among other things, has to see to it that the curtains in the windows are correctly opened and closed so that the few great works of the tradition are more or less properly illuminated for the randomly gathering spectators. Without the picture—I only read and work on the history of philosophy; i.e., I attempt to lay out what seems important to me for loosening up philosophizing without considering the economy of the lecture."[102]

The job offer from Berlin allowed Heidegger to improve his working conditions in Freiburg: "I have obtained the same dispensation, reducing my duties to a very precise weekly schedule; and moreover, something Berlin did not give me, the assurance that in the coming years I will be granted *two* (nonconsecutive) semesters of leave."[103] Thus he was able to stay longer at Todtnauberg, thanks to his sabbatical in the autumn of 1932. Despite its pleasures, despite the identification with Alemannia, Swabia, or Baden to which he sometimes laid claim,[104] the city at the foot of the Black Forest was not his city of choice, because he had experienced the wandering and exile of someone who did not have the strength to stand firm in Berlin, so as to govern philosophically his homeland and his people there. Freiburg was only a starting point, but he remained there for the rest of his life. That was not so surprising for a thinker who had said, "Perhaps philosophy demonstrates more clearly and forcibly than other disciplines what *beginners* we all are."[105]

This thwarted move to the metropolis of Berlin can be contrasted to the much more frequent traveling the philosopher was doing because of the global success of *Being and Time.* Heidegger, who was trekking around Germany and Europe, opened himself to a larger world, a source of previously unknown sensations as well as greater celebrity. In September 1928, he went to Latvia to speak on the subject of "Kant and metaphysics." "These days spent in Riga," he wrote, "were for me rather difficult, but people there are very friendly and accommodating."[106] "The boat ride from Stettin to Riga was magnificent—the sea was a mirror—so I hardly felt anything of the ocean's vastness. I must say, all in all, the sea strikes me as boring and unimportant—but that is just the one-sided impression of a mountain-dweller."[107] In 1929 the pace accelerated: on 24 January he spoke before the Kant Society of Frankfurt;[108] in March, he was at a meeting in Davos, Switzerland; on 4 December he gave a talk in Karlsruhe titled "The Current State of Problems in Philosophy" before the Kant Society. He repeated this talk in Amsterdam on 21 March 1930, adding another, "Hegel and the Problem of Metaphysics," delivered the following day; finally, there was a lecture tour of Germany in the autumn of 1930:[109] Köln, Wiesbaden, Frankfurt, Göttingen, Bremen, and Beuron.

Of all these trips, the most important was his stay in Davos. Dedicated to pleasure and the treatment of pulmonary disorders, including tuberculosis, since the preceding year this Swiss spa had also offered university courses intended as much to bring together people of different nations, first of all those of Germany and France, as to offer its wealthy clientele high-level entertainment. And it was at the urging of Elfride, who was always enterprising, that the philosopher had gone there.[110] On arrival, he found Davos "dreadful," with "boundless vulgarity in the architecture, a completely random hotchpotch of guest houses & hotels. And then the invalids—."[111] Heidegger was there to give three lectures titled "Kant's *Critique of Pure Reason* and the Task of a Laying of the Ground for Metaphysics"; he could have given more, but since his primary motivation was the skiing[112] (or so he wanted to believe) and the lectures were "strenuous,"[113] he declined to do so in order to ski as much as possible. To the same end, the lectures were pushed back to 5 p.m.[114] so that he could take full advantage of his days in the mountains.

Even though the ski-runs were in poor condition because it had not snowed for weeks, Heidegger was enthusiastic, wholly absorbed in his discovery of the high mountains, accompanied in particular by Kurt Riezler, the registrar[115] at the University of Frankfurt whose acquaintance he had made in January.[116] "Yesterday we did the Parsenn tour; it was indescribably beautiful. [. . .] We climbed to 2,700 and had a descent to 800 m. [. . .] It's wonderful, the wealth of scenery, the views that change completely every 50 m."[117] Physical altitude does not always lead to moral elevation; and society often encourages its members to compare themselves to one another. In this way, skiing with new companions raises the question of each person's relative level. But the philosopher, worried about his ego, was able to reassure himself regarding his incomparable mastery of skiing: "At the beginning I was rather anxious about how it would go, but after the first 100 m. I realized that I was superior to them all, even Riezler, who has skied a lot in the Alps."[118] Heidegger took pleasure in depicting himself as a mountaineer thinker, a philosopher on skis, breaking with the urban elegance of the conferencegoers, with whom he did not feel at ease, perhaps a remnant of his modest, rural origins: "Exhausted by a good fatigue, the sun, and the restored freedom of the mountains, and our bodies completely overwhelmed by the steep descent, the speed of which still whistled in our ears, in the evenings we always barged in, dressed in our ski gear, interrupting the elegance of evening clothes. For most of the lecturers and listeners, this fusion between a research project carried out with rigor and joyous and perfectly relaxed ski excursions was something unprecedented."[119]

Heidegger caused a sensation by his manners as well as his remarks. From the outset, he thought he could tell his wife-impresario that his mission would be accomplished: "I think the non-Germans probably will be as impressed as you hope them to be."[120] Subsequent events seemed to him to confirm this initial feeling: "My third lecture, in which I spoke for 1 1/2 hours without a manuscript, was a great success."[121] The success he enjoyed came less from what he elaborated in these three lectures than from the general attention that surrounded him and the working group in which he participated with Ernst Cassirer, a brilliant representative of neo-Kantianism—still the dominant trend in Germany, from which Heidegger, as Rickert's student, had himself come. Cassirer, a Jew, a Social Democrat, and a defender of the Weimar Republic, belonged to the tradition of universalist, rationalist philosophy issuing from the Enlightenment. He sought to pursue Kant's critique of reason by producing a philosophy of culture and symbolic forms, basing himself on numerous works in the positive sciences, ethnology, linguistics, psychology, and the history of ideas. A few years earlier, he had published the second volume of *The Philosophy of Symbolic Forms,* which was devoted to "mythical thought,"[122] a work that Heidegger had criticized in a note in *Being and Time,* rejecting its use—naïvely positivist in his view—of a multitude of ethnographic studies.[123]

In Davos, Cassirer dealt with philosophical anthropology, taking on the line of thought Heidegger had developed in *Being and Time:* as the summary of his lecture puts it, "basing himself on the problems of space, language, and death, he showed that the human world and thereby man's being undoubtedly have their point of departure (*terminus a quo*), their original foundation, in the world of hard-working action," as Heidegger had developed it, "but that they reach their end (*terminus ad quem*) only in the autonomous, free realm of spirit, and it is there alone that they can unfold their authentic meaning."[124] Cassirer honored Heidegger by making him the point of departure for his remarks, and he was not the only one to do so: "Since [Cassirer] focused his lectures on my book and others also positioned themselves with regard to it, I have become the focal point, in any case too much so for my taste, within the context of a meeting in which the protagonists are present in person. [. . .] The whole thing often took a turn that came dangerously close to a sensational event."[125]

Heidegger himself took part in the general emotion caused by a spirited but civil intellectual confrontation: as the title of his lecture suggested, he accused neo-Kantianism of seeing the *Critique of Pure Reason* merely as a theory of cognition, whereas he saw it as the vanguard of a refoundation of metaphysics on the basis of the existence of *Dasein*. Resuming his attack on Cassirer's project of understanding man through a study of culture, during the discussion he said: "A metaphysics of Dasein directed at the possibility of metaphysics as such [. . .] must pose the question concerning the essence of human beings in a way which is *prior* to all philosophical anthropology and cultural philosophy."[126] The discussion bore chiefly on Heidegger's thinking, and he too took part; finitude, anguish, and the task of philosophy were central to the discussion. Cassirer, a humanist and an optimist, maintained that philosophy should "allow man to become sufficiently free, to the extent that man can just become free," thereby permitting a radical liberation from "anxiety as mere disposition."[127] By contrast, Heidegger, the hard-nosed existentialist, posited that philosophy's task consisted of "throwing man back [. . .] into the hardness of his fate from the shallow aspect of a man who merely uses the work of the spirit."[128]

Heidegger found this discussion satisfying, and afterward he wrote: "I've just got a two-hour public discussion with Cassirer over with, which went very well &—quite apart from the content—made a big impression on the students."[129] Indeed: one of them, Otto Friedrich Bollnow, found it "breathtaking," the audience having "the exciting feeling of witnessing a historic scene,"[130] the kind one recounts years later to one's posterity. All the same, Heidegger regretted his opponent's good will and openness to dialogue: "Cassirer showed himself to be very distinguished and almost too obliging in the discussion. As a result, I met with too little resistance, which prevented me from giving the problems we took up all the necessary complexity in their formulation."[131] To be sure, he loved to strike a pose, to point out the inadequacy of the debates and the nullity of their contribution for himself and others. Nevertheless, his assessment of his visit to Davos was excellent: "Although there's basically nothing for me to be learnt here—I'm still very glad to join in with such things now & again—one's versatility, one's handling of people & a certain outward assurance do benefit."[132] In addition, he had the feeling he had made a true friend, Kurt Riezler: "The registrar, with whom I've become really good friends, would like to keep me on here afterward. Perhaps he's the man I'm looking for as a friend—& if that were the outcome of this conference—it'd be a matter of great inner happiness to me."[133]

In Davos, where he was the center of attention, Heidegger's celebrity reached an initial high point. That celebrity opened the way to France and Holland. Among the French people present were Léon Brunschvicg, a professor at the Sorbonne who gave lectures there, and three students: Jean Cavaillès and Maurice de Gandillac, who were seeing him for the first time; and Emmanuel Levinas, who already knew him. For Cavaillès, "it was with a genuine intellectual joy that the audience was able to listen to Heidegger, whose ardor, seemingly stimulated by the objections, [led him] to define in impressive formulations the meaning of *Dasein* in his doctrine, to situate the place and function of truth in metaphysical reality, and finally, to bring out the role of anguish as revealing man's finitude and the presence of nothingness."[134] Probably on the basis of the account Brunschvicg had given him, Georges Gurvitch, who had taught a course on contemporary philosophy at the Sorbonne, was able to complete his survey by including Heidegger, even going so far as to present him as "the most influential philosopher in Germany today."[135]

In Davos, Heidegger had made the acquaintance of Dutch colleagues,[136] including Hendrik J. Pos, who participated somewhat in his debate with Cassirer; these colleagues invited him to Amsterdam on 21 March 1930, and again the following summer.[137] Heidegger indulged in some tourism, visiting Nordwyik and The Hague. An afternoon spent in Zandvoort led him to exclaim: "The sea & the dunes—but the beach! You're right, I wouldn't have stood it for long & above all I wouldn't have got down to any work."[138] And yet, despite moments of friendship with his hosts Pos, Vanoli, Van de Hoop, and the Van der Horsts, his overall assessment was negative: "This time, Holland in general gave me much more an impression of self-satisfaction and indolence."[139] Nonetheless, in Amsterdam he spent two mornings in the museum looking at a Van Gogh exhibition. His taste for storm scenes, combined with the quality of the work, led him to prefer a wheat field in a storm to *Irises*. He also had the "really big surprise" of suddenly finding himself "in front of one of Rodin's

'Burghers of Calais'—the one clasping the key in his hands." During these years, Heidegger had acquired a true aesthetic love for the French sculptor, which further increased his interest in this visit to the museum, so that "the two mornings spent with these works" were for him "what was most rewarding & lasting."[140]

For a rooted philosopher, Heidegger moved around a lot. His roots deeply sunk in the Swabian-Alemannic soil allowed him to visit places as far away as Davos, Amsterdam, Berlin, and Riga. From the outset, he followed Elfride's lead: the first lecture he gave outside the city where he lived was delivered in Wiesbaden, where his in-laws lived—lectures on Spengler that he considered "burdensome"[141] because of his subject, which suggests they were given at Elfride's urging. Next, she became enthusiastic about the idea of going to Japan; her motivation was probably her desire for a "broadening of horizon,"[142] a desire her husband did not share to nearly the same extent. The discussion in Davos, or in any case the attempt to find there an international audience and opening, also originated with Elfride.[143] Conversely, her husband, needing tranquility for his work, liked to remain far away from her and the children. In September 1922, he had stayed in Freiburg alone while his family was in Todtnauberg: "My Dearest Soul, I'm really longing to see you—& it *isn't at all nice*—alone in the flat—but marvelous for working—I have to come to terms with this contrast. Fortunately I don't have much time to ruminate on it."[144]

Elfride saw to material comfort, the proper running of the household, the calm necessary for his work—without which, Hermann said later, Heidegger would not have become such an important man.[145] The boys were not allowed to make noise in the house, or to shout in the garden, or to invite friends over to play.[146] Elfride shared character traits with her mother-in-law, as her husband himself noted, considering her similar to the portrait of his mother that he had sketched in "The Fieldpath."[147] Like Johanna Heidegger, Elfride was cheerful, but not always easy to get along with, because she was authoritarian, severe, and overprotective. Her younger son felt free only in his tent, when, as a preadolescent, he went to youth camp.[148] Her husband needed other women to hold up flattering mirrors that gave him the additional confidence and energy he would need if he hoped to change the course of things with his intellect, but it is likely that these extramarital relationships also gave him an authority and freedom he lacked at home.

His mistresses' influence could be seen in the flighty philosopher's travels: in early August 1926, Hannah Arendt seems to have made him stop in one of the cities (Weinheim, Mannheim, or Heidelberg)[149] that the express train passed through on his way from Marburg to Switzerland, where Husserl had invited him to spend a week. In January 1928, at the urging of Elisabeth Blochmann, Heidegger considered going to Berlin.[150] Each of his mistresses' hold on him reached its limit in the temperament of the philosopher, who moved from one woman to another: when in early January 1928 he wrote *Volo ut sis* to Blochmann, echoing Saint Augustine, his pen merely formed the same letters of the same Latin phrase he had addressed to Arendt a month earlier.[151] Elfride was, in a way, only *prima inter pares,* as she learned to her sorrow in the summer of 1930. This caused a fissure in their relationship, and Heidegger, who was supposed to join his family in August on the island of Spiekeroog, in the Baltic, in the end did not do so.[152] Henceforth he felt compelled to address his wife with greater distance and so wrote "My dear Elfride," and no longer "My Dearest Soul."

In this game with countless players, Elfride remained the pivot of her husband's existence. She succeeded all the better in holding onto him because she benefited from the help of her two sons. Hermann's memories are inconsistent, but they agree on one point: Heidegger was "cheerful and affectionate." In 1996 the first memory relating to his father that occurred to Hermann[153] was the habit of meeting him for lunch and dinner, because "busy as he was with studying and thinking," meals were the only opportunities for his sons to see him; they talked about soccer, skiing, and what the boys or their friends were doing. In 2014[154] Hermann was more expansive, remembering a ride with his father when he was three years old, sitting in the basket of his father's bicycle. He added that Heidegger was what a father ought to be, playing with his sons, swimming with them in the Lahn River in Marburg, skiing with them. These late memories confirm the impression that emerges from Elfride's letters: Heidegger, though leaving the care of the boys chiefly to their mother, sometimes took pleasure in spending time with them.

Encountering the Ascendant Nazi Movement in Berlin

Rumor, an amorous specter throwing her loose-fitting, shape-shifting, filmy veil over everything and peddling by word of mouth the most diverse gossip, transmitting it faithfully or treacherously, fell in love with Heidegger in 1932 and wended her way far beyond the halls of the University of Freiburg. René Schickelé, an Alsatian author who wrote in German, reported in his diary the rumor that "Heidegger no longer associated with anyone but National Socialists" at the time[155]—which astonished the writer. Another, similar rumor reached Hannah Arendt's ears: the philosopher, driven by a fanatical anti-Semitism, was alleged to be excluding "Jews from the seminar invitations" and no longer saying hello to Jews[156]—which Heidegger expressly denied. A few months earlier, his former teacher Husserl had taken it for established fact that Heidegger had converted "to National Socialism and to a sudden anti-Semitism."[157] One final rumor: he was said to be a Party member, and Rudolf Bultmann questioned him about it. Heidegger strongly denied the rumor: "That I'm a member of the NSDAP is a latrine rumor—as we said in the army—that has lately been spread by all and sundry, seeing that I've already received numerous questions of this kind. *I am not a member of that party* and will never be one, any more than earlier I was a member of any other party."[158]

These rumors may have some foundation in truth that the historian can hope to discern in hindsight, if the sources allow it. The rumor Schickelé heard—that Heidegger no longer associated with anyone but National Socialists,[159] was clearly an exaggeration, but it denotes the broadening of his relations to academics closely connected with the NSDAP, which probably occurred following Fatherland Day in Baden, held in Karlsruhe from 11 to 14 July and organized by the Badische Heimat e.V. association. This patriotic event celebrated the withdrawal of French troops from the left bank of the Rhine, the premature end to one of the most important provisions of the Treaty of Versailles. The honorary president of the organizational committee was Eugen Fischer (1874–1967), a physician and eugenicist who since 1927 had been the director of the Kaiser Wilhelm Institute of Anthropology, Human Genetics, and Eugenics (Kaiser-Wilhelm-Institut für Anthropologie, menschliche Erblehre und Eugenik) in Berlin. It may have been at that point that Fischer established friendly ties with Heidegger, which were severed only after the war, with Fischer's death.[160] Among the speakers was Ernst Krieck, a schoolteacher who had become a university professor specializing in pedagogy and an early Nazi for whom Heidegger had limited esteem, but whom he saw as an ally when the Third Reich was being established. Another relationship of uncertain origin, but which began in the early 1930s and was more important for the philosopher, was that with Alfred Baeumler, who had been one of the founders of the Combat League for German Culture (Kampfbund für deutsche Kultur), under the leadership of the Nazi ideologist Alfred Rosenberg, who put him in charge of a scholarly institute.[161] Since 1930, Baeumler had been trying to enlist, post mortem, Friedrich Nietzsche as a Nazi philosopher, by writing *Nietzsche, Philosopher and Politician*[162] and editing Nietzsche's writings, letters, and accounts[163] to make them serve this scholarly falsification. In 1932, Baeumler was an essential source of information and indoctrination for Heidegger, who held in great esteem his "very fine little booklet"[164] on Bachofen; Erich Rothacker, who had included this sixty-page collection in his series,[165] had perhaps introduced the two men, unless it was Niemeyer, the publisher they shared, who had done so.

The rumor Schickelé had heard was based on the reality of Nazi relationships that Heidegger had established at that time, whose number is difficult to determine, and that reflected his newfound affinity with the NSDAP. As Heidegger wrote of the Party in December 1932 to his friend Bultmann, "I consider many things about it *very positively*."[166] This affinity for "Nazi radicalism" had begun early on; without saying why, his disciple Hans-Georg Gadamer traced it back to "well before 1933."[167] We can infer that it made its appearance in 1930, based on the invaluable *terminus ad quem* provided by a letter the philosopher sent to his wife as he was passing through Wiesbaden in early October: "I happened to have a *Völkischer Beobachter* with me. Father was very interested in it."[168] The *Völkischer Beobachter* had been the Nazi Party's official newspaper since 1920; Heidegger might have obtained an issue out of curiosity. But no, he "happened to have" an issue because it was not unusual for him to have one: the philosopher was reading the Nazi daily because it was his newspaper, even though he might sometimes go without reading newspapers, as when he was staying at Beuron.[169] Moreover, as he had done with his brother, to whom he gave a copy,[170] Heidegger proselytized, showing one to his father-in-law, who was "very interested in it."[171] Thus, only a few months after Fatherland Day in Baden in July 1930, the philosopher was in all likelihood an NSDAP voter, as suggested by the fact that he read the Party's newspaper regularly.

On 25 September 1930, the front page of the issue of the *Völkischer Beobachter* that Heidegger gave his father-in-law rejoiced that, in the Reichstag elections of 14 December, the Nazi Party "took 1,380,000 votes away from the Marxists."[172] This figure was false, but served to spark the imagination: although the SPD (Social Democratic Party) had lost 600,000 votes since the elections of 20 May 1928, when voter participation had increased, the KPD (German Communist Party) had gained 1,300,000. The electoral success of the two revolutionary parties, the NSDAP and the KPD, was striking: the Communist Party's representation rose from 54 to 77 seats in the Reichstag, while that of Hitler's party rose from 12 to 107 seats. This remarkable electoral breakthrough resulted from a conjunction of factors, crises that favored extremism on the left as well as on the right.

In 1930, the Weimar Republic was taking a harder line: a day after the Social Democratic Chancellor Hermann Müller resigned on 27 March, the monarchist president, Hindenburg, named Heinrich Brüning to be chancellor, because, although he belonged to Zentrum, one of the three Weimar coalition parties (along with the SPD and the DDP) that had founded and supported the new German democracy, he was on the conservative fringe closest to the views of the president and his entourage; he did not shrink from an authoritarian interpretation of the constitution based on the regular use of the president's extraordinary powers, such as legislation by decree and the dissolution of the Reichstag.

Fresh elections took place in September 1930, because the president had dissolved the Reichstag in the hope that elections would produce a legislative majority that would support him, despite the poor economic and social situation: unemployment had been high since 1929 and was increasingly exacerbated by the indirect effects of the American stock market crash. In January 1930, 3.2 million Germans, or 14 percent of the active population, were unemployed; if short-term unemployment is included, the number stood at 4.5 million.[173] This desperate situation favored the extremes, and many voters, worried, were tempted to turn to alternative, radical solutions to remedy the country's woes. The NSDAP took advantage of this all the more because it had benefited from the 1929 campaign against the renegotiation of the Young Plan, a program that arranged Germany's reparations for the First World War. Hitler, who was still relatively little known in 1928, had increased his audience throughout Germany by traveling all over the country to demand the cancellation of reparations pure and simple. This campaign was financed by Alfred Hugenberg, a media magnate and the head of the DNVP (German National People's Party), who also gave Hitler a prominent place in the columns of his newspapers.[174]

Heidegger's conversion to Nazism took place in the summer of 1930 and was part of a groundswell: many voters, especially on the right, including the elites, turned toward Hitler's party. It remains for us to understand why.

A regular reader of the *Völkischer Beobachter,* the philosopher was not unreceptive to Nazi propaganda. Thus, in the brief review he wrote for his wife on the issue of 25 September 1930 that he had shown to his father-in-law, he pointed out the reference to the Leipzig trial. This trial involved three Reichswehr officers whose Nazi inclinations led to their being indicted for conspiring with the NSDAP; it was feared that the Party might stage another putsch to overthrow the government with the help of the army. Hitler was called as a witness, which gave him an opportunity to vigorously protest that his party was committed to legality in its efforts to take power. As in the case of his trial in 1924, the courtroom was an ideal platform from which to advocate his ideas before numerous attentive journalists. The partisan *Völkischer Beobachter* further magnified Hitler's performance as a people's spokesman seeking respectability, a brilliant media success that Heidegger believed was already "recoiling upon its notorious prosecutors."[175] Transported in his mind to the courtroom by the Nazi daily, the philosopher took no distance from it, admiring the reversal achieved by the peerless orator that Hitler could be, though in reality the three officers were all found guilty a few days later.[176]

Propaganda was one of Hitler's main assets; he knew how to deploy considerable means for impressing voters. Leni Riefenstahl would move closer to Nazism after attending Hitler's speech at the Sportpalast on 27 February 1932.[177] Already won over to the cause, Heidegger was greatly impressed by the preparations for the celebration in honor of Hitler that was to take place in Wiesbaden in 1930: "Everywhere huge placards saying 'We're on the attack!' "[178] Besides, according to Karl Jaspers's testimony in his *Philosophical Autobiography,* written during the 1950s, his friend was also drawn to the demagogue's hands. "How could a man as uncultured as Hitler govern Germany?" Jaspers is supposed to have asked Heidegger. The latter, fascinated, is said to have replied: "Culture isn't important at all, [. . .] just look at his marvelous hands!"[179] Hitler's virtuoso use of his hands was one of his chief rhetorical assets: he knew perfectly well how to play a scene, skillfully using hand gestures like an actor to heighten his expressiveness. The American journalist William Shirer, who had gone to hear Hitler's speech to the Reichstag, which was convened in the Kroll Opera House on 19 July 1934, made this laudatory and therefore instructive comment: "I've often admired the way he uses his hands, which are somewhat feminine and quite artistic. Tonight he used those hands beautifully, seemed to express himself almost as much with his hands—and the sway of this body—as he did with his words and the use of his voice."[180]

Heidegger, who allowed himself to be impressed, ended up reading *Mein Kampf,* which he gave as a Christmas present in 1931 to his brother, who remained loyal to Zentrum, as did most of the residents of Meßkirch.[181] In his letter conveying his good wishes, Martin stressed, to be sure, how "weak"[182] he found the autobiographical chapters at the beginning; but he did not have praise high enough to express his approval of "the sure and extraordinary political instinct" of the author as it emerged in the rest of the work: "He already had it when we were all still lost in the fog, no lucid person can contest that. It is no longer a matter of petty partisan politics, but of the salvation or collapse of Europe and Western culture. Anyone who still does not understand that deserves to be crushed in the chaos."[183] Unlike the decisive remedy and protection that Hitler brought to the West, the debates of the time on the future of the German university seemed to him contemptible. Criticism of the universities was a commonplace in Germany, especially on the right: under the title "Is There Still a University?" the *Frankfurter Zeitung* published in December 1931 a series of opinion columns by Eduard Spranger, Paul Tillich, and, notably, Karl Jaspers, with whom Heidegger had been discussing the question since the early 1920s. Although the intellectual convergence ought to have made him look with favor on the columns that Fritz had sent him, Heidegger threw them in the wastebasket, condemning them with a lapidary judgment: "These things are not to be decided in a newspaper."[184] Conversely, repeating Nazi slogans, trusting in Hitler, he concluded: "It seems that Germany is waking up, understanding and seizing its destiny."[185]

Books counted for Heidegger, a man of letters; but more than propaganda or *Mein Kampf,* which he read only later, Heidegger's conversion to Nazism resulted from Elfride's direct influence, just as she had led him to discover the Youth Movement and cultivate a form of anti-Semitism. A close disciple who had come to visit the Heideggers in Todtnauberg, where they resided continuously from Christmas 1931 to March 1932,[186] Hermann Mörchen wrote in his diary that they had conversations in the early evening, before retiring at 8:30 p.m. in a "cabin truce."[187] The subject of discussion, which was unusual, astonished him: not philosophy, but "especially National Socialism." He was surprised that Elfride, "who used to be such a liberal imitator of Gertrud Bäumer"—hence a feminist who wanted to promote women's emancipation, especially through education, something she had wanted for herself—"had become a National Socialist." This despite the fact that the Party assigned the traditional Protestant role to women, the three "K's," *Kinder, Küche, Kirche* (children, cooking, church), as the saying went, and even though Gertrud Bäumer herself was hostile to the NSDAP. What surprised Mörchen even more was that "her husband follows her!"[188] Mörchen's account is clear: Elfride Heidegger went so far as to induce her husband to sympathize with Hitler's party; as Mörchen tells it, Elfride directed the discussion, while Martin followed. Mörchen's account corroborates what we can discern elsewhere: completely absorbed by his philosophical relation to the world, Heidegger depended heavily on his wife for everything that had to do with "natural life"[189] and the world outside philosophy, tending to withdraw into his intellectual pursuits: in June 1932, he wrote to his wife that he was keeping "everything at arm's length."[190]

Because we do not have free access to the sources, we know relatively little about Elfride herself. According to Günther Anders's testimony, she started supporting the NSDAP in December 1923, when the Heideggers were moving into the cabin in Todtnauberg.[191] This cannot be ruled out, but in the absence of a corroborating source it is best to be cautious. *Testis ullus, testis nullus.* She had long been filled with a *völkisch,* anti-Semitic nationalism propitious for Nazism: the choice of Germanic first names for her sons, Jörg and Hermann, was consistent with that—especially Hermann, a German form of Arminius, the Germanic hero in the struggle against Rome, equivalent to the victorious Vercingetorix in the national mythology of France or his English counterpart, Boudica.

A letter dated 12 January 1932 and addressed to Elfride's best friend, Elfriede Lieber, nicknamed "Friedel," provides some sense of when Heidegger's wife began to sympathize with the NSDAP—1926 or 1927, a time when its national audience was tiny—and to understand the reasons with a force and clarity that her husband's motivations lacked, given his political ignorance.

Elfride began by pointing out what was at stake in these "questions," namely, the "most serious and most exciting things" in their life, "connected with the destiny" of their people.[192] She vigorously objected to the Weimar government's policy of fulfilling the terms of the Treaty of Versailles (*Erfüllungspolitik*); in domestic policy, she denounced the "reign [*Regiment*] of the lower classes," the "masses."[193] While at the same time suspecting him of having the dissimulation of a "Jesuit," she wanted to be conciliatory toward Chancellor Brüning, who was "perhaps the best man" that Germany had, though his actions were restrained by the influence the left had on him, so that he could not act as he wished.[194] Fundamentally, however, she shared the views of the far right, of Hugenberg's DNVP and Hitler's NSDAP, which she equated with the right; everything they had prophesied, everything against which they had warned "for the past five or six years or even more"[195]—all that had come to pass. "We are a totally disarmed people—threatened on all sides and economically absolutely ruined." Fiercely hostile to France, which had inspired this iniquitous treaty, she also held the Germans responsible for their misfortune: "We didn't say 'no' at Versailles and that [. . .] triggered the curse [*Fluch*] like an avalanche."[196]

That mistake, that cowardice in foreign policy, was, however, only secondary compared with the danger that Bolshevism posed for Germany and "Western culture as a whole." In fact, "Bolshevism is not a new social order, flexible, capable of making compromises, like the age of the French Revolution or so-called 'Western democracy.' It is just as subversive as Christianity was for Germanic antiquity—though in the opposite direction."[197] This letter illuminates the discussion reported by Hermann Mörchen, in which Elfride's influence on her husband was discernible even in his formulations: a Nazi dictatorship was necessary, because "only through such a dictatorship can an even worse one be avoided, namely, communism, which would destroy the whole culture of the individual personality, and subsequently, all culture in the Western sense."[198] The concern about the "culture of the individual personality" was more closely related to the ideals of the Youth Movement than to phenomenological ontology, which was a sign of the role played by Heidegger's wife in the very choice of terms in the conversation.

An ideological hodgepodge, Nazism had borrowed this theme all the more easily in that, during the First World War, the Youth Movement had taken a heroic and military turn. And in *Mein Kampf,* Hitler discussed at length the incontestable role of the person in human history, particularly in relation to art, culture, and politics:

> The movement must promote respect for personality by all means; it must never forget that in personal worth lies the worth of everything human; that every idea and every achievement is the result of one man's creative force[. . . .]
>
> Personality cannot be replaced; especially when it embodies not the mechanical but the cultural and creative element. No more than a famous master can be replaced and another take over the completion of the half-finished painting he has left behind can the great poet and thinker [*der große Dichter und Denker*], the great statesman and the great soldier, be replaced.[199]

This celebration of the role of the genius in human history served as the argument in an anticommunist diatribe, probably based on the fact that the driving force of Marxist history is not competition among exceptional personalities, but merely the changing relations of economic production. Hence, Hitler concluded, "by the categorical rejection of the personality and hence of the nation and its racial content," Marxist doctrine "destroys the elementary foundations of all human culture, which is dependent on just these factors. This is the true inner kernel of the Marxist philosophy insofar as this figment of a criminal brain can be designated as a 'philosophy.' With the shattering of the personality and the race, the essential obstacle is removed to the domination of the inferior being—and this is the Jew."[200] Confronted by this horrific peril, Hitler concluded his work by sowing the seeds of hope: if the NSDAP "becomes more and more aware of the profoundest essence of its struggle, feels itself to be the purest embodiment of the value of race and personality and conducts itself accordingly, it will with almost mathematical certainty someday emerge victorious from its struggle."[201]

Elfride's *völkisch,* ultranationalist, anti-Semitic, and personalist anticommunism won the support of her husband, who, since his Catholic youth, had never shown much sympathy for Marxism either; the "Reds" were not very popular in Meßkirch at that time or afterward. His break with Catholicism did not make him like them any better: in January 1919, Heidegger had been disturbed by the Spartacist attempt at a coup d'état and the "crazy situation" that his "dear homeland" was experiencing;[202] later on, the Bolshevist danger became spectacularly obvious to him in Riga in 1928: "The city has still not overcome the years of war and Bolshevist domination. One senses the strong imprint of the Russians there in many regards, imperceptibly and all the more profoundly. The destiny of the Balts is distressing."[203] If they weren't careful, the Germans would suffer the same distressing fate, all the more surely because communism was well served by an extremely powerful philosophical bedrock: "Behind it is the systematic dialectic founded upon Hegel, which for the moment is still superior in comparison with all the vague & seething stuff of the Nazis."[204] Following the example of the lecture on social democracy that he gave in Meßkirch on 13 April 1913, in which he focused on the "true foundation of this party, its origin," which could be discovered, beneath the superficial appearances of the everyday life of politics, only by a philosophical examination attentive to fundamental concepts, in 1932 Heidegger feared the intellectual power that served as communism's philosophical base, the Hegelian dialectic, which Marx had adopted for his historical materialism.

Bolshevism was primordial not only for Elfride, but also for Baeumler, who accordingly encouraged his friend's fear of the Red peril: "B[aeumler] [. . .] does not consider communism to have been repelled at all—only fragmented for the time being—if a man comes who pulls the cause together he'll be a terrible force."[205] Anti-Marxism was a bridge between Catholicism and Nazism: thus for Baeumler, the standard work had been written by a Catholic and issued by a Catholic publisher: "The best & most informed book on communism is said to have been published here by Herder."[206] He may have been talking about the book by the Jesuit Viktor Cathrein, a thick, frequently reprinted volume titled

Socialism: An Inquiry into Its Foundations and Its Feasibility.[207] But it is more likely to have been Waldemar Gurian's *Bolshevism: An Introduction to Its History and Its Doctrine,*[208] which was more in touch with the Soviet reality of communism that Baeumler was relaying: "Each week Trotsky has a twenty-pfennig booklet published in Germany, in which he gives his opinion on the situation, makes observations, & points the way ahead."[209]

Since 1916, Heidegger had tended to assimilate Marxism and the Jewish spirit, observing the "horrifying" "jewification" of the culture of German universities ("The question of capital though!").[210] That seemed still to be the case in 1932, when he adopted without reservations Baeumler's assimilation of Jews and communism: "B[aeumler] [. . .] does not consider communism to have been repelled at all [. . .] the whole Jewish intellectual world is going over to it now."[211] Elfride also made this conflation of Jews and Marxism, which was a commonplace on the right and far right. Thus she mentioned in her letter the "Judeo-Marxist preparatory work of the SPD in Germany."[212] True, Nazism criticized Marxist materialism in the name of "Idealism," sustained by the German people, but above all it proposed the idea that, by its intrinsically Jewish nature, Bolshevism was working like a parasite to destroy the Aryan race and the German people. One of the most painful examples of that effort was said to be the "stab in the back" perpetrated by the Revolution of November 1918. In a paradox that seemed not to bother anyone, many NSDAP and KPD sympathizers or activists moved from one party to the other. For the German far right, Bolshevism was in any case only one of the faces of the global Jewish conspiracy; another was Jewish international finance, which was particularly powerful in Anglo-Saxon countries. In his *Myth of the Twentieth Century,* Alfred Rosenberg claimed that the "great mission of the new German Workers' Movement" was to "uproot Marxist materialism and financial capitalist backing [*die finanzkapitalistiche Rückendeckung*] as an alien, Syrian Jewish plant."[213]

This theory of a conspiracy bringing together largely unrelated men and ideas led Baeumler to say that "the *Berliner Tageblatt* has been a communist paper for a year now."[214] Liberal and noncommunist in its leanings, the daily *Berliner Tageblatt* was edited by an assimilated Jew, Hans Lachmann-Mosse, the father of the German-American historian and specialist in Nazism, George Lachmann Mosse. Despite its liberal orientation, ideologically incompatible with communism, Baeumler and then Heidegger did not reject the idea that what Baeumler considered a Jewish paper was in fact communist: the idea of a global Jewish conspiracy, popularized especially by the forgery known as *The Protocols of the Elders of Zion,* allowed them to endorse the plausibility of the implausible, especially since—if we are to believe Karl Jaspers's account after the fact—Heidegger was convinced of the reality of that conspiracy by 1933 at the latest.[215] This can be easily explained by the fact that he had been reading *Mein Kampf*.

The Heideggers thought that communism posed so great a danger for Germany that Chancellor Brüning's moderate politics would not be sufficient. In the letter to her best friend, Elfride said that the peril was so great that only the NSDAP could cope with it: "In my opinion, the Bolshevik danger has already become so enormous—as has that of the Judeo-Marxist preparatory work of the SPD in Germany—that it can no longer be overcome with decrees, large or small, of a state of emergency—police decrees or objective, rational considerations like those that Brüning represents—but can be controlled—if that is ever possible!—only by a fanatical nationalist movement [*eine fanatische Volksbewegung*] that is ready, at the risk of its own life, to counter violence with violence. And where else could this movement be today, if not with Hitler?"[216] This letter tallies with Hermann Mörchen's account: since "democratic idealism and the conscientious measures taken by someone like Brüning can no longer be effective," it was necessary to turn to the Nazi Party, because "a dictatorship that is not afraid to resort to drastic measures, such as the Boxheim documents," was necessary to thwart communism.[217] These secret Nazi Party documents, revealed in late November 1931, caused a scandal. Written by members of the administration of the Gau Electoral Hesse, they were shown to the police by a renegade *Kreisleiter* (midlevel official).[218] They outlined the steps to be taken by the Party once it was in power: nationalist paramilitary leagues such as the SA were to take over the ministries and apply state-of-emergency measures; in a great many cases, enemies of the German people were to be executed as a way of imposing arbitrary rule by bloodshed and crushing any opposition.

The recourse to dictatorship, force, and even murder by the state, considered normal even in peacetime, was a clear sign of how brutalized European societies had become during and after the war: that was the conviction George Lachmann Mosse developed in *Fallen Soldiers*. This idea is not without foundation: in the 1920s, intellectuals on the revolutionary right advocated dictatorship and violence. The historian Ernst Kantorowicz praised Frederick II's use of force in Sicily, where he restored with the greatest rigor his power over his barons and imposed on his people a unity it lacked. At the end of his account of this Sicilian restoration of royal control, Kantorowicz concluded in these terms: "The example of Frederick II shows everything valuable that a legislator can accomplish by force and violence, on the condition that he knows what he wants."[219] Drieu La Rochelle also saw violence as the only means for doing away with humanity's cultural decadence: "A few men isolated in the modern world, in America, Asia, and Europe, frightened by deficiencies on a continental scale which are not masked by the weak constructs erected on all sides by the consortium of the forces gone astray that we name at random—democracy, capitalism, agnosticism, mechanization, communism—dream of ceasing these half-measures, and are no longer afraid of the word 'destruction.' They do not shrink from desperate means: arming madmen, brutes, these millions of enemies lurking within humanity. Material destruction in a world that is now only material."[220] In the early 1930s, the thinking of German intellectuals of the revolutionary right had become even more radical. For example, according to Carl Schmitt in *Concept of the Political* (1932), it was no longer the time for reflections on dictatorship focused on the use of Article 48 of the Weimar constitution; German democracy was tottering, violence was taking over the streets, and a profound transformation of the government seemed to be under way. Radicalizing the reflections in *On Dictatorship* (1921), *The Concept of the Political* saw the discrimination between friends and enemies as a reality preexisting the state.

Favorable to a violent dictatorship, Heidegger did not see communism as the only enemy of the German people and its salvation: definitely anticommunist, he was even more irreligious and anti-Catholic. In early October 1930, he did not mention the votes supposedly taken from the "Marxists" to which the *Völkischer Beobachter* referred; by contrast, he paid considerable attention to the hostility to Zentrum, the Catholic party of the "center"; thus he reported that "in the *Völk. Beobachter* even Hindenburg is warned not to get too involved with Brünning [*sic*]. All in all, the front against the Center is fierce."[221] Chancellor Brüning, a member of Zentrum, was a special target for the NSDAP, which had within it an irreligious group; above all it wanted to bring down the government, using all available means to feed the fire that would consume this reviled democracy.

The anti-Zentrum violence that he read about in the *Völkischer Beobachter* seemed not to displease Heidegger, whose political anti-Catholicism took a violent turn in June 1932 in a heated debate with Blochmann; the philosopher had legitimately given his friend "the impression that he was politically biased."[222] As a later letter to Fritz shows, a month afterward Heidegger was still feeling a strong, cold scorn that suggests his furious wrath when confronted with Blochmann's esteem for the chancellor: "I don't know how much your political opinions have evolved—but I suppose you are not among Brüning's admirers and that you leave Zentrum to the women and Jews as their refuge."[223] The target of this caustic remark, Blochmann supported the chancellor, whose second cabinet collapsed on 30 May,[224] because she was also afraid of the communist threat. In the later letter he sent her, Heidegger made his position clear a posteriori:

> I was not targeting thereby Zentrum's policy over the past two years—but rather the Zentrum that I have come to know to my detriment ever since my earliest childhood—along with the Catholic Church and its material possessions, which is something else again. There is no need to dilate on that subject. Thereupon, Bismarck wrote in his *Thoughts and Memories:* "I have acquired the impression that the partisan, sectarian spirit *that providence has given to Zentrum instead of the national feeling imparted to other people* is more powerful than even the pope."
>
> Communism, for example, may certainly make us tremble, but what is clear is that Jesuitism is—excuse the expression—diabolical.[225]

Inspired by Bismarck, whom the Nazis claimed to follow, and breaking with memories of his Catholic boyhood, Heidegger now adopted a view typical of *Kulturkampf,* seeing the Catholic party as a foreign agent more dangerous than communism because it had been at work for decades and continued to try to weaken the German people spiritually by favoring liberalism and intellectual mediocrity. In the face of this forgetting of the essential distress of *Dasein* and the increasing mediocrity of the culture of the time, and in view of the need to repeat the great early days of philosophy in Greece, Catholicism, with which he had broken long before, was a danger even greater than the threat of communism his wife painted for him.

Whereas Heidegger's rejection of religion brought him closer to Nazism and to Baeumler, it distanced him from the DNVP and the German nationalists, who saw themselves as Christians: "What seems most dangerous & obstructive to Baeumler is the *Christian* affectations of the German nationalists. Yet we want to try to bring together the people who share an inner bond."[226] Heidegger shared Baeumler's anti-Bolshevism, as well as his hostility to Christianity; and like Baeumler, he was aware of a deep affinity between the Nazis and these anti-Semitic, reactionary ultranationalists.

The alliance between the two parties was strategic; Hitler did not want to tolerate any party other than his own once he had come to power, because in his view "the philosophy [*Weltanschauung*] is intolerant; it cannot content itself with the role of one 'party beside others,' but imperiously demands, not only its own exclusive and unlimited recognition, but the complete transformation of all public life in accordance with its views."[227] The Nazi Party wanted a right-wing revolution that would sweep away political parties, the bourgeoisie, Marxism, and Jews, by appealing to the resolute and disinterested commitment of young people. "Above all," Hitler trumpeted in *Mein Kampf,* "we appeal to the mighty army of our German youth. They are growing up at a great turning point and the evils brought about by the inertia and indifference of their fathers will force them into struggle. Someday German youth will either be the builders of a new folkish state, or they will be the last witness of total collapse, the end of the bourgeois world."[228]

Heidegger shared the antibourgeois[229] cult of youth[230] and the rejection of political parties that were so strong in Nazi ideology. He was "apolitical" even if he didn't use the word, which did not mean that politics was of no interest to him. As he wrote to Blochmann two weeks later, he was "very far from affirming that 'politics' and debates of this kind are unfettered and subsidiary in themselves."[231] He simply rejected liberal democracy, the role of parliament, and the participation of the masses and political parties in political life. In *Being and Time,* he left no room for democratic discussion or parliamentary debate; authenticity required decision as an instantaneous rejoinder, the seizing of a destiny. In his view, therefore, the Weimar Republic was the reign of *das Man.* The vehemence of Heidegger's reply to Bultmann regarding his supposed membership in the NSDAP proceeded from his rejection of the idea of being a member of any party whatever, and not from an aversion to Nazism itself: quite the contrary. Because he and Bultmann were great friends, Heidegger admitted to him in confidence that, though he was not a member of the Party, he was also not hostile to it, and even on the whole approved of the orientations of Adolf Hitler's movement: "Indeed, I consider many things about it *very* positively, entirely along the lines of what you write." In his letter of 14 December 1932, the theologian had in fact communicated his view of Nazism, which he initially saw as a movement unlike the ruling parties, which were corrupt and sources of disorder and division.

This radical critique of the Weimar government was one of the main elements in Nazi ideology, and more broadly in that of the reactionary right. In the preamble to its twenty-five-point program made public in Munich on 24 February 1920, the NSDAP accused the other parties of trying to ensure above all else their own perpetuation, and to that end, to multiply programs artificially maintaining "the masses' dissatisfaction." In point 6, it said it would "combat the corrupting parliamentary economy, officeholding only according to Party inclinations without consideration of character or abilities"; and in point 25 it concluded by indicating the manner in which the preceding measures were to be carried out: "the formation of a strong central power in the Reich."[232] The future projected for the Germans' imagination was that of a prosperous people welded together in a popular community (*Volksgemeinschaft*), directed with energy, competence, and devotion by its leaders (*Führer*).

The hostility to democracy, parliament, and political parties, said to be responsible for all Germany's ills, had been central to Nazi propaganda since the elections of 1930,[233] and though the NSDAP, like all the other parties, now agreed to use the ballot box to fight for control of parliament, it did not support the regime. Hitler made that clear in his speech in Munich on 16 September of the same year. Unlike the parliamentary parties that saw the parliament as an "end in itself," for the NSDAP it was merely a "path toward [its] goal," a detour made obligatory by the constraints of the constitution. This first great electoral victory, in which the Party increased its share of the vote from 2.6 percent in the Reichstag elections of 1928 to 18.3 percent in 1930, was for the Nazis only a new "weapon"[234] to be used in their struggle, merely a strategy for seizing power through the parliament that would ultimately be its victim.

Heidegger's political attitude, like that of many academics and writers hostile to political parties and parliamentary democracy, extended to "intellectuals." In a letter to Blochmann, he lambasted "this kind of 'politics' that provides such ample materials for discussion among the ranks of the 'intellectuals,' " for whom he had in general very little esteem. The expression "intellectuals" (*Intellektueller*) referred mainly to men of letters who were active on the left; in referring to their "liberalism," Heidegger was probably designating two things: liberal political positions favorable to individual liberties, democracy, and human rights on which the Weimar Republic was founded; and a laxity in spiritual matters, a lack of rigor and courage in the face of the distress of *Dasein,* which led to lukewarm and ill-founded positions and then became the source of this political liberalism. What "intellectuals" called "politics" was thus merely "a literary pretext" resulting from a liberalism interested in things only insofar as they seemed to belong to the "cultural domain,"[235] because the torrent of their writings sought to escape, through a politics of culture, the harshness of being in which the life of the people had to be grounded. Heidegger, the promoter of an essentially philosophical political project that sought precisely to revolutionize the German people's spirit, thought he could distinguish himself from these intellectuals because he did not seek refuge in culture, but rather rooted himself powerfully in his own existence.

Perhaps in referring to "intellectuals" Heidegger was thinking of Thomas Mann, whose *Magic Mountain*[236] he had read and liked. Although the second volume of this novel had somewhat disappointed him,[237] he had "read the first volume straight through."[238] Mann, who had won a Nobel Prize in 1929, was a famous writer and a particularly influential intellectual who had joined the DDP (center-left republicans). On 17 October 1930, he had given, in Berlin, a speech titled "An Appeal to Reason" that denounced Nazism, whose political project seemed to him contrary to the spirit of a cultured people like the Germans. He addressed an "economically ill people" that was losing "healthy political thinking"[239] and beginning to vote en masse for a radical nationalism that was turning its back on the German nationalism of the nineteenth century, shot through with "strong cosmopolitan and humanistic subtleties,"[240] in order to embrace a "barbarism"[241] and "fanaticism" in a grotesque style[242] of militarism that was the opposite of German culture.

Contrary to Thomas Mann, in 1932 Heidegger was an ardent supporter of Nazism: his political sympathies were all the more in evidence in his letter to Bultmann of 16 December because his criticisms concerned only " 'cultural' matters" regarding which the "spirit" and the "standards" of the Nazi Party inspired "great reservations"[243] in him. By contrast, his theologian friend was severe in judging the turn taken by the NSDAP, which was now playing the electoral game in order to establish itself on the political scene:

> Personally, I do not understand why the National Socialist movement has become a "party." The authentic movement was and perhaps still is something grand, with its instinct for details, the feeling of solidarity and discipline. But must these strengths be used for the Party's electoral battles? Was it necessary to return to speeches and publications on the same lamentable level as in other parties? Is it necessary, where the Party wins, as in my region of Oldenburg, to now go back to the same corruption that is once again inherent in political parties? Can we be surprised if the voter base—whom the Party, precisely *qua* party, is compelled to win over—is a rabble like the voter base of the other parties?[244]

The relative disappointment Bultmann expressed coincided with that of a certain number of voters: whereas in the elections held on 31 July 1932 the NSDAP had won 230 seats out of 608, its best showing in a free election, it obtained only 196 seats in the elections of 6 November. To Bultmann's dismay, he discovered that it was a party not unlike the others, corruptible and worried about its base. Many voters also had questions about the Party's strategy, which seemed a dead end: Hitler, intransigent, could not take over the chancellery so long as Marshal Hindenburg refused to appoint him; the Nazi practice of obstruction seemed purely negative, preventing the country from functioning without being able to lead it in another direction.

For his part, Heidegger saw the obstacles that separated the NSDAP from power, and he adopted a partisan, anti-Semitic point of view. After the shock of the major electoral success in July, Hindenburg's humiliating rejection, on 13 August, of a cabinet headed by Hitler, and the unrest at the time sparked by the murder in Potempa, a village in Upper Silesia (five members of the SA had killed a Polish Communist worker in front of his own mother and were later sentenced to death), it "was clear that all the Jews [. . .] were regaining control and gradually freeing themselves from the state of panic in which they found themselves."[245] These episodes of conservative resistance, in the face of the National Socialist danger, and of Marxist agitation, which Heidegger interpreted as a Jewish reaction, were followed by another, similar episode on the eve of the November elections: when Chancellor Franz von Papen received the public support of 339 industrial magnates acting together under the slogan "With Hindenburg for the people and the Reich!" Heidegger concluded: "The fact that the Jews succeed with a maneuver like the Papen episode shows how hard it will be in any case to overcome everything connected with big capital and everything that is big in general."[246] Pessimistic, Heidegger also saw hindrances in the NSDAP itself: "In addition, there are the ahistorical aspects of the 'Nazis.' And despite that, despite all the excrescences and dissatisfactions, we have to cling to them and to Hitler. I'm sending you his latest speech."[247]

Even as he pinned his hopes on the Nazi movement, Heidegger himself could not help seeing its limits: he pointed out to his spouse, as he had to Bultmann,[248] how much effort the Nazis required.[249] Intellectually, they had nothing solid, only "vague & seething stuff."[250] He took his criticisms in part from Baeumler: "According to his reliable sources, the Nazis are still very narrow-minded in all cultural-spiritual matters—technical college & school of character [*Fachschule und Charakterschule*]—this formula is meant to solve everything & of course means ruin."[251] The Nazis' cultural project was remote from Heidegger's philosophical conceptions of an ontological return to the Greeks. Higher education as it was supposed to be reformed (notably according to Ernst Krieck, "an upstart elementary teacher full of resentment"), around "technical college" and "schools of character,"[252] reproduced in part what Heidegger objected to in the university's organization: its splintering into specialized, compartmentalized disciplines that uprooted the fundamental unity of science grounded in ontology. In addition, these "schools of character" must have seemed to Heidegger similar to the planned gymnastics courses in Marburg in 1928: they would produce nothing but a hollow nationalist ferment around athletic activities, when what was needed was an education in courage in the face of the distress of *Dasein*.

Heidegger found little comfort in the work of Hans Grimm, whose colonialist novel *A People without Space* (1926)[253] he had liked: "*Grimm*—unsure in his intentions now—he lacks the great *material* appropriate to his new novel."[254] As for the *Völkischer Beobachter,* which Heidegger continued to read, its "standard" was then "again beneath contempt at the moment—if the movement didn't otherwise have its mission, it'd be enough to fill one with horror."[255] Baeumler himself disappointed him "to the extent that philosophically he really is rather weak—good as a historian—excellently informed in the latest movements."[256] Heidegger was not the only one who sympathized with the Nazis while remaining critical of them; for example, at the same time, Wilhelm Stapel wanted to reorient the NSDAP in a Protestant direction.[257] Such views did not run counter to their wishes for the Party's success.

Heidegger did not feel as great an affinity for the NSDAP as he did for *Die Tat* (*Action*), a monthly magazine edited by Hans Zehrer (1899–1966). A Conservative Revolutionary imbued with the Youth Movement's ideals of personality and sacrifice, Zehrer wrote in October 1932 a critique of Nazism of which Heidegger approved. Beginning his article by referring to "the great doubt" that the period's political confusion inspired in him, Zehrer raised "the crucial question" that "troubles the whole personality": "Is what we are experiencing today the result and the goal of a development that consummated the monstrous sacrifice and shook men from head to foot? Is it the end [. . .] of a revolution that began on the first day of August 1914, which annihilated millions of men in the war, in the postwar period, and in the economic crisis, which could have meaning only if it formed new men and new ways of life, and which seems today to have arrived at its goal?"[258] This uncertainty was all the more oppressive because the revitalization of the German people's life as a whole was becoming urgent, and required a revolution to "eliminate this state and establish something new and perhaps creative": in the grip of a mediocre present, would the NSDAP be capable of bearing the heavy burden of leading Germans toward their future? Alas, the NSDAP exhibited "tragic flaws" that disqualified it.

Zehrer thought that the fight against liberalism by means of elections, that is, by liberal means, could lead to nothing but a "dead end." It was necessary to adopt an apolitical strategy, to do away with party politics, in order to have an "authentic discussion" on two levels, institutional and ideological. The first presupposed "gaining a foothold within this state and trying to take part in its work, at least to keep an eye on it." But since Hitler was taking an "all or nothing" stance, rejecting any government of which he was not the leader, Zehrer concluded that the NSDAP had "refused to gain a foothold in the state" and thus "to inform itself about what was actually going on." Because of its extremist strategy, the Party therefore still remained a novice in politics, a common criticism made of it, which Heidegger adopted following Zehrer: "The Nazis don't have any trained [*geschulten*] & experienced people."[259] Recruiting mainly young people, the Party had not the slightest experience of government; for the time being, it hardly knew how to do anything but produce propaganda and intimidate people in the streets.

Ill-informed, it failed even to arouse public opinion; its antigovernment propaganda to mobilize voters for the legislative elections could only be "fruitless," because "the parliament" could "not win anymore." As vague in its goals as it was fiery in its criticism, the Nazi Party lacked the necessary programmatic clarity that alone would have allowed it to enlighten and educate the people "regarding three or four clear objectives" so as to prepare it for incorporation in an "authoritarian state."[260] The Party's organization itself had room for improvement in that regard; but though the NSDAP needed to restructure itself in this way, Zehrer doubted it would have the strength to do so, any more than it would be able to stop talking and finally take action.

Although he felt closer to the *Action* group than to Hitler's party, Heidegger was not in complete harmony with the group. "To be sure, it has become fashionable these days to attack the ancients, even among men whose work and objectives deserve all our approbation; I am thinking in particular of the group around the review *Die Tat*. Even with the best will in the world, I cannot believe in the alleged reform of Protestantism. And so far as antiquity is concerned, it's almost grotesque to see these people confuse the archaic period with the later Roman culture of the pre-Christian era, which would set the tone for the 'world' of the German Gymnasium."[261] Heidegger thus found himself quite alone, without a group or organization that he could join without betraying what seemed to be the future of the German people, the great Greek beginnings of philosophy, from the pre-Socratics to Aristotle, which was so distant from the spiritual decadence of "Roman culture of the pre-Christian era," from which the German and European educational tradition had emerged. As for his own irreligiousness, it could hardly lead him to believe that the future lay in the "reform of Protestantism" that *Die Tat* was promoting.

Critical of the NSDAP, Heidegger was aware that a treatment as radical as a Nazi dictatorship would cause serious damage to culture and science, which might not be able to recover from it; but their condition was so degraded, so mediocre, that there was nothing left worth saving. He based himself on Bismarck's *Thoughts and Memories,* and "above all" on the Greek historians: "I constantly ask myself what we've come to—not only that there's nothing great & essential here—but there's a lack [. . .] of all feeling for standards & rank." The university was at the center of his preoccupations and disappointments; thus he condemned it irrevocably "as a mere institution" that had "long since ceased to have any right to itself—so long as it doesn't change from within. And I no longer believe in that happening."[262]

Heidegger's reflections were also based partly on his experience as a teacher. He had the feeling that he had "lost all contact with youth—not as a straggler—but as one who runs on ahead—." In the vanguard, he felt alone at his outpost, which was certainly a sign of the new life he was breathing into philosophy, but also of how his listeners "here in Freiburg" struggled to follow him so far and so fast: "Even though I have the large lecture hall firmly in my power, I cannot rid myself of the feeling that it passes them by, and if it does hit the mark it's hardly worthwhile."[263] Henceforth, somewhat disillusioned, he thought that the things he had to accomplish "cannot have any effect at all through direct contact—but only through the proper intermediate stages. And these one can perhaps help prepare through one's teaching activity,"[264] but it wasn't at all a sure thing.

Heidegger remained a revolutionary of the spirit and even grew more radical. His teaching would not suffice to transform the German university, nor would his secret, concerted philosophical activity with comrades-in-arms such as Jaspers; he needed to employ superior means. Only a political revolution in Berlin could make a spiritual revolution at the universities possible. Convinced that philosophy was the quintessence and goal of all politics, Heidegger was concerned neither about freedoms nor about civil peace nor about the economic crisis and its tragic consequences for society: the spirit of the age favored mediocrity, and an energetic remedy was required. "However much of an effort the Nazis require of one, it's still better than the insidious poisoning to which we've been exposed in recent decades under the catchwords of 'culture' [*Kultur*] & 'spirit.' "[265] Nazism would allow a clean sweep of modern German culture and its mediocrity, a purely negative though necessary function, because then it could rebuild a culture in contact once more with the grandeur of the earliest days of philosophy in ancient Greece. The establishment of a Nazi dictatorship might introduce the "proper intermediate stages" from which philosophy studies throughout Germany would return to their rootedness in being.

It must be said that Heidegger's political culture and thought were as simplistic as they were radical; they struggled to free themselves from the narrow circle of the university and philosophy. Mörchen had the same intuition, which led him to conclude, regarding his teacher's conversion to Nazism: "I would not have suspected it, but to be frank it's not very surprising. He doesn't understand much about politics, and his disgust with mediocrity and half-measures makes him pin some hopes on the party that promises to do decisive things [. . .]. When one lives at such lofty heights, one doesn't have the same criteria of evaluation."[266]

Although Heidegger sympathized greatly with the Nazi movement, it took him a long time to develop a real inner motivation to become involved; and despite the urgency of a revolution that would take place only through the Nazis, he was reluctant to be distracted from his philosophy. His 1932 summer vacation was extended by a semester of sabbatical leave, of which he wanted to make good use: "This autumn I don't want to interrupt my work time in any way. To that end I've not only declined all invitations and anything that resembles them, but also postponed the trip to Meßkirch until spring."[267] In fact, since June he had done what he could to concentrate on what really counted: Baeumler had arranged to have the German Student Union (Deutsche Studentenbund)—which had recently been taken over by the German Federation of Nazi Students (Nationalsozialistische Studentenbund)—invite Heidegger to its congress, which was to take place in late June at Blankenburg am Harz. Heidegger had declined, believing that because of his work, he could not possibly go for the time being. This led him to the more general awareness of "how necessary it is to undertake wholly primordial & appropriate reflection & work here." He realized "that the immediate necessities of the day—however important they may seem—must take second place."[268] Similarly, he is said to have declined to attend the speech Hitler gave at Freiburg's Mösle Stadium on 29 July, though his wife took their two sons to hear it.[269] Active support for Nazism certainly had its importance, but far less than the preparations for a philosophical revolution that would otherwise have no hope of occurring.

Heidegger remained passive for a long time. Hitler's appointment as chancellor on 30 January 1933 did not lead him to abandon his wait-and-see attitude. With only two other Nazis in the government (Göring as air force minister and Frick as interior minister), the Nazi Führer seemed to be the hostage of the conservatives who, for their part, were counting on manipulating him. The same day, Heidegger's brother, Fritz, wrote to him: "Today, Weimar was buried."[270] The philosopher remained circumspect: "If Hitler succeeds in holding onto his position and thus escaping Papen's control, then that will be the case."[271] This end of the republic seemed to him indispensable because of the Red peril: "Because 'muddling through' [*Gewurschtel*] must come to an end—Weimar—has failed completely against the danger of Bolshevism—which your average Joe of today [*heutige Spießer*] does not always see."[272]

When a fear borders on obsession, there is every likelihood that its object will be realized, not necessarily by an external necessity, but by the psychological force of the conviction sustaining it. When, on 27 February, the Reichstag was set on fire by an unhinged leftist, it was said that this was a Communist effort at subversion, and there was already such widespread belief in its imminence that this seemed obvious to almost everyone. The next day, to thwart the potential for large-scale destabilization, Hitler managed to persuade President Hindenburg to sign a decree concerning "the protection of the people and the state" that suspended fundamental freedoms. The first paragraph of this decree authorized, "even beyond the limits usually set by law," "attacks on individual freedom, on the right to free expression and freedom of the press, and on the right of assembly; violations of the privacy of correspondence and of telegraph and telephone messages; search and seizure orders; as well as restrictions on ownership."[273] The legal foundations for the Nazi dictatorship were laid, particularly since Frick was the Reich's minister of the interior and Göring, who had been president of the Reichstag since the summer of 1932, was minister of the interior for Prussia, a Land that held two thirds of the German population. Members of the SA and the SS, which had recently become auxiliary police units, had complete latitude to violently take over the streets and stop their adversaries from campaigning, on the pretext of maintaining order. Heidegger was in full agreement with Nazi leaders: for his friend Jantzen on 3 March 1933[274] he inscribed a dedication in a copy of Martin Harry Sommerfeldt's *Hermann Göring: A Portrait of a Life,* hagiographic propaganda written in honor of Hitler's quintessential loyalist, Göring.[275]

The elections held on the following 5 March marked a turning point and took place in a coup d'état atmosphere. With the opposition muzzled, Nazi propaganda was particularly effective: the NSDAP benefited from state resources and generous gifts from business moguls worried about instability and the power wielded by Marxist labor unions. Although not brilliant, the election results were good for the movement (43.9 percent); with the help of its ally, the DNVP (8 percent), it won an absolute majority in the Reichstag. Even as the "German revolution"[276] seemed to have definitively brought down the old order and Germany was now covered with red flags bearing a black swastika on a white disk, Heidegger felt a growing need for action: "These days difficult tasks are looming on the horizon, and people are not making things easy for you—even if most of them think that now everything is settled."[277]

As he often did in times of crisis, on 18 March Heidegger went to Heidelberg to see Jaspers, who found him changed. As Heidegger reported to his wife the next day, "he thought that my countenance & general demeanor showed a quiet harmony as never before."[278] Heidegger wanted to believe that this was because of the approach of their sixteenth wedding anniversary and the "inner help" Elfride gave him. It would be more accurate to say that, carried away by the euphoria of the establishment of the Nazi dictatorship, this "quiet harmony"[279] resulted from Heidegger's faith in the forthcoming realization of the philosophical revolution that he had been hoping for since 1918, and that was supposed to revitalize the German people's spirit and root it once again in the soil. At first, Jaspers seemed to share the main lines of his vision: "We—J. & I—have had the old contact & are already immersed in all questions of concern"; his friend was "also quite receptive to the real happenings that constitute the current German revolution."[280] Against the background of a renewed consensus regarding the "inner failure of the university as a unified world capable of exerting an influence," they were both "at a loss" about the "positively practical (the immediate)" effects that Nazism would have. Heidegger attributed their remaining differences to two factors: first, Jaspers's wife was Jewish and he was "tied down" by her, though he saw Germany's "destiny" and the "tasks" incumbent upon it "in a thoroughly German way & with the most genuine instinct & the highest demands"; and second, Jaspers's "intellectuality" had not yet "quite shaken off the Heidelbergian in him." This liberal side caused him to believe that their political engagement should take the form of publications of occasional texts: in this case, he tried to "persuade" Heidegger "to write a pamphlet on the university," whereas Heidegger had a true aversion to such writings subordinated to a "false topicality."[281]

Heidegger did not want to be distracted from the philosophical inspiration that had come to him over "these months of leave," and that made him feel he had found the "most characteristic spiritual form" he needed.[282] "Even though action must be taken as resolutely as hitherto—& more so—in all coming individual decisions in the university," Heidegger did not feel he could "allow a type of action that is 'political' in the narrow sense somehow to become the yardstick for philosophical action. The appearance of being on the outside will stay & yet *only in this way* will it be possible for the metaphysics of German existence [*Dasein*] to become an effectual work in its original affinity with the Greeks."[283] The philosopher, who wanted to pave the way for the great philosophical revolution he had been planning for fourteen years, retained his conviction that his words, if exposed to the current situation, would be drowned out in idle talk: "On the great matters one must keep silence as long as possible."[284]

Heidegger's euphoria was further buoyed by the Enabling Act (Ermächtigungsgesetz) of 24 March, a "law to remedy the distress of the people and the Reich" that gave Hitler complete latitude to enact laws for four years, even in contravention of the constitution (Article 1), with the sole reservation that he could not undermine the president's powers or those of the Reichstag or the Reichsrat, the upper legislative body, as institutions (Article 2).[285] "The process under way is for me—precisely because many things in it remain obscure and uncontrolled—a powerful and unusual occasion for contemplation. It increases my will and the certainty that I am working in the service of a great mission and contributing to the construction of a world grounded in the people. The washed-out, ghostly character of a 'culture' and the unreality of so-called values long ago became, in my view, null and void, whence my search for a new ground in *Dasein*. We will find this ground, and with it the Germans' vocation in the history of the West, only if we expose ourselves to being itself, in a new way and through a new appropriation."[286]

It was a time for new converts. "Everything is 'political,' "[287] they were discovering, and this annoyed Heidegger. They were like blind men who recovered the sight in one eye: did they not understand that this was nothing more than "one path among others of the first revolution?"[288] What was "assuredly for many people the way to a first awakening" was to be followed by a second awakening that would be "far more profound."[289] The political revolution that had just come into being bore within it the seeds of the philosophical revolution, since regenerated matter was not an end in itself but held out the hope that its virtual, consummate forms would see the light of day. The philosopher would be there for this second revolution, which was largely unrelated to the one desired by Gregor Strasser and the SA, aimed at removing the elites from power; it would take place through a dialogue with its two enemies, which, though authentically political, could not be narrowly so: "The debate with 'Marxism' and Zentrum can only get bogged down, in the literal sense, if it does not mature into a twofold debate, first with the sin against the spirit coming from the communist world, but no less with the moribund spirit of Christianity."[290] Whereas journalists and politicians usually care only about the ephemera of events at work in history, it takes a philosopher to discern the true, subterranean forces at work and to combat them; otherwise it was to be feared that "everything would be confined" "to the level of purely fortuitous events,"[291] and that this first awakening, this initial attempt to stand up and root oneself in the German soil and destiny, would fall back, "all other things being equal," into the spiritual torpor of the Second Reich. Brave in the face of these perils, Heidegger wanted to appear confident: "Such fears, in our view, must not reduce all the importance of the process under way, but neither must we consider it certain that our people has already conceived in this way the mission that has secretly been assigned to it—and in which we believe—and found the strengths that will ultimately give it a new energy."[292]

True to the idea of his exceptional destiny, the philosopher thought he bore within himself "a distant readiness"; he would be able "to succeed in providing philosophy with ground and space for decades to come."[293] Nonetheless, he was now alone, abandoned by his old comrade in arms. Whereas at the beginning of Heidegger's stay in Heidelberg, he had believed Jaspers excited about the process under way, in fact his friend had reservations. Piqued, Heidegger now denounced the generational difference: "I've seen that it is possible to write about 'the spiritual situation of the age'[294] without even being affected by the real process under way—indeed, without even noticing it. Although the age difference between us is barely ten years, we belong to different generations; in addition, Jaspers's world has no place for the Greeks—which, in my opinion, amounts to a catastrophe at this point in the world's Western adventure. But from a human point of view, his class and the integrity of his will compensate for these shortcomings at the root of our philosophical antagonism."[295] Nazism was a young people's movement; of the great philosophers, only an old man like Jaspers could fail to see what the fountain of youth being offered Germany was: the Greeks! Heidegger did not know how else to explain the reservations of his friend, with whom he had been in a philosophical duel for ten years; furthermore, this disappointment may have hastened a reorientation of Heidegger's efforts to revolutionize his people's spiritual life. The old were not up to the coming battle; young people had to prepare for the fray on their own, come together, and strike. "So far as the university is concerned," Heidegger wrote, the priority was "to ensure that the torch is passed and to unite the younger generation in the will to form a genuine educational community in which the global destiny of our people will become an extremely urgent task and a mission, the most far-reaching possible. Where everything is alive, not only the right but even the obligation to withdraw into the solitude of one's own hardest work can grow, in order to be able to have a grip on one's time."[296]

When Baeumler seemed to be angry, when Krieck said nothing, and when the ministry in Karlsruhe remained deaf to Heidegger's requests,[297] the philosopher entered into discussions with Nazi academics and students in Freiburg; he would have to take the rectorship by force when the current rector, the theologian Joseph Sauer,[298] finished his term and a new rector, the Social Democratic anatomist Wilhelm von Möllendorf,[299] was about to take office, wholly against the grain of the history of being. The battle promised to be strenuous, because on 12 April Heidegger still felt sidelined, and the environment was not particularly favorable for a philosophical revolution. He "justifiably distrusted the universities," where the "reaction" was becoming more active. But, he wrote, that should not "lead us astray in the opposite direction and induce us to assign missions only to Party members." In any case, he had the bitter pleasure of venting his spleen in front of his university colleagues: "The one and only question—'the most vital (literally!) of all'—that my colleagues are discussing in the university senate is, you'll never guess—the question of salaries. But even those who are a little more alert think first and exclusively in terms of organization and care nothing about the enormous work demanded for an internal reconstruction of the university, which alone can once again give rise to a spiritual world capable of rooting itself in the people as a whole."[300] Heidegger was too much a philosopher to be a good politician; for him, events and institutions in their being had little more substance than the shadows projected on the wall of Plato's cave. All that counted was the sun of being that shone outside, and he claimed he could release all these prisoners who had never known anything but the reign of darkness.

Against all odds, Heidegger managed to become the leader of the University of Freiburg, swept into office by the nazification of the whole of German society, as is suggested by the inscription on his official portrait as rector: "In the course of the general coordination [*der allgemeine Gleichschaltung*] [of Germany], on 21 April 1933 Professor Dr. Martin Heidegger was elected rector of the University of Freiburg im Breisgau."[301]

Under two laws in particular bearing its name, the first passed on 31 March and the second on 7 April, *Gleichschaltung* was supposed to be literally a "coordination" or a "synchronization" of the Länder with the Reich, intended to make the provincial authorities march to the beat of Berlin and thus in fact impose Nazism there. The second law therefore stipulated the appointment of *Reichsstatthalter* (imperial governors or lieutenants), who, being assigned to oversee in the Länder "the political directives issued by the chancellor of the Reich," had control over the government, the parliament, the administration, and the courts. These laws served to legalize and establish in perpetuity the takeover the NSDAP had embarked upon starting in early March, when, on the pretext of unrest that it had itself fomented with its SA and SS, it seized control of the streets and official buildings and raised the Nazi flag over them. Wilhelm Frick, minister of the interior, declared a state of emergency in one Land after another, as the conservatives had done the preceding year in Prussia. Once the provincial institutions had been abolished, *Reichskommissars* (imperial commissioners) were named and assumed power at the local level. In this way, during March and April the NSDAP brought the German people as a whole and all its institutions to heel, silencing its opponents and placing its men in key positions, resorting to intimidation when necessary. On 11 March, Robert Wagner (1895–1946), who had taken part in the Beer Hall Putsch in 1923, became head of the Land of Baden, first as commissioner and then, on 5 May, as imperial governor; he proceeded to nazify public office in Baden. From 11 March on, the Ministry of Religion, Education, and Justice was run by Dr. Otto Wacker (1899–1940), a member of the SS who had previously directed the Party's press office in the region. Dr. Eugen Fehrle (1880–1957), a professor of classical philology in Heidelberg, was placed under his command as director of higher education, while on 10 April Dr. Franz Kerber (1901–1945), the editor-in-chief of the Nazi newspaper *Der Alemanne,* was appointed mayor of Freiburg. Like the municipal authorities, the immediate oversight of the University of Freiburg had been coordinated with the Reich; the university could no longer be run by a Social Democrat who resisted the new regime.

Under these favorable circumstances, Heidegger, who did not belong to the Party, succeeded in establishing himself as its trusted ally at the University of Freiburg, where there were few members of the NSDAP. When, on 3 March, an appeal to vote for the NSDAP was signed by 300 German university professors, only two were from Freiburg, the philologist Wolfgang Aly and the surgeon Alexander Ritschl.[302] In this context, a man with no partisan affiliations could be accepted most easily. Heidegger maneuvered simultaneously in Berlin, Karlsruhe, and Freiburg; his worldwide fame, as well as his allegiance to the new regime, recommended him. In early April, Eugen Fehrle, the director of higher education at the ministry in Karlsruhe, went to Freiburg to meet the outgoing rector, Josef Sauer, and the man elected to succeed him, Wilhelm von Möllendorff. Fehrle did not, however, limit himself to these official representatives of the university, but met with the small group of local Nazi professors. Hugo Ott has found an account one of them wrote referring to the negotiations concerning the future leadership of the university, from which Möllendorf was to be excluded, because he was a "notorious democrat":

> To take the first point raised at our recent discussion, concerning the alliance of National Socialist university teachers, we have ascertained that Professor Heidegger has already entered into negotiations with the Prussian Ministry of Education. He enjoys our full confidence, and we would therefore ask you to regard him for the present as our spokesman here at the University of Freiburg. Professor Heidegger is not a Party member, and he thinks it would be more practical to remain [unaffiliated] for the time being in order to preserve a freer hand vis-à-vis his other colleagues whose position is either still unclear or openly hostile. He is quite prepared, however, to join the Party when and if this should be deemed expedient on other grounds. But I would particularly welcome it if you were able to establish direct contact with Professor Heidegger, who is fully apprised of all the points that concern us. He is at your disposal in the coming days, but I should say that there is a meeting in Frankfurt on the 25th which he could usefully attend as the spokesman for our university.[303]

On 20 April, Möllendorff and the university council resigned in response to pressure resulting from an article in *Der Alemanne,* an unofficial mouthpiece for the NSDAP in Baden. The new rector was ordered to do his part in the nazification of the Land and the Reich as a whole, and not to obstruct the new policy in "staff-related matters":

> [We cannot] imagine how a common ground of trust could ever be established between Professor von Möllendorff and the student body, which is overwhelmingly National Socialist in its sympathies. But even if these differences could be overcome by honest hard work, the resistance to official government policy in Baden, and indeed in Berlin, would lead to the kind of friction that is best avoided in the interest of steady progress. Unnecessary time and energy would also have to be spent in easing

> strained relations. The whole point of *Gleichschaltung* is to avoid this kind of thing: men with a shared aim and purpose are supposed to pool their resources and work together for the attainment of the common goal. There must be no more pulling in different directions, no more dissipation of resources. Nobody who wishes to play his part should be excluded: all the more reason, therefore, to ensure that the common enterprise is not hindered or disrupted by unnecessary opposition. We urge Professor von Möllendorff to seize the opportunity—and not to stand in the way of the reorganization of our university system.[304]

Refusing to collaborate with the new authority by following a political line of which he disapproved, and the object of a veiled threat in the reference to "the kind of friction that is best avoided," Möllendorff withdrew. These were not empty threats: at several points in his diary, Josef Sauer mentions the "unprecedented terror perpetrated against left-wing parties and Zentrum."[305] On 21 April, the day after Möllendorff resigned, he nominated as his successor Heidegger, who was elected by a near-majority of the electoral board. Thirteen of the ninety-three members had been excluded because they were Jewish.[306]

A few days later, on 3 May, Heidegger joined the Nazi Party; his membership card bore the number 3 125 894, backdated to 1 May,[307] which was the last day for joining, registration having been closed to stem the rising tide of applications since March. The elections of 5 March had shown what the new ruling power in Germany would henceforth be, and a great number of *Märzgefallene,* Nazis who "fell in line in March" (just as in France there were the *républicains du lendemain,* "next-day republicans" after the establishment of the Second Republic), joined the Nazi movement, convinced that it was obviously opportune to do so: 1.6 million people joined at that time, and 2.5 million had joined since 30 January 1933.[308] The first of May was also the day when Erich Rothacker and, notably, Carl Schmitt joined the Party. These two new members, Heidegger and Schmitt, were important recruits whose prestige was to serve the NSDAP: in Freiburg, *Der Alemanne* was overjoyed.[309] Karl Bossler, a liberal intellectual, was aware of this and wrote to the Italian philosopher Benedetto Croce: "Heidegger, and along with him Carl Schmitt, the author of books on public law and politics, and a disciple, up to a certain point, of Georges Sorel, have been revealed as the two intellectual disasters of the new Germany."[310] Less critical of the Nazi Party, on 4 May 1933 Heidegger explained to his brother his reasons for joining: "Yesterday I joined the Party, not only because of an inner conviction, but also because I realize that it is only by following this path that a reform and clarification [*Läuterung und Klärung*] of the movement as a whole is possible."[311] By becoming part of the NSDAP, Heidegger wanted nothing less than to change its spirit and become its chief ideologue; his personal work had to be put on the back burner: "At present we do not have the right to think of ourselves, but only of the German people as a whole and its destiny, which hangs in the balance."[312]

III

Is Nazism Germany's Destiny? (1933–1945)

7 • The Rector's Address, or a Self-Portrait of the Philosopher as *Führer*

These opinions and these passions had become for them a kind of new religion which, while encouraging some of the important effects produced by religion, snatched them from selfish egoism and impelled them toward heroic action and devotion.

Alexis de Tocqueville, The Ancien Régime and the Revolution, *trans. Gerald Bevin, p. 157*

The "Horst Wessel Song" resounded in the auditorium, the *aula,* of the University of Freiburg, which had become unrecognizable:

Raise the flag! The ranks tightly closed!
The SA marches with calm, steady step.
Comrades shot by the Red Front and reactionaries
March in spirit within our ranks.
Clear the streets for the brown battalions,
Clear the streets for the storm division!
Millions look upon the swastika full of hope,
The day of freedom and of bread dawns!

The "craggy faces" of Nazi Party officials in "Hitler uniforms"[1] predominated even on the dais, where they eclipsed the elderly wives of the professors, while "the medieval robes, the uniforms, and the flag of the student associations" were mixed with the "grey" and "black of the men of the SA and the SS."[2] When they reached the refrain in the last stanza, the audience gave the Nazi salute, supporting, if not the party whose anthem they were adopting, at least the new Germany that had been imposed so brutally over the past months, the Germany of Adolf Hitler, who seemed to be reconnecting the German people with its destiny. All these worthy professors and their spouses raising their arms made for a curious scene in this often conservative milieu far removed from both the SA's plebeian ideas and the memory of activists who had died in battle against communist or conservative militias. What a tragic contrast with science and scholarship, this evocation of the march in which militants blindly fell in under the constraint of a paramilitary discipline, even as the passage from John 8:32, "The Truth Shall Set You Free," written in gilt letters on the façade of the aula, was seemingly effaced. On that Saturday morning, 27 May 1933, the ceremony during which the new rector was installed in office seemed to announce the end of a world, that of a liberal university devoted to pure knowledge; a new world was coming into view, invoking violence by uniforms and speeches, imposing an allegedly German revolution at the very heart of the university.

The ceremony had begun with the entrance of high Nazi officials of Baden who had held their offices for only a short time: the mayor of Freiburg, Dr. Franz Kerber, and Dr. Eugen Fehrle, director of higher education at the Ministry of Religion, Education, and Justice. These middle-aged men were joined by the determined, baby-faced new minister, Dr. Otto Wacker, who was also a member of the SS. Next, Vice-Rector Sauer said a few words, professing allegiance to the "new situation," while at the same time bidding farewell "to olden times," when they had "fought valiantly for national dignity and the law."[3]

Then it was time for the new rector's address. He moved forward, grave and pale in a red robe.[4] It was a solemn moment. In the auditorium of the university where he had studied after earning his Abitur, and where he had taught continuously up to that point, many people important in his own life were assembled before his eyes. They embodied the three temporalities of his *Dasein:* his students, his wife, and his sons,[5] present along with their close friend Elisabeth Blochmann. His past as a young seminarian was in evidence, not only in the master of ceremonies, Josef Sauer, who had been his professor and had supported his first philosophical efforts, but probably also in his old friend Engelbert Krebs, who was now the dean of the Faculty of Theology, and Conrad Gröber, the archbishop of Freiburg and a "paternal friend" who, having torn him away from their native Meßkirch, had set him on the path of philosophy. His future could also be seen there, with the conspicuous presence of the new authorities, the two other rectors in Baden, Wilhelm Groh from Heidelberg and Hans Kluge from Karlsruhe, as well as his colleagues, some of them, like Walter Eucken, hostile to him and others, like Wolfgang Aly, who had been won over.

The philosopher, like other local supporters of the new regime, wanted to give this transfer of power as much publicity as possible. He had concerned himself personally with the slightest details in this regard. A microphone was supposed to transmit his address: the leaders of the local Nazi district (Kreisleitung), accompanied by "numerous colleagues,"[6] supported the idea of broadcasting it, but this proposal was rejected by Robert Wagner, the Gauleiter and imperial governor, who, as such, had supreme control over the Party and the state in Baden. At least, Heidegger had made sure he would be heard as best he could be. He had rejected the lecture of a biologist colleague, Konrad Guenther, who had proposed to speak on the subject "The Doctrine of the *Heimat* and Germanness" (*Heimatlehre und Deutschtum*);[7] Heidegger had told him that this lecture was not appropriate for the situation, a convenient way of keeping most of the attention on his own address, which was not to be that of an ordinary rector in ordinary times. It had to break new ground by the very pomp that surrounded it. To that end, Heidegger had asked the mayor of Freiburg to bring in forty-five musicians to provide the volume of sound necessary for this historic moment, a volume that would not have been reached by the city's theater orchestra. Thus the ceremony opened, fittingly, with Brahms's *Academic Festival Overture*,[8] sweeping and joyous, and ended with Wagner's *Homage March* (*Huldigungsmarsch*), which was supposed to produce an "impression corresponding" perfectly "to the era,"[9] grandiose and heroic like the late Romantic music of which the new regime was particularly fond.

Imbued with the solemnity of the event, Heidegger then invoked both Greek authors and paramilitary training in a manifesto of an academic philosophy that was as Nazist as it was personal; by teaching his audience what the education of the future *Führer*[10] of the German people should be, he sought to assume the spiritual leadership of the revolution from his lectern. Thus spake the new rector.

Leadership, Leaders, and Followers

"Assumption of the rectorship entails the *spiritual* leadership of this university [*ist die Verflichtung zur* geistigen *Führung dieser hohen Schule*]."[11] By closely intertwining rhetoric, philosophy, and politics, Heidegger applied to the university three inseparable concepts on which the new regime was built: leadership, leaders, and followers (*Führung, Führer,* and *Gefolgschaft*).

Since his student days, Heidegger, who had shown the greatest interest in apologetics, had considered himself an orator and a leader of souls. This interest had become philosophical in his course on Aristotle's rhetoric, given in 1924–1925, in which he described the art of oratory as "leadership of the soul [*Seelenleitung*]," "a guiding of the lives of others by speaking with them and addressing oneself to them."[12] Then the term *Führung* (leadership)[13] appeared, along with its derivatives (*Seelenführung, Führen der Existenz*),[14] used in the rhetorical sense to translate the Greek *psychagogia* (*ψυχαγωγία*).[15] This conception, which was educational in the first place, took, with Nazism, a political turn: in the course he gave in the winter semester of 1933–1934, he declared that "the science related to the power of speech, rhetoric, is the fundamental human science, political science."[16]

When, in his address as rector, he described his task as "*spiritual* leadership," Heidegger showed by his text itself what he might mean by that: the power to speak to everyone from a podium, and thanks to the skill and energy of one's rhetoric, to make oneself fully understood in order to direct minds or spirits. Combining subtle arguments with oratorical figures—metaphors, hyperboles, oppositions, accumulations, and rhetorical questions—the rector's address was one long exhortation, a harangue intended to incite in his listeners the German university's self-assertion, a will to realize its own essence, a resoluteness in achieving "a true and shared rootedeness [*Verwurzelung*] in the essence of the German university."[17] Also used by Alfred Baeumler,[18] Ernst Krieck,[19] and Ernst Horneffer,[20] "self-assertion" was one of the fashionable expressions usually characterizing the community of the people (*Volksgemeinschaft*) putting itself forward as collective will. Adopted by Heidegger to refer to the university, it designated a will to assert oneself not separately or against the rest of the nation, but rather spontaneously and in harmony with it: it expressed the Freiburg academic community's voluntary adherence to the fully German project that its spiritual *Führer* presented to it.

Heideggerian rhetoric was expressed as a polemology that exalted courage and combat (*Kampf*), because "only combat [. . .] implants in the entire faculty and the entire student body the fundamental disposition on the basis of which self-assertion, in defining itself, makes possible a resolute self-meditation to achieve authentic autonomy."[21] Heidegger returned to the martial tone of his conception of philosophy, now transposed to the community of professors and students. Each of them was a *Dasein:* they could make authentic decisions in light of their own deaths, in an inner struggle in the face of their own existence and the distress peculiar to it. And if they did not do so, if they preferred to just go along in a comfortable state of unconsciousness, they would devolve into a mere herd at the mercy of *das Man,* closed off from all true knowledge. The university was a "community of fighters," shot through with tensions between teachers and students. Only these tensions would bring every individual's disposition for struggle to its state of incandescence and thereby hone, necessarily, the "self-assertion"[22] of the whole community.

To reach the high point of his speech, Heidegger enlisted Plato in his military-intellectual brass band: he concluded his exhortation with a quotation from the *Republic,*[23] translating it in such a way as to leave it open to all kinds of interpretations: "Alles Große steht im Sturm."[24] One of these interpretations, "everything great is exposed to storms," was inspired by Nietzsche, who had written similarly: "Examine the lives of the best and most fruitful people and peoples and ask yourselves whether a tree that is supposed to grow to a proud height can dispense with bad weather and storms."[25] Another, "Everything great stands firm under attack," might be understood as both a valorization of war (*Sturm* was the title of one of Jünger's war stories)[26] and an incitement to join the SA, the NSDAP's "storm troopers."

Extremely well developed, this rhetoric of combat placed Heidegger among the Nazi intellectuals.[27] His polemological depiction of Plato was like that of the commentators at the time, who saw the Greek philosopher as a warrior.[28] The glorification of voluntarism and an often soldierly courage was also a commonplace: Leni Riefenstahl's film of the 1934 Party rally was titled *Triumph of the Will;* like other Nuremberg rallies, it put on display not only the dignitaries and their speeches, but also the paramilitary organizations, which filed by in battalions, marching behind their flags to the sound of songs, drums, and trumpets. Dedicating his *Myth of the Twentieth Century* to the "two million German heroes who fell in the world war," Alfred Rosenberg stated that the "task of our century" is to "create a new human type out of a new view of life [*Lebensmythus*]. And for this, courage is needed, courage of each single individual, courage of the entire generation growing up, indeed of many following generations. For chaos has never been mastered by those without courage, and a world has never been built by cowards. Whoever wishes to go forward must therefore also burn bridges behind him. Whoever sets out on a great journey must leave old household goods behind. Whoever strives for what is highest must turn his back on what is lesser. And to all doubts and questions the new man of the coming great German Reich knows only one answer: I alone will triumph!"[29]

In Heidegger's inaugural address as rector, this unsparing rhetoric sought to incite a community of scholars to rally around its rector. Nonetheless, *Führung* as he conceived it now went far beyond the purely rhetorical meaning it had had in the 1920s; it had an authentically political dimension, as did rhetoric itself.

Heidegger knew that the very term *Führung* had taken on a full-fledged political meaning: already on 6 May, welcoming new students when the Third Reich had been making inroads for a few months, he had pointed out the "unusual" character of the moment when they were entering the university: "The German people as a whole has found itself again under a great *Führung*. In this *Führung*, the people, which has come to itself, is creating its own state."[30] Heidegger described his task as rector and the bond that was to connect him with the university community by using the same term he employed to praise the government of Germany under the Third Reich. In that way, from the first sentence on, the philosopher inserted himself into the totalitarian frameworks of the NSDAP's thought. In its political meaning, *Führung* was borrowed from the Nazi vocabulary; as Carl Schmitt noted the same year, "this concept of leadership [*Führung*] proceeds completely from the concrete, substantial thought of the National Socialist movement."[31] This mode of thought structured the *Führerstaat*, the "leader state," and the *Führerprinzip* that Hitler had defined in *Mein Kampf* to impose his authority on the Party when it was still being contested by Gregor Strasser and the left wing of the NSDAP. This principle can be summed up in one sentence: "Any man who wants to be leader bears, along with the highest unlimited authority, also the ultimate and heaviest responsibility."[32] Committees, rather than being collegial bodies, had only an advisory function, and had no part in decision making; the supreme leader's competence and his election by Party members were supposed to legitimate his total power. One of his essential attributes was that he could delegate his full authority to other persons who, being subordinate to him, exercised it in the framework of a defined mission or territory, for which he was answerable only to his superior within a pyramid structure. Described in *Mein Kampf* to justify Hitler's domination over his own party, this organization had the authority to be transposed "for the entire state,"[33] which is what happened with *Gleichschaltung*, which Heidegger, among others, embraced.

The Nazi *Führerprinzip* was based on one of Heidegger's old convictions. Since 1918, he had thought that only a *Fuhrer* would be able to lead the German people out of the spiritual "poverty" in which it found itself.[34] For Hitler, it was also the means that Germany needed in this interwar period in which the Reich felt humiliated by the Treaty of Versailles, and where his people seemed to him weakened by its bastardization by the Jewish "parasite."[35] For the German people to return to its "greatness and power," it had to break with the mediocrity of parliamentary democracy by exalting the "personality of the leader" and reestablishing it "in its rights."[36] This was the value of personality translated into politics: like the brilliant artist, whose work cannot be completed by someone else, the exceptional leader is irreplaceable and has to take power for the greater good of his community. This cult of the leader reflected an aristocratic conception hostile to the masses and was by no means original to the right: Hitler wrote that "the progress and culture of humanity are not a product of the majority, but rest exclusively on the genius and energy of the personality."[37] Heidegger was moving in the same direction: "Only the individual is creative even in leadership, the masses never."[38] The celebration of heroism was a natural corollary of this cult of the leader, so that the demagogue maintained that a *Führer* vested with "unlimited authority" bore "the ultimate and heaviest responsibility," and "only the hero" was "cut out for this."[39] Whereas the view of action in *Being and Time* was already heroic,[40] in 1933 Heidegger believed that, in order to assume its function as *Führer,* the teaching staff had to become "strong [enough] for leadership [*Führerschaft*]." "Such a strength" "selects the best" (*die Auslese der Besten*) and binds them "to the essential."[41] With the inaugural address, Heideggerian heroism had taken an aristocratic turn tinged with social Darwinism. This idea of "selecting the best" anchored Heidegger in Nazism, which postulated that the life of human societies was a war of all against all among peoples, races, and individuals, and that in this universal struggle the best and strongest were selected. For Hitler, as for others, a rejection of this principle was a factor of decadence, a sign of jewification.[42] Heidegger thought that this selection came about through an aptitude for leadership, thanks to a spiritual strength up to the scholarly mission that academics were supposed to carry out.

The German university had a decisive role in the spiritual leadership of its people: it was the "highest institution of spiritual and political education,"[43] which, "on the basis of science and through science," trained the "*Führer* and guardians of the German people's destiny."[44]

With the term "guardians" (*Hüter*), Heidegger was partially following the model of the ideal commonwealth that Plato imagined in the *Republic,* aristocratic and philosophical, giving power to the best, who were both leaders and philosophers: "To them by their very nature belong the study of philosophy and political leadership, while it befits the other sort to let philosophy alone and to follow their leader."[45] The followers are the workers, whose task it is to produce the commonwealth's means of subsistence, and the warriors, who have to protect it with their weapons; all of them must obey the guardians, those who, combining an excellent nature and education, are the city's intelligence, cultivating wisdom and trying to safeguard justice within the commonwealth by keeping in mind the good—the loftiest idea, the shining sun outside the cave in the allegory, accessible only to philosophers, who are freed from the chains that keep the ordinary prisoner in his darkness, weakly lit by a fire that he takes for the sun itself.

The guardians Heidegger imagined were not necessarily professional philosophers: alongside "the statesman and professor" there were also the "physician," the "judge," the "pastor and the architect." All of them were guardians, because in German society they were trained to assume the role of philosophers within their fields of expertise, and they remained under the influence of the received knowledge they preserved. In this way, contrary to a utilitarian conception such as the one promoted by the regime, "knowledge is not in the service of the practice of a profession, but the other way around: the professions obtain and administer this highest, essential knowledge of the people regarding its whole *Dasein*."[46] Although they were specialized—the statesman in politics, the professor in teaching, the physician in care of the body, the judge in the maintenance of justice, the pastor in the guidance of souls, the architect in construction—in Heidegger's view all these figures in German society required knowledge that extended far beyond technical skills to embrace the whole of the people's existence, insofar as their areas of specialization concerned one or several "powers" shaping the "world" of the people: "nature, history, language; the people, morality, the state; poetry, thought, religion; illness, madness, death; law, economics, technology."[47] Their knowledge therefore being also political, they were all guardians of the people's knowledge.

These notables were not only guardians but also *Führer*, leaders, entrusted within the orbit of their profession to lead the German people toward its destiny within a history in the making. Heidegger therefore characterized as *Führer* professionals who did not necessarily have an institutional role as commanders and who were related in that respect to the "anonymous *Führer* without the status of civil servants"[48] that he mentioned a few months later in reference to the new type of student. He may have been remembering his first stint at the training camp in 1918, during which he had been treated not as befitted his rank, but out of consideration for his person; his value was already expressed in his status as the holder of a doctorate and his position as a teacher at the university. Or perhaps, on the contrary, he was remembering the humiliation of his second stint at the camp, which was so important for his evolution toward a revolutionary temperament, when he was treated only as befitted his rank.

The power of *Führerschaft*, a term that designates both a group of leaders viewed collectively and the quality of leadership they share, lay less in marching ahead than in "being able to go it alone," an inner aptitude that proceeded from an existential aptitude, that of "wanting the essence of knowledge," which required exposing themselves to the "farthest outposts of the danger of the constant uncertainty of the world." Then, in the distress of forgetting, "communal questioning and the word bestowed in accordance with the community [*gemeinschaftliche gestimmte Sagen*] were awakened in the leaders."[49]

Like Plato, Heidegger placed professors in a realm apart from the other professions, giving them an eminently political function. In his reference to the professions to which university study leads, he wrote "the statesman and professor," without repeating the definite article. This had the effect of portraying them as uniting two sides of a single function in the commonwealth: "The statesman and professor, the physician and the judge, the pastor and the architect."[50] This argument by way of form is coupled with another concerning content: inasmuch as they trained the other *Führer*, inasmuch as, more than others, they had in view the "historical spiritual mission of the German people," which was to attain "knowledge of itself in its state," academics were entrusted with "safeguarding our people's will to knowledge."[51] Heidegger made this explicit on 11 November, on the occasion of the oath of allegiance to Adolf Hitler sworn by university professors. The statesman and professor had all his fellow citizens participate in the life of the state, on the basis of a knowledge that was both political, because it had to do with the state, and existential, because it was rooted in the communal existence of each individual. "Spiritual guidance," as Heidegger conceived it, was thus political in the highest degree, in conformity with his long-held notion that all true politics is cultural, the rest being nothing but inessential busyness. Professors were statesmen, in the same way that in Plato's *Republic* the guardians were the leaders of the commonwealth; and, just as from the point of view of the intransigent Catholicism of his youth, priests had to govern the life of the state, Heidegger's new learned men had to combine knowledge and power in the most elevated sense of those terms. As a "guardian of [his] people's will to knowledge," Heidegger exercised his spiritual *Führung* outside the university, seeking to lead his people by means of his knowledge, in that way following in the footsteps of Plato's guardians. In possession of the loftiest political knowledge and placed in the vanguard of the spiritual guidance of the German revolution vis-à-vis his academic colleagues, he tried to reveal to his people the profound essence of the process under way: "The National Socialist Revolution is not simply the assumption of a power already existing in the state on the part of a different party that has grown large enough to do so; instead, this revolution is producing *a complete and radical change in our German existence* [*die völlige Umwälzung unseres deutschen Daseins*]."[52] Contrary to the Weimar Republic, where one party succeeded another when it had acquired enough power to do so, the Third Reich was a revolution that actually affected the very being of every German in his relation to the state, giving him the means to assume authentically his people's destiny by resolutely following his leader, Adolf Hitler; and everyone had to feel growing within the will to give a growing role to this political knowledge of an extraordinary urgency.

Conceiving the new education that was to train the nation's future elite as a whole, enlightening the people through a strong and repeated public discourse, the rector of the University of Freiburg bestowed on himself a special role, that of a new Plato, that of the modern philosopher par excellence and the true inspiration of the coming revolution, an ambition that was in evidence even before his inaugural address. Two weeks earlier, Josef Sauer had written in his diary: "Heidegger clearly feels that he is a born philosopher and the spiritual leader [*Führer*] of the new movement, as the only exceptional great thinker since Heraclitus."[53]

Represented by the best minds and spirits, that is, those that were most resolute and most rooted, the academic *Führerschaft* was supposed to be so strong that it awakened "the authentic *Gefolgschaft* of those who have a new kind of courage":[54] organized by the *Führerprinzip,* the University of Freiburg, as presented in the address given by its rector, was a community following its leaders.

Before the Nazi period, the term *Gefolgschaft* was rare, limited to the history of institutions interpreted in the light of Tacitus's *Germania:* "The word describes the military leader's group of armed companions, the *comites* in Latin, the *Gefolgsleute,* a group of free men that follows its prince to war, remaining only loosely attached to him in peacetime, and whose size confers on this prince power and reputation. The relation between the prince and his

Gefolgsleute, his *leudes,* was based on an oath of loyalty, and that is why nineteenth-century French legal historians translated *Gefolgschaft* as 'truste' [a group of men bound to the king by a loyalty oath]. The words *antrustiones* and *comites* designated the members of the *truste,* the loyal."[55] For the Nazis the *Gefolgschaft,* far from being a past reality, was the incarnation of the juridical national spirit, and the model on which the German people should be organized: clearly referring to this idea (without, however, adopting the term), point 19 in the NSDAP's program demanded the "substitution of a German common law in place of the Roman Law serving a materialistic world-order,"[56] thus replacing the contracts and rights impersonally guaranteed by Roman law with the racial value of each individual and the living relation of loyalty uniting a people with its leaders.[57]

The use Nazism made of the term *Gefolgschaft* makes it difficult to translate. The term *truste,* which is interesting for the ancient and medieval periods because of the importance of the reference to Tacitus, is not suitable for the Third Reich, where *Gefolgschaft* became an ordinary word used to emphasize the idea of following (*folgen*), the word's root, which Heidegger, among so many others, allowed to resonate with *Führer,* leader. *Gefolgschaft* became such a key word in the "language of the Third Reich" (LTI, *lingua tertii imperii*) that Victor Klemperer devoted a whole chapter to it in his book by that name, because it contained "the whole emotional mendacity of Nazism, the whole mortal sin of deliberately twisting things founded on reason into the realm of the emotions, and deliberate distortion for the sake of sentimental mystification."[58] On the basis of the "law regulating national labor" of 20 January 1934, businesses, like the rest of German society, were subject to the *Führerprinzip.* Their managers were designated as *Führer,* and the employees as *Gefolgschaft.* As Klemperer noted, everything in their relationship was governed by the law: "And now, in the *Gefolgschaftssaal* [the followers' room, that is, the staff room used for breaks], they were all divested of this regulatory instance, only to be dressed up and transfigured by the single word *Gefolgschaft,* which burdened them with the old Germanic tradition, it turned them into vassals, into weapon-bearing liegemen forced to keep faith with their aristocratic, knightly masters." The everyday use of the term *Gefolgschaft* did not make it anodyne, and as Klemperer noted, "it twisted a peaceful relationship into a belligerent one; it stifled criticism; it led directly to the cast of mind expressed in that sentence emblazoned on every banner: 'Führer, command and we will obey [*folgen*]!' "[59]

Within the university as Heidegger conceived it, the academic *Gefolgschaft* was to follow its leaders: finding its unity in the will to be "genuinely, collectively rooted in the essence of the German university,"[60] the university community was hierarchical, calling for a distinction between the student body and the teaching staff, but especially between *Gefolgschaft* and spiritual *Führer,* because it was the latter alone who bore the ultimate responsibility for success or failure: "However, this essence achieves clarity, rank, and power only if the leaders are themselves guided—guided by the inflexibility of this spiritual mission that forcibly places the destiny of the German people in the character of its history."[61] Guided by history more than anyone else, Heidegger proclaimed at the beginning of his inaugural address the duty of spiritual *Führung:* he positioned himself, without any possible ambiguity, as the leader of this Freiburg *Gefolgschaft* that he was forcing his colleagues to join, despite the university's tradition of collegiality that saw the rector as only *primus inter pares,* the first among peers.

Heidegger did more than proclaim himself spiritual guide and the students his followers; he also used seduction and diplomacy. Acknowledging that students were the vanguard of Nazism at the university, he found it pointless to try to "begin by awakening the followers," because the "German Student Union" was already "on the march."[62] For Heidegger, the *Gefolgschaft* was not to be passive, any more than it was so for the jurists Schmitt, Forstshoff, or Koellreutter. However, he went beyond voluntary submission by referring to the followers' resistance: "All leading [*Führung*] must recognize the *Gefolgschaft*'s own strength. But all following bears within itself resistance. This essential opposition between leading and following must not be erased, even less extinguished."[63] Heidegger justified his remarks philosophically by referring to the disposition for struggle, which alone allowed self-assertion and self-meditation. But another, political reading was also possible: he was handling the German Student Union carefully by recognizing its legitimacy and autonomy, the better to ensure its cooperation in the work of the academic revolution to which they all aspired, in spite of their differences regarding the details.

With his academic philosophy tinged with ontology and a historical mission, Heidegger went beyond the vulgar, everyday, propagandistic sense of the term *Gefolgschaft.* He appropriated it, like the jurists for whom this concept had become central for understanding and legitimating *Führung,* the relationship between *Führer* and *Gefolgschaft* that was supposed to be the principle of the totalitarian (or "total")[64] state. Despite the magnitude of the means of repression deployed by the NSDAP, Nazi ideology conceived the union of the community of Germans under the *Führerprinzip* as being primarily the result not of constraint but rather of voluntary support. Otto Koellreutter, reflecting on the authority of the total state, saw its foundation in a "communitarian ethics," the "idea of community," "the idea of 'us' as the totality of a people," conceived in the "conscious political fusion of the people with the state." For him, it was the NSDAP's duty to spread among the people this idea, which involved "recognizing the *clear* [*offen*] *Führerprinzip*."[65] For an individual, collective assent to a leader's total power was to be based on the feeling of being an indissoluble member of a moral organism of which the *Führer* was the head; this conception was rooted in the ideological corpus defined by the Party and its leader. Thus Koellreutter was repeating what Hitler had said at the Nuremberg rally in late summer 1933, when he characterized Nazi *Führung* as "seeing the people not as an object of its action," but rather as its natural prolongation, since it was "living in the people, feeling with the people, and fighting for the people."[66]

Führung, a "union of the soul" (*seelische Verbindung*) for Koellreutter, was for Carl Schmitt based more profoundly on an "identity of kind": it meant being of the same blood, belonging to the same race, the same people, again conceived primarily spiritually. Thus the concept of *Führung*, neither an image nor a general idea, made it possible to "grasp the absolute identity of kind [*Artgleichheit*] between the *Führer* and his following [*Gefolgschaft*]. Both the seamless contact between the leader and his followers and their mutual trust are based on this identity of kind, which alone can prevent the leader's power from being transformed into tyranny and caprice and mark the difference from the domination—still so intelligent or still so advantageous—of a foreign kind of will [*eines fremdartigen Willens*]."[67] Schmitt seems to place in opposition the national will expressed by the *Führer* guiding his *Gefolgschaft* and communism, a domination "still so intelligent or still so advantageous" that was subjecting the Russian people to the totalitarian power of communist democratic centralism at a time when the USSR was establishing itself as a model to be followed, even though the will that drove it was of a foreign kind and therefore incompatible with the German national genius, its history, and its customs.

Even when the technical, juridical terms *Führung* and *Gefolgschaft* were not adopted, they tended to turn up in speeches, like those of the eugenicist Eugen Fischer, who justified his support for the Third Reich by praising the new *Führerstaat*, the leader state, anchored in the German race, which he contrasted to the seducer (*Verführer*) characteristic of the Weimar Republic; and he strongly stressed the national character of the *Führerstaat* and its origin in the feeling of collective belonging, which shaped what he could not have known to call *Gefolgschaft*: "Once again, we are experiencing [*wir spüren wieder*] the great *Führer,* far from the *Verführer* who opens gulfs between classes, makes promises, and shows images that cannot be realized. Instead, we have a true *Führer,* who offers us a plan that can be carried out, and that is built on a *völkisch* foundation, on the idea of the identity of kind [*Gleichartigkeit*], on the same blood, the same race, the same spirit, and on national membership in the German people [*völkischen Deutschtum*], from which German culture has drawn its growth over all the centuries [of its history]."[68] With the new *Führerstaat* the German people thus recovered its own history by building once again on a *völkisch* foundation.

Heidegger also justified his conception of *Gefolgschaft*—in this case, academic—by postulating its strict Germanic nature: "The *Gefolgschaft,* teachers and students, are awakened and strengthened only on the basis of a true and shared rootedness [*Verwurzelung*] in the essence of the German university."[69] The idea of "awakening" already connoted a *völkisch* perspective on the *Gefolgschaft* insofar as it was one of the major themes of Nazi propaganda: *Deutschland erwache!* ("Germany, awake!") was the motto emblazoned on the NSDAP's banners as early as 1925.[70] Above all, Heidegger was paying attention to the essence of the *German* university, not to the universal essence of the university, because he was addressing the German academic community, which he thought was concerned, like him, about the bond with its people: "*We* consider the *German* university to be the institution of higher learning that seeks to provide, on the basis of knowledge and through knowledge, education [*Erziehung*] and training [*Zucht*] for the leaders and guardians of the German people's fate."[71] Rather banally and too rapidly, this sentence might be summed up in two simple, neutral propositions: the university has an educative function; and it is the site for the training of the elites. In that case, we would not be departing from the ground of a universal essence of the university. But Heidegger thrice insisted on Germanness: that of the university, that of the people as seen by a community embedded in a concrete history, and that of the state. For German professors and students in 1933, year I of the Third Reich, a new and authentically German regime characterized by the leader state (*Führerstaat*) required that the university educate and train leaders and guardians.[72]

For Heidegger, the German people was the one and only raison d'être of the German university. And yet, hadn't he had foreign students ever since the early 1920s? Wasn't the education of the Japanese Tanabe Hajime, Kuki Shūzō, and Seinosuke Yuasa,[73] the Germano-Italian Ernesto Grassi, and the Franco-Lithuanian Emmanuel Levinas of any interest for a university, even if it was German? This narrow focus on the national function of higher education was related to a characteristic of the whole inaugural address: ultranationalism, insofar as the glorification of the nation tended to obscure the prospect of a broader membership in the human race. This is also shown by the authorities Heidegger invokes, who are exclusively German (Nietzsche, Clausewitz) or Greek (Aeschylus, Plato), Greek civilization being conceived as the beginnings of a Western history considered from the German point of view.

This narrowing of the focus on the essence of the university to Germany reflected Heidegger's conception of the common destiny at the end of the 1920s: in paragraph 74 of *Being and Time,* he had already closely linked community, people, and destiny, to the exclusion of higher levels of political allegiance, such as civilization or humanity.[74] This narrowing was also characteristic of the Third Reich's ultranationalism at the time: as soon as it was established, the regime took anti-Semitic measures that expressed its aversion to Jews, its racist hatred, and the identitarian fantasy that was the beating heart of its ultranationalism, not simply a love for one's own people, but a hatred of the other, an other who was largely imaginary and whom the Nazis tended to blame for all the world's woes.

Established by the laws of 22 and 25 April, the new student regulations were anti-Semitic. The first law concerned the "formation of student associations in schools of higher education"[75] and reserved membership in student associations (Article 1) to "students whose origins and native language are German," while the others, foreigners or German citizens who were of non-German origin (that is, who were Jewish), were represented by the associations but could not belong to them (Article 2). The second law, targeting overcrowding in German schools and universities,[76] promulgated in its fourth paragraph a *numerus clausus* for "citizens of the German Reich of non-Aryan origin," who were not to constitute a proportion of the student body greater than their proportion in the general population, though those whose fathers had fought for the Central Powers during the Great War, or whose grandparents were Aryan, had the right to enroll. The implementation decree, dated the same day, set at 1.5 percent the total proportion of Jewish students.[77] The new law regarding students changed the conditions of study in Germany, making them far more restrictive for students considered to be Jews, that is, those who had at least one parent or grandparent who was of the Jewish religion.[78]

The fear of "jewification" that Heidegger saw at work in German culture and the nationalist definition he gave of the essence of the university were consistent with the spirit of these laws that sought to give a *völkisch* turn to higher education by expelling foreigners and those the Nazis considered non-Germans, despite their citizenship status. Thanks to these new laws, "the German Student Union [*deutsche Studentenschaft*] has placed itself under the law of its essence,"[79] as Heidegger put it in his inaugural address: only authentic Germans could now be members and the association had truly rooted itself "in the essence of the German university,"[80] whose goal was to train the future leaders of Germany.[81]

For Heidegger, *Gefolgschaft* did not proceed from Germanness alone; in order to be a real community, it also had to be united by communication (*Mitteilung*), which was, along with struggle (*Kampf*), one of the two ways that "the power of destiny" became free.[82] Communication and not concertation: the communication of information, of an injunction, an assent, in each case an expression of the resoluteness through which one accepts the common destiny without falling into the weakness and inauthenticity of deliberation. Heidegger clarified this idea in the course on Aristotle he gave in 1933–1934: citizens, as he described them, could not only speak to and understand one another, but could also listen to an exhortation or an order.[83] This emphasis on vertical communication, from a leader to a subordinate and vice versa, was characteristic of the *Gefolgschaft*, playing an essential role in uniting individuals behind a leader. But for the leader's discourse to be understood, his followers had to be prepared for it, which made their education indispensable.

Heidegger was working to that end. This spiritual *Führung*, this comprehensive education that he exemplified at the university and elsewhere, was the duty of academics as "guardians of [their] people's will to knowledge," because it was only by giving the people knowledge of itself, in its state, that each citizen would be a willing element of the *Gefolgschaft* and would resolutely assume his common destiny by unquestioningly following his leaders. In asserting that the responsibility for the people's destiny lay with each of its members, despite their inequality, Heidegger moved closer to the totalitarian conceptions of the jurist Ernst Forsthoff, who wrote:

> The totalitarian state must be the state of total responsibility; it represents the oath of loyalty to the nation sworn by each individual. This oath elevates the private character of individual existence. Always and everywhere, in his attitude and in his public activity as well as within the family and the community, each person is responsible for the destiny of the nation. What matters is not that the state extend its directives and its laws even to the nation's most minuscule groups, but that here, too, a responsibility can be asserted, the individual who does not completely

> subordinate his personal destiny to the nation can be called to account. This demand made by the state, total and addressed to every citizen, determines the new essence of the state.[84]

For Nazi ideologues, the question was: how to make everyone swear an oath of loyalty to the nation, how to ground concretely the assent of the *Gefolgschaft?* Forsthoff thought in moral and especially in legal terms: the state demanded a loyalty oath from everyone, and those who failed to swear it could be "called to account." In this respect, he remained within the state framework of legal obligation. Another jurist, Koellreutter, was more aware of the historic change brought by the advent of the Third Reich, which established a hybrid regime closely linking the Nazi Party to the state. The role of the NSDAP was to elicit the ideological adherence of the *Gefolgschaft* by means of propaganda:

> The German *Führerstaat* must [. . .] imbue the people as a whole with the National Socialist idea of the state as a unitary attitude [*Haltung*]. Therein lies the peculiar task of the "Party" as a movement—because *qua* "party" it no longer has anything in common with the old parties. [. . .] In the National Socialist state, the "Party" has a unity-shaping power [*eine einheitsbildende Kraft*]. The Party is the political "movement" to which, under the *Führer,* the responsibility for the establishment, maintenance, and safeguarding of the German people's political training is assigned.[85]

Despite his NSDAP membership card, Heidegger remained loyal to his apolitical conception (i.e., his hostility to political parties), which was a crucial element in his sympathy with Nazism: the knowledgeable and existential assent of the people to the state was the mission of the university, which displaced the Party as propagandist and made way for the professors. To the exclusion of the Party, the university was the new Germany's supreme spiritual authority, at least potentially, so long as its leaders were up to their mission; and even if he hoped to win allegiance through his speeches, Heidegger was aware of the difficulty of actually converting all of his colleagues. Thus on 9 May he replied to Eugen Fehrle, the director of higher education at the Ministry of Education for Baden, who had congratulated him on joining the NSDAP: "I thank you from the bottom of my heart for your good wishes on the occasion of my joining the Party. We must now do everything to win over [*erobern*] the world of the educated [*Gebildeten*] and scholars [*Gelehrten*] to the new national political spirit. That will not be an easy fight."[86]

One might think that the spiritual character of Heidegger's *Führung* distinguished it from the purely political *Führung* that characterized ordinary conceptions favorable to the Third Reich. But such a belief would underestimate the profoundly ideological nature of this regime. Nazism sought to be a total revolution, simultaneously political, racial, and national, social to a certain extent, and in any case spiritual, because changing people's minds was the very condition for shaping a new man and a new society, rid of the modern decadence that had characterized the earlier period.

The idea of spiritual *Führung,* leadership by discourse and by knowledge or science, and not by the pure power of command that Heidegger stressed at the beginning of his speech, was embodied in Hitler.[87] Above all, it was a constitutive element of Nazi ideology, which liked to play on the two meanings of the term *Führer:* commander and guide. Hitler himself wanted to be the intellectual guide of his movement; in writing *Mein Kampf,* he sought to consolidate his role as leader of the Party while he was imprisoned in the Landsberg fortress; once Hitler was in power, his magnum opus was given to newlyweds in place of the Bible, and was supposed to anchor his power as Führer deep within Germans' minds and spirits.

Hitler based his spiritual *Führung* on a kind of scientism: he claimed to justify the revolution he was planning by a worldview drawing lessons from science, in particular from history and biology. "Historical experience," he wrote, "shows with terrifying clarity that in every mingling of Aryan blood with that of lower peoples the result was the end of the cultured people."[88] The Führer appealed to an "almost mathematical certainty" to justify the effects, as grandiose as they were ineluctable, of the politics glorifying race and personality that the state was to impose on its people:

> If, in the world of our present parliamentary corruption, it becomes more and more aware of the profoundest essence of its struggle, feels itself to be the purest embodiment of the value of race and personality and conducts itself accordingly, it will with almost *mathematical* [my emphasis] certainty someday emerge victorious from its struggle. Just as Germany must inevitably win her rightful position on this earth if she is led and organized according to the same principles.
>
> A state which in this age of racial poisoning dedicates itself to the care of its best racial elements must someday become lord of the earth.[89]

Even more than Hitler, Rosenberg stressed the necessity of a spiritual revolution: as he indicated in his preface, he wanted to "create a new human type out of a new view of life."[90] With the advent of the Third Reich and the rising sales of his book, Rosenberg, who had denounced the "enormous and unique intellectual chaos of present-day life,"[91] went so far as to observe, on the occasion of the sale of the one-hundred-and-fifty-thousandth copy, that the intellectual revolution he was hoping for was being realized:

> Today, the *Myth* has left a deep, indelible mark on the German people's affective life [*Gefühlsleben*]. The new editions that keep coming out are clear testimony that a decisive upheaval in the spirit and mind [*ein entscheidender geistig-seelischer Umbruch*] is growing into a historic event. [. . .] The political and state revolution is over; the transformation of minds is only beginning. In its service, *The Myth of the Twentieth Century* is already in the vanguard.[92]

The idea of spiritual *Führung* was also found among academics such as Eugen Fischer, the famous eugenicist in Freiburg, who, on the occasion of the oath of allegiance to Adolf Hitler, described the role of scholars in the construction of the new state: "At the same time, we, the student body and the teaching faculty [. . .] are constructing, directing [*führen*] the life of the German spirit, just as we have directed, regulated—constantly regulated—it, following the new state wholeheartedly and completely."[93] Fischer agreed with Heidegger and his conception of the university: guided by their professors, students were being prepared to direct the people's spiritual life, at least in the future, by virtue of the eminent position they would take in Germany's society and state. Despite his scientism, Hitler denied academics and intellectuals any legitimate role in leading the revolution; intellectuals were to theorize the revolution made by others, not lead it. Hitler insisted that "the greatest revolutions in this world have never been directed by a goose-quill!"[94] A writer, like a philosopher, was, even in his way of speaking, "neither born nor chosen" for leadership.[95]

Hostile to the party's ideological role, to which he contrasted the university's scientific and political role, Heidegger distinguished himself by also according a leading role to philosophy: his political revolution was to be a spiritual revolution.

Creating the German People's "True Spiritual World"

Heidegger wanted to revolutionize his people's spiritual world; whereas professors suffered from a defective leadership (*Führerschaft*), students were, for their part, prepared to follow. "We do not need to awaken the followers

[*Gefolgschaft*]. The German Student Union [Deutsche Studentenschaft] is on the march. And *whom* it seeks are these leaders through whom it wants to elevate its own vocation [*Bestimmung*] to a well-founded, well-informed truth, and to put it in the clarity of an interpretive, active language and body of work."[96] With these words, Heidegger established that the setting in which his educational project was to be developed was not just different from but better than that of the German Student Union, a group dominated by the Nazis, who were federating all of Germany's student associations: thus he exercised his intellectual leadership over these followers who were waiting like a thoroughbred eager to be mounted by a rider who knew how to be its master.

Heidegger thought that an academic education was not enough; it was necessary to break with the model of the university derived from Humboldt, in which knowledge was cultivated for its own sake. But it could not be limited to a political education without a philosophical foundation. Thus the ambivalence he had shown in Marburg with regard to physical exercises resurfaced: he opposed the gymnastic societies based on a purely ideological nationalism without philosophical rootedness; at the same time, one had to rethink the whole of academic culture, in which the cult of the body and being-with-others (*Mitsein*) would have their function, assigned by philosophy. This union, in which "science and German destiny" "come to power at the same time in this will to essence," required not only that science be exposed "in its most innermost necessity" through a return to the philosophical essence of science, but also that "German destiny" be endured in "its most extreme distress" through a resolute acceptance of the communal *Dasein* heroically facing death. This alliance between science and destiny in university teaching would be expressed in the indissoluble pairing of "education and training."[97]

Whereas philosophical education distanced Heidegger from the anti-intellectual ideas of Nazi ideologues such as Hitler, Rosenberg, and Krieck, training brought him much closer to them, since they emphasized character building. In *Mein Kampf* the leader of the NSDAP certainly gave priority to the "training [*Zucht*] of absolutely healthy bodies" with a view to the "shaping of mental abilities"; but of these he preferred "the development of character, especially the promotion of will-power and determination, combined with the training of joy in responsibility," to "scientific schooling." Hitler's principle was that "a man of little scientific education but physically healthy, with a good, firm character, imbued with the joy of determination and with will-power, is more valuable for the national community than a clever weakling."[98] Rosenberg, who was less anti-intellectual, maintained that "the first task of education is not the mediation of technical knowledge but formation of character. It must strengthen racial values such as once slumbered in the Germanic essence. These values must be carefully cultivated. [. . .] State-controlled schools must educate soil-rooted citizens of state. The citizenry must become aware of what they are fighting for in life. The citizenry must understand the totality of values that are theirs, irrespective of any individual features."[99]

Despite subtle and even major differences regarding the greater or lesser importance of purely physical education, these ideologues agreed on the importance of character building as a way of shaping a new man, a project characteristic of totalitarian regimes, whether fascist or communist. Heidegger, despite his relative originality, did not differ from this overall project that sought to create a cultural breach by educating the people. In the same way, the means he imagined for implementing the pedagogical pairing of "education and training"[100] were the same as those urged by the Third Reich, in particular the German Student Union, which he wanted to lead back to its truth.

As the rector himself observed, the Deutsche Studentenschaft had come into being with the new law regarding students: "Thanks to the new student law, the German Student Union places itself under the law of its essence and defines this essence with it."[101] In Heidegger's view, the importance of this new legislation resided in the fact that, in contrast to the Prussian institutions of higher education, for which "the festive proclamation of the new student law" had been set for May Day, it had been decided that in his university it would be "incorporated in a suitable way into the celebration of the transfer of the rectorship."[102] A new regime required a new student law and a new rector, which it was fitting to display in a spectacular fashion.

Student regulations had quickly been changed by the regime in Berlin, in particular with two laws dating to 22 and 25 April. To be sure, the Reich had no educational jurisdiction (and thus no Ministry of Education), because the Weimar constitution reserved that jurisdiction for the Länder. These two laws had their legal foundation in the Enabling Act of 24 March, and were part of the general process of *Gleichschaltung,* which tended to subordinate everything to the Nazi government in Berlin. Paragraph 2 of the law of 22 April laid the legal foundation for a totalitarian organization of the students by defining the principle whereby there would be only one representative body for them within each institution, a student union recognized as a "part of the school of higher education" representing "the students as a whole" and which would also supervise the latter by "collaborating" "in the fulfillment of [students'] obligations to the people, the state, and the school."[103] The German Student Union had been subject to the *Führerprinzip* since 1932,[104] and that principle, "conceived for a type of student that no longer has anything in common with the liberal era," was "strictly implemented in the organization of the student association."[105]

For Heidegger, the German Student Union in Freiburg placed *itself* under the law of its own essence. He did not see this law as an effort to subject students to the regime, but rather as the recognition of what was an organic part of the university, whose function was to contribute to the common work: the association was therefore to see to it that the students would no longer be "free" in the sense of being able to behave capriciously, as they liked, but rather "free for"[106] their spiritual vocation within the German people. The autonomy permitted by this totalitarian law went so far as to confer on the student union the capacity to define its own essence.[107] In fact, paragraph 3 of the law of 22 April stipulated that the "details of the organization and work of the student associations" would be regulated not only by "the decrees of the federated governments regarding the student law and the bylaws of the institutions of higher education," but also by "the bylaws of the student associations."[108] The student unions were thus encouraged by the new legislation to promulgate measures valid for themselves in order to play their concrete role in the reform of education in Germany.

The measures taken concerned chiefly the establishment of a labor service (*Arbeitsdienst*) and a "defensive" sports (*Wehrsport*) program.[109] Such sports, a paramilitary activity that could not be prohibited by the terms of the Treaty of Versailles, were actually practiced as preparation for war. In Freiburg, students had set up, in February 1931, a military sports camp near Umkirch, where they were trained, notably, to throw grenades; the neighbors did not appreciate the noise and danger, and defensive sports were therefore banned by the government of Baden.[110] A quintessential method of physical education, defensive sports were a perfect way to train "absolutely healthy bodies,"[111] the principal goal of education for Hitler, a way of creating physiques that could face enemy fire in the vengeful struggle against the Treaty of Versailles.

Whereas defensive sports training was the rather humdrum outcome of the regime's paramilitary spirit, the labor service was more complex. The idea was not new: in 1931 the Brüning government had set up a voluntary labor service that the Nazi regime began to implement more broadly in April 1933. The German Student Union demanded that it be made compulsory, even as, using the new prerogatives granted by the law of 22 April 1933, it required all university students to perform ten weeks of service, and high school graduates six months.[112] On 29 April, the Reichskommissar for the labor service ordered that preparations be made to establish a compulsory labor service that would take advantage of the NSDAP's and the *Stahlhelm* (Steel Helmet) veterans league's installations in localities with populations under 100,000, to be used as labor camps.[113] Finally, the law of 26 June 1935, which made labor service compulsory for all young Germans, justified its measures by arguing that it was necessary "to give German youth, in the spirit of National Socialism, training in the community of the people and a true notion of work, above all the respect that is owed to manual labor."[114]

While they were building roads or draining swamps, young people were indoctrinated; and, subjected to a military discipline and a military organization, they wore uniforms, lived in camps, and marched with their spades held high like lances or rifles. The labor service had at least two objectives: to respond to the massive unemployment and to circumvent the limits imposed by the Treaty of Versailles on the number of soldiers in the German army. It also expressed Nazi ideology, which not only prized the salutary culture of the body, but also saw this collective work as a way to cement young people's community spirit, making them feel that they belonged to a people that was classless because bound together by common tasks and leaders. Anti-intellectual and often hostile to the traditional elites, Nazism included a dose of social utopianism that brought it closer to the far left in its glorification of the community and the valorization of manual labor. Thus we can understand why the celebration of the promulgation of the new student law, which included the introduction of the labor service, took place in Prussia on May Day. The establishment of this service complemented the law against overcrowding in schools and institutions of higher education in Germany, and the decree of 28 December, which limited the right to pursue advanced studies in 1934 to 15,000 high school graduates, 10 percent of them women,[115] henceforth allotting only one place for every two men and for every seven women.[116]

The new student law was steeped in ideology. The military spirit animated it through and through. On the occasion of its ceremonial promulgation on May Day, Klaus Schickert, the "vice-*Führer*" of the German Student Union, enjoined all the members of the university community to become "soldiers of science."[117] In his commentary on the new measures, the jurist Arnold Köttgen stated that "the political student is the objective that an academic education with new goals ought to seek, supported by defensive sports [*Wehrsport*] and the labor service."[118]

Heidegger approved of the overall project of a "spiritual and political education."[119] To mold a "political student," and beyond that a new man, Heidegger appropriated *Wehrsport* and the labor service, incorporating them into his own philosophical and political project. In his remarks, the major tasks of the students were all called "services": the essence of the German university—the training of the guardians and *Führer* of the German people—required that students serve the community even in their studies. There were three such services: labor, defense, and knowledge, corresponding to three sorts of obligations toward the people.

Defensive service corresponded to students' obligation with regard to "the honor and destiny [*Geschick*] of the nation amid other peoples," while military service was to develop through knowledge and discipline the "availability for engagement even unto death."[120] Theoretical studies and paramilitary exercises were to be combined for this purpose, an indication of Heidegger's conceptions, which went beyond mere military sports. The knowledge service, for its part, proceeded from the German people's spiritual mission, which "constantly reconquers its spiritual world"[121] and requires new knowledge. The labor service, an obligation to the community of the people (*Volksgemeinschaft*), demanded participation "in the suffering, aspirations, and capacities of all the professions and of every member of the people,"[122] because, as he explained the following year in his course on logic, "work as such, even if performed by a single individual, transports man into being-together with the other and for the other."[123] Whereas the philosopher marked his distance from the social elitism that he saw among the students and from their aspiration to have a "distinguished profession,"[124] the anti-intellectualism that presided over the *Arbeitsdienst* set in place by the regime found expression in certain overtones in his speech, when he denounced "empty subtlety" (*leerer Scharfsinn*)[125] or the love of science for its own sake that seeks only the progress of knowledge.[126]

Expressing the Nazi conception of work, the labor service as Heidegger saw it also retained its military turn within an education wholly conceived as "combative."[127] This combative education tended to make students into *Führer,* though anonymous ones because they lacked official recognition; only its pedagogical power mattered to Heidegger, who saw it precisely as one of the goals of university training.[128] *Gefolgschaft* gives rise to comradeship, which makes some individuals rank-and-file heroes whom he describes as "anonymous *Führer* without the status of civil servants," who "do more, because they endure and sacrifice more" and bear a characteristic stamp (*Schlag*): "Comradeship shapes the individual beyond himself and stamps him in the mold of a type completely characteristic of a group of young men. We know the firmness of his features, the hard clarity of his gaze, the resoluteness of his handshake, the brutality of his speech."[129]

Heidegger had probably been convinced of the educational value of these groups of young men less by the Nazi militias than by the Youth Movement, which sought to reinvigorate the German nation by this means. Nonetheless, because the swastika seemed to point the way to the future, groups of young Nazis, both adolescents and adults, were the structures in which the leaders and guardians to come had to be educated and trained. Between the lines, Heidegger sketched out an educational model for his own sons: Hermann, thirteen, was old enough to belong to the "Cubs" (*Pimpfe*) of the German Young People (Deutsche Jungvolk) and he was in fact a member.[130] Jörg, who was fourteen, was old enough to join Hitler Youth proper (Hitlerjugend) before enlisting in the SA four years later.

The combative education conceived by Heidegger was inspired by the youth organizations of the time; nonetheless, he wanted to reach a higher cultural level by means of a philosophical foundation resting on the three services—labor, defense, and knowledge—which, despite their differing names, overlapped. All three were connected with the people, in which they found their meaning and their obligation: students were linked "through the people to the state's fate [*Geschick*], in a spiritual mission." The unity of the services was not just a detail, insofar as it proceeded from the unity of knowledge Heidegger desired: "Knowledge of the people that collaborates with it, knowledge putting itself at the disposition of the state's destiny, bound together with the knowledge of the spiritual mission, the original and full essence of science whose realization is entrusted to us."[131] The third service was the ground for the other two, insofar as it was the pure essence of knowledge that had become aware of its mission for the German people.[132]

In this process, science and politics were inseparable: as Heidegger put it a few months later, the "claim [*Anspruch*] to knowledge gains power only if the great powers establish their authority in the state itself," meaning that knowledge "is realized in the process of a people becoming a state," to the point of merging with it: "This knowledge is the state."[133] This once again presupposed that the university would respond to its vocation as the guardian of the people's will to knowledge; and contrary to the party's simple role in propaganda, the university's activity had to be authentically scientific, nurtured through and through by science even in the training it provided.[134]

At the foundation of this educational revolution, closely linking science to the people, to its work and its destiny, professors were to revolutionize science,[135] not only by forging ahead with it, which would have simply prolonged the earlier movement toward specialization and the groundless accumulation of knowledge for its own sake, but rather by basing it in the first place on a clear principle: all science is philosophy, whether it knows it or not, whether it wishes to be so or not,[136] because it presupposes an understanding of being, of its own foundations, and therefore must be related to the whole of existence. Led by philosophy, German science had to show it could live up to its principles and, in doing so, "conform to the distant injunction from the beginning of our spiritual and historical *Dasein*."[137] Postulating the close relationship between the Greeks and the Germans, Heidegger thought that a spiritual mission in the history of the West was incumbent on his people: reproducing the great beginnings of philosophy by returning to the "two preeminent properties of the original Greek essence of science"—the "creative weakness of knowledge" (*schöpferischen Unkraft des Wissens*),[138] which required a combative courage in the face of the distress of existence; and an "authentic" practice of theory, which presupposed that it be understood not as an activity "for its own sake," but as "the highest modality of *energeia* [ἐνέργεια], of man's 'being-at-work.' "

Heidegger reduced science to its political essence, to his conception of national "socialism": it was not a leisure activity, something beautiful and empty reserved for an elite, but a kind of work that associated the theorist with the working activity of the whole community of the people, in that it was the "innermost, determining center of the whole *Dasein* of the people and the state" (*die innerst bestimmende Mitte des ganzen volklich-staatlichen Daseins*) and "the power that keeps all of *Dasein* sharp and seizes it wholly."[139] As for the weakness of knowledge, Heidegger illustrated it with a quotation he drew from Aeschylus: " 'But knowledge is far less powerful than Necessity.' This means that all knowledge of things remains at the mercy of the superior power of destiny and fails in the face of it."[140] Behind the reference to destiny, the philosopher was pointing to science's distress at taking on the distress of existence in its relationship to knowledge: all knowledge is caught up in forgetfulness, *lethe,* against the backdrop of which truth appears like the spectacle of a veil torn away thanks to our inner strength.

By adopting the two major properties of Greek science as Heidegger conceived it—theory considered a task for the people, and the uncertainty in which all science and all existence dwell—the university could create for the

German people "its world of the innermost and outermost [*äußersten,* most extreme] danger, that is, its true *spiritual* world."[141] It is a "true spiritual world" because it is founded on the originary essence of truth, the manifestation of the powers shaping the world against the backdrop of forgetfulness and human distress in the face of *Dasein,* instead of on modern spiritual dispersal and decadence.

That expression, "spiritual world," was at the heart of Heidegger's political and scientific reflections, and, indirectly, of his academic thinking as well, the central issue itself. To understand the expression, we might provide a simple equivalent, namely, "culture": science, revitalized, was supposed to change the culture of the German people. But that would be to underestimate the complexity of this concept borrowed from Dilthey, who connected it with history and set it in opposition to nature. For Dilthey, man "is located in the midst of this nature, to adopt an expression of Spinoza's, as *imperium in imperio.*"[142] He is an empire of consciousness in a natural empire, a spiritual world in a material world, and though part of this larger whole, he enfolds it within himself and for himself: nothing exists for human consciousness except what is within it, so that nature, though surrounding consciousness, turns out to be merely a part of it, an object among others, alongside the goals and values of life enclosed along with it in the "spiritual world that acts independently"[143] in man. Consciousness guarantees man freedom within the empire of necessity, that is, within nature; that freedom to think and establish a spiritual order gives rise to history and the ability to produce novelty, through which human life is distinguished from the realm of nature.

For Heidegger, the interest of the expression "spiritual world" lay in the fact that it was based on a conception of the world compatible with the ontology of *Being and Time,* accentuating the collective perspective of that ontology and its connection with the spirit of a people. The spiritual world, then, is not only the world in which a people lives, but also the one it is, starting with the "manifestation [*Offenbarkeit*] of the superior powers shaping the world."[144] On the ground of Dilthey's thought, Heidegger's rejection of the topic his colleague in biology proposed took on an intellectual meaning: with his desire to speak about "the doctrine of the *Heimat* and Germanness," by "transposing the common life of the animal and plant world onto the future of the [German] people,"[145] Konrad Guenther had put the cart before the horse, trying to understand spirit on the basis of nature; instead, he should have considered spirit without reductionism, an empire within an empire, as a historical consciousness endowed with freedom whose world is shaped by several "worldly powers of human historical *Dasein*,"[146] nature being only one of them among others.

In his inaugural address, Heidegger took care to clearly mark the importance of the spiritual world for a people: thus he explained that this world was not "a culture's superstructure," as a Marxist-inflected approach might have led one to think; nor was it "an arsenal of useful knowledge and values," as the technological and militaristic utilitarianism so widespread in Nazism would have described it. Instead, it was the innermost "power of excitement [*Erregung*] and the broadest disruption [*Erschütterung*] of the people's *Dasein*," because of its simultaneously ontological and total essence. If in this way Heidegger distinguished his philosophy from Nazi utilitarianism, which was a very reductive way to understand culture, he nonetheless did so in order to penetrate further into the *völkisch* thought that was shaping Nazism by asserting that a people's spiritual world was consequently "the power to preserve the deepest of its blood-and-soil strengths [*erd- und bluthaften Kräfte*]."[147]

Blut und Boden ideology, which had appeared for the first time in a letter to Elfride in 1920, was finally asserted publicly in one of the philosopher's major philosophical texts, whereas, in his speeches around the same time, it also structured the depiction of the mountainous soil of the Black Forest and the Alemannic blood of its inhabitants. During the student registration ceremony on 6 May 1933, Heidegger described in these terms the educational framework that was being offered them: "But you have no need to achieve everything that must belong to university life and cleverly seek it out. It's there, and it's waiting for you: the superb city, the Alemannic country, the mountains and the Rhine, the Alemannic ethnic group [*Volkstum*]."[148] In the autumn, describing Todtnauberg in "Why Do I Stay in the Provinces?" Heidegger referred to the "gravity of the mountains and the hardness of their primeval rock, the slow and deliberate growth of the fir-trees, the brilliant, simple splendor of the meadows in bloom, the rush of the mountain brook in the long autumn night, the stern simplicity of the flatlands covered with snow—all of this moves and flows through and penetrates daily existence [*Dasein*] up there."[149] Severe but nourishing, exposing one to the "distress"[150] (*Not*) of existence, this natural beauty formed the "creative landscape" that he had chosen as his "work-world."[151] It was also the milieu most propitious for training a fighter like Albert Leo Schlageter, to whom he had referred on the eve of his inaugural address, mentioning that the "staunch will" of this fighter had been forged by the mountains of "primitive rock" and "granite," whereas the "lucidity of his heart" had been nourished by "the autumn sun"[152] on the Black Forest. Depicting his chosen region, Heidegger described nature there as a force molding the spiritual world: it was an *Umwelt,* an environment or surrounding world that shaped the spiritual world in which Schlageter had been brought up, a world Heidegger offered the students in Freiburg.

Without great originality, Heidegger adopted the conceptions of the Youth Movement: modern young people, largely corrupted by the modern, urban sprit, would recover authenticity and responsibility toward their people in contact with the landscape that had shaped it since time immemorial. That was why the city did not appear on the list of "powers" Heidegger drew up. In the speech given on 6 May, Freiburg was, as it were, swallowed up by the nearby Black Forest; inversely, the metropolis of which Berlin was the archetype seemed unable to form an environment, a power shaping the spiritual world: it was an abyss for the latter, a squalid and fallacious un-world. In this respect, Heidegger was approaching what he touched on in *Being and Time:* in contrast to the city and its perpetual, uprooting movement, the familiar sojourn in the *Heimat* corresponded to the profound sense of being-in-the-world.[153] Conscious or not, this supplanting of the metropolis reflected the view Heidegger had always had: big cities concentrated modern giddiness, superficiality, and decadence, whereas the *Heimat* was a crucible of courage, lucidity, and authenticity. Instead of the opposition between the Meßkirch way and the Freiburg way found in his very first writings, he set up a Todtnauberg way, a condensation of the Black Forest, the *Heimat,* and a place of thought, looking proudly down on an ignoble Berlin way. Thus he retained the intuition he had had in 1918, even if it had been secularized and militarized.

This conception was deeply rooted in the culture he had grown up in: Conrad Gröber, in the diary he wrote in Rome, referred to the Meßkirch musician par excellence, Conradin Kreutzer,

> who came into the world more than a century before, in the valley's mill, and who, in the solitude of his native land, heard no music other than the whistle of the wind, the rumble of thunderstorms, the rustle of leaves on the trees, the murmur of streams, the squeak of millstones rubbing against one another, the hoarse bark of the chained-up farm dog, the cock's crow, and the song that a lark chimed out as it rose into spring and the summer sun.[154]

The environment, here nature, shapes man; musical genius is born of the sounds of the elements, in a natural determinism typical of a Romantic conception of Catholicism that valorizes the countryside.

Heidegger's view of nature was not as schematic as that of his former mentor. His description of the Black Forest showed that it was not enough simply to be present in this exceptional region in order to draw from it all its virtues, because despite the importance of the physical and human environment for human existence, its effect was not automatic. To receive it, it was not enough to be a tourist, an outside observer, a winter skier or a summer hiker; on the contrary, one had to "take it into oneself and let it resound inside the affective disposition [*Stimmung*] of one's whole *Dasein*."[155] Therefore one had to live in this region as in one's native country, whose effect would be all the greater the longer one had resided there and would bind one's ancestors to this soil, as Heidegger imagined it had done for him: "The inner relationship of my own work to the Black Forest and its people [*Menschen*] comes from a centuries-long and irreplaceable rootedness [*Bodenständigkeit*] in the Alemannian-Swabian soil."[156]

The effect of the soil on a man's sensibility depended on his blood, that is, his ancestry, as a spiritual legacy that opened one fully to the power of nature. History, another power shaping the world through the continual presence of his ancestors in this region, had made Schlageter the depository of the *genius loci:* a student in Freiburg and a fighter for German destiny, he was "the son of a peasant,"[157] and thus came from a bloodline that concentrated the virtues of this landscape. It was for that reason that Heidegger proposed him as an example for the new students at the university, so that he might change their perspective in these times of German revolution: "The Black Forest is not *solely* the territory that gives rise to winter sports and a superb area for excursions and summer vacations. Henceforth, we who are from the University of Freiburg come to know *first of all:* the native mountains, the native forests, and the native valleys of Albert Leo Schlageter."[158]

By selecting Schlageter from Germany's recent past and holding him up as a model, the philosopher was continuing a line of thought from *Being and Time:* for him, heroes were at the heart of the tradition that discovers a destiny. He wanted to promote among his students the imitation of past heroes, taking for granted their "anticipatory resoluteness," "for the choice made in authentic repetition is above all the one that makes one free to continue the battle and to take up the torch."[159] He also had his own example in mind, as he showed in the fall in his speech "Why Do I Stay in the Provinces?" He saw himself as the depository par excellence of the spirit of the place, elevated to the highest degree of lucidity by philosophy. To be sure, he was a native of Swabia, born into a family that had been established for centuries in the area around

Meßkirch; since he had fully appropriated the mountains of Todtnauberg, he mentally extended this little homeland of his ancestors to include all of the Alemannic region, with Freiburg and the Black Forest. That was how he conceived this "rootedness in the Alemannian-Swabian soil," the name for the union of the bloodline from which he was descended and this soil he had chosen for his work and leisure. Thus the choice of Todtnauberg for a science camp was not an accident, but rather stemmed from a theory of man's spiritual world and its historicality.

Heidegger set great store by blood and soil, which he saw as the "strengths" of a people's existence. His relative originality within Nazism took the form of a strong emphasis on soil understood as a natural and historical environment, making him in this respect similar to thinkers such as Jakob von Uexküll (1864–1944), Ludwig Ferdinand Clauß (1992–1974), and Erich Rothacker (1888–1965), who stressed the importance of the environment in the development of animals and men, pointing out their historicity in one way or another. In contrast to this radically historical conception of living beings in general, other ideologues postulated the immutable, substantial permanence of racial characteristics. The most polemical of these was the eugenicist and raciologist Hans Günther (1891–1968), the student of Fischer's who had the greatest influence under the Nazi regime, and who opposed, in his magnum opus (which sold 270,000 copies between 1922 and 1943),[160] "theories of the environment that see development, determination, dependency all around, whereas [the historic change under way], in contrast to all these negative intuitions, emphasizes the essence itself, the ahistorical being of things."[161]

Those who refused to give the environment a role in shaping race followed Gobineau in trying to explain the improvement or degeneration of races by the combination of good or bad blood alone; and though the theory was more fully worked out as science advanced—August Weismann (1834–1914), the founder of neo-Darwinism, postulated the existence of immutable characteristics inherent in the germ cells that gave blood its racial properties—the central idea remained the same. Thus Hitler maintained that "nationality [or ethnicity, *Volkstum*], or rather race, does not happen to lie in language but in blood";[162] and, since he considered the Aryan race—that is, the Indo-European race—to be superior, he thought that by mixing with other races it was committing a sin against the law of nature. For him, the policy to follow was logical: "The German Reich as a state must embrace all Germans and has the task, not only of assembling and preserving the most valuable stocks of basic racial elements in this people, but slowly and surely of raising them to a dominant position."[163] The conquest of power thus had to entail a biological revolution; this moment would be a "nobler age" in which "men" would no longer be "concerned with breeding up [*Höherzüchtung*] dogs, horses, and cats, but with elevating [*Emporheben*] man himself."[164]

As for Rosenberg, though he posited the priority of blood, he was not opposed to other factors: "We on our side do not deny very diverse influences: landscape and climate and political tradition; but all this is outweighed by blood and the blood-linked character. Things revolve around the reconquest of this order of rank."[165] This did not prevent him from recognizing the role of the environment: "The majority of basic myths have a fixed point of radiation—their place of creation. Thus, in their outward form, they appear to be comprehensible only on the basis of a completely distinct environment [*Umwelt*]."[166] That environment was the far north, the "prehistoric Nordic cultural center" where, as was common at the time, he located the origin of the Aryan race, which then spread through the world to create all kinds of civilizations: "Ahura Mazda says to Zoroaster: only once a year does one see the rising and setting of stars and sun and moon; and the inhabitants hold to be a day, what is a year. This must be for the Persian god of light a distant memory of the Nordic homeland, for only in the far north do day and night each last six months."[167]

Despite the great attention it gave to the physical characteristics of the races, Nazism wanted to be seen as a kind of Idealism, not materialism: race was also understood as spiritual, particularly by Rosenberg, who closely associated the two dimensions by claiming that "soul means race seen from within. And, conversely, race is the external side of a soul."[168] Although he praised Darwinism and nineteenth-century positivism for having been the "first powerful, though still wholly materialistic, protest against the lifeless and suffocating ideas that had come from Syria and Asia Minor and had brought about spiritual degeneracy," these modern scientific movements had considered blood the "symbol of real life," while depriving it of a soul, reducing it to "a chemical formula," allegedly to explain it.

In Rosenberg's work, blood was the key idea in an anticonceptual and antiuniversalist irrationalism which, valorizing the instinct originating in the people and the race, was similarly opposed to religious or philosophical universalism. Rejecting racial mixing and detachment from the "racial environment" (*artlichen Umwelt*),[169] he advocated the "values of the racial soul that stand as the driving forces [*treibende Mächte*] behind this new image of the world," but had "not yet become a living consciousness [*lebendiges Bewußtsein*]." His political and spiritual project was thus to "awaken the racial soul" in order to "recognize its highest value" and, under its dominance, to allot to other values their organic position "in the state, in art, and in religion" so as to "create a new human type out of a new view of life."[170]

Although Heidegger agreed with other Nazi ideologues on many points, in particular Rosenberg's idea of a spiritual revolution or the term "powers," which he adopted to conceive the spiritual world of a people, his point of view was particularly rich and incomparably more scientific; and, by positing that a people's spiritual world was the "power to preserve the deepest of its blood-and-soil strengths [*erd- und bluthaften Kräfte*],"[171] he emphasized the primacy of the spiritual world, which he conceived within his philosophical ontology, and he was far from reducing it to soil or blood.

When Heidegger developed his theory of race in his winter-semester 1933–1934 course on the essence of truth, he therefore criticized the summary Nazi theory proposed by Erwin Guido Kolbenheyer (1878–1962), an Austrian-German novelist, dramatist, and poet. In January 1934, Kolbenheyer had come to give a lecture at the university, entitled "The Value of the Art of Poetry for Life and Its Effect on Life." He developed the role of poetry for a people in its "battle to adapt to life"[172] (*Anpassungskampf*) by using, like Hitler, the ideology of the Aryan race to understand the politics of the time. The day after this lecture, Heidegger, though fond of Kolbenheyer, applied a malicious Platonic perspective to him: "Every period and every people has its cave and the inhabitants who belong to that cave";[173] Kolbenheyer seemed to him to be an example of such an inhabitant. Recalling the lesson he had learned from the august Dilthey, and in line with his own ontology, Heidegger pointed out that "corporeality" (*Leiblichkeit*) could not explain reason, but on the contrary, was to be founded on "existence" (*Existenz*) in the same way that, in Dilthey, consciousness, though enclosed within nature, guarantees man his freedom, however slight. Even as an infant, man is not primarily an animal who later receives reason, but "immediately a man."[174]

At the end of the semester, Heidegger concluded with the question of the status of blood and soil in its relation to the spiritual world insofar as that world is driven by the will of the people to attain self-knowledge in its own national state. He took a critical stance: "The will to knowledge and spirit is thus the will by which we stand or fall. Today, there is much talk about Blood and Soil as frequently mentioned forces [*vielberufener Kräfte*]. Intellectuals

[*Literaten*], who still exist today, have already mastered these forces. Blood and soil are certainly powerful and necessary, but not a sufficient condition for a people's *Dasein*. Other conditions are knowledge and spirit, not as a supplement in juxtaposition, but insofar as only knowledge leads the flow of blood in a certain direction, only knowledge leads the soil on a path to the gestation of what it is able to bring forth: knowledge acquires nobility on the soil even in the resoluteness it could achieve."[175]

By not reducing spirit to body, Heidegger made room for the latter, which contributes to fashioning the world through the power of blood understood racially, through nature, or through illness: "What we recognize as our body is not in itself present there-in-front, it is not what constitutes the source of *Dasein,* but rather is, in a way, suspended amid the affective dispositions and their power."[176] And "it is precisely by virtue of its entanglement in the affective disposition that corporeality has for us what makes it oppressing and calming, troubling and protective."[177] As a result, illness is not "the perturbation of a biological process, but an event that occurs in the history of a man, something that is based on, among other things, a way of being disposed affectively."[178] Illness makes you feel this way or that, a state that is physical but not limited to the physical: *qua* fact of consciousness, it shapes my world in a particular way. Heidegger, who was reading Plato at the time, must have been thinking more or less obscurely about the passage in the *Theaetetus* where Plato has Socrates say that wine does not taste the same when we are ill: sweet to the tongue when we are healthy, it seems bitter when we are indisposed.[179] Returning to the question of the physical and moral influence of blood, an ideological commonplace of the period, the philosopher concludes: "Thus blood as well as ancestry can determine man on an essential level only if they are determined by affective dispositions, never solely by themselves. The voice of blood proceeds from man's fundamental affective disposition. It is not suspended above for itself, but has its own place in the unity of the affective disposition."[180]

This consideration of the German people from the point of view of racial biology was also found in the idea of returning to the Greek beginnings of philosophy. In the inaugural address, Heidegger asserted that he wanted to take his inspiration from Greek antiquity, "the beginning of our spiritual and historical *Dasein,*"[181] a cultural and historical conception that identified Greece as the spiritual antiquity of Germany, closely linking the two. Through its thought and poetry, Greece had laid out Germany's principles of culture. Moreover, in the course he gave in the summer semester of 1933, which was contemporaneous with his inaugural address, he went further, referring to "the Greek people, whose racial stock [*Stammesart*] and language" had "the same origin"[182] as the German. He adopted sporadically the commonplaces of the Nazi doctrine of the races, as they had been expressed by Rosenberg, for example. The Nordic race was the common origin of all the great civilizing peoples, so that "the march of world history has radiated from the north over the entire planet, determining, in vast successive waves, the spiritual face of the world [*geistige Gesicht der Welt*]—influencing it even in those cases where it was to be halted." "These migration periods—the legendary march of the Atlanteans across north Africa, Persia, and India, followed by the Dorians, Macedonians, and Italic tribes; the diffusion of Germanic folkish migration—culminated in the colonizing of the world by the Germanic west [*das germanisch bestimmte Abendland*]."[183]

Thus the goal of the strong assertion that "only a spiritual world guarantees a people greatness"[184] was in fact to show the importance of the spiritual revolution it was calling for, not to reject Nazi conceptions of blood and race.

"God Is Dead"

"God is dead." In his inaugural address, Heidegger repeated the remark made by Nietzsche, who, "passionately seeking God,"[185] had made this observation regarding what seemed to him "the greatest recent event—that 'God is dead,' that the belief in the Christian God has become unbelievable."[186] Heidegger understood this as an "abandonment of contemporary man amid beings," which had to be taken seriously in order to ponder: "What of science?"[187] From there, it was necessary to go back to truth and freedom, and then to being. He wanted a secularized science that accepted the distress of existence without affording itself the fallacious refuge of a belief in God that guaranteed science and truth. Beyond the reference to Nietzsche, which was very much of its time, he returned to the essential point of his 1929 discussion of Plato's cave allegory: religion is a "basic stage"[188] of knowledge, it belongs to the cave one must leave behind in order to face the light of truth and its blinding uncertainty.

By repeating Nietzsche's remark, Heidegger relegated Christianity in general—and even more, corrupting Catholicism—to an obscurantist past. His thesis, though it remained implicit, was particularly hostile toward Catholicism, and yet the rector was not teaching a course limited to a small number of students; delivering a formal inaugural address was in essence a program for a university that included a Faculty of Theology, an address he was presenting in front of the people who, deep down, he saw as embodying religious science: his vice-rector, Sauer, and probably also his old friend Engelbert Krebs, and especially his first mentor, Conrad Gröber, archbishop of Freiburg. His friend Elisabeth Blochmann noted how moved the philosopher was: "Little M., in a red robe, was so pale as to be almost rather touching."[189] This emotion went beyond mere nerves: he was going against the core of his family's cultural heritage, rejecting it in a speech that moved beyond false pretenses with such power that perhaps only coming out as gay under such circumstances might have produced a greater effect on him. This stance hostile to Catholicism and uncomfortable for the rector was why, at the dinner following the address, at a restaurant fittingly called "Der Kopf" ("The Head"), he "spoke with somewhat icy, formal coldness." The vice-rector tried to lighten the mood by making "humorous remarks," asserting the "necessity of collaboration" among the three rectors in Baden and the "great cultural and political significance of the three universities" for Germany as a whole. It was only then that Heidegger relaxed and "warmed up," speaking of the protection that Sauer had accorded him in the old days, and even being "amiable"[190] toward Möllendorf, despite their opposing political and academic views.

Heidegger's growing hostility toward Catholicism did not erase all traces in him of his former religious beliefs; he still held onto large remnants of a profoundly Catholic culture.

On 12 April 1933, he sent Blochmann a copy of Augustine's *Confessions* as a birthday present, accompanied by a rather long commentary for the occasion: "I think the *Confessions* are most appropriate for this day and I hope you draw a rich and lasting benefit from this great book; the force of existence that pours forth from it is in fact inexhaustible. The most fruitful way to read it still seems to me to begin with Book 10, followed by Book 11—and only afterward take up the 'biographical' elements, if they can even be called that. You have to read the original text, if only because of its admirable Latin—which defies all translation. And the best way is to read the text provided by the great edition by the Benedictines of Saint-Maur—only in that way can the whole atmosphere peculiar to the book unfold."[191] Heidegger had probably consulted the Benedictine edition—ancient, monastic, precious—in the rich library of the Abbey of Beuron, if only on the occasion of his lecture on time in Augustine's work, given on 26 October 1930. The abbey must have surrounded any reference to the *Confessions* with its atmosphere of spiritual contemplation. The Benedictine edition achieved an apotheosis, leading Heidegger to touch, through memory, not only the book he had read there but also the setting, propitious for introspection, of the little cell where he had felt at home and which seemed inseparable from the text itself. Consciously or not, the philosopher experienced Augustine's theological autobiography the way Proust experienced the taste of the madeleine that, when dipped in tea, caused the Combray of his early years to emerge with an overwhelming truth. This is not surprising, because the memories connected with Beuron went back a long time, to his childhood walks with his mother, but they were also almost contemporary, because he had made his last visit to the monastery only two years earlier, before the archbishopric forbade him to enter.[192]

Above all, despite his hostility to religion and his desire for a science without God, Heidegger retained a mode of thought that was largely theological. Central to his academic and political thinking, the theme of destiny was religious in nature, because, being closely linked in the public sphere to a mission or vocation, it returned to a way of thought that implicitly included the ideas of predestination or a divine plan, completely consistent with his earlier mode of thought.

Heidegger had done a close study of Protestant theology, notably in Luther's work, where the concept of vocation played a major role: by practicing his trade (*Beruf*), man was responding to the call (*Ruf*) of God, who asked him to do it as his vocation (*Berufung*). This vocabulary appeared in several texts from this period, such as the speech given on the occasion of the matriculation of students on 6 May 1933,[193] which dealt with "the fundamental question of philosophy" in the form of the call of history: "University students are well aware of the greatness of the historical moment through which the German people is passing at present. [. . .] And in this process under way, university students are part of this awakening, and they are responding to their vocation [*Berufung*]."[194] Through their involvement in the German revolution, "university students," that is, the Deutsche Studentenschaft, showed the resoluteness to which history called them, in a resolute response that became a destiny, similar to the acceptance of the earthly vocation to which each person is called by Luther's God. For Heidegger, history, the people, conceived with regard to being, henceforth replaced God: university students responding to their vocation "live by the will to find the training and the education that will make them ripe and strong for spiritual and political leadership [*Führerschaft*], which, having come from the people, for the people, has to be administered to by the people."[195] The vocation of university students referred more broadly to the core of the inaugural address's program, the German people's "spiritual mission,"[196] a historical mission, to be sure, but with an implicit eschatological foundation: every mission supposes someone who assigns it. So who, beyond history, gave the German people its mission, if not something or someone like a God guaranteeing a form of salvation?

The conception of truth and freedom played a role in the complexity of this religious relation to destiny. Heidegger proclaimed to the students at Freiburg that freedom consisted in being not "free from" but rather "free for."[197] Contrary to the liberal conception of freedom that allows us to choose one thing rather than another and, in so doing, to use our freedom vis-à-vis our environment or ourselves, and contrary to the "much-touted 'academic freedom' " that emerged from the Humboldtian university—which, being "inauthentic" and "solely negative," consisted only in "a lack of concern, an arbitrariness of views and inclinations, license in action and inaction"[198]—Heidegger's conception of freedom was first of all ontological. It was a question of making oneself free for truth conceived as *aletheia,* the unveiling or revelation of being that indirectly makes us free for resoluteness in the face of death and a resolute assent to the common destiny. Going beyond a conception of truth in terms of revelation, which is religious rather than Greek in origin, Heidegger inverted John's "The truth shall set you free," rephrasing it as "Freedom shall make you true," in order to ground a phenomenon of truth that would allow us to embrace destiny. Freedom thus conceived justified voluntary, ontological participation in the *Gefolgschaft,* the following, for whom authentic existence requires making oneself free in order to follow the common destiny embodied by the Nazi *Führung.* Resolute assent to destiny led to a voluntary servitude, though it was conceived, thanks to ontology, from the point of view of a higher freedom. In that way, Heidegger adopted a position similar to that of Luther regarding the two kingdoms: if man is free in the kingdom of heaven (or, in Heidegger's case, of ontology), in his earthly kingdom, he is a slave, by God's will, to which he must submit.

In Heidegger's relation to the established discourse, the continuity with the Catholicism of his youth is striking: from his very first texts, there were not several possible choices with regard to the world and God, because one had to have the strength to conform to a cold logic that demanded obedience to the Roman Catholic religion and to its science, by denying one's subjectivity and rejecting any cult of the self. During the Nazi period, instead of following the Vicar of Christ to be in harmony with divine providence, he had to approve of the Nazi *Führung* in order to follow German destiny. Freedom, truth, vocation, mission, and destiny thus converged to provide a foundation, religious in origin, for a secularized political thought. "What came in the beginning always remains yet to come"[199]: although de-Christianized, theology, the Christian religion, the Catholicism of his childhood, and the Protestantism with which he began to be imbued toward the end of the second decade of the twentieth century continued to structure his philosophical and political thought, even when he repeated Nietzsche's remark in his address: "God is dead."[200]

This political theology discernible in Heidegger's writings at this time was commonplace under the Nazi regime. The NSDAP's victory had greatly strengthened in his contemporaries the sense of a mission given to the German people by history. Erich Rothacker wrote: "In the meantime, the victory of the national revolution, with the erection of the Third Reich, has simultaneously erected a new image of man. The accomplishment and realization of this image is the world-historical task of the German people [*die weltgeschichtliche Aufgabe des deutschen Volkes*]."[201] Even beyond the upheaval of consciousnesses produced by the Third Reich, which for many Germans was a national revolution, this strong persistence of religion in a secularized, indeed irreligious way of thinking had its roots deep in the foundations of the main ideologues of the Nazi movement, even before the advent of the new regime.

Rosenberg, who was similarly hostile to Christianity and especially to Catholicism, also retained the idea of a historic mission:

> Past and present suddenly appear in a new light, and for the future there results a new mission [*Sendung*]. History and the task of the future no longer signify the struggle of class against class or the conflict between one church dogma and another [*Kirchendogma und Dogma*], but the settlement between blood and blood, race and race, folk and folk. And that means: the struggle of spiritual values [*Seelenwert*] against each other.[202]

On this supposed historical mission of his people, Rosenberg erected a veritable secularized religion:

> The collapse of 1918 tore apart our very vitals, but at the same time laid bare to the searching soul the threads which had woven their fabric of mixed blessings. From the tribal consciousness of ancient Germania, by way of the ideas of the German kings, through the new leadership of Prussia and the faith in a united Germany, there is born today, as the greatest flowering of the German soul, a racially based folkish consciousness [*artgebundene Volksbewußtsein*]. On the basis of this experience we hail as

> the religion of the German future the fact that, though lying now politically prostrate, humiliated and persecuted, we have found the roots of our strength, and have actually discovered and experienced them anew with such force as no previous generation has known.[203]

This intellectual schema is also found in Hitler, who frequently refers in *Mein Kampf* to destiny, mission, and predestination. Considering "the highest unlimited authority" and the "ultimate and heaviest responsibility" incumbent upon the *Führer,* he asserts that "only the hero is *called*"[204] to be a *Führer.* This heroic vocation that Hitler thought he had was coupled with a consideration of his birthplace, which he saw as a symbol of his mission, whose crucial importance for his future he indicated by beginning *Mein Kampf* with these words: "Today it seems to me that it is my vocation [*Bestimmung*] that *Fate* [*Schicksal*] should have chosen Braunau on the Inn as my birthplace. For this little town lies on the boundary between two German states which we of the younger generation at least have made it our life's work [*Lebensaufgabe*] to reunite by every means at our disposal."[205] The *Anschluß,* the annexation of Austria to Germany, was not the sum total of the duties that fell to him: more broadly, he had to fight against the Treaty of Versailles, which prevented the German people not only from uniting, but also from finding the means of establishing its power among the other nations of the world. And, as a result,

> if the National Socialist movement really wants to be *consecrated* by history with a great mission for our nation, it must be permeated by knowledge and filled with pain at our true situation in his world; boldly and conscious of its goal, it must take up the struggle against the aimlessness and incompetence which have hitherto guided our German nation in the line of foreign affairs.[206]

Propaganda was one of the Party's most important duties in the accomplishment of its mission. Playing with religious beliefs, it had to morally rearm the German people by making it ardently desire a war experienced and conceived under the aegis of God:

> For this, to be sure, from the child's primer down to the last newspaper, every theater and every movie house, every advertising pillar and every billboard, must be pressed into the service of this one great mission, until the timorous prayer of our present parlor patriots: "Lord, make us free!" is transformed in the brain of the smallest boy into the burning plea: "*Almighty God, bless our arms when the time comes; be just as thou hast*

> *always been; judge now whether we be deserving of freedom; Lord, bless our battle!*"[207]

Hitler did not limit his comments on political theology to the state alone: he saw nationality or ethnicity (*Volkstum*), rather than the state, as embodying a "higher" political mission (*Mission*), because in his view the state's mission "lies essentially in the nationality whose free development the state must merely make possible by the organic force of its being [*Dasein*]."[208] The prohibition of marriages that defiled the race was supposed to allow the union of a man and a woman to be once more the "*consecration* [*Weihe*] of an institution," because it had returned to its purpose of creating "*images of the Lord* and not monstrosities halfway between man and ape."[209] Humanity itself also had a mission, that of creating and dominating, which would come to an end, for lack of being fulfilled, with the definitive disappearance of the Aryan as a result of the dissolution of his blood in that of inferior races. Against "our present notorious weaklings," sheep bleating about human rights, Hitler vigorously asserted the existence of a single, unique, "*holiest* human right" (*heiligste Menschenrecht*), a right but also a duty: "to see to it that the blood is preserved pure and, by preserving the best humanity, to create the possibility of a nobler development of these beings."[210]

Heidegger was not to be outdone in this political theology that competed directly with the religion inherited from his parents by positing an immanent eschatology. In the seventh session of his seminar in winter 1933–1934, he developed in these terms the union of the *Führer* with the people against "two menacing powers," death and the devil.

> It is only when the *Führer* and those he leads [*Geführte*] are united in *one* destiny and fight for the realization of *one* idea, that the true order grows. [. . .] In each new moment, the *Führer* and the people will unite more closely to realize the essence of their state, and thus of their being; growing together, they will stand up to the two menacing powers of death and the devil, that is, the transience and decay of their own essence, by means of their sensible and historical being and will.[211]

The devil, an essential figure in the religion of his childhood who had haunted Heidegger during his mother's last days, was, like death, contained spiritually by the union of a people and a guide fighting resolutely for the realization of an idea, of a destiny that was accepted on the basis of their own history and which became salvation.

"Alles Große steht im Sturm."[212] "Everything great is exposed to storms," and also "everything great stands firm under attack." Basing himself on a quotation from Plato reinterpreted by Nietzsche and by the Sturm Abteilung (SA), Heidegger had just finished his inaugural address as rector. He had outlined his plans as rector by situating them in the new history that was in progress and that heralded a profound revolution from which Germany would emerge changed forever. In so doing, he had glossed over certain details that were less consensual: Hitler, the institutional power of *Führer* that he wanted to arrogate to himself, and the anti-Catholic battle he expected to wage, as the rest of his rectorship was to show.

Sometimes elliptical or prudent, expressing himself as usual in a language that quickly became hermetic and self-referential, Rector Heidegger thus laid out the main lines of his program and the conceptions underlying it. Suffering from a headache, drowsing near him during a large part of his speech, his vice-rector, Sauer, sensed his former student's programmatic ambition, though he considered him "almost unintelligible." "He talked about almost everything," Sauer wrote in his diary: "God is dead, the Greek spirit must be passed on to the Germans. The new age requires three things of students: labor service, military service, and study service."[213] In the audience, Heidegger's friend Elisabeth Blochmann found his speech "very beautiful," a true "philosophical discourse" whose closing impressed her: "Everything great is exposed to storms." "Quintessential M.H.," she concluded in her letter written the next day to her other mentor, Hermann Nohl, "and so serious that one was really very grateful to him for it."[214]

Far from being heard only by those present at the ceremony, Heidegger's inaugural address received favorable attention even abroad. The rector took care to have numerous offprints made and to send them out so that the speech would have the largest audience. To do this, he had chosen the Korn-Verlag publishing house in Breslau, which specialized in far-right militant works like Arthur Moeller van den Bruck's *Third Reich*.[215] Among those receiving offprints were allies, such as leaders of the German Student Union,[216] and enemies, such as Richard Kröner—Heidegger had wanted to see Kröner's authorization to teach withdrawn in July 1923.[217] He accompanied the offprints with a "Heil Hitler" when the addressees were "Aryans" supporting the regime, and with "cordial greetings" when they were not, as in the case of Karl Löwith, who judged this screed with moderation and distance:

> Compared to the numerous speeches and pamphlets that "aligned" professors made public after the revolution, Heidegger's address is of great

> philosophical import and great ambition, a little masterpiece of formulation and composition. From the philosophical point of view, it is a masterpiece of ambiguity, it manages to make useful to the historical "moment" (*Being and Time,* §74) the existential categories of ontology, in a way that gave the impression that their philosophical intentions could and should be reconciled with the political situation, just as freedom of research should be reconciled with the constraint of the state. "Labor service" and "military service" are now of a piece with "knowledge service," so that at the end of the presentation one isn't sure whether one ought to study Diels's pre-Socratics or march with the SA.[218]

Among Heidegger's friends, Karl Jaspers, who had read excerpts of the address in the newspapers, praised the text in late August, when he received the offprint: "The great stroke of your inception in the early Greeks affected me again like a new, but at the same time obvious, truth. In this, you come together with Nietzsche, but with the difference that one may hope that you will at some point realize, through philosophical interpretation, what you are saying. In this respect, your address has genuine substance." Of course, he had a few reservations, noting "the qualities of this address that are of the time," and "something in it" that struck him "as a little forced," "statements" with a "hollow ring"—all reservations that nonetheless did not prevent him from declaring himself, "all in all," "only happy that someone can speak in such a way that he touches upon genuine limits and origins."[219]

Although just as friendly, Rudolf Bultmann did not manage to appear overcome with joy. Reacting on 18 June to the inaugural address based on an inexact review of it he had read in the *Freiburger Tagespost,* the theologian expressed his incomprehension at the philosopher's accession to the rectorship itself. He wrote that he was so "deeply disturbed" that he had not found the strength to congratulate his friend until he had read the review of his speech. Influenced by Nietzsche and Kierkegaard, but resistant to Hitler and Rosenberg, Bultmann was happy to see Weimar swept away, but was worried by the atmosphere of "ὕβρις [*hubris*] and repressed fear" that was spreading "oppressively." He therefore communicated his circumspection and expressed his regret, kindly, that he was not enthusiastic like his friend, who was now the new regime's rector. " 'We do will ourselves!' you say, if the newspaper reports it correctly. How blind this will seems to me! What a risk this will poses that every instant will fall short of itself. What *hubris* this about-turn has already produced, deaf to the demand that the 'spiritual world be ever renewed in the extreme exposure to the powers of being.' "[220] Like Heidegger, Bultmann perceived Nazism's fundamental and absolute brutality; like him, he was aware that it was possible to elevate oneself through philosophy to a level far above the Nazi movement, as his friend was doing; but, not being obsessed with the idea that philosophers shape the spiritual world of their time, he could harbor no hope that the person swept up to that altitude could thereby become more visible or audible to the common man.

Perhaps Bultmann thought that his friend should have meditated on Nietzsche's remark, which would have given Heidegger more gravity and weight in the coarse world of the Third Reich: "The more we rise, the smaller we appear to those who cannot fly."[221] Believing he was an eagle of thought blessed by the sun of the new Reich, Heidegger not only came to suffer the scorn of a few vulgar spirits jealous of him, but soared so high that his own hubris cast him down to the depths of the abyss when the star that had guided him was consumed in the gigantic inferno of war.

8 • An Albatross Tries Out the Goose Step

(1933–1934)

Le Poète est semblable au prince des nuées
Qui hante la tempête et se rit de l'archer;
Exilé sur le sol au milieu des huées,
Ses ailes de géant l'empêchent de marcher.
Charles Baudelaire, "L'Albatros" (1861)

The Poet is a brother of this prince of clouds,
Familiar of the storm, he laughs at bows and slings.
But exiled on the earth among the hooting crowds,
He finds his walk is hobbled by his giant wings.
"The Albatross," trans. William H. Crosby

Under the Third Reich, Heidegger increasingly linked in his own mind the figure of the poet and that of the thinker. And, though he does not seem to have been familiar with Charles Baudelaire's "Albatross," which depicts the poet's clumsiness and unhappiness in the prosaic life he leads with his fellows, the poem could have been written to predict, with the superhuman art of the poets, what Heidegger's situation as a thinker in Nazi Germany would be. As the "prince of clouds," he would attempt to use his mind to establish himself as king of the geese, only to experience a humiliating failure. It was not that Heidegger did not apply himself to marching in goose step and making others march with him. By virtue of his position, his prestige, and his discourse, he became a zealous promoter of the new regime. He publicly supported its entire policy, which he implemented and sometimes even anticipated.

A Rector Philosopher in the Vanguard of the Nazi Regime

Heidegger conceived of his *Führung* as a mastery of speech. He therefore spoke a great deal. He spoke in Freiburg, on occasions that were traditional for a rector: ritual occasions such as his inauguration as rector in May and the student matriculation celebration in November;[1] or special occasions, for example, the fiftieth anniversary of the establishment of the Institute for Pathological Anatomy in August 1933[2] and the death of his colleague, the obstetrician-gynecologist Otto Pankow, in February of the following year.[3] He spoke out on other occasions, dictated by the circumstances of the new regime: the broadcast of a speech by Hitler in the university stadium on 17 May,[4] the celebration in honor of Bismarck and the solstice on 24 June,[5] the opening of university courses to the unemployed of Freiburg,[6] and the call to join the Labor Service in January 1934. He also traveled a great deal to speak outside Freiburg, a sign of his desire to make himself heard throughout Germany. Berlin, which until recently had served as a foil, became more than ever a center of attraction, because it was from there, whether he wished it or not, that Heidegger could truly hope to wield influence in an increasingly centralized state. But he also traveled, in June, to Heidelberg, the other major university in Baden, and to Leipzig, for the meeting of the Nationalsozialistische Lehrerbund (NSLB; National Socialist Teachers League), which in November 1933 issued a declaration of allegiance to Adolf Hitler that was translated into many languages and widely disseminated. Held shortly before the plebiscites in favor of leaving the League of Nations and the election of a single, Nazi slate to the Reichstag, the declaration prompted Heidegger to appeal publicly to the German people to approve that radicalization of the regime.

The students, more malleable than the faculty and fervent supporters of the Third Reich, represented the future, both near and more distant, of the university and of Germany. They were therefore the Reich's privileged target. Under the new laws, students were under the control of the German Student Union, with which Heidegger was already in touch. In June 1932 the German Student Union had invited him to its congress in Blankenburg am Harz, but he had preferred to focus on his work.[7] Now, however, after being named rector on 21 April 1933, Heidegger entered into contact with its leadership in Berlin on the 24th, to propose a national seminar for its *Führer*. The seminar was held on 10 and 11 June and, in addition to Heidegger, probably included Alfred Baeumler and Ernst Krieck.[8] On 26 September Heidegger also participated at a student camp in the suburbs of Berlin, on the Döberitz parade ground.[9]

Because the bonds between him and the Deutsche Studentenschaft were strong, the student union even considered printing one of Heidegger's courses (GA 16, 106),[10] probably the one he had taught on the fundamental question of philosophy during the summer semester.[11]

In his speeches, the philosopher proved to be as radical as usual. Invited to Heidelberg on 30 June by the local student union to deliver the first talk for its political education program, he struck hard: "A revolution is going on in Germany, and we must ask ourselves: *is there a revolution going on in the university as well?* No. The fighting still consists of preliminary skirmishes, and up to this point it has launched only one attack: through the training for a new life in the work camps and in the educational association [*Erziehungsverband*] alongside the university, the latter has been relieved of these educational duties, which it had up to this point thought were its exclusive domain."[12]

Heidegger was persuaded of the importance of the camps, which were particularly well suited to ensure that students would be "taken hold of" (*ergriffen*) by the "concept" (*Begriff*)[13] of political science, which he was promoting with his words. The most notable camp he organized was in Todtnauberg and took place between 4 and 10 October 1933.[14] For what he described to the Freiburg university community as a "vacation camp" (*Ferienlager*),[15] students left the university on foot, in close ranks, wearing "the SA or SS uniform, or possibly the *Stahlhelm* uniform with an armband." They charged up the mountain, where reveille was scheduled for 6 a.m. and taps for 10 p.m.[16] The troops came from Freiburg but also from Kiel and Heidelberg; each of the three groups was headed by a privatdozent. All were under the *Führung* of Heidegger, who had defined the spirit of this science camp with national ambitions: "The actual work of the camp consists in reflecting on the ways and means of winning the battle for the future university of the German spirit." To that end, the philosopher prescribed:

> The camp's work [*Lagerarbeit*] must not follow an empty program. It must grow out of genuine leadership and allegiance [*Gefolgschaft*] and it should produce its own order therefrom. A few talks given before the whole camp community should produce the basic mood [*Grundstimmung*] and the basic attitude [*Grundhaltung*]. The crucial discussions in the groups must carry and ignite the collective discussions.
>
> The camp's success depends on the ability to find fresh courage, clear-sightedness, and vigilance for the future, on the will to loyalty, sacrifice, and duty. It is from these strengths that a true *Gefolgschaft* will

> arise. And only it will support and consolidate a genuine German community.[17]

In his speeches, Heidegger followed Germany's new orientations, while grounding them in his own philosophy. On 26 May 1933, for example, on the eve of his inauguration as rector, he presided at the tribute to Albert Leo Schlageter, a veteran and Freiburg graduate who had become one of the martyred heroes of the NSDAP for his acts of resistance against the French in 1923. Heidegger elaborated not only his notion of blood and soil but also that of the single direction of destinies, as he had formulated it in *Being and Time*.[18] Referring to the path that would lead Schlageter to his death, Heidegger noted: "He had to [*er müßte*] go the Baltic countries; he *had to* go to Upper Silesia; he *had to* go to the Ruhr. He was not allowed to escape his destiny, to die the most painful and greatest death with a hard will and a lucid heart."[19] Like the destiny described in *Being and Time,* Schlageter's successive destinies bore in advance a direction, which he resolved to take: to go fight in the Baltic states, then in Upper Silesia, and finally in the Ruhr, where he passed from life to death, seeing that death delivered from the barrels of French guns.

The speeches Martin Heidegger delivered in Leipzig in early November were similarly imbued with his philosophy. On 11 November he appealed to the Germans to approve the plebiscite authorizing Germany's exit from the League of Nations, which Hitler had decided on, and the single slate of legislators for the Reichstag: "The German people is called upon to elect the Führer; but the Führer is asking nothing from the people, instead, he is giving the people a direct opportunity to make the highest free decision, whether the whole people wants its own *Dasein* or *not*."[20] Heidegger's injunction, following Hitler's, called for the Germans to communicate their assent and thereby take responsibility for their own being-with-others. In that way, they would "free" the "superior power" of fate,[21] despite the fact that the direction of fate was clearly traced in advance: it consisted of leaving the League of Nations and sending only Nazi legislators to the Reichstag. For Hitler, exiting the league was a way to set the conditions for a return to the policy of military expansion, by leaving that body charged with promoting peace through dialogue, in Europe and the world. For Heidegger, it was above all a decision in harmony with his notion of the authenticity of a people, as set out in paragraph 74 of *Being and Time*.[22] It was a manner of once more taking full responsibility for one's own destiny, by leaving that cosmopolitan body, which was hampering authentic resoluteness in the face of one's own destiny, in the same way that parliamentarianism within the state itself could do. It was therefore necessary as well to vote overwhelmingly for the new, entirely Nazi, chamber of the Reichstag, which was subject to the Germans' approval at the same time. In following their leader in unison with Heidegger, Germans were able to will their own *Dasein:* the plebiscite was approved by 95.1 percent of the voters and Nazi candidates garnered 92.1 percent in the election.[23]

Heidegger repurposed certain elements of his philosophy to make them serve the regime's propaganda. Even so, he did not remain insensitive to the spirit of the times. He was so filled with the Nazi notion of work that, in his 1934 course, he expatiated on joy as the fundamental affective disposition, appropriating without ironic distance the title, in the form of a slogan, of the Nazi organization in charge of leisure activities: *Kraft durch Freude,* "strength through joy." As the philosopher put it: "That is why having a joyous heart at work is so important. That is not an affective disposition that merely accompanies our work, it's not a supplement to work; but joy as a fundamental affective disposition is the foundation of true work, whose accomplishment is the only thing that makes man apt for *Dasein.*"[24] That Nazi "socialism" made sense to the philosopher, who was intent in this course on distinctly marking the break with Marxism: "It does not mean a simple change in the way of thinking about economics, it does not seek a distressing leveling down or the glorification of inadequacy. It does not refer to the pursuit, without ever making choices, of a well-being for everyone without any goal other than itself." All the latter referred to what Heidegger reviled: the Marxist understanding of socialism. On the contrary, for him "socialism" meant "concern about standards and the essential configuration of our historical being, and that is why it wants an order of precedence based on the vocation [*Beruf*] and the work done, it wants the inviolable dignity of each kind of work to be recognized and unconditional priority granted to the service imperative and to the fundamental relation to the inescapability of being."[25]

The appropriation of Nazi ideology had greater political consequences when it came to eugenics. The major law on the matter, concerning "the prevention of offspring with hereditary diseases," was promulgated on 14 July 1933. Because its aim was to improve the "race" by prohibiting its "degenerate" members from reproducing, paragraph 1 of the law established the principle of sterilizing individuals affected by various pathologies of the body (deafness and visual impairment, significant physical deformities) or mind (mental retardation, hereditary epilepsy, schizophrenia, manic-depressive disorder, Huntington's disease, severe alcoholism).[26] The law went into effect on the following 1 January; by August 1939, it would affect about 300,000 people, who were forced to undergo surgical sterilization.[27]

Being no more clairvoyant than anyone else, Heidegger could not have known these figures in advance. But he approved the principle, which required a Spartan courage, spurned by Christianity and unattainable for bourgeois liberalism. At the informal talk (*Tischgespräch,* literally "table talk") he gave in early August at the Institute of Pathological Anatomy, he noted: "What is decisive and surprising is that the essence of health has in no way been defined in the same way in every period and among every people."

To support his views, he compared what he saw as the Greek, Christian, and modern bourgeois notions of health. In the same spirit that he had discussed Spartan eugenics in Plutarch's *Life of Lycurgus,* which condemned fragile infants to death and promoted robust births through flexible marriage laws, Heidegger presented the Greek notion of health from the exclusive angle of the state. Ultimately, the state justified the passive euthanasia of patients who had become useless: "For the Greeks," he believed, " 'healthy' means neither more nor less than ready and strong enough to be active in the state. Doctors were not allowed to treat anyone who no longer satisfied these conditions."[28] Conversely, Christian doctrine considers "an excess of suffering and affliction to be equivalent to health, that is, to the condition that makes someone eligible for and worthy of salvation in the next world," whereas "earthly happiness and well-being, if they rely on themselves, are diseased and unhealthy." The "modern bourgeois world," finally, defines health as "the sedate enjoyment of bodily well-being" and thus tends to reduce medicine and medical practice to a "simple technique of eliminating and relieving medical conditions."

Heidegger thereby relativized historically the determination of the essence of health: "So far as what is healthy and what is not, a people and a period determine their own law, depending on the inner greatness and extent of their *Dasein.*" He did not do the same, however, for that essence itself. The principle of medical autonomy, by which a people bestows on itself the measure of health according to its own spiritual greatness, was inserted into a law of history that decided every aspect of the greatness or decline of a people: "For every people, the first guarantee of its authenticity and greatness is in its blood, its soil, and its bodily growth. If this is lost or even allowed to weaken extensively, any effort made by state policy, any economic and technological knowledge, any spiritual action, will ultimately remain null and void."

He thus fully adopted Nazi principles of eugenics as well as the principles of euthanasia, which he attributed to the Greeks. The body, by means of blood, soil, and its own growth, is primary and decides in great part the greatness of a people, even its spiritual dimension, though that dimension cannot be reduced to the body alone. As a result of Heidegger's absorption of Nazi ideology, with this theory the informal talk marked a shift away from the rector's address, which had placed greater emphasis on the "spiritual world" and its preeminence over blood and soil. The two ideas were not incompatible, of course: blood, soil, and the growth of the body were primary when compared to consciousness; and consciousness, though secondary, had primacy as *imperium in imperio*. The shift in emphasis was nonetheless notable.

Heidegger concluded his informal talk by saying that the Third Reich, having supplanted the smallness of the Christian and modern bourgeois ages, was a great era, and that, under Hitler's leadership, the German people would regain the conditions of its historic longevity and greatness. "The German people is about to rediscover its own essence and make itself worthy of its great destiny. Through the National Socialist Revolution, Adolf Hitler, our great *Führer* and chancellor, has created a new state through which the people will once again guarantee its history a long and stable life."[29] Heidegger's approval of the regime from the standpoint of its racial policy was not abstract. The circumstances of his remarks, not only the time but also the place (the Institute for Pathological Anatomy, the center for eugenics in Germany), clearly indicate that he was aware of the spirit of the law, whose harshness, totalitarianism, and antiliberalism were in complete harmony with his valorization of resoluteness and courage. In the context of molding the new teacher and *Führer* at the university, that led him to call for "a hard breed" (*ein hartes Geschlecht*), one that does not think of itself but lives by a "constant self-challenge" in the pursuit of the "goal to which it is devoted."[30] That hardness necessary for shaping leaders at the university was no different in essence from that required if the people was to become "worthy of its great destiny." The people would cultivate not only its mind or spirit, by means of a philosophical revolution, but also its body, through a fully courageous policy that would dare stand firm, even to the point of embracing the extreme measures indicated by Adolf Hitler.

The emphasis placed on blood and on support for the regime's eugenics policy was not an anomaly in Heidegger's texts. Witness, a year after his talk at the Institute of Pathological Anatomy, the course on logic he taught in summer 1934 and his argument regarding "the voice of blood."[31] In parallel, his meditation on the essence of the people led him to mention, among the occurrences of the word *Volk*, a number that seemed positive to him, such as the actions of the "*völkisch* movement," which sought to "bring the people back to the purity of its racial origin [*zur Reinheit seiner Stammesart zurückbringen*]," as well as "measures taken for the improvement and protection of the people."[32] Above all, his embrace of the regime's eugenics policy explains his investment in the creation in Freiburg of a "tenured professorship in racial doctrine and hereditary biology." The ministry was slow to respond to his request, however. On 13 April 1934, only ten days before he resigned, Heidegger complained to the ministry that, for months, he had been calling in vain for the position. The subject he had chosen for his letter clearly indicated the heart of the matter: "instruction in racial hygiene,"[33] that is, racist eugenics.

The rector of Freiburg did not limit himself to a mastery of speech: he also conducted himself as a loyal and even zealous official of the regime. "Following leaders (*Führer*)": these were not empty words for Heidegger, who himself lived his life as a follower of leaders. When Robert Wagner was named *Reichsstatthalter* of Baden, Heidegger congratulated him in a letter of martial tribute: "Rejoicing in this appointment, the rector of the University of Freiburg salutes the *Führer* of his native borderland with a martial *Sieg Heil!*"[34] *Sieg Heil,* a bellicose variant of the "German greeting" *Heil Hitler,* which became standard with the advent of the Third Reich, evoked the victory (*Sieg*) one boasted of achieving. In saluting one's leader with a "martial *Sieg Heil,*" one fell in line as a follower, armed with resolute words, like a combatant ready to fight on the front lines in the battles to come. The tribute to Wagner was akin to those Heidegger paid to Hitler in various public speeches, as when, on 17 May, addressing students and faculty, the philosopher marked the end of the radio broadcast of the chancellor's speech in the university stadium with these words:[35] "The chancellor of the Reich, our great *Führer,* has spoken. Other nations and peoples must now decide. We *have decided.*" And he concluded with a "German *Sieg Heil*" to "our great *Führer* Adolf Hitler."[36]

Heidegger was fascinated by Hitler. On 13 April, he shared his enthusiasm with Fritz. "From one day to the next we see the greatness with which Hitler is now becoming a statesman. The world of our people and of the Reich is caught up in change, and anyone who still has eyes to see and ears to hear and a heart to act is swept along and moved by an authentic and profound excitement [*wird mitgerissen und in eine echte und tiefe Erregung versetzt*]."[37] A charismatic leader, Hitler was accorded by Heidegger, as by so many other Germans of the time, an extraordinary status as a messiah who had come to save them. Like so many others, Heidegger approved of what he saw: even the Nazis' anti-Semitic policy did not pose a problem for him. A few lines later, he pointed out that, as a result of the law for the restoration of the professional civil service, three Jews had "disappeared"[38] from his department, but only to complain about the increase in his workload. Obsessed with his project for a philosophical revolution, he was ardently hoping for the realization of what he equated with the hidden plans of a providence addressed to only a few initiates: "Once again, we encounter around us a great reality and, at the same time, the great necessity of constructing that reality within the spiritual world of the Reich and in the secret mission of the German essence [*deutschen Wesen*]."[39]

Three weeks later, he replied to his brother, who had complained about the Nazi Party, that he should not "consider the movement as a whole from below but from the point of view of the Führer and his grand aims."[40] Enthralled, Heidegger wished in September to be appointed to a chair in Munich, closer to his idol: "A tenured chair is vacant there. That would have the advantage of a great scope for action and would not be as out of the way as Freiburg is now. The opportunity to approach Hitler."[41] He went so far as to make his mustache resemble Hitler's, small and almost square, an extension of his nose. Heidegger also imitated Hitler's gaze and the poses he struck, so much so that Hitler reminded Fritz of his brother: "I don't know if it's just an illusion or not. Many of Hitler's attitudes, as well as his gaze on the recent posters, often make me think of you. That comparison alone leads me at times to the conclusion that Hitler must be a splendid fellow."[42] The philosopher's Hitlerism grew over time, and, pushing even further his philosophy of *Gefolgschaft*, with the appeal of 3 November to German students, he swept aside "doctrines and 'ideas' " as possible rules for their being, the better to insist: "The Führer himself, and he alone, *is* the present and future German reality and your law."[43] In something between an observation and an injunction, an ideology and an ontology (with his emphasis on "is"), Heidegger maintained that the German people was grounded in its supreme leader, who ought to be the only law observed by the German students. On 23 February 1934, as the regime was consolidating itself ever more, the philosopher even concluded his seminar "The Essence and Concept of Nature, History, and State" by proclaiming that the Third Reich was the clear endpoint of German history: "The leader state [*Führerstaat*]—as we have it—signifies the completion of historical development [*die Vollendung der geschichtlichen Entwicklung*]: the realization of the people in its leader [*die Verwirklichung des Volkes im Führer*]."[44]

The realization of the *Führerstaat* had to come to the university; otherwise, that realization would not be complete. Heidegger was thus the first to endeavor to introduce the *Führerprinzip* into academia. The proclamation of his spiritual leadership during his rector's address was meant to be part of the nazification of all German institutions, as the caption to his official rector's photograph announced.[45] And, not satisfied with mere symbols, Heidegger in fact adopted the organizational principles of the new regime. In the telegram he sent on 20 May to Chancellor Hitler, Heidegger asked him to postpone the reception for the board of the Association of German Universities until it had submitted fully to *Gleichschaltung,* which was "particularly necessary" there.[46] When, as rector, he composed that telegram, he was conducting himself like an authentic Nazi *Führer,* trampling underfoot traditional academic collegiality. He did not submit the telegram to anyone, which caused a scandal. "That's what's known as 'collegial,' "[47] Sauer wrote ironically. For the inaugural celebration of his rectorship, he treated the deans as *Führer,* having them take a step forward in front of their respective faculties.[48] The invitations to the rectorship celebration illustrated even better that change of governance style. Although the printed text followed the traditional formulation: "The rector and the Senate of the Albert-Ludwigs-Universität Freiburg hereby invite . . . ," Heidegger had modified it in his own hand to read: "The rector of the Albert-Ludwigs-Universität Freiburg hereby invites . . . ,"[49] making the senate nothing more than a council stripped of the dignity proper to it, with its leader effaced.

Moreover, Heidegger neglected to convene the university senate. This omission was the easiest way to bring the senate to heel, whatever the problems to be settled, and whatever the resistance that might arise from that tactic of seizing power. When Walter Eucken from the Faculty of Jurisprudence and Möllendorff from the Faculty of Medicine rebelled, Sauer tried to push his former disciple in the direction of greater collegiality. (Möllendorff had earlier been elected the new rector, but had been forced to resign.) Both men urged Heidegger to convene the university senate to discuss the institutional changes under way. The jurist Sauer had the sense that the rector was acting as if he just wanted "to roll along on his own, following the system of the leader principle."[50] That application of the *Führerprinzip* by the new rector caused such a scandal that it henceforth became known as the "Heidegger affair,"[51] a name that has remained, even as the dossier has grown thicker over time.

In the following months, Heidegger continued to spark complaints of abuse of power because of the role he played in drawing up the constitution of 21 August governing the universities in Baden. Heidegger was the main force behind the constitution, if not its author. According to the new bylaws, the *Führer*-rector was appointed by the ministry for an unlimited term. The university did not have the right to suggest a name or to reject the one imposed on it. The rector then chose as he pleased the *Führer*-deans of the faculties,[52] adopting the absolute command structure of the *Führerprinzip*. With that conception of how institutions of higher learning were to be organized, Baden once again sought to be in the vanguard of the regime, as it had been regarding the status of the Jews. In the privacy of one of his black notebooks, Heidegger was able to express his delight: "The *parliamentarianism* of the university senate and of the faculties has indeed been eliminated."[53] The next day he replied to Carl Schmitt, who had mentioned in a letter the famous fragment by Heraclitus: "Combat is the father of all things, and of all things king." Heidegger said that the letter had "given him great pleasure," because he had not forgotten "the king," the Greek βασιλεύς (*basileus*), behind which his Nazi ear heard *Führer,* a word so prevalent at the time. He went on to say that he found himself "in all-out *polemos* [πόλεμος, combat or war],"[54] mentioning the Faculty of Law, which had to be converted to the regime's new spirit in the matter of jurisprudence. That was why he was hoping for his correspondent's collaboration. The rector of Freiburg was pessimistic: "Here, the situation is desperate. The gathering of the spiritual powers that are supposed to lead us to what is coming is becoming increasingly urgent."[55]

The University of Freiburg was in fact a long way from uniting behind the man who aspired to become its *Führer.* Josef Sauer, the vice-rector marginalized by his rector, learned through the press the content of the new constitution. Filled with resentment, he lamented in his diary the same day: " '*Finis universitatis*': the end of the university. And we're in this mess because of that fool Heidegger, whom we elected to the rectorship in order to bring about a new spirituality of the universities. What an irony! For the moment we can do nothing except hope that the other German universities, particularly in Prussia, will not take this step into the abyss, even though they are being urged in no uncertain terms to do so; that will soon put paid to Baden's little aberration."[56]

At the same moment, Karl Jaspers, who was a professor at Heidelberg and was thus affected by the new university constitution, also learned of the text that would govern his university: "It is an extraordinary step,"[57] he wrote to Heidegger on 23 August. "Because I know from my own experience how the outgoing constitution works, and because for years I have consciously withheld all initiatives because everything fails against this wall, I cannot do otherwise than to find the new constitution right."[58] Expressing the sort of nostalgia we feel when confronted with signs indicating that, good or bad, an era is coming to an end and that a part of us is dying with it, Jaspers had only one criticism: "Whoever has such powers at his disposal would also have to take responsibility for mistakes, of character or of insight, in his actions—if the constitution is to accomplish something *in the long run*. The form in which a critique of *appearances* and of *actions* can come to a deciding court of appeals is, it seems to me, not laid down."[59] Rightly fearing that, over time, "a racket in intrigue, dependent on particular circumstances," would be the result, he nevertheless judged such criticism a secondary matter. He predicted that "the first test" would be to learn "to what extent the leaders of all ranks, those designated by each subordinate one, possess the *gift of discerning spirits*." And he concluded by wishing "success" to that "aristocratic principle."[60]

With that fully Nazi university constitution, which served as a model for the "coordination" of German universities, Heidegger was officially named *Führer*-rector by the ministry in Karlsruhe on 1 October.[61] He chose his deans himself (Möllendorff among them),[62] as well as a university chancellor who could receive a full delegation of powers, a system he had set up on 28 June, anticipating the adoption by special dispensation of that new law.[63] He expected all his academic colleagues to follow him and anticipated that those he had chosen as leaders would assist him.

Heidegger's proclamation of his *Führung*—his leadership over the university—and his role in elaborating new university bylaws that entitled him to almost absolute power as *Führer*-rector, did not mean he would actually possess such power. He had to overcome opposition, which in some cases came from his natural ally, the German Student Union. Heidegger was determined to impose his own notion of the new educational system by means of three "services": knowledge, defense, and labor, strongly united through philosophy. That rigorous conception of the new university organization was at the heart of his public criticism of the German Student Union in May, when he pointed out that it did not want "unified education, combining spirit, defense, and labor," but rather "SA military training along with labor service, also consisting of drills, and the associated specialized technical knowledge."[64] To impose his own views, he had made inquiries about the way the introduction of defensive sports to the universities had been discussed in Berlin on 7 and 8 April.[65] And, a few days before his speech, to ensure that the defense service in Freiburg had "strict and experienced leadership,"[66] he requested the assistance of the local police. That was probably a way for him to control the establishment of the defense service, which would have eluded him had it been overseen by the SA.

Heidegger put a great deal of effort into his paramilitary organization, entrusting it to Dr. Georg Stieler, a former navy officer active in the *Stahlhelm*. Stieler therefore led exercises for students equipped with wooden weapons in the clay pits of a brickyard near Freiburg, at the foot of the Schönberg. An eyewitness, a veteran of the First World War and professor of medicine at the time, reported to Hugo Ott that, "prompted by curiosity," he was watching "these rather childish war games" when he suddenly saw the rector's automobile arriving. Heidegger promptly leapt out, like a general going to inspect the troops on a parade ground. Then, "Professor Stieler, as the 'commanding officer,' stood to attention in front of the great philosopher, who was short in stature, and made his 'report' in the correct military manner." The two men were very dissimilar: one very short, the other a giant, over 6 feet 7 inches tall. "It was a touching, and at the same time slightly farcical scene, given the considerable difference in the two men's physical size."[67]

Heidegger was clearly exceeding the limits of "*spiritual* leadership." He wanted to impose his authority, and that included using the administrative power he possessed. He enlisted students and faculty as his followers, which led to a sort of conflict of authority in his relations with the student body. Granted, the student union at each university was supposed to "collaborate" to ensure that students "fulfilled their duties concerning the people, the state, and the university,"[68] which placed them in a form of relative subjection to, notably, the rector of their institution. Nevertheless, each local union, recognized as a branch of its school, was included in the structure governed by the *Führerprinzip*, which is to say, the German Student Union. According to the university bylaws and the law, therefore, the students were not placed in the *Gefolgschaft* of their rector, but ultimately in that of the *Führer* of the Deutsche Studentenschaft. Furthermore, they were under the "protection" of the Reich's minister of the interior, Wilhelm Frick.[69] One of the characteristic aspects of Nazism was in evidence here: behind the unity of leadership that supposedly presided over the new Germany, governed by the *Führerprinzip*, *Gleichschaltung* led to the establishment of centralized, hierarchical, and competing Nazi powers. Although they were organized in accordance with the leader principle, their anarchical proliferation would gradually undermine the actions of the German state. In addition, Heidegger ran into a problem that had arisen much earlier for Hitler himself: the lack of discipline of young people, particularly those in the SA.[70] The Führer succeeded in definitively quelling the SA by killing off its leaders on 30 June 1934, the Night of the Long Knives, a radical measure to which the *Führer*-rector could not resort.

Nazism at the University: A Purge Policy

By taking charge, by being elected rector of his university as the Third Reich was getting under way, Heidegger accepted a situation in which the regime's anti-Semitism was already finding expression. Even before the new student regulations, established across the Reich by the laws of 22 and 25 April, and which elicited the philosopher's approval in his rector's address,[71] Reichskommissar Robert Wagner had issued a radical decree in Baden. On 6 April, in advance of the rest of Germany, he ordered that all non-Aryan civil servants, including retirees, be stripped of their titles. At the university, the deans and the members of the senate were relieved of their duties.[72] Edmund Husserl himself, though a convert to Protestantism, was subject to the regime's anti-Semitic measures. The Reich did not consider the Jews members of a religious faith that they could adopt or abandon to embrace a different one. It saw Jews as a well-established race distinct from the Germans, by virtue of its Asian blood and its parasitical nature.

As a result of the law adopted in Baden, Husserl lost his emeritus status. His retirement from active teaching became an expulsion from the university. The next day, the law of 7 April on the restoration of the professional civil service established a higher and less harsh standard, inasmuch as its article 3a allowed exceptions for civil servants already employed on 1 August 1914, for veterans who had served on the front lines under the flags of the Central Powers, and for the sons and fathers of soldiers who had died in battle.[73] The Ministry of Education for Baden nevertheless required that the Reichskommissar's order be implemented, an expression of a radicalism very much in line with the spirit of the regime. Edmund Husserl was informed of his suspension on 11 April. This local initiative did not prevent the order from being abrogated fourteen days later, on the grounds that it was illegal.[74]

Heidegger had had a falling-out with his former teacher, but Elfride still remembered her past friendship with the great phenomenologist's wife, Malvine Husserl. Although very anti-Semitic, Elfride was upset about the Husserls, to whom they had been very close. She wrote Malvine a letter, both to end the friendship and to offer consolation. In it she conveyed the remnants of affection and esteem she still felt, but also the force of her racist and anti-Semitic ultranationalism. Elfride did not express the slightest regret regarding Husserl's suspension. But perhaps that was because, writing on 29 April, she knew that the decree behind it had been abrogated the previous day. She said, however, that "in these difficult weeks," she wanted to write the Husserls a few words to acknowledge their past kindness and to express compassion for their son Gerhardt, a professor of law in Kiel: the Heideggers had learned in the press that he had been dismissed in accordance with the law of 7 April, even though he was a veteran of the First World War. Even so, Elfride considered the law "harsh but sensible from the German point of view."[75] The measures that affected the Husserls, father and son, were necessary for a higher cause, the national revolution that would restore all the German people's strength and authenticity. Such a sentiment may well have sparked Malvine Husserl's ire and resentment. Had not Husserl and his family proved that they were not Jews but truly Germans, patriots who had paid with their blood in the First World War, Protestants and staunch conservatives, as any German university professor worthy of the name had to be? Elfride wrote that letter in her own name and in that of her husband. Granted, of the two she was the more anti-Semitic. Her husband, however, had moved closer to her in that respect, just as he had done with Nazism. For Martin Heidegger, the advent of the Third Reich coincided with the development of his own anti-Semitism.

In the 1920s Heidegger's students, as well as his friend Jaspers,[76] had not perceived any disposition on his part unfavorable toward the Jews. Max Müller believed that, at a personal level, Heidegger had never shown himself to be "hostile" [*gehässig*] toward a Jew.[77] As Karl Löwith remembered it, "*Sein und Zeit* is dedicated to the Jew, Husserl, the book on Kant to the half-Jew, Scheler, and in his courses at Freiburg, Bergson and Simmel were taught."[78] Hans Jonas pointed out that "No—Heidegger wasn't a personal anti-Semite. Presumably it felt a little uncanny to him that so many of his students were Jewish, but more in the sense that it was somewhat one-sided, that there weren't enough others who were more like him. The only discussion of antisemitism in his immediate surroundings came up when word got out that his wife belonged to the nationalist youth movement. Perhaps she nagged him occasionally, saying, 'Martin, why do you act deaf and dumb? Why are you constantly surrounded by young Jews?' There were rumors that Elfride Heidegger had antisemitic leanings, but I can't say how people knew this."[79]

By the end of the decade, her husband too tended to understand the mediocrity of German culture in terms of a general movement of Germany's "growing jewification." In a letter of 2 October 1929, which caused a scandal when it was published sixty years later, Heidegger wrote to Viktor Schwoerer: "What is involved is nothing less than the overdue reflection on the fact that we are faced by a choice between once again supplying our German spiritual life with autochthonous strengths and educators, or ultimately surrendering it to the growing jewification in the broad and the narrow sense. We will find our way back to the [right] path only if we are capable, without agitation or fruitless conflict, of helping new strengths to develop."[80] Jonas was right: in the late 1920s Heidegger seemed inclined to regret the weakness of authentically German and rooted forces more than the existence of Jewish students or faculty. Equally if not more so, he was worried about the dissemination of a spirit that he considered Jewish, and that was corrupting German culture: "jewification" "in the broad sense" referred to the Catholics in particular, and we have seen the extent to which Heidegger deplored their "progress" in Freiburg. That equating of Catholicism with the Jewish spirit was perfectly in keeping with the letter of 8 September 1920, in which Heidegger judged Georg Moenius's *Hölderlin* "so grotesque" that it made him want to be "a spiritual anti-Semite," because that superficial and cosmopolitan book written by a Catholic priest seemed so remote from the "primordial freshness & rootedness of life."[81]

The Nazis were quick to conflate the word "Jew" with other expressions and to use it metaphorically. Everything, or almost everything, they opposed quickly became Jewish or Marxist, which more or less amounted to the same thing. In *Mein Kampf* Hitler described the "bourgeois world" as "Marxist," except for the fact that it believed "in the possibility of the rule of certain groups of men (bourgeoisie)," while Marxism itself planned to "hand the world over to the Jews."[82] Rosenberg frequently likened Catholics to Jews. In the preface to the third edition of his *Myth of the Twentieth Century,* the fiercely anti–Roman Catholic ideologue found in the negative reactions to his book a further argument in favor of its relevance: "The wild unrestrained abuse by Roman churchish circles has shown how deeply justified the assessment of the Roman Syrian dogma in fact is in the present work."[83] Considering Meister Eckhart one of the heroes of the Nordic soul in Germany, Rosenberg praised him for his struggle against that Judeo-Roman spirit, which he identified with Christianity:

> With his anti Roman religion, his moral teachings and his critique of cognition, Eckhart consciously separated himself, indeed abruptly, from all basic tenets of both the Roman and the later Lutheran churches. In place of the static Jewish Roman outlook, he asserts the dynamic of the Nordic Western soul; in place of monistic violence he demands the recognition of the duality of all life; in place of the doctrine of subjection and blissful slavery, he preaches belief in freedom of soul and will; in place of ecclesiastical arrogance by the representatives of God, he places the honor and nobility of the spiritual personality; instead of enraptured,

> self-subjecting love, he offers the aristocratic ideal of personal spiritual detachment and loneliness; in place of the violation of nature appears its perfection. And all this means that in place of the Jewish Roman view of the world, the Nordic spiritual creed appears as the inward side of German Teutonic man—of the Nordic race.[84]

Perhaps Heidegger had read *The Myth of the Twentieth Century* or had become familiar with its theses through his discussions with Baeumler. In any case, in 1932, when he had become Baeumler's friend, he developed in class a vision of European history inspired by Rosenberg. The origin of philosophy was confined to Greece alone. "Western philosophy began in the sixth century B.C.E. with the Greeks, a small people with a closed mode of behavior that was based purely on itself."[85] Rooted, autarkic, and philosophical, the Greek people "naturally knew nothing about the 'occidental' or 'the Occident.' "[86] The "occidental" is understood linguistically only in reference to the "oriental." It was thus the result of a geographical expansion unrelated to the original mode of thought, which was narrowly Greek: "This expression designates first of all a geographical concept, as a delimitation from the Orient, the oriental, the Asiatic."[87] The adjectives "oriental" and "Asiatic" led implicitly to the idea of the Jewish people, which was understood to be Asiatic in the theory of races of that time. Heidegger made explicit this importance of the Jew for the Occident, a paradoxical importance because the Jews were conceived as being Orientals by virtue of history, not geography: "But at the same time, the term 'occidental' is a historical concept and denotes the history and culture of today's Europe, appearing with the Greeks and especially with the Romans, determined and borne in its essence by Jewish Christianity. Had the Greeks known something about this occidental future, we would never have arrived at a beginning of philosophy. Romanness, Judaism, and Christianity have completely altered and falsified the initial philosophy, that is, Greek philosophy."[88] The history of the Occident as Occident was therefore a decline. The late Greeks and, to an even greater extent, the Romans were certainly the agents of that decadence, but its essence was intrinsically Jewish, in that Christianity was a religion indissociable from the Semitic people, amid whom it had emerged.

As the letter to Schwoerer shows, Heidegger's extended or metaphorical usage of "Jewishness" coincided with everything that in one way or another was "groundless" (*bodenlos*) or "uprooted" (*entwurzelt*), far from the solid and circumscribed ground of the Greek origins of philosophy. The concept of Jewishness therefore referred to Western decadence, the narrative of which

Heidegger developed three years later. Jewification in the broad sense was a synonym pure and simple of the general uprootedness at work in modern culture, whether that meant the growing influence of the Catholics at the University of Freiburg or the uprootedness, in Heidegger's view, of science in general: divided into competing disciplines, science took no interest in the essential question of being and confined itself to accumulating positive data without challenging the epistemic fundamentals on the basis of which they were accumulated. Heidegger therefore maintained that "the rootedness of the sciences in their essential foundation is moribund."[89]

Notably, he opposed the neo-Kantian tradition, arguing that "*Dasein* has had its historicality so thoroughly uprooted by tradition that it confines its interest to the multiformity of possible types, directions, and standpoints of philosophical activity in the most exotic and alien of cultures; and by this very interest it seeks to veil the fact that it has no ground of its own to stand on."[90] This criticism of uprooted philosophy in the opening pages of *Being and Time* took as its target Cassirer in particular, whom Heidegger reproached on two counts: first, for adopting Kantian concepts without questioning them; and second, for using ethnological studies to develop his ideas, for example, in volume 2 of *Philosophy of Symbolic Forms,* which is devoted to mythical thought.[91] Heidegger did not deny that studies of primitive peoples might be attractive for a philosopher seeking to return to the origins of man's everyday existence, since such studies might disobstruct his view of everything the tradition of interpretation had placed before his eyes.[92] His major objection was that the ethnological content available to the philosopher is not neutral but already skewed from the outset by the sociological and psychological concepts and interpretations of Western science, which "the ethnologist brings with him."[93] Furthermore, "*everydayness does not coincide with primitiveness,* but is rather a mode of *Dasein*'s Being, even when that *Dasein* is active in a highly developed and differentiated culture—and precisely then. Moreover, even primitive *Dasein* has possibilities of a Being which is not of the everyday kind, and it has a specific everydayness *of its own.*"[94] Western or occidental man does not have the same everyday *Dasein* as primitive man: the two do not live in the same environment (*Umwelt*), and each of their cultures is that of a place, a history, a "there" that conditions the very being of *Dasein.*

For Heidegger, then, when Cassirer inserted himself into the Kantian tradition without authentically reworking it on the ground of his own existence, but instead developed his thinking through ethnological studies of foreign populations, he was displaying a misdirected curiosity, an uncontrolled appetite for knowledge, which Augustine in his *Confessions* had already vilified with the expression *concupiscentia oculorum*. This "concupiscence of the eyes" is not limited to sight alone or to the desire to know. It is distinguished from philosophical wonder by its vacuity, in that it seeks diversion in the ever-new. It is thus characterized by a superficial agitation, as a result of which *Dasein* is "everywhere and nowhere" and is "constantly uprooting itself."[95]

Of all contemporary philosophers Heidegger's most frequent target was Cassirer, because of his uprootedness, even aside from his Jewish ancestry, which was present in Heidegger's mind.[96] In addition to the central place Cassirer implicitly occupied in *Being and Time,* Heidegger had debated him in Davos in March 1929, a few months, therefore, before the letter to Viktor Schwoerer. He had also taken great care to point out to his students and to Elfride the role of his own peasant background, a spiritual inheritance that stood in stark contrast to Cassirer's urban, modern, and intellectualist uprootedness.[97] The importance of Cassirer, however, did not mean that he was the exclusive embodiment of the philosophical jewification to which neo-Kantianism gave rise. That same year, the philosophers Siegfried Marck and Fritz Heinemann, both neo-Kantians of Jewish descent, were the targets of virulent criticism from Heidegger. A report on Marck's candidacy for the professorship in Breslau is dated 7 November, a month after Heidegger's letter to Schwoerer. In this report, Heidegger reviewed Marck's *Dialectic in Philosophy of the Present Time.*[98] Although he approved of the pages devoted to *Being and Time,* he harshly condemned the book as a whole:

> As the preface explicitly states, the book aspires to be simply an "introduction to the philosophy of the present time." Such ventures, which are proliferating at the moment, are more literary and editorial in nature—but not necessities and serious and scientific tasks. What this book lacks, therefore, like the one of the same kind [*dem gleichgearteten*] by the privatdozent Heinemann of Frankfurt,[99] is any substance and all focus [*jede Substanz und alles Schwergewicht*]. [. . .] It is superfluous for me to continue to discuss this book, for it absolutely does not belong to the body of publications to be taken into account as qualifications for a chair.[100]

In a second report on Marck, written in February 1930, Heidegger was even more caustic in discussing the same book: "Such literature is not to be taken into account as a serious explanation. M[arck] will always be able to talk capably about what is modern at the moment, but he will never have the necessary gravity to contribute real questions in the tasks of philosophy. This type of philosophy teacher is our ruin."[101] As Emmanuel Faye points out,[102] Heidegger uses here the term *gleichgeartet,* akin to *gleichartig,* "of the same kind," which at the time commonly had anti-Jewish connotations. Nonetheless, as in his discussion of Cassirer, Heidegger focused on a moral and intellectual portrait of what seemed to him to express the superficiality, the flippancy, associated with the uprootedness of modern times, and which gave the "jewification in the broad sense" of German universities its particular coloring. Moreover, Marck's other publications showed that he was drawn to the Enlightenment, pacifism, Marxism, and social democracy, all of which Heidegger held in contempt.[103]

Heidegger also seems to have experienced "jewification" in the "strict sense" in Marburg itself. In February 1928, during major maneuvering for a position, he reported to Elfride: "Indeed the best are—Jews."[104] His own students were in many cases Jews, by religion or descent. Some, such as Günther Stern, whom Heidegger seems always to have treated "with a great deal of contempt," embodied the uprootedness he abhorred: he was an avid traveler, an "asphalt man of letters." One evening, when Heidegger had received him at home, Stern reproached him "for having set aside man's dimension as a nomad, a traveler, a cosmopolitan, for having represented human existence, in fact, merely as that of a plant, as the existence of a being rooted in a place and never leaving it," and for "considering man at bottom a rooted being" and in that way not even granting him "the mobility of an animal."[105] In addition to valorizing the city and travel, Stern had, in Heidegger's view, the flaw of being one of the few politicized students—and politicized in the worst way. He "was developing into a leftist social critic," and, as Jonas noted, "that alone would have alienated him from Heidegger, who had nothing to say about the burning problems in contemporary society and politics."[106] A leftist and a Jew who rejected all rootedness, his student Stern was for Heidegger one of the most despicable figures of the jewification of German universities, in both the strict and the broad sense. In his winter-semester seminar of 1933–1934, after he had become rector, Heidegger went further in his appropriation of the cliché of the Jew as rootless Oriental, even doubting that the Jew would ever develop German patriotism: "For a Slavic people, the nature of our German space would certainly manifest itself differently than it does for us; for Semitic nomads, it will perhaps never manifest itself absolutely."[107]

With that idea of a Jewish threat looming over culture, Heidegger was repeating a hackneyed theme. Hitler, referring in *Mein Kampf* to the prominence of Marxism in higher education, spoke similarly of "jewified universities."[108] Yet he targeted more the jewification of popular culture and, with his typical violence and vulgarity, made it one of the notable moments in the narrative of his conversion to anti-Semitism:

> What had to be reckoned heavily against the Jews in my eyes was when I became acquainted with their activity in the press, art, literature, and the theater. All the unctuous reassurances helped little or nothing. It sufficed to look at a billboard, to study the names of the men behind the horrible trash they advertised, to make you hard for a long time to come. This was pestilence, spiritual pestilence, worse than the Black Death of olden times, and the people was being infected with it! It goes without saying that the lower the intellectual level of one of these art manufacturers, the more unlimited his fertility will be, and the scoundrel ends up like a garbage separator, splashing his filth in the face of humanity. And bear in mind that there is no limit to their number; bear in mind that for one Goethe Nature easily can foist on the world 10,000 of these scribblers, who poison men's souls like germ-carriers of the worse sort, on their fellow men.[109]

Unlike the Nazi demagogue, with his predilection for mass culture, Heidegger limited himself for the most part to science and the universities. That was already the case in 1916, when he repeated in part the fears formulated by Richard von Kralik, namely, that too many university graduates were Jews, compared to the number of Protestants and Catholics. Heidegger now adopted a *Blut und Boden* phraseology, like Count Yorck, whom he admired. Making the connection between physical and mental ground and anti-Semitism, Count Yorck thanked Dilthey "for all the particular cases in which you keep teaching posts away from the meager Jewish routine [*die dünne jüdische Routine*], which lacks consciousness of the responsibility of thought, just as the race as a whole lacks the sense of a mental and physical ground [*Boden*]."[110] The Jew was a cosmopolitan, without a physical soil in which to take root, and was as a result without a mental ground to stand on in the practice of science, which required a "consciousness of the responsibility of thought." The Jew was incapable of such a consciousness, and that led him to a routine and anemic philosophy. This was an academic variant of the commonplace that attacked the rootless Jew. The Jew was the emblematic resident of the metropolis, with no roots in a familiar countryside. Instead, the Jews were scattered nearly everywhere over the surface of the planet and were quick to support a universalist ideology, whether liberal or Marxist. For Heidegger, Stern was an everyday example of that rootlessness.

Although anti-Semitism was muted in the Nazi speeches of the early 1930s,[111] it structured in great part the NSDAP's view of politics. Such was the case with regard to Marxism, as we have seen. Such was also the case with respect to antiparliamentarianism, which was understood in anti-Semitic terms, and was extremely important in Heidegger's intellectual adherence to Nazism. Point 6 of the Nazi Party's program, the denunciation of the "corrupting parliamentary economy," was inserted within a series (points 4 to 8) whose aim was to remove the Jews from the German nation. Jews were considered not members of a religious faith but a different bloodline. Point 4, for example, stated that "only a member of the race [*wer Volksgenosse ist*] can be a citizen. A member of the race can only be one who is of German blood, without consideration of creed. Consequently, no Jew can be a member of the race." Point 6 had the more particular aim of excluding Jews from the life of the state: "The right to determine matters concerning administration and law belongs only to the citizen. Therefore, we demand that every public office, of any sort whatsoever, whether in the Reich, the county [*Land*] or municipality, be filled only by citizens." So it was that, just before mentioning in point 7 the possibility of expelling foreigners, and therefore the Jews, if the state could not sustain the German population, the Nazi program denounced "the corrupting parliamentary economy, office holding only according to party inclinations without consideration of character or abilities."[112] In the Nazis' eyes, then, that practice appeared to be Jewish, first in terms of custom and ultimately in terms of blood. It would come to an end when an authentically German power was set in place. Did Heidegger, like the NSDAP, equate democracy with the "Jews"? There is reason to doubt such a crude and unequivocal conflation. By contrast, given the philosopher's tendency to ascribe to "jewification" everything that was not rooted, to see metaphorically a Jewish spirit but without necessarily focusing on the presence of "Jews" (or persons reputed to be Jews), we can only conclude that the Nazi denunciation of a jewified democracy was not incompatible with his ideas.

Multifarious and omnipresent for Heidegger, the "growing jewification" of German spiritual life justified in his view the issuance of a special grant from the Berlin ministry to support the work of Dr. Eduard Baumgarten (1898–1982), who would become his assistant. It also justified allowing Franz Josef Brecht to earn his habilitation under Rickert in Heidelberg. Already in February 1932, Heidegger had written: "We need such colleagues in the universities, now more than ever."[113] These two young academics had very different focuses of interest: Baumgarten was an Americanist and a specialist in pragmatism, while Brecht was concerned with Greek literature and thought. They had one point in common, however, which recommended them to Heidegger: both had a nationalist sensibility. Baumgarten, who had volunteered to fight in the war, had written a short work, *Nationalism and Social Democracy,* in 1919,[114] while Brecht had just published a pamphlet titled "Plato and the George Circle."[115]

Heidegger was aware that, despite its strong presence in German universities, anti-Semitism was not an article of faith that could be professed without harm. Longstanding trust in the interlocutor was required: "What I could only allude to in the certificate, I can say more clearly here," he wrote to Schwoerer, whom he had known since the early 1920s and with whom he maintained a cordial relationship, discernable in this same letter. The solid institutional and scholarly position Heidegger had acquired, the pointlessness of being considerate toward Edmund Husserl, who had arranged for Heidegger to succeed him, seemingly allowed the philosopher to express his anti-Semitism outside a purely private sphere, while still remaining cautious.

Despite these precautions, Heidegger's anti-Semitism was the subject of rumors. In the winter of 1932–1933, he wrote ironically to Hannah Arendt: "I am now just as much an anti-Semite in university issues as I was ten years ago in Marburg, where, because of this anti-Semitism, I even earned Jacobsthal's and Friedländer's support." The better to refute these "slanders," which claimed that, in 1932, he was excluding "Jews from the seminar invitations" and did not "say hello to Jews," he asserted that he was no longer extending seminar invitations. Furthermore, though he was on sabbatical during the winter semester and did not wish to be disturbed, he had granted an interview to a Jewish man who urgently wanted to "write a dissertation" and was perfectly capable of doing so. He had allowed another candidate, also a Jew, to visit him every month "to report on a large work in progress," and had received from a third Jewish student "a substantial text for urgent reading." To show how far his graciousness toward Jewish students extended, he listed those for whose work he had sought financial assistance: "The two fellows of the Notgemeinschaft [Emergency Society] whom I helped get accepted in the last three semesters are Jews. The man who, with my help, got a stipend to go to Rome is a Jew." He concluded, finally, with his good personal relationships with Jewish colleagues, who had nothing to do with these "university issues," "e.g., Husserl, Misch, Cassirer, and others," adding, with respect to Arendt herself, a woman he knew intimately: "Above all it cannot touch my relationship with you."[116]

It is not possible to verify all the details put forward by Heidegger, though some are questionable. For example, his relationship with Husserl had greatly deteriorated, against the background of an intellectual divorce, after the teacher arranged for his former student to succeed him at the University of Freiburg. But though Heidegger was an anti-Semite, we can only agree with him when he defended himself against the accusation of "raging anti-Semitism." His friend Blochmann was a "half-Jew"; he was directing or had directed the dissertations of a number of Jewish students, including Karl Löwith, Helene Weiss, Hannah Arendt, Hans Jonas, Herbert Marcuse, and Werner Brock, and he had the greatest respect for all of them. He felt the same about Brock, who replaced Eduard Baumgarten as Heidegger's assistant after Baumgarten disappointed him. Perhaps Heidegger was unaware of the Jewish ancestry of some of them, Brock or Löwith, for example, who was Protestant,[117] but that was not the essential thing. Although averse to the uprootedness of Jewish thought, Heidegger had friendly feelings for Jewish people and consideration for them or for their writings, when he found them to be of high quality.

He looked favorably on *Jüdische Rundschau,* a publication to which Baeumler had drawn his attention, and which Heidegger found "excellently informed & of a high standard."[118] A newspaper published by the Zionist Federation of Germany (Zionistische Vereinigung für Deutschland), it was oriented toward the Jewish people's emigration to Palestine, which was of a nature to please an anti-Semite hostile to the jewification of Germany. Heidegger had encountered Zionism for the first time through Jonas, who in his *Memoirs* pointed out that the idea that the "standing" of his teacher "might suffer as a result of so many Jews leaving or being forced to leave apparently didn't occur to him. Heidegger was in no way prepared for such a thing."[119] Apart from its excellent orientation, which was congruent with that of Jonas and with what may have looked to Heidegger like a solution to the jewification of Germany, the philosopher was able to assess the Zionist review's high standards. They were evident even in the portrayal of Nazism in the issue of 3 June 1932, which was probably among those Baeumler had ordered for him. The article, which critiqued several books on the NSDAP, always maintained the neutrality and accuracy of a rigorous analysis, attempting to shed light on the rise of the movement. After its lightning-fast ascent beginning in September 1930, and with the fall of the Brüning cabinet on 30 May 1932, Nazism was "for many serious Germans a distressing phenomenon, which is occurring in every circle of one's worldview and way of life. One has the sense that, in the coming period, National Socialism will determine the nation's destiny, not only in its politics but also in its spirit."[120] These measured words, the awareness of a political culture peculiar to Nazism that extended largely beyond the narrow sphere of partisan life, were of a nature to please Heidegger, a Nazi sympathizer at the time.

His anti-Semitism was in no way "raging." But very few anti-Semites were relentless enough to be fully coherent. The value recognized in a person individually could render secondary, even to the point of denial, the fact that he belonged to the Jewish "race," which was otherwise considered absolutely and universally bad. Joseph Goebbels, a fanatical anti-Semite, was also a great admirer of Fritz Lang, to whom he offered the position of president of the Reichsfilmkammer, the public corporation that oversaw German filmmakers. When Lang retorted that his mother, though born a Catholic, had Jewish parents, Goebbels is said to have replied that he was the one who decided who was Jewish and who was not, and that Lang could become an honorary Aryan (*Ehrenarier*).[121] The Führer himself had his "decent Jews." In 1938 Eduard Bloch, a Jewish physician from Austria who had cared for Hitler's mother when she had cancer, enjoyed the Führer's protection when Bloch's country was annexed to the German Reich, a protection Bloch continued to enjoy until he emigrated two years later. Hitler maintained that, "if all the Jews were like him, there would be no anti-Semitism."[122] As late as 1940 the Führer had Heinrich Himmler intervene in favor of Ernst Hess, despite his four Jewish forebears. Hess had been Hitler's comrade in arms in the First World War, and had even become his company commander. The German leader thus sought preferential treatment for him.[123] Even among staunch Nazis during the Second World War, many had a "good Jew," a "decent Jew," as Heinrich Himmler himself lamented on 4 October 1943 in Posen, attempting to justify the extermination without mercy of the Jews: "And then along they all come, all the 80 million upright Germans, and each one has his decent Jew."[124]

The "raging anti-Semitism" against which Heidegger defended himself was a very rare thing. Anti-Semitism often entailed exceptions and—in 1933, in any case—did not reach the extreme radicalism Himmler manifested ten years later. Like a number of anti-Semites, Heidegger displayed a deep ambivalence toward the Jews and the Jewish spirit, a phenomenon also evident in his relations with the Catholics. Although he worried about their "progress" in Freiburg and considered waging a struggle against them, the philosopher enjoyed the company of the monks of Beuron and his stays at their monastery.

The nazification of the University of Freiburg, like that of German society in general at the time, entailed a purge policy that affected all its members, in the first place Jews or those of Jewish descent and potential political opponents of the Third Reich. In that case as well, Rector Heidegger implemented the regime's policy and was even sometimes in the vanguard.

It is not certain that the rector covered up for the students who looted the Jewish student fraternity building or that he authorized a poster calling for the denunciation of Jewish students,[125] but Heidegger's attitude toward the implementation of the law of 25 April "against overcrowding in German schools and universities" leaves little room for ambiguity. On 3 May, he wrote the deans that a quota of 1.5 percent for new students and of 5 percent for returning students would be applied to "non-Aryans."[126] On 6 May, he sent around a circular, composed on the 4th of the same month by Eugen Fehrle, secretary for higher education in Baden, which established that students who had been in the SA, the SS, or other nationalist militias would be given priority for financial assistance from the university, discounts on tuition, and scholarships, whereas Jewish and Marxist students would be ineligible.

A sign of the importance Heidegger attached to the anti-Semitic policy: while he was *Führer*-rector and hence endowed with total power over his university, he lent this measure further publicity in the 3 November issue of the Freiburg student newspaper, going beyond what the ministry prescribed. "Jewish students," he explained, "are students of non-Aryan stock in the sense of §3 of the law for the restoration of the professional civil service and of subsection 2 of §3 of the first implementation decree of the law for the restoration of the professional civil service of 11 April 1933."[127] He took care to broaden on his own initiative the field of application for that measure, outside any legal framework other than his own power as *Führer*-rector: "This ban on granting financial aid applies *as well* [my emphasis] to any student of non-Aryan stock, one of whose parents and two of whose grandparents are Aryan, and whose father fought during the First World War on the front lines for the German Reich and its allies. The only exceptions to this ban are students of non-Aryan stock who themselves fought on the front lines or whose fathers died during the First World War while fighting on the German side."[128] For Heidegger, then, it was not enough for a Jewish student to have had a father who fought for the Central Powers; he had to have died for the fatherland and in the German ranks, unless the student himself had been on the front lines, as had been the case for his former student Löwith. It is possible to think that, for Heidegger, only military service on behalf of Germany, by the student himself or by his father, could be the guarantee of an authentic disposition toward the community of fighters that the German people had to be, in order to respond to its destiny—and, moreover, of a true disposition toward a resolute science that took upon itself existence even in the face of death. The philosopher illustrated the "cumulative radicalization" (in Hans Mommsen's expression)[129] characteristic of the regime. Great latitude was left to Nazi leaders at every level, and a first radical measure, the law on the professional civil service, was the starting point for a second, that against educational overcrowding. The latter was in turn the basis for a measure ordered by the Karlsruhe ministry to cut off financial aid, a measure whose field of application was further broadened by the *Führer*-rector Heidegger and made possible by the implementation of a university constitution modeled on the *Führerprinzip*. The totalitarian structure of power opened the way for a cascading radicalization, each step tending to increase the scope of the measures taken higher up.

The purge of the student body was accompanied by that of the faculty. Although sometimes purely symbolic—for example, Heidegger's refusal to allow "non-Aryans" to sign the "appeal to scholars throughout the world,"[130] in which Nazi academics swore their allegiance to Hitler—the purge was also juridical and professional. Under the supervision of the Karlsruhe ministry, it was up to Heidegger to ensure the enforcement at the University of Freiburg of the law of 7 April 1933 concerning the restoration of the professional civil service. Its aim was to exclude Jewish faculty members (though it tolerated a few exceptions) or those suspected of opposing the new regime, as stipulated in its paragraph 4.[131] Heidegger was not single-minded. His ambivalence appeared in the letter he wrote on 12 July to the Karlsruhe ministry. Affirming that he was "fully aware of the necessity of applying the law on the restoration of the civil service," he weighed it against the university's interests on a case-by-case basis. He asked that two of his colleagues with worldwide renown be spared, the Latinist Eduard Fraenkel and the chemist Georg von Hevesy, out of consideration for the consequences their expulsion might have on Germany's position in the world, and also for the service these "exceptional spiritual forces" had rendered to the university.[132] Fraenkel was dismissed but Hevesy was not, probably because of the practical importance his research might have and the considerable resources provided him by a Rockefeller grant, resources he had invested in equipment for the new institute of physical chemistry.[133] On 19 July, when the ministry's decision became known, the rector once again pleaded in very laudatory terms on behalf of his Latinist colleague, in the name of the Faculty of Philosophy.[134] The great esteem he had for Fraenkel did not prevent Heidegger from making use of the regime's anti-Semitic contempt for the Latinist to sully the reputation of Eduard Baumgarten, the philosopher's former assistant, who had disappointed him. Heidegger wrote a hateful report on Baumgarten for the Göttingen faculty association: "By his relationships and his frame of mind, Dr. Baumgarten belongs to the Heidelberg group of liberal, democratic intellectuals that gravitates around Max Weber. During his stay here, he was anything but a National Socialist. [. . .] After failing with me, he formed a close bond with the Jew Fraenkel, who used to work at Göttingen and has now been dismissed from our university."[135]

Whereas Nazi ideology had a tendency to conflate social democracy and communism, to view them as a coherent whole without consideration for the deep cleavage between them, Rector Heidegger did not think that way. The SPD, the Red peril of his Catholic youth, had given way to its renegade offspring, the KPD. When, therefore, one of his colleagues, a geophysicist named Königsberger, was denounced in December 1933 because he had belonged to the Social Democratic Party until early 1932, Heidegger replied to the ministry the following 16 January, pleading for discreet leniency on both political and practical grounds. He argued that Königsberger had ceased all political activities and was devoting himself fully to his research, then concluded that "the equipment of the Institute of Mathematics and Physics was almost all Professor Königsberger's private property and that in the event of his early retirement, the department would disappear."[136] The geophysicist was therefore not to be harassed in the slightest.

Heidegger was not always the champion of his implicated colleagues, even becoming at times their prosecutor. In contrast to the leniency he recommended for Königsberger, he demonstrated the greatest severity toward the chemist Hermann Staudinger, who, despite his signs of goodwill toward the regime, had a history of pacifism. The rector seems to have gotten wind of these tendencies from a young Freiburg physicist, Alfons Bühl. A veteran in the last months of the war, Bühl, as a member of the Iron Division *Freikorps,* had fought the Spartacist uprising in Berlin before taking part in the battle in the Ruhr against the French. In late September 1933, on the strength of the evidence Bühl had gathered, Heidegger denounced Staudinger to Fehrle, secretary of higher education, as an administrative note from the Karlsruhe ministry attests: "On the occasion of his visit to Freiburg on 29 September 1933 the secretary for higher education was briefed by the rector of the university, Professor Heidegger, whereupon he instructed the rector to inquire into the existence of circumstances pertaining to article 4 of the law for the reestablishment of a permanent civil service in the case of Professor Staudinger."[137] On the 30th Fehrle lodged a complaint, which was investigated by the Karlsruhe Gestapo. Heidegger received the dossier thus constituted on 6 February 1934. He was asked to form an opinion about it, which he delivered promptly, on the 10th, in order to fall within the enforcement period for paragraph 4 of the law, which ran until 31 March.

His judgment, based on several indications of antipatriotism, was caustic. In the first place, there were Staudinger's actions: he had "passed German processes for manufacturing chemical products on to foreign (enemy) countries"; "in January 1917, that is, at the moment when the greatest peril was threatening the country, Staudinger applied for Swiss nationality"; and "on 1 September 1919, that is, immediately after the defeat of Germany, Staudinger renewed his application for Swiss citizenship, 'out of consideration for the changes that had occurred in Germany's internal and external situation,' as he himself put it." Second, there were the positions he had taken: "Staudinger never hid the fact that he was actively opposed to the German nationalist movement and repeatedly declared that he would never support his country either by bearing arms or by other service"; "In 1917, from Zurich, Staudinger wrote a petition on behalf of the pacifist Nicolai, who had refused to pledge allegiance to the flag." Hinting at Marxist sympathies on Staudinger's part, Heidegger wrote: "It is significant that the ambassador, Adolf Müller, who subsequently became a Marxist, designates Staudinger as an idealist!" And the rector concluded in very harsh terms: "These facts themselves require the application of §4 of the law on the restoration of the civil service. Inasmuch as, after the debate on Staudinger's appointment in Freiburg in 1925–1926, these facts have become known to broader German circles and have remained so, the reputation of the University of Freiburg also requires an intervention, especially since Staudinger now boasts of being 110 percent favorable to the national uprising. Dismissal, rather than retirement, ought to be considered. *Heil* Hitler."[138]

A month later, Heidegger relented, alluding on 5 March to Germany's image in the world, which might suffer from too tough a measure: "On mature reflection," it seemed to him advisable to adopt a "course of action" similar to that taken in the case of Franz Keller, a professor of moral theology who had been forced into retirement for his pacifism, but without being dismissed. Heidegger's change of heart resulted exclusively from the damage that the University of Freiburg's image might suffer abroad because of Staudinger's "international standing within his professional field": "I need hardly point out that this in no way alters *the facts of the case*. It is simply a question of avoiding fresh difficulties in our foreign relations if at all possible."[139] Perhaps he had remembered the Cannizzaro Medal awarded to the chemist by the Reale Accademia Nazionale dei Lincei, Rome, for his work on rubber and cellulose, about which Heidegger himself had informed the ministry the previous year.[140] In early March he had probably received indisputable evidence of Staudinger's reputation, namely, his participation at the international chemistry colloquium in Madrid in spring 1934, the expenses for which Heidegger mentioned to the ministry on 12 March.[141] Staudinger, for his part, protested that he supported the national revolution, and on 25 February 1934 published an article in the *Völkische Zeitung* titled "The Importance of Chemistry for the German People." Because his work on the structure of rubber and cellulose could prove to be of the greatest importance in the regime's quest for economic self-sufficiency, Staudinger finally managed, not without humiliation, to hold onto his post without being further harassed.

What were Rector Heidegger's motivations in the Staudinger case? In the first place, he was probably influenced, if not manipulated, by Alfons Bühl, who may have hoped to take over Staudinger's chair if the chemist were relieved of his duties. Bühl, a student of the founder of *völkisch* physics, Professor Philip Lenard (1862–1947) of the University of Heidelberg, in 1934 succeeded Wolfgang Gaede, who was dismissed because of his opinion on the importance of the Jews for German science: he is reported to have said that "Germany would be finished" without them.[142] Beyond the role of Bühl, whose service record and combative determination must have impressed Heidegger, the philosopher's severity toward Staudinger should probably be attributed to the warrior ethos that Heidegger was cultivating, and which was the exact opposite of the chemist's pacifism. Heidegger wanted the university to create for the German people "its world of the most intimate and most external and extreme [*äußersten*] danger, that is, its truly *spiritual* world."[143] To that end, everyone had to "hold fast to the German destiny in its most extreme distress."[144] In his course during the winter semester of 1933–1934, Heidegger, appropriating Heraclitus's thinking, went even further, claiming that "the essence of being is struggle [*Das Wesen des Seins ist Kampf*]; every being [*Sein*] passes through decision, victory, and defeat."[145] Staudinger had wanted to flee his destiny as a combatant and had even taken a stand against patriotic struggle during a period of extreme distress, the world war. For the rector, that behavior was antinational and antiscientific, because the absence of courage in the face of the enemy denoted modern spiritual dissipation and decadence, concealing human distress in the face of *Dasein* itself. Furthermore, the new rector was somewhat receptive—at least indirectly, through his wife[146]—to the idea of revanche and to the revanchist ambience of the Third Reich. A month later, he called a brief rally against the Treaty of Versailles, at the end of the defensive sport exercises on 28 June,[147] to mark with the requisite resoluteness the fourteenth anniversary of the reviled *Diktat*. Between Alfons Bühl's self-interested influence, Heidegger's own meditation on the essence of being as struggle, and his militant support for a policy aimed at revising the Treaty of Versailles, Heidegger was caught up in dispositions that all converged to make him condemn an academic with a pacifist past.

Harsh toward the chemist Staudinger, Heidegger displayed even greater virulence toward Richard Hönigswald, a neo-Kantian philosopher and professor in Munich, on whom Dr. Einhauser, adviser to the Ministry of Culture in Bavaria, had asked him to write a report. Hönigswald's family was Jewish and, as such, he was subject to the law on the restoration of the professional civil service. In no other extant text of Heidegger's is the denunciation of uprootedness stronger than in this letter, which the philosopher wrote on 26 June 1933:

> Dear Herr Einhauser,
>
> I gladly respond to your request and offer you my judgment below. Hönigswald comes from the school of neo-Kantianism, which defended a philosophy made to order for liberalism. It completely dissolved man's essence in a free-floating consciousness and ultimately diluted it in a general, logical world-reason. In this way, with an apparently rigorous philosophical and scientific foundation, the focus was shifted away from man in his historical rootedness [*in seiner geschichtlichen Verwurzelung*] and in his popular transmission of his origins in soil and blood [*in seiner volkhaften Überlieferung seiner Herfkunft aus Boden und Blut*]. This was accompanied by a deliberate repression of any metaphysical questioning, and man was reduced to nothing more than a servant of an indifferent, general world culture [*einer indifferenten, allgemeinen Weltkultur*]. All of Hönigswald's writings, and apparently also his whole activity as a teacher, grew out of this basic attitude.
>
> And it must be added that Hönigswald champions neo-Kantianism's ideas with an especially dangerous subtlety and an empty dialectic. The danger consists above all in the fact that this activity gives the impression of being extremely objective and rigorously scientific, and has already deceived many young people and led them into error. Even now I consider the appointment of this man at the University of Munich to be

> a scandal that can be explained only by the fact that the Catholic system prefers to give priority to such people, who are apparently ideologically indifferent [*weltanschaulich indifférent*], because they pose no danger to its own efforts [*den eigenen Bestrebungen*] and, as is well known, because they are "objective-liberal."[148]

Drawing the portrait of an uprooted scholar, Heidegger's indictment made no place for vulgar anti-Semitism, even if it was implicit in his intellectual and political hostility toward "Jews." Hönigswald's neo-Kantian and liberal philosophy was for Heidegger a universalist and rootless rationalism, a mode of thought cut off from history, the people, the blood and soil in which every man is rooted, a philosophy whose extreme danger lay in its apparent scientific rigor and impartiality. For Heidegger, therefore, Hönigswald constituted one of the most advanced and perverse forms of the rootlessness of the age, the "jewification" of German universities "in the strict and the broad sense." The report that he wrote against Hönigswald, and which played a role in the latter's expulsion from the university, must therefore be understood within a context that extends beyond the enforcement of the law on the restoration of the professional civil service. It was among the charges the philosopher led in the struggle against the "un-German spirit" of the time.

On 12 April 1933 the German Student Union sent out a poster with the title "Against the Un-German Spirit," to be put up in the universities. On a large white sheet measuring 47.5 by 70 centimeters,[149] bordered on the left with a bright red double stripe, the student union had printed in Gothic script, and in the same blood-red color, its twelve theses. Thesis 7 stated, notably: "We regard all Jews as foreigners, and we intend to take our national identity [*Volkstum*, popular culture] seriously." Thesis 10 expected students to go beyond "Jewish intellectualism and the symptoms of liberal decadence previously associated with it in German spiritual life." Thesis 11 demanded that students and faculty be selected "on the basis of the reliability of their thinking in terms of the German spirit"; and thesis 12, finally, that "German schools of higher learning" be "the refuge for *Volkstum* and the battlefield resulting from the strength of the German spirit." These aspects of the twelve theses of the German Student Union were consonant with the views of a rector who, hostile to liberalism and intellectualism, worried about the "jewification" of the German universities and wanted to revive the German spirit by relying on the disposition toward struggle.

The campaign conducted by the student union against the "un-German spirit" culminated in the book burning of 10 May, for which the union issued an appeal in the *Breisgauer Zeitung*. The call to mobilize was cosigned by the Combat League for German Culture (Kampfbund für deutsche Kultur), headed by Alfred Rosenberg. It read: "The German Student Union is determined to lead the spiritual battle against the Judeo-Marxist corruption of the German people, to the point of complete annihilation [*den geistigen Kampf gegen die jüdisch-marxistische Zersetzung des deutschen Volkes bis zur völligen Vernichtung durchzuführen*]. As a symbol of that struggle, Judeo-Marxist writings will be burned publicly on 10 May. Germans, assemble for that battle! And display the community of struggle [*Kampfgemeinschaft*] in public. [. . .] The fire of annihilation will thus become the fiery flame of our enthusiastic struggle for the German spirit, German mores, and German customs."[150]

That Freiburg campaign against the un-German spirit, Jewish in the strict or the broad sense (anti-intellectual, antiliberal, anti-Marxist, even anti-Christian), was the local version of a vast movement at work in all the university cities of Germany. On 10 May in Berlin, Alfred Baeumler, having concluded his inaugural lecture, justified the campaign under way, then led a torchlight procession to a pile of books. He was the first to brandish a torch, which gradually consumed in flames volumes that for him symbolized the un-German spirit, freedom of knowledge, and individualism, all "poisons" that had "accumulated in an age of false tolerance."[151] It is not known whether Heidegger delivered a speech similar to that of his friend at the time, who, alongside Elfride, had initiated him to National Socialism. In any event, the libraries of Freiburg were purged, the un-German books burned. Ernesto Grassi, an Italian philosopher then living in Freiburg, later described that tumultuous period: "Then suddenly, the destructive outburst of the years beginning in 1933: Heidegger's rectorship, his inaugural address; under his rectorship, the burning of Jewish and Marxist books, tokens of science 'in a state of decay.' The fire crackled outside the university library."[152]

That book burning and those that followed complemented the measures taken against Jewish civil servants or those resistant to the new regime. Just as the law of 7 April claimed to restore the professional civil service, the campaign to destroy books was intended to work toward cultural recovery, by waging a battle of spiritual annihilation. At the university, after the expulsion of all or part of the "non-Aryan" faculty and students came the removal of "un-German" books. The regime's takeover of culture, the censorship it exercised, affected all the media. It was an old preoccupation of the Nazis, who were persuaded by their ultranationalism and their understanding of propaganda that, in the conquest and exercise of power, it was indispensable to reduce their opponents to silence. The cultural struggle was part of an overall strategy that placed the primary emphasis on elimination. Hitler wrote in *Mein Kampf*: "For it will take a struggle, in view of the fact that the first task is not creation of a folkish state conception, but above all elimination [*Beseitigung*] of the existing Jewish one. As so frequently in history, the main difficulty lies, not in the form of the new state of things, but in making place for it. [. . .] And so, unfortunately, the fighter for such a new idea, important as it may be to put positive emphasis on it, is forced to carry through first of all the negative part of the fight, that part which should lead to the elimination of the present state of affairs."[153]

In the Nazi Party's program, that notion was applied to culture. After point 4 stipulated that Jews could not be German citizens because of their foreign blood, point 23 had the aim of creating a "German press" to battle "known lies." It demanded in particular that all journalists at German-language newspapers be German citizens, to the exclusion, therefore, of "Jews" or those presumed to be Jews, and that no non-German be able to influence such newspapers one way or another. Organs of the press acting "counter to the general good" were to be banned, and the law would prosecute (without further specifications being given) "artistic and literary forms which exert a destructive influence on our national life." Finally, following from the preceding points, point 24 stated that "the Party" "combats the Jewish-materialistic spirit within and around us."[154]

The struggle against the un-German spirit was not the work of a few isolated fanatics. Set in place by the student union in particular, it reflected the deep-seated notions of the Nazi movement itself, though it distinguished itself from the program in one detail. Whereas the Nazi program stipulated that non-German newspapers could appear in German, the twelve theses sought to restrict the use of the national language and Fraktur script to Germans alone. That struggle was a major aspect of the NSDAP's cultural conquest of power. The monopoly on writing and on ideas would give complete latitude to the total revolution under way, particularly at the university, whose function was to mold the future leaders of the German people. The destruction of books was the negative counterpart of the contribution to be made by the science camps, which Heidegger played a role in organizing. As Georg Plötner, head of the central department for political education of the German Student Union, wrote to Heidegger's liegeman Rudolf Stadelmann, the training seminar held in Berlin was to demonstrate the "awakening of the German spirit," understood as a "logical extension of the first campaign," the campaign against "the un-German spirit."[155]

That dual dimension, positive and negative, was evident in the speech Heidegger delivered in front of the blazing fire at the university stadium for the celebration of solstice. He concluded in revolutionary terms a succession of symbolic ceremonies[156] to destroy "un-German" books:

> Fire! Say to us: "You mustn't become blind to the struggle, but you must remain lucid for action."
>
> Flame! Your blaze tells us: "The German revolution is not dormant, it has recently flared up everywhere and lights our way along a path from which we can no longer turn back."[157]

The militant fire that had sprung up in all the university cities of Germany, to ensure that the corruption of the "un-German" spirit would perish in its flames, aspired not only to purify but also to serve as the luminous torch of the revolution under way. The equivalence established between fire and political awakening was a commonplace of the Nazi Party, which, avid for references to antiquity, used the figure of Prometheus to personify its role as fire-bringer.[158] Hitler resorted to the same metaphor, characterizing the Aryan as "the Prometheus of mankind from whose bright forehead the divine spark of genius has sprung at all times, forever kindling anew that fire of knowledge which illumined the night of silent mysteries and thus caused man to climb the path to mastery over the other beings of the earth. Exclude him—and perhaps after a few thousand years darkness will again descend on the earth, human culture [*Kultur*] will pass, and the world turn to a desert."[159] Heidegger was so attuned to the ideological importance of Prometheus that, in quoting in his rector's address one of the lines Aeschylus had attributed to the Titan, the philosopher deliberately distorted it, proclaiming, "Knowledge is, however, far less impotent than necessity," whereas the Greek text referred not to knowledge but to technicity (τέχνη, *techne*).[160] The philosopher was thereby able to support his argument by referring to this figure of antiquity prized by the new regime.

The fire speech was not only a celebration of the work of the German Student Union, the Combat League for German Culture, or the Party as a whole. It was also a way for the rector to assert his revolutionary mastery, by delivering a sort of neopagan prayer that invoked Fire and Flame, for which Heidegger became the oracle: "Fire! Say to us [. . .] Flame! Your blaze tells us [. . .]."[161] The general convergence of his views with those of the German

Student Union did not mean, however, that they were absolutely identical. The student union's twelve theses lacked subtlety and philosophy. In his rector's address, Heidegger therefore maintained that the Deutsche Studentenschaft sought "the *Führer* through whom it wishes to elevate its own vocation to a grounded and learned truth and place it in the bright light of an interpretive, active word and work."[162] The German Student Union's thesis 7, for example, the longest and most concrete, and not the least fanatical, demanded that "Jewish works [. . .] appear only in Hebrew. If they appear in German, they must be clearly labeled as translations. We want tough action against the abuse of German or Gothic script." Heidegger seems to have clearly distanced himself on that point, as Hans L. Gottschalk later reported. Thesis 7 could be summed up as obliging Jewish professors to publish in Hebrew; Heidegger is said to have retorted that "everyone is making a fool of himself as best he can."[163] The critical approval the philosopher bestowed on the student union and on organizations in the Nazi movement as a whole was also audible in the speech about fire. As in the rector's address, Heidegger did not doubt the students' combative resoluteness, nor, a fortiori, did he doubt their "lucidity,"[164] which required strengthening by his authoritative word.

In the course he gave on the essence of truth in the winter semester of 1933–1934, Heidegger in fact had his students meditate on combat, so as to develop the lucidity they still lacked. To that end, he turned to Heraclitus's fragment 53: "Combat is the father of all things, and of all things king." He began by pointing out that the Ephesian had in mind not competition but truly combat, "standing up to the enemy."[165] Contrary to what he had done in the 1920s, when he emphasized the combatant and his resoluteness in the face of his own death, the Nazi rector, imbued with the spirit of the new regime and probably also with Carl Schmitt's *Concept of the Political,* focused on the enemy and the threat he constituted: "Whoever he might be, the enemy is he who constitutes an essential threat to the *Dasein* of the people and of its individuals."[166] Far from being an evil, in Heidegger's judgment the enemy was so important for ensuring that human existence retain its cutting edge that it was sometimes necessary to create him: "And it might even seem that there is no enemy. For that reason it is a fundamental necessity to find one, to bring him to light, or even to create one so that this standing-up-to-the-enemy takes place and *Dasein* does not lose its edge."[167] The difficulty of finding the enemy is all the greater in that he may actually lie within, so close that he disappears from view. That proximity redoubles the danger because the enemy within is by that very fact the one best able to threaten a people in its very essence: "The enemy may have established himself on the innermost root of a people's *Dasein* and may oppose and contradict the latter's own essence. Then the combat is all the sharper and harder because only a tiny part of it consists in mutual strikes; often it is far more difficult and laborious to locate the enemy as such, to lead him to unmask himself, to avoid having illusions about him, to remain ready for attack, to cultivate and increase constant availability, and to launch a long-term attack with the goal of complete annihilation [*den Angriff auf weite Sicht mit dem Ziel der völligen Vernichtung anzusetzen*]."[168]

Brutality in politics was at its height under Nazism, in both its acts and its discourse, seemingly replicating the extreme violence of the world war, but within the state itself. Every opponent, every non-Nazi element, could be turned into an enemy within who had to be eliminated. The idea of annihilation was a commonplace of Nazism. For Hitler before the Nazis took power, for example, it designated the danger posed to Germany by various internal maleficent powers, the party system ("after thirteen years during which [the parties] have totally destroyed Germany, the time has finally come now to eliminate [*Beseitigung*] them, too")[169] or communism ("fourteen years of Marxism have ruined Germany; one year of Bolshevism would destroy her"). In that "inner struggle"[170] that the Führer saw ravaging the country, after the Decree for the Protection of People and State of 28 February, which enlisted all law enforcement resources to that end, the watchword became "Annihilation of Marxism."[171] A large number of arrests followed: about 25,000 were tallied in Prussia in late April;[172] in Bavaria, a much less populated Land, the total reached 10,000 at that date.[173] Beginning on 22 March, some of the arrested were detained in the concentration camp that, at Himmler's instigation, had opened in Dachau. Finally, the SPD was banned on 22 June as an "enemy organization of the people and the state" (*volks- und staatsfeindliche Organisation*).[174] That ban was the prelude to the rapid end of all the other parties. Hence, on the following 14 July, the "Law against the Reconstitution of New Parties"[175] completed a campaign of institutional annihilation that far surpassed the ban on the Marxists.

The vagueness of Heidegger's remarks takes into account the difficulty of simply designating the enemies within, those whose "complete annihilation" eventually had to be sought. It was a hard task to flush out the enemy within, even when, in 1936, the regime simply wanted to draw up a list of Jewish authors: "The necessary bibliographical work is very difficult," Carl Schmitt said at the time, "because, of course, we have to establish with the greatest possible accuracy who is a Jew and who is not."[176] This was an even more serious problem for Heidegger, who proposed a great variety of enemies within, including the Jews in the strict sense, conceived as a separate ethnic group in Germany, even though it intermingled intimately with the German people.

In the known sources Heidegger left behind, the neo-Kantian Hönigswald was the person he most identified with that enemy within, considering him a particularly depraved example. By his intellectualism and liberalism, Hönigswald uprooted and corrupted young people, concealing himself behind the respectable appearances of disinterested science. The rector, however, had an even more devious and dangerous enemy in mind: Catholicism. In his eyes, the power of "objective-liberal" ideas of the kind held by the neo-Kantian philosopher came from a different movement of thought, the "Catholic system."[177]

In his rector's address, despite quoting Nietzsche, Heidegger moderated the expression of his philosophical irreligion, saying almost nothing about it. He wanted, of course, to expound the principles of his actions as rector, but he probably did not wish to cause a scandal, which would have been inopportune and damaging. He could easily imagine such an outcome, given that his audience included the archbishop of Freiburg, as well as members of the Faculty of Theology and his vice-rector, Josef Sauer. His silence was circumstantial. The speech he gave in autumn as *Führer*-rector at the science camp, before an audience that was more in agreement with his thinking, showed the particular direction that the "clear-sightedness" and "fresh courage"[178] he required of participants ought to take. They had to take aim against Christianity, in order to combat the false assurances provided by belief, in the face of the insecurity and distress of existence. Heinrich Buhr, a student in theology at the time who later became a Protestant minister, bore witness to what he heard.

> As a young student in Protestant theology, I heard Heidegger speak for the first time in Todtnauberg, in autumn 1933, before student representatives of the universities of Heidelberg, Freiburg, and Tübingen. In that group I was the only theologian, the only one who adhered to theology. Martin Heidegger delivered a speech against Christianity, against Christian theology, against that interpretation of being, of reality—that was all I was able to understand at the time. According to him, if one wanted to attack Christianity, it was not enough to limit oneself to the second article of the doctrine (that Jesus was the Christ). Even the first article, according to which a God had created and continued to sustain the world—so that a being [*Seiende*] was only a product [*Gemachtes*], fabricated, as it were, by

> a craftsman—was, in the first place, what had to be rejected. According to him, the reason for a fallacious devaluation of the world, a contempt for and negation of it, resided therein, and it was also the cause of the false sense of security and safety based on artificial and deceitful representations of the world, in contrast to the great and noble knowledge relating to the insecurity of being. That is what I vaguely understood at the time and remembered. It was not unfamiliar to me, for I was reading Ernst Jünger (I'm thinking of *The Adventurous Heart*).[179]

Heidegger had thus not lost his antireligious feelings. On the contrary, they were given freer rein than ever before. But Catholicism was not only a baneful intellectual system, concealing the distress of existence with its promise of salvation, culpably uprooting the science that devoted itself to the Catholic religion, uprooting the faithful as well, who thereby lost their authenticity. It was also a political and academic power whose great strength formed an obstacle to the new regime's educational control of its people.

On 22 December 1933 Heidegger wrote to the ministry about filling the vacant chair in ecclesiastical history, an opportunity to give his opinion on the place of the Church in the new state. "As in all future proposed appointments, the first question is which candidate—assuming that he possesses the scientific and psychological aptitudes—offers the greatest guarantee of imposing the National Socialist educational will." Heidegger thus adopted as an indisputable principle the new political and ideological canons with respect to teaching, as he himself had expounded them in his rector's address. To mold the future "leaders and guardians of the German people's destiny," an adequate political science and adequate training were absolutely needed.[180] That made the employment of Catholic professors problematic, because of Catholicism's dogmatic subordination of the state to the Church: "Since according to Catholic dogma the Church stands *above* the state, in all Catholic education, so long as it truly seeks to be what it claims to be, *the state's popular will* is necessarily *subordinated* to the ecclesiastical. Consequently, the Church still forbids priests to belong to the Party. Therefore any evaluation of candidates from a political point of view is irrelevant."[181] In his desire for an educational monopoly by the Nazi state at the expense of the Church, Heidegger was in full agreement with Rosenberg. Positing that "the first task of education" was to mold character, that is, to "strengthen racial values such as once slumbered in the Germanic essence" and which must be "carefully cultivated upwards," Rosenberg concluded that "the national state" had to "lay claim to sole control of schools without compromise." It was only in that way that it could "educate soil rooted citizens of state," who had first to "become aware of what they are fighting for in life," and "understand the totality of values that are theirs, irrespective of any individual features,"[182] whether religious, cultural, or political.

Catholicism was thus a check on the totalitarian state, an obstacle to the revolution under way, and it had to be suppressed. Furthermore, it was par excellence the enemy within, against which one therefore had to "prepare the long-term attack with the goal of complete annihilation."[183] Catholicism was in fact the most dangerous institution and system of thought, a foreign body firmly attached to the *Dasein* of the German people. According to the rector of Freiburg, the liberal neo-Kantian Hönigswald owed his chair to the Roman Church alone. The Church was therefore the power underlying intellectual and political liberalism, as Heidegger had written in a letter to Blochmann the previous year. Inquiring into the concrete accomplishments of Zentrum "as a Catholic cultural force, over recent decades," he replied: "It has encouraged liberalism and a general leveling down—whether that took the form of the lowering of standards or—and this is much more dangerous and was the result of a concerted policy—of the *raising* of standards to a certain level of mediocrity kept well in hand."[184] The former case probably corresponded to the rapid expansion of a mass culture typical of modernity; Weimar may have served as the paradigm here. Hönigswald represented the latter case, because of his rigor and apparent objectivity. Ultimately, such universalism did not greatly trouble the Catholic Church, which was able to recognize in it one of its own ambitions. The Church, moreover, by virtue of its academic power, had that universalism well in hand.

The anti-Catholic struggle was longstanding and entailed both victories and defeats. Among the victories in the rector's eyes was the implementation of paragraph 4 of the law on the restoration of the professional civil service, which forced the retirement of the professor of moral theology, Franz Keller,[185] the only full professor implicated by that paragraph. We do not know what role Heidegger played in the affair, but one thing is sure: he had no dearth of motives for approving the action, because Keller, in addition to being a Catholic, was a pacifist. Among the setbacks: in early 1934 a Catholic guild in Freiburg managed to have repealed the suspension that Oskar Stäbel, the *Führer* of the German Student Union of the Reich, had imposed on it. Despite the deterioration of the rule of law, everything was not yet legally possible in Germany, especially since the Catholics' right of association was guaranteed by the concordat with the Vatican signed on 20 July 1933. Heidegger experienced that judicial regularization as a defeat for Nazism and a victory for Catholicism: "In any case, this public victory by Catholicism must not stand, especially here in Freiburg," he wrote to Stäbel on 6 February 1934. "It does all our work harm, *the greatest harm imaginable* at the present time. I have known for years, in detail, the local conditions and powers. We *still don't know* Catholic tactics. And one day we will pay heavily for that."[186]

A Growing Personal Isolation

The purge policy that Heidegger conducted in tandem with the regime had repercussions for his personal relationships, particularly with "non-Aryans." The rector, whose anti-Semitic policy was in conformity with that of the Reich, no longer accepted thesis students whom the government deemed to be "Jews." He wanted his Jewish students to write and defend their theses, but not with him. He made an arrangement, it appears, with his Catholic colleague Martin Honecker, who was happy to accept them.[187] Helene Weiss, for whom Heidegger had the greatest respect, had to go to Basel, Switzerland, to complete her thesis under the directorship of Herman Schmalenbach. The uneasiness Heidegger felt with his "non-Aryan" students did not necessarily prevent him from being kind to them. He obligingly received Karl Löwith when he came through Freiburg for two days. His former student attended Heidegger's class, in which, Löwith noted, the philosopher analyzed the "different types of silence, for which he had a profound sense and expertise." Heidegger invited Löwith to have dinner with him while Elfride was out. They avoided sensitive subjects, limiting themselves, as Löwith reported, "to the question whether I should give up Marburg and follow up the chance of a post in Istanbul. He invited me to spend the night in his house, and seemed a little surprised when I declined and instead went to stay with a former student friend who taught in the medical faculty."[188] Heidegger did not confine himself to dispensing advice; he also helped some of his students emigrate. Such was the case for Paul Oskar Kristeller,[189] who, according to Hans Jonas, "later said in New York that he had nothing against Heidegger because when he emigrated to Italy, Heidegger sent letters of recommendation[190] that helped him find a position there."[191]

Heidegger's own assistant, Werner Brock, was also harassed by the Nazi state. Unaware that Brock was Jewish,[192] the philosopher had recruited him in summer 1931. His previous assistant, Oskar Becker, had been appointed to a chair, and Heidegger had not wanted to lose him, Becker being associated with the first philosophy seminar Heidegger had been assigned, thanks to

Husserl's kindness. Jaspers warmly recommended Brock. "I had great joy in every conversation with him," he had written to his friend. "He understands the latest things, and the slightest allusion finds in him an accommodating understanding. He has the advantage of being no one's *pupil*. There is a free atmosphere around him. If I had an assistantship to fill, I would certainly choose Brock from among all the young people I know at this time."[193] Heidegger recruited him and did not regret his choice: "Brock is very eager, conscientious, and still a bit too excitable and insecure; he takes the Heideggerizing cackle of a few fellow-traveling pupils too seriously."[194] Jaspers rightly saw "kindness"[195] for Brock in these remarks, friendly feelings that arose in the face of the Nazi peril, as he himself attested at the end of the war: "Heidegger's assistant in the Department of Philosophy, Dr. Brock, was a Jew. Heidegger was not aware of this at the time of Brock's appointment. When the National Socialists began to take measures against the Jews, Brock had to leave his post. According to Brock—and I have this from his own lips at the time—Heidegger behaved impeccably toward him."[196] His assistant had already been targeted by the Baden decree of 6 April, but he was reinstated when the law of 7 April on the restoration of the professional civil service took effect.[197] He was now threatened with having his habilitation taken away from him. Heidegger, who knew he would thereby lose Brock in the fall, wrote again on 11 August to his colleague in Basel, Paul Häberlin, to warmly recommend him.[198] It was no easy task to assist Brock effectively: "In the flood of current events, it is still in vain that I seek a place for Brock; this is where one sees the immediate uselessness of philosophy."[199] Ultimately, Heidegger "helped him to get established in England by writing him very warm references."[200]

Of Heidegger's friends, Elisabeth Blochmann was also affected by the regime's anti-Semitic policy, and she sought help and comfort from Heidegger. Although Protestant, she was reputed by the regime to be a "non-Aryan," because her mother had Jewish parents.[201] She submitted in despair to the law: "The strictness of this law is so pitiless that it excludes you not only from the work of the moment, but, in a foreseeable future, from any work in German education. So that no private school can hire you anymore." The tragic irony was that she had at first been sympathetic toward the regime. Blochmann was a fervent nationalist, as attested by the doctoral thesis in history she had defended in 1923, written on an anonymous pamphlet from the seventeenth century, "Remember That You Are a German."[202] She was deeply wounded by the measure of which she was the victim, whose aim was to exclude her from the body of the German nation: "I have very painful days behind me," she wrote to Elfride on 18 April, "I would never have imagined that such an expulsion would be possible. Perhaps I've lived too naïvely in the certainty of a deep solidarity of mind and feeling—and that is why I found myself initially defenseless and prey to despair."[203] The despair that now took hold of Blochmann led her to seek any means possible to escape the law and keep her position: "The fact that I completed my initial training by Easter 1914," she explained to Heidegger, "which makes me eligible for employment in the civil service, and that the school in Weimar is eager to hire me, as I have been assured, makes things much easier in view of the new situation. Maybe I will no longer need to plead that my great-great-grandfather was elevated to the nobility and to a knighthood by Frederick the Great."[204] Heidegger seems to have intervened, as the card he sent her suggests: "At present, things depend on the decision-making authorities."[205] Whatever this intervention may have entailed, it was without effect. Blochmann held a grudge, even doubting that the intervention had taken place. Finally, in January 1934, this close friend of the Heideggers also emigrated to England, where she was hired by the University of Oxford.

Therefore, though Martin Heidegger participated in the regime's anti-Semitic measures, and though that disposition was noticed by contemporaries such as Edith Eucken-Erdsiek,[206] he was far from being driven by "raging anti-Semitism."[207] Nonetheless, the assistance he granted to certain close friends was not incompatible with a strong anti-Semitism, inasmuch as the issue at the time was not the perpetration of genocide but the restoration of the German people's racial purity through the exclusion of foreign elements, foremost among them the Jews. Before the advent of the Third Reich, Heidegger, like other anti-Semites, seemed favorably disposed toward the Jewish emigration to Palestine, in which the interests of the Zionists converged with those of the Nazis and rested on the same principle: the Jews were not a cultural or religious community that belonged to various European peoples, but a people in its own right and destined as such to establish itself in its own state. In facilitating the emigration of those of his close friends who were non-Aryans in the eyes of the regime, which, moreover, he held in esteem, the philosopher was thus fully coherent.

Heidegger had had many students who were Jewish or of Jewish descent. The emigration of a large number of them would now contribute toward isolating him emotionally and intellectually. The relations he had maintained with some of his closest friends ended at that time. The correspondence with Arendt was interrupted and that with Blochmann became much less frequent. At the same time, the letter Elfride had written to Malvine Husserl did not lead to a reconciliation between their husbands. The letter was in fact a self-justification in the form of a farewell. Implicitly, the entire anti-Semitic policy of the time, though "harsh" and causing psychological wounds to people who had devoted themselves to Germany, and who, on an individual basis, might deserve the greatest respect, was "sensible from the German point of view."[208] It was difficult for the two sides to revive a friendship on such divisive foundations.

The friendship between Heidegger and Jaspers also suffered from the effects of time. They had both changed a great deal since 1933. After the decisive Reichstag elections of 5 March 1933, Heidegger, visiting Jaspers in Heidelberg, had exclaimed in a letter to his wife: "I find it unsettling how this man [. . .] is tied down by his wife." Gertrud Jaspers, who was Jewish, prevented her husband from fully adhering to the new regime. Furthermore, Jaspers was still faithful to the national liberalism of Max Weber.[209] Heidegger gradually took his distance from his friend, whom he saw for the last time in late June 1933, when he was invited to Heidelberg by the local student union. Contrary to his habits, he did not consider staying with Jaspers, even though, upon learning of his lecture, Jaspers had warmly invited him to do so.[210] In his *Philosophical Autobiography,* written after the war, Jaspers drew a frightening picture of their discussion: "I spoke of the Jewish question, of the pernicious nonsense of the *Elders of Zion,*" to which Heidegger supposedly replied: "There is, however, a dangerous international alliance of the Jews." When Jaspers saw the admiration his friend had for Hitler, he was "distraught": "Heidegger had said nothing about his inclinations toward National Socialism before 1933."[211] After that last visit, they exchanged a few letters and a few books, including the rector's address, which Jaspers praised.[212]

As Jaspers understood it, Heidegger had tacitly broken off their friendship. The fact that he did not announce to his friend his lecture in Heidelberg of 30 June was a first sign of that breakup and would be a further cause of it. The presence of Jaspers's "non-Aryan" wife beside him at the lecture, even as Heidegger was elaborating at length his aversion to the "Jew," probably dissuaded Heidegger from going to see his friend. Later, their political and intellectual exchanges made the growing distance between them even more obvious. A further fracture occurred in 1934,[213] when Jaspers happened to read the report Heidegger had written on Baumgarten.[214] The use of the anti-Semitic expression "the Jew Fraenkel"[215] could not have failed to upset Jaspers. Heidegger's attempt to discredit Baumgarten by mentioning Max Weber's circle could only have had the same effect, since Jaspers himself was part of it. The sense of betrayal must have been all the stronger given that, in late 1932, Heidegger had judged a text Jaspers had written on the famous sociologist "grand, beautiful, simple, and clear,"[216] greatly pleasing its author.[217] Jaspers's estrangement from Heidegger occurred against the background of Jaspers's reversal, in his own mind, vis-à-vis Nazism. It was his father in 1934, "eighty-four years old at the time," who had opened Jaspers's eyes to the new Germany, telling him: "My boy, we have lost our fatherland!" Since then, as he confided to Heidegger in 1949, "a sadness lies like a veil over everything," from which he no longer emerged, "despite the cheerfulness of the façade."[218]

9 • An Oracle Facing the Storm

(1934–1945)

The enthusiasm of the early days of the rectorship waned. As he was seeking to inspire the course of the Nazi revolution, Heidegger lost his illusions but not his faith in the historical necessity of Nazism. From the lofty heights of Todtnauberg, sensing the Third Reich's rush toward power and toward the abyss, the philosopher became an oracle in the face of the storm unleashed by Berlin.

From the Resignation to Disillusionment (1934–1936)

Heidegger's rectorship had no fixed term. The philosopher himself did not seem in any hurry to leave his position, as he showed in September 1933, when he was once again offered a chair in Berlin "connected with a political mission."[1] He turned it down, preferring to continue his work as rector in Freiburg. He explained himself publicly, both in writing in autumn 1933, and on the radio in spring 1934, in a text that vaunted his "Swabian-Alemannic roots" and the "creative landscape" he found in that "province."[2] In the position he was offered, teaching would have been a secondary matter, in which he would have been led to " 'direct' the Prussian lecturers," but in a manner not his own—administrative and not intellectual—and in a place unfamiliar to him. All that gave him the sense of being groundless and of feeling he would be taking on more than he could handle. When he turned down the job in Berlin, he was relieved of that agonizing outlook. At the same moment, a chair in Munich had to be filled, since Hönigswald, who had previously held it, was targeted by the law on the restoration of the professional civil service, with the cooperation of Heidegger himself. Were Heidegger to accept it, he believed that this chair—like Berlin—would provide him with "more influence" than he had in Freiburg and a greater proximity to the center of political life (to Hitler, in this instance). The university itself did not appeal to him very much. It seemed "dead" to him, and he feared that, if he left Freiburg, all the work he had undertaken "would collapse."[3] So he stayed.

And yet, on 27 April 1934, slightly more than a year after Heidegger was elected to the position (21 April 1933), his resignation was accepted. His retreat was not a disengagement from the Third Reich; he had simply realized the limits of his power as *Führer*-rector. Outside the university, Heidegger, though unenthusiastic, was not particularly negative. In late February 1934 he noted in one of his black notebooks that while the NSDAP was not moving in a direction contrary to his wishes, it was falling short of his hopes, which prompted him to note: "The structure of ethnic-national [*volklich-staatlichen*] *Dasein* is creating the movement according to a mode of organization determined by soldiers and engineers."[4] It therefore remained impregnable to philosophy. Considering the abstract intellectual principles on which Nazism rested, he expressed a view more favorable than the one he had had before the advent of the Third Reich: "The instinctive ideological disposition is as certain as the concomitant spiritual world is confused. This disposition rests largely on a problematic repetition of nineteenth-century forms and its positivistic biologism, without seeing or grasping that for the last fifteen years this change of the whole of being has been prepared, a change in which the movement must quickly take root if indeed it is to be able to impose a creatively spiritual world of its own on the planet."[5] Conversely, his judgment of the situation at his university had become more negative: "The powers that are capable of effectiveness, that sustain, and that are becoming rooted, are all with the *youth*," he wrote, but not with the student union, because its development had proceeded "not constructively" but "only polemically."[6] Heidegger had not succeeded in imposing his spiritual leadership on the Deutsche Studentenschaft; he had not managed to become its spiritual *Führer*. And, despite the convergences in their points of view, the student union had remained undisciplined and had become an obstacle to the Nazi revolution as Heidegger conceived it. The students were not really subordinate to him. They were unruly and answered to other hierarchical Nazi organizations (especially the Deutsche Studentenschaft and the SA), over which he had no authority. They were autonomous revolutionaries. Most of the faculty, for its part, was committed to the academic traditions of freedom—of knowledge, of teaching and learning—and had no appetite for the spiritual revolution Heidegger was attempting. Finally, the rector was under the close supervision of the ministry. Perhaps he was in denial at first, refusing to see this everyday powerlessness or hoping that the consolidation of the Third Reich and the force of his ontological discourse would give his power a stronger foundation. Later on, he may have realized that the situation would not change. In any event, he resigned after a controversy that was in itself minor.

Adolf Lampe stood at the center of this controversy. Lampe had held an interim position since the winter semester of 1933–1934, filling a vacant chair in political economy. He was a nationalist war veteran whose conservatism kept him hostile to Nazism. That lukewarm attitude toward the new regime had estranged him from the student union as well as from Erik Wolf, *Führer*-dean of the Faculty of Jurisprudence and Political Science, and his faithful ally, Rector Heidegger. During the summer semester of 1934, finding Lampe too liberal and not nationalist enough, the *Führer*-dean opposed the extension of his interim appointment.[7] In late March, Lampe appealed directly to the ministry, bypassing the Freiburg chain of command. The minister heeded him: in a letter to the rector dated 12 April, he overruled Wolf,[8] about whom many members of his faculty had long complained, alluding to "very considerable misgivings, which I am inclined to think are not entirely without foundation." And he concluded: "I wish to bring this to your immediate attention, and ask you to consider whether it might not be expedient to appoint a new dean for the start of the summer semester."[9]

The *Führer*-rector's powerlessness in the face of the faculty's opposition, the insubordination of the student leaders allied with the local SA,[10] and the minister's rather offhand attitude toward him, on this point and others, led Heidegger to submit his resignation to the ministry two days later: "After careful examination of the university's current situation, I have arrived at the conviction that I must return to direct educational work, freed of administrative tasks, among the student body [*Studentenschaft*] and the young teaching staff [*jüngeren Dozentenschaft*]. The new regulations are in effect; thanks to them, the restructuring of educational institutions has been accomplished and work has begun. I therefore take the liberty of asking you to appoint a new rector of the University of Freiburg for the 1934 summer semester."[11] Heidegger was persuaded of the paramount importance of individuals; the institutions that governed them were secondary. His actions as rector had encountered their limits precisely in such individuals, who had been unable to answer the call of history. At least he himself had gone as far in his actions as the ambient mediocrity allowed, stationing himself in the vanguard of the revolution of academic institutions. Henceforth, his task was to work once more toward changing the German people's spiritual world, by attempting to root in being those who could receive that lesson, the students and young professors who had followed him since the beginning, those who had placed themselves in his *Gefolgschaft*.

Heidegger had already decided to resign, but for the moment he kept it a secret. His resolution did not keep him from becoming enraged when he learned that the ministerial letter concerning Wolf had been inspired by Lampe's direct appeal to the ministry. "I consider it deeply inadmissible that the ministry should receive, without the rector's knowledge, professors who take steps to obtain a vacant position, while an appointment procedure is ongoing. After this incident, I decline all responsibility in the matter of the attribution of the chair of political economy."[12] The same day, 23 April, he informed the *Führer* of his university that he was resigning.[13] The minister accepted his resignation on the 27th,[14] once he had found someone to succeed Heidegger, namely, the criminal lawyer and jurist Eduard Kern. The next day, Heidegger wrote in his private notebook: "My resignation tendered, because a justification no longer possible. *Long live mediocrity and noise!*"[15] The minister informed the local press on 30 April, with a warm acknowledgment of the first Nazi rector of Freiburg: "The Minister of Culture, Education and Justice, Dr. Wacker, has accepted the resignation tendered by the present rector of the Albert-Ludwigs Universität in Freiburg, Professor Martin Heidegger, and has expressed to him his thanks and special appreciation for all the hard work he has done during his leadership of the university."[16]

It was a painful succession. Heidegger had given some thought to the words he would deliver upon his departure: not " 'collegial' farewell speeches," but "a *companionable* word on the spur of the moment."[17] He would have spoken of a "*foundered* year" for him, "a lost one." He would have indicated his disappointment, greater than ever, in the university. The "void" there had become manifest "very swiftly and from all sides," with a "disoriented educational power," an "anemic ideological power," and an "erratic scientific power." In the future, the "danger" was not "reactionism": "the supposed 'revolutionaries' are even *more* reactionary, since in decisive matters they are less experienced and less capable than those who are 'old.' "[18] There are biting words that resentment dictates to us; but, when our anger has been cooled by the passage of time, by fear, or by shame, we are ultimately induced to hold our tongues. Heidegger retreated into silence. As Josef Sauer noted in his diary on 29 May 1934, when the rector's successor was inaugurated, "during the entire ceremony, including the meal at [the restaurant] *Der Kopf,* Heidegger seemed to be attending the funeral of a suicide; he did not utter a word."[19]

For a long time, the philosopher was haunted by the failure of his rectorship. The error he had made in committing himself returned again and again in his writings.[20] He blamed himself, first, for having turned down a blind alley, for having gotten stuck between "obedience to a minister," his "own law," which he was trying to follow, and "justification in the face of history." He had deluded himself about his colleagues' capacity for asking questions: "My rectorate was based on a great mistake, namely, my wanting to bring *questions* into the temperament and regard of my 'colleagues,' questions from which they were at best *excluded,* to *their* advantage—and undoing."[21] Later, in the same bilious mood, he reconsidered the very terms of his rector's address, situating within the long history of an intellectual decline his error in introducing a reform of academic knowledge:

> "The Self-Assertion of the German University," or—the little entr'acte of a great error.
> *For,* already decades ago that which is striving for these goals has been prepared:
> The natural sciences are becoming completely technologized.
> The human sciences are becoming instruments of politics and ideology.
> The *science* of jurisprudence is becoming otiose.
> Theology is becoming senseless.

And the university? Not any more a wretched fig leaf for the nakedness of this unstoppable disintegration: a sad occasion for pompous ones (*Wichtigtuer*) who have come too late.[22]

Despite this desire to show he was a philosopher and to pick up his work where he had left it before the advent of the Third Reich, Heidegger did not succeed in completely pushing away that bad dream, which added to the pain he felt at having broken with Catholicism. "With me," he confided to his friend Jaspers in July 1935, "it is [. . .] a laborious groping about. Only a few months ago, I was able to resume work on the text sketched out in the winter of 1932–1933 (sabbatical semester), but it is a thin stammering and, besides, two thorns—the confrontation with the faith of the tradition and the failure of the rectorate—already contain enough of what must actually be overcome."[23]

Despite the persistent bitterness left by his rectorship, Martin Heidegger's opinion of Nazism had hardly changed, as Karl Löwith came to realize. The former disciple was staying in Rome when his teacher came to that city in 1936 to give two lectures, accompanied by his wife and sons. This reunion was not entirely joyful. Löwith had been one of Heidegger's first students and had looked after Jörg and Hermann when they were little. He was the first on whom Heidegger had conferred the habilitation, and the philosopher had worked hard to secure him a chair in Marburg itself. But Löwith, though a Protestant, was a "half-Jew" in the eyes of the regime. He was in Rome because he had lost his chair: the Nuremburg Laws of September 1935 had made the anti-Semitic laws more stringent, eliminating the clause that protected war veterans. The moments the two men spent together were marked by "undeniable reservations" because, "even on this occasion, Heidegger did not remove his Party insignia from his lapel." He wore the insignia, displaying his support for the regime that was persecuting his disciple "during his entire stay in Rome." "It had obviously not occurred to him that the swastika was out of place when he was spending the day with me."[24] Returning from a "glorious" excursion to Frascati and Tusculum with the Heideggers and Löwith's wife, the former disciple made up his mind to bring up the question they had been carefully avoiding, the situation of Germany at the time. The two men then spoke of what were among the first public moments of the "Heidegger affair."

Neither disciple nor master seems to have been aware of the very first episode in that affair. It had traveled beyond the walls of the University of Freiburg in 1934, when one of Heidegger's former students, Herbert Marcuse—in exile because of his Jewish ancestry—published a first article in a German review that had taken refuge in France.[25] A model of insight, the article placed Heidegger's engagement within the context of an intellectual struggle against liberalism, alongside other Nazi ideologues such as Baeumler, Krieck, Schmitt, Forsthoff, and Koellreutter. Pointing out the essential role, for his former teacher, of the question of the historicality of human existence, Marcuse quoted the rector's address and other passages destined to fuel the scandal even in our own time, such as the infamous "The Führer himself, and he alone, is the present and future German reality and your law,"[26] a line Marcuse was able to read in the university's student newspaper.

Heidegger and Löwith were aware of the first debate, again in German and again outside Germany, since it was only there that the controversy was free to rage—this time in German-speaking Switzerland. In early 1936 (a few months, therefore, before the reunion of the master and his disciple), a debate took place in the *Neue Zürcher Zeitung* between the philosopher and journalist Hans Barth and the Germanist Emil Staiger. It had arisen from the lecture

Heidegger had just given, on 17 January, titled "The Origin of the Work of Art." On 20 January Hans Barth noted that Heidegger, after dedicating his first book to a Jew and his second to a half-Jew—*Being and Time* to Husserl, the book on Kant to Max Scheler—was now one of the philosophical spokesmen for the new Germany. He understood that shift in psychological terms: "As a general rule, men are not heroes—nor are philosophers, though there are exceptions."[27] On 23 January Emil Staiger, "a Heidegger enthusiast," responded, denouncing the lack of objectivity of Barth's review.[28] Barth, said Staiger, had gotten caught up in basely political reflections. Staiger defended Heidegger, asserting that he ought to be placed not among contemporary philosophers such as Spengler or Tillich but among the greats, alongside Hegel, Kant, Aristotle, and Heraclitus.

In his discussion of these two positions with the key player, Löwith was in agreement with Marcuse's interpretation, though he does not seem to have read it. He explained to his former teacher that he agreed "neither with Barth's political attack nor with Staiger's defense," because he was of the opinion that Heidegger's "partisanship for National Socialism lay in the essence of his philosophy."[29] Heidegger agreed "without reservation, and added that his concept of 'historicity' formed the basis of his political 'engagement.' He also left no doubt about his belief in Hitler." The philosopher maintained that he had "underestimated only two things: the vitality of the Christian churches, and the obstacles to the annexation of Austria." Despite the failure of his rectorship and of the Prussian Academy of Professors, "he was convinced now, as before, that National Socialism was the right cause for Germany; one had only to 'hold out' long enough." The only aspect that "troubled" him was "the ceaseless 'organization' at the expense of 'vital forces,' "[30] at the expense of "anonymous *Führer* who are not government officials."[31] The apolitical Heidegger had himself suffered the effects of administrative and political impediments to his initiatives and did not seem to be aware that these were inextricably linked to the organization of a complex society. And, as Löwith pointed out, he seemed not to see "the destructive radicalism of the whole movement and the petty bourgeois character of all its 'strength-through-joy' [*Kraft-durch-Freude*] institutions,"[32] which were precipitating Germany toward mediocrity, chaos, and crime.

A study of the contemporary sources left by Martin Heidegger confirms most of Löwith's statements. His resignation from the rectorship marked a break in the philosopher's academic engagement but not in his support for the regime, which the Night of the Long Knives on 30 June 1934 did not change, despite what Heidegger led people to believe after 1945.[33] His speeches in the spring and summer of 1934 were in line with those of his rectorship. By contrast, the episode of 30 June left no trace in his writings. An important event in the consolidation of Adolf Hitler's power, the Night of the Long Knives laid to rest the specter of a second revolution—socialist this time—after the national revolution. It strengthened in a lasting manner Hitler's alliance with the army against the SA, which was aspiring to supplant that arm of the military.

Heidegger kept intact his polemology, his belief in the German people's mission, and he still believed that the *Führerprinzip* was salutary. On 26 and 27 May, he went to Konstanz for a reunion with his schoolmates from the Gymnasium, to mark the twenty-fifth anniversary of their graduation. Addressing his former classmates, he chose not to recollect their schooldays as eighteen- and nineteen-year-olds. Instead, he invoked the memory of all their fellows who had died on the front lines. The military defeat of the past did not seem to Heidegger to be the essential thing. For the future, history required that the Germans have "enduring courage, clear knowledge, the maintenance of genuine standards, and belief in the people's mission. We must win the Great War *spiritually;* that is, *combat* must become *the innermost law* of our *Dasein.*"[34] With this idea of a mission dictated by history, Heidegger reiterated the task he was assigning to his people, that of imbuing its world with "danger."[35] In fact, "for the essential man, combat is the *great test* of every being, which determines whether we see ourselves as slaves or as masters."[36] The idea of winning the Great War spiritually was one of the major ideas in Moeller van den Bruck's *Third Reich.*[37] For Heidegger, that spiritual victory implied an inner greatness: "Man must first become great in the ground of his essence, and see the great things and join their following [*Gefolgschaft*]." The idea of following led necessarily to that of the leader: "Following, binding oneself in the *Führer's* will, first creates community." Like the evocation in the "Horst Wessel Song," for example, this typically Nazi community of struggle glorified its dead heroes, who remained in one's thoughts: "Our generation [*Geschlecht*]—in our mysterious comradeship with our dead companions—is the bridge to the historical and spiritual victory in the Great War."[38]

Heidegger was not simply repeating Nazi notions. He explicitly justified the "new German reality" of the Third Reich, which he interpreted as follows: "The new movement, which runs through this people, is the deepest and widest concern of the people's liberty." He then took up the notion of freedom he had elaborated in the rector's address: "Freedom does not signify the absence of an obligation [*Ungebundenheit*] to act and to allow [*lassen*]; instead, it means: *a connection with the inner law* and with the orders of our essence. Freedom signifies: a gathering together of these strengths, which guarantee the people its continued historical and spiritual existence. Freedom means: the awakening and realization of the people's will to fulfill its most distinctive mission."[39] He saw freedom thus understood as "the authentic meaning of German socialism," that is, National Socialism grasped philosophically. This idea allows us to understand the deeper meaning of the remark Heidegger made at the start of his course on Schelling in 1936: "The profound untruth of those words that Napoleon had spoken to Goethe in Erfurt was soon to come to light: politics is fate. No, Spirit is fate and fate is Spirit. The essence of Spirit, however, is freedom."[40] Ontological freedom marked the authentic return of politics as destiny, which for the German people merged with Nazism.

Late June marked no break at all, as attested by the lecture on the German university that Heidegger gave twice, on 15 August 1934 and again the next day. The context was less the consequences of the Night of the Long Knives than the institutional changes that took place in August, with which Hitler laid the final totalitarian foundations of the Third Reich. On 2 August, President Hindenburg died. The same day, the Führer combined the duties of president with that of chancellor. Soldiers swore personal fidelity to him. On 19 August, the Germans approved by plebiscite that institutional upheaval, with 89.9 percent of the vote. How did Heidegger view this new Germany in the midst of the plebiscite campaign? "The essence of the National Socialist revolution," he proclaimed, "consists in this, that Adolf Hitler has raised this new spirit of community and made it a power shaping a new order of the people." Taking up the regime's ideological principles, he added that "the rule [*Herrschaft*] of this state is the responsible fulfillment of the will of the leader [*Führerwillens*], on whom the confidence of the people as a followers [*das gefolgschaftliche Vertrauen des Volkes*] confers leadership [*Führung*]."[41] The Führer, followed by his people, was bringing about the consummation of history. Hitler's state visit to Mussolini on 14 June 1934 met with the philosopher's enthusiasm. He would see it as the beginnings of the reattachment of Austria to Germany, as the Führer—and, following him, the philosopher—hoped: "When the airplane freely transports the *Führer* from Munich to stand beside Mussolini in Venice, then history is made [*dann geschieht Geschichte*]."[42] On 29 October 1934, when Heidegger, his left hand on his heart, his right hand raised, swore the service oath that was expected of him as a civil servant, the words he uttered proceeded from his deep convictions and were not merely the formal fulfillment of an external obligation: "I swear: I will be faithful and obedient to the leader of the German Reich and people, Adolf Hitler, to observe the law, and to conscientiously fulfill my official duties, so help me God."[43]

In his resignation letter, Heidegger wrote that he wanted to focus on his teaching. Perhaps he thought so at the time. Perhaps it was simply a convenient excuse, easily acceptable to his supervisors, to explain his desire to leave a position that he had initially taken on with such passion. In any event, he agreed to be part of the Academy for German Law,[44] founded the previous year and headed by Hans Frank (who, as the Nazi governor-general of occupied Poland, would play a decisive role in the Holocaust). The actions of that organization were essential in the drafting of the anti-Semitic Nuremburg Laws of September 1935. Heidegger's participation in the academy tended to increase his anti-Semitism, to imbue him further with Nazi intellectual frameworks. He even participated in elaborating these frameworks, so much so that, in a letter to Kurt Bauch of 7 February 1935, he pictured his Freiburg colleague's students as follows: "Of course, I don't know your 'audience,' but I fear you too will be holding classes and will be exerting yourself in front of those who, from the start, are determined not to work for National Socialism—a few scattered Jews, half-Jews, if not failures [*Mißglückte*], Jesuits and Blacks [i.e., Catholics] in layman's clothes, and a few wits."[45] Heidegger was adopting the different categories composing what, in his letter to Schwoerer of 2 October 1929, he had denounced as "jewification" "in the strict and the broad sense."[46] He understood "jewification" in the strict sense in terms of the concepts of the time. He distinguished between "Jews"—"scattered" because of the anti-Semitic laws that had restricted their numbers at the university and had impelled some of them to emigrate—and "half-Jews" like Löwith, considered to be of mixed blood because his father was "Aryan" and his mother, though Christian, had parents who practiced the Jewish faith. The representatives of jewification in the broad sense remained, as before, diverse: Catholics, liberals, and "failures." A year later, in a letter to Bauch, Heidegger again mentioned a racial separation between true Germans and Jews. Referring to Werner Brock, his former assistant whom he had helped get to England and who seems to have asked to work in his seminar once again, Heidegger concluded with a maxim: "Remarkable how the Jew is lacking something there. It would never occur to one of our own to ask such a question."[47]

He was still working to build the Third Reich, including its racial policy; that policy did not keep him from continuing to commit himself more than ever in that direction, though he aspired to be an educator first and foremost. On 11 August 1934 he mentioned the science camp that would take place in the Black Forest beginning on 26 October, and which he would lead, as he had done the previous year.[48] Above all, he was approached to take over an institution in its formative phase, the Prussian Academy of Professors, a project he had in mind when he submitted his resignation as rector. He had written to the minister that he had to return "to direct educational work, unhindered by administrative tasks, with the student body and the young teaching staff."[49] This training school for academics was to have its headquarters in Berlin. More seriously than ever before, Heidegger considered moving to the capital. The Prussian academy,[50] about which he was already thinking in autumn 1933, had the advantage of being a new project he could hope to mold as he liked. In a report of 28 August 1934, he laid out the principles that ought to govern the new institution, in order to "realize the future German university." Its professors were to be trained in accordance with three considerations: pedagogy, aimed at molding real teachers and not merely researchers; political science, leading to a rethinking of "traditional *science* on the basis of the questioning orientations and strengths of National Socialism"; and a desire to create a community of life and of struggle resting on "a unitary worldview [*Weltanschauung*]."[51] Borrowing the language of the Church, Heidegger insisted on the "*vita communis* of students and professors,"[52] proposing not an educational camp but a secularized monastery, a philosophical Beuron transplanted to a Berlin draped in swastikas, one that would place itself in the intellectual service of National Socialism.

Alas, that merging of the Berlin way, the Meßkirch way, and the Todtnauberg way did not take place. Aspersions were cast on Heidegger's character, and the project failed. Standing in his path were Ernest Krieck, an ally in 1933 who by the next year had turned into an adversary, and especially Erich Jaensch, with whom relations had already been poor in Marburg.[53] Jaensch wrote a vicious attack, saying it would be irrational "if what is possibly the most important post in the intellectual life of the nation in the weeks and months ahead were to be filled by one of the biggest scatterbrains and most eccentric cranks we have in our university system: a man about whom men who are perfectly rational, intelligent, and loyal to the new state argue among themselves as to which side of the dividing line between sanity and mental illness he is on." The gray zone Heidegger supposedly inhabited between health and mental illness was coupled with a hyperrational Jewish spirit that was as seductive as it was dangerous: "Heidegger's thought is characterized by the same obsession with hairsplitting distinctions as Talmudic thought. That is why it holds such an extraordinary fascination for Jews, persons of Jewish ancestry, and others with a similar mental make-up. If Heidegger acquires a decisive influence over the formation and selection of young academics, this will mean with absolute certainty that the selection criteria in our universities and intellectual life will favor those of Jewish stock who remain in our midst."[54]

The Third Reich was no stranger to violent confrontations between individuals or institutions. Heidegger, whose ambition was to reshape the German university under his leadership, could not fail to be confronted with ferocious jealousies and rivalries. The fact that the philosopher's language was esoteric, so idiosyncratic that it was comprehensible to only a few initiates, made the clash with the age all the sharper, as Jaensch's report and Sauer's notes on the rector's address attested. Furthermore, the speculative discipline of philosophy could hardly hope to inspire a regime whose principal dignitaries had for the most part not pursued higher education. True, Joseph Goebbels, minister for public enlightenment and propaganda,[55] held a doctorate in philology;[56] Wilhelm Frick, minister of the interior, had earned a doctorate in law; and Alfred Rosenberg, a major ideologue for Nazism, had a degree in architecture. Even so, few of the most prominent Nazi figures were university graduates, and none were academics. Nazi anti-intellectualism marginalized the role of universities in the formation of the elites. Granted, with the advent of war, many young university graduates played a key role in the German presence in Eastern Europe, especially in the Holocaust. But from 1934 on, the SS, the Nazis' elite corps par excellence, trained its own pool of high-level recruits in its own institutions, the *Ordensburgen*, even as the Party gradually set in place, beginning in 1938, the "Advanced School of the NSDAP," under Rosenberg's direction.

Heidegger's introductory course on metaphysics for the summer semester of 1935 seemed to be an admission of failure. He addressed "the impression that philosophy can and must provide a foundation for the current and future historical *Dasein* of a people in every age, a foundation for building culture." Although "philosophy always aims at the first and last grounds of beings," it "can never *directly* supply the forces and create the mechanisms and opportunities that bring about a historical state of affairs, if only because philosophy is always the direct concern of the few." Heidegger construed these limitations of philosophy as the reason it was disparaged at the time: "One says, for example, that because metaphysics did not contribute to preparing the revolution, it must be rejected." He nonetheless clung to the hope that, "indirectly, on back roads that can never be charted in advance," philosophy might spread "and then finally—sometime, when it has long since been forgotten as originary philosophy," degenerate into the banal self-evidence of *Dasein*.[57] It was therefore necessary to arm oneself with concepts, resoluteness, and patience.

Heidegger knew that only a very few in his audience could understand him and that Nazism, though his preference, was not intellectually superior to liberal bourgeois culture, whether that of the Weimar Republic or a form prior to it. His rectorship had sustained the illusion that the Todtnauberg way dominated at close proximity those of Berlin and Meßkirch, but the philosopher grasped rather quickly the great distance that separated them. He realized, moreover, that the influence that the mountain of philosophy could exert over the country's fate could be felt only in the long term—if, indeed, it ever had any effect on human fate. In the end, though his underlying support for the regime did not suffer as a result, Heidegger's idolatrous love for Hitler seems to have died out by the end of 1935, at which time he stopped ending his letters to Kurt Bauch "*Heil* Hitler." His friend had shown him the crudeness of the Nazi press,[58] while Heidegger, for his part, was fully convinced that his dream of an immediate spiritual leadership for the new Germany would never be realized.

An Emotional and Philosophical Transformation (1934–1939)

For Heidegger, the changes came less from his political choices than from his private life. Elfride's enterprising feminism had spurred her to learn to drive, one of the first women in Freiburg to do so. From the time of Heidegger's rectorship, she had driven her husband to the university.[59] And, though the practice was still rare at the time, the Heideggers had purchased an automobile, one sign among others of how much their material situation improved once the philosopher held an academic chair. Their affluence had its limits, of course. When they took the train, they traveled in third class rather than the more comfortable but more expensive second.[60] How remote, however, was that painful time when Heidegger wondered whether he ought to change careers and enter the civil service.

Profoundly damaged by Elfride's discoveries of the philosopher's infidelities, the trusting intimacy between husband and wife was difficult to rebuild. Significantly, in the salutations of his letters to her, Heidegger hesitated between his traditional and loving "My Dearest Soul" (*mein liebes Seelchen*) and the more distant "My dear Elfride," which now became the more common.

There was a reason for that: he continued to have extramarital affairs, which he justified, sheepishly, as an addiction to sex with other women, even though he knew the harm they caused his wife; and indecently, describing the affairs with an irresponsibility at odds with his philosophical odes to courage and authenticity. While staying in Todtnauberg with Elisabeth Schmid, a relative[61] who may have become his mistress, Heidegger accompanied his birthday wishes to his wife with the following words:

> You know that I'll perhaps never be fully able to make good the early suffering that came your way from me; and this pain grows greater by the year. But I can endeavor, with what remains to me, to do things right and thank you every day for your kindness & love. I don't want anything for myself, but everything for the task. And if—as it appears—I now once again have to go through a spiritual crisis so severe that it even leaves its mark upon the body, here too you will be my strongest & most silent help, even without specifically involving yourself in philosophy.[62]

Words, words, words, his wife must have thought. Increasingly, she suffered from living in the shadow of the Work to Come and of the Thinker's mistresses. She cultivated her own intellectual and political interests, combining feminism and Nazism. She became closer to the woman who served as her model, the liberal Gertrud Bäumer.[63] From 1934 on, Elfride threw herself into her work in the Zähringen neighborhood, organizing "Mothers' Evenings" on behalf of the Nationalsozialistische Volkswohlfahrt (NSV),[64] the Nazi charitable organization.[65] Above all, in 1936 she became friends with Erika Semmler, who subsequently took charge of culture, education, and training in the Women's Nazi League (the NS-Frauenschaft)[66] and persuaded Elfride to accompany her on trips to Berlin.

That estrangement between husband and wife was not absolute. Elfride, who still managed the everyday affairs of the household, continued to bestow little favors on her husband, who was receptive to them. Having gone up to Todtnauberg by himself in August 1936, sad at being alone, the philosopher found comfort in the way his wife had prepared the cabin, which made him feel her kind and heartening presence, thanks to which he was already less lonely.[67] He in turn continued to play the role of spiritual protector. Upon the death of his father-in-law in 1938, he wrote a letter to Elfride that belonged to the ancient genre of philosophical consolation. What remains of a cherished father after he has died? He responded by emphasizing not only memories but the life model her father had been. "You bear the unlosable figure of your father within your heart. And if what is fragile in the human being has now been taken from you, this only means that what can never be stolen from you will remain in your possession as all the more precious and radiant. For what belongs to you is not only the memories of the dear departed, but the whole living fabric of your own nature is filled with the constant presence of your beloved father."[68]

The children too were changing, growing up. Jörg, the elder, showed a strong inclination for railway engineering and carpentry.[69] In 1932, at the age of thirteen, he had built a large watermill so elaborate that his father was prompted to say: "I can't keep up at all even when he draws a sketch of the plans."[70] Jörg, said Heidegger, spent time "hammering away in the workshop."[71] His son showed much less enthusiasm for the liberal lessons dispensed at the Gymnasium. Two years later, he was sent to Stuttgart, to the first Waldorf-Steiner school, which devoted a great deal of attention to the trades but without dispensing with intellectual disciplines. We do not know what that year at a new school was like for Jörg, staying first with a teacher, then with friends, the Magiruses. For one reason or another, he did not spend a second year there. In early 1935 he was placed as a boarding student at a Hermann-Lietz School in Bieberstein;[72] its alternative pedagogy also gave great importance to the manual occupations. Jörg remained there for several years, and his parents feared he would fail his *Abitur* exam because of his poor performance in foreign languages and history. German, mathematics, and the natural sciences were easier for him. His father visited Bieberstein in late February 1937 and was reassured to find that, though the history teacher expressed dissatisfaction, the other instructors were encouraging: "He really is one of the boys who makes the best impression now. And barring really rotten luck, they'll pass him."[73] Shortly thereafter, Jörg did in fact earn a *Notabitur* (emergency secondary school diploma), which allowed him in April to join the Labor Service in Melsungen, where he remained until October.[74] Only then did he go to the Karlsruhe University of Applied Sciences to study mechanical engineering.[75] The previous year, he had in fact continued to display his practical dispositions: his mother taught him to drive[76] and, thanks to a special dispensation she arranged for him, he was able to take the driving test and had his license by the age of seventeen.[77]

The younger child, Hermann, followed a life course more traditional at the time for the son of a prominent Nazi. He studied at the Friedrich-Gymnasium in Freiburg,[78] where he was—as he still is—his father's son first and foremost. And because he had some difficulty with Greek and Latin, his father helped him after dinner, explaining linguistic points better than the boy's teachers were doing. In addition to skiing and canoeing, which father and son engaged in together,[79] Heidegger was interested in Hermann's activities in the Jungvolk, the branch of Hitler Youth for boys ten to fourteen. In 1934,[80] rather than join the Hitlerjugend proper, Hermann remained in the Jungvolk, an enthusiastic *Führer* who rose in the ranks, from *Jungenschaftsführer* to *Jungzugführer,* and finally to *Fähnleinführer.*[81] This earnestness in conforming to his parents' educational outlook did not rule out a certain whimsy, which even at the age of fifteen led him to find pleasure in collecting pine cones in Todtnauberg. He stowed the cones, probably meant to feed the fire in the fireplace, in his father's bed, which Heidegger did not appreciate. "Hermann should collect the pine cones on the floor & not in my bed,"[82] he wrote to Elfride.

More than Jörg, Hermann cultivated his relationship with his father. As it happens, his mother had informed her younger son at age fourteen that Martin Heidegger was not his biological father, making him promise to keep quiet about it.[83] It is not pleasant news to learn one is illegitimate, a bastard. It is likely that his mother told Hermann in order to unburden herself of that heavy family secret, and that the prohibition on speaking about it extended to his father, who thus did not know that his son knew. Far from estranging him from the philosopher, that news brought Hermann closer to him. In March 1936 he stayed at the cabin with his father, who found it "very nice with Hermann."[84] The boy applied himself to excelling at skiing, the sport his father was so fond of. In 1939, after participating in a competition organized by the Jungvolk, from which he had "returned very satisfied," Hermann took part in the university championships at Feldberg. Above all, having earned his secondary school diploma, he studied philosophy in Freiburg, where, to his father's delight, he was Heidegger's student: "Hermann makes me very happy—he's now, I think, kindled an interest in philosophy after all—at any rate he understands that it involves something that cannot simply be equated with 'science' & 'worldview.' "[85]

Sometimes life brings surprises. The Heidegger family no longer had two children but three. In addition to Jörg and Hermann there was now Erika Birle, a distant young cousin of Elfride's who joined them in July 1935, at the age of fourteen, following the successive deaths of her parents.[86] Even aside from that critical period of adolescence, there are more favorable circumstances for moving to Germany after leaving São Paolo, Brazil, where Erika had lived until that time. The relationship between her and her new family was all the more complicated in that there was a difference in educational level between them. Hermann kindly tried to bridge the gap after he began his university studies and had acquired sufficient intellectual legitimacy to give lessons to the girl, who was only a year younger than he—Heidegger called her "the lass." Hermann's commitment to teaching tended to bring him even closer to his father, who spoke to him with a great deal of freedom, man to man: "I told him recently in a conversation one evening that we fail to take enough account of what an uncultured environment the child grew up in; for then there's so much more scope for inconstancy."[87] Erika had neither the temperament nor the intellectual abilities to pursue studies like her two adoptive brothers. She was soon called up for the Labor Service, for which she worked in the Black Forest, as a household aide for a Protestant minister's family. It was a positive experience and, upon her return to Freiburg, she took a training course offered by the city. In 1939 she earned a certificate qualifying her for that occupation.[88]

The Heidegger children, even the "lass" Erika, had reached adulthood, an often exhilarating time when one makes one's own choices and when parents are sad to see their young charges leave them. Such was the case for Heidegger, who tried to console himself in the face of the new emptiness of the house in Freiburg: "I'm going through strange times at the moment with Hermann & Erika often away. The growing of the children into independence & a world of their own—this is a new task for us as well, to acquire the proper free attitude yet indirectly still give them something on their way."[89]

In addition to the changes in his family, there were some in his friendships as well. Under the Third Reich, Heidegger gradually became isolated. He lost touch with the friends who were "non-Aryans" or the spouses of "non-Aryans." His last contact with Arendt was in 1932, with Jaspers in 1936, with Löwith in 1937, with Blochmann in 1938. True, he wrote now and again to Bultmann; he still had Jantzen in Freiburg; and in March 1933 he became friends with Kurt Bauch, another art historian from the same university, to whom he grew close because of their shared Nazism. And he established a cordial relationship with another colleague, the Romanist Hugo Friedrich. But that changed little as to the paucity of his friends, which led him to write to Kurt Bauch on 7 February 1935: "It is nice when there is still a human being outside the family whose existence can delight us."[90] The last letter he wrote to Jaspers tended in the same direction: "The *Jaspers* envelope on my desk is getting thicker and thicker. In other respects, it is lonely."[91] In the last missive he sent to Blochmann, he spoke at length of the loneliness of creative people, which he tried to understand as a feature of the age: "We are entering an age when, in a different way and more roughly than before, everything that is essential has to confront solitude. [. . .] I believe that an age of solitude must take over the world if it wants to recover fresh energy to work on restoring the native vigor of things."[92]

In Todtnauberg, as he had always done, Heidegger experienced the loneliness of a thinker in Romantic terms, combining the sense of the fragility of human existence in nature with the intoxication of immersing oneself in it, secure in the knowledge that "the simple things all around one provide for the continuity & steadiness of work & its broad direction." "Everything ordinary" disappeared, even as he was surrounded by the little things that make up life in the mountains: "This evening I'm sitting in the cabin with the shutters closed, & outside there's a 'pig' of a storm raging once again. What's more, there must be something wrong with the standard lamp, yesterday it suddenly flickered & a fuse blew in the shed; I replaced the fuse—but I don't dare use the lamp anymore. The new stove is very nice."[93]

Following his rectorship, Martin Heidegger changed the orientation of his philosophy. In the months after his resignation, he "felt drained" and "was afraid of a long barren period." He found new inspiration by working to elaborate a language that, though "new," would still be "without affectation," claiming that "what's worn out is no good anymore & only leads one astray."[94]

German literature was the field he had pursued most extensively at the Gymnasium, a field "in which he proved to be extremely well read," and to which he devoted himself even "at the expense of his other subjects,"[95] as the rector of the minor seminary of Freiburg averred. In recovering that youthful passion for literature, Heidegger definitively concluded the long period of logical positivism and Scholasticism, the attention to ontological categories that had characterized him in the 1910s and 1920s. He now devoted himself fully to language, ever more often considering his thinking to be a saying, a poetic and philosophical act that transcended both simple communication and abstract conceptual reflection. Hence, on 10 January 1945, at the age of fifty-six, he compared himself to Kant, who, at the same age though under "quieter circumstances," had written the *Critique of Pure Reason*. Heidegger believed he himself had "the clear knowledge" that he was standing "right on the threshold to a more experienced and simpler mode of expression."[96] Beginning in 1934, he returned to the dynamic of linguistic creation he had pursued in the 1920s, which had culminated in the neologisms of *Being and Time*. This time, however, the inspiration no longer came from his own existence and his relation to his native region, but from his reading of Hölderlin, and then, increasingly from 1935 on, of Nietzsche. Associating these two authors had become commonplace through the George Circle, as Heidegger himself noted.[97] He adopted a new philosophical posture, now akin to prophetic exegesis.[98] The philosopher believed that the spiritual revolution in the history of the West, with which the German people was charged, could come from meditation on Hölderlin and a confrontation with Nietzsche; this exegesis was prophetic because it would open the new path that he thought Germany had to follow to fulfill its mission within the destiny of the West.

Heidegger saw Nietzsche as the "last of the great Western thinkers,"[99] in that he was the last to have thought hard about being, considering it an empty word, "the final wisp of evaporating reality."[100] Nietzsche was fundamentally opposed to the idea of an ontology. He wanted to bring philosophy back to earth, at a time when it tended to stay in the "backworlds" to which being belongs and in whose name earthly life was devalued. For Heidegger, however, Nietzsche's observation that being was a "vapor" or an "error" was the sign of an age, the completion of metaphysics; having been exhausted, metaphysics had lost the meaning of what constituted it at the start, the questioning as to being. It was therefore imperative to sort things out with the thinker who was sounding the end of a long history, that of Western philosophy, which Nietzsche himself had recognized as metaphysical.[101]

The divergence between Heidegger's and Jaspers's interpretations of Nietzsche precipitated the end of their friendship. Their correspondence during the Third Reich was interrupted in 1936, after an exchange of two letters written on the same day, 16 May. The two men felt they were in the same philosophical frame of mind: "Your attitude toward philosophy in this age is probably also my own," noted Jaspers, adding: "Your high estimations—Nietzsche, Hölderlin—bring us close together."[102] Heidegger for his part acknowledged receipt of Jaspers's book on Nietzsche with friendly words of praise: "In February of this year, I announced for the coming winter a lecture course on Nietzsche's *Will to Power;* it was to be my first. Now that your work is out, I don't need to make this attempt, for my intention was precisely said simply and clearly in the Foreword: to show that the moment has come to move from reading Nietzsche to the work. Now in the first hour I can simply refer to your book, which additionally is manageable for the students—and, for the winter, I will choose another lecture course."[103]

As a frame of reference shared by the two philosophers, the study of Nietzsche ought to have become common ground; instead, it became a bloody arena. Heidegger followed through on his course on Nietzsche's *Will to Power* and in it engaged in a summary execution of the man who until then had been his friend:

> In Jaspers, all philosophy is impossible, to put it clearly. Philosophy is ultimately an "illusion" in the service of the ethical illumination of the human personality. Philosophical concepts lack the power of truth, not to mention the power of truth that essential knowledge has. Insofar as in the final analysis Jaspers does not take philosophical knowledge seriously, there is therefore no longer any genuine questioning in his work. Philosophy becomes a moralizing psychology of man's existence. That is an attitude that prevents him, despite all his efforts, from ever penetrating a world in Nietzsche's philosophy that questions and explains.[104]

Parallel to the Freiburg philosopher's unfriendly disposition toward him—of which Jaspers was probably unaware—Jaspers's situation deteriorated. In 1937 he was expelled from the university and prohibited from publishing. He lived in growing dread because of the ever-increasing threat to his wife, Gertrud, who, as a Jew, was at risk of being killed. He did not receive the slightest sign of compassion from Heidegger, who was therefore the reason for the complete rift between them.

Because Hölderlin was the "poet of the Germans"[105]—not an eminent member of the Germanic literary heritage but the future of his people of few words, for whom he became the precious spokesman—Heidegger believed it was imperative to meditate on him alongside Nietzsche. And, "*philosophically*," Hölderlin seemed "far beyond even his friends Hegel & Schelling." The Romantic poet, he wrote, was "in a quite different place, which for us is still unspoken & which it will be our task to *say*—not to talk about." Hölderlin's hermeticism lent itself to creative interpretations, though these were not easy. It was "difficult to be alone with Hölderlin," Heidegger wrote, and he wanted to reassure himself through thought that it was "the difficulty of everything great."[106] Considering the line "Was bliebet aber, stiften die Dichter" (But what remains, the poets find), he sought to place the poet's saying "into the *Dasein* of a people, and thus to erect this *Dasein* for the first time, to ground it." Then the poet would become a "a force in the history" of the German people. And Heidegger, contributing to that work, believed he was engaged in " 'politics' in the highest and most authentic sense."[107] The poetic turn of Heidegger's philosophy proceeded from his notion of thought, which was not pure reason. Thanks to Hölderlin's poetry, the fundamental tone, the underlying mood of the German people had to be changed, and with it, its spirit. Heidegger was not sure what reception his prophetic exegesis would find among his people. "I wonder if the Germans will ever grasp that [Hölderlin] was not a weakling unable to cope with life who took refuge in verse, but a hero facing up to the gods of the future—without any followers, 'rooted fast to the mountains for days on end.' "[108]

The poet's writings exerted a great influence on Heidegger. He adopted certain orthographic oddities: *Schicksaal* for *Schicksal* (destiny), *Seyn* for *Sein*. He found encouragement for his own political theology, taking up the flight of the gods or the evocation of the gods to come. He developed that political theology even further, by painting the Third Reich in fateful and religious colors: "To be a *Führer* is a destiny,"[109] he said in his course on Hölderlin's *Germania* and *The Rhine,* and "destiny" was the name for "the beyng of the demigods."[110] In that way, the leader state (*Führerstaat*) acquired a mythological brilliance from the Hölderlinian way Heidegger had of looking at it, while his reading of the poet also gave new force to his rooted and ontological patriotism: "The 'fatherland' [*Vaterland*] is beyng [*Seyn*] itself [. . .], the historical *Dasein* of a people,"[111] he explained in his course for the winter semester of 1934–1935, broadening to "beyng" itself the thesis he had outlined in *Being and Time,* which equated the profound meaning of man's *Dasein* with dwelling alongside.

In extolling the solitude of the thinker and poet, Heidegger, in his return to Hölderlin and Nietzsche, in no way broke with the ambient Nazi culture: on the contrary. Granted, it seems he had read the great Romantic poet in his early youth and had spent his free time on the front lines perusing "Socrates and Alcibiades" in particular, a poem he quoted in a letter to Elfride.[112] His affair with Hannah Arendt had led him to *Hyperion,*[113] which filled him with enthusiasm. But it was only during the Third Reich that Hölderlin became an influence of the first order on Heidegger's thought. The same was true for Nietzsche, who really became essential in his writings only with the rector's address, and even more with the many courses he devoted to the philosopher beginning in 1936. Baeumler had also set his sights on Nietzsche, preparing an edition of his works in twelve volumes, an undertaking in which Heidegger participated. And, despite the boredom the editorial work seemed to cause him,[114] he was so appreciative of the result that he advised his students to employ the volume devoted to *The Will to Power,* alongside the biography oriented in a *völkisch* direction that Nietzsche's sister had written about her brother—

with the reservation, however, that she did not go beyond the biographical to penetrate to the heart of Nietzsche's thought.[115] This did not mean that, overall, Heidegger held Baeumler in high esteem. In 1934 he described in one of his notebooks the man who had been his ally and friend as espousing, philosophically, a "neo-Kantianism rehashed with National Socialism."[116]

The Nazi regime salvaged as much of the earlier Germany as it could, the Germany it found authentically German and not jewified. For example, the mysticism of Master Eckhart was consonant with the irrationalism of the Third Reich, which earned him the honor of being quoted on the title page of Rosenberg's *Myth of the Twentieth Century.* And lines from Hölderlin appeared as an epigraph to the preface for the third edition: "O companions of my age! Do not question your doctors or your priests when you pass within."[117] Romanticism held an even larger place in Nazi Germany than it had in Weimar. The cultural avant-garde, rejected as degenerate, faded away in favor of the glorification of feeling, heroism, and the fatherland by artists such as Wagner, the Führer's favorite musician.

Like the recuperation of large spans of German culture by other Nazis, Heidegger's rendering of Hölderlin was hardly faithful. Despite his injunction that the poem not be freely at one's disposal, and the claim that he and his contemporaries were in fact at the disposal of the poem, in such a way that their *Dasein* became "the living bearer of the power of this poetry,"[118] he seems to have been deaf to the poet's cosmopolitan humanism, inherited from Roman antiquity and the Enlightenment. And yet, Heidegger quoted in class a letter Hölderlin wrote to his brother in 1799 which bore witness to that cosmopolitanism: "Above all else we wish to adopt, with all love and with all seriousness, the great saying *homo sum, nihil a me alienum puto;*[119] it is not meant to make us frivolous, but only to make us true to ourselves and perspicuous and tolerant toward the world."[120]

In the same way, Heidegger tended to read Nietzsche in terms of Ernst Jünger's *The Worker* (1932),[121] by virtue of which he increasingly understood the spiritual decline assailing Europe in light of technology and its will for global domination. Science and the modern world as a whole seemed to Heidegger to be part of "machination" (*Machenschaft*), a system of thought and action oriented exclusively toward making (*machen*) by means of technological calculation. The world, increasingly concerned with calculation and turmoil, having become more than ever the world of the masses, the media, and the abolition of space and time, seemed to know less and less about philosophical reflection, despite its essential necessity:

> When the farthest corner of the globe has been conquered technologically and can be exploited economically; when any incident you like, in any place you like, at any time you like, becomes accessible as fast as you like; when you can simultaneously "experience" an assassination attempt against a king in France and a symphony concert in Tokyo; when time is nothing but speed, instantaneity, and simultaneity, and time as history has vanished from all *Dasein* of all peoples; when a boxer counts as the great man of a people; when the tallies of millions at mass meetings are a triumph; then, yes then, there still looms like a specter over all this uproar the question: what for?—where to?—and what then?[122]

That general metaphysical decline was a rootlessness that Heidegger understood within the frameworks of his anti-Semitism. More than ever, the philosopher was hostile to the "Jew." In his black notebooks, he repeated the stereotype of the calculating and manipulative Jew, which could already be found in his writings of the 1920s.[123] He made it a theme of metaphysical reflection: "One of the most concealed forms of the *gigantic,*" one of the emblematic forms of machination (*Machenschaft*), "and perhaps the oldest, is a tenacious facility in calculating, manipulating, and interfering; through this facility the worldlessness of Judaism receives its ground."[124] Heidegger even viewed that calculating Jewish spirit as the reason that his former teacher Husserl could not reach the zone of the essential philosophical questions[125] but instead was confined to a positive science oriented fundamentally toward a mathematical mastery of nature. That contempt for the man who had initiated him to phenomenology and who had acted as his protector during his career, even yielding his own chair to him, manifested itself one last time in spring 1937, when Heidegger failed to attend Husserl's funeral. Heidegger was foremost among the many colleagues and disciples who declined to give a last farewell to the man who, only a brief time earlier, had been a global celebrity at the University of Freiburg.

In consonance with the time, Heidegger considered the "Jews" to be a race apart because they were of a different blood. That blood expressed itself as an affective disposition, an underlying mood specific to the Jews, which favored a spiritual uprootedness so contagious that it was also affecting a number of "his own." The spiritual and metaphysical result of that "jewification" was nonetheless dire, as his introductory course on metaphysics implicitly portrayed it: "This Europe, in its unholy blindness always on the point of stabbing itself in the back, lies today in the great pincers [*in der großen Zange*] between Russia on the one side and America on the other. Russia and America, seen metaphysically, are both the same: the same hopeless frenzy of unchained technology and of the rootless organization of the average man [*der bodenlosen Organisation des Normalmenschen*]."[126] That metaphor of a suicidal Europe stabbing itself in the back repeated the legend that accused the Jews of stabbing Germany in the back, of causing its defeat, a commonplace of the regime. Heidegger, who in 1934 had said he wanted to win the Great War spiritually,[127] had in mind this anti-Semitic reconstruction of history, but he adapted it for his own use. Europe, uprooted, jewified, was "always on the point of stabbing itself in the back," an expression that for him designated a spiritual suicide, a rejection of philosophical meditation in favor of technological calculation alone. The danger was all the greater in that Europe found itself "in the great pincers"[128] constituted by "Russia" on one side and "America" on the other. Heidegger was reiterating in metaphysical terms the commonplace of the global Jewish conspiracy. Gilbert Kahn's 1958 French translation of *Introduction to Metaphysics,* in rendering "in der [. . .] Zange" as "dans un étau" (in a vise), masks that commonplace.[129] Apart from the fact that *Zange* is a military as well as an instrumental metaphor (*Zange* means both "pincers" and "stranglehold"), which is lost in the translation of the word as "vise," the substitution of the definite article (*die* in German, *la* in French, "the" in English) for an indefinite one (*un,* or "a") wrongly suggests that Heidegger invented the image out of whole cloth. In fact, he was alluding to a commonplace, which he specified as "*the* great pincers" of the Soviet Union and America.

In appearance, the two states were opposing models of ultramodernity. One, Bolshevik, under Stalin's leadership, was the Communist beacon, which through central planning and economic socialization committed itself to the "regulation and mastery of the material relations of production."[130] The other, a paradigm of liberal and capitalist democracy, was the home of gigantism, of the state,[131] of cities, finance, and Taylorized factories, in which, as Charlie Chaplin showed in *Modern Times* (1936), man was becoming nothing more than a flesh-and-blood cog in a great machine of standardized mass production. Beyond their apparent differences, however, Russia and America were the leading edge of the modern will to global technological mastery, the cause and effect of a metaphysical uprooting that would ultimately seal the spiritual fate of those devoted to them.

In thus representing these two states, seemingly opposed in every way but in fact one and the same evil threatening Europe with its groundlessness, Heidegger was repeating on the metaphysical level the idea of the global

Jewish conspiracy, which he had mentioned to Jaspers in 1933, using the expression "dangerous international alliance of the Jews."[132] That idea was central to Nazism; inspired by the *Protocols of the Elders of Zion,* it wanted to see a hidden unity between Judeo-Bolshevism, which had conquered Russia, and international Jewish finance, which dictated the policy of the United States and England. Hitler wrote that, parallel to the misdeeds of Judeo-Bolshevism in Russia and Germany—even where it had stabbed the army in the back—in the Anglo-Saxon countries "the annihilation of Germany" in 1918 "was not an English interest" "but primarily a Jewish one,"[133] and the Jews governed "the stock exchange forces of the American Union."[134] Heidegger made Hitler's structure of thought serve his own metaphysical outlook, but the structure in both cases was exactly the same—except that, for Heidegger, the global Jewish threat was less a sinister conspiracy than a metaphysical uprooting. It came about, in particular, at the two extremities of the modern world, which were even more "jewified" than Europe itself. The outcome, however, was more favorable, because the "spiritual decline of the earth," its jewification according to the letter to Schwoerer, "has progressed so far that peoples are in danger of losing their last spiritual strength," which made it possible at least "to see the decline [. . .] and to appraise it as such."[135]

What recourse could exist against such an evil? The political regime was one condition: a right-wing totalitarian regime like Nazism was needed to fight against that modern decline. In his *Contributions to Philosophy* (1936–1938), Heidegger insisted on the need to erect and maintain, against the unbridled license characteristic of modernity, "sovereignty over the masses who have become free (i.e., groundless [*bodenlos*] and self-serving)." To that end, the "shackles of 'organization' " would provide "resistance to the inexorable uprooting."[136] That task of the Nazi dictatorship was purely preliminary; it was not sufficient to transform uprootedness (*Entwurzelung*) into rootedness (*Verwurzelung*). Heidegger's idea in this book can be expanded and clarified through a passage from his course on Schelling, taught at the same time. In reference to Schelling, Heidegger meditated on uprootedness with the Nietzschean term "nihilism": "Moreover, it is well known that the two men who, in Europe, on the basis of the political form given to the nation and thus to the people—different ways of telling the truth—unleashed countermovements, both Mussolini and Hitler, [then], have, again in different ways, been influenced in an essential manner by Nietzsche, without the authentic metaphysical domain of Nietzsche's thought being thereby recognized directly."[137] The trip Heidegger had taken to Rome in 1936 had convinced him of the kinship between the two regimes, each of which he saw as being, in its own way, under the influence of the German philosopher. Both regimes had good leadership, but it needed to be strengthened by a true metaphysical knowledge acquired on the authentic ground of Nietzschean metaphysics.

Heidegger believed that the struggle against nihilism was a result of Nietzsche's influence. But, in his thinking about uprootedness, when he placed the Germanic or the Western in opposition to the "Asiatic," he was under the influence of the anti-Semitic logorrhea of the time. On 30 November 1934, in his lecture "The Present Situation and the Future Task of German Philosophy," he proclaimed that "the true historical freedom of the peoples of Europe is, however, the *precondition* for the West to return once more to itself spiritually and historically and to secure its fate in the earth's great decision against *the Asiatic*."[138] By "true historical freedom" he meant the union of individuals in a true political community, a *Gefolgschaft* united by the assent given to its leader and the rejection of the irresolute idle talk of a parliament or league of nations. In his eyes, that is what the Germans had succeeded in obtaining with the advent of Nazism. It was now imperative not to stop midway but to work for the historical and spiritual revolution that would decide the rootedness or uprootedness of being, on the scale of the earth itself.

Hölderlin was the subject of Heidegger's meditation in autumn 1934. In his course that semester on the poem *The Rhine,* he placed in opposition a German, Western destiny and an "Asiatic" one, conceived as a *fatum,* a blind "fatality" deprived of will. Heidegger pointed out that a "first overcoming of the Asiatic sense of *fatum*" had occurred among the Greeks, especially with the conceptualization of *polemos* in Heraclitus, who made it "the name of a primordial power of Western-Germanic historical *Dasein*."[139] The philosopher noted that this overcoming was predicated on a "fundamental experience," the experience and knowledge of death.[140] As in *Being and Time,* rootedness in existence, expressed as resoluteness, required an authentic relationship to one's own finitude. The resoluteness to meditate deeply on the experience and knowledge of death would ultimately make possible the earth's great decision against "the Asiatic."

Heidegger's concept of the Asiatic, like that of jewification, was plastic, capable of taking various forms depending on the occasion. In Greek antiquity, it entailed the struggle between Greeks and Persians; in the modern age, it designated the opposition between Germans or Europeans and Jews. In that respect, the philosopher proceeded in the same way as Hitler, who in *Mein Kampf* wrote of "the world empire of Jewish satrapies" (*das jüdische Weltsatrapenreich*).[141] This theme was even more present in Rosenberg's thought. *The Myth of the Twentieth Century,* for example, linked "Jews," the "Christian church," and "Syrians," understood as the cause of the decline of the Aryans—which is to say, the Persians, driven by the "spirit of Zarathustra." As a result, "the Nordic disposition and Nordic racial breeding are the answer today to the Syrian East, which has diffused itself throughout Europe in the form of Jewry and the many varieties of raceless universalism [*in der Gestalt des Judentums und in vielen Formen des rasselosen Universalismus*]."[142]

Although powerful, Heidegger's hatred of the "Jew" did not take away his free will. For example, he criticized Julius Streicher, one of the most notorious anti-Semites, founder of *Der Stürmer,* an extremely crude satirical weekly. In 1936, when Heidegger discussed his relationship to Nazism with Löwith in Rome, his former disciple remarked that Heidegger was a member of the Academy of German Law, alongside Streicher himself. The philosopher replied, after an embarrassed silence—followed by a general defense of the need for engagement—that "one need not waste words over Streicher; *Der Stürmer,* after all, was no more than pornography." Heidegger said, "he could not understand why Hitler did not get rid of this fellow; maybe Hitler was scared of him."[143] The philosopher's distaste for Streicher tended in the direction of what Jaspers wrote after the war: even after 1933, when Heidegger's anti-Semitism was becoming increasingly obvious, it could happen that, "in other cases, [. . .] anti-Semitism went against his conscience and his inclinations."[144]

Heidegger's consonance with the regime did not prevent him from criticizing other Nazis or the standard ideology. These criticisms were not rare and would serve as the grounds for his defense after 1945. But he would misrepresent them: made from within Nazism, they were put forward by a philosopher aspiring to show the way toward a Nazism coherent with its metaphysical essence, whereas Heidegger would try to portray them as absolute criticisms of Nazism. He had nothing but contempt for Ernst Krieck and Alfred Baeumler, the two philosophers who, when the Nazis took power, were initially his allies, and who pursued enviable careers within the regime. Inspired by Nietzsche, who honored the enemy by choosing one worthy of himself, Heidegger did not deign to give the two men such an honor. Thus, in order to explain why he did not reply to Krieck's reproaches, he wrote in one of his black notebooks that he would wage battle only against an "opponent, not someone who champions mediocrity."[145]

With the example of Kolbenheyer, we have also seen Heidegger's view of biologism. He did not criticize the role of race in history, but rather the fact that this role was not conceived ontologically. Seemingly correcting the errors in racial analysis of scientists of the time, in his *Contributions to Philosophy* of 1936–1938 he railed against theories that equated the "Nordic and Germanic" spirit solely with experimental research and which considered rational and mathematical research Jewish: "*Sheer idiocy* to say that experimental research is Nordic-Germanic and that rational research, on the contrary, is *racially foreign!* We would then have to resolve to number Newton and Leibniz among the 'Jews.' It is precisely the projection of nature in the *mathematical sense* that constitutes the presupposition for the necessity and possibility of *'experimentation'* as measuring."[146] A little more than 150 pages later, he criticized the non-ontological nationalism of his time, arguing that "*only on the basis of* Da-sein *is it possible to grasp the essence of a people,*" which meant that the people could not be "a goal" or "a purpose," because such thinking was merely "a 'popular' expansion of both the 'liberal' thought of the 'I' and the economic idea of the conservation of 'life.' "[147] In that respect, ordinary Nazi ideologues—unlike the Nazi regime, which resulted from the German revolution—had not broken intellectually with liberalism; they conserved its principles, simply broadening them to the dimensions of the people.

This type of ultra-Nazi criticism of Nazism could also be found in a letter to Bauch of 1936: "National Socialism would be fine as a barbaric principle—but it should not be so bourgeois."[148] One sign of how central that idea was to his thought: Heidegger had written nearly the same thing in 1934 in one of his notebooks. "National Socialism is a *barbaric principle*. That is its essential character and its possible greatness. The danger is not National Socialism itself—but, rather, its trivialization into a sermon on the true, the good, and the beautiful."[149] Democracy for its part held the promise of a "historical death"[150] for Europe, against which, precisely, Nazism was fighting.

It was indispensable that the German people break with bourgeois science and the bourgeois spirit, in order to confront the danger and challenge of the time. With the same cultural ultranationalism as in his rector's address, but with a more patent anti-Semitism, in his introductory course on metaphysics Heidegger assigned to his own people a distinct historical role as well as a central and perilous geographical position: "We lie in the pincers. Our people, as standing in the center, suffers the most intense pressure—our people, the people richest in neighbors and hence the most endangered people, and for all that, the metaphysical people."[151] In the same manner as the Romantic commonplace,[152] he called the Germans the "metaphysical people,"[153] because of the mission incumbent upon it to revive the great Greek beginning of philosophy, through the reiteration of the questioning of being.[154] Appropriating the Fichtean idea that Germany was placed "in the midst of nations," he added the idea of the global Jewish conspiracy and the encirclement prevailing before and after the First World War, when Germany was trapped between the East (Russia) and the West (France and the United Kingdom). However dangerous they might have appeared to Heidegger in 1935, these "pincers" gripping the German people would be felt with ever-increasing force when, four years later, Germany was led by its Führer into war.

The Ordeal of a New World War (1939–1945)

Hitler had wanted war for a long time. It was imperative to seek revanche against the French; it was essential to unite all Germans in a single state and to conquer the *Lebensraum* (living space) they lacked. Struggle itself, the driving force of life, without which everything was just decline and death, had to be given its due: "Mankind has grown great in eternal struggle, and only in eternal peace does it perish."[155] The revision of the Treaty of Versailles and of the measures that obstructed the revival of German power was only the beginning of a march toward war, in pursuit of a new imperialism. The fighting would be fiercer than ever. On 16 March 1935, the military draft was reestablished, with the objective of constituting an army thirty-six divisions strong. A year later, Hitler sent troops into the demilitarized zone of the Rhineland. On 9 September of the same year, he decided to implement the "Four-Year Plan," to prepare the country materially for a war. The *Anschluss,* the annexation of Austria to the Reich, took place on 13 March 1938. Ceding to Hitler's pressure, the Munich Agreement of 29 and 30 September accepted the annexation of the Sudetenland, where German speakers were in the majority. On 14 and 15 March 1939, German armies invaded what remained of Czechoslovakia, imposing a protectorate and partition. Slovakia became a satellite state. In the same push, on 23 March the Reich's armies entered the Memel Territory, occupied by the Lithuanians.

Heidegger reacted to his country's foreign policy like many Germans, approving of the strong-arm policy conducted by Hitler and worrying about the risk of war, even though he did not really believe in it. The decision to massively rearm in March 1935 was probably one of the inspirations for the statement he made in his course, that the Germans were "the people richest in neighbors and hence the most endangered people."[156] Rearmament against all these neighbors was imperative, whereas the concertation promoted by the

League of Nations could only be a trap. The annexation of Austria was a matter close to Heidegger's heart; he had been disappointed by the first, failed attempt of 1934.[157] Most likely, he joined the more than 99 percent[158] of Germans who in 1938 voted in favor of the annexation and of the slate of legislators for the Reichstag the Führer submitted. The threat of war during the crisis in Sudetenland deeply frightened the philosopher, leading him to write to his wife: "It's almost a comfort to know that dear Father no longer has to endure all these confusions." He reflected more and more, in the wake of Nietzsche and Jünger, on technology's will to power as the force driving the West toward its end. And, though he was not sure that the grave international crisis would culminate in a global conflagration, he increasingly felt it was the future destiny of modern man: "I really am very worried, not about particular things but about the West as a whole—even if worst doesn't come to worst—when I reflect upon the level on which everything now moves."[159] As always, what mattered to Heidegger was to see not the ephemera of events, to which other men attached themselves exclusively, but the underlying principles activated in secret and accessible only to the philosopher.

Heidegger was convinced of the historic role that Nazism had to play, that of an "active nihilism"[160] pushing modernity toward its end, in order, finally, to begin a new history, with the assistance of a new philosophical saying with which he identified himself—a grandiose role both for the regime and for him. In a letter of early 1939, he railed against the intellectual mediocrity of the Third Reich and its façade of Romanticism, while pointing to the true force at work: pure technological mobilization, which, he lamented, lacked a spiritual refoundation. "The internal situation [of the country] worries me more than the external one—for the latter is but the consequence of the former. What's the point of things like 'customs' & 'symbols' anymore in view of the actual realities and the inexorable dynamic of the military-technological organization of the people as a whole; why, they're just smokescreens [*Vor-wände*]—Romantic—historicist—attempts at Romanticism—more academic than all that is 'academic' today, which after all is working everywhere for the Four-Year-Plan."[161] The Four-Year Plan, established in 1936, was supposed to make the economy and the army capable of sustaining a long war. Granting priority to strategic innovations and the development of substitutes (*ersätze*) that would guarantee Germany's economic self-sufficiency—the absence of which had been deadly during the First World War—that plan had given a technological and utilitarian orientation to German science. According to Heidegger, German science ought to be known for being the active nihilism by means of which modernity would end, and beside which everything he saw of "Romantic—historicist—attempts" seemed an outmoded and false academicism.

Science and scholarship, not being equal to the task of supporting the regime spiritually, were the focus of most of Heidegger's criticisms of Nazism. A year later, he wrote that he considered "the whole operation of the university (apart from medicine & nat. sciences) to be pointless,"[162] wondering when his own work would have an impact. In a letter to Bauch the next year, he vituperated against "the absolute prostitution of 'science' today."[163] And in his course on Hölderlin's poem *The Ister* in the summer semester of 1942, he railed against the scientists who believed that all the ancient Greeks were already "National Socialists." Far from honoring the principle that governed the German regime at the time, these scientists, in establishing such a historical bridge, did "no service whatsoever" to "the historical singularity of National Socialism."[164] Nazi Germany had a role in history that no longer called for the obligatory reference to the Greeks. It was transforming itself from an epigone into a paragon.

On 1 September 1939, Germany attacked Poland, having laid claim for months to the Danzig Corridor. This time, the Western powers reacted, confronting the reality of Nazi imperialism. What would become the European part of the Second World War was launched.

Hermann Heidegger was mobilized in the reserve battalion of the Seventy-Fifth Infantry Division, stationed in Donaueschingen, not far from Freiburg. He began to consider a career as a military officer,[165] which was consistent both with the family tradition inherited from his recently deceased maternal grandfather and with the ethos professed by his father. Seeing loved ones go off to war is always a source of anxiety: "Where do you think Hermann will end up now?" Heidegger wondered, then added: "We'll probably be without any news for a while, there's talk here of a three-week postal ban for these convoys."[166] He sent Hermann a letter and a package; Hermann replied with lines that Heidegger himself would not have disapproved of under similar conditions: "One must 'draw thought from within oneself, I'm glad to be able to do this; so though I miss the spiritual encouragement, at the moment I'm replacing it myself.' "[167] In addition, the Karlsruhe University of Applied Sciences closed its doors as a precaution; a French offensive was feared, though it did not come. Jörg was forced to pursue his studies elsewhere. He went to Munich[168] for a short stay; by mid-December, he too was mobilized.[169] Their adoptive sister, Erika, was not greatly affected by the events. That autumn of

1938 she was able to take a course at the residential school for foreign girls in Stuttgart, to complete her training as a domestic aide.[170] She moved to that city in 1942 to be a social worker.[171]

Their father also faced the closure of his university, since Freiburg too was within immediate range of the French armies. He therefore took refuge in Meßkirch, which was farther from the French threat. The war led him once again to tread the ground of his ancestors, which he had not often done in the previous decade, though in 1936, on the occasion of his Aunt Gertrud's eightieth birthday, he had celebrated his home region.[172] The changes that had come to the town of Meßkirch imbued him with the paradoxical sense of being a stranger in his native land: "In one's home town—and yet not at home; this is another of the many conflicting situations arising from the essential insecurity of the universally armed West."[173] In appearance, the war changed everything: more than ever, the men wore uniforms, and the quest for power reached new heights. Heidegger found himself hoping that the time was coming for "great transformations in thought & human existence," the shape of which could hardly be guessed. Both the new era seemingly heralded by the war and the presence in Meßkirch of his writing "workshop" gave him the needed "impetus to work."[174]

Released from the pressures of teaching, Heidegger could concentrate on his writing. It made him forget the university and the canceled semester, which now seemed "unreal" to him.[175] He was busy with the tedious process of editing his manuscripts, which took up hours and whole afternoons of work, for him and his brother. When Heidegger had finished "looking through & comparing the extremely substantial—previous transcripts & the original manuscript in question," his brother typed out the definitive text.[176] At the same time, the philosopher was working to collect his ideas, probably in a black notebook, a task he managed best when he strove for the "simplest" way of saying "what is essential."[177] The editing of his texts made that job easier, since his previous efforts were thereby more present to his mind.

In the evening, the brothers relaxed by taking ritual walks "on the paths through the fields and woods." The "phony" war was palpable in Meßkirch, where everything had grown calmer: "The deer now come out into the snow-covered fields & meadows; with the restricted traffic the countryside has fallen quite silent again. [. . .] As far as provisions are concerned, the people here still hardly notice this strange war. And many of them think it'll soon come to an end by itself."[178] Sunday broke up the uniformity of days with visits to his extended family, and All Saints' Day, with the tribute paid to the dead, contributed to the sense of rupture. His youth in Meßkirch was gone, as attested by the "older graves," whose inscribed names reminded him of the people from the past whom he had lost. For the most part, the faces of the living were already unknown to him, giving him, "at a glance," only a vague sense of familiarity, whose origins were shrouded in mystery. That did not prevent him from rediscovering spiritual dispositions that he knew well. Sometimes he disapproved of the "perplexity & refuge in the faith of the Church," which seemed to him as prominent as ever; at other times, by contrast, he approved of the people's "willingness to make the sacrifices that are necessary."[179]

Heidegger did not understand all the changes at work, though he himself bore the mark of them. He remained convinced of the ever-present danger that Bolshevism—another name for "communism," "nihilism," "uprootedness," the "Asiatic," "jewification"—posed to the world. In his "Koinon: On the History of Beyng" of 1939–1940,[180] he posited that "communism is the metaphysical constitution of peoples in the final phase of the completion of modern times."[181] He was surprised that, "on the teacher's instructions," pupils at the school in Meßkirch had to "cross out the words 'Bolshevism, the world enemy' in their readers from 1938."[182] These new manuals had become outdated within a year, not by the decision of an isolated teacher in Meßkirch but by the Reich's foreign policy. Since the signing on 23 August 1939 of a nonaggression pact that contained a secret clause stipulating the division of Poland, the Soviet Union had become, if not an ally of Germany, in any case a friend. This was affirmed by the German-Soviet Treaty of Friendship, Cooperation, and Demarcation on the following 28 September, signed after the two powers had invaded Poland, a country abandoned by its own allies: the British had hunkered down on their island, the French behind the Maginot Line. And, though Heidegger did not go so far as to cross out the words "Bolshevism, the world enemy" in his own mind, his understanding of the movement changed with that war. The enemy par excellence turned out to be someone else. With the USSR and the United States at peace with the Reich, while the United Kingdom had declared war on it, the "great pincers" eased their grip somewhat, even while remaining real. True, the English and the American spirits were united in an "Anglo-American world," which, despite the opposition between capitalism and anticapitalism, was related to Bolshevism by its "sheer *rationality*."[183] Nevertheless, for Heidegger, the most dangerous form of "Bolshevism" now seemed to be embodied not by the USSR but rather by the bourgeois-Christian form of "English 'Bolshevism.' "[184]

Heidegger went back and forth between Meßkirch and Freiburg. He missed his wife's "silent presence,"[185] an integral part of his work; and, though he worried about his library and manuscripts, the threat did not seem very great. During that period of instability and material difficulties, he wondered: should he not go teach at the Meßkirch Gymnasium, or at the school in Todtnauberg? Finally, in the summer semester of 1940, the university reopened.[186] Elfride for her part was spinning the wool from her Angora hare[187] and trying to save money.[188]

All things considered, everything was going peacefully, even though the border was close by. Then, all of a sudden, the war stopped being "phony," especially for the Allies. The return of the swallows also marked the return to military operations. The German sword had initially been directed against a frail enemy, Poland, leaving to the west only a thin shield of German forces, which the Western powers might have quickly shattered to strike Germany at its heart. In April 1940 the sword was turned against Denmark and Norway, to guarantee the delivery of Swedish iron. At the time, Heidegger greatly admired the technological and military might of his people, which was hastening the coming of a new metaphysical era. He gave his attention to the invasion of Scandinavia, filmed for propaganda purposes, a procedure he understood not as an element of the madness of cinema but as a weapon mobilized to increase power: "When today, during the most audacious military operations carried out by airborne debarkation troops, an airplane films the drop of paratroopers, this has nothing to do with the 'sensational' or with 'curiosity'; the broadcast a few days later of the images of these procedures, making a whole people aware of them, is in itself part of the overall activity and a factor in armament. This 'filmed reporting' is a metaphysical procedure and is not subject to the judgment arising from everyday representations."[189]

Barely blunted by its northern campaign, the German sword turned with the greatest force against the Netherlands, Belgium, and France beginning on 10 May. They were quickly brought to heel. France resigned itself to signing the armistice, which it did on 22 June, in the Rethondes clearing of the Forest of Compiègne, in the same train carriage where, on 11 November 1918, the armistice ending the First World War had been signed. Heidegger was in Meßkirch for the midsemester vacation when the German armies struck to the west. By 18 May, he was aware of the speed of the French defeat, which contrasted so sharply with the resistance of France during the First World War: "Our enemies, even though they have their aircraft & armored cars, still think along the old lines & have to rethink matters from one day to the next. With us, however, the complete mastery of technology has in advance produced a quite different kind of strategic thought. [. . .] The ruthless 'operation' is in itself also an unconditional commitment to the inner lawfulness of the unconditional mechanization of warfare."[190] When he meditated on the events under way, he once again contrasted a deceptive appearance—that Nazi Germany was engaged in an ordinary nihilism, ordinary because "bourgeois," "materialistic"—with the metaphysical greatness of its undertaking to achieve power. "On the basis of the horizon of 'spirituality' and of bourgeois culture, one might consider the total 'motorization' of the Wehrmacht, from top to bottom, as unlimited 'technologism' and as 'materialism.' In reality, it is a metaphysical act,"[191] metaphysical because of the conscious will to become an active nihilism and to usher in a new era, a second flowering of thought. Across the Rhine, after the defeat of 1940, the French people was no longer equal to the task of metaphysics that Descartes had founded in its midst.[192] By contrast, that Nazi victory showed how, with the motorization of the Wehrmacht, the Germans, thanks to the Third Reich, would ultimately embody a "new humanity that transcends the man of today" and which, corresponding "to modern technology and its metaphysical truth," was destined for "unconditional domination over the earth."[193] Heidegger was impressed by the attitude of the United Kingdom toward the French fleet at Mers el-Kebir. On 3 July 1940, fearing that the French ships would be salvaged by Hitler in spite of the signed accords, the Royal Navy sank them in that port near Oran, causing 1,297 deaths. The philosopher reflected on the justice or injustice of that act of war between Allies, still and again under the sign of the will to power. "When, for example, as they are now doing, the English bombard French naval units at anchor in the port of Oran and destroy them, that is perfectly 'just' from their point of view of power: whatever serves to increase their power is 'just.' "[194] Political morality was only a trap, a clever instrument serving the interests of states. Law had no validity beyond the people who had instituted it; universalism could no longer be much more than a weapon of propaganda, destined to be polished up to serve in the war of all against all: "But in no case is it possible and licit *for us* to justify this behavior; each power, conceived metaphysically, has *its own* law [*Recht*]. And it is only out of impotence that it falls into injustice [*Unrecht*]. However, it is part of the metaphysical tactics of each power to not consider the behavior of the opposing power from the latter's point of view, precisely, but rather to evaluate this adverse behavior on the basis of a universal human morality, which nonetheless has only a purely propaganda value."[195]

Heidegger was torn between astonishment and elation at the speed of the German victory, coupled with anxiety about the absence of suffering that resulted: "The storm that is now breaking over our enemies is worrisome,"[196] he wrote, because the French war might not be the ordeal the Germans needed in order to start anew. "Yet other forces are necessary, especially those that prevent the war from becoming dependent [?] on the war, but find their way out of it to another beginning. Yet these forces are still without space & without shape; but I believe *that they* are there."[197] It was imperative to overcome metaphysics by sinking to the depths of one's bitterness. But the overcoming of the nihilism of that era, resting on the void of thinking about being, could not occur on its own, by means of pain in the face of the earth's devastation and nothing else. It required an escort (*Geleit*)[198] to show the way. Therein Heidegger recognized his own destiny, which entailed meditation on Hölderlin and a confrontation with Nietzsche.

Until the end of the conflict, the philosopher held onto the idea that National Socialism was a historical necessity, commanded by the history of metaphysics, of which he alone perceived the authentic meaning. That meaning led him to approve of every aspect, including racial, of the strong-arm policy adopted by the regime. In his eyes, "the thinking about race" elaborated by Nazi Germany, and especially by his friend the eugenicist Eugen Fischer, was a form of calculation that consisted of "taking race into account." It was not "something political," which one could choose or not choose, any more than it was the arbitrary product of biology. Rather, it was a reality inextricable from the modern history of metaphysics. The implementation of that thinking through "selective breeding of the race" (*Rasse-züchtung*) was in essence "an avenue of self-assertion [*Selbstbehauptung*] with a view to domination."[199] Because modernity found its end with the full realization of the nihilism at work, and because technology rested on nothing but the pure will to power, the "cultivation of the race" (*Rassenpflege*) pursued by Germany was in the philosopher's eyes "a necessary measure toward which" "the end of modernity" was tending.[200] Heidegger confirmed these views, dating to the late 1930s, in his course "Nietzsche's Metaphysics" for the winter semester of 1941–1942: "The *principle* of the institution of racial selection" was "metaphysically necessary."[201]

As Fischer's friend, Heidegger had detailed knowledge of the regime's racial policy. Having approved in summer 1933 of the mass forced sterilization of patients suffering from pathologies understood to be hereditary, the philosopher also gave his approval to the sterilization of the "Rhineland mongrels," those who had a black father and a German mother. The sterilizations were perpetrated in 1937 by the institute his friend directed.[202] Heidegger later assented to the mass murder of the disabled that began in 1939 and lasted until the scandal touched off by Bishop von Galen of Münster, who denounced the crimes in a sermon of 3 August 1941. The following autumn, Heidegger implicitly sought to justify from his lectern these deaths of more than 70,000 people who, in the space of less than two years, were victims of Aktion T4.[203] The only distance the philosopher took from the criminal policy of the Third Reich lay in his outlook, which was based on principles, on metaphysics. His aim was less to condemn these crimes than, on the contrary, to show they were ineluctable and desirable if the will to power at work during the era was to reach its climax in Germany.

Heidegger, then, approved of Nazi eugenics. Given the current state of the sources, however, it is not obvious whether he also approved of the policy conducted against the "non-Aryans" in Germany and Western Europe, a policy of persecution and later extermination. It may be that he simply had partial knowledge, limited to the persecution policy. Although the Freiburg synagogue, like so many others, was burned down on *Kristallnacht,* 9 November 1938, and the majority of "non-Aryans" remaining in Freiburg were deported on 22 October 1940, in 1941 Heidegger referred only to "world-Judaism, incited by the emigrants allowed out of Germany [*die aus Deutschland hinausgelassenen Emigranten*]."[204]

After the defeat of France in 1941, only the United Kingdom still opposed the Third Reich, which did not succeed in invading the country or bringing it to its knees. Hitler decided to attack the Soviet Union, the home of "Judeo-Bolshevism," whose conquest would allow him to resume the drive to the east, the Teutonic knights' *Drang nach Osten.* After the conquest of southeastern Europe as far as Greece—a measure that was intended to assist the struggling Italian ally and open the way to the invasion of Russia—the German armies launched Operation Barbarossa on 22 June, a year to the day after the armistice of Rethondes. Hitler opened up to his people about the operation, beginning his speech with the following words: "Oppressed by many cares, and condemned to months of silence, I can now at last speak openly; the hour for me to do so has come."[205] In his black notebook Heidegger recopied that incipit, which announced a complete reversal in German policy and sparked his irony: "*The outbreak of the war against Bolshevism* has finally relieved many Germans of a burden, insofar as they were concerned over what they saw as an overly close bond to Russia."[206]

Like the Führer whose words he was glossing, Heidegger found the global politics of the time to be a three-player game. Germany, he believed, was in contention with the United Kingdom and the USSR, two countries he united into an oriental whole, denying that the U.K. had a "Western outlook" and placing it within the global Jewish conspiracy: "Even the thought of an agreement with England, in the sense of a division of the imperialistic 'franchises,' does not touch the essence of the historical process which England is now playing out to the end within Americanism and Bolshevism and thus at the same time within world-Judaism."[207] Radical as usual, Heidegger ruled out the idea Hitler had mentioned regarding a division of the world between imperial powers, which would have recognized zones of domination belonging to Great Britain and Germany. Taking a polemological approach, he saw the metaphysical principle of the will to power at work in the world, which made any peace between empires an illusion. Heidegger also adopted the idea of a global Jewish threat, with Europe caught between the Soviet blade of the pincers to the east and the Anglo-Saxon blade to the west. "English Bolshevism,"[208] which in that new world war had been the leading edge of the struggle against Germany—at a time when the United States and the USSR were still staying out of it—had reached the end of its preeminent role in history. That role now passed to Soviet Bolshevism, against which the Reich was taking up arms.

The regime understood the increasingly arduous war as an enterprise of annihilation directed against the East. Even before the advent of the Third Reich, the Nazis may have had an extreme though vague notion of annihilation. Examining the struggle of the Romans against the "Semitic Jewish centers" of Carthage and Jerusalem, Rosenberg argued that the "destruction of Carthage" was "a deed of superlative import in racial history [*eine Rassengeschichtlich ungeheuer wichtige Tat*]," because, thanks to that deed, "the later cultures of central and western Europe were spared the infection of this Phoenician pestilence." That explained his regret at the belatedness of Titus's actions against the Jews, who had already spread to Egypt, Greece, and even Rome itself. The destruction of the "Semitic Jews" had not annihilated their race, an outcome that Rosenberg proposed for future meditation on the part of the Germans: "World history might well have taken a very different course had the obliteration of Carthage been accompanied by a total annihilation [*Zerstörung*] of the other Semitic Jewish centers of the Near East."[209]

In launching an attack against the USSR, the Nazis adopted a new radicalism, which went well beyond the military annihilation suffered by France less than a year earlier, and even further than the tens of thousands of summary executions to which the Poland campaign had given rise.[210] On 19 May 1941, in anticipation of the launch of the invasion, the "directives for the conduct of the troops" depicted Bolshevism as "the mortal enemy of the National Socialist German people," requiring, therefore, "ruthless and energetic measures against the Bolshevik agitators, the partisans, the saboteurs, and the Jews, as well as the total elimination [*restlose Beseitigung*] of all resistance, active and passive." And on 6 June, the "directives for the treatment of the political commissars," who were denied the status of combatants, explicitly exhorted that they be murdered.

These directives, which expressed an ideology as summary as it was racist and murderous, were widely disseminated among the troops,[211] and, alongside a preliminary indoctrination, contributed toward shaping the view they had of the local populations and how they were to be treated. A noncommissioned officer, for example, mentioned Julius Streicher's newspaper, *Der Stürmer,* in a letter of August 1942: "I've now received *Der Stürmer* three times. It fills me with happiness. [. . .] You could not have made me happier. [. . .] I had detected the Jewish poison among us for a long time. It is only with this campaign that we are realizing how far it might have gone at home. Every day we are witness to what the Jewish regime in Russia has done. Even the most skeptical are cured in the face of the facts. Our duty is to liberate this world from this scourge, and we will succeed; that is the reason the German soldier is defending the eastern front, and we will not return before we have extirpated the evil and destroyed the heart of Judeo-Bolshevism, 'benefactor of humankind.' "[212]

The German troops on the Soviet front, followed by *Einsatzgruppen,* engaged in many crimes—that was in fact the special task of these "task forces"—in a war understood to be a fight to the death. It translated into a scorched-earth policy that ravaged entire regions, a struggle against the "partisans" that killed hundreds of thousands of civilians on the grounds of their "race," the execution of more than 500,000 prisoners of war as biological and political enemies of the Reich, and the detention of prisoners of war under appalling conditions, leading to the death by starvation, cold, disease, and ill treatment of more than 3 million[213] people considered to be "subhumans."

Unlike the activity of the death camps, which was kept secret and did not entail a large number of perpetrators, the campaign against the Soviet Union involved the majority of young Germans, who were therefore witnesses to or participants in the atrocities, whether up close or at a distance. The Heidegger sons advanced with the German troops: Hermann to Russia,[214] Jörg to Greece with his motorized division.[215] In one way or another, they were caught up in that violent rampage against civilian populations and prisoners of war. It is even possible that the younger son, named a *Bataillonsadjutant*[216] with the rank of officer,[217] ordered massacres.

Although there is nothing to corroborate the account Hermann gave in a recent interview in *Die Zeit,* it does have the merit of clarity. He could not say whether his father knew anything during the war about the extermination of the Jews, but Hermann himself learned of it on the night of 21 June 1941, while in Romania with his unit, set to invade Ukraine. Either the massacres perpetrated in Poland in 1939 or, more likely, those following the invasion of Romania and Transnistria must have been at issue.[218] Later, he said, an SS officer and former fellow Scout spoke of the murder of Jews in Russia, though Hermann did not tell his father about them.[219]

To learn what the Heidegger sons did, we would have to read all the letters from the philosopher to Fritz during that period, when the brothers were particularly close to each other. I wrote to Hermann's son, Arnulf Heidegger, asking permission to consult the manuscripts held in Marbach. He replied that this correspondence—which is essential in more than one respect, and which probably contains disturbing details about Jörg or Hermann—cannot for the time being be made freely available to researchers, because its content "touches on the private sphere of many living persons who ought to be protected."[220] One may take offense, in the name of truth, that texts essential for understanding what a family did, thought, or experienced seventy years ago are sealed in order to remain concealed; one may approve of a son who, administering a legacy of private texts, behaves in such a way as to protect his declining father, whose last days are already tinged with painful revelations.

Although the conduct of Heidegger's sons in the war remains hidden, it is now possible to have an accurate idea of what the philosopher thought of the Soviet war. A recently published short excerpt of a letter from Heidegger to Fritz, dated 20 July 1941—that is, nearly a month after the launch of Operation Barbarossa—bears witness to an at least vague awareness of the unheard-of brutality of the fighting in the USSR, which contrasted sharply with the start of the conflict: "*The war is only now beginning* [Heidegger's emphasis]. The brutality [*Brutalität*] of the fighting in the East is obviously of 'world-historical' 'dimensions' [*offenbar von 'welthistorischen' 'Ausmaßen'*]."[221] The philosopher was cognizant of all or part of the criminal spirit and actions of the Wehrmacht in the East, of the genocide under way. Such more or less vague knowledge of that aspect of the extermination of the Jews was in fact commonplace.[222] The war of annihilation, new in its radicalism, seemed to Heidegger to be a good thing, equal to the task required; it would probably lead to the victory of Germany in the battle with the USSR, a particularly jewified power. With the United States and the United Kingdom, the Soviet Union constituted the great pincers that were squeezing Germany. The idea of annihilation haunted Heidegger at the time, even in his meditation on thought as such. In the winter semester of 1941–1942, speaking of the constructive action of thought, which could also become destructive, he uttered this sentence: "Annihilation ensures against the establishment of all the conditions of decadence."[223]

Heidegger's assent to the annihilation of the Judeo-Bolshevik enemy, including its physical annihilation, had an aim that eluded other Nazi doctrinaires, such as Hitler and Rosenberg. For the philosopher, the essential annihilation was not physical, material, or political but spiritual, ontological, and metaphysical. Annihilation was "machination" (*Machenschaft*) that had reached its end, nihilism unveiled, the consummation of metaphysics. As Heidegger wrote in 1938 or 1940, "here, annihilation does not mean elimination [*Beseitigung*]" or "destruction [*Zerstörung*]." "Here, annihilation leads 'positively' to nothingness," which, when it is permanent, finds expression in "devastation [*Verwüstung*]." Consequently, devastation is not the void, the absence of things, but a sui generis order in which "beings no longer come into the decision of being."[224] That does not mean that there are no acts of destruction on earth, but they are only a preliminary to devastation.[225] With lucidity, in early August 1941 Heidegger provided an overview for his friend Kurt Bauch of the hierarchy he saw among these three phenomena brought by war: "Devastation is more essential than destruction and annihilation. The latter lead only to nothingness, the former realizes the absence of decision."[226] In his text "Koinon" of 1939–1940, he had introduced a further distinction, also illuminating: that of *Selbstvernichtung,* self-annihilation. After positing (probably in 1940) that "the Christian and bourgeois form of English 'Bolshevism' is the most dangerous one," and "without the annihilation [*Vernichtung*] of the latter, the modern epoch will continue," he qualified the statement by adding that "definitive annihilation can only take the form of essential self-annihilation [*wesenhaften Selbstvernichtung*]."[227] Only England could definitively annihilate England; only the USSR could put an end to the USSR; only Germany could do the same for Germany. Granted, the war of annihilation waged in the East had the aim of annihilating a dangerous spiritual power. Above all, however, its aim was to allow the German people to reach, through an active, deliberate nihilism, both the heights of material power and the abyss of ontological self-destruction. It was imperative to pursue to the end the process under way, since it could not be checked but only hastened. The end through self-destruction, combined with world conquest, would allow the question of being to be posed anew. This task of active nihilism fell to Germany. The declaration of war against the USSR was a way for the country to assume its mission for the spiritual salvation of the West and of the world. Only in this way, in the ruins of modernity, could the German people, caught up in the distress of existence and in its mission within the history of the West, emerge from the nothingness of the will to power, truly meditate on Hölderlin, rediscover the path of being, and spiritually revive humanity as a whole.

The mission that Heidegger recognized for Germany did not rule out a global competition among the peoples driven by nihilism. He wrote in his notebook what he believed was truly at stake in the confrontation between Germans and Jews: "The question of the role of *world-Judaism* is not a racial question, but a metaphysical one, a question that concerns the kind of human existence [*Art von Menschentümlichkeit*] which in an *utterly unrestrained way* can undertake as a world-historical 'task' the uprooting of all beings from being."[228] This was more than a war of destruction or domination, a struggle for the survival of one race that entailed the submission or annihilation of another. The war was a metaphysical pursuit coursing toward the ontological uprooting that occurred by means of a total war. And that metaphysical war was secret, invisible. As he wrote to his friend Kurt Bauch, who was on the general staff of the Kriegsmarine (German Navy) in Berlin, on 10 August 1941: "At present the Russian war is there; but its meaning transcends it. I do not need to elaborate, since you know more about it. But I know enough."[229]

At the start of the Russian war, Heidegger was not optimistic. He drew up a ten-point balance sheet that hardly seemed reassuring about the future. He pointed out that, after two years of one victory after another, Germany now found itself without any new potential allies, caught up in a war with multiple fronts—something it had wanted to avoid with the German-Soviet Pact, and which was now a reality because of Germany's "own resolution."[230] In addition, the power of "world-Judaism, incited by the emigrants allowed out of Germany," was all the greater in that world-Judaism could not be "held fast anywhere" and did not require war operations in order to act. All that remained for the Germans was "the sacrifice of the best blood" of the best of their people,[231] which he could easily identify with his own sons. Hermann, in fact, had suffered a serious leg wound in September 1941 and had to be repatriated from the Russian front.[232]

That sacrifice would be an ordeal allowing the return to being. By means of the worry, grief, or despoliation it could occasion, war would make possible a radical change in the mentality of the German people. Already at the end of the First World War, Heidegger had judged that the war had not yet "become frightful enough for us,"[233] because it was unable to lead the people to contrition and meditation. In 1943 he wrote similar words in a letter to his friend Kurt Bauch: "Two world wars" were "necessary to raise again, in Germany, the question of the being of beings."[234] Again and again, Heidegger embraced the observation he had made in 1929, even before the Third Reich was established. The German people, the West, suffered from only one source of distress, the distress of the absence of distress, the forgetting of finite existence, which led to uprooted thought, an uprooted life.[235]

The war had become truly global by late 1941. The principal danger was no longer English or Soviet but American. Four days after the surprise Japanese attack on the American naval base at Pearl Harbor on 7 December, Hitler, on his own initiative, declared war on the United States. The two major regions of the world that had been at war—Asia since 1937, with the beginning of Japan's conquest of China, and Europe since 1939 and the German offensive against Poland—were now bound by shackles of fire passing through the Americas.

Germany's declaration of war on the United States changed Heidegger's perception of that conflict within the history of being. Noting the Americans' desire not to seek compromise, he said in his summer semester course of 1942: "We know today that the Anglo-Saxon world of Americanism has resolved to annihilate [*vernichten*] Europe, that is, the homeland [*Heimat*], and that means: the commencement of the Western world. Whatever has the character of commencement [*das Anfängliches*] is indestructible. America's entry into this planetary war is not its entry into history; rather, it is already the ultimate American act of American ahistoricality [*Geschichtslosigkeit*] and self-devastation [*Selbstverwüstung*]."[236] Ahistorical and destined for self-annihilation in that war against Germany, the United States once again assumed the appearance Heidegger had conferred on it in 1935, in the introductory course on metaphysics: a mortal danger, one of the blades of the "great pincers" gripping the German people. Except that now, minimizing the risk posed by "English Bolshevism," he learnedly explained in his course on *The Ister* that

"Bolshevism is only a derivative kind of Americanism,"[237] making Americanism the root of the evil of the age.

It is within this context that we must understand the pages, newly revealed with the publication of a fourth volume of black notebooks, in which Heidegger speaks of the struggle against the "Jewish," which he saw as a "principle of destruction."[238] "Only when what is essentially 'Jewish' in the metaphysical sense combats the Jewish [*das Jüdische*] is the apex of self-annihilation in history reached; on the condition that the 'Jewish' has seized full domination everywhere, so that the battle against 'the Jewish' is also successful first and foremost in its dominion [*Botmäßigkeit*]."[239] Once again, Heidegger was designating not a person but a phenomenon: the "Jewish" (*das Jüdische*) and not the "Jews." He put into play both a "broad sense" ("metaphysical" in this case) and a strict sense (that which for him was in fact "Jewish": Christianity, the jewified West, and especially, at that time, Americanism, Judeo-Bolshevism). For Heidegger, uprootedness had conquered even the right-wing totalitarian states, engaged in a race for power for its own sake, which obscured more than ever the distress of being; in parallel, the United States too had entered the war. Meanwhile, the "Jewish" "has seized full domination everywhere,"[240] so that the struggle Nazi Germany and its allies were waging against their enemies was a war between what was metaphysically Jewish and what was intrinsically, if not racially, Jewish. Blossoming into a global conflict, the diseased flower of "machination," the principle of destruction—racially or metaphysically Jewish—was reaching the point of no return: self-annihilation. The overcoming of metaphysics was near at hand; the oracle would be able to be heard in the nothingness of the will to power.

In summer 1942, when Heidegger wrote these lines on the annihilation of the Jewish by the "Jewish," he was thinking primarily, if not exclusively, of the battle of Titans between Germany, " 'Jewish' in the metaphysical sense," which was taking upon itself destruction as a principle, and the USSR and England, joined by the United States, the quintessence of "machination." The recently published letter to Fritz of 29 January 1943 goes in the same direction. The German defeat in Stalingrad seemed inevitable (Paulus's Sixth Army would surrender just a few days later), and Heidegger had already lost there "one of his best students from the years 1930–1934."[241] But what he judged to be particularly decisive was "the great threat" constituted by the union of Bolshevism and Americanism "in one and the same form of essence [*zu einer einzigen Wesengestalt*]," working "*themselves* to destroy, on the basis of that unity, Germanness [*Deutschtum*] as the center of the West."[242]

At the same moment, the death camps were going about their sinister work, which remained more or less hidden from their neighbors. Whether Heidegger knew or did not know what was being perpetrated there seems to me in no way to change the overall assessment: the philosopher, still and always radical, tended to approve of all the measures taken by the Nazi state to guarantee itself world domination and to precipitate the self-annihilation of modernity. For him, that undertaking was not the effect of a policy desired by his people but the necessary outcome of the history of a jewified West, so much so that the Germans were becoming more "Jewish," more uprooted and destructive,[243] than the Jews themselves. After that self-annihilation of the "Jewish," of which they were ultimately the unwitting agents, the Germans could return to rootedness, thanks to their meditation on Hölderlin: " 'The return to the homeland' [*Heimkunft*] is the future of our historical essence. There, 'goals' are not affirmed [*bestimmen*]. Thus only the beginning is uttered with truth [*stimmt*]."[244] Far from a genocide, devastation was thus a necessary step in the return home; the necessary ontological asceticism made it possible to disregard beings in order to accede to being.

Against that "return to the homeland," against that revival of the question of being, a Jewish system[245]—Catholicism—was being erected in Freiburg, again and always. Heidegger retained for the religion of his youth a violent aversion, which, though remaining ontological and metaphysical, increasingly fed on the black legend propagated by a number of German Protestants and liberals: Rome, the shackles of the Catholic spirit, wanted to extend its dominion to the whole world, just as the city of Romulus had conquered the civilized world. That is how we must understand a passage from the course on Parmenides Heidegger gave in 1942–1943. The forcefulness of his denunciation gave voice to the muted and corrosive feelings he had come to have about the Church: "The 'imperial' here emerges in the form of the curial of the curia of the Roman pope. His domination is likewise grounded in commandment. The character of commandment here resides in the essence of ecclesiastical dogma. Therefore this dogma takes into account equally the 'true' of the 'orthodox believers' as well as the 'false' of the 'heretics' and the 'unfaithful.' The Spanish Inquisition is a form of the Roman curial *imperium*."[246] Even before Roman civilization, the Jewish spirit, finding expression in Greek in the Septuagint, had made the concept of the true lose its sense of an opening to the phenomenon that conceals or discloses itself, the properly Greek representation of truth as *aletheia* (*ἀλήθεια*). Quoting John 14:6 in Greek ("I am the way, the truth, and the light"), Heidegger provided his students with this commentary:

"Only the sound of this phrase is Greek."[247] Later conceived in Latin as "a quality of the mind or soul in the inner man," "the essence of truth as *veritas* and *rectitudo* is without space and without ground."[248] *Aletheia,* used moreover as an instrument of imperial domination, had been distorted throughout the Middle Ages and continued to be so even in modern times, because it was obstructed by "an enormous bastion of the essence of truth determined in a manifold sense as 'Roman.' "[249] That violent warping of truth contributed strongly to ontological uprootedness, the spiritual "jewification" from which the West was suffering. It was therefore imperative to destroy the bastion of the essence of truth that was maintained by Catholicism and was still obstructing the German spirit.

In one of his black notebooks, Heidegger probed even deeper, to the root of the "spiritual jewification" of the West itself. Under the name "Europe," the West had seen its intrinsically Greek essence overshadowed by Christianity, which appropriated it for its own ends and dismissed ancient Greece as paganism: " 'Europe' is the modern form of forgetfulness, in which the West [the 'Evening Land,' *Abend-land*] is restrained. *Christianity,* that is, the Pauline, gnostic, Roman, and Hellenistic organization of Jesus's evangelical life, is a prefiguration of Europe. It has nothing to do with the West, because it denies Greek culture in the most dangerous way possible—namely, exploitation, which distorts its meaning—in order to achieve its own goals, in which respect Greek culture is taken to be pagan."[250]

The war, having become global, was increasingly terrible for everyone, the Germans included. Temporarily discharged from the service, Hermann gradually recovered from his leg wound and in 1942 attended his father's courses.[251] His presence in the lecture hall made the philosopher inclined to feel for his audience of student veterans all the tenderness of a father. Although a number of his students were women, including Princess Margot von Sachsen-Meiningen, who became Heidegger's mistress,[252] he had written to the rector of the university, on 16 October 1942, that teaching ought to be structured exclusively for the students discharged from the front lines, and that he would henceforth refuse to give any lectures abroad, in Rome, Madrid, or Lisbon, as he had been invited to do: "Because of the prolonged duration of the war, the studies of these students returning from the front take on a significance that far transcends mere education. It does not suffice to give special consideration to these students alongside the others. These students have to be recognized as our most cherished audience and everything that transcends the instructive dimension of education must be conceived in relation to their needs."[253]

Concern about his combatant sons also found expression in his lecture in Freiburg on 6 June 1944, on Hölderlin's poem "Return," in which he linked the idea of the return home to that of the resoluteness of the German soldiers, who were fighting far from the soil of the homeland, but whose eyes were riveted on it:

> The sons of the country, then, who are far away from the soil of the homeland, but whose eyes are turned toward the serenity of the homeland, which gleams at them, put their lives in the service of the treasure trove still in reserve and do not hesitate to sacrifice themselves. Are they not, then, these sons of the homeland, the poet's closest relatives? Their sacrifice holds within it the appeal that the poet addresses to the dearest in the homeland, so that the treasure in reserve might still be spared. It will be, if "those whose worries are in the homeland" become the worried ones in an essential way. Then there is a relationship with the poet. Then there is a return home. And this return is the future of the Germans' historical being.[254]

Despite the concomitance of his lecture and the Allied landing in Normandy, Heidegger probably had in mind the eastern front, where Jörg was fighting, where Hermann had also battled and to which he might shortly return—as he in fact did the following August. Heidegger distinguished between two levels of patriotism, one ordinary, the other ontological. Ontological patriotism, which he ardently wished for, meant being worried about the homeland "in an essential way," and it was that form of patriotism that he sought to develop in his students in the courses he gave. More than ever, Heidegger conceived of the German soldiers' combat as a "sacrifice."[255] The Battle of Stalingrad, far from being a brilliant testament to German technological domination, ended in defeat on 2 February 1943 and marked the ebb tide of the Reich's armies. It seemed to expose the civilized regions of Germany to the nomadic hordes from Asia, against whom it was imperative to hold fast to the bitter end. Heidegger, far from defeatist but heeding the change in the course of the war, noted in his black notebook at the time: "The only one who will win this war is the one who *can* lose it and in this loss grasp the call of a unique change in the essence of man, and stand ready for it."[256]

It was a time of ordeals and privations. Elfride no longer confined herself to spinning the wool from her Angora hare. She put her garden on Rötebuckweg to good use, cultivating fruits and vegetables and raising bees. Potatoes grew in the former swimming pool, which had been filled in and turned into a bomb shelter. Even the garage in Freiburg had lost some of its pretentiousness: no longer housing an automobile, it was now filled with goats.[257] The urgency of the times also spread to family events: in December 1942 Jörg married Dorothee Kurrer in Berlin, so quickly that his parents were unable to be there.[258] Somewhat later, his young wife, nicknamed "Dorle," moved in with her parents-in-law in Freiburg.[259] The philosopher, for his part, was having trouble getting his article "Plato's Doctrine of Truth" accepted for publication; in the end, it was published solely because of an intervention at the highest level.[260]

These ordeals, privations, and humiliations did not undermine the philosopher's support for the regime. In the light of metaphysics, he revisited the totalitarian power of the leaders operating within Nazism, a power characteristic of ultramodernity: "The moral outrage of those who do not yet know what *is* often takes aim at the arbitrariness and the claim to dominance of the 'leaders' [*Führer*]. [. . .] One believes that the leaders had presumed everything of their own accord in the blind rage of a selfish egotism and arranged everything in accordance with their own will. In truth, however, they are the necessary consequence of the fact that beings have entered the way of wandering, the place of extension of the void, which demands a single order and guarantee of beings."[261] The void is that in which thinking about being is located. Being is forgotten in the calculation of beings, which occasions the wandering of modernity. In the system of machination, *Führer*—necessary, all-powerful, but far from expressing their own whims—turn out to be "the suppliers who have decision-making power and who oversee all the sectors where the wearing away of beings is kept secure: because the whole of the circle (of the districts) is before their eyes and thus they dominate wandering to the extent that it is calculable."[262] The leaders performed their leadership function, that of expressing the will to power, even if their subordinates would suffer as a result.

Heidegger remained imbued with Nazism even in his way of philosophizing about Hölderlin and Nietzsche. In his 1944 lecture, he referred to the Germans as the "people of the poem and of thought,"[263] because of the German people's essential connection to Hölderlin, the "the poet who thinks," and to Nietzsche, "the thinker who poetizes."[264] Heidegger was repeating in part a statement Hitler had uttered on 21 March 1933, during the Day of Potsdam: Hitler characterized the Germans as "a people of singers, poets, and thinkers" (*Volk der Sänger, Dichter und Denker*), to whom only "the path of interiority" (*der Weg nach innen*) still remained open in the end.[265] And, as Heidegger noted on a page in one of his black notebooks, the Führer, in his speech of 30 January 1940, had recognized "poets and thinkers" as "workers."[266] The philosopher could only have acquiesced to the "path of interiority" that ultimately awaited the Germans, a path that he himself ardently wished for. The striking literal resemblance of Heidegger's statement, even in its word order, to Hitler's speech of 21 March 1933 invites us to consider it a truncated and concealed quotation close to plagiarism. Further confirmation of the great interest Heidegger found in that speech is provided by a passage from a letter to his wife, whom he asked: "Have the copies of the Potsdam speech on Fr[ederick] the Gr[eat] arrived?"[267]

Heidegger, who did not repudiate that national identity inspired by Hitler, also had not lost his anti-Semitic prejudices. In his interrupted course for the winter semester of 1944–1945 titled "The Completion of Metaphysics and Poetry," he critiqued the following quotation from Nietzsche: "Germany produced only one poet apart from Goethe: that was Heinrich Heine—and moreover, a Jew." Heidegger commented: "This remark casts a strange light on the poet Goethe. Goethe-Heine, 'the' poet of Germany. Where is Hölderlin?"[268] He not only regretted that Hölderlin, whom he obviously believed to be "the" poet of the Germans, had been forgotten; he also regretted the association between the Jew Heine and the German Goethe, which tended to devalue the latter, to "jewify" him in one way or another.

The war pursued its course, which was no longer favorable to Germany. Since the Allied landing in Sicily on 10 July 1943, and especially in Normandy on 6 June 1944, the country was in fact caught in the pincers and suffered ever-increasing damage. The intense bombardment of German cities came to Freiburg. On 27 November, the old city center lay in ruins, with the exception of the cathedral. On the following 15 January Martha Petri died, apparently from fright, in her apartment in Wiesbaden, which had been hit by the bombing.[269] The American-Soviet pincers were tightening around Germany, so much so that they seemed to be realizing a providential destiny acting against the Germans. That destiny was incomprehensible to Heidegger, who noted three days later, in a letter to Fritz: "What the 'world spirit' [*Weltgeist*] holds in store for the Germans is a mystery. Equally obscure is why it is using the Americans and the Bolsheviks as henchmen."[270]

The Third Reich was working hard to muster its last forces and throw them into the fray. Fritz was mobilized in the army in early 1945.[271] Called up for the

Volkssturm on 8 November 1944,[272] Martin Heidegger was put to work digging trenches in Alsace, which reminded him of the First World War, even as it cost him a great deal of effort.[273] He was finally discharged in December.[274] He came up with a plan to rent and restore one of the towers of Meßkirch Castle and to store his manuscripts there. As Berlin was teetering, only his native region seemed able to ensure him safe ground. The project required resources—men and materials—that were no longer easily available as the war ended, and winter made the work all the more difficult. He had to resign himself to abandoning it.[275]

Heidegger was increasingly alone. The war sapped his strength and led him to fear he would be unable to store safely his thousands and thousands of pages of manuscripts, which he had to read over, type out with his brother's help, and safeguard against the terrible destruction the country was suffering. The bombing of Meßkirch on 22 February 1945 not only caused thirty-five deaths and left more than 120 wounded, it also destroyed the bank in whose safe he had stored his texts. Fortunately, the texts were buried under the rubble without being ruined.[276] The decision was made, ultimately, to seal them up in a cave above the Danube, alongside manuscripts by Hölderlin.[277] Heidegger, the oracle of the poet—and, beyond him, of destiny—held onto a providentialist vision of history nurtured by the Hölderlinian word, which led him to write, in the margins of his notes for the class on *The Ister* in 1942:[278] "Perhaps the poet Hölderlin must become the fateful figure who will determine the development of a thinker whose grandfather was born on almost the same date as the *Hymn to the Ister* and the poem *Memory*, according to the birth certificate *in ovili* [in the sheepfold], in the upper valley of the Danube,[279] near the riverbank, on the rocks. There is nothing of chance in the secret history of the legend. Everything is the effect of providence."[280] Providence seemed to be showing by multiple signs—in particular, geographical and historical coincidences between the life of Hölderlin, the "poet of the Germans," and the lives of Heidegger's family—the connection between the great Romantic poet and the philosopher of Meßkirch, whose family had been rooted in his home region for many generations. Full of mystery, God appeared to announce in that way the fate of the Swabian philosopher, whose thinking would take the great poet of his region as its source. It was from there, he felt, that the renewal of beyng would come: "Ever more clearly, the idea comes to me that our native country, the heart of southwestern Germany, will be [*seyn wird*] the historical birthplace of the Western essence."[281]

The sense of his destiny, though exhilarating, was also a weighty obligation for Heidegger, an anxiety that sometimes turned to panic. He absolutely had to find a safe place for his manuscripts, so that his destiny could be realized. The philosopher worked in great haste, seriously overtaxing himself, tormented as he was by the metaphysical destiny of his people.

> In the process I probably rather overdid it, as I was working at night again too, above all on the more external business of listing and collating the material. I haven't wanted to write to you about it up to now, as I thought it was just temporary fatigue—but the insomnia is continuing, the faint spells & headaches & strange depressions. Since Fritz left, I have no one around me with whom I can talk or go for a walk in between whiles. Yet what really wears one down is the fate of this people, especially when thinking beholds it in its Western essence & with a destiny such as this.[282]

Overworked, depressed, Heidegger had to concede that, despite his prophetic pose, the long-awaited awakening of the Germans had not come about and his words had been spoken in vain. "Over everything there now lies a rubble of incongruity and strangeness, which is all the more disconcerting because it was heaped by one's own people over the hidden striving of its own essence to grope its way to its truth."[283] Perhaps the suffering still had not been great enough? That is the question he asked himself. "Perhaps even now, in spite of the unspeakable misery, there is little pain in the world because everything is only hardened by the power of the will."[284] The will to power everywhere at work made spirits nearly impervious to suffering. The distress of being still remained inaccessible to them. Heidegger thus wanted to take refuge in the expectation of an event sent by destiny but still concealed: "What is now taking place over the entire planet is of such a kind that an essential event [*wesenhaftes Ereignis*] must be concealed within, even if we cannot yet see it & cannot yet speak of it."[285]

IV

A Nazi Bound to Remain Silent? (1945–2017)

10 • In Distress over Germany in Ruins

(1945–1949)

The Denazification of Martin Heidegger (1945–1947)

The denazification period was particularly painful for Heidegger. Even before the start of the university proceedings, he faced a first ordeal with his house. The French military government had demanded that the municipality provide accommodations, which were in short supply because of the widespread destruction of Freiburg. Homes were to be seized as a first priority from members of the Nazi Party, who thus found themselves temporarily deprived of all or part of their residences. In mid-May 1945, three weeks after the French troops entered the city, the Heideggers' house on Rötebuckweg was placed on a requisition list. And, after an inquiry as to its amenities, it was provisionally confiscated, along with the philosopher's personal library. Because Heidegger was in the Upper Danube Valley, where part of the Faculty of Philosophy had taken refuge, it was Elfride who, on 10 June, first appealed the decision.[1] The mayor replied on 9 July: "The military government requires the city to make available a large number of homes for the needs of the government and the accommodation of priority categories. The directive issued by the military government states that the homes of former Party members are to be requisitioned first. In view of the fact that Professor Heidegger was a member of the Party, all the criteria for the issue of a requisitioning order have been met."[2]

On 16 July, upon his return from the Upper Danube, Heidegger responded in a vehement letter. "On what legal grounds I have been made the target of such an unheard-of proceeding I cannot imagine," he wrote to the mayor. "I wish to protest in the strongest possible terms against this attack on my person and my work. Why should I have been singled out for punishment and defamation before the eyes of the whole city—indeed, before the eyes of the world—not only by having my home requisitioned in this manner, but also by being obliged to give up my workplace altogether?" Heidegger, then as before, was particularly sensitive to the question of the image created abroad, by Nazi Germany under his rectorship, and now by the opprobrium heaped on him in the new Germany. He raised an outcry, stressing his noninvolvement in the Party, despite the membership card he kept to the very end: "I never held office of any kind within the Party, and was never active in the Party or in any of its organizations. If there are those who regard my rectorship as politically compromising, then I must insist on being given an opportunity to defend myself against any charges or accusations, made by whomsoever—which means being told, first and foremost, what *specifically* has been alleged against me and my official activities."[3]

The philosopher's letter and the mobilization of loved ones on his behalf had a limited effect. Although his library was not confiscated for the moment, the Heideggers had to share their house with a French military family, who lived on the ground floor, a periodic occupation that lasted several years. It was enormously uncomfortable, not only because of the lack of privacy resulting from forced cohabitation with strangers, but also because of the number of occupants of the house during this time when Germany was in ruins. Also living in the house were Dorle, Jörg's wife since 1942,[4] as well as friends—Elfilede Pagels and one of Theophil Rees's sons.[5] They were joined in 1948[6] by Heidegger's childhood friend Ernst Laslowski and his wife, Lene, refugees from Silesia[7] who had fled in advance of the Soviet occupation. Then, in late July 1945, they had to take in former concentration camp prisoners, which did not exactly delight the philosopher.[8]

In his letter to the mayor, to insist on his indignation at the partial requisition of his house, Heidegger asked for the chance to explain himself. The denazification proceedings conducted by the university gave him that opportunity, but they were only a long descent into hell. The denazification commission, formed by the University of Freiburg under the military government's authority, was composed of Constantin von Dietze, Gerhard Ritter, and Adolf Lampe, resisters in the *Freiburger Kreis* who had been arrested after the failed conservative plot to assassinate Hitler on 20 July 1944,[9] along with the theologian Arthur Allgeier and the botanist Friedrich Oehlkers. Of all these members, the most important was Lampe, an upstanding individual and a close friend of Walter Eucken,[10] the person most firmly opposed to Heidegger's introduction of the *Führerprinzip* at the University of Freiburg. Lampe had personally been treated badly by Heidegger and had played a tenuous but decisive role in his resignation, that of the straw that broke the camel's back, as Ott analyzes it.[11] He had been subjected to the arbitrariness of the *Führer*-rector, and he was determined to see to it that Heidegger's transgressions were judged.

On 23 July 1945[12] Heidegger appeared before the denazification commission, as the most prestigious of the cases it had to adjudicate. The commission listened to witnesses; Heidegger explained himself. The same evening, he reported to Fritz: "Everything went well. What the French are doing is still undetermined. But it does not appear that they wish to eject me. The hunt here is conducted primarily by the politicians from Zentrum, and the theologians and all reasonable people are speaking out against it."[13] His hostility toward political Catholicism provided him with a simple interpretation, counterbalanced by the actual behavior of his theologian colleagues. And though the war from which the Germans were emerging had been hard, Heidegger yearned for that time, which for him had been easier and exhilarating: "Everything is sinister and worse than in the Nazi period."[14] He looked back fondly on the weeks of calm and the fruitful work in Meßkirch, but Freiburg in ruins seemed "frightening" to him.[15]

Heidegger had accurately assessed the commission's mood. The report was ready in September 1945, and its conclusion—that he was guilty—was expressed in particularly benevolent terms, repeating the arguments he had honed for his defense. He was said to have lived "prior to the revolution of 1933 [. . .] in a totally unpolitical intellectual world"; "he looked to the National Socialist revolution to bring about a spiritual renewal of German life on a national-ethnic basis, and at the same time, in common with large sections of the German intelligentsia, a healing of social differences and the salvation of Western culture from the dangers of communism. He had no clear grasp of the parliamentary-political processes that led up to the seizure of power by the National Socialists; but he believed in the historical mission of Hitler to bring about the spiritual and intellectual transformation that he himself envisaged." Despite his support of the Führer, Heidegger was said to have protected the university in a certain measure from the excesses of the time, in preventing "the crude campaign of persecution against the Jews mounted in April 1933 from being carried on to the university premises."

The report focused especially on the rector's inaugural address, pointing out that it had "caused a considerable stir both at home and abroad." It was "his own program for the reform of the university system," in which Heidegger "eschewed any discussion of 'racial policy' and other Party slogans, and chose instead to develop his own concept of true science and scholarship, which at bottom was far removed from mere subservience to the tactical dictates of the day. But insofar as he placed 'labor service' and 'military service' on an equal footing with the 'knowledge service' for the student, he himself provided Nazi propaganda with the lever it needed to exploit his speech for party political purposes." A review of the policy Heidegger had conducted noted that the students had become "insolent and arrogant," that "the majority of the professors were deeply offended by his decrees, which were frequently seen as heavy-handed and overbearing," that the rector had played an "active part in transforming the university constitution in line with the 'leadership principle' and in introducing the outward forms of Hitlerism [e.g., the Hitler salute, the so-called *deutscher Gruss*] into academic life," and finally, that he had "penalized or sacrificed persons who were opposed to the Nazis, and even contributed directly to National Socialist election propaganda by issuing proclamations to the press." The report went on to mention the mutual estrangement between the philosopher and the Party, leading up to the divorce of his resignation. It ultimately concluded: "There can be no doubt that in the crucial year of 1933 Heidegger consciously placed the full weight of his academic reputation and the distinctive art of his oratory in the service of the National Socialist revolution, and thereby did a great deal to justify this revolution in the eyes of educated Germans, to raise the hopes people had placed in it, and to make it much more difficult for German science and scholarship to maintain its independence amidst the political upheaval. The label 'Nazi' ceased to be applicable to him after 1934, and there is no danger that he would ever again promote the ideas of Nazism."[16] Although sensitive to the loss that his removal from the faculty would represent for the university, the commission determined that Heidegger ought to be punished for his involvement. Despite Lampe's opposition, it proposed that he simply be forced into early retirement; his emeritus status would allow him to teach but would bar him from taking part in university administration.

That prospect led Heidegger to consider who his successor ought to be, a question of importance both for the continuation of his work and for his self-image, because only a brilliant successor can fully honor the person who yields his chair. As he wrote to Rudolf Stadelmann on 1 September, he therefore wanted his successor to be Gadamer, one of his very first students: "Among all the others, he is the one who is the most valuable for his intellectual scope, as a teacher and as a colleague. I would wish him to be my successor, should it come to that."[17]

The report was extremely lenient. The rumor spread that the military government had simply granted Heidegger a leave of absence and that he was invited to Baden-Baden to give lectures to the French. Furthermore, a disproportion existed between the fate that awaited him and that to which other Nazis, less compromised but also less influential, had already been subjected, that of being removed from the faculty or even interned in French concentration camps. In view of these factors, Vice-Rector Franz Böhm, backed by Lampe and Eucken, wrote a letter to the rector's office on 9 October, in the hope of derailing the accommodating report. In it he concluded: "In view of the fact that in a whole series of cases the military government has imposed harsher penalties than were recommended by the university and the examining commission, it makes me very bitter to think that one of the principal intellectual architects of the political betrayal of Germany's universities, a man who at a critical moment in time, from a position of prominence as the rector of a leading German borderland university and a philosopher of international standing, became the vociferous spokesman of an intolerant fanaticism, charted the wrong political course and preached a catalogue of pernicious heresies, heresies which to this day he has never repudiated—that a man such as this should merely have been subjected to the stricture of '*disponsibilité*' [leave of absence], and clearly feels no need at all to answer for the consequences of his actions."[18]

The commission was compelled to reconsider the Heidegger case, to pursue its inquiry in greater depth, and to propose a penalty more in keeping with that imposed in similar instances. Sensing the growing difficulty of the situation, on 15 December the philosopher wrote a letter to Constantin von Dietze, chair of the denazification commission. Heidegger weighed each argument to give it the greatest appearance of truth, consolidating the foundations of the defense he would maintain until his death: "In 1933–1934 I was already opposed to the National Socialist worldview," he claimed, transforming his philosophical disgust at the ontological weakness of Nazism into an opposition on principle, already akin, it seemed, to a sort of spiritual resistance realized as a courageous but naïve engagement: "At that time I believed that the movement might, on a spiritual level, be directed toward other paths, and I considered this attempt compatible with the movement's social and political tendencies." Displaying a naïve Hitlerism, disassociating the Führer from his party, he had believed that "Hitler, after taking responsibility for the people as a whole in 1933, would rise above the Party and its doctrine, and that everything would come together on the terrain of a renewal and union toward a Western responsibility." That illusion quickly dissipated, he said, because of the bloody Night of the Long Knives, during which the leadership of the SA and of the NSDAP's left wing was wiped out. It opened his eyes: "This belief was a mistake that I recognized after the events of 30 June."[19] The argument that Heidegger broke with Nazism because of the bloody purge in the early summer of 1934 was backed by Ritter, a member of the commission, who claimed he "knew for a fact" that the philosopher "was secretly fiercely opposed to National Socialism after the Röhm putsch and had completely lost his faith in Hitler," who had led him so disastrously astray in 1933.[20]

According to Heidegger, his short-lived belief had a harmful effect: "In 1933–1934, it placed me in the intermediary position of approving of the Party's social and national (and not National Socialist) views, while at the same time denying its intellectual and metaphysical doctrine (its biologism), because its social and national views, as I saw them, were not inherently connected with its biological and racial worldview."[21] He cleverly adopted the terms Hitler had chosen for his party, "national" and "social," but bestowed on them connotations that were anything but Nazi. He justified that usage based on his opposition to biologism, which he claimed to reject, while making it the indubitable and exclusive intellectual foundation of Nazi doctrine. In doing so, he seemed to forget that, twelve years earlier, he had stated that the importance of the "spiritual world of a people" lay in the "power for preserving at the deepest level the strengths it draws from earth and blood."[22] Furthermore, these forces were said to act on human existence by shaping one's affective disposition to the point that, "for every people, the primary guarantee of its authenticity and greatness" was "in its blood, its soil, and its bodily growth."[23] The totalitarian *Führerprinzip* was by no means an ideological detail of Nazism, but one of its founding principles, which Heidegger shared without reservation. He succeeded in concealing that aspect by conceding he had been at fault "in the technical and personal aspect of the university's administration," but only to better protest the political and intellectual purity of his intentions, in view of the fact that he had never exchanged pure and simple his philosophy for the more cursory ideology prevailing in the NSDAP: "I never sacrificed to the Party the spirit and essence of a renewal of science and the university." He then concluded, with dignity and erudition: "I sought to bring about a renewal of the *universitas*."

When he wrote to von Dietze on 15 December, Heidegger was already, if not broken, in any case seriously dejected. He feared for his sons; he feared for his career; he feared for his work. He believed that, one day, he "would truly still have something to say to the West and the world." "Taking part in the general and spiritual destiny," and preoccupied as he was by the fate of his two sons, "who had disappeared in Russia," his abilities were "in any case in a condition" that might barely suffice "to complete part" of what he longed to do "for the future of philosophy."[24] He was, moreover, facing a profound personal crisis: since 1942 he had been involved with Margot von Sachsen-Meiningen,[25] the mother of two children, and she was demanding that he choose between her and Elfride.[26] Above all, perhaps, the course of the regime that had plunged the country and Europe into chaos thwarted the plans he thought he was able to recognize in history. Was this the sign of his weakness, he who saw himself as the new oracle of Germany, the interlocutor of Hölderlin and Nietzsche, whose new saying would bring about a return to the questioning of being? In one of his black notebooks, Heidegger wondered whether he had not come 150 years too late—the Hölderlin era might have been more favorable—or 300 years too early, since metaphysics had not reached its end through the world's self-destruction. As a supreme mark of uncertainty in despair, he concluded with an "or else?"[27] indicating his total lack of an answer. Taken together, these reassessments of various kinds undermined the philosophical mountain he was scaling to consider from its summit the destiny of Germany within history.

Heidegger, who since the 1920s had philosophized about *Not,* distress, experienced that sensation at the time in an incomparably stronger and more personal way than he had done during the storms at his cabin. At the end of the year, he found himself in the inner state when distress turns to panic, and when a man, hanging from the edge of a chasm, tries with all his might to catch hold of anything within his reach, roots or crevices in the rock, which, good or bad, may either serve as a reliable support and save him from peril or give way under his weight and send the poor soul plummeting into the abyss. In addition to sending a letter to the chair of the denazification commission, Heidegger therefore asked to call two witnesses to testify, if not to his good conduct, in any event to his good character: Conrad Gröber and Karl Jaspers, old friends whose footing had become firmer in that Germany in ruins, and who allowed him to hope they would each lend a helping hand. That was true for one but not the other, who, on the contrary, precipitated his fall.

Heidegger's last contact with Gröber was lost in a misty past. Gröber had been named archbishop of Freiburg in 1932,[28] and, anxious to smooth the way for the signing of a concordat and thus avert the resurgence of *Kulturkampf,* he so actively supported the vote to give Hitler plenary powers in 1933 that he was nicknamed the "Brown bishop."[29] But these good feelings toward the regime changed so thoroughly[30] that in 1945 he was viewed as "a cornerstone of the Church's resistance" and held "an unimpeachable authority, particularly vis-à-vis the French military government."[31] When Heidegger went to the archbishop's palace, embarrassed but determined to take his destiny into his own hands by reminding his "paternal friend" of their past friendship, he hoped that the archbishop would not only have sufficient influence to help him but would also forgive him for his apostasy and his fight against Catholicism. Marie, the archbishop's sister and a native of Meßkirch like Heidegger himself, received him with great affability, speaking the local dialect they shared. The sister's warm welcome was complemented by her brother's kindness. Heidegger's first mentor may have been moved by the force of their common memories, or perhaps by Christian charity. Perhaps as well that prince of the Church was hoping for a spectacular conversion of the world-renowned philosopher who, though certainly compromised by Nazism, might nevertheless rejoin the Catholic intellectual vanguard and display to everyone the edifying spectacle of conversion. On 8 March 1946, a few months after the pitiable visit the philosopher made to him, Gröber wrote a letter to that effect to Father Leiber, Pope Pius XII's advisor for German policy: "It was a great consolation to me when he came to see me at the start of his misfortunes and conducted himself in a most edifying way. I told him the truth, and he listened with tears in his eyes. I shall not break off relations with him, because I am hopeful of a spiritual change of heart within him."[32] Although the actual wording of the text is lost to us, we do know that Gröber sent the French military government a report favorable to his former disciple, in the interest of mitigating the severity of a measure the university was proposing. But Abbot Virrion, serving in the Department of Education for the occupation authority, warned Gröber on 2 January 1946: "It will be difficult to get Heidegger reinstated at the university if the rector votes against it."[33] The abbot promised to do whatever he could, given that the archbishop had commended his former protégé to him.

Heidegger also asked Jaspers to come to his assistance. Because he had not compromised himself under the regime, of which he was ultimately the victim, Jaspers was one of the philosophical figures with whom the new university authorities could hope to rebuild Germany. Heidegger knew this and counted on Jaspers's philosophical intelligence and the memory of their friendship to provide him with the protector he so needed. In addition, Jaspers had become the friend of one of the members on the Freiburg denazification commission, Friedrich Oehlkers, who like him had endured the painful condition of being the spouse of a non-Aryan under the Third Reich.[34] However great his crisis of conscience, Jaspers, torn between loyalty to his old friend and the political and philosophical reasons for condemning him, resolved to write a report. In a postscript of 24 December appended to his letter, he confided to Oehlkers: "Because a Sunday came in between, the letter remained here. I was able to consider whether, in respect to my earlier relations with Heidegger, I should ask you to forgo an answer from me. To answer and not to answer are both, in this case, against my nature. Finally, the summons of an official authority prevailed and, above all, the summons of Heidegger himself. So I am sending the letter."[35]

The former *Führer*-rector had overestimated the support he would get from Jaspers. Inspired by the spirit of justice, that typed letter, dated 22 December, was truly an indictment of Heidegger, whose interests would have been better served had it never been written or sent. The long letter was organized into six substantial points.

First, Jaspers summarized his reluctance to express himself on the subject, referring to his relations with the accused since 1933, and to their last conversation that year: "At our last meeting," he wrote, Heidegger himself had remained silent, had "ignored awkward questions altogether or gave vague answers—particularly on the Jewish question."[36]

Second, Jaspers weighed Heidegger's report on Baumgarten against the rector's attitude toward his assistant, Werner Brock, reaching a state of confusion that reflected the contradictions of his subject: "In the 1920s Heidegger was not an anti-Semite. That thoroughly uncalled-for remark about 'the Jew Fraenkel' shows that by 1933 he had become an anti-Semite—in certain contexts, at least. He did not always exercise restraint in this matter. This does not rule out the possibility that in other cases, as I must assume, anti-Semitism went against his conscience and his inclinations."[37]

Third, Jaspers addressed Heidegger's philosophical value, calling the philosopher "a significant figure." And though he could not refrain from noting that he judged Heidegger "a long way removed from 'science' " and "uncommonly uncritical," Jaspers considered him perhaps "unique among contemporary German philosophers" in occasionally "hitting the nerve of the philosophical enterprise in a most mysterious and marvelous way."[38]

Jaspers sought, fourth, to place the question of Heidegger's denazification within the broader context of the time. Because Heidegger was "one of the few university professors" who contributed to putting "National Socialism in the driving seat," justice required that he not go unpunished, given the large number of people subjected to denazification. Although he might be allowed to publish because of his philosophical genius, he still ought to be barred from teaching, especially since inaction on the matter would be deleterious to the postwar reconstruction efforts. "Heidegger's mode of thinking, which seems to me to be fundamentally unfree, dictatorial, and uncommunicative, would have a very damaging effect on students at the present time. And the mode of thinking itself seems to me more important than the actual content of political judgments, whose aggressiveness can easily be channeled in other directions. Until such time as a genuine rebirth takes place within him, and is *seen* to be at work within him, I think it quite wrong to turn such a teacher loose on the young people of today, who are psychologically extremely vulnerable. First of all the young must be taught how to think for themselves."[39]

Fifth, Jaspers revisited Heidegger's Nazism, willingly conceding a certain originality, a naïveté on his part, the better to contrast him with philosophers such as Baeumler and Schmitt. Each of the three, though "very different" from one another, "strove for the intellectual leadership of the National Socialist movement. To no avail."[40] In Jaspers's view, the best touchstone for judging a person's Nazism was the date at which a reversal took place and the motives behind it: 1934, with the Night of the Long Knives; 1938, with the major pogrom of *Kristallnacht;* or 1941, with the start of the war against the USSR. Jaspers might have added 1943 or 1944, the turning points in the war, with the German defeat at Stalingrad and the Normandy landing, which accelerated the Germans' general retreat. In his opinion, "a change of heart that postdates 1941 is virtually meaningless—and indeed means very little unless it occurred decisively after the events of 30 June 1934."[41] Jaspers had changed his mind that year. As it happens, Heidegger claimed that his views changed precisely on that date, which placed him in the right position in his old friend's chronology. Based on a note from the 1960s, however, we may presume that Jaspers did not give credence to that assertion: "On what foundation, that end in 1934? No document. In any case no fight against the Nazis, no remorse, but an objective political uselessness. He was like a marionette tossed into a corner after being found useful at the start."[42]

Sixth, and by way of conclusion, Jaspers suggested that, if "special measures" were to be applied to "special cases" such as Heidegger's, he might receive "a personal pension to enable him to pursue his philosophical studies and publish his works," but should be suspended from teaching for several years, long enough to reexamine the situation prevailing at the time, in light of his publications. If a "special arrangement of this kind" were rejected,[43] in the interest of the equal treatment required by justice, Heidegger ought not to benefit from preferential treatment but ought to be subject to the full force of the denazification procedure, as other, more obscure Nazis had already been. Jaspers opened the possibility of Heidegger being removed from his position or even interned, like Hugo Friedrich, the great Romanist of Freiburg.[44]

As the outcome of the proceedings approached, Heidegger, having probably gotten word of Jaspers's report—Jaspers had given permission for its partial release—felt obliged to show further proof of humility in his requests. In early 1946, he offered to abstain from teaching, until such time as the university would request that he return to it, a way to reduce further the benefits of early emeritus status. The senate rendered its verdict on 19 January 1946: it was harsh. Heidegger was forced into retirement; had no right to teach; could not hope to have his case reexamined at a later date, as Jaspers had proposed; and finally, had to "maintain a low profile at public functions and gatherings of the university."[45]

Heidegger's situation continued to deteriorate, because the conditions of denazification changed in the course of 1946. In order to treat all cases equally, the French occupier established a "regional denazification commission,"[46] which did not feel bound by the decisions made by each university and conducted its work based on the different categories of defendants. Heidegger was judged as a Nazi rector, and, as he learned provisionally on 5 October and definitively on 28 December 1946, he was simply pensioned off and not granted emeritus status. He was barred from teaching and from holding a position at the university.[47] He was thus stripped of his standing as an academic, being considered merely a worker who had reached retirement. As a further punishment, painful and humiliating though temporary, he was sentenced to clear rubble from the streets of Freiburg,[48] which the carpet bombing by the Allies had transformed into a carpet of ruins. Finally, one more threat loomed over him in 1947: the confiscation of his library, which, it was rumored, was to become part of the collections of the University of Mainz, an institution newly created by the occupier. This threat was averted, thanks to the effective intervention of Gröber, among others.[49]

Shortly thereafter, the measures taken against Heidegger were eased. The times were favorable. The Cold War, palpable since 1947, served as encouragement to definitively put an end to quarrels with the defeated former enemy. In 1949 the Federal Republic of Germany came into existence. In addition,

Heidegger's sixtieth birthday attracted media attention, and three volumes of miscellanea honored him. The key aspect that changed was the possibility of having the ban on teaching lifted. Heidegger would thereby not only recover the right to public speech but could ultimately earn emeritus status. Resistance remained strong at the University of Freiburg, but the intellectual merit and international fame of a former colleague resulted in a reinstatement of sorts. The Faculty of Philosophy, which had energetically supported Heidegger from the start of the denazification procedure, now found a context much more favorable from its perspective, which was disciplinary. Did the Nazi philosopher deserve to be reinstated, out of consideration for his importance and prestige? By all means yes, replied the Faculty, which was able to advance its viewpoint by suggesting an appeal to an international committee of experts, composed, in Germany, of Romano Guardini (Munich), Nicolai Hartmann, and Werner Heisenberg (Göttingen); in Switzerland, of Karl Jaspers (Basel) and Emil Staiger (Zurich); and in France, of Charles Bayer.[50]

In 1949 Heidegger was granted permission to teach again. The reexamination procedure was approaching its end, when, on 1 April 1950, a minority of professors from the Faculty of Philosophy, judging the moment opportune, proposed that he be quite simply reinstated. This was technically possible because his chair was officially held only temporarily by Wilhelm Szilasi, a close friend from the 1920s. That initiative delighted Heidegger, who, in a letter to the rector dated 6 April, judged that solution "the one best suited to the situation, particularly after five years during which I have been subjected to sanctions that went far beyond what the university's denazification commission had recommended in 1945."[51] But Heidegger had to agree to forgo that hypothetical solution: it was unrealistic, because it would have given rise to an intolerable outcry at the university. He had to be content with what the rector and dean, favorably disposed toward him, thought they could actually give him, a lifting of the ban on teaching, the assignment of courses, and guaranteed emeritus status when he reached retirement age.[52] Because his reinstatement was partial, Heidegger found it quite insufficient to compensate for the injustice of which he believed himself the victim. In a 1949 letter to Fritz, he did manage to joke about the decision by the high commissioner for political denazification, which had classified him as a *Mitlaüfer* (fellow traveler) of Nazism,[53] an expression he judged "stinging." He added: "A fellow traveler of Beyng I have always been and would also like to remain."[54] But he still referred to the "smear campaign"[55] against him, and the previous year, as the idea of his rehabilitation was beginning to be tossed about, he had written, filled with resentment, that "how the University dealt with its shame was its own affair."[56]

The Reconstruction of a Philosopher (1946–1949)

In 1945 Germany was in ruins. Its territory was drastically reduced in comparison to 1919. The Prussian Königsberg had become the Russian Kaliningrad, the other regions east of the Oder and the Neiße had been handed over to Poland, and their German residents had been forced en masse into exile. Laid low, *Germania* and her barbarous swastika yielded her place to two dissimilar and rival daughters born in 1949. One of them, East Germany, brandished the hammer and sickle in the Soviet style, trying to look like a people's democracy. The other, West Germany, a federal republic under the protection of the United States, draped herself in the three colors of liberal Germany—black, red, and gold—those of the Weimar Republic. The Federal Republic also adopted Weimar's gold coat of arms, with an imperial eagle "displayed sable beaked langued and membered gules," in the language of heraldry. A new future was taking shape: an economic miracle on one hand, a collectivized life on the other, in a troubling context of Cold War and the fear of nuclear holocaust. Only a few years after the fall of the Third Reich, West Germany had rebuilt its cities, factories, roads, and railways. Its fields were cultivated, just as they had been before the war, and its soldiers had gone back to being workers. Heidegger too was reconstructing himself.

The philosopher had made up his mind to spend the first part of 1946 in Badenweiler, in the Schloss Haus Baden psychiatric clinic, run by the psychiatrist Viktor Freiherr von Gebsatell. An essential part of Heidegger's psychological reconstruction came from the intellectual exchanges he had with Gebsatell, who practiced *Daseinsanalyse,* the anthropological-existential current of psychology developed by Ludwig Binswanger and Medard Boss.[57] The psychiatrist admired Heidegger, and, along with the rest cure, the walks, and the injections of glucose every other day, this greatly helped the German philosopher to assuage his ego:

> It was a good decision to come here; for along with the distance from everything connected with Freiburg, the pleasant humanity & spontaneous friendliness of Herr v. G. is helping me greatly. He is 63 years old now, has experienced much, has come from philosophy & remains within it despite his basic theological orientation, which is by no means narrow. He knows my stuff in great detail & tells me how much he & his

> friends have for years been waiting & pinning their hopes on my thinking. [. . .] He thinks I should leave the university now whatever happens; for what is essential in my thinking, which he sees very clearly, will be constantly distracted & held back by didactic constraints. [. . .] In his eyes, philosophy itself, & what I think & say & seek, is much too fundamental & central for him to assume the role of someone simply dealing with an interesting "case" here.
>
> So I think the days I spend here will be very invigorating & clarifying.[58]

It was a propitious time for Heidegger to write in his personal notebook. Volume 97 of the *Gesamtausgabe,* which comprises the black notebooks for the years 1942 to 1948, has little to say about the end of the war but contains many pages on this period difficult for the author. The import of his masterpiece and his ego figure prominently: "1807: *Phenomenology of Mind* [Hegel]. 1867: *Capital* [Marx]. 1927: *Being and Time* [Heidegger]."[59] The tone of wounded metaphysical pride is evident in passages sometimes astonishing in their despair, in which he compares thought to a shipwreck: "The *sinking ship* on the sea of *Beyng* is thought. Only when the rats desert the ship does the ship's time come—*it sinks,* it belongs to the element, to beyng itself. Then there remains only the one, the only one, who entrusts himself to the ship: and he goes down with it."[60]

Heidegger felt great ire toward university professors,[61] toward the "terrorism of the international press,"[62] and toward his compatriots, who were guilty of betraying their metaphysical mission by barring the prophet of their destiny from teaching: "How far have we gotten with the Germans? Only as far as they were already—which they now deny only more stupidly, and their own souls even more stupidly; and, sharing the mockery of foreigners, they naïvely assess the most hidden essence. Just as terrifying to endure is the destruction and devastation that have befallen the Germans and their country. All that has not reached the self-annihilation that, in the betrayal of thought, now threatens *Dasein.*"[63] In cutting out Heidegger's tongue—he was henceforth forbidden to express himself and to work toward the salvation of his people—the Germans were annihilating themselves, and that self-annihilation was undesirable because it did not make the machinery of "machination" collapse on itself. Instead, it definitively impaired any hope of spiritual renewal. That betrayal, he believed, could not invoke "the inevitable consequences of the rule of terror of the system" that had just disappeared. For him, it was a behavior "more furious and more destructive" than the "devastation" of contemporary

Germany visible everywhere, worse too than the devastation that was "manifest in posters intended to create horror."[64] As Peter Trawny has shown, Heidegger was alluding here to a poster produced by the Psychological Warfare Division of the Supreme Headquarters of the Allied Powers of Europe. Illustrated with photographs of liberated concentration camps, it bore the caption: "These vile acts: you are to blame!"[65]

Angered by the Germans' betrayal of him, Heidegger grossly reduced the estimation of guilt that the Allies and the era as a whole had attributed to his people after the discovery of the death camps. About twenty pages later, the vehemence of his denunciation intensified, reaching a fever pitch that only the immense pain of an overweening vanity seems able to explain:

> Might not the failure to recognize this destiny [. . .], considered from the point of view of destiny, be an even more essential "offense," an even more essential "collective offense," whose magnitude could not in any way—be measured in its essence by the horror of the "gas chambers"—; an offense—more disturbing than all the publicly "reprehensible" "crimes"—which certainly no one would have the right to excuse in the future? Can "one" imagine that right now the German people and its country are a single concentration camp [*Kz*]—a camp unlike any the "world" has ever "seen" and that "the world" will not see either—and that not-willing is even more deliberate than our absence of will with regard to the barbarization [*Verwilderung*] of National Socialism.[66]

That rageful episode of depression also led him to reassess his past actions. Heidegger revisited the error he made in 1933, using the language—typical of him at the time—of the will to power, but without adding a great deal of substance to the matter at hand.[67] He even considered moving to a different place. He recorded in his notebook: "Forty years ago, in 1906, I came to this city as a Gymnasium student. It is now time that I leave it."[68] And on 15 March 1946 he wrote a long letter to Elfride to that effect. Did he want to remain in Freiburg, whose material destruction echoed the intellectual and emotional destruction of his ties to the university? He believed it necessary "to get away from the university atmosphere entirely," so that his thinking and work could retain their "clear style and grounding."[69] Did he want to move to Todtnauberg? No, because it was lacking the modern conveniences. Above all, the cabin had the disadvantage of being too close to Freiburg, and his "break" with the university also affected his "relation to the city & everything else,"[70] which was also broken. Heidegger actually wanted to move to Meßkirch, with which he had reconnected during the war and where his brother was living. The two men had built a new relationship around the philosopher's writings, which Fritz was hard at work editing and typing out, in dialogue with Martin. For that reason, Heidegger understood that "having Fritz nearby would be a further boon." And he particularly felt how much he needed this bond when he was absorbed in his work.[71] Fritz was a loyal, admiring brother with a lowbrow sense of humor. He liked to say, in a play on words that is difficult to translate: "Mein Bruder ist der Philosoph, ich bin der viel sooft"[72] ("My brother is the philosopher, I'm the boozer"). Furthermore, the town where Heidegger had grown up seemed to be exactly what his future work required: "Messkirch, i.e., home, calls me for the single reason that I need this close environment as the supporting & driving element in the great loneliness of the work to come & I feel quite vividly that a collected, settled, rooted way of life [*Bodenständigkeit*] for the years still remaining is part & parcel of the work."[73] But did he really want to add complications during that difficult postwar period? Did he really want to force Elfride to leave? Freiburg was the boys' home, the family's house was there, a house Elfride had designed, decorated, and managed for eighteen years. Heidegger was therefore thinking of passing it on to his sons rather than selling it. Furthermore, moving somewhere else would have been "a further strain with existence now strenuous enough as it is."[74] Despite his desire to leave, he came to his senses on his own. He would have liked to convince Elfride to leave, he would have liked her to decide of her own accord, in the higher interest of the work to come; he did not want to bear the responsibility for the decision. It was a bad idea and he knew it. So they stayed.

Three years later, Heidegger could only congratulate himself for having resisted that impulse in the strained context of the denazification process he was subjected to in Freiburg. During a stay in Meßkirch, his letter to Elfride displayed no enthusiasm for his home region or for his university city: "I collect myself again in thought; this way the other things vanish of their own accord. In the long run of course there'd be no circle to live among here; a great deal slips into trivialization in the little town; but the professorial environment is no longer a circle either; if indeed it every seriously was."[75]

Although he did not move away physically, did not leave Freiburg for Meßkirch, Heidegger did take his leave in thought, opening himself intellectually to the world. He found translation a demanding and effective way to forget somewhat how his great destiny had been shattered by the fall of the Third Reich. After a translation of Paul Valéry in June 1945, in collaboration with Hugo

Friedrich, his colleague in Freiburg,[76] Heidegger attempted during his psychiatric treatment to translate Lao Tze,[77] whom he had discovered during the war through a Chinese student[78] and whose Zen practice invited him to philosophical meditation.

Heidegger opened his mind to Asia on his own initiative, but France came to him. For a long time, without ever going there, he had been acquiring an enviable renown across the Rhine. The French occupation encouraged intellectual exchanges, though Heidegger's past positions were hardly favorable toward the "Great Nation." Under the Third Reich, a regime hostile to France, the philosopher had repeated the black legend of Napoleon. In 1936, introducing his course on Schelling's 1809 treatise on human freedom, Heidegger had explained to his students: "Eighteen hundred and nine: Napoleon ruled, that means here, he oppressed and abused Germany."[79] He saw France as the homeland of Descartes, the nation where modern metaphysics had originated. This was the beginning of the technological and mathematized mastery of nature, which Heidegger believed demanded a "confrontation,"[80] a conceptual battle. With the French occupation, his disposition toward the neighboring country became more amenable. The immediate danger of the denazification commission came from those of his colleagues who were on it or from those who, seeing the former Nazi in him, tried to push the commission toward more severity. The occupiers, ingenuous and fascinated, tended to allow the ex-Nazi to be eclipsed by the lofty stature of the philosopher and his still-extraordinary word. As a result, Heidegger, who professed to despise fashion, the modality of *das Man*, was beholden to it for the friendly interest manifested by those who might have treated him like the henchman of a barbaric regime.

Frédéric de Towarnicki and Maurice de Gandillac were among the first Frenchmen to come to see him. Each wrote an account of the experience, published in *Les temps modernes* in January 1946.[81] Gandillac was already a pioneer, having heard Heidegger in Davos in 1929. He met the philosopher again in very different times, in Zähringen, a neighborhood that, though on the fringes of the "pile of ruins"[82] that the center of Freiburg had become, also bore the traces of war. To compensate for the lack of provisions, the residents had planted "cabbage and potato patches" on the side of that "slightly wooded hill."[83] Heidegger lived in a wooden house, and his "study" was "almost monastic in its bareness."[84] Gandillac found the master of the Black Forest "short and squat." He also took note of Heidegger's mustache, cut into a square like Hitler's, which had a disconcerting effect. Refusing to accept the first model that came to mind, he opted to laugh off his first impression, speaking of the German philosopher's "Charlie Chaplin mustache, [which] irresistibly evokes certain meek aspects of the Führer."[85] To see Heidegger as a fan of Chaplin's mustache in *The Great Dictator*—ridiculous but innocuous—was much more acceptable for a Frenchman overwhelmed by his host's prestige than to see the actual original, who still had Heidegger's allegiance. When Gandillac wrote his memoirs in extreme old age, after time had erased the shock of that disturbing sight, denial took hold of him even more forcefully, and he managed to persuade himself that he had perpetrated a "rather foolish joke."[86] Neither a fool nor a malicious joker, impressed without being servile in his interview with the great philosopher, the younger Gandillac (he was under forty) brought up politics, sensing that he was being "indiscreet": "What does Heidegger think of the reeducation of the young, of the responsibility of his people? He readily acknowledges that the detoxification treatment will be long and difficult, that Hitlerism was in a sense only the historical explosion of a 'structural' malady of man generally. But he refuses to incriminate the 'German' man by name, to confess a sort of collective *Verfallen* of the Germanic community. The philosopher's only hope is to cultivate the true sense of freedom among his disciples."[87] The Frenchman did not understand that Heidegger, having remained a Nazi, rejected the idea of German guilt. Heidegger had quickly changed the subject, not because he felt ill equipped to awaken consciousnesses to freedom as he understood it, but because he was ill at ease and knew he would not be understood. He therefore took refuge in "everyday banality,"[88] attempting to make Gandillac forget the German philosopher's involvement and to mask his own ever-present support for the very principle of Nazism. Gandillac concluded there was a divorce of sorts between Heidegger's theory and practice: "Whatever his genius, how can one fail to measure the gap between the very rigors of his philosophy and the weakly, evasive attitude of the 'man in situation'?"[89]

Towarnicki, having gone to see Heidegger in autumn 1945, viewed himself as a "philosophical liaison officer." He brought writings by Sartre, Merleau-Ponty, and Beaufret and returned to France with a letter to Sartre inviting him to meet Heidegger in Todtnauberg. The meeting never happened. In the article he drew from his visit, Towarnicki repeated, with no distance whatever, the master's discourse on his Nazi involvement. Because Heidegger was a seducer, and not only of women's bodies—far from it—he set out to seduce France through Towarnicki: "With great emotion, Martin Heidegger spoke to me of [. . .] France. 'The spiritual life of that people,' he told me, 'is indispensable to the world, now more than ever. That is why, amid all the other peoples, it has such a large share of responsibility.' "[90]

Jean Beaufret was a philosophy teacher at the Lycée Condorcet in Paris and prepared students for the entrance exams to the *Grandes Écoles*. It was he with whom Heidegger formed a friendship, unequal to be sure, but profound and decisive for the German philosopher's reception in France. Beaufret had the significant role of becoming the first of Heidegger's disciples in that country, his obligatory interlocutor, the teacher of generations of young Heideggerians who took his second-year classes in the arts (*la khâgne*). Toward the end of 1945, Heidegger and Beaufret began corresponding. On 23 November, in response to a letter, the German philosopher wrote to tell the Frenchman how much he thought of him. "The now almost classic comparison between 'Jaspers and Heidegger' is *the* misunderstanding *par excellence* [in French in the text] that is circulating in our philosophy," he wrote, but Beaufret had clearly distinguished between the two. Agreeing with the remark, "but if German has its resources, French has its limits," Heidegger also approved of Beaufret's criticism of Henri Corbin's rendering of *Dasein* as *réalité humaine,* a very bad translation. Heideggerianizing himself, the German philosopher made a counterproposal that extended beyond his own language, "no doubt in an impossible French": "être-le-là" (to-be-the-there).[91] That intellectual rapport, the uncritical assumption of the value of Heidegger's thought and the language in which he expressed himself, was the basis for the German philosopher's relationship with his French disciples. The prophet of the Black Forest found himself understood by Beaufret; he sensed in him devotion to his language and his thought. For that reason, while still at the Badenweiler clinic, Heidegger wrote to Elfride on 4 March 1946: "Of important Frenchmen, above all Prof. Beaufret from Paris, whom I don't want to miss under any circumstances, could be considered [for a visit]. He can easily come here."[92] He had to wait till the end of summer, 12 September 1946, to see Beaufret for the first time, in Todtnauberg.[93]

The disciple also influenced his master. Whether coincidence or the influence of his new friend, one of the most visible changes of the postwar period was in Heidegger's handwriting. In October 1946[94] he abandoned the German (Gothic) cursive script, understood to be national, and adopted Latin characters, like the vast majority of publications in Germany. That change did not come easily: his hand, dexterous when tracing the characters learned in childhood, suddenly became clumsy when he had to submit to a new discipline. As a result, Heidegger felt obliged to ask Blochmann to "excuse" his handwriting, because he could not manage to get used to "this script."[95]

On the intellectual level, in autumn 1946 the exchanges with Beaufret gave rise to the "Letter on 'Humanism,'" the most famous of Heidegger's texts from the postwar period. The disciple had asked him how to raise anew the question of humanism, which was fashionable at the time. Despite the fall of Italian and German fascism, liberal humanism was still being contested by totalitarianism, given the great appeal of Marxism for a number of intellectuals. Within that context, on 29 October 1945 Sartre had delivered his famous lecture "Existentialism Is a Humanism," in which he used the term "existence" in a sense different from Heidegger's. Whether this was a misconstrual or the freedom of a thinker responsible for his own concepts, "existence" for Sartre was the basis for the notion of freedom. In man, existence preceded essence; he was a being before being something, and he had to make a choice, define himself on his own. Man thus found himself "condemned to be free," by which means he found his human dignity. From there, Sartre developed a philosophy of history, both individual and general, that was radically opposed to determinism and the notion of destiny. With a touch of provocation, he therefore proclaimed: "Those who hide their total freedom from themselves, behind a sense of seriousness or deterministic excuses, I will call cowards; those who try to show that their existence was necessary, though it is the very contingency of man's appearance on earth, I will call bastards."[96]

Despite Sartre's references to Heidegger, the German philosopher was quite far from that position, which from his standpoint overlooked the question of being and limited itself to a philosophical anthropology inspired here and there by *Being and Time*. Positioning himself within the perspective of being, Heidegger repeated for the most part what he had argued in his 1942 version of "Plato's Doctrine of Truth."[97] Humanism was an obstacle to the question of being, a last vestige of metaphysics that had to be overcome:

> The beginning of metaphysics in the thought of Plato is at the same time the beginning of "humanism." Here the word must be thought in its essence and therefore in its broadest sense. In that regard "humanism" means the process that is implicated in the beginning, in the unfolding, and in the end of metaphysics, whereby human beings [*das Mensch*],[98] in differing respects but always deliberately, move into a central place among beings, of course without thereby being the highest being. Here "human being" sometimes means humanity or humankind [*ein Menschtum oder die Menschheit*], sometimes the individual or the community, and sometimes the people [*das Volk*] or a group of peoples. What is always at stake is this: to take "human beings," who within the sphere of a

> fundamental, metaphysically established system of beings are defined as *animal rationale,* and to lead them, within that sphere, to the liberation of their possibilities, to the certitude of their destiny, and to the securing of their "life." This takes place as the shaping of their "moral" behavior, as the salvation of their immortal souls, as the unfolding of their creative power, as the development of their reason, as the nourishing of their personalities, as the awakening of their civic sense, as the cultivation of their bodies, or as an appropriate combination of some or all of these "humanisms." What takes place in each instance is a metaphysically determined revolving around the human being, whether in narrower or wider orbits. With the fulfillment of metaphysics, "humanism" (or in "Greek" terms: anthropology) also presses on to the most extreme—and likewise unconditioned—"positions."[99]

This text criticized all notions of time—intellectual, moral, and above all political, including that of Nazism—which in Heidegger's eyes did not make Nazism less necessary, since it was imperative to push to its extreme point that ideology founded on the subjectivity of a community, a people, and a race, understood as a "group of peoples," in the hope of building something new against the backdrop of the earth's devastation. The humanism Heidegger was rejecting was thus very broad, extending far beyond what is ordinarily called "humanism," the value granted to the human being as such, independent of any consideration of gender, color, or culture. Designating by the term "humanism" any worldview centered on humankind in one way or another, be it practical, moral, political, or theoretical, Heidegger discredited humanism in the strict sense, but also racism, nationalism, individualism, rationalism, and asceticism. Humanism, despite its diversity, was always a retreat from the distress of *Dasein,* a refusal of being, in an impulse directed toward the "liberation" of its possibilities, "the certitude of [its] destiny," and "the securing of [its] 'life.' "[100]

The letter on humanism did not diverge at all from the ideas Heidegger had developed in 1942. After pointing out that the idea of humanism appeared with Roman civilization, during an age dominated by the translation of Late (and therefore decadent) Hellenism, rather briefly discussing Sartre, whose humanism, like Marx's, had the originality of not requiring a return to antiquity, Heidegger sought to get to the root of the question: "Every humanism is either grounded in a metaphysics or is itself made to be the ground of one. [. . .] In defining the humanity of man, humanism not only does not ask about the relation of being to the essence of man; because of its metaphysical origin humanism even impedes the question by neither recognizing nor understanding it. On the contrary, the necessity and proper form of the question concerning the truth of being, forgotten in and through metaphysics, can come to light only if the question 'What is metaphysics?' is posed in the midst of metaphysics' domination."[101] Although he wanted to distance himself from Sartre, Heidegger was influenced by him, in that he somewhat rehabilitated man. Whereas the French philosopher conceived of man's dignity in terms of the fact that he has to be free, Heidegger saw man as a "shepherd of being." Having returned to an inner pastoral poverty, having rid himself of a cumbersome and alienating metaphysics, man finds his dignity in the safeguarding of being, which in turn keeps him under its protection.

With such arguments, which created a sense of delving deeper than any other philosophy, written in an esoteric, difficult language that suggested even more than it said, Heidegger had a better reception in postwar France than anywhere else in the world. Since the nineteenth century, the French had been very fond of German metaphysics—Kant, Hegel, Marx, Husserl—whose technical language or jargon was an added attraction, absent from the overly classic and less appealing clarity of representatives of the French national tradition, such as Bergson or Alain. Heidegger was the latest fashion, but the German influence went back a long time.

Quite a few French young people arrived to make the acquaintance of the sage of the Black Forest. Roger Munier left behind one of the iconic accounts of a Frenchman who had discovered Heidegger in his little cabin in Todtnauberg. Twenty-six years old in 1949 and anxious to improve his German after studying philosophy, Munier was staying in Sankt Blasien, in the Black Forest. Since the early 1940s he had been reading *Being and Time* and some of Henri Corbin's translations of Heideggerian texts, for example, "What Is Metaphysics?" Having learned that their author had a cabin not far from his own vacation resort, Munier treated himself to a little adventure, heading to Todtnauberg to meet Heidegger. The Frenchman did not send word he was coming and did not know how he would be received. He knocked on the wooden door of the little cabin overlooking the valley. Elfride opened it, welcomed him kindly, and, after having him wait for a brief moment, showed him in.

> The dwelling was very austere. Whether it was because of the sun shining outside, I have a vague memory of semidarkness, in which I could barely make out the most basic furniture, as one may expect to find in a mountain cabin. Heidegger was there. He held out his hand to me, giving me a piercing look but one filled with gentleness and, it seemed to

> me, a certain warmth. He was sixty at the time. I was taken aback by his size; I had imagined him taller. His tanned complexion was that of a mountain man, as was his outward appearance: green collarless jacket with a button adorning each lapel, knee socks, low-cut shoes. On his head was a sort of skullcap, also white.
>
> He showed me into the little room he used for his office. It too was cramped and sparsely furnished. Apart from the table where he was working, opposite the window and right up against it, I saw nothing but a modest shelf on the wall, with just two or three books on it, including *Critique of Pure Reason*. On the table were papers, all the same size, like pages cut in four, on which he had jotted down a few words in pencil—and on which he continued to write here and there, as we were talking. An old-fashioned pocket watch, suspended across from him in the narrow space that separated the table from the open window, marked the time.[102]

This infatuation of French intellectuals was not without ambivalence, and it was in France that the Heidegger affair resurfaced in the immediate postwar period, in two reviews: *Critique*[103] and *Les temps modernes,* which is to say, Sartre's review. The influence of the Freiburg philosopher on Sartre's existentialism led the French thinker to pay attention to the debates surrounding Heidegger. In 1946 Towarnicki relayed the former Nazi rector's self-justifying discourse.[104] The following year, the affair turned into a sparring match between the Belgian Alphonse de Waelhens and Karl Löwith, a former friend and well-regarded disciple of the master, whose position, now critical, established a strong connection between *Being and Time* and Heidegger's later political engagement. Löwith published essential passages from texts such as "The Self-Assertion of the German University," the speech in memory of Schlageter—delivered on the eve of Heidegger's inauguration as rector—and the appeal the following November in favor of leaving the League of Nations and in support of the Reichstag elections. With its theses and antitheses, its arguments and counterarguments unfolding in an article, the responses to the article, and the response to the response,[105] the polemic on Heidegger's Nazism acquired a liveliness it had not previously had and which has continued to this day, with some moments of respite.

Three major ways of understanding Heidegger's Nazism took shape at the time: the first, orthodox, repeated the discourse of self-defense developed in 1945 (Towarnicki); the second, informed by a detailed knowledge of Heidegger's philosophy of the 1920s, understood his Nazi involvement as a logical consequence—though difficult to imagine before the fact—of his notion of the radical historicality of decision within a human existence (Löwith); and the third, lying between the first and the second, sought to set aside or condemn Heidegger's Nazism while safeguarding his philosophy. This was the perspective adopted by de Waelhens and Éric Weil, a synthesis destined for a long future and which it is interesting to examine more closely.

In his article "The Heidegger Case," published in the July 1947 issue of *Les temps modernes,* Weil, observing with mild irony that the "Heidegger dossier" was still growing thicker, sought to draw up his own balance sheet based on the exchanges. His critical assessment worked to the advantage of philosophy but not of Heidegger as an individual. In making his case, Weil gave a virtuoso performance that strove to distinguish between the two. On the intellectual level, not hesitating to separate philosophical activity from the rest of the mind, he pointed out: "It is Nazi language, Nazi morality, Nazi thought (*sit venia verbo*), Nazi feeling. It is not Nazi philosophy." Heidegger was not "a biologistic materialist," because, for him, "the logos took precedence over nature as science understands it." For that reason, Weil said, "M. Heidegger believes he should prevail." Regarding Heidegger's political opinions and involvement, he noted: "M. Heidegger approved of Hitler's assumption of power, he was not overly upset by the entire history of the first year of the Thousand-Year Reich, he publicly approved of the break with the League of Nations, he brought all his moral weight to bear on his students and on public opinion in his country so that Hitler would be the future of Germany, and he was disappointed to find that the Reich could dispense with his services, since it needed no philosopher at all. The only thing he can complain about is that Nazism was an ingrate toward him." Firmly condemning how Heidegger compromised himself under the regime, the French philosopher concluded: "He is the only important philosopher who spoke out in favor of Hitler, and the most burning question is therefore whether his political decision is tied up with his philosophy and, through his philosophy, with philosophy pure and simple."

To respond on a personal level, Weil went beyond the Freiburg speech Towarnicki had reported, basing his judgment on an empty, abstract, and ahistorical view of decision, while ignoring its fateful character, though this was particularly important in Heidegger's conception of politics:[106] "The flaw in Heideggerian existentialism, if one asks philosophy to direct man to historically and politically concrete conclusions, is therefore that it does not lead to any decision because it leads only to decision in general. The act of placing it in the service of radical nationalism is entirely arbitrary and gratuitous, though not forbidden, licit, not prescribed, comprehensible, since that philosophy radically disassociates the philosopher of possibility from the man, who must live in a reality which, as a philosopher, he must abstain from understanding otherwise than in its form. There are philosophies that bind the philosopher: Heidegger's is not one of them. It is neither reactionary nor revolutionary, it has no politics." Wishing to complete his demonstration with a Heideggerian critique of Nazi engagement, which was also intellectual in nature, Weil vociferated: "And because M. Heidegger falsified his philosophy, because he abused it to extort from it a political response it cannot give, in view of the fact that it cannot even ask the question, precisely for that reason one can say that this philosophy, in its pure form, is true in part, true in the sense that Hegel gives to that word: it reveals a part of German reality. It does not justify National Socialism, but it expresses that German reality in which National Socialism was possible, without, however, being necessary."[107]

The reconstruction of Heidegger was not confined to France. Another noteworthy relationship of that period was with Ernst Jünger, whom the philosopher had read and admired but had never met in person. He did so on 16 September 1948, thanks to the publisher they shared, Vittorio Klostermann. The writer went up to the cabin to see Heidegger and came away with a strong impression. More than ever, the philosopher was adopting the pose of the sage of the mountain, peasant and philosopher by turns:

> From the first, there was something there—not only stronger than word and thought but stronger than the person himself. Simple as a peasant but a fairy tale peasant, capable of metamorphosing himself at will. [. . .] He was the one who knows, the one whom knowledge does not simply enrich but to whom it brings joy, as Nietzsche required of science. [. . .] I had the opportunity to feel such a direct impression of strength only one other time, though I met many contemporaries who, rightly or wrongly, bore illustrious names. In the second case, I am thinking of Picasso. When it comes to his creations as well, I am less a connoisseur than an amateur. In both cases, I felt the undifferentiated spiritual power that engenders the differentiated, in the form of thoughts, actions, or images—in short, works.[108]

Jünger and Heidegger considered publishing a review together, a project that Jünger ended up pursuing alone. Despite a will to "discover and to make visible in an original way what is authentic in the Western tradition, to gather together those who wait, to strengthen those who seek," Heidegger displayed little appetite for the plan. He spoke of the "tyranny of public opinion," which "cannot be broken from within. The joint appearance of our names, even under the simple form of a regular collaboration, would be transformed into a political event that would perhaps either shake our last secure position, or in the end confuse it." Directing a review would entail playing a role in the national media, getting mixed up with *das Man,* novelties, and everything the era might want to find interesting. In that context, Heidegger, harsh as he often was toward the culture of the time, mentioned a letter received from an émigré, who, as it happened, was his former student Hans Jonas. "A few days ago," he said, Ernst Laslowski, "my friend, a refugee from Upper Silesia who lives with us, received a letter from a Jewish émigré (a professor in the USA) who wrote that *he* (that is, is to say, *one*) is extremely anxious to learn what was going on with Jünger's and Heidegger's new journal."[109] The "Jewish" émigré, as Heidegger described him, proved to be, beyond his own individuality—which the philosopher designated by "he"—a henchman of *das Man,* the uprooted and uprooting turmoil that Heidegger for his part refused to get mixed up in.

The discreetly anti-Semitic character of that portrait clearly mirrored the letter from Jünger to which Heidegger was replying: "I hold Hiller as one of those principally responsible for the Jewish pogroms; it was he who furnished material for the *Stürmer* by besmirching everything German for decades. Hiller and Streicher, they are two sides of the same coin."[110] Jünger was rewriting history, and in unflattering terms. The essayist Kurt Hiller (1885–1972), active since the Weimar Republic, was of Jewish descent and had attacked Jünger after the war at a conference in London on 20 October 1945, while taking a stand on the ban on Nazi writers. What does "Nazi" mean? he asked. "Noble nationalist literature, more discreet, more politic, more civilized, is by far the most dangerous. Ernst Jünger is more dangerous than Adolf Hitler. Thomas Mann's *Reflections of a Nonpolitical Man* is more dangerous than Jünger."[111] Although Jünger adopted the same polemical attitude Hiller had displayed, he went well beyond a quarrel between individuals. According to Jünger, Streicher, a crude anti-Semite, was merely a response to Hiller. The persecution of the "Jews," even to the point of genocide—which Jünger wanted to see simply as pogroms—was partly an effect of the writings of essayists such as Hiller. Although more discreet than Jünger, Heidegger once again joined the fight against jewification. Far-right commonplaces remained favorable soil for new friendships, even after the collapse of the Third Reich.

A few months later, Heidegger was able to speak freely at the Bremen Club, with complete confidence that he was among his own. He had been invited by his former student and friend Heinrich Wiegand Petzet, the son of shipowners and patrons of the arts. Nineteen years earlier, he had visited the club with them and had expressed his thoughts on the essence of truth.[112] On 1 and 2 December 1949, he delivered not one but four lectures. His ontological negationism surfaced in two of them. He spoke of *Das Ge-stell* (enframing), a new term to designate "machination" (*Machenschaft*)—and even more obscure in German. The enframing or system of the time was entirely oriented toward global technological mastery. The extreme, horrific scope of the phenomenon extended even to the roots of Heidegger's familial imaginary: agriculture, he said, was becoming "a motorized food production industry." To truly convey the horror of that uprooting by modern technology and the gradual loss of home occasioned by the massive use of tractors and machine tools, integrated into increasingly vast circuits of production and distribution thanks to the growing use of modern modes of transport, the philosopher posited that "in its essence," mechanized agriculture was "the same thing" as "the fabrication of cadavers in gas chambers and extermination camps, the same thing as blockades and the reduction of countries to famine, the same thing as the manufacture of hydrogen bombs."[113] In that way, Heidegger slipped into Holocaust denial,[114] not so much in denying the genocide itself—or the reality of mass deaths—as in denying its historical, moral, and political importance, to which German guilt was indissolubly linked. Setting up a hierarchy that granted first priority to the question of modern agriculture in its essence, he placed genocide on the same level as blockades and the manufacture of hydrogen bombs. The Soviet Union had imposed a blockade on Berlin from 24 June of the previous year to 12 May 1949, while the Americans had become involved in the production of H-bombs, also in 1949. The global Jewish conspiracy remained quite present in Heidegger's mind. In that Cold War context, his metaphysical negationism fed on both a visceral anticommunism and a revived anti-Americanism, which, though he did not say so, had together reconstituted the "great pincers" of 1935. He was far from seeing the Americans as liberators, or even as a shield and sword against the USSR. Two years earlier, when the Cold War was still in limbo, he had even shone the spotlight on the American danger: "The destruction of Europe, no matter how it may be carried out, with or without Russia, is the work of the Americans. 'Hitler' is only a pretext. However, the Americans are on the whole Europeans. Europe is destroying itself."[115]

In another lecture at the Bremen Club, titled "The Danger," Heidegger reflected in greater depth on death in the camps, saying it was less a death—the end of the existence of a mortal whose life finds its being in its relation to death—than an artificial perishing caused by an industrial system: "Hundreds of thousands of people are dying. Are they dying? They are perishing. They have been killed. Are they dying? They are becoming the elements of an inventory held in store for the fabrication of cadavers. They have been liquidated in extermination camps without being noticed. And also without all that—millions of people now living in China are experiencing poverty, starving to death like animals [*Millionen verelenden jetzt in China durch den Hunger in ein Verenden*]."[116] The Holocaust was an industrial deprivation of death and ranked its objects among the beasts. As early as his course for the winter semester of 1929–1930, titled "The Fundamental Concepts of Metaphysics," Heidegger had meditated in similar terms on the absence of death among animals: "Is the death of the animal a *dying* or a way of *coming to an end*? Because apathy belongs to the essence of an animal, the animal cannot die in the sense in which dying is ascribed to human beings but can only come to an end."[117] Modern technology had reached the point of confusing categories, at times reducing man from his essence as hero and soldier, a being that resolves to be itself in the face of death, to the status of the subhuman victim incapable of being his own essence.

Once again, this observation of a dehumanization of man's death in the extermination camps went hand in hand with Holocaust denial. Heidegger understated the number of victims in the camps. He spoke of "hundreds of thousands" dying, when there were actually millions—at least 3 million in the camps of Chelmno, Sobibor, Belzec, Treblinka, Majdanek, and Auschwitz-Birkenau,[118] and a total of 6 million victims of the genocide. Yet he knew the actual scale of the killing. Marcuse had written him in a letter of the "millions of Jews" killed by the Third Reich, a number Heidegger repeated in his own letter of 20 January 1948.[119] He further minimized the Holocaust inasmuch as he contrasted the supposed "hundreds of thousands" of victims to the "millions" who had succumbed to famine in China. A major phenomenon that occurred after the fall of the Qing Dynasty in 1911, caused by civil and foreign wars and by the destruction of or failure to maintain the hydraulic network during that period, famine did not end with the proclamation of the People's Revolution on 1 October 1949. Historically speaking, the comparison made no sense. The famine in China did not stem from the use of superpowerful technology, but rather from the lack thereof. To make Heidegger's claim plausible, it must be supposed that this famine was the conscious deed of Chinese Communists, who knowingly applied a deadly policy against their own people. This could not have been the case in 1949—the civil war was not the Great Leap Forward. But that mattered little to Heidegger, since he was pointing to the mortal danger raised by communism.

In denying the importance of the Holocaust and the German people's responsibility for it, Heidegger behaved like other former Nazis or members of the German far right, who refused to take on the crushing burden of Nazi crimes. While Jünger was speaking of "pogroms" and dismissing Streicher and Hiller in the same breath, Carl Schmitt, on 23 August of the same year, transferred the guilt for the Holocaust onto "the democratic spirit." He wrote in his *Glossarium:* "Who is the true criminal, the real instigator of Hitlerism? Who discovered that individual? Who gave that abominable episode to the world? To whom are we beholden for those 12 million [*sic*] murdered Jews? I can tell you very precisely. Hitler did not discover himself. We are beholden to the pure democratic spirit, which concocted for us the mythic figure of the unknown soldier of the First World War."[120] Gottfried Benn was less crude, writing to his publisher in April 1949: "Even today, I think that N.S. [National Socialism] was an authentic and profound attempt to save the teetering West. The fact that, later, inappropriate and criminal elements gained the upper hand is not my fault and was not by itself predictable."[121] These intellectuals—and Heidegger was one of them—were like the Nazis whom George Mosse encountered after the war, nostalgic for the Third Reich, silent in public most of the time, but opening up to one another: "In listening to those former Nazis, I truly had the feeling that they had not changed, that they could not change."[122] In Heidegger's case, the circumstances carried a decisive weight: filled with a muffled anger against the denazification process to which he had been subjected, observing that the USSR and the United States, having become superpowers, were clamping down on Europe and fighting over it, he experienced in his private life the consequences of the Soviet policy toward Germany. His childhood friend Laslowski and his wife, refugees from Silesia, were still living in the house on Rötebuckweg. Although Hermann had been released in September 1947,[123] his father worried about Jörg, who was still being held in Russia. Only a few days after the Bremen lectures, the news of his elder son's liberation reached the philosopher while he was in Meßkirch. And, as an indication of how much the Russian detention mattered to him beyond his own child, he wrote: "I always think now with particular sympathy of the prisoners who must still remain behind. We're still 12 short here, and 60 are missing."[124]

Reunions after the Genocide

Heidegger's propensity for Holocaust denial was not conducive to reunions with friends who had been victims of the Nazi regime. Very early on, however, his friendship with the Szilasis, interrupted during the Third Reich because of their "non-Aryan" race, resumed. Despite the fact that the two men were the same age, Wilhelm considered himself a disciple of Heidegger. "Sz.'s concern & devotion is touching," wrote the Freiburg philosopher. And it was in that capacity that Szilasi became Heidegger's replacement, though not his successor, at the university. Szilasi's wife, Lili, seemed unaffected by the war and even by the turn Heidegger's thought had taken in the 1930s. The philosopher therefore found that one of her letters, probably typed, came from "a 'world' that has stood still in time & no longer 'is' at all," the world of modernity and the cultural and philosophical intellectualism of the Weimar Republic. "Whereas there the typewriters clatter away, here the hand with the pen falters in the face of everything dark & painful & unfathomable yet at the same time great & uncanny—& thought hardly dares turn itself to word. We've long since ceased to ek-sist [*eksistieren*] in order to produce 'philosophy' & 'culture'—but rather to find the site where the dwelling human being is again touched by Beyng [*Seyn*] as what is whole and healing [*das Heile/n*], & disaster [*das Unheil*] does not lapse into a mere meaninglessness to be ignored 'once the war is over.' "[125]

In his course on Parmenides for the winter semester of 1942–1943, Heidegger had already spoken ill of typewriters. He himself rarely used the devices, leaving that to his brother's agile hands. On the basis of that ignorance, not imagining that a typewriter—like a computer nowadays—could, similar to a quill or fountain pen, be an extension of the hand and the mind that command it and could disappear in the act of writing, he preferred to fasten onto the idea that, with this instrument, the hand no longer traces the letters itself. In that course, therefore, the typewriter appeared as the "triumph of the machine" pure and simple: "The typewriter veils the essence of writing and of the script. It withdraws from man the essential rank of the hand, without man's experiencing this withdrawal appropriately and recognizing that it has transformed the relation of Being to his essence."[126] Although a longtime friend, Lili was for these reasons a figure of the uprootedness of the era, of the jewification Heidegger had fought alongside the Third Reich, a figure perverted by technology, carried away by the superficiality of a culture that was not coming back to the essential, to the prophetic pain of beyng.

Marcuse, who was tackling head-on the question of Nazism and the extermination of the Jews, had difficulty for that reason finding common ground with Heidegger. In a letter to his former teacher, Marcuse had painted a picture of the Third Reich in three points: as a genocidal and anti-Semitic regime; as a totalitarian regime relying on terror; and as a regime driven by a perverse ideology, adopting common and essential terms from the German language—foremost among them "spirit," "freedom," and "truth"—only to give them meanings contrary to their usual ones. In the reply Heidegger sent to Marcuse on 20 January 1948, he tried to be conciliatory but allowed his Holocaust denial and anticommunism to find expression: "Regarding the serious, justified grievances you have 'against a regime that killed millions of Jews, that normalized terror, and that has turned into its opposite everything that was ever really associated with the idea of spirit and freedom and truth,' I can only add that in place of 'Jew,' we must now put 'East German,' and then that the same holds for one of the Allies, with the difference that everything that has happened since 1945 is known to world public opinion, whereas the Nazis' bloody terror was hidden from the German people."[127] Heidegger, who had himself contributed philosophically to that conceptual perversion, continued to do so by referring to the "Nazis' bloody terror," no longer, as Marcuse did, to denote the terrorism of the Third Reich—consubstantial with its totalitarian nature—but rather to designate the Holocaust. The regime came out looking better, and the genocide was reduced to mere pogroms, like the many that history had already known, particularly in the East. In speaking of the "serious, justified grievances," Heidegger was in fact only making a pro forma concession, because it was important to him to shift the specter of guilt onto the USSR. Granted, Nazi Germany had been guilty, especially vis-à-vis the Jews, but the USSR was even more guilty vis-à-vis the East Germans, whom it had subjected to the same fate, by violently occupying their territories. And because the Soviet Union was doing so before the eyes of the world and with its knowledge, the world itself bore a share of the guilt. During the Third Reich, by contrast, ordinary Germans were unaware of "the Nazis' bloody terror." Heidegger weighed the Holocaust and its 6 million victims against the East Germans, despoiled, exiled, raped, and in some cases killed by the Soviet armies, whose advance marked their annihilation—but not extermination—in that part of Europe.[128] The philosopher indulged in a negationist, nationalist, and anti-Bolshevik sophism, a mark of the strong ideological continuity of his thought between the Nazi period and the present. The totalitarian regime as such was whitewashed, and its criminal deeds, of which the Germans (kept at a distance) knew nothing, were portrayed as ultimately less serious than those of the Soviets, in that they were hidden rather than open. Heidegger, who believed he had been irreproachable during the Third Reich, had difficulty making reproaches against that regime, the enemy of freedom, culture, and humanity.

The question of guilt was not an insurmountable obstacle to Heidegger's reunion with Marcuse. It was for Jaspers, however, despite his goodwill. Jaspers wrote a first letter on 1 March 1948 but did not send it. It expressed the desire to write to Heidegger and the difficulty of doing so after all the time that had passed, after the long silence from his friend, after the darkness of the Third Reich and the crisis of conscience connected with the denazification proceedings. Jaspers was a sentimental man, who could not make up his mind to definitively draw a line through a past friendship.[129] But the weight of Heidegger's silence was still too heavy. It was not until the next year that Jaspers managed to face up to it. On 6 February 1949 he wrote a letter that he did send, and which began with these painful words: "I have wanted to write to you for a long time now. Today, on a Sunday morning, the impulse finally came to me. I will attempt it. There was once between us something that bound us together. I cannot believe that it has been extinguished without remainder." After mentioning the denazification commission and the report on Baumgarten, in which Heidegger spoke of the "Jew Fraenkel" and the circle of intellectuals around Max Weber, Jaspers tried to set out how he and Heidegger might feel toward each other. With a great deal of dignity and simplicity, he explained how he had experienced their friendship during those terrible years: "I don't know what you will reproach me for, perhaps with justification. For myself, I may say that I don't blame you because your conduct in this world-upheaval does not lie primarily at the level of moralizing debates. The infinite sadness since 1933, and the present situation, in which my soul only suffers more and more, have not bound us together but silently separated us. In the long years of banishment and danger to my life, the monstrousness, which is something completely different from mere politics, allowed no corresponding word to be spoken between us. We have slipped further away as human beings. My wife is present to me at every moment, about whom I said in our next-to-last meeting that she is decisive for all of my philosophizing (I still see the look of amazement on your face)."[130]

Heidegger replied with a brief, falsely ingenuous letter, which made no promises. He had not, it seems, received the letter, but he knew that Jaspers had written to him. He spoke of the happiness of their friendship, as if they had never been estranged, as if he, Heidegger, had never put an end to their conversation as friends and philosophers.[131] As it happened, Jaspers had kept a copy of the letter of 6 February, which he was thus able to send to Heidegger a second time. The letter bothered Heidegger, and, despite his jocularity, he evaded the question, refusing to examine his conscience, presenting himself in a favorable light as the opponent of Nazism: "I found no way toward dialogue. This became even more difficult for me since the spring of 1934, when I went into opposition and also internally severed myself from all matters at the university, for my helplessness increased. [. . .] If I do not go into explanations pertaining to your first letter, it is not because I want to pass over anything. Mere explaining will immediately go awry by becoming interminable. Coming to terms with the German disaster and its entanglements in world history and modernity will take the rest of our lives!"[132]

The exchanges continued, cordial and intellectual. Finally, Heidegger managed to find a few words about his friendship with Jaspers and his wife: "Since 1933, I no longer came to your house, not because a Jewish woman lived there, but *because I simply felt ashamed*. Since then, I have not entered your house, but I have also never again entered the city of Heidelberg, which is what it is to me only because of your friendship."[133] This discourse pleased Jaspers, who claimed it meant a lot to him that Heidegger had expressed shame. Jaspers was therefore encouraged to give his personal opinion of his friend's Nazism, a view that went deeper than "stupidity"—as Heidegger characterized it—while being less favorable toward him: "You seemed to behave toward the manifestations of National Socialism like a boy who dreams, who doesn't know what he is doing, who doesn't know how blindly and forgetfully he gets mixed up in an undertaking that looks to him like something completely different than what it is in reality, and then stands before a pile of rubble and allows himself to be driven further."[134]

Heidegger relaxed, used the language of conciliation, was falsely contrite about his political involvement and the rest. Then he launched into a diatribe against Stalin, fueled by Jörg's long-delayed return from the USSR, coupled with a denial of the pertinence of political action: "The matter of this evil has not come to an end. It has now entered a genuinely global phase. In 1933 and before, the Jews and the politicians of the left, as those directly threatened, saw more clearly, more sharply, and more broadly. *Now* it is *our* turn." Heidegger did not want to see what might have been specifically German about the Nazi evil. Evil was not about the involvement of individuals or of nearly an entire people, who, consenting, coerced, and manipulated, took part in a regime of terror and crime. It was a question of global technology pure and simple, of which Soviet communism was the leading edge. He believed, therefore, that "Stalin doesn't need to declare war any longer. Every day he wins a battle, but one doesn't see it. For us, as well, there is no avoiding it, and every word and every piece of writing *is* in itself a counterattack, if all of this does not play itself out in the *political*, which itself has long been outplayed by other relations to being and leads a pseudoexistence."[135]

Heidegger still made the link between anticommunism, uprootedness, and spiritual decadence, a link that also appeared in the draft of a public letter in the summer of 1950. He concluded by expressing surprise that "the constitution authorizes anyone to be a member and an activist in the Communist Party," whereas a "peculiar blindness thus leads to the erosion and internal dissolution of our people's last substantial strengths."[136] The liberalism of the postwar Bonn government, like that of the Weimar Republic, was guilty of not ending by force the deleterious action of a foreign party, the party of uprootedness itself. Unlike fascism and its active nihilism, conducive to hastening the final catastrophe and the overcoming of metaphysics, liberal democracy was a weak, indifferent system and thus of a nature to let the evil rot away, until the last spiritual forces in Germany were definitively snuffed out. Toning down his anti-Semitism and anti-Americanism, as he was encouraged to do by the opprobrium hanging over anti-Jewish sentiments and by the need for American military power, Heidegger in fact repeated the portrayal he had given in his introduction to metaphysics in 1935, though he effaced one of the two blades of the great pincers assailing Europe. All that remained was the Soviet blade.

His Nazi apoliticism was transmuted, acquiring a global dimension. It was no longer a question of parties but of states whose policies—war or peace—were immaterial. Five years after this letter to Jaspers, Heidegger stated with the greatest clarity his view of the radical impotence of any political party at the time. "No individual, no human group, no commission, even if composed of the most eminent statesmen, scientists, or technicians, no conference of the leaders of industry and of the economy, can slow or direct the historical development of the atomic age. No purely human organization is capable of taking in hand the government of our period."[137] After the fall of Nazism, the history within which other men moved, having become ordinary, seemed to have lost its meaning and its interest. History seemed to lie only in *das Man,* and so Heidegger now read a newspaper "only rarely."[138] What was the point, in fact, when nothing in it bore the grandiose mark of destiny any longer?

In his letter to Jaspers, Heidegger completed the portrait of that metapolitical struggle against *das Man* and the uprootedness of being, the import of which went well beyond the power relations between two blocs. He added a touch of his characteristically vague prophetism: "Despite everything, dear Jaspers, despite death and tears, despite suffering and horror, despite misery and affliction, despite groundlessness [*Bodenlosigkeit*] and exile, it is not nothing that occurs *in this homelessness* [*Heimatlosigkeit*]; instead *an advent is concealed in it,* distant whiffs of which we may, perhaps, still experience in a light breath, and which must be captured in order to preserve them for a future that no historical construction, especially today's, which thinks technologically throughout, will decipher."[139]

After a few inconsequential letters, Jaspers was silent for two years. Heidegger's political arguments had troubled him, borrowing too heavily as they did from the intellectual notions that had favored Hitler's coming to power. And Heidegger had said nothing about Jaspers's little book *The Question of German Guilt,*[140] which had been sent to him in the expectation of a real exchange. Jaspers was haunted by the survivor's guilt he felt after the horrors of the Third Reich: "We survivors did not seek [death]. We did not go into the streets when our Jewish friends were led away: we did not scream until we too were destroyed. We preferred to stay alive, on the feeble, if logical, ground that our death could not have helped anyone. We are guilty of being alive."[141] The perspectives of the two philosophers were radically opposed. The Nazi Heidegger, without remorse or regret, located the blame in an abstract and global principle, whose primary concrete threat lay outside Germany and had been one of the many motives for his former involvement in support of the NSDAP. Jaspers, more humane, a victim and the husband of a victim, saw how human these horrors were and how they implicated everyone. To refuse to die fighting them was to accept them and thus to carry a crushing guilt after the war. For Jaspers at least, that stark difference in viewpoint in such an existential realm could only give rise to a mute anger—tempered by embarrassment[142] by virtue of his civility and feelings of friendship—especially since it was sharpened by the memory of Heidegger's misconduct during those terrible years and the clear dissonance between his behavior and the account he gave of it after the war. Despite the best of intentions on both sides, their renewed friendship fizzled out, without their even seeing each other again. The missives they exchanged subsequently were only a pale reflection of their friendship before 1933.

Jaspers had finally sensed that, despite Heidegger's protests of friendship and understanding, they were still in opposing camps: victims versus executioners.

True, his friend had not murdered anyone, but he had supported the regime that had done so and on a scale beyond imagining. Jaspers had ultimately come to understand what Heidegger's basic posture had become: Holocaust denial dressed up in metaphysics, respectable in appearance but fundamentally intolerable.

The resumption of relations with his women friends, mistresses, or female disciples was a simpler matter. This is understandable, given the difference in his behavior toward women and toward men. In his later years, he was as quick to compete with men as he was to seduce women. Little information is available about Heidegger's relationship with his former student Helene Weiss, except for the philosopher's remarks to reporters from *Der Spiegel*. He said that, in April 1948, she had sent him her habilitation thesis, which included a grateful acknowledgment of her teacher: "The attempt at a phenomenological interpretation [. . .] is indebted to Herr Heidegger's novel interpretations of Greek philosophy." In the postwar period and until her death in 1953, he visited her frequently in Basel, where she had settled after living in Scotland and Germany.[143] As for Elisabeth Blochmann, she resumed her relationship with her former mentor, friend, and lover on the occasion of his birthday in 1946, with a brief text accompanied by a small volume of sonnets by Rilke. Elfride had been in touch beforehand, and the two women subsequently exchanged several letters. Heidegger waited until March of the following year to reply to Blochmann; it was difficult for him to resume an epistolary relationship before seeing her again, before speaking to her again, before a word in person reestablished "what time had interrupted, without ever being able to snuff out friendship or memory."[144] Denial of the breakup was a condition, perhaps indispensable, for the reestablishment of the relationship. It was a way of denying the Third Reich, which Heidegger had supported to the end and which had not encouraged the kindest of feelings toward friends considered to be "non-Aryans." In the following years, they exchanged a few letters, a few gifts. Their friendship was renewed.

11 • End Paths

(1950–1976)

Happiness Regained? (1950–1969)

For Heidegger, the 1950s and 1960s were years of happiness regained. The life of his family normalized, at least in part. The Heideggers gradually regained sole possession of the house on Rötebuckweg. By 1949 French military personnel were no longer billeted there,[1] though their friends Ernst and Lene Laslowski were still living in the house in 1952, because of the enduring housing crisis.[2]

The Heideggers' two sons, finally back from Russia, could resume their lives. The elder, Jörg, found his wife changed: since summer 1949[3] she had been suffering from schizophrenia.[4] When her husband returned, her father-in-law privately displayed little philosophy and a great deal of anger: "It's deeply regrettable & irresponsible of Dorle to spoil this harmony of joy & the will to make a new start like this. Her foolish fantasies are just an escape from the serious path of life that is now beginning. I won't even mention her ingratitude toward us."[5] Dorle and Jörg's marriage was at an impasse, which did not prevent Jörg from resuming his studies in mechanical engineering in Karlsruhe in the summer semester of 1950.[6] After graduating in 1952,[7] he took his first job, in Bad Homburg, on 1 August of the following year.[8] Hermann, the younger son, having come back two years earlier, had chosen history as his career path and had even undertaken a thesis titled "German Social Democracy and the National State between 1870 and 1920,"[9] which he defended in 1953. Like his father before him, he received his doctorate from the University of Freiburg, though in a different discipline. He chose to pursue his career not in higher education but in the primary schools. Once he was trained, he became a teacher in the village of Wieslet,[10] located in the Black

Forest of the Wiese Valley, not far from the family sheepfold in the Danube Valley. He did not teach for long; the Cold War, which threatened the freedom and even the existence of West Germany, led the nation to join NATO in 1954 and to sign the treaty establishing the European Defense Community. An army had to be reconstituted. Hermann received an offer to be part of it,[11] which he accepted. In late 1955 he therefore joined the Ministry of Defense to participate in the creation of the Bundeswehr.

On 10 April of the previous year, Hermann had married Jutta Stölting,[12] a native of Lower Saxony in northern Germany. His brother's second marriage followed shortly thereafter: on 12 August, Jörg took as his wife Hedi Veidt, the daughter of one of his mother's former classmates. The wedding did everyone good: "I look back fondly on Jörg & Hedi's quiet wedding. The occasion has helped us too."[13] Weddings were followed by births, a great number of them, in fact, during the baby boom. Erika, Martin and Elfride's adopted daughter, led the way in September 1945, giving birth to a little Martin,[14] quickly followed by Ursula and Christoph, then, later, Johannes. Hermann followed suit in 1955, with Ulrike, then Almuth, twins Detlev and Dietrich, and the baby of the family, Arnulf. Jörg's first child, Gertrud, who many years later would edit her grandfather's letters to her grandmother, was also born in 1955, followed by Friederike, Burghard, Imke, and Dorle.[15] All these births were a great joy to Elfride, who could reinvest her maternal feelings in the care lavished on her children, daughters-in-law, and grandchildren, especially when Jörg returned, in autumn 1954, and moved with his family into the house on Rötebuckweg.[16] Two years later, he moved out, but remained in the same Zähringen neighborhood.[17]

As for the philosopher, he often spent long stretches in Meßkirch working with his brother, which gave him great satisfaction, given the assistance and intimate understanding Fritz provided: "As ever, work with Fritz is 'fruitful' & full of agreement. He isn't at all 'narrow'—He said it'd be only right if they placed me on the Index in Rome."[18] As was their habit, they took many walks on the "fieldpath," which began at the castle and wended its way through the fields and woods. The philosopher also came to Meßkirch for major family events, some happy, like the ordination party for his nephew Heinrich in June 1954, and others unhappy, like the funeral for his nephew Franz in May 1955: "Silent but composed grief pervades the little house here," he reported. "Liesel is much calmer & more collected than Fritz, who hides it all with painful humour."[19]

In addition, Heidegger had kept in touch with his former classmates, who in November 1949 celebrated his sixtieth birthday, slightly after the actual date.[20] Meßkirch made a fuss over him: the following month, for the jubilee marking the centennial of the death of the local musician Conradin Kreutzer, Heidegger told his wife that, "at the actual ceremony," he had "the seat of honor next to the mayor in front of all the others."[21] He involved himself in the life of the town by delivering speeches. For example, on 30 October 1955, he gave one titled "Releasement" ("Gelassenheit") for the 175th anniversary of Kreutzer's birth; he gave another on 27 September 1959, having been made an honorary citizen of Meßkirch on the occasion of his seventieth birthday; and on 2 May 1964, the reunion of classmates from 1894 and after[22] gave him an opportunity to speak on Abraham a Sancta Clara, as he had done fifty-five years earlier for the bicentennial of the local holy man's death.

Heidegger liked to celebrate the *Heimat* and rootedness. In "The Fieldpath," he depicted himself as a young student with his books, walking along the path of the title and drawing his thoughts from the land that surrounded him, just as a peasant would harvest its crop:

> Sometimes there lay on the bench this or that volume of the writings of great thinkers, which an awkward youth was trying to decipher. When the enigmas multiplied and no way out was in view, the fieldpath was of great help. For it silently guided our feet along the winding path across the expanse of this parsimonious country.
>
> Ever anew, thought, struggling with the same writings or with its own problems, followed the trail the fieldpath traced through the meadow. It remained as close to the thinker's steps as those of the peasant going out to mow hay in the early morning.[23]

Referring to his "awkward youth" in Meßkirch, the philosopher unconsciously rewrote his past, to make it better correspond to the portrait of a thinker rooted in his native soil. As he had written Elfride in 1920, it was she who, through their walks, had suddenly opened his mind to the beauty of his home region. As a student, he "had no 'time' for it."[24] Home was the landscape with kitsch scenes and metaphysical colors against which he liked to paint his self-portraits: "When one is a philosopher, then one is what Nietzsche said [. . .]: 'The philosopher is a rare plant,' that is, it requires its own soil . . ., whose growth and secret powers of surviving no chemical soil science will ever discover. A rare plant needs a rare soil. And if something is [rare] here, even a little bit, then the rarity of our local soil here lies in the fact that this land, the earth, and the sky over it, are in no way striking, unusual, or outstanding."[25] In gratitude for having just been granted honorary citizenship in

Meßkirch, Heidegger praised the very ordinariness of this soil (*Boden*), an aspect that was becoming rare in an age attentive to the latest innovations, the latest technologies. His home region, having kept its distance from the uprootedness of modernity, had nothing extraordinary about it, and that was precisely what made it extraordinary, what made it the land suited to bring forth a philosopher.

Heidegger had reached the age of reaping rather than sowing, an age when it is difficult to make a new life, especially if one is firmly convinced one is right, about and against everyone and everything else. And, because he liked to celebrate rootedness, he was still inclined to deplore the uprootedness at work in modernity and the danger posed to the native region in a time of global technology. What was most notable in this postwar period came from the philosopher's new tone, which he first adopted in Meßkirch under the sign of *Gelassenheit*. The warrior ethos was thus succeeded by serenity, release, which he conceived as a healthy relationship to technology:

> We can use technical devices, and yet with proper use also keep ourselves so free of them that we may let go of them any time. We can use technical devices as they ought to be used, and also let them alone as something which does not affect our inner and real core. We can affirm the unavoidable use of technical devices, and also deny them the right to dominate us, and so to warp, confuse, and lay waste our nature. [. . .] I would call this comportment toward technology which expresses "yes" and at the same time "no," by an old word, releasement [*Gelassenheit*] toward things.[26]

The many long stretches spent in Meßkirch did not exhaust Heidegger's love for the native soil. He also reappropriated the places of his childhood a few kilometers away. The family farm in Göggingen had been through the war, which wiped out the Kempf line. And, though the farm had been sold, Heidegger often returned to visit it, engaging in discussions with the new owners. In this carefree place he had lived in the midst of his family, "with no thought of the world wars that were to come." The farm brought to his mind the following words, which he attributed to the Church Father Hegesippus: "A joy it is to linger among the familiar domestic things of our forefathers and to study their words and deeds in fond remembrance."[27] He reestablished contact with the Beuron monastery and, accompanied by his brother Fritz, returned there for the first time in November 1949,[28] visiting his old friend Father Anselm. The priest's death on 27 November 1951 did not mark the end of Heidegger's relationship with the monastery of his *Heimat.* He became friends with the abbot and the new librarian. Fritz, himself a friend of many monks at Beuron, went there for St. Martin's Day. Heidegger's attachment to this place from his childhood is indicated by his return there in August 1963, accompanied by Jean Beaufret. They spent several hours in the abbey church. It was the philosopher's last documented visit to the monastery.

Heidegger's thought conserved a religious dimension, and he even returned to the faith, if not to the Church. *Gelassenheit* was one mark of it, in that he had come across the notion while reading Martin Luther in 1919.[29] In October 1951, while attending a service in Beuron, he was touched by the liturgy, just as he had been as a child: "A dwelling within the praise of God transpires in the liturgy; but there's often also a doubt as to what extent a fruitful closeness is still alive. On the other hand, neither in the Catholic nor in the Protestant Church can a creative or history-making piety be enforced by a liturgical movement—unless the God speaks himself. This is why it may after all be that a proper way to reach it is to prepare and awaken in the individual attentiveness to the word, the presentiment of its realm."[30] That piety, a pensive waiting for God, can be heard in exemplary fashion in Heidegger's lecture "The Question Concerning Technology," which he concluded with these words: "Questioning is the piety of thought."[31]

Although farther away, Konstanz, where he spent the first three years of Gymnasium, was still looked on favorably, because it was there that the Heideggers had become engaged to be married, and because he kept in touch with former classmates in that city. The couple went there in October 1954 for the 350th anniversary of the Heinrich-Suso-Gymnasium. With a few days' hindsight, Heidegger wrote to Elfride: "And now you've caught a small reflection of what surrounded me as a little boy at grammar school; only you must imagine everything much quieter & almost sleepy. For me of course they were the first foreign parts I knew, & seen from here a residue from them lies over everything even now."[32]

Supplanted by Meßkirch, the Todtnauberg cabin was now less suitable for the philosopher, who was getting old and no longer saw it as the ideal place for his work. He went there less often, even as their house in Freiburg recovered a charm for him that it seemed to have lost a few years earlier. "Our wonderful cabin years remain in our memory & perhaps the best thing really is if we venture once more to preserve our inseparableness purely within its ownmost root—in order to be all the better able to do so. It gladdens me how in the last few years I've subsequently become increasingly fond of the Freiburg house too, in spite of its city location."[33] Near Freiburg, and the place where his postwar renewal began, the Badenweiler clinic still held an undeniable importance for Heidegger. In spring 1949 he met Lina Kromer there, a regionalist poet with whom he corresponded in the Alemannic dialect.[34] Having come to the clinic on 4 and 5 October 1952, for a celebration to honor the poet Georg Trakl, he made the acquaintance of Ludwig von Ficker, who had published poems by Trakl in the review *Der Brenner,* which Ficker had founded in 1912.[35] A friendship began at that time and lasted until Ficker's death in 1967.

The normalization of the postwar years also affected the universities. Of those people close to Heidegger, Löwith returned from the United States to accept a chair in Heidelberg in 1952, while Blochmann left England and was named a professor in Marburg. That made possible a reunion between her and the Heideggers the following year.[36] Although the relationship between the philosopher and the educationalist did not recover the intensity it had had before the war, their reunion was so warm that they began to use *du,* the familiar form of the second-person pronoun, to address each other.

Even as the "non-Aryans" Blochmann and Löwith resumed their academic careers—lost during the Third Reich—Heidegger was partially reinstated in Freiburg. Although his name was not cleared, his retirement in 1950,[37] and then the emeritus status he was accorded on 26 September 1951,[38] freed the philosopher and his family from the financial difficulties into which the war and immediate postwar period had plunged them. Their restored material comfort allowed them to purchase a new car in 1951.[39] Having been reinstated at the German university, Heidegger was able to resume teaching, first seminars, and then, in the summer semester of 1952, a lecture course. The question it asked, "What Is Called Thinking?" (*Was heißt denken?*) filled the hall to capacity. During one session, the young Hugo Ott, a student of theology at the time, was in the lecture hall, as he later confided to me. Heidegger could again participate in the major events of his university. On 27 June 1957, for its five hundredth anniversary, he gave a lecture to which he attached the greatest importance,[40] on the principle of identity. Nearly ten years later, during the winter semester of 1966–1967, he conducted a seminar on Heraclitus with Eugen Fink, also a former student of Husserl's. This was Heidegger's last notable activity at what had been his university for fifty-eight years.

The university had become a secondary matter for the philosopher, who over time was showered with public honors. In 1957 he became a member of the Heidelberg Academy of Sciences and Humanities and of the Academy of

Arts in Berlin. In 1959 he was made an honorary citizen of Meßkirch. The following year, the Land of Baden-Württemberg awarded him the Hebel Prize; in 1969 he was accepted to the Bavarian Academy of Fine Arts.[41] He did continue to teach, however, giving many lectures or holding private seminars. In late March 1957, for example, invited to Darmstadt by his friends Egon and Dory Vietta, he assembled a small elite around him, composed of Alfred Guzzoni, Kōichi Tsujimura, Hartmut Buchner, and Hildegard Feick.[42]

Heidegger's second career unfolded abroad more than it did in Germany. His psychiatric treatment at Badenweiler in 1946 had laid the foundations for one of the new directions of his work after 1945. Moving closer to Medard Boss around *Daseinanalyse* beginning in 1947, Heidegger held seminars with him in Zollikon, near Zurich, between 1959 and 1969. The psychiatrist, though a close friend of the philosopher's, did not inspire boundless esteem. Heidegger found him "still awkward in his thinking about the fundamental questions."[43] Nonetheless, the philosopher assisted Boss as he was writing *An Outline of Medicine and Psychology*, which appeared in 1971.[44]

Heidegger increasingly chose the French as his privileged interlocutors. In 1955 he went to France for the first time, with Elfride, for the Cerisy-la-Salle colloquium in Normandy. In Paris, accompanied by Beaufret, he met René Char "under a Ménilmontant chestnut tree."[45] Beaufret, his principal French disciple, lived in the capital, but it had the disadvantage of being a big city. It was therefore in Provence that the thinker rooted in Baden really found a second home. From 1956 on, the Heideggers discovered together that region of France,[46] and the philosopher returned by himself many times subsequently, especially for three summer seminars in Le Thor between 1966 and 1969, at Char's invitation.[47] A strong friendship formed at the time between the philosopher and the poet, against the backdrop of a Provence identified with Greece. Surrounded by "lovely old things," Char lived near L'Isle-sur-la-Sorgue in "a simple country house" with an "enchanting garden." He seemed "very rich" to Heidegger and behaved quite "amicably" with him and his companions: "At once the right spiritual atmosphere was created, as indeed only those French know how."[48] Later, they had "a good conversation about the technological world of today and saving the countryside," a theme that could only have brought them closer together, since Char proved to be "full of despair."[49]

Beaufret's students François Fédier and François Vézin pampered their illustrious guest. This was especially true of Fédier, who took care of everything at the hotel and whose fascination with the modern Heraclitus led him to take a large number of photographs, many of them of poor quality. He nevertheless published them subsequently,[50] so captivated was he by the philosopher. Heidegger was very favorably impressed by his students: "Altogether, these young people, with whom I always read Heraclitus in the mornings [. . .] it's an elite."[51] The pleasures of the table and conversation about the cuisine complemented the pleasures of teaching: "At table much eating is done & just as much talking about la cuisine; but I keep a low profile."[52] As he noted two years later, "all in all, eating takes up a lot of time for the French."[53] Made up of traditions, whether continued or abandoned, cuisine was an occasion for reflection. And, in a time of technology and the standardized man, even in one of the most typical regions of France, the cuisine was undergoing changes characteristic of modernity: "As Beaufret says, the food no longer has the specific character of the landscape—by agreement of the hoteliers there are internationally uniform regulations—but there are melons & grapes in abundance & the plain table wine."[54] Further evidence of the misfortunes affecting the region: Marcelle Mathieu, a widow, farmer, and partaker at the Heideggerian feasts, was "thin and rather careworn," because agriculture was going badly.[55]

Heidegger enjoyed himself in Provence, a region that made him think of Greece and could create the illusion that he was a new Plato surrounded by his disciples. He liked it so much that, when invited to speak at the University of Aix on 20 March 1958, he declared his love, mingling the impression produced by the landscape, the memory of Cézanne, and his own convictions about the links between greatness of spirit and rootedness in a soil:

> Why am I talking here in Aix-en-Provence?
> I love the gentleness of this land [*Land*] and its villages.
> I love the harshness of its mountains.
> I love the harmony of the two.
> I love Aix, Bibémus, Mont Sainte-Victoire.
> Here I've found the path of Paul Cézanne, which, from its beginning to its end, corresponds, in a certain way, to my own thought's path.
> I love this land [*Land*] with its seacoast, because it heralds the proximity of Greece.
> I love all that because I am convinced that there is no essential work of the mind that does not have its root in an original rootedness [*Bodenständlichkeit*].[56]

More prosaically, Heidegger's new love for Provence showed the extent to which he had recovered a certain material comfort, to the point of being able to make a foreign region his own through travel. The postwar period was that of the German economic miracle: a large portion of the population, like the Heideggers, had the means to engage in tourism, both national and international. The couple had a predilection for the Mediterranean. Accompanied by Boss and his wife, they went on vacation to Sicily in April and May 1963,[57] then to Greece in April 1966.[58] On three other occasions, in 1962, 1964, and 1967, the Heideggers went to that region on their own.[59] Their house too became more comfortable: the pool, which had been renovated after the war, was heated by 1968, extending the season for swimming.[60]

The philosopher's regained happiness was not without its shadows, even in his greatest joys. The resumption of his affair with Hannah Arendt in 1950 contributed to that chiaroscuro effect. It should not have resumed: unlike Blochmann before her exile, Arendt had not sympathized with Nazism. She did not feel she had a common destiny with the German people. And, though her life was filled with the German language and its poets, that was hardly a foundation for a favorable view of a criminal regime's henchman. Besides, she judged her former lover and mentor severely:

> This living in Todtnauberg, grumbling about civilization and writing *Sein* with a "y," is really a kind of mouse hole he has crawled into because he rightly assumes that the only people he'll have to see there are the pilgrims who come full of admiration for him. Nobody is likely to climb 1,200 meters to make a scene. And if somebody did do it, he would lie a blue streak and take for granted that nobody will call him a liar to his face. He probably thought he could buy himself loose from the world this way at the lowest possible price, fast-talk himself out of everything unpleasant, and do nothing but philosophize.[61]

"Love," however, "can forgive a great deal": years later, that is what Jonas explained to a student who had come up after a reading to ask how Arendt had "forgiven Heidegger for his anti-Semitism so quickly."[62] In 1929 she had written to Heidegger: "Our love has become the blessing of my life."[63] During the last letters they exchanged in 1932, Heidegger was forty-three, Arendt twenty-six. Now a new relationship was established, more equal and deeper, between two older adults, so different from who they had been in the 1920s, a still-young professor and a former student who had only recently become a young woman. They saw each other in early February 1950, during a tour of Europe Arendt had undertaken. She got his address from Hugo Friedrich and sent Heidegger a note. In a letter, he invited her to come to the house on Rötebuckweg, informed

Elfride of their past relationship, then went to Arendt's hotel a few hours after mailing his letter.[64] As Arendt wrote to him later, she was not expecting him, because she had not yet received his note. "When the waiter spoke your name, [. . .] it was as if time suddenly stood still." Seduction prevailed over every other consideration, at least for Heidegger, whereas for Arendt, "the power of the impulse" had mercifully saved her "from committing the only really inexcusable act of infidelity."[65]

Elfride did not know that her husband had once more given in to adulterous impulses, only that he had done so in the past with Arendt. She proved to be understanding, evoking "something indestructible" that prevailed and endured between them. Having been put at ease, the philosopher tried to confide in his "dear Wife" a week later, by letter: "A moment has come when I must tell you what has moved me particularly in the last few years." Thanks to the distance afforded by a missive, he could write what he had been unable to say to her face. First, he assured her once again that the role she played as a wife was not only practical—allowing the philosopher to live in a well-kept house without having to worry much about it. It was produced, "right down to the slightest and inconspicuous detail," by her "inner belonging" to the path of the philosopher's thought. Reminding her that he had promised to dedicate a text to her dealing "specifically with Plato's thought," he wanted his wife to believe that she was not merely a housewife but his intellectually irreplaceable partner. This first mollifying remark was a sort of *captatio benevolentiae,* by means of which he wanted to make her favorably disposed toward what followed, which was less consensual and which his pen had difficulty putting to paper. Just as Socrates sensed the influence of a spirit, a daemon, who, though invisible, communicated with him, Heidegger, because of his philosophizing itself, was possessed by a god. He was in some sense "erotomaniacal," mad for Eros, "the oldest of the gods according to Parmenides"; the beat of Eros's wings moved him "every time" he ventured onto "untrodden paths" in his thinking. "To live up to this purely and yet retain what is ours, to follow the flight and yet return home safely, to accomplish both things as equally essential and pertinent, this is where I fail too easily & then either stray into pure sensuality or try to force the unforceable through sheer work." Heidegger, who thereby went to confession by means of a letter, concluded by showing the contrition prescribed by such an exercise: "My disposition and the manner of my early upbringing, instability and cowardice in the ability to trust & then again inconsiderateness in the abuse of trust, these are the poles between which I swing & thus only too easily & only too often misjudge & overstep the measure with regard to Hera and Eros."[66]

After a sin, a lapse that led him to have sex with another woman, contrition was a necessary moment in a moral cycle within which the philosopher was caught up, and which did not last long enough to keep him from falling again. Heidegger continued the relationship of seduction uniting him with Arendt. On the 19 March following his confessional letter to Elfride, he declared to his lover: "I need her [Elfride's] love, which bore everything in silence through the years and still has room to grow. I need your love, which, mysteriously maintained in its early seeds, brings hers from its depths."[67] That relationship was based on physical attraction, at least for the philosopher, who began his letter of 12 April with these words: "Hannah—What is more beautiful—your picture or your letter? Only you yourself, and your having sent them both."[68]

Arendt responded to these romantic entreaties all the more easily in that they were accompanied by an intellectual attraction: she considered him a genius.[69] In 1950 Heidegger's *Off the Beaten Track* was on her bedside table, and she had begun to read "with great pleasure" his *Heraclitus*.[70] It is likely they talked together about the Holocaust. In *The Origins of Totalitarianism,* Arendt seems to have been inspired by the thesis Heidegger had developed at the Bremen Club two months before their reunion, about the people who reached the end of their lives in the camps, without having experienced their own death. The following year, the political scientist referred to an "insane mass manufacture of corpses," preceded by the preparation of "living corpses"[71] that had lost all human rights. She wrote that "the concentration camps, by making death itself anonymous (making it impossible to find out whether a prisoner is dead or alive), robbed death of its meaning as the end of a fulfilled life. In a sense they took away the individual's own death, proving that henceforth nothing belonged to him and he belonged to no one. His death merely set a seal on the fact that he had never really existed."[72] Arendt's critical reiteration of the same idea Heidegger had developed in the context of Holocaust denial shows the extent to which arguments can be reversible, able to serve one perspective or another—a major phenomenon in the Heidegger affair.

Hannah's affair with her former teacher continued steadily afterward, but was sometimes infused with irony, frustration, or anger. In late 1957, after reading his "Identity and Difference," she pointed out that he "quotes himself and interprets himself, as if he were a text taken from the Bible."[73] In 1960, when she sent him a copy of her book *The Human Condition,* which, she said, "came directly out of the first Freiburg days and hence owes practically everything to you in every respect,"[74] he said nothing about it for five years. In

November of the following year, she wrote of her disappointment to her other teacher, Jaspers, who was a kind of father to her, while the other had been a lover: "I know he [Heidegger] finds it intolerable that my name appears in public, that I write books, etc. All my life I've pulled the wool over his eyes, so to speak, always acted as if none of that existed and as if I couldn't count to three, unless it was in the interpretation of his own works. Then he was always very pleased when it turned out I could count to three and sometimes even to four."[75]

Her husband's reunion with Arendt was not easy for Elfride. She managed to put a good face on it the first time, in 1950, accepting the past, but could not contain her rage upon Arendt's second visit, in May 1952: "The wife is mad with jealousy," Arendt told her own husband, "a jealousy that only increased during the years when she'd hoped he would quite simply forget me. This was expressed in a more or less anti-Semitic scene when we were alone together, she and I. It must be said as well that the lady's political convictions [. . .] have remained intact, despite the experience of the past years. Their stupidity is so narrow-minded, so vicious, so resentful, that one can understand what happened to Heidegger."[76] Jealousy had revealed something of Elfride's temperament and her undiminished Nazism. Arendt rightly saw how great Elfride's political influence could have been on her husband. She was probably unaware of the extent to which Elfride's jealous rage was fueled over and over again by Heidegger, who, more than ever, remained a seducer, continuing to have a string of extramarital affairs well beyond Arendt.

Among the names of his lovers after 1945 that have come down to us: Countess Sophie Dorothee von Podewils, Dory Vietta, Hildegard Feick, Marielene Putscher, Andrea von Harbou. Their ages varied, an indication of how avidly he sought the favors of women: in 1955, when he went to Tübingen to see Putscher, a doctor, art historian, and former student, she was thirty-five,[77] thirty-one years younger than he. He sometimes traveled with them, around Provence with Vietta, for example, in September 1957.[78] Often they were students, former students, or collaborators: Feick helped him type up his manuscripts.[79] Others came from more remote circles—for example, the neurologist von Harbou.[80] Heidegger acquiesced to these relationships as much as he sought them out. From time to time, he was obliged to confess them to his wife, but found himself unable to vary a great deal the expression of his contrition. "However insistent these women are," the almost septuagenarian conceded in late April 1958, "I was still to blame—Because—even in their own right—there's nothing sustaining or really significant about these encounters.

The clear recognition of what still remains for me to do, the unpublished texts, the lectures—the real task—has been helping me increasingly for months—to live calmly for work & break free from earlier bonds of the past. All this will also make me quite free again for you for the important years we may yet have in store." He ended another letter on the same day with a rather mild "With all best wishes, constantly thinking of you, your w. Bl. [white Blackamoor]—white, but not yet wise."[81]

The philosopher, who had meditated a great deal on the need for a soil adequate to his thought, publicly covered with a veil of shame these many mistresses. Yet they were supposed to keep the flame of his cult alive; without them, his word would have been less forceful. The adulation that surrounded him required more than one priestess. And, because one woman was not enough for him, he brought unhappiness to the woman he married. The rage at Arendt that seized Elfride in 1952 soon turned to despair, when she began to suspect her husband was having an affair with Countess Podewils.[82] Elfride's condition deteriorated over time, and she was diagnosed with major depression in 1960. From January to March, she was in treatment in Hinterzarten,[83] and she continued to take tranquillizers and sleep aids prescribed by their psychiatrist friend Boss,[84] which led to memory loss. As usual, Heidegger made her promises that bound only the person who really wanted to believe them: "And now this my love: one of the main remedies is me—in whom everything will be all right—and the good years are still ahead of us, when I hope to succeed in producing the counterpart to B[eing] & T[ime]."[85]

Despite his efforts, the philosopher did not succeed in writing that second great book, producing instead a string of coherent but scattered writings that lacked the systematic structure of his magnum opus. He likewise failed to exercise self-control in his sex life. As a result, the relationship between Heidegger and his wife continued to fluctuate. Sometimes things were calm, and he began his letters with his ritual "My Dearest Soul." Other times they were tumultuous, and he used a more distant "Dear Elfride." His wife's jealousy was all the more acute because Heidegger often spent long weeks away from her. Despite the proximity of their son Jörg and his family, she did not have a sympathetic ear in which to confide her unhappiness. Elfride tried meeting her rivals Arendt and Harbou: perhaps she hoped to make them her allies, or perhaps she wanted to intimidate them. In late April 1958 Vietta and Harbou decided to leave their lover, shortly after meeting with his wife.[86] At the same time, Elfride wrote many letters to her husband, in which she vented her spleen but which she rarely sent, such as this one from 28 June 1956:

Dear Martin
Thank you for two letters and for the nice cards by Braque. I hope by now you've made a good start with work—yes, you have your work, which is the centreeof your entire life—but then what happens on the sidelines anyway! This is why you cannot understand how—through you—I've been cast out from my center. [. . .] I *know* of what you do, of the inspiration you need, & even now I've striven once more to see what makes you happy & her as the one who can give it. But that all this should be bound up not only with "*lies*"—no, with the most inhuman abuse of my trust, this still fills me with despair. [. . .] How would you bear [infidelity]? And I'm supposed to be able to endure it—not *once*—but again & again throughout 4 decades? can any human being do so if he isn't superficial or made of stone? Time & again you say & write that you're bound to me—what is the bond? It isn't love, it isn't trust, you look for " 'home' " in other women—oh Martin—what is happening to me—this icy loneliness.

But I won't write anything more; you don't like hearing it anyway; there are many letters I've started here, but I haven't posted any.—Have you ever thought about what empty words are—hollow words? What *is lacking* in such words?[87]

A Philosopher Facing the Destiny of His Nazi Past (1950–1976)

Heidegger had made Nazism his destiny, which now weighed heavy on him, and he struggled to extricate himself. When he began a relationship with someone, the question of his Nazi involvement always lurked behind their exchanges: "In September 1969," recounted Barbara Cassin, "I was twenty-two and was invited to the seminar Heidegger was giving at Le Thor, in René Char's home. There were fewer than ten participants, and we were staying at the Hôtel du Chasselas, where we took our meals together. Heidegger liked to hold his seminar in the morning, and there were sometimes hikes in the afternoon. I was lucky to be able to participate in the seminar. We all knew he had been a Nazi, rector of the university, but we were at the home of René Char, Captain Alexander in the Resistance. Heidegger taught us about the Greeks and poetry's importance for thought."[88] However kind people were toward him, the question did not always remain unexpressed. Towarnicki mentions a scene that unfolded in Freiburg: "We were in the garden and were talking about Greece. I suddenly said to him, with a sharpness in which the evil spirit of Baden wine played no small part, that his disastrous involvement in 1933 had placed his French friends in a real bind. Why had he done it during that time? I remember Mrs. Heidegger looked at me, petrified. After a moment of silence, Heidegger, surprised, leaned toward me with the grave air of someone who is preparing to reveal a great secret: '*Dummheit.*' He repeated the word, as if he wanted to give even more weight to the obvious: '*Dummheit.*' Stupidity."[89] In private, with his French friends Towarnicki and Fédier[90] and with others, including Petzet,[91] Heidegger spoke of his Nazism—which he reduced to his rectorship—as being stupidity, the greatest stupidity of his life. He must have been remembering that, in one of his black notebooks of 1934, he had deemed his rectorship an "error,"[92] because the idea of the self-assertion of the German university was meaningless. His error was not that he had played a role in the installation of the Nazi regime, as he now wanted people to think, but that he had believed a philosophical revolution at the university was possible. In hindsight, he was able to think that this "stupidity" was ultimately the source of considerable annoyance, in exchange for the decidedly slim satisfaction of having temporarily introduced the *Führerprinzip* at the University of Freiburg. It was not worth it: the faculty was too hostile to revolution, the students too restless. It would have been better to concentrate at once on Hölderlin, Nietzsche, and the pre-Socratics.

In the immediate postwar period, the Heidegger affair was taken up again in French reviews, but these episodes were too far away to bother the figure at their center. Nevertheless, because he himself helped fuel the affair after the fall of the Third Reich, it returned to Germany in the 1950s. His views about Nazism had hardly changed since the collapse of the regime, as he intimated to anyone with ears to hear it. In 1954 he published "Overcoming Metaphysics," in which he argued for the necessity of *Führer*[93]—no one noticed. The same could not be said of the publication the previous year of his 1935 course *Introduction to Metaphysics,* which, on page 152, celebrated "the inner truth and greatness of National Socialism."

Hartmut Buchner, who was helping Heidegger correct the proofs for the book in his writing studio in Freiburg-Zähringen, came across the original expression and warned the teacher that his intentions might be misinterpreted and might prompt comments. Heidegger protested against changing it: "I cannot do that: it would be a falsification of history. I said it that way at the time, and if the readers of today do not want to understand what that really meant within the course as a whole, I also cannot help them."[94] Despite that energetic and haughty refusal, Heidegger did modify his text, without informing his assistant. He replaced "National Socialism" with "this movement," less explicit but nonetheless clear to his contemporaries, since the NSDAP, the antiparties party, liked to call itself "the movement." In using a demonstrative adjective rather than the definite article, Heidegger simply took a slight verbal distance, which would fool no one.[95] He felt the need to spell out the philosophical meaning of his praise of Nazism, by adding a comment in parentheses. It introduced an idea from a later time, one that originated in the meditation on Nietzsche in light of Jünger. Henceforth, page 152 of the forthcoming book read: "the inner truth and greatness of this movement [namely, the encounter between global technology and modern humanity]."[96] The preface stated that the content of the original text had not been tampered with but simply made more accessible through minor corrections and clearer through the addition of parentheses.

Even modified, the text did not go unnoticed. The polemic was launched in the *Frankfurter Allgemeine Zeitung* by a twenty-four-year-old student, Jürgen Habermas, whose stated objective was to "think with Heidegger against Heidegger."[97] Celebrating *Being and Time* as "the most important philosophical event since Hegel's *Phenomenology*," Habermas wondered "how a thinker of that rank could have fallen into such an obvious primitivism, as the ungainliness of the style in this appeal for the self-assertion of the German university indisputably shows the sober-minded observer."[98] Above all, with a great deal of clarity, force, and aptness, he asked the disturbing question raised by the conditions of that publication: "The fact that these sentences were published for the first time in 1953, without commentary, gives us grounds to suppose that they express without modification the view Heidegger holds at present. It would be superfluous to cite this expression on the inner truth and greatness of National Socialism if it could not be surmised from the course as a whole. But it can. Heidegger explicitly asks the question of questions, the question of being, together with the historical movement of those times."[99] Facing a polemic he probably had not anticipated from the mountaintop of the history of Beyng, Heidegger was surprised and dismayed, even if, in response to Habermas's precocity, he could do no more than exclaim: "The author of the article in the Frankf. Allg. [. . .] is a 24-year-old student!!"[100] From then on, he deliberately stopped looking at newspapers. And spurning that question after the fact, so as to feel better in control of it, he wrote to Elfride, "Basically these things are of no consequence."[101]

Scorn does not always allow one to sweep aside definitively one's humiliations, especially when they are repeated. Habermas was not the only one troubled by that celebration of the greatness and truth of Nazism. After the *Frankfurter Allgemeine Zeitung, Die Zeit* took up the discussion launched by the brilliant young student, before formulating the problem in its own terms. If, in speaking of the " 'inner truth' (which Hitler himself is said not to have perceived)" and "greatness"[102] of National Socialism, Heidegger was not giving "his political and moral assent to the program and practice of the NSDAP," then it was up to him, "in 1935 as in 1953, to elaborate on their meaning—that is, to uncover their vulnerability as to the obsession with persecution."[103]

With the growing accusations, it became increasingly difficult for Heidegger to remain silent. He responded to the weekly a short time later, claiming that he was justified in retaining the original text as it was, in an era when it was becoming anachronistic, even scandalous: "It would have been easy to remove from the printed text the above-mentioned sentence, along with others that you quote. But I did not do so, and I will keep it in the future."[104] Pointing out that the sentence belonged historically to the course, he asserted above all that his life path after 1934 was known to all, and that his audience in 1935 perfectly understood what there was to be understood. He made the same argument in 1966, during the interview he granted to *Der Spiegel,* simply adding that, during his course, he had not read aloud the parenthetical comment, convinced as he was that, even without it, "his audience would understand correctly."[105]

This sentence from *Introduction to Metaphysics* also caused a shock outside Germany. Three years after the book's publication, Jean Wahl, who had contributed considerably to the French reception of Heidegger, offered a critical commentary that agreed with Habermas's editorial. "But there is a page 152, which is very troublesome for anyone who admires the philosopher Heidegger. [. . .] What is characteristic and somewhat worrying both for Heidegger and for Germany is that he saw fit to reprint this sentence as it was."[106] Later, this passage continued to loom like a shadow, reminding readers of Heidegger's past convictions, which were never repudiated but simply set aside because of the change of regime. In a letter to Stefan Zemach in Jerusalem on 18 March 1968, Heidegger characterized his position when he was teaching "Introduction to Metaphysics" as being "clearly opposed [*eindeutig gegnerisch*]" to Nazism, but argued that he had to avoid being understood by those who were watching him. By way of conclusion, he used the example of his course on Nietzsche between 1936 and 1940, which "each listener clearly understood as a critical and fundamental confrontation with National Socialism."[107] After the Habermas episode, Heidegger deliberately chose to distort the historical record, with, ultimately, the unexplained disappearance of the original page from the manuscript, which is nowhere to be found in his Marbach archives.[108]

Contrary to the principle Heidegger announced in 1953 in *Introduction to Metaphysics,* he was selective in what he published, making additions and especially cuts. Supposedly, his *Nietzsche,* published in 1961 and translated into French in 1971,[109] an essential work for the popularization of Heidegger's late thought, reprinted in two volumes texts running from the Nazi era until 1946, with only minor corrections: "In the text of the lectures unnecessary words and phrases have been deleted, involuted sentences simplified, obscure passages clarified, and oversights corrected."[110] In actuality, the text was rewritten, its historical references stripped out, to such a point that it is a different book. It now forms part of the *Gesamtausgabe,* along with the texts in their original version.[111] Among other things, the laudatory references to the Nazi-inflected studies of Baeumler[112] and Hildebrandt disappeared,[113] as did the consideration of the victory over France in 1940, which showed how the Germans, going to the extremes of nihilism, seemed destined for "unconditional domination of the world."[114] Similarly, the first edition of Heidegger's 1936 course on Schelling, published in 1971, omitted the brief but clear passage on Hitler and Mussolini as "countermovements" to "nihilism," a passage that was later restored.[115]

Heidegger's dissimulation occurred against the backdrop of his growing rejection of both history and historical studies. No longer believing in the promises of history, he wanted nothing to do with current affairs. He took refuge in pure thought and everydayness, in stark contrast to his notions about the Third Reich. Back then, history had a grandiose meaning, and it was imperative to take an interest in it. The biographies of philosophers were of interest if, as in the case of Dilthey, they provided an understanding of the "spiritual world" in which the individuals had been formed. The course "Germania and the Rhine" of 1934–1935 used Hölderlin's letters to shed light on the poet. Heidegger indicated his preference for the critical and chronological edition of the works and letters overseen by Norbert Hellingrath,[116] precisely because of its erudition.[117] Although the philosopher rejected pure erudition detached from a meditation on the poet, the former had to shore up the latter. Even Hölderlin he introduced in terms reminiscent of his introduction to Aristotle ten years earlier: "We are beginning immediately with a poem and are thus neglecting to mention: Hölderlin was born on March 20, 1770, in Lauffen on the Neckar as the son of [. . .] and so forth. He published something like a novel, and in addition wrote this and that. From the nineteenth century to the present, his poetic work has been assessed in such and such a way." That done, however, Heidegger marked a clear change of direction: " 'Life and work,' as they are called, and the history of their treatment are not something we wish to slight—quite to the contrary. In no other poet are the *historical Dasein* of the *poet, his* need to create, and the destiny of *his work* so intimately one as *they* are with Hölderlin. [. . .] We shall encounter the *Dasein* of the poet in his own time and in each case from his own locale, and do so directly from out of the magnificent treasure of his letters, this *Dasein* without official position, without hearth and home, without success and renown—that is, without that entire sum of misconceptions that can accrue to a name."[118] What was true in 1934–1935 remained so in 1936, in the course on Nietzsche's *Will to Power*[119] and in the one on Schelling's treatise *On the Essence of Human Freedom* (1809). Heidegger began his course on Schelling with a substantial introduction, bibliographical, biographical, and historical.[120] He spoke at length of the French occupation of Germany and began in that way to paint the backdrop for Schelling's writings, which he laid out in resolutely historical terms: "Kant's philosophy, the French Revolution, the Greeks, and the argument about pantheism, which was occasioned by Jacobi's essay on Spinoza, determined the spiritual world of Tübingen down to the daily customs."[121]

Heidegger dropped these historiographical tendencies, which were very different from the image he later left of his relationship to philology, biography, and history. After the war, he cultivated convictions likely to divert the gaze from a philosopher's engagement with history. A remark attributed to him,[122] purportedly an introduction to Aristotle, became popular: "He was born, he worked and died," a sentence that seems to have originated in the course for the summer semester of 1924: "In a philosopher's personal life only this is of interest: he was born on such and such a date, he worked, and he died."[123] After 1945, the apparent condemnation of biography was accompanied by that of historical studies, in favor of the adventure of philosophers within the advent of Being: "It is a matter of sparking the debate on the question that is the business of thought," Heidegger expounded in a posthumous outline for a preface to his complete works. "It is not a question of communicating the author's opinion or of characterizing his position or of ranking it within the series of other philosophical, historically observable positions."[124] That position was not a calculation, or could not be reduced to one. At a time when their son Hermann had already begun his thesis, a 1950 letter to Elfride harshly condemned historical studies for being unable to transmit a tradition authentically, an essential matter if philosophy is to remain alive and agrees to confront continually the essential problems:

> Tradition [or transmission, *Überlieferung*] is not made by *historiology*, [. . .] but at most is disguised & confounded by it; especially by the research & archive activity of modern scholarship. That the human sciences—the philologies too—are unable to find or offer any real tradition is one of the main shortcomings of our university education & its whole activity. [. . .] Of course tradition, even when great & simple, is nothing in itself if nothing answers to it & if it isn't brought to speak in action & thought. [. . .] If it were expressed, the whole elaborate apparatus of the professors would cave in on them & they'd be forced to think about things & not only go into what is essential, but *remain with it* all the time. They're afraid of this. And in these conditions anyone who pursues his own course is eventually worn down.[125]

Heidegger, who placed history in opposition to the problems of thought, was again confronted with the problem of the recent past, which is to say, Nazism. An admirer of the writings of Paul Celan (1920–1970), he had the opportunity to meet the Jewish poet at a public reading at the University of Freiburg in 1967. The reading was organized by the Germanist Gerhart Baumann, who informed the philosopher about it. "For a long time now I have wished to make the acquaintance of Paul Celan," responded Heidegger, who, as early as 1956 or even 1954, had sent inscribed copies of his own works to the poet's home in Paris.[126] "He has advanced very far and usually stands back. I know everything about him; I also know that he went through a grave crisis, from which he has recovered as much as a man can do."[127] It was not an easy meeting, because of the poet's tormented personality and the philosopher's history of anti-Semitic remarks. Nevertheless, Celan agreed to pay a visit to Heidegger the next day in Todtnauberg. Unfortunately, their budding friendship died in the face of the philosopher's silence. The disappointed poet, hoping perhaps that Heidegger would break, wrote these words in the visitor's book in Todtnauberg: "In the cabin book, with a glimpse at the star of the fountain, with, in the heart, the hope of a word to come."[128] Despite the silence he endeavored to adopt, Heidegger did not succeed in hushing up the affair, which even tended to intensify when some of his books began to be published, from 1959 on. Increasingly scrutinized, they often gave rise to reviews and responses in newspapers and journals. After the pioneering work of Löwith's *Thinker in Impoverished Times*,[129] a string of books came out, more or less notable. By their sheer volume and their appearance one after another, they amplified the affair: Paul Hühnerfeld's *On the Heidegger Case: Essay on Demythologization*,[130] Guido Schneeberger's collection of documents[131] (on which the American Dagobert D. Runes relied for his *German Existentialism*),[132] Theodor W. Adorno's *The Jargon of Authenticity*,[133] and Alexander Schwan's *Political Philosophy in Heidegger's Thought*.[134] Associated with the figure of Hitler, who was born the same year, the philosopher even became a character in Günther Grass's novel *Dog Years*, which portrayed him as the spiritual counterpart to the *Führer* of the Thousand-Year Reich. "Get this straight, dog: he was born in Messkirch. That's near Braunau on the Inn. He and the Other had their umbilical cords cut in the same stockingcap year. He and the Other Guy invented each other."[135] A few articles in scholarly reviews were published in France as well, written by a new generation of polemicists: Jean-Pierre Faye brought out translations of Heidegger's texts from the Nazi period, including the profession of faith in Adolf Hitler;[136] Fédier adopted the discourse—if not the robes—of a lawyer, to energetically formulate his first responses.[137] More important were the writings of Robert Minder,[138] a Germanist and professor at the Collège de France who, writing with equal fluency in German and French, had a mainstream audience on both sides of the Rhine. Jean-Michel Palmier published the first book in French on the affair.[139]

Without overlooking philosophical reflection, the polemic became multilayered, enriched by questions of translation, language, psychology, and biographical and historical facts. The writer and critic Hühnerfeld, for example, conducted a fairly broad inquiry in his book of barely 100 pages. Seeing Heidegger's rejection of biography as a way of concealing his own life, he demonstrated the philosopher's opposition to neo-Kantianism beginning in the 1920s and outlined connections to Romanticism and expressionism. He also pointed out his "barbaric provincialism," his irrationalism, and the germ of Nazism in *Being and Time*, a germ that may have been the necessary reason for Heidegger's Nazi involvement. On that score, the philosopher Ludwig Marcuse, who reviewed Hühnerfeld's book for *Die Zeit*, expressed his skepticism, pointing out that Stefan George, despite his cult of the leader, remained immune to Nazism, chose exile in 1933, and, unlike the rector of Freiburg, did not say: "The Führer himself, and he alone, is the present and future German reality and your law."[140]

Heidegger paid little attention to these books, though some were foisted on him by his friends or the German press. He could not avoid the book by the famous Frankfurt School sociologist Theodor Adorno, who, like Hühnerfeld, based his case on the irrationalism of Heidegger's philosophy: "Irrationality in the midst of the rational is the working atmosphere of authenticity,"[141] and that atmosphere, Adorno argued, predisposed one to Nazism. Heidegger, quick to detect conspiracies, made a connection with Grass's novel: "It now seems clear who is behind the nastiness of the 'Dog Years.' "[142] A few years later, when Jünger spoke to him about Grass, Heidegger had the same grievance about Minder, saying he wanted no "further knowledge" of his "agitations," which consisted of inviting Adorno to the noble institution of the Collège de France so that he could "rail against" the German philosopher there.[143]

Not all of Heidegger's friends turned a deaf ear to the revelations coming from publishing houses at the time. Despite his estrangement from his former friend, Jaspers continued to have conversations about him with Arendt, which led them to speak of Alexander Schwan's book, reviewed in *Der Spiegel* in February 1966.[144] As is common when a great deal of time has elapsed, Jaspers was rewriting history in his fashion: whereas *Der Spiegel* stated that Heidegger had stopped visiting him because of his wife's Jewishness—which is likely—Jaspers tried to convince himself of the opposite: "In fact, it was Gertrud and I who displayed increasing indifference toward him."[145] As for Arendt, she, like Heidegger regarding Grass, suspected that Adorno might be the source of that attack in one way or another, that, through his "people," he might have been "behind the scenes."[146] Another of Heidegger's friends, Erhart Kästner, urged him to respond to *Der Spiegel:* "I have no more urgent wish," Kästner wrote on 4 March, "than that you stop not defending yourself. You don't know all the sorrow you are causing your friends in stubbornly refusing to do so until now. [. . .] Slander becomes fact when one does not defend oneself against it."[147]

Heidegger himself read the *Spiegel* article and was infuriated by it. He finally agreed to write a clarification of the facts, which he sent to the weekly and a number of his friends.[148] It consisted of five points, the first two being: "It is untrue that during my rectorship (from the end of April 1933 to February 1934), I forbade Husserl, my professor, from entering the university in any form whatever. It is untrue that in 1933 relations with Husserl and Jaspers were broken off by me."[149] When he was forced to speak up, Heidegger readily adopted the genre of the list of corrections, which tended to undermine the credibility of its object while providing little foundation for a response, even when his interlocutor—Jean-Michel Palmier, for example—was well disposed toward him.

Palmier's theory about Heidegger's relationship to Nazism was very much in the spirit of the philosopher's 1953 edition of *Introduction to Metaphysics.* "The encounter of modern man and global technology, a theme in Ernst

Jünger's *Worker,* is the historical meaning that Heidegger thought he was able to recognize in the German National Socialist movement."[150] Palmier first got in touch with Jünger and ultimately succeeded in reaching Heidegger, but without inspiring any enthusiasm in him. "I have only just begun to read his book," Heidegger wrote to Jünger. "It certainly represents a great deal of work and the efforts at 'objectivity' are clear. The author, however, has a greater gift for journalism than for thinking. He has already written too much for his age. But perhaps he can learn to learn. I do not appreciate this sort of literature—whether for or against or in-between. Nevertheless, it tends to run wild, and meets a need arising from boredom."[151] A few months later, Heidegger found the time to deliver a short report to Palmier, which began with many factual corrections and ended with a historical perspective that was both vague (the different situations of universities) and inaccurate (1934 or 1938 would have been understandable, but why 1937?). It appealed for understanding and especially relativization: "It is very difficult for the present generation really to imagine after the fact the situation of the world and the state of German universities [at that time], which was very different in different places. National Socialism is judged from the point of view of the period after 1937, viewing 1933 retrospectively. It is seldom mentioned that back then, the new government in Germany was immediately recognized by other countries, and that even the invitation to come to Berlin for the 1936 Olympics was rejected by none of them."[152]

Heidegger's reluctance to expose his person and his Nazi past in the media was overcome in only one instance, for *Der Spiegel,* once again after friendly pressure from Kästner. The latter knew Rudolf Augstein, founder and director of the weekly, and suggested in late February 1966 that he interview the philosopher. Heidegger refused at first: "In no case will I lend myself to any form of organized interview with *Der Spiegel.*"[153] Augstein wrote him about it on 23 March,[154] well aware of the journalistic interest such an interview could have, if the great world-renowned philosopher and former *Führer*-rector of Freiburg deigned to play along. Heidegger's defenses gradually fell. He set his conditions, such as having his friend Petzet assist him. Finally, on 23 September, a team arrived from *Der Spiegel,* including the journalists Augstein and Georg Wolff, accompanied by a script, a technician to record the interview on tape, and the photographer Digne Meller Marcovicz,[155] who would return two years later to take photos of the Heideggers in Todtnauberg. The well-known interview they produced would appear only after Heidegger's death, a final word from beyond the grave.

The questions were polite, deferential even, including those about the philosopher's involvement with Nazism: "Professor Heidegger, it has been repeatedly noted that your philosophical work has been somewhat darkened by certain incidents in your life that did not last very long, but were never cleared up, either because you were too proud or because you considered it inadvisable to discuss them."[156] In the case of this interview in *Der Spiegel*, as with that of the complete edition of Heidegger's Nazi texts, the misrepresentations would be only temporary and partial. Heidegger was able to portray himself as he intended, as a critic of Nazism rather than a critical Nazi. He said he had believed at the time that "in the confrontation with National Socialism a new path, the only one still possible, toward a renewal might be opened up."[157] Although he disassociated himself from a vulgar Nazism, he still affirmed that, unlike democracy, which offered "no real critical analysis of the technological world"[158] and was thus unable to provide a satisfying response to the challenge of modern technology, "National Socialism did in fact go in [the right] direction." He only regretted the intellectual level of those "people,"[159] who were by no means equal to the task. Consistent with the views he held during the Third Reich, he spoke of "the special, inner relationship of the German language to that of the Greeks and their thought," then added: "Today, the French confirm this again and again. When they begin to think, they speak German: they assure me that they can't do it in their own language."[160] Heidegger understood this intellectual and linguistic self-abnegation characteristic of disciples as an awareness of the impasse in which the French found themselves, an impasse linked to the metaphysics that originated with Descartes and which the French were striving to overcome: "Because they see that with all their great rationality, they can no longer cope with today's world when it comes to understanding it in the provenance of its essence."[161] Moving closer to the Meßkirch way, Heidegger said that, in the face of global technology, "only a god can save us."[162] Thought and poetry had to prepare the way for that god's coming. And, anxious to celebrate over and over again the virtue of rootedness, he hammered in what had seemed completely obvious to him since his Catholic youth: "According to our human experience and history, at least so far as I am aware, I know that everything essential and great has its origin in the fact that man had a homeland [*Heimat*] and was rooted in a tradition."[163]

Heidegger remained radical. In "Releasement," he had explained to his fellow residents of Meßkirch that hydrogen bombs were not really dangerous unless they did *not* explode,[164] because, unexploded, they would not hasten the end of metaphysics. And he did not like liberal democracy much more than he ever had. A few months after his interview with *Der Spiegel*, he was at Boss's house in Zollikon and, though he refused to have a television at home, he watched alongside his Swiss friend an electoral debate, with both interest and contempt: "Yesterday evening we watched all that election to-do from Bonn on German television; Kiesinger extremely unpleasant; Brandt & Mende very tight-lipped & annoyed; Schröder no less so. Let's hope the SPD & FDP stick together so the conservatives don't make any headway. Strauss wangled the electoral procedure. He appeared too; nasty."[165] His usual apoliticism, his view of elections as mere "to-do" and "wangling," always went hand in hand with his irreligion, which made him look kindly on the coalition between the Social Democrats and the liberals, inasmuch as it created a united front against the Christian Democrats.

The anti-Semitism that had played a role in the sympathy Heidegger developed for Nazism and which was again forcefully expressed around 1949 had since that time been strangely quiet—if, that is, we are to believe the sources currently known, which will have to be confirmed by the forthcoming publication of the journals Heidegger kept during this period. There was one last occurrence—questionable, however, because the statement only hints at its meaning—in a letter he wrote to his wife on 4 July 1961: "Yesterday evening we heard Jaspers's latest lecture on Swiss radio; he spoke about the 'Jew Jesus,' the greatest man in Western civilization & the founder of its history.—"[166] Heidegger could not have failed to react against that focus on Jesus; without a doubt, he would have preferred Heraclitus or Parmenides. Beyond this quarrel over individuals and the vision of the history of the West, Jesus's Jewishness probably did not work in his favor. At most, Heidegger's anti-Semitism was now only an aversion to the disproportionate historical role given to the "Jew Jesus." That change can be understood in light of two factors: in 1949 Heidegger was still facing the denazification proceedings, and his son Jörg was still being detained in the Soviet Union, the land of "Judeo-Bolshevism." In 1950 he resumed his relationship, profound but intermittent, with Arendt. In 1961 the relationship faced a crisis, when Arendt sent him her book *The Human Condition*. Their affair was thus unable to silence completely his hostility to the "Jew."

Last Gleams of a Thinker (1969–1976)

Heidegger lived to old age, long enough to see a large number of his loved ones die. To survive is to see others die, not only to suffer their loss but also to see one's own death reflected in theirs. His sister, Marie, passed away in 1956,

Jaspers in 1969, Blochmann in 1972, Arendt in 1975. The visits to Todtnauberg became increasingly rare and brief. "At our age—and that of the cabin—we can no longer venture to go there for a long stay, especially because of the danger of dampness. The cabin is built right on the ground."[167] Even the house on Rötebuckweg was not suited to their old age. After designing the two homes in which they had spent the greater part of their lives, Elfride was busy "making preparations for the construction of a little one-story house" in their back yard for the "two old people" they had become. Preparing for his death as well, Heidegger no longer wrote very much, focusing on "putting his manuscripts in order"[168] and on the publication of his complete works, which were to comprise more than 100 volumes. Because of her age, Elfride gave up driving in 1968, even as senescence got the better of the "not yet wise" philosopher's misbehavior. On 10 April 1970 he had a heart attack in Augsburg, during another tryst. That indiscretion at age eighty-one was his last: beginning the next year, cared for and watched over by Elfride—for whom these were some of the best years of her life—he spent the rest of his days in their new little house at no. 25, Fillibachstraße, which looked out on a little dead-end street.[169]

The last private seminar, in 1973, took place in Zähringen rather than Le Thor, because the old teacher could no longer make such a long trip. If we are to believe Jacques Taminiaux's account of that last seminar, Heidegger was not always pleasant. He could even be very "authoritarian" and "arrogant." Was this the effect of old age, or a character trait that had remained invisible to his captivated disciples? After reading out a summary of the previous session of the seminar, the philosopher questioned Beaufret about the difference between the notion of consciousness in Husserl and Heidegger's own notion of *Dasein*. "Faced with such an outrageous question, Beaufret was hesitant: 'Finitude?' '*Nein! Nein!*' replied Heidegger sharply. 'Mortality?' whispered Beaufret. '*Nein,*' exclaimed Heidegger, adding: 'Come on, we're not in kindergarten here!' " Taminiaux then intervened, proposing as an answer: "Consciousness is essentially immanent, whereas *Dasein* is characterized by transcendence." Heidegger, finally satisfied, "looked at him as if he were a child" who had found the "right answer" and concluded with these words: "Indeed. And what is essential to transcendence is the projection toward a future!" If he really did utter these words, Heidegger was becoming a cruel master, because Beaufret's answer, though less precise, was altogether accurate: what is proper to man's existence, finite in its essence, makes him a being-toward-death, who, moving beyond the present, defines himself between past and future by accepting or rejecting the certainty of his own end to come. Nevertheless, as Taminiaux later told it, "these words fell on them like a revelation." And Heidegger himself "assumed the posture of the prophet."[170]

When one's hair has long since turned white and the body weakens, the mind knows that the end, ineluctable, is approaching, though death does not immediately announce when it will come. The arrival of old age can be seen and felt: it can also be counted. Like the golden wedding anniversary that the Heideggers celebrated in 1967, the philosopher's eightieth birthday symbolically marked the transition to this age of the greatest uncertainty. In anticipation of the momentous occasion in 1969, Elfride planned a major celebration for her husband, and Gadamer organized a large colloquium in Heidelberg for his teacher, who received expressions of friendship or veneration from all quarters.

Slightly ahead of the anniversary, Blochmann placed under the banner of both events the letter she wrote him on 23 March 1969, expressing her "twofold gratitude": "The fact that in the course of a long-term spiritual project, following directly from a youth spent studying, the young 'weather balloon specialist,' a budding philosopher in the First World War, was able to become a well-known philosopher who is one of the few wholly autonomous thinkers of our time, who has already acquired a stature in the history of the European mind, and who in addition has been capable, in his peaceful old age, of bringing his life's work to its own completion—all that is amply sufficient to incite gratitude. The philosopher Martin Heidegger can no longer fall into oblivion. But I am equally grateful, in a very personal way, that our paths crossed a half-century ago—and what a half-century!" It is common for old friends to invoke memories of their early days. Blochmann went further, declaring, albeit with modesty, her intellectual preference for the first Heidegger she had known, the one from the first half of the 1920s: "Even if your later philosophical work was to be more highly esteemed, by readers better qualified than I," she confessed, "and indeed by their author himself—you remain for me the friend who was very good at interpreting Plato in such a fascinating way, at a time when *Being and Time* and the studies on Kant were in gestation, the friend who revealed to me, in discussions during our long hikes through our beloved Black Forest, the intensity, gravity, and boldness of his thought. Those were unforgettable days! They gave me forever a model of what philosophizing could mean." And she recalled a line attributed to Heidegger at the Davos debate: "To philosophize is to be prepared to make the leap into *Dasein*." His friend Hermann Nohl had reacted to the statement in the following terms: "One doesn't completely understand, but if one thinks of the way he had of holding himself on his skis, one can only love him for having said that."[171]

That year, estranged students reestablished contact with their teacher. Löwith participated in the birthday colloquium Gadamer held in late June. And, though Löwith had become critical of Heidegger's political thought and political involvement, and had distanced himself from Heideggerian philosophy in general, he too remained grateful for the extraordinary teacher the Freiburg philosopher had been and for the friendship showed him. They had been of decisive importance for Löwith's formation as a philosopher: "On this unique occasion I should first like to express my personal thanks for being allowed to take part, although I do not belong to those students who have developed philosophically the direction which you began. If I nevertheless feel like one of your students, the reason does not lie in my positive acceptance of your inquiry into Being. It lies, rather, in the fact that you were the only teacher who permitted me to experience what a philosophical lecture can offer in forcefulness and concentration, and that during the confusion following the First World War, you gave me decisive incentives for self-reflection, made stiff demands, set standards, and opened up perspectives."[172]

Löwith was not the only one who, with the approach of old age, at a time when the thought of the Third Reich was becoming a memory, wanted to reestablish a peaceful relationship with his teacher. The same was true of Hans Jonas, who came to visit Heidegger a few weeks later, during Boss's seminar. Did Heidegger still harbor the anti-Semitic tendencies he had displayed toward Jonas twenty years earlier in a letter to Jünger? If we are to believe Heidegger himself, he did not give Jonas a warm welcome: as the philosopher wrote to his wife, he was "cautious."[173] He must have appeared less distant than he wanted to admit to her. Either that, or Jonas, eager to reconnect with his teacher, was impervious to that coolness. For, upon his return to Zurich, Jonas appeared to his friend Arendt "overjoyed by the meeting in Zurich," of which he gave "a thorough report."[174] It was an occasion for disciple and master to recall the past. Jonas, who was now sixty-six, had taken Heidegger's classes in Freiburg "in his first semester," back in 1921. He had now "completely abandoned the theolog. philos. problems & turned his attention to the fundamental questions of biology." It seemed to his teacher that he wanted "to regain a positive relation" to Heidegger's thinking. Their discussion also addressed "the situation of philosophy" and "the sudden change in attitude" in the United States toward Heidegger's thought.[175] The philosopher was probably delighted with his audience in that country, where some of his former students had had brilliant careers, and, though often critical, had helped lay the foundations for his renown. Arendt, Jonas, Herbert Marcuse, Löwith, and Strauss were pursuing an intellectual dialogue with their teacher. And they were heeded, especially since American students after the war were quite taken with European thought, both French and German. As George L. Mosse, then a professor at the University of Wisconsin in Madison, attested: "The students liked all the ideas coming from Germany. I joked with them at times that they liked anything that had a German accent."[176]

In this dithyramb competition, Arendt was the clear winner. Even though she was Jewish and had had to leave Germany because of Nazism, in the speech she wrote for her teacher's eightieth birthday she spoke of his Nazi involvement with a great deal of understanding, even complaisance, in the most flattering and frightening paean possible: "We who want to honor thinkers, even if our residence is in the middle of the world, can hardly help but find it striking and perhaps even irritating that, when they got involved in human affairs, both Plato and Heidegger resorted to tyrants and führers. This must be attributed not simply to the conditions of their respective times, and even less to innate character, but, rather, to what the French call a 'déformation professionnelle.' Theoretically, the tendency to the tyrannical can be detected in almost all great thinkers (Kant is the great exception)."[177] Heidegger was compared to Plato and was said to be one of the few great philosophers to have become involved in world affairs, thereby demonstrating the temptation tyranny represented for everyone. What Heidegger had sought, after the war, to present as the greatest stupidity of his life was for Arendt one of the sure signs of his philosophical greatness. Added to that admiration was a pure, unaltered love, which led her to dedicate her panegyric to him in these words:

For you
for September 26, 1969
after forty-five years
as ever.[178]

Eternal love sometimes comes up against its limits shortly before death. In 1975 Arendt, paying Heidegger one last visit, was shocked and very depressed by the metamorphosis that the proximity to death had worked on the man she had loved so much: "Heidegger is now suddenly really very old, very changed from last year, very deaf and remote, unapproachable as I never saw him before."[179]

In the solitude of his notebook on Heidegger, Jaspers, close to the end himself, drew up his own balance sheet of his relationship with his old friend, whom he situated not far from the Todtnauberg way, on the mountaintop of philosophy, in that landscape with its rarefied and cold air, overlooking the valleys where the lives of ordinary men played out. With regret, he noted: "It would seem there is no longer anyone up there now. Searching in vain for men who would attach importance to the eternal speculations, I thought I had come across one. He was the only one. That man was my enemy, with perfect civility, for the powers we served were irreconcilable. It soon appeared that we could no longer speak to each other. Joy turned to sorrow, a distinctly hopeless sorrow, as if we had been unable to seize an opportunity that was within reach. Such was my encounter with Heidegger."[180]

In January 1976, sensing the approach of death, Heidegger invited in one of his fellow residents of Meßkirch, Bernhard Welte,[181] a professor of theology in Freiburg. The philosopher was eager to talk about the preparations for his funeral. He wanted to be buried in the cemetery of their shared *Heimat,* following a Catholic ceremony, and he asked Welte to deliver a speech near the grave. Heidegger's death, on 26 May, was peaceful. Just the day before, he had walked in his garden. Elfride, having left him after her morning ministrations, returned to find he had fallen into eternal sleep.[182] Two days later, he was buried in Meßkirch. Someone read a word of salutation Heidegger had written in a final expression of devotion to his native region, which sought to erase the actual remoteness of the philosopher, who belonged more to the big city of Freiburg or to the ski resort of Todtnauberg than to the small farming town he wanted to see in Meßkirch. From beyond the grave, Heidegger invoked the memory of the mentor and fellow native of the town, Conrad Gröber, who had died in 1947 and had done so much for each of them. He hailed Welte, also named an honorary citizen, along with the mayor, the town council, and the entire community of Meßkirch, before giving a final assessment of the era, full of pessimism and astonishment: "May concord reign among all those who take part in it. That will in fact require reflection on the question whether and how a *Heimat* can still exist in the period of a world civilization subjected to the standardization of technology."[183]

12 • The Heidegger Affair after Heidegger

(1976–?)

The disadvantage of reading books written by people belonging to a certain party or a certain set is that they do not always contain the truth. Facts are disguised, the arguments on both sides are not brought forward in all their strength, nor are they quite accurate; and what wears out the greatest patience is that we must read a large number of harsh and scurrilous reflections, tossed to and fro by serious-minded men, who consider themselves personally insulted when any point of doctrine or any doubtful matter is controverted. Such works possess this peculiarity, that they deserve neither the prodigious success they have for a certain time, nor the profound oblivion into which they fall afterwards, when the rage and contention have ceased, and they become like almanacks out of date.

Jean de la Bruyère, The Characters, *trans. Henri van Laun, 1, 58*

The death of Heidegger the man did not do away with Heidegger the philosopher, whose thinking, continually read, discussed, and taught, remained all the more alive in that the 102 volumes of the *Gesamtausgabe,* having heretofore remained largely unpublished, have been delivered to readers so gradually that, even now, not all the volumes are available. Similarly, the Nazi destiny that pursued Heidegger after the fall of the Third Reich only tightened its grip. In 1976 he was an indisputable authority on the European continent and a major figure of contemporary thought everywhere else, his Nazism forgotten by the vast majority of readers in favor of his philosophy of human existence and the concealment of being in the era of global technology. By degrees, however, he came to personify the Nazi philosopher par excellence, the very figure of the thinker led astray, straight into the inhuman horror of the twentieth century. By no means did his death quell the Heidegger affair, the principal impetus of his posthumous destiny.

The scandal with its many twists and turns, composed of accusations against the Freiburg philosopher and the reverberations, repetitions, or replies to which they gave rise in the media—scholarly reviews, newspapers, radio, television, even blogs—actually reached its height after the master's death, first with the publication of Victor Farías's book in 1987 and, to a lesser extent, of Ott's biography the next year;[1] then with Emmanuel Faye's book in 2005;[2] and finally, in 2014, with the beginning of the publication of the black notebooks, philosophical journals the philosopher had kept from 1930 on. The scandal tended to spread out from the principal countries that took an interest in Heidegger: Germany and France first and foremost, then Italy and the United States.[3] Ideas and texts circulated in their national and linguistic space, while often extending beyond it at particularly fraught moments, as the example of Farías clearly demonstrates. A Chilean academic, Farías was a former student of Heidegger's living in Germany; his book, though written in Spanish and German, was originally published in French translation.[4] It had not, it seems, managed to find a publisher in his adoptive country,[5] until its colossal success in France led to wide global distribution. The German translation even had a preface written by Habermas.[6]

Like Farías, Heidegger's critics were often former Heideggerians who had turned against him: after Marcuse and Löwith, they included Günther Anders, Jean-Pierre Faye, Karl Ulmer, Otto Pöggeler, and Alain Renaut, among so many others. Lines of descent played a major role: consider the biological and intellectual relationship between Jean-Pierre Faye and his son Emmanuel.[7] They shared the conviction that Heideggerian thought was dangerous insofar as, being essentially Nazi, it was not recognized as such. Among Heidegger's defenders, intellectual relationships played a crucial role: in France, for example, generations of Heideggerians educated in the *khâgne* classes[8] followed one after another, descended from the disciple of disciples, Jean Beaufret. At the Lycée Condorcet, Beaufret begat Vezin and Fédier; Fédier, a teacher at the Lycée Pasteur de Neuilly, had France-Lanord as a student; and France-Lanord now teaches at the Lycée Jeanne d'Arc in Rouen. The role of this preparatory class in the arts in transmitting Heideggerian devotion cannot be overestimated. Whether or not to join in: that is one of the things at stake in these years, when students, often malleable because young and anxious to conform to the model of the competitive entrance exams for the *écoles normales supéri-*

eures, find themselves for many hours in the company of a single teacher per subject. Such teachers, who are not ordinarily researchers, nor, in many cases, do they hold doctorates, are more or less cut off from academic research and its critical demands, but they may have the sense that they are dispensing a revealed truth because, precisely, they are the teachers and their students drink up their words, provided the teacher in question has the necessary charisma.

As a long-term global phenomenon, the Heidegger affair after Heidegger's death, a vast and complex subject, would deserve a book all its own.[9] Let us make do with an abbreviated version.

A Media "Bombshell," a "Definitive Study," and Continued Denial

Essentially a narrative in three parts—before, during, and after the rectorship—Farías's *Heidegger and Nazism* was easy to read, supposing it is possible to write a book on Heidegger that is so. And, apart from some personal research (concerning, in particular, the plan for the Prussian Academy of Professors), the book relied on the texts published by Schneeberger[10] and on Ott's research, which first became known through academic articles, usually published in scholarly reviews with a limited circulation.[11] According to Farías's thesis, Heidegger had become rector because of his Nazi sympathies, which reflected the convictions of a lifetime. Given that the oldest text published in the *Gesamtausgabe*, as well as the last to be published while Heidegger was alive, both had to do with Abraham a Sancta Clara, Farías assimilated the philosopher's ideas to the preacher's nationalism, anti-Semitism, and conservatism. The Chilean academic, seeing Heidegger's political engagement as a desire to become the official philosopher of the regime, reassessed Heidegger's post-1945 discourse about why he had taken his distance from it. His decision, according to Farías, was attributable to the elimination of Röhm and the SA and, with it, of student Nazism, following the Night of the Long Knives on 30 June 1934. The sentence at the end of the introductory course on metaphysics, on "the inner truth and greatness" of National Socialism, is said to have referred to Röhm and the SA, whom Farías understood to be Heidegger's allies against Krieck and Rosenberg, henceforth the regime's leading intellectuals.

Farías's book became widely known through the mainstream press, where it received an enthusiastic reception—from Roger-Pol Droit, for example, who bestowed effulgent praise in his review for *Le Monde*:

> It has been claimed that Heidegger had only an accidental, temporary, and entirely external relationship to Nazism. Driven solely by the desire to regenerate the German university, he believed, fleetingly, that a national revolution under way could make that rebirth possible. [. . .] During these twelve months of purely "administrative" cooperation with a recently vested power, Heidegger confined himself to delivering a few speeches, which, though certainly unfortunate, were simply tailored to the circumstances. After his resignation, over the course of some ten years of political silence, he lived under the surveillance of the authorities, facing censorship of his publications and harassment by a power that held him in greater and greater disgrace. [. . .] That version is no longer tenable for anyone who has read Victor Farías's meticulous investigation. For several years, this forty-seven-year-old Chilean academic, who was Heidegger's student, delved into all the accessible archives, combed through the press of the Reich, scrutinized the magazines of the Nazi Party and affiliated organizations, examined the internal reports of the university and ministries, and collected statements. His conclusion is simple, perhaps too simple: Heidegger was, in every fiber of his being—in his acts, his texts, his thinking—an eminent and resolute member of the Nazi Party, whose fundamental convictions he never abandoned. Relentlessly documented, the book is a bombshell.[12]

The response to Farías's book was enormous, in both the support it received and the rejection it met with. Even before further translations came out, the scandal rapidly reached other countries, including Italy. It was bitterly disputed there, soon after the article in *La Repubblica* of 18/19 October 1987: "New Accusations against Heidegger: 'He Was a Nazi.' "[13] In the later part of that year, no fewer than twenty-five articles appeared in ten different organs of the press, throughout the entire peninsula. Gianni Vattimo vigorously defended Heidegger in *La stampa*.[14] Germany did not stay out of the fray, and the reactions there were less favorable. Granted, Rainer Marten, a philosophy professor at the University of Freiburg, found Farías "altogether correct when he discovers Heidegger's 'racist conception,' " which "pays homage to a 'true fascism.' " Not surprisingly, however, Hermann Heidegger averred that it was all nothing but "lies and slander." Hartmut Tietjen, one of the editors of the *Gesamtausgabe*, expressed the belief that Farías's book was "philosophically ignorant, incomplete, and documentarily deficient."[15] Jürgen Busche waxed ironic: "All right then, Heidegger was a Nazi."[16] In the important volume edited by Günter Neske that appeared in response the next year, Gadamer was intent on thwarting what he saw as the book's superficiality and ignorance. To do so, he gave his own view of Heidegger's involvement:

> In any case: no surprise should be expected from those of us who, for fifty years, have reflected on [that] [. . .] when we hear that in 1933—and for years previously, and for how long after?—he "believed" in Hitler. But Heidegger was also no mere opportunist. If we wish to dignify his political engagement by calling it a "standpoint," it would be far better to call it a political "illusion," which had notably little to do with political reality. [. . .] In 1933 and 1934, he thought he was following his dream, and fulfilling his deepest philosophical mission, when he tried to revolutionize the university from the ground up. It was for that that he did everything that horrified us at that time. For him the sole issue was to break the political influence of the Church and the tenacity of academic bossdom. Even Ernst Jünger's vision of "the worker" [*der Arbeiter*] was given a place beside his own ideas about overcoming the metaphysical tradition via the reawakening of Being. Later, as is known, Heidegger wandered all the way to his radical talk of the end of philosophy. That was his "revolution."[17]

In France, contempt sometimes combined with laziness. Because the reports or accusations of Heidegger's Nazism went back a long time, they seemed so stale that inquiries about the debate no longer seemed necessary. Everything had already been said, everything was known—at least, that is what some wanted to believe. For example, Jacques Derrida, refusing to comment on Farías's book, declared to the *Nouvel Observateur* that he had "found nothing in this investigation that has not been known for a long time."[18] Lacoue-Labarthe, who for his part made the effort to read it, claimed: "This book is profoundly inaccurate and I even find it—I am weighing my words—dishonest."[19] He gave three major reasons. First, Farías indiscriminately understood everything Heidegger did after 1933 as the actions of a militant, with no sense of nuance or spirit of inquiry, even as the sources that might provide a defense were played down. Second, in the guise of history, Farías's method of reading the texts consisted of conflation, and his commentary on the connection between the young Heidegger and Abraham a Sancta Clara was based less on the future philosopher's rather brief text than on a long discussion of the seventeenth-century preacher himself and of anti-Semitism in southern Germany and Austria, including that of Karl Lueger, mayor of Vienna. Without textual evidence, merely by juxtaposition, the precept of guilt by association was applied, to make Heidegger "responsible for what he did not say." Third, Farías was weak in philosophy, passing over in silence the critique of Nazi biologism that Heidegger pursued in the courses on Nietzsche.

The circle of orthodox Heideggerians also struck back forcefully, under the leadership of Fédier, in the January 1988 issue of *Le Débat*.[20] Their point of view was classic, a combination of the Towarnicki version and the Weil/De Waelhens option: Heidegger's involvement was confined to 1933–1934, part of a general movement by millions of Germans; and, not being "philosophical," it left unscathed his works from both before and after the rectorship. It was an unfortunate but philosophically insignificant episode. One voice spoke out against that view, but it did not carry beyond the Rhine: Gadamer, the master's favorite disciple, criticized the ease with which some French had long separated philosophy from politics. "It has been claimed, out of admiration for the great thinker, that his political errors have nothing to do with his philosophy. If only we could be content with that! Wholly unnoticed was how damaging such a 'defense' of so important a thinker really is."[21] In a case of historical irony, Gérard Guest invoked Ott's authority against Farías (as did Fédier, in his *Heidegger: Anatomy of a Scandal*,[22] then on the talk show *Apostrophes*, and even later in his edition of Heidegger's political writings)[23] and, in a later issue,[24] translated Ott's review. Never mind that Ott was convinced of Heidegger's deep-seated Nazism and had inspired Farías: the latter had to be discredited.

Ott had also become Farías's chief critic at the *Neue Zürcher Zeitung*, basing himself on the French edition[25] (and, two years later, the German edition).[26] With a touch of bitterness, he made fun of the French philosophers, who seemed to be discovering for the first time the Nazism of their thinker of choice:

> In France, a sky has fallen—*le ciel des philosophes* [in French in the text]. In the absolutely dazzling mise en scène assured him by the *nouvelle philosophie*, the book on Heidegger by the Chilean Victor Farias, with a preface by Christian Jambet, recently arrived on the market, shaking the French intellectual world. There is talk of a national scandal. Clocks run differently in France than elsewhere. We know that. There is thus nothing surprising about the delay with which results of research long known (and in great detail) in the German-speaking world have only now come to the attention of the French public, with the consequence, it is true, that the orderly world of the dominant philosophical schools has now been turned upside down.[27]

The French intellectual world was in fact in an uproar. Farías's book was featured on television programs, a sign of its colossal impact. First there was *Océaniques* on the French channel FR3. Two episodes, on 7 and 14 December 1987, served as a bridge between the broadcast of a 1975 German film by Walter Rudel called *Heidegger: Speech and Silence* and a debate assembling a prestigious panel of participants around Michel Cazenave: George Steiner, Jean-Pierre Faye, Fédier, and André Glucksmann. Then came *Apostrophes* on Antenne 2, on 20 May 1988. In the last half-hour of a program titled "Must We Condemn Them?" Luc Ferry and Alain Renaut, the authors of *Heidegger and the Moderns*,[28] debated Fédier, who had just issued a book in response to Farías: *Heidegger: Anatomy of a Scandal*.[29] The Chilean was subjected to harsh criticism. Fédier characterized his book as "rubbish" and claimed that "its author is out of his mind." Ferry and Renaut did not hold the book in much higher esteem, but they believed the scandal it had caused raised a real question, namely, the place in France of Heideggerianism as a substitute ideology for Stalinist Marxism, a way of pursuing a critique of the modern world and modern democracy.

Indeed, Heideggerianism, buoyed by Sartre's Marxism and the lineage of disciples originating with Beaufret, was in fact becoming an alternative to Stalinism and Maoism, which had previously captivated French intellectuals. In France, Heidegger remained one of the major influences of the philosophical avant-garde: Derrida, Michel Foucault, Paul Ricoeur, then Alain Badiou, Glucksmann, Philippe Lacoue-Labarthe, Jean-Luc Nancy, and perhaps, to a lesser extent, Alain Finkielkraut. Ferry and Renaut, however, did not take into account the importance that the Catholic reception of Heidegger may have had (though its voice was heard less in the media). After the war, at a time when the Church was seeking paths to modernization—which led to the Second Vatican Council (1962–1965)—Heidegger's modern ontological thought had seemed a felicitous choice to replace neo-Thomism in seminary classes on philosophy. This approach was favored by many of Heidegger's Catholic students, including the theologian Karl Rahner, who had taken the philosopher's courses in Freiburg in the 1930s. As a result, the baby boom generation to which both Ferry (b. 1951) and Renaut (b. 1948) belonged also included the Catholic Heideggerians Philippe Capelle (b. 1954)[30] and, especially, Jean-Luc Marion (b. 1946), a prolific author from 1970 on.[31] They arrived after the pioneers:[32] Henri Birault; Roger Munier, who had belonged to the Society of Jesus;[33] the *académicien* Jean Guitton;[34] and the Christian existentialist Gabriel Marcel. Heidegger's legacy is even more significant when his immediate students are taken into account: Arendt, Gadamer, Jonas, Strauss, Emmanuel Levinas. A great deal was at stake intellectually in the efforts to keep Heidegger shielded from condemnation for Nazi convictions, all the more so because the philosopher of Todtnauberg had found a place in the minds of the educated general public. Also in 1988, the cartoonist Claire Bretécher chose to illustrate the cover of the first volume of her *Agrippine* with a depiction of her protagonist sitting on her bed in ripped jeans, headphones in her ears and a sullen look on her face, reading a copy of an improbable *Heidegger in the Congo*.[35]

The criticisms Farías's book received were in some cases deserved. He was not inspired by the greatest rigor. His footnotes made it impossible to check the sources to which they supposedly referred. His translations of Heidegger were questionable.[36] The book contained factual errors and mistakes in personal names,[37] and it sometimes truncated quotations. A second edition came out in 1989, partly correcting these problems.[38] Even more than these flaws in scholarship, the very material in the book was dubious. One of its central ideas, the connection between Abraham a Sancta Clara and Heidegger, was in fact based on a conflation. Granted, the preacher was anti-Semitic. But what proof was there that, from his earliest text, the future philosopher was receptive to that aspect of his predecessor's character? What proof, likewise, that he had a pronounced sympathy for the SA and Ernst Röhm, apart from what Heidegger said about them in 1945 to lead people to believe in his break with the regime at that time? In his review of the book in the *Neue Zürcher Zeitung*, Ott showed that the book's so-called method very often consisted of mental associations, which led to many serious misinterpretations: "It appeared, at the end of my own research, that Rector Heidegger actually found himself in conflict with the SA students toward the end of his rectorship. It is thus a construction pure and simple when Farías presents the day of 30 June 1934 (the Röhm putsch) as Heidegger's major political turning point, as if Heidegger's revolutionary thinking ended with the defeat of the SA."[39]

The reception of Farías's book gradually changed, becoming less enthusiastic. Droit, the same critic who had spoken of "Victor Farías's meticulous investigation" and had called the book "relentlessly documented" and a "bombshell,"[40] became much less laudatory. He now pointed out the problem in the reception of Heidegger's Nazism: "In France over the last twenty years, Heidegger ultimately took the place of Marx as a sort of new 'insuperable horizon.' That may be why Victor Farías's book, despite its philosophical flimsiness and its overreductiveness, has been so upsetting. For, in spite of its flaws, it necessarily leads to the only fundamental question that is worth the trouble of dwelling on: how are we to understand the connection between Heidegger's thought and his embrace of Nazism?" Not satisfied with the irenic reception that reduced that connection to nothing, Droit now rejected Farías as well: "The other way of getting around the problem consists of seeing that connection everywhere, of portraying Heidegger as a caricature, a Nazi through and through—already [. . .] in 1910, still [. . .] in 1964—whatever he may do, think, and say. That is the exaggerated and overly facile character of Farías's conclusion."[41] The polemic, then, took a completely different turn; the Chilean, at first effusively praised, was later banished.

The blast of his intellectual "bombshell" continued to make the Heideggerian fortress tremble, its force all the stronger in that the book was readable and spoke more to the imagination than a dry conceptual discussion would have done. Although Farías's book lost some credibility, the position of the orthodox Heideggerians was by no means completely reinstated. On 20 May 1988 Bernard Pivot, at the end of *Apostrophes*, could not help but find—without scorn but rather with compassion—that Fédier's person and his book were pitiable, because they struggled so hard, and in vain, against something that had become glaringly obvious: "I find there is something pitiable both in your book and in your person, because, when it comes right down to it, you are trying to save Heidegger from dishonor through this book, even though there are many things that damn him all the same—and it's very clear why; it's because you yourself have all the same devoted part of your work, your toil, to Heidegger. There is something terrible about seeing that the man you so admire, this philosopher of genius, is all of a sudden someone who is, well, in many respects despicable."[42]

In lifting the veil on Heidegger's past in such a troubling manner, Farías's book conferred on the scandal a popularity and intensity it had been lacking, and which it never completely lost subsequently. One sign among others of that French tumult: the program *Océaniques* devoted to it, available for viewing at the Bibliothèque Publique d'Information in Beaubourg (along with the other episodes of *Océaniques* and *Thalassa*), was at the time the video most often consulted. In a month and a half of the installation's operation, there were 200 requests for it, out of a total of 3,133 viewings.[43] A flood of books intended for an audience beyond the narrow circle of Heidegger's readership hit French bookstores: reissues of notable books, such as those by Pierre Bourdieu[44] and Adorno;[45] French translations of sources like Löwith's memoir;[46] and, finally, new essays by Ferry and Renaut,[47] Janicaud,[48] Lacoue-Labarthe,[49] Jean-François Lyotard,[50] Henri Meschonnic,[51] and Habermas.[52]

The English-speaking world remained more in the position of an observer. There, the storm occasioned in France by Farías's book was of little more consequence than a light summer breeze. The newspapers remained nearly silent. The work had been published in French, and its English version had not yet come out, which severely limited the interest of journalists, especially since Heidegger did not have the same importance in that area of the world as he had in France or even Germany. It was a matter for specialists, such as Thomas Sheehan, who reviewed the book and the Heidegger case more generally in a landmark article, published in the *New York Review of Books* in June 1988. In a brief historical overview, Sheehan, a professor at Loyola University in Chicago,[53] pointed out that Farías's book, "written in Spanish," had been rejected by a German publishing house and was "finally published in French translation" in October 1987, when it proved to be "explosive": "Over the last six months virtually every French philosopher of note has taken a very passionate stand, one way or the other, on l'affaire Heidegger."[54] Combining criticism and praise, he maintained that, "although his historical method and political analysis come under sharp fire from critics (particularly his association of Heidegger with the SA leader Ernst Roehm), it would be wrong to say that one cannot learn from this book. Farías has assembled much if not all of the available data on Heidegger's relation to the Nazi regime between 1933 and 1945."[55] Some documents, drawn from the East German archives or the West Berlin Documentation Center, were even "of enormous value."[56] The rest of the article, taking the long view, relied on Ott's studies and on a vast bibliography to draw a picture of Heidegger's activities during the Third Reich, which seemed to the author both "deeply disturbing and frequently disgusting"—from his crucial role in the nazification of the University of Freiburg's bylaws to his silence about the Holocaust. "For the hundreds of pages that he published on the dehumanizing powers of modern civilization, for all the ink he spilled decrying the triumph of a spiritless technology, Heidegger never saw fit, as far as I know, to publish a single word on the death camps."[57] In his conclusion, Sheehan called for "revisiting Heidegger's involvement with Nazism," not primarily "to pass judgment on the past" or to "attack the man because one cannot attack his work," but rather to sift through his thought in order to determine "what might still be of value, and what not."[58] "We now know how greatly he 'erred.' The question remains how greatly he thought," which meant it was necessary to "start demythologizing him."[59]

A few months later, England, largely unreceptive to "Continental" philosophy—to which Heidegger belongs—proved to be not altogether unresponsive to the storm unleashed by Farías across the Channel. In early October 1988, Michael Zimmerman, relying not only on Farías but also on Pöggeler, Lacoue-Labarthe, Bourdieu, and Lyotard, wrote a few pages devoted to Heidegger in the *Times Literary Supplement*. Having restated the generally accepted discourse on Heidegger's Nazism, Zimmerman ended by pointing out the relevance Heidegger's questioning could have for our own modernity: "Heidegger's own question remains valid: how are we to assess the technological mobilization of humanity and the earth at the end of the twentieth century?"[60]

In their books, scholars in the Anglo-American tradition rushed to reflect on the connections between Heidegger's political engagement and his thought,[61] or even to give an overall picture of his body of work. Tom Rockmore followed the affair closely, including its French version.[62] In his wake, Richard Wolin published a monograph,[63] then edited a collection of studies.[64] These two authors, after Löwith, developed the thesis of the continuity between the political philosophy of *Being and Time* and Heidegger's engagement with Nazism. General-interest books also came out.[65] As in France, the philosophical interest of Heidegger's texts caused some to try to "denazify" the philosopher. This was attempted several years later, with subtlety but a certain naïve optimism, by Julian Young, a professor from Auckland, New Zealand, who was published in England.[66] He set out to show that, though Heidegger's involvement in Nazism was not superficial, his philosophy was fully compatible with liberal democracy.

Farías's book came out in English in 1991.[67] The few resulting newspaper columns emphasized how much it changed the image one might have of Heidegger. According to Thelma Z. Lavine in the *Washington Post*, "the significant achievement of Farias's Heidegger and Nazism is that it establishes beyond doubt Heidegger's commitment to Nazism and his involvement in the activities of the Nazi regime."[68] Allen Lacy noted in the *New York Times*: "Although Martin Heidegger's philosophical writings have their partisans in the United States, his influence here has been much less weighty than it has been on the Continent. Mr. Farias's book accordingly is of less moment here. It does provide, however, fascinating material for a case study of a philosopher who would seem to have cooperated eagerly with the false promises of tyranny."[69]

The scandal set off by Farías gave rise to an increase in historical research in Europe. As *Le Monde* reported,[70] the Germanist Jacques Le Rider went to the archives at the Ministry of Foreign Affairs in Paris to check the Heidegger dossier,[71] which confirmed that the philosopher was not perceived as an opponent of the regime. And, in the record established by the Freiburg branch of the NSDAP in 1938, the "overall assessment" of Heidegger simply stipulated: "Great capabilities as a scholar, fierce adversary of Catholicism. As for the rest, scholar cut off from the world." In the matter of whether he was "politically reliable or politically suspect," the dossier indicated: "reliable."

A few historians of varied sensibilities published their studies: Ernst Nolte,[72] Domenico Losurdo,[73] and especially Ott, who, spurred by the publishing situation, finally assembled his research into a biography, which appeared in Germany in 1988, meeting with an enviable international reception. Translated into French and Italian in 1990,[74] it was afforded a second German edition in 1992, then translations into English,[75] Spanish,[76] and Polish,[77] as well as a Japanese adaptation.[78] The two German editions received forty-five reviews, thirty-two of them in the German-speaking world, three in the United Kingdom, two in the United States, two in France and Spain, and one each in Sweden, Italy, the Netherlands, and Hungary. The most reviewed translations were the French edition, with nineteen reviews in Francophone Europe, and the English-language edition, with sixteen, primarily in the British Isles. Curiously, the Italian edition was reviewed only three times. Is that a miscount, or was the problem poor promotion on the part of the publisher?[79]

Ott had encountered the question of Heidegger's Nazism for the first time while writing a chapter on the history of Baden under the Nazi regime.[80] The 1983 publication of the rector's address and of Heidegger's postwar discourse of self-justification elicited Ott's keen interest, and he therefore set out in the following years to deconstruct that dishonest defense, conducting a thorough investigation. His first results, though published for the most part in scholarly reviews, did not remain completely unknown, even outside Germany. In 1984 an article in *L'Espresso* reviewed them, under the headline "Heil Heidegger!"[81] In the United States in June 1988, Sheehan claimed that Ott's book, which would come out in Germany that September, would be "the definitive study of the topic."[82] The work by the Freiburg historian marked a major milestone in the Heidegger affair, less by the scandal it may have sparked than as the inescapable biographical frame of reference for the philosopher's relationship to Catholicism and then to Nazism. Like so many others published after 1988, the present book owes a great deal to it.

There were a few minor reverberations when the German edition came out in France: a book review by Nicolas Tertulian;[83] and a few dozen lines in *Le Monde* before its publication, in one paragraph of a long article,[84] as a counterpoint to the scandal caused by Farías's book. The following year, the Romanist Joseph Jurt published two articles focusing on his colleague from the University of Freiburg. The first was a scholarly book review,[85] the second a solid popular article that placed Ott's work within a historical Freiburg school, to which the historian had given the impetus, taking Bernd Martin (and now Bernd Grün) along with him:[86]

> Hugo Ott and Bernd Martin, historians at the University of Freiburg, have devoted themselves for some time to thorough research on the author of *Sein und Zeit*. After the 1983 publication of the report written by Heidegger in 1945 (*The Rectorship from 1933 to 1934: Facts and Reflections*), Ott has examined the validity of the philosopher's theses in a richly documented book. He had access to unpublished documents held in the archives of Baden-Württemberg, to the very extensive correspondence between Jaspers and Heidegger, to unpublished letters from Husserl, and to the diary of Joseph Sauer, Heidegger's predecessor in the Freiburg rectorship. In the face of these documents, many of the philosopher's assertions regarding his attitude toward the Third Reich no longer hold up.[87]

When the French translation was published, its reception was balanced but flattering, beginning with Jean-Michel Palmier's long afterword to the book, which ended as follows:

> In portraying the major phases of his life and of his relationship to history, [Ott] also takes no position on [Heidegger's] philosophy and on what about it may have determined his political engagement. There is a historian's modesty that we must know how to praise. What [Ott] brings us is not a further synthesis of "Heidegger and National Socialism" but a rigorous study of his political engagement. Written without hatred and without indulgence, this book strives to achieve objectivity, even though passion and personal investment are not absent from it. It constitutes a decisive contribution to the questions raised by Heidegger's relationship to history, though it is impossible to respond to them solely through historical analysis, as Jürgen Habermas has pointed out. Assuredly, this study by Hugo Ott is the first to reconstitute the facts for us on such a grand scale, and no one can now ignore them.[88]

The high academic quality of a book often receives the honors it deserves in scholarly reviews more than in newspapers. Hence it was in *Vingtième siècle* that Michel Trebitsch bestowed laurels on his German colleague, rewarding the "unassailable monument of erudition"[89] resulting from "research on an impressive volume of public and especially private archives (correspondence)."[90] And, even though Ott had produced "terrible documents" on the rectorship, his judgment remained "measured."[91] Without limiting himself to the time period that had been raked over so often but was still poorly known, the critic rightly recognized that "the newest part of this book certainly has to do with the intellectual youth of this student from a modest background."[92] The newspapers, by contrast, did not pay attention to this major work in a manner commensurate with its importance; they were much less interested in it than in Farías's more sensational book. Nevertheless, *Le Monde*, in a review by Thomas Ferenczi, was laudatory: "The study by the historian Hugo Ott, published in Germany in 1988, offers a great deal of new information that confirms Farías's version and contradicts the one Heidegger's friends have imposed since 1945. Rigorous and well documented, it sheds new light on the conditions under which Heidegger acceded to the position of rector, the way he exercised it, and the reasons he left it."[93] "The German historian Hugo Ott confirms that, from 1933 to 1945, the philosopher remained loyal to Hitler's regime."[94] A certain caution seemed to have temporarily prevailed, after the excessive enthusiasm about Farías's book: neutral though positive, this review showed that, after a great deal of agitation in the media for three years, the Heidegger affair was running out of steam. And, though critical, the book itself, with its seriousness, level-headedness, and altogether academic erudition, did not incite either bitter polemics or the panegyrics of disciples.

The very soundness of Ott's biography made it dangerous. In the extremely long preface to the French translation of Heidegger's political writings (*Écrits politiques*) that Fédier published in 1995, he noted the less laudatory reception *Heidegger and Nazism* was receiving at the time, saying that "no reader acquainted with real history has taken Farías's book seriously."[95] But Fédier was forced to acknowledge that Ott's book was a different species, more difficult to discredit: "Another book, Hugo Ott's *Martin Heidegger. Unterwegs zu seiner Biographie*, has met with a totally different reception since its publication in late 1988."[96] Vague insinuations can usefully cast some doubt, however, leading readers to receive a book unfavorably, in order, ultimately, to make them believe an interpretation of the facts much more consistent with a disciple's wishes:

> I do not have the time to explain how it proceeds, the prejudices on which it is built, or above all the *image* of Heidegger it conveys. Hence I will say only this about it: any attentive reader sufficiently familiar with

> Heidegger's thought is perfectly capable, in the face of every one of Hugo Ott's interpretations, and on the basis of the same documents, of responding with a different if not completely opposite interpretation of his own. This already has the virtue of being true to one of the most indispensable legal principles: *in dubio pro reo* (if there is any doubt in the interpretation of Heidegger's rectorship, let that doubt work in his favor) and not, as is the case for inquisition trials, *in dubio contra rem* (everything that is not immediately comprehensible must contribute toward sullying the figure of the accused).[97]

Fédier, understanding history as a court of law, once again deployed the rhetoric of a lawyer. It was not useful to think like a historian, in terms of degrees of truth, from possibility to probability to certainty. A judge issues a verdict—conviction or acquittal—and, in a state under the rule of law, one can obtain an acquittal by giving the accused the benefit of the doubt. Against the inquisitorial will of prosecutors with evil intentions, or ignorant of Heidegger's philosophy, Fédier invoked doubt in favor of the defense.

In response to the success of Ott's biography, Hermann Heidegger belatedly made up his mind to critique it in *Études heideggeriennes*.[98] The philosopher's son, who holds a doctorate in history, does not have the prejudice against or disdain for that discipline shared by a number of his father's followers. Laying claim to his own formation as a historian,[99] he did detailed critiques directed at the man he called "a historian of economics," in partial reference to the designation of the chair Ott occupied,[100] thus engaging in an ad hominem attack whose aim was to better discredit his adversary on a matter of political, religious, and cultural history. "When they were written up, the results of his research were unfortunately treated with a casualness unbefitting a scholar. That, and narrow-mindedness, led him at times to prejudices, faulty judgments, suspicions, inaccuracies, and unfair expositions."[101] This often dubious content was accompanied by a deficient form, at least from the standpoint of linguistic purism. Hermann Heidegger had inherited his mother's *völkisch* sensibility: "In his text, foreign words often appear for which there are good German words."[102] Noting that the book had already been published in six languages, he wished to counter that international success with 163 marginal annotations: "7 pirated editions" of unpublished texts reproduced without his consent; "64 objective mistakes or unauthorized reprints, including unindicated omissions from quotations; 21 missing source citations; 49 *assertions that are not true;* 22 important facts that were not unknown have been suppressed by Ott, while many speculations are written down without proof."[103] Hermann Heidegger's successive readings led him to conclude that a total of 243 passages from the first edition were false, ill-founded, or illegitimate. And, alongside displays of temper in the face of certain sources published without his agreement, he made remarks that, though nitpicking, were not in some cases without pertinence or interest. For example, he corrected the date on which Martin Heidegger joined the NSDAP from 1 May to 3 May, based on the letter to Fritz of 4 May (which he subsequently published in GA 16), a day earlier than the *Breisgauer Zeitung* indicated.[104] In addition to these many remarks, Hermann Heidegger's wrath found expression in his refusal to allow Ott access to the philosopher's unpublished writings, a prohibition H. Heidegger had formulated the previous year as director of the Deutsches Literaturarchiv in Marbach. Those who fear scholarship or science attempt to silence it, or, failing that, to dry up its source.

The years that followed the Farías/Ott episode were in appearance calmer, because less spectacular, but they were also essential. Gradually, the newly issued or reissued Heidegger texts changed the philosopher's image. Consider the now-infamous letter of 2 October 1929 to Viktor Schwoerer: published by Ulrich Sieg in *Die Zeit* in 1989, it revealed for the first time evidence of Heidegger's anti-Semitism in the evocation of "the growing jewification in the broad and the strict sense" that threatened "our *German spiritual life.*"[105] The publication of these texts actually continued a movement dating back to the 1970s, which accelerated at the time, gradually undermining the walls built around the philosopher to conceal his past.

The strategy of concealment had been at work in the publication of the texts themselves, which gave rise to a series of scandals. Although of secondary importance, they cast doubt, by dint of repetition, on the *Gesamtausgabe* as a whole. The public had already learned of particular statements about the Third Reich that had been omitted from one major text or another. In *Der Spiegel* in 1977, for example, it was revealed that the publication of the 1936 course on Schelling[106] was missing the mention of Hitler's and Mussolini's policies as "countermovements" against nihilism.[107] Later, the differences between the book assembled in 1961 based on the courses on Nietzsche, which was devoid of any reference to the regime, and the courses as they were later published in their original version became apparent. The conditions governing the production of that complete (or supposedly complete) edition itself caused a scandal in the 1990s, but without extending beyond the academic sphere.[108]

Editions of previously unpublished or forgotten texts would prove to be of even greater consequence. Already in 1983, Hermann Heidegger had reissued the rector's address, previously almost inaccessible, accompanied by his father's self-justificatory text on the rectorship.[109] Martin Heidegger's complete works continued to bring their share of revelations. In 2000, volume 16 reprinted most of the occasional texts from the Nazi period, and in 2005 the letters to Elfride were published. This correspondence included the 1916 comment about "the jewification [*Verjudung*] of our culture & universities."[110]

Heidegger had prepared the way for the concealment, and his son Hermann pursued it. But he could not continue to do so unobstructed, once his niece decided to publish the letters, which Elfride herself had entrusted to her. Half-compelled and half voluntarily, Hermann Heidegger wrote an afterword on 3 July, revealing that his father by law, by spirit, and by love was not his father by blood: "At the age of just 14 I was told by my mother that my natural father was a friend from her youth, my godfather Dr. Friedel Caesar, who died in 1946. My mother made me promise at the time to mention this to *nobody* except my future wife, as long as she herself was alive. I have kept this promise. Now I am grateful to my niece for allowing me to make this declaration, in so doing freeing myself from a burden that has weighed upon and tormented me for 71 years and confessing the historical truth."[111] Likewise, after long maintaining the fiction of a philosopher totally ignorant of Nazism before the installation of the Third Reich, he acknowledged that his father had voted for the NSDAP in the elections of 6 November 1932 (in the elections of 31 July Martin Heidegger is said to have voted for the small wine grower's party of Württemberg).[112]

At first sight difficult to dispute, these works often prompted violent counterattacks, the question of interpretation being so hard to separate from the publication of the texts. Before publishing his own book on the subject,[113] Arno Münster made his views known in *Libération*, drawing out what seemed to him most "compromising" in GA 16, the letter of 13 April 1934, in which Heidegger expressed his wish for the creation in Freiburg of a "tenured professorship in racial doctrine and hereditary biology."[114] He thereby pointed out, following Ludger Lütkehaus's article in *Die Zeit*,[115] that "the philosopher [had] not been content to approve the Nazi political myth of the 'rebirth of the German people, under the political direction of the charismatic leader Adolf Hitler,' " but had also, "in his letters from the years 1933–1935, approved and explicitly defended the Nazi eugenics ideology as well as the plans to establish 'racial hygiene' in the German Reich."[116] In order to excavate a part of the intellectual foundations of this wish, Münster mentioned the August 1933 *Tischgespräch* held at the fiftieth anniversary of the Institute for Pathological Anatomy, in which Heidegger asserted that "for every people, the primary guarantee of its authenticity and greatness" was "in its blood, its soil, and its bodily growth."[117] "Is this not," asked Münster rhetorically, "an adherence without reservations to the Nazi ideology of 'blood and soil'? Does not Heidegger, once again, take a position as a philosophical sycophant for a regime that, in its practices, did not hesitate for a second to link that doctrine of 'greatness' in 'blood and soil' to the exterminationist vision of an ethnic cleansing that cost six million European Jews, among others, their lives?"[118]

The reply came two months later from the sharp and subtle pen of Christian Sommer, a young doctoral student at the time. He expounded his notion of the relationship between scholarship and interpretation:

> In "the Heidegger affair," the positivist frenzy, the mere historiographical compilation of the facts, runs the risk of missing what it claims to discern: the place of Heideggerian thought. [. . .] This volume is interesting, in that it makes accessible the documents that have fueled the polemic for forty years. As for thinking about Heidegger's relation to Nazism, that is another matter—the matter for thought, precisely. Is it necessary to recall that the historical facts do not think in our place? Even if an exhaustive dossier on Heidegger's National Socialism had been assembled, it would still have to be interpreted philosophically, even as the historico-political dimension of his thought is reconstituted, [which] cannot be done in a day.[119]

Beyond that appeal for prudence and perspective, Sommer repeated the commonplace that had originated in the discourse of self-defense that Heidegger produced after the fact. Roughly, he was not a "blood and soil" thinker; always, or after 1934, he challenged Nazi biologism. And the young scholar concluded with a consensual, "You see, things are not simple."[120]

In fact, things are not simple. It is all the more difficult to interpret Heidegger in that his language is obscure, his texts innumerable, in some cases still unpublished and in others perhaps still poorly edited, if we are to believe the recent history of the critique of the texts. Their literal comprehension is an arduous task, and an overall synthesis, though not impossible, is particularly beholden to the philosophical choices of the interpreters. Since specialists in Heidegger are usually Heideggerians, they have a personal interest in a mode of thought that they assimilate to their own. The interpretation of this type of passage, moreover, requires a broad and precise knowledge not only of the Heideggerian corpus but also of his life, his historical context, and the methods of historiography themselves. And yet, again and again, the naïve notion has persisted that there are "irrefutable,"[121] "undeniable," or "indisputable" facts,[122] expressions that are ultimately very handy when pounding out one's opinions on the matter, all the more so in that the claim to be uttering "indisputable facts" is frequently the sign of factual errors to come.

A specialist who moves among texts written at different times by the same apologist can sometimes meet with surprises, which may astonish, annoy, or amuse. Such is the case for Fédier's comments on the anti-Jewish poster. In 1995, he mentioned what he called, following Heidegger alone,[123] the "only too infamous *Judenplakat*." His master claimed he had banned it. Fédier honestly acknowledged that there was probably "no direct means for offering proof of this assertion," a way of recognizing that there was no textual source or even oral statement except from Heidegger himself,[124] whose text of self-defense Fédier cited: *The Rectorship 1933–1934: Facts and Reflections*. He then continued in a purely speculative mode: "For anyone who has endeavored to reconstitute how Heidegger viewed his action, there is no solid reason for calling into doubt that ban."[125] It took only eight years to starkly alter the past. What was first without proof and had to be the object of a generous hypothesis became an "indisputable" and "undeniable" "fact," while its author was now "irreproachable":

> One of the measures taken by Rector Heidegger is an indisputable fact and very significant in and of itself: the prohibition, on the university campus of Freiburg im Breisgau, on posting a "sign against the Jews," composed by the National Socialist student organizations (and which would be posted at almost all the universities in Germany). That undeniable fact (which Heidegger's detractors, in defiance of the most basic honesty, pass over in silence, or whose significance, though obvious, they seek to minimize) allows us, in my opinion, to get a clearer idea of the conditions under which Heidegger believed he could assume the post of the rectorship.[126]

Beyond the mere restatement of the master's factual discourse, the basic interpretation given by Heidegger's defenders rested on euphemism, the minimization in one way or another either of the reality of Nazism in general or of the philosopher's Nazism in particular. This entailed, in the first case, a restrictive, arbitrary, and ahistorical definition of Nazism designed to except

Heidegger from it (as Marcel Conche did in declaring his desire to "cleanse Heidegger of the suspicion of National Socialism, for the simple reason that he is absolutely exempt from what is essential to National Socialism: racism and anti-Semitism").[127] In the second case, it involved an assimilation pure and simple of Heidegger's Nazism to the Conservative Revolution,[128] a movement less well known, more intellectual, and less frightening than the Nazi movement, or a disassociation of philosopher and philosophy, action and thought.

Even critical Heideggerians, despite their intellectual distance, held onto the desire to keep Heidegger at a safe distance from too great an involvement in the Nazism of his time. Jeffrey Barash was among them. An American living in France and a recognized specialist on the German philosopher, he was critical of Heidegger's rejection of universal validity (for Heidegger, validity does not extend beyond the historicality of the people),[129] irritated by his position regarding the entry of the United States into the war,[130] but at the same time reluctant to place him within an era and an ideology to which Heidegger in fact belonged. Conceding that there were "affinities" between his philosophy and Nazism, which arise "especially" "with respect to the interpretation of history,"[131] Barash refused, in *Heidegger and His Century*, to view Heidegger as a radical Nazi as well as an original philosopher. Even in an article published much later, in *Les temps modernes*, Barash held that "despite the fact that Heidegger's thought distinguished itself from the Nazi ideology of biological race in the late 1930s"—in that he adopted a fatalistic position toward the racial policy of Nazism, conceived as "a necessary measure to which the end of modernity is driven"[132]—the philosopher continued to "manifest a certain partiality in favor of the Hitlerian regime and its war effort."[133] But what, then, was that "partiality" if not a form of Nazism, though—granted—not purely and simply reducible to the era?

Denial by the majority of French Heideggerians did not prevent the general public from becoming more familiar with the master's Nazism. Rüdiger Safranski wrote a balanced, readable, synthetic biography that helped disseminate the state of the research in the matter. Having appeared in German in 1994, it was published in French in 1996 and in English in 1998. Its underlying restraint did not allow for scandal: its reception was therefore laudatory but also barely perceptible.

France, so attached to anything that might fuel the Heidegger affair, granted Safranksi's book only a short article in *L'Express*: "Neither hagiography nor indictment: Safranski attempts to retrace the thinker's singular destiny, while placing him within the intellectual and political history of his time, and thus undertakes to 'recount in terms of good and evil, and beyond good and evil,' what he takes to be 'the most captivating chapter in the history of the German spirit in the twentieth century.' "[134]

The English-speaking world was less stinting in its welcome. The *Times Literary Supplement* found the biography "thoughtful, sensitive and sympathetic."[135] In the United States, Richard Rorty's review in the *New York Review of Books* bore the apt subtitle: "One of the greatest Western philosophers was also a Nazi."[136] The book was "equally successful at illustrating its subject's pettiness and at displaying the vast power of his imagination."[137] In the *Boston Sunday Globe,* Dietrich Orlow found that this "superb work of synthesis" "places Heidegger's thought and life in the volatile context of 20th-century German and European politics and philosophy" and went on to recommend it as "the best introduction to Heidegger's complex philosophy."[138]

Heidegger's Nazism tended to become known across the Atlantic through his student and mistress Hannah Arendt, whose brilliant career as a political theorist and essayist had earned her lasting renown. Relayed by the press, the Arendt biographies of Elisabeth Young-Breuhl[139] and, especially, Elzbieta Ettinger[140] (the first scholar who was able to read the Heidegger-Arendt correspondence, but without being permitted to quote it),[141] then the correspondence itself,[142] indirectly informed the educated American public about the philosopher's Nazism.

In the United Kingdom, the BBC devoted an important documentary to Heidegger, within a trilogy titled *Human, All Too Human,* which placed him between Nietzsche and Sartre as major figures of contemporary philosophy. This balanced film running under an hour did not conceal Heidegger's Nazi involvement, which an educated public, often still unaware of it, now discovered for the first time. Broadcast in 1999, in the early stages of the massive spread of the internet, it was mentioned in a long post the next year, which noted the shock the documentary had caused certain viewers. One of them, for example, said he was dismayed that "the depth of [Heidegger's] collaboration with the Nazis has only recently [. . .] been brought out."[143] The documentary became even more accessible in subsequent years: referenced by Wikipedia,[144] it was even posted on YouTube several times.[145] Thanks to this new medium of mass communication, the Heidegger affair was reaching a major turning point: an extraordinary number of documents, bits of information, and analyses, consultable at modest cost, anywhere, at any hour, and often indefinitely, were made available to the public.

Cyberspace, Globalization, and *Heidegger: The Introduction of Nazism into Philosophy*

> When the farthest corner of the globe has been conquered technologically [. . .]; when you can simultaneously "experience" an assassination attempt against a king in France and a symphony concert in Tokyo; when time is nothing but speed, instantaneity, and simultaneity, [. . .] then, yes then, there still looms like a specter over all this uproar the question: what for?—where to?—and what then?
>
> GA 40, 41; *Introduction to Metaphysics*, 40

> Many thoughts [. . .] are also more difficult to express in an age when men are losing the true relationship to language and becoming slaves of the computer.
>
> Letter to Blochmann, 8 October 1966

Heidegger knew computers—which were at first enormous military calculators—only from a distance. He knew nothing of personal computers, smartphones, or any of the electronic devices that allow access to the network of networks, which, thanks to language transformed into data, in that instantaneous and global communication, gives an ever more planetary dimension to human culture. The internet did not invent globalization, as the passage from *Introduction to Metaphysics* reminds us if we have forgotten. Conversely, it participated greatly in the acceleration of exchanges of information throughout the world, which is one of the characteristics of globalization. In the 2000s the Heidegger affair reached its planetary stage, not only because of the overall development of the media and the internet in our time, but also because the protagonists, who more than ever sought to emancipate themselves from national borders, took the global dimension of their audience into account.

The first of these protagonists was Emmanuel Faye, son of Jean-Pierre Faye. Born in 1956, an associate professor (*maître de conférences*) at the University of Nanterre, the younger Faye belongs to the generation that already took a great interest in Heidegger's Nazism. And, even while following the tendency to pursue a philosophical critique of Heidegger, he reflects the historical turn taken with Ott's writings in the 1980s especially, in whose line Farías too had placed himself. In France[146] and the United States,[147] the historical dimension of some of the research was confined to its philosophical aspect. In Germany,[148] however, it also included the publication of sources and biographical scholarship.

Unlike Farías's *Heidegger and Nazism*, there is nothing narrative about Faye's *Heidegger: The Introduction of Nazism into Philosophy*. More than anything, it is based on a commentary of the texts and courses from the early Nazi period (volumes 16, 36/37, and 38 of the *Gesamtausgabe*), even as it sheds light on the earlier and later periods. More than his predecessor, Faye cultivates a patent academic seriousness, compiling many recent studies and original sources, providing a substantial bibliography, and accompanying his arguments with notes in which the passages he translates to serve his demonstration are given in the original languages. His ambitious book strives to place Heidegger's political and philosophical positions within the Nazi or *völkisch* ideology of the 1920s and 1930s: for example, the racial and phenomenological theories of Ludwig Ferdinand Clauß, who, like Heidegger, was Husserl's student in Freiburg. As indicated by its subtitle, "In Light of the Unpublished Seminars of 1933–1935," the occasion for the book was provided by the transcriptions of little-known seminars that Heidegger held during the years when his teaching was supposed to serve the political education of the students of Freiburg. These texts are manuscripts held at the Deutsches Literaturarchiv (German Literature Archive) in Marbach, and as such are inaccessible to anyone not certified by Hermann Heidegger. Faye therefore worked from "summaries and quotations published in a number of studies" (to which he refers imprecisely), on the basis of which "it is now possible [. . .] to form an idea of some of the unpublished seminars."[149]

The great success of the book in the media, both in France and abroad, can be attributed to its strong thesis: Heidegger's philosophy was not a philosophy, it was a form of Nazism, overlooked and lurking in philosophy even in our own time. That is the meaning of the title, *Heidegger: The Introduction of Nazism into Philosophy.* Seen from a distance, Faye, like Farías, belongs to the interpretive tendency introduced by Löwith and Marcuse: Heidegger had become involved with Nazism because his own philosophy involved him in it. From closer up, it appears that Faye created a fourth, more radical means of understanding. Heidegger's thought was less a philosophy than a masked Nazism, which had to be combated as such. He therefore began his book in martial terms:

> We have not yet grasped the full significance of the propagation of Nazism and Hitlerism in the domain of thought and ideas—that mounting tidal wave that sweeps up minds, dominates them, possesses them, and eventually overcomes all resistance. Against it, the military victory was

> but the winning of a first battle—a vital one, to be sure, and a costly one for humanity, since it took a world war. Today a different battle, more protracted and sinister, is unfolding: a contest in which the future of the human race is at stake. It calls for a heightened awareness in all areas of thought, from philosophy to law and history.
>
> Whether we are considering the case of Heidegger, Schmitt, Jünger (in many respects), or Nolte, these main propagators of Nazism in the life of letters have taken the time to refine their strategy of reconquest after the defeat of the armies of Hitler's Reich.[150] [. . .] Soon the 102 volumes of the so-called complete works (sixty-six volumes have appeared to date), in which the same assertions are repeated over and over through thousands of pages, will encumber by their sheer bulk the shelves reserved for twentieth-century philosophy and continue to spread the fundamental tenets of Nazism on a worldwide scale. It is therefore of the utmost importance to see clearly into that undertaking, to react and resist its influence before it is too late. Such heightened awareness is indispensable if we are to return to what philosophy truly has to contribute to the thought, overall evolution, and achievement of mankind.[151]

Rhetoric is one of the strong points of the book, which frequently hammers away at its thesis: Heidegger's thought, being Nazi, is unworthy of a philosopher. Faye adopts a vehement and dramatic tone, seeking to elicit fear, disgust, and indignation by relying on one of the rare ideological commonplaces still strong in France and in the West generally, namely, hostility to Nazism, a horrible, barbarous, and criminal regime, responsible for the extermination of the Jews and against which no honorable person can fail to stand up with the greatest violence, by taking up either arms or the pen.

The quasi-omnipresence of the Holocaust in the author's mind made him want to find as much confirmation as possible of Heidegger's support for or even responsibility in this crime. He overinterprets a number of sources in this direction. Upon reading the passing mention in a 1933 course of the "total extermination" (*völlige Vernichtung*) of "the enemy," who "may have grafted himself onto the innermost root of the existence of a people,"[152] Faye concludes: "It is important that we realize that that doctrine of the enemy and *polemos*, however 'ontologized' it may be by Heidegger, is in no form or fashion a simple theoretical view or intellectual game but indeed a radically murderous doctrine, the translation of which into the real world cannot but lead to the war of extermination and the concentration camps."[153] The philosopher's interpretations thus clearly tend toward the teleological, according to which history has an end toward which it is necessarily moving. In this case, the Holocaust is the logical and inevitable outcome of the advent of Nazism, which was its premise, and, farther up the line, of the First World War, and even, why not, German Romanticism, which Nazism made its own. Even so, Faye might have resisted the temptation of that teleological reading had he not forgotten or omitted to place the passage from Heidegger's course in relation to the appeal of the German Student Union of Freiburg, which was speaking rather of a "spiritual battle," a text Faye had quoted more than 100 pages earlier.[154] Because he does not base his commentary of Heidegger's course on that source, even though it was contemporaneous and close to the rector of Freiburg, for Faye there can be no doubt whatsoever: "It is indeed nothing short of a call for the physical, moral, and spiritual destruction of the enemy, who is identified by Heidegger and Schmitt with what is foreign to the racial 'essence' of the people."[155] In the preface to the second edition, he repeats the same idea, speaking of a "very clear" "murderous aim" and of an incitement "to exterminate the assimilated Jews and political opponents."[156] Conversely, following Wolfgang Benz's interpretation of the book burnings of 10 May 1933, I believe it is more accurate to see Heidegger's brief comment as a legitimation of the appeal by the Deutsche Studentenschaft to "kill thought,"[157] to completely purge German culture and German universities, from which all Jewish authors and Jewish thoughts—in the strict and the broad sense—all those "enemies" within accused of corrupting the German spirit, would henceforth be absent. No need to kill people: they must simply disappear from academic positions and libraries, in the same way that the Nazi program wanted to silence Jewish newspapers. It is true that the mere incineration of books pulled from henceforth "purged" libraries now appears to us a very weak "total annihilation" of Judeo-Bolshevism, because our minds are filled with the awful images of the extermination camps. Nevertheless, the book burnings fulfilled their spiritual function, that of annihilating the non-German spirit, Judeo-Bolshevism, liberalism, individualism, even Christianity.

Wanting to establish Heidegger's complicity in the criminal policy of the Third Reich, Faye advances a hypothesis as original as its foundation is rickety: Heidegger, not content to be steeped in Hitlerism, may have participated in elaborating it as one of Hitler's ghost writers.[158] At the very least, the Führer was paying heed, more or less closely, to professors such as Schmitt and, of course, Heidegger:

> Hitler announces on 30 January 1939, in his most frightful speech, that the world war will mean "the extermination of the Jewish race in

> Europe." He calls it "his prophecy," which he will carry out with the "Final Solution," decided upon in January 1942. Now, this is quite simply the ultimate translation into action of what Heidegger theorizes in 1933, at which time he already spoke, as we have seen, of a "total annihilation."
>
> Therefore we must take seriously what authors such as Heidegger or Schmitt spell out in their writings or express in their lectures and classes. When they use the word "extermination" (*Vernichtung*), it is no mere idle fancy. Coming from much-heeded sources, these statements catch on and prepare the future, pending their translation into deeds, and history has shown how rapidly these fatal statements are implemented in Hitlerism.[159]

The circle was complete. Heidegger not only called for genocide in 1933; Hitler heard him. It was therefore necessary to break up that insidious offensive of someone who was—among others, to be sure—at the origin of the greatest genocide in history.

Supported by an effective publishing house, *Heidegger: The Introduction of Nazism into Philosophy* was widely reviewed in the press. It received seventeen French-language reviews, twelve German, two Italian, and four in the English-speaking world.[160] And just as Droit had at first been taken in by Farías's book, eighteen years later he gave Faye's a warm reception, being the first to review it and adopting his main idea: Heidegger had introduced Nazism into philosophy. The Hitlerian evil that was believed vanquished in 1945 persisted in the reception given the philosopher:

> The war against Nazism continues. Since the crushing of the Wehrmacht, that war has come through words, images. [. . .] Emmanuel Faye's impressive work, pursued on the basis of the seminars of 1933–1934 and many other sources, some of them wholly unpublished, shows that it has become impossible to separate Heidegger's thought from his resolute involvement in the Third Reich's political action. It becomes laughable and deceitful to speak of an accident or an aberration, when one observes how the "master" himself expounds, at length and explicitly, the fusion of his major philosophical intuitions and Nazi ideology. [. . .] May philosophers and exegetes assess the risks to come. So long as books conveying Nazi themes are published, translated, taught, and commented on without a warning, the worst may yet return.[161]

Like Droit, the press often repeated Faye's theses without disputing them, sometimes even exaggerating them. Both *Télérama*[162] in France and *Corriere della Sera*[163] in Italy stated as an established fact the hypothesis that Heidegger was one of Hitler's writers. At the same time, critics spoke up, including Thomas Meyer at *Die Zeit*,[164] Joseph Hanimann at the *Frankfurter Allgemeine Zeitung*,[165] and Éric Loret at *Libération*. The latter's weariness with the Heidegger affair led him to dip his pen in ink whose malice was not always devoid of a somewhat crude sarcasm:

> No doubt Faye has laudable intentions, but his thinking is already discredited in the preface to this second edition, even more quickly than it was gunned down in the conclusion to the first, in spring 2005: "If his writings continue to proliferate without our being able to stop this intrusion of Nazism into human education, how can we not expect them to lead to yet another translation into facts and acts, from which this time humanity might not be able to recover?" Faye must therefore be read to (not) be believed. We can always be accused of manipulation, truncation, but a longer quotation gives an idea of his (tauto)logical system. Wishing to show that Heidegger glorified "destructive fire," he writes: "In 1942 we again find the call for fire, this time placed in the center of his teaching. He in fact devoted his course of summer 1942 to a commentary on Hölderlin's hymn *Der Ister,* and quite particularly its first line, quoted several times in the course: 'Jetzt komme, Feuer,' 'Come now, fire.' That call is tragically disturbing because, in the summer of 1942, the crackling and rising fire was that of the extermination camps: Belzec, Sobibor [. . .] where the corpses of the exterminated Jewish victims—and sometimes live children—were burned by the thousands in giant infernos." No need to attend the École Normale to see how the "course" spent "commenting" on *Der Ister* has bizarrely become a "call" for fire, with the transfer of Hölderlin's line into Heidegger's mouth. Is Hölderlin responsible for the Holocaust? Suddenly, we're worried: how did Bachelard, author of a *Psychoanalysis of Fire* in 1938, escape Nuremburg?[166]

Faye's book faced not only criticisms of his method but also the old habits of thought of the orthodox Heideggerians, like Éric Weil's minimization from 1947, which could still be discerned in Maxence Caron's remarks: "If the man Heidegger assuredly compromised himself, his thought, whether we like it or not, escapes the usual indictment. We must not deny anything about the reality of his involvement, but we must acknowledge the political innocuousness of his oeuvre. We can read, work on, and love Heidegger's thought, without fear of being sneakily splashed with subliminal Nazi messages, just as we can read, work on, and love Plato's works without fear of becoming a retrospective henchman of the tyrant of Syracuse."[167]

The criticism—albeit biting—and the sarcasm did not prevent *Heidegger: The Introduction of Nazism into Philosophy* from having a considerable impact. Even more than Farías, Faye was able to prevail in the battle of images, by systematically using his right of reply, by drawing up a petition to open the Heidegger archives, and by taking a firm stance against Heidegger's inclusion in the curriculum for the *agrégation*[168] in philosophy[169] or on the philosophy shelves of libraries, rather than "in the historical archives of Nazism and Hitlerism."[170] It was a large-scale media event, well served by the industry its author applied to publicize it in interviews and to respond when criticisms arose. The number of media platforms and the energy he expended allowed him to further the propagation of his theses in France and abroad. He was also well served by events: shortly after the publication of his book, Heidegger's letters to his wife came out,[171] a particularly rich source that bore witness to the philosopher's Nazism and made it more comprehensible. Faye was able to take them into account in his petition of January 2006 and then in the preface to his second edition.

The response the book received was further strengthened by the counterattack of the radical Heideggerians in *Heidegger, Now More than Ever.* Although it offered nothing new, it gave a new urgency to the affair. Rather than managing to ridicule its target, the force of the denunciation mounted by Fédier and his coauthors tended to rouse interest in the book they opposed so violently:

> Here, then, is the general layout of the book: carefully swing back and forth between the enormity of the accusations and the emotional charge of revulsion we naturally feel when the Nazi crime is mentioned; don't leave readers confronted with a "revelation" that might appear to them to have gone too far, without having conditioned them beforehand by evoking the very real horror that Nazism was. The technique of E. Faye's book thus consists of connecting, by every imaginable bridge, the words "Nazism" and "Heidegger's thought," so that, in the mind of a reader unfamiliar with the German philosopher, a sort of conditioned reflex is created.[172]

This bitter polemic was not confined to books and newspapers, but also included notable radio and television broadcasts. On France Culture, on

9 May 2005, Faye participated in Marc Voinchet's radio program *Tout arrive,* with Jean-Édouard André, Philippe Lacoue-Labarthe, Pascal Ory, and Bruno Tackels. And on 23 February 2007, he took part in a landmark "Bibliothèque Médicis" broadcast on the Public Sénat television network with Fédier, Pascal David, and Édouard Husson.[173] On that program, the place of history within philosophy was an essential question, whether through Husson 's comments about the *Judenzählung* (Jewish Census) as a context for interpreting the letter to Elfride of 18 October 1916 on "the jewification of our culture & universities,"[174] or through David's caricatural rejection of history. Explaining Heidegger's rectorship in his introduction to the discussion, Jean-Pierre Elkabbach noted that the philosopher was elected rector by his peers and was then named "*Führer* of the university" by the ministries. David feigned incomprehension: "I may have misunderstood, but I thought I heard a slip in your introduction just now, at the beginning of the broadcast, when you said that, in 1933, Heidegger was *'Führer'* of the university. Perhaps I misunderstood, but it's 'rector.' "[175] Whether out of laziness, contempt, or cowardice, David apparently did not read Ott or Bernd Martin. He had probably simply rejected Ott's book after Hermann Heidegger's review of it.[176]

Another noteworthy broadcast, in Germany this time, was the program *Forum* on radio Südwestrundfunk 2 (SWR), on 30 June 2005. Moderated by Werner Witt, with Kurt Flasch, Rainer Marten, and Holger Zaborowski, it was more interesting and balanced than the others. In particular, Flasch's comments provided a German glimpse at a fundamentally French affair, pointing out how Faye called into question Beaufret's legacy of Heidegger interpretation, an exegetical and uncritical mode of reading:

> In France, there is a very common style of philosophizing in the Heideggerian manner, which often depends on translations, and which often also uses the older texts, for example, the 1961 edition of *Nietzsche,* and not the version corrected and prepared on the basis of the manuscripts, that is, the edition of the complete works. And it is part of Faye's protest to say: you are working on secondhand texts, you have not yet captured the whole movement. In France, there is also, I should say, a rhetorical posture of Heideggerianism, and it is imprecise, not directly connected to the text. And Faye is a philologist who reopens the subject anew, based on the texts. It must therefore be said that this is, in the first place, a polemic against the enthusiasm for Heidegger that does not proceed historically or philologically, and which was founded in France by Jean Beaufret.[177]

The affair also took a more popular turn. On 11 September 2005, the Fête de l'Humanité hosted a debate titled "Heidegger, Nazism, and Philosophy," with Faye, Jean-Pierre Cotton, Lacoue-Labarthe, and Nicolas Tertulian.[178] Above all, a new mass medium allowed amateurs to speak freely: with the web, everyone could give an opinion, in the comments sections of newspapers, on social networks, or on their own site or blog. Even as a very popular online forum opened a thread on the question,[179] Pierre Assouline relayed the affair on *La république des livres*, with several posts, all of them followed by many readers' comments: 179 for "The Heideggerians Counterattack!"[180] 164 for "What to Do about Heidegger?"[181] 192 for "Free-for-All on the Margins,"[182] so many that these articles were transformed into a Heidegger forum in which all positions found expression. Although some contributions—such as those of Pierre Teitgen, my fellow student in the *khâgne* who has perpetuated the long line of radical Heideggerians—were of academic caliber, many were written at a level not customary for the affair. Consider the last comment added to Assouline's article of 23 June 2005 by "Heil Heidegger," posted on 30 June 2010, and that unites linguistic nonsense with historical absurdity: "If he causes so much of reaction at least he'd have had the merit of opening the horizons of many people who were accustomed to thinking the way 'they' have always thought. In my opinion, the genius of Heidegger was to know how to play with the etymology of words in order to go on about a theory as monstrous as the nazi [*sic*]. With philosophers like Nietschze [*sic*] and Heidegger the nightmare of the Holocaust could happen only to humanity."[183]

Two amateur sites were set up, one to defend each of the camps. They were very successful: paris4philo.org,[184] founded by "Ritoyenne" and also run by "JP," hewed to a pro-Heidegger line; phiblogzophe,[185] run by "Skildy," was anti-Heidegger. Announcing it was a "research blog on Heideggerian Nazism," phiblogzophe adopted an extremist line, publishing articles with suggestive titles: "Bambach, Heidegger, and the Killer Greeks," "Heidegger: Klostermann the Rogue," "The Logic . . . of Heidegger: A Treatise on Nazism." Having opened in November 2004, it proudly announced it had 601,170 (705,911 at the time of writing)[186] page views and proclaimed: "Heidegger's Nazism is not a detail in the history of philosophy." Set up in opposition to that site, paris4philo.org, as its name might suggest, expressed a form of Heideggerianism current at the Sorbonne, the hub of Heidegger's influence since Jean Wahl's time. Beginning in the 1980s, philosophers of various sensibilities (Pierre Aubenque, Jean-François Courtine, Jean-Luc Marion, Claude Romano, but also Alain Renaut) taught there; some teach there now. The founder of the site had an interesting career that demonstrates the appeal the Freiburg philosopher could exert over a decent man. As he confided to me in an e-mail, Ritoyenne studied computing before moving on to philosophy and writing a master's thesis on Heidegger. It seemed to him and his friend that "the attacks in the various media" were "very vicious": "Consigning Heidegger to the rubbish heap, brushing him aside with 'he was a Nazi,' always seemed incredibly sad to me. And the arguments on certain sites that made it their mission to smash Heidegger to pieces (1 of them still in service) seemed absurd."[187] These internet users were receptive to Fédier's influence. The Sorbonne is not a temple of science closed upon itself: the other editor, known as "JP," which is to say, Joseph Plichart, a former student of Fédier's, recorded a long interview with his teacher in 2008[188] and the next year edited one of his *khâgne* courses.[189]

The Wikipedia pages devoted to Heidegger were and remain sites of the polemic and among the things at stake. A count on 12 March 2014 of the bytes devoted to the philosopher's Nazism in the principal Western languages gives a glimpse of the popularity of the affair, based on the length of the articles devoted to it: 147,472 bytes for the German edition,[190] 83,227 for the English,[191] 75,403 for the French,[192] 13,038 for the Italian.[193] The length of the Spanish text, confined to a single article on Heidegger, is similar to that of the Italian. The passion this theme inspired is also revealed by the number of revisions made to the articles. Whereas the overall mean on Wikipedia for these four languages ranges between 16.34 corrections for the French edition and 28.53 for the German,[194] the modifications of the articles devoted to Heidegger's Nazism are much more numerous: 52 for the Italian version, 387 for the French, 785 for the English, 1,106 for the German. A study of the text of the articles shows that this variation in the number of modifications is the direct result of the seriousness shown by the compilers and the prominence of the critical approach. The Italian version, the most apologetic, states, among the facts not open to discussion, that during the rectorship Heidegger was briefly a member of the Nazi Party,[195] an assertion unaccompanied by a footnote. By contrast, the German version begins with this information-packed sentence, supported by two references: "In 1930 [Martin Heidegger] started reading the *Völkischer Beobachter*; in 1932 he voted for the NSDAP. After the seizure of power by the Nazis he wanted to participate in the transformation of society, especially through the introduction of the leadership principle at the universities."[196] A noteworthy fact, and a sign of the extent to which the Heidegger affair is not a mere juxtaposition of national scandals: each of the articles includes a number of French references, to both critics and apologists. Furthermore, the three most modified articles—the German, the English, and the French—all received the greatest number (by far) of corrections from a single user with the online identity "Filinthe": 655 for the German,[197] 321 for the English,[198] 83 for the French.[199] An active user since 26 April 2012, Filinthe gives only his online identity on the French site,[200] but indicates on the German site that he is a French philosophy teacher at the secondary school level;[201] on the English site, he goes so far as to reveal that he lives in Germany and that his name is—Joseph Plichart,[202] the same Plichart who runs paris4philo.org under the handle "JP." Since 2012, the three main Wikipedia articles on the Heidegger affair have therefore been the target of a "Fédierist" offensive. Satisfied with the state of the French article—barely presentable but conforming fairly well to Fédier's professed doctrine—it reserves the greatest share of its attention for the English and, especially, the German article, both of which make the mistake of presenting a line that is not "orthodox" enough.

That mobilization of amateurs by the internet reached its height with Stéphane Zagdanski's website paroledesjours. It posted replies from the radical Heideggerians[203] as well as videos from Gérard Guest's free seminar. Zagdanski was so committed to the cause that he became fully integrated into their circle and contributed to the *Martin Heidegger Dictionary*, published in 2013.[204] The philosophy teachers, because of their profession and average age, were unfamiliar with the modern means of communication; Zagdanski gave them not only a forum but also energy and invention for their common struggle. Compiling a manifesto in fifteen languages, he managed to have it sent, according to his statement, to 150,000 recipients throughout the world, ensuring that "this original use of the Internet in the world of the debate of ideas has also had a success that no traditional mass media could have ensured. Several hundred people have come every day to consult the dossier since it was posted online on 10 May 2005."[205]

Faye was not caught napping after leading that first, strong charge. As the new publications of sources continued to bear witness to Heidegger's Nazism, his media savvy, the rhetorical force of his book, and the countless lectures, scholarly review articles, and chapters in collections he produced in French, German, English, and Italian[206] combined to place *Heidegger: The Introduction of Nazism into Philosophy* at the center of the debate. The book, though weak, was translated into several languages: German, English, and Spanish in 2009; Italian in 2012; and Brazilian Portuguese in 2015, with plans for a Chinese translation as well. The polemic was relaunched in these countries, but with greater balance overall than in France, as the reception of the American edition demonstrates.

True, the reception was initially similar to that of the Heidegger affair in France. Even before the book was issued by a well-known publisher on 24 November 2009,[207] an article, tritely titled "Heil Heidegger!"[208] sounded the charge: "How many scholarly stakes in the heart will we need before Martin Heidegger (1889–1976), still regarded by some as Germany's greatest 20th-century philosopher, reaches his final resting place as a prolific, provincial Nazi hack?"[209] The hour of reckoning may have finally come, thanks to the imminent publication of Faye's "scrupulously documented study," which would launch "the latest, most comprehensive archival assault."[210] This article, by a denigrator without nuance, drew more than 150 comments, divided between champions and accusers, more than any other book review published that year by the *Chronicle of Higher Education*.[211]

The reactions posted on the book's Amazon web page were also divided: the middling average, three stars out of five from twenty-three customers, can be explained by their profound disagreement. Nearly half were satisfied (30 percent gave the book five stars and 13 percent four stars), while the other contingent, only slightly more numerous, was negative (22 percent gave it two stars, 26 percent one star). The proportion of mixed reviews was very low (9 percent).[212] The enthusiasts celebrated the truth (or what they took to be the truth) finally unveiled. Peter N. Nevraumont, for example, called his post "Heidegger the Nazi" and spoke of "a brilliant book," concluding that "no one can read Heidegger again without knowing his sordid 'philosophical' past."[213] The critics, though harsh in their ratings of the book, strove to remain balanced: Terence Kuch, for example, justified his low rating by acknowledging that, to be sure, Faye had done "an astonishing amount of research," but that his "hateful, obsessive attitude toward his subject ruins what would otherwise be a very good book."[214]

Faye's book drew divergent reactions from academics. One of his warmest readers, Gregory Fried, had at first reacted negatively upon reading Carlin Romano's polemical article.[215] And, using his favorite Czech word, *zmrzlina*, as his handle,[216] he wrote in his comment that "to a large extent," the furor surrounding the work and the article that praised it was "a repeat of the scandal that erupted 22 years ago when the work of Victor Farías and Hugo Ott was published." There was "nothing really new here, except perhaps an increase in the 'data' of Heidegger's loathsomeness as a human being."[217] Reading *The*

Introduction of Nazism into Philosophy changed his mind. He still had reservations: it was "primarily a work of history and biography" and not of philosophy. Faye did not "engage Heidegger philosophically, except perhaps in a negative sense," as when he defended Descartes.[218] In addition, Fried did not share the desire to exclude Heidegger from philosophy; it was precisely on that battleground that he had to be combated.[219] He nevertheless saw great value in the book, whose "most important contribution may be to serve as a wake-up call to Heidegger scholars," in two ways. In the first place, "we simply cannot ignore Heidegger's political biography and its relation to his thought"; and, he believed, "there are likely to be more disturbing revelations in the coming years." Second, it no longer sufficed to be satisfied with an "explication or transliteration of Heidegger's German idiom"; it was "high time that Heidegger scholars working in English begin to do in earnest what he did himself, namely, to address enduring questions through our own language and through its literature and philosophical traditions."[220]

One of the sharpest critics, Peter E. Gordon, found few virtues in Faye's book, "one of the most single-minded and unrestrained political attacks on Heidegger's philosophy ever written," whose "immoderate" tone and misguided approach made it the equivalent of a "jeremiad."[221] In addition, the method Faye followed was problematic: "Faye interlaces the most damning evidence with far less convincing documentation concerning Heidegger's contemporaries, not infrequently indulging in an easily refuted strategy of guilt-by-association."[222] Even in his interpretation of the philosopher's own texts, Faye went too far and, stating that "Heidegger furnished the theory which *necessarily* reached its ultimate realization in the Holocaust," misconstrued the reality of philosophical interpretation: "Any genuinely philosophical texts are open rather than closed in their interpretative possibilities."[223] A discursive and dialectical process, philosophy is in its essence the least capable of giving concrete marching orders, for a genocide, for example.

Unlike in France, where the debate was still whether Heidegger had or had not been a Nazi, or whether his philosophy could still be separated from his involvement, in the United States the essential question was how much faith to place in the quality of Faye's study. Tom Rockmore, who had written the foreword to the American edition and who saw the book as confirmation of his own thesis of an indissoluble link between Heidegger's political engagement and his philosophy,[224] lavished praise on the "fullest review so far in the literature in any language of the relation between Heidegger and National Socialism."[225] Faye showed himself to be "unusually well informed" about Heidegger, mastering both the philosopher's texts and "the full range of Heidegger studies as they bear on this theme in a variety of languages."[226]

Convinced that the opposite was true, Thomas Sheehan, a critical Heideggerian who was among the very first both to praise Ott and to criticize Farías, belatedly took Faye to task. Dishonest or inept? He let the reader decide whether his adversary was not both, denouncing his "sloppy scholarship."[227] He detailed with pugnacity many errors in the translations or interpretations that formed the basis of Faye's thesis that Nazism had been introduced into philosophy. To better make Heidegger a fundamentally proto-Nazi thinker from the early 1920s on, Faye conflated him with Ludwig Clauß, author of the racialist treatise *The Nordic Soul,* without any evidence of an exchange or acquaintance between the two men, only the frail arguments that both had taken Husserl's courses and that Max Niemeyer was their publisher.[228] Extending his critique to Faye's later studies, Sheehan zeroed in on his interpretation of the letter to Kurt Bauch of 1 August 1943, which characterized "the being of beings" as a "formula," a "*mot couvert*" or "code word" (*Deckname*).[229] Faye assimilated it to the "Nazi Fatherland,"[230] even though the letter did not refer to Nazism. The Frenchman based himself on a misquotation from the course of winter semester 1934–1935 on Hölderlin's hymns "Germania" and "The Rhine." Through a displacement of the scare quotes, "Das 'Vaterland' ist das Seyn selbst,"[231] "The 'Fatherland' is beyng itself," was transformed into "The Fatherland is 'being' itself."[232] As Sheehan noted, being is the name of the *Lichtung,* the clearing in which beings come to unveil themselves, to make themselves accessible to vision and thought. Furthermore, Hölderlin links it poetically not only to the fatherland but also to the sacred, nature, chaos, and destiny, among other things.[233] According to Sheehan, therefore, there was at best ineptitude, at worst, fraud.

In his brutal critique, Sheehan targeted not only Faye but also his followers. Faye was now a full professor at the University of Rouen, basking in the glory of the worldwide influence of his writings. Behind the polemicist, there were now critical or even caustic researchers, who recognized his authority and formed a new sect within Heidegger studies, one that was not idolatrous but iconoclastic. The collection Faye edited in 2014[234] had attracted to him these specialists from various backgrounds, including the Franco-German Sidonie Kellerer and François Rastier, director of research in linguistics at the Centre National de la Recherche Scientifique (CNRS). Kellerer revealed to the general public, on both sides of the Rhine, that the text of Heidegger's 1938 lecture "The Age of the World Picture," published in *Off the Beaten Track* in 1950, had been rewritten to appear anodyne or even critical of Nazism.[235] In October of the following year, Rastier would publish a book focused in great part on decoding a work he considered the "monologue of a murderous doctrine."[236] Both Keller and Rastier, like other epigones such as Gaëtan Pégny, adopted Faye's term *Deckname* and idea of a coded language. Sheehan therefore targeted them as well in the notes.[237]

A brutal attack calls for a brutal response. Faye's followers replied in two articles,[238] preceded by an over-the-top open letter that proclaimed: "This title ["The Introduction of Fraud into Philosophy?"] borrows the structural pattern of the work of Emmanuel Faye published in 2005. The word *Nazism* is replaced by *Fraud*. Thus the accusation of fraud is used to obfuscate the question of Nazism in the philosophy of Heidegger."[239] This was an irony of fate for Sheehan, who very early on—beginning in the late 1980s—had acknowledged Heidegger's Nazism,[240] and who, in his article, spoke of the black notebooks[241] as "proof positive of his most despicable convictions."[242] He was cast in the inglorious role of an orthodox Heideggerian, intent on concealing a Nazism that was nevertheless obvious. In a further sophism, Rastier reduced the singularity of philosophical thought by not distinguishing it from the language of the far right at the time: "He denies that *Bodenlosigkeit* means *absence of soil*, holding to the translation *lack of foundation*. It matters little, here, that by means of the English term *ground* Dr. Sheehan manages to conflate the German terms *Grund* and *Boden*. There is no evidence adduced to confirm that linguistic initiative. By contrast, *Bodenlosigkeit* has been a major theme in Nazi and anti-Semitic discourse since the 1920s."[243] Then he continues: "Heidegger having been compromised, to say the least, Dr. Sheehan thinks he can defend him by attacking the reputation of Emmanuel Faye and by thus jeopardizing his honor."[244]

The letter, written by Rastier, was signed by twenty-one academics, philosophers, and linguists, often closely associated with Faye, living primarily in France, secondarily in neighboring countries (Germany, Belgium, Spain, Italy), but also, in five instances, in North America and even, in the case of Johann Fritsche, Turkey. Published in English in the American review *Philosophy Today*, this text attested to the scale of the polemic, which encompassed the West if not the entire globe. In addition, with the rise of the internet and the use of English as a handy lingua franca allowing a vast public to communicate instantaneously, Heidegger studies were tending to become anglicized. Ordinarily, scholarly works remained in their authors' mother tongue,[245] while mainstream publications on the internet were more and more systematically written in English, particularly on social networks such as Facebook. In the summer of 2017, there were five groups (forums) devoted to Heidegger, four of them in English,[246] a single one in French, and none in German: the Martin-Heidegger-Gesellschaft, an international, German-language organization federating the Heideggerians, has traded the master's language for that of the web.[247] And, though not absolutely all the messages posted in these groups are in English, that language dominates.

Black Notebooks at the End of the Affair?

In the early 2010s, buoyed by the rise of the internet and the translations of Faye's book, the Heidegger affair reached a vast scale. Books, sometimes vicious, flourished in French,[248] German,[249] and Spanish.[250] They were met with replies from moderate Heideggerians: Holger Zaborowski,[251] a German living in Washington, D.C.; and Alfred Denker,[252] a Dutchman living in France but with a strong presence in Meßkirch. Both were very active in producing editions of the sources and in holding debates in their high-quality *Heidegger Jahrbuch*, and, in French, in the *Le dictionnaire Martin Heidegger* (*The Martin Heidegger Dictionary*),[253] which is orthodox in its approach. The Heidegger affair, though it was penetrating into regions where it had previously been less present, such as the United States and the Spanish-speaking world, had on the whole lost a little of the vehemence it had when *Heidegger: The Introduction of Nazism into Philosophy* was first published in France. And, despite the widespread acceptance of a critical position, the orthodox Heideggerians, especially the French, were still managing to depict Heidegger as resistant to Nazism in one way or another, to varying degrees depending on the interpreter.

What cemented this reading was the commonplace that Heidegger was critical of Nazi biologism and that he was not anti-Semitic. That view was shared by all, well beyond the orthodox circle. Richard Wolin, for example, said that Heidegger "never subscribed to the racial anti-Semitism espoused by the National Socialists. To him this perspective was philosophically untenable, insofar as it sought to explain 'existential' questions in reductive terms. For Heidegger, biology was a base exemplar of nineteenth-century materialism—a standpoint that needed to be overcome in the name of '*Existenz*' or 'Being.' "[254]

Hadrien France-Lanord, who belongs to the latest generation of orthodox Heideggerians, began his article on anti-Semitism in *The Martin Heidegger Dictionary* by assuring his readers that "in Heidegger's entire body of work published thus far (84 of 102 volumes)," there was not "a single anti-Semitic sentence."[255] The anti-Semitism of the master of Freiburg was merely a "rumor sometimes deliberately sustained and which has contributed toward surrounding Heidegger with a cloud of suspicion."[256] To support his view, the author offered a contorted interpretation of the two occurrences of *Verjudung*, which, like Fédier, he translated as *judaïsation* (judaization) rather than *enjuivement* (jewification): "As for the word 'judaization' (*Verjudung*), which Heidegger used at the time, and which will be found only one other time in a letter to Schwoerer of 2 October 1929 [. . .], it is not impossible that it is to be understood as a risk of sorts that the specifically Greek ontological problematic will be absorbed by a reflection of an essentially moral nature. [. . .] In that sense, the word would carry the weight of a relationship to ontology that Heidegger had not yet fully elucidated at the time."[257]

Everything, or nearly everything, changed when the rumor spread of the forthcoming publication of Heidegger's black notebooks. Far from showing once and for all the philosopher's antagonism toward Nazism, as Fédier had promised in his sparring match with Faye (he quoted an unpublished and supposedly negative passage[258] about Nazism, described as a "barbaric principle"),[259] these notebooks would shake even the small cell of orthodox Heideggerians.

In November 2013 an Italian online cultural magazine first relayed a rumor that black notebooks with "clearly anti-Semitic notes" were to appear in March 2014. The author had obtained the information from the "official editorial oversight board for the notebooks."[260] In accordance with Heidegger's wishes, these texts were supposed to have appeared at the very end of the complete works, as their crowning achievement (*Krönung*); but, oddly, their publication was accelerated. The ninety-three-year-old Hermann Heidegger had left the management of the rights to his youngest son, Arnulf. When the son learned of the existence of these notebooks and the nature of their content, he decided that they ought to be made public: "The world must know." In Gertrud's wake, the new Heidegger generation was breaking through the fog of obfuscation. Coming from the supreme authorities of Heideggerianism, the effect would be devastating. For the first time, the evidence made clear that anti-Semitism and Nazism were not a historical accident—this belief had saved the thinker while abandoning the private individual to an unfortunate but external involvement. No, they were truly at the heart of his thought itself, so much so that even the French cell of diehard Heideggerians felt the blow. Previously, all the efforts of the orthodox Heideggerians had been directed at minimizing

Heidegger's Nazism. Granted, he had for a time believed in Nazism and had kept his Party card until 1945, but he had not embraced the regime's biologism or its racism or its anti-Semitism. Now the fiction was no longer tenable; it was no longer possible purely and simply to adopt Heidegger's discourse of self-defense in its entirety. More than ever, these disciples found themselves in the pitiable situation Bernard Pivot had spoken of in reference to Fédier in 1988: pitiable, not because it was contemptible, but because it was so inextricable and painful that it elicited compassion.

From the beginning, the resumption of the affair was rooted in globalization and in cyberspace. The rumor was published on the internet, in Italian, in an article that adopted an anglicism ("gossip") to report on a German scandal. It proceeded in the same manner, further unfolding in the other two countries that, along with Italy, had from the beginning been at its heart: France and Germany. In early December Nicolas Weil, a journalist for *Le Monde*, relayed the rumor on his blog without many details.[261] On 13 December Jonathan Derbyshire cited Weil's post, "Heidegger, Proof of Nazism by the 'Black Notebook'?" in English, in the magazine of ideas *Prospect*.[262] An amateur then translated the post into Spanish on the 26th of the same month.[263] Éric Aeschimann, who knew more details about what was going on, reported them in *Le Nouvel Observateur*. He mentioned a "memo" written by Peter Trawny, editor of the notebooks, who had communicated it to the radical French Heideggerians, with whom he had defended the master against Faye a few years earlier. "Do the philosopher's unpublished notebooks provide proof of his anti-Semitism? That is, in any case, the opinion of Peter Trawny, the specialist who is preparing them for publication in Germany next March. Having arrived in France, his 'memo' is causing an uproar in the little circle of Heideggerians." Why such anxiety? When questioned by the journalist, France-Lanord said he was in fact "profoundly distressed" and found what was emerging in these notebooks "appalling." The journalist asked him what was at issue. "Remarks can be found there that are critical of Judaism, Christianity, and nihilism, but also of Americanism, English imperialism, and Bolshevism, as well as Nazism—all these 'isms' being caught up, in places, in the same critique of *Machenschaft* (the reign of total efficiency). Which is obviously not unproblematic."[264] Seeing before his eyes the contentious quotations, the journalist observed that, "in the first sentence, 'Jewry' (*Judentum*) is associated with 'the absence of land' and, in the second, with 'calculation' and 'trafficking'—extremely negative terms in Heidegger's writings, but which appear throughout his entire oeuvre and are not reserved for Jewry. More particularly, an excerpt that François Fédier translated for us could fuel the polemic: the German thinker wanted Jewry to 'exclude itself on its own.' . . . Read: exclude itself on its own from the German people."[265] Fédier, true to his vocation as Heidegger's chief counsel, once again took up his defense, clarifying, as Aeschimann reported:

> Such sentences, taken out of their theoretical context, may in fact appear despicable. But, placed within the logic of Heidegger's thought, they may not express any anti-Semitism. On the contrary, in a digression where he criticizes the Jewish prophets, the philosopher stipulates: "Note for jackasses: these remarks have nothing to do with 'anti-Semitism.' Which is so stupid (*töricht*) and reprehensible (*verwerflich*)."[266]

Fédier's defense could not put out the fire lit by such firebrands and hurled by the editor of these disturbing texts, which an unfortunate young disciple was repeating. Spreading like wildfire on the web, the *Nouvel Observateur* article was reproduced the next day on an Italian blog, which inquired: "Heidegger's Unpublished Notebooks: Nazism or Eternal 'Anti-Semitism' "?[267] A few days later, the press around the world followed suit. The Spanish-language scholarly review *Alea* soberly noted the "forthcoming publication of Heidegger's 'black notebooks,' "[268] while the Italian daily *Libero* spoke of the "Franco-German War over the anti-Semitic philosopher."[269] The blogger Stefano G. Azzarà published this Italian article, having already done the same with the French.[270] The internet once again demonstrated its enormous, potentially infinite power of replication, since print articles were not only published online, they were also reproduced there in various ways by amateurs, and sometimes even translated.

The misfortune of one camp is sometimes the good fortune of the other. Like the Chernobyl cloud, the crisis of the French Heideggerians did not stop at the Rhine. Faye granted an interview to *Die Zeit* on 27 December. With the black notebooks, "the crowning achievement of the complete works," he found confirmation of the thesis he had developed in *Heidegger: The Introduction of Nazism into Philosophy* concerning the reality of Heidegger's "radical anti-Semitism."[271] On the 13th of the same month, the *Frankfurter Allgemeine Zeitung* rejoiced, speaking without nuance of the "debacle of philosophy in France." When France-Lanord affirmed that his article on anti-Semitism was out of date and would have to be rewritten, Jürg Altwegg added ironically: "But by preference in Paris, under the supervision of the French Heideggerians."[272]

Altwegg's sarcasm should not fool us: outside France, the little world of international Heideggerianism was also in upheaval. Günter Figal, professor of philosophy at the University of Freiburg and president of the Heidegger Society, acknowledged on 18 December that these notebooks did in fact contain anti-Semitic passages.[273] Later, he said in an interview for *La Stampa* that they were a "burden" to him. These "sentences of my Heidegger," he added, were "disgusting and awful," even though "twentieth-century philosophy is not conceivable without him."[274] The vice president of the Heidegger Society, Prof. Donatella Di Cesare at the Sapienza University of Rome, who, as it happens, is Jewish, granted an interview to *La Reppublica*, also on 18 December. She commented on the expression *Weltjudentum* (world Jewry), pointing out that it invoked "dark contexts, international conspiracies, the antechamber of the worst anti-Semitism."[275] Trawny, editor of the black notebooks and director of the Martin Heidegger Institute at the University of Wuppertal, suffered a deep blow to his beliefs. He opened up about his discoveries for the first time on 27 December for the weekly *Die Zeit*, reiterating the last conversation between Heidegger and Jaspers during the Nazi period, as Jaspers had related it in his *Philosophical Autobiography*, a conversation riding on the conspiracy of the Elders of Zion. Where Jaspers spoke of the absurdity of that supposed global conspiracy, his friend retorted that there was, all the same, "a dangerous international alliance of the Jews." Trawny believed that the publication of the first black notebooks would show that there was "a kernel of truth" in the account given by Jaspers. For Trawny, the anti-Semitism found there was *seinsgeschichtlich*, "ontohistorical," participating essentially in philosophical history, that is, in the history of being. The black notebooks did not mention *Kristallnacht*, when the Freiburg synagogue near the university was set ablaze. By contrast, "global Jewry" appeared in the notebooks as "one of the powers that, submitting to 'machination' [*Machenschaft*] (that is, to modern technology), fought for global domination. 'Global Jewry' is said to have adopted the aim of thwarting what Heidegger claimed to be the distinctive role of the Germans in the philosophical destiny of the West. An idea that can be understood only through the *Protocols of the Elders of Zion*."[276]

The new scandal created an increasingly loud uproar, even though neither the offending volumes nor their editor's essay had yet appeared. They were published in Germany beginning on 12 March 2014. The publication by Klostermann of the first three of the nine volumes, covering the 1930s in 1,200 pages, finally allowed these black notebooks to become better known.

Their surprisingly unphilosophical title came from Heidegger himself, who named these texts after the black covers that protected the dozens of notebooks,[277] containing forty years of writing, from 1930 to the early 1970s, with few deletions. Depending on his mood of the moment, he had given them names: the first fourteen were called "Ponderings" (*Überlegungen*), followed by nine "Annotations" (*Anmerkungen*), two "Four Notebooks" (*Vier Hefte*), two Latin "Vigilae" (*Vigilae*), one Italian "Notturno" (*Notturno*), two "Intimations" (*Winke*), and four "Provisional Remarks" (*Vorläufiges*). Their state of preservation was uneven. The first, *Überlegungen I*, dating to 1930, has been lost. Thirty-four of them were deposited at the Deutsches Literaturarchiv in Marbach in the mid-1970s.[278] A last notebook, *Anmerkungen I*, was found after the fact by journalists from *Die Zeit*, in the possession of Silvio Vietta,[279] the son of one of Heidegger's former mistresses, and was finally published in volume 97 in 2015. In addition to these texts, there are two notebooks, *Megiston* and *Basic Words* (*Grundworte*), whose uncertain status led the editor of the black notebooks to doubt thc appropriateness of publishing them.[280]

Heidegger had incorporated these notebooks into his long-term publishing strategy, which in a first phase entailed concealment. Intended to be revealed at the very last, the notebooks stored in Marbach, where access to the Heidegger collection was already discretionary, were moreover kept secret, out of sight. Our distress increases when we read a Latin quotation from Leibniz at the beginning of Heidegger's *Annotations IV*,[281] "Qui me non nisi editis novit, non me novit," "He who knows me only by my publications knows me not." It intimates the existence of a Janus-faced Heidegger: one public and published, but fallacious; the other private and unpublished, but authentic. This sentence involves more than a simple opposition between exoteric and esoteric teachings, depending on whether Heidegger was addressing the general public or initiates. It can be interpreted in the light of his strategy of concealment followed by belated publication, which profoundly changes the interpretation of his thought. Having once been known, his thinking now seems almost strange to those who have become specialists in it. The formal novelty of the black notebooks within the Heideggerian oeuvre moves in the same direction, alternating between aphorisms, philosophical chronicles, and intimate diary. Although his German has little in common with the Latinizing French of Montaigne's *Essays*, Heidegger's undertaking recalls that of the sixteenth-century writer: in both instances, a philosophical meditation caught up in an era also paints the portrait of its author, with the same ambiguity vis-à-vis the reader. Neither writer cared about "serving"[282] the unknown reader, to whom, however, they offered their texts (posthumously in Heidegger's case). This allows the expression of a great sincerity, there more than elsewhere, which can be disturbing in the case of the Nazi philosopher.

The edition of the black notebooks was accompanied by the little book written by their editor, with a title shocking from an orthodox Heideggerian: *Heidegger und der Mythos der jüdischen Weltverschwörung* (Heidegger and the Myth of the Global Jewish Conspiracy).[283] Trawny's thesis was the same one he had announced in *Die Zeit* in December: in his philosophical journals, Heidegger developed an "ontohistorical anti-Semitism" in which he incorporated vulgar prejudices, such as the conspiracy of the Elders of Zion, into a reflection on the history of metaphysics. And, as Trawny clarified a few months later in his preface to the French edition, "in one phase of his thought, Heidegger, within his narrative of the history of being, transformed anti-Semitic stereotypes that were very widespread at the time. My impression is that the end of that phase must be linked to his reunion with Hannah Arendt."[284] After Farías's lack of rigor and Faye's polemics, the affair was returning to the moderation and nuance of Ott's book. That prudence did not prevent Trawny from painting an uncompromising picture of the philosophical situation of Heidegger interpretation: "As I see it, on one hand, the extreme positions have become more entrenched, both the apologetic and the hostile position; on the other hand, a cautious and balanced interpretation of the *Notebooks* has begun to take the stage. Only that third voice is philosophical. It thinks it can clearly name Heidegger's 'error' and, at the same time, point out the unfathomably philosophical spirit of the *Black Notebooks*. It requires that, each time, it agree to put its own position to the test as well."[285]

The conclusion of his book opened the question of Heidegger's uncertain destiny after the latest revelations: "The *Black Notebooks* from the 1930s and 1940s will make a revision of our confrontation with Heidegger's thinking necessary. [. . .] Even if Heidegger's thinking survives that revision, the statements treated in the foregoing considerations will disfigure it like broke-open scars. A 'wounding of thinking' has occurred."[286]

The publication of the first black notebooks, as well as the essay that shed light on them, was the occasion for many reviews in the principal Western languages, and for television[287] and radio broadcasts.[288] For the global press, the matter was settled. The *Frankfurter Allgemeine Zeitung* ran the headline: "Martin Heidegger's Black Notebooks Prove the Philosopher's Anti-Semitism."[289] The *Guardian* followed with "Heidegger's 'Black Notebooks' Reveal Antisemitism at Core of His Philosophy."[290]

The *New York Times* ceded the floor to specialists. According to Richard Wolin, a professor at the Graduate Center of the City University of New York, "The evidence now isn't just undeniable, it's over the top." Likewise, for Richard Polt, who teaches at Xavier University in Cincinnati, the "presence of anti-Semitic comments in the so-called black notebooks [. . .] should not come as a surprise to anyone who has been paying attention to the evidence," such as the 1933–1934 seminar "On the Essence and Concept of Nature, History, and the State," published in Germany in 2009[291] and only recently published in English.[292] This is the text on which Faye had already written at length in *Heidegger: The Introduction of Nazism into Philosophy*, in which Heidegger evoked the "nomadic Semites" who would never understand the nature of "our German space."[293] Finally, Sheehan, a professor at Stanford, believed that too many Heideggerians "have swallowed the Kool-Aid and bought in wholeheartedly to his story about modernity" as decline, which Heidegger used to "launder" his anti-Semitism. The scandal of the black notebooks was an opportunity to "rethink, from scratch,[294] what his work was about."[295]

In a long and clear article published in the *New York Review of Books*, Peter E. Gordon was able to place the black notebooks within the perspective of the Heidegger affair and the philosopher's thinking about being: "The black notebooks may nonetheless help us to understand how a philosopher consumed with a question of such generality could come to see in the Third Reich a realization of his own ideas. In one of the earliest entries (circa 1933, though precise dating is difficult) he wrote: '*The metaphysics of Dasein* must deepen itself into its innermost structure and broaden into a metapolitics of the historical people.' "[296] As for the anti-Semitism that surfaces in some passages, it seems banal at first glance, like the Jews' talent for finance; but, Gordon averred, "it was Heidegger's singular genius to interlace these *idées reçues* with themes from his own philosophy."[297]

More than anyone else, it was Trawny who was featured in the press, where he could summarize his theory, recount the surprise of his discovery, confide his resolution to publish the manuscripts without modifying them, and note the pressures he had endured from the French Heideggerians to stop the publication of his essay and to strip him of his editorial responsibility. He could also pay tribute to the Heidegger family, which was standing firm.[298] In addition, supported by his publisher[299] and the Goethe Institute, Trawny, speaking with admirable elegance in both French and English, gave a series of lectures around the world. Colloquia, roundtables, and seminars were held in Meßkirch,[300] Siegen,[301] Paris,[302] Pisa,[303] New York,[304] and Bogota;[305] the publicity was done on websites and social networks or through mailing lists, and the events were then often filmed and posted online. The internet continued to disseminate the affair more inexpensively, because this type of event, limited in time and space, was becoming indefinitely accessible for zero marginal cost.

The Heidegger affair may have seemed to be at an end in late 2014. At that time, Trawny's book was followed by one by Donatella Di Cesare, vice president of the Heidegger Society. Published in Italy in November, her *Heidegger and the Jews*[306] embraced that same moderation and that same desire for a critical rereading of the former master, wishing above all to place his personal anti-Semitism within the general anti-Semitic tendency pervading the history of philosophy. A new dominant opinion thus took root even among the moderate Heideggerians. Heidegger was a Nazi and an anti-Semite, not by accident but in his very thinking itself. What more could be added? Then, in March 2015, came the publication of volume 4 of the *Black Notebooks*, which, dealing with the period between 1942 and 1948, would have revelations about the quintessential taboo of our time: the extermination of the Jews during the Second World War.

Di Cesare went public with the question on 8 February, advancing a shocking thesis. Contrary to Heidegger's supposed silence on the subject, he had expressed the view that the Jews "self-destructed" and that the Allies committed a crime more grave than the "gas chambers"[307] in preventing the Germans from pursuing their destiny. "Rigorous and coherent, Heidegger does no more than draw his conclusion from everything he has said previously. The Jews are agents of modernity" and "have besmirched the spirit of the West, undermining it from within."[308] "The Shoah is presented as playing a decisive role in the history of Being because it coincides with the 'supreme fulfillment of technology,' which consumes itself after devouring everything else."[309] The Jews ultimately "self-destructed," leaving the field free for the " 'purification of Being.' " The Allies, for their part, "failed to understand the Germans' mission and stymied their global project. This crime is held to be more serious than all the other crimes. This guilt has no term of comparison, not even the 'gas chambers' (an expression placed in quotation marks!)," because the German people was supposed to "save the West."[310] After such statements, what are we to make of the black notebooks? What are we to do with a Heidegger surrounded in a cloud of deadly poison gas? The philosopher Di Cesare refused to separate these texts from the rest of his oeuvre, to which in fact they do belong. They are not mere "historical documents" like those of Victor

Farías. They even make it imperative to reread in a new light Heidegger's entire body of work, as far back as *Being and Time*. Their author, she said, ought not to be proscribed or banished, as Faye wished. Very much to the contrary, it was necessary, without forgiving him, to deal with "the complexity of his thought in an open, critical fashion."[311]

Attentive reader, you will have understood that I do not share Di Cesare's interpretations, because they rest on false evidence, namely, that "annihilation" necessarily meant "mass murders," which would have been known to all at the time, just as they are at present.[312] Whatever reading is given to these passages, they distress us; published in Italy in a large-circulation newspaper and even translated online into English, Di Cesare's article had a tremendous impact. Notably, it was reprinted a month later in an opinion column in *Le Monde*.[313] Two days later, Di Cesare granted an interview to a German magazine, which soon relayed her theses to the German-speaking world.[314] On 23 February, Faye seized the opportunity to restate his theses in the *Corriere della Sera*, under the suggestive title "Heidegger, Prophet of the Fourth Reich."[315] Later, the American Richard Wolin told the German magazine, without a great deal of nuance, that "Heidegger considered the 'Final Solution' necessary." Wolin thus aligned himself with Faye, who had professed that idea since 2005, and with Daniel Goldhagen,[316] an American political theorist who had sparked an enormous polemic by explaining the Holocaust in terms of the Germans' "eliminationist" anti-Semitism. Wolin harked back to well before the Second World War, to Richard Wagner, who had wanted the elimination of the Jews as the "solution to the Jewish question,"[317] but without having a specific method.

Despite the variety of interpretations given to this fourth volume of black notebooks, their publication sank Heidegger. Through them and without being aware of doing so, he seems to have self-destructed for posterity. The historical irony is that the greater part of these final revelations come from the infamous *Annotations I*, the notebook that was thought to be lost. Although particularly contingent, the final catastrophe was nevertheless spectacular.

In early January, even before volume 97 came out, Figal resigned as president of the Heidegger Society.[318] Although he had argued the previous year that it was not a "society of hero worshipers,"[319] he had reached the point, in the words of the *Corriere della Sera*, of "no longer wanting to represent in any way an individual capable of assertions of a pathological nature."[320] As he confided to the *Badische Zeitung*, the black notebooks change one's relationship to the author, because "Heidegger is present there in person." Because he "constantly" wrote "I," his name was no longer simply the "label for a philosophical oeuvre." For Figal, then, it was the "end of Heideggerianism," and Heidegger's texts had to be "read in their context," so that he was not placed "on a pedestal."[321]

Heidegger's texts were called into question in other spheres as well. Even as the very principle of the "definitive edition" the philosopher desired was more than ever vehemently challenged,[322] the Klostermann publishing house, concerned about its reputation, came to doubt the authenticity of certain readings that had governed the preparation of Heidegger's texts. How was it that his anti-Semitism surfaced so late, having seemed to be absent, or nearly so, from the other works of the 1930s and 1940s? And there were regrettable precedents that could not be repeated if the publisher's image of seriousness was not to be further impugned. Volume 39, on Hölderlin's "Germania" and "The Rhine," even in its third edition, had transcribed the abbreviation "N.soz"—which is to say, "National Socialist"—as *Naturwissenschaft*, "natural science."[323] And as Trawny told *Die Zeit* in 1995, because of the opposition of Hermann Heidegger, who held the rights, and of Friedrich-Wilhelm von Herrmann, the philosopher's last private assistant and general editor of the *Gesamtausgabe* since that time, Trawny could not restore a passage from 1938 in volume 69 that prefigured the revelations of the black notebooks. In it Heidegger wondered "wherein lay the grounds for the predestination for planetary criminality characteristic of Jewry."[324]

At the University of Freiburg, Figal's academic chair, which was Heidegger's former chair, was to be done away with upon the retirement of its current holder. It was to be replaced by a mere lectureship—in analytic philosophy, the movement long in vogue in Germany and one radically critical of the propensity by metaphysics to create false problems with words.[325] Truly in the era of globalization, which has affected even Heidegger studies, a major online petition to oppose eliminating that chair collected 3,379 signatures in August 2015.[326] Also disseminated on social networks, the petition, though German, was written in English: "Save Phenomenology and Hermeneutics in Freiburg." So far, it has been unsuccessful. The calling into question of Heidegger also came to Meßkirch, where there was talk of stripping the philosopher of his honorary citizenship and renaming the Martin Heidegger Gymnasium.[327] Like a fallen Roman emperor, Heidegger faced *damnatio memoriae*, having his name chiseled off all the public inscriptions and being condemned to an ignominious oblivion.

The last and damning revelations, contained in the excerpts from the correspondence with Fritz,[328] would have caused a major scandal had they come out before the black notebooks. As it was, they only confirmed Heidegger's deep-seated, longstanding Nazism, which appears there in a more everyday, less metaphysical light than in his philosophical journals. On 13 October 2016, *Die Zeit*[329] quoted excerpts in which, in plain, nonontological language, Heidegger's Hitlerism and anti-Semitism, as well as his anti-Catholicism, were clearly expressed. The philosopher thought he recognized an "extraordinary and sure political instinct" in Hitler;[330] and, after the Nazi success in the legislative elections of July 1932, he wrote that "as early as the month of August [it] was clear that all the Jews [. . .] were regaining control and gradually freeing themselves from the state of panic in which they had found themselves."[331] He also wrote to Fritz: "I don't know how much your political opinions have evolved—but I suppose you are not among Brüning's admirers and that you leave Zentrum to the women and Jews as their refuge."[332]

Notwithstanding the interest of this news, its propagation was relatively limited. These quotations from *Die Zeit* were later reprinted by other organs of the press: *Il Corriere della Sera*, with an article by Di Cesare;[333] *Le Monde*;[334] and *Le Nouvel Observateur*,[335] which translated the original article in full (a translation later referenced[336] or immediately copied[337] on two French blogs). It was then mentioned in English for the first time in the *Paris Review* of 18 October.[338] This article itself received comments the next day on a blog in the same language.[339] In German, it was not until 25 October that a new newspaper (provincial, in fact) spoke of these letters;[340] in Spanish, they were at first mentioned only in a Málaga newspaper[341] and an online magazine,[342] before being cited, in January 2017, in *El Mundo*,[343] then *La Razón*,[344] and in two other online magazines.[345] In English, it was only after the translation of the article in *Die Zeit* in the prestigious *Los Angeles Review of Books* of 25 December[346] that it received more attention.[347] The titles were usually divided between distress ("A Moral Disaster," *Die Zeit*) and banality ("Heidegger, the Philosopher-Führer," *La Razón*), while weariness also made its appearance ("Heidegger and Anti-Semitism Yet Again," *Los Angeles Review of Books*), on a theme that was now beyond doubt ("Newly revealed letters from Heidegger confirm his Nazism—not that there was any doubt," was the subtitle of the *Paris Review* article).

More and more, the Heidegger affair is becoming common knowledge. Every year confirms somewhat more the philosopher's Nazism, clarifies it, shows its considerable scope. There is no longer any sensational news to be expected that would change the picture. At most, certain secondary features might be retouched. It is time for a return to pure academic debate, far from the reporters' cameras and microphones, and for publications, whether that entails the rest of his philosophical journals, the other writings in the so-called complete works, or, above all, the some 10,000 letters that Karl Alber is to bring out, in more than forty volumes. Once all these texts have been published, there will be not just solid ground but a bedrock on which academics will be able to build their scholarly edifices. Better than ever, the biographer will retrace in minute detail Heidegger's life, friendships, loves, choices, and aberrations. Better than ever, the historian will place him in his time, which will itself be illuminated. And better than ever, the philosopher will interpret his thought.

In addition, the moderns must no longer wish to worship or despise the master of Freiburg. More than ever since the publication of Faye's book, what is at stake is the right to read Heidegger, a right involving all the authors of the tradition, as Michael Marder wrote with conviction on a *New York Times* blog: "Now, if canonical philosophers were blacklisted based on their prejudices and political engagements, then there wouldn't be all that many left in the Western tradition. Plato and Aristotle would be out as defenders of slavery and chauvinism; St. Augustine would be expelled for his intolerance toward heretics and 'heathens'; Hegel would be banned for his unconditional admiration for Napoleon Bonaparte, in whom he saw 'world spirit on horseback.' "[348]

The ancient authors constitute a pantheon. If posterity honors them, or makes every effort to expel those it reviles, that is not the matter of philosophy. It does not recite catechisms, old or new. It does not achieve its aim either in venerating saints or in hunting witches. Rather, seeking to gain knowledge and wisdom, it attempts to return to the foundations of the human world through a sincere, rational dialogue that philosophers engage in, with others and with themselves. This dialogue, this sincerity, require recognizing, understanding, and respecting alterity. Without an other, there is only repetition of the same, pure ideology. Heidegger's being a Nazi is an opportunity for thought. Idolatry will diminish, and critical dialogue will be all the more productive in not lapsing into hatred. For that to happen, however, his Nazi destiny must not definitively kill him. Yet that may be how his story will be written: Heidegger adulated; Heidegger abhorred; Heidegger forgotten.

For the time being, if journalists and the public seem to be wearying of this thirty-year-old scandal, the black notebooks themselves continue to inspire torrents of scholarly ink,[349] but not always the best controlled. Recently published opinion columns[350] perpetuate again and again the errors in the media characteristic of the Heidegger affair since Farías's *Heidegger and Nazism* came out in 1987: on one hand, a negationism intent on minimizing or concealing the philosopher's Nazism; on the other, a sensationalism that, at the cost of dubious manipulations, paints a portrait more true to their authors' desires than to historical reality as it can be reconstituted.

The most common methods of negationism (the denial or the relativization of Heidegger's Nazism) have been to dissociate the man and the thinker, to understate the length of his engagement, or quite simply to assert that the new publications contribute nothing new to the subject and that the emphasis on his Nazism is a way of not having to read him. In a recent opinion column for *Libération,* Jean-Luc Nancy has given one of the most subtle examples of such negationism. The Nazism of the rector of the University of Freiburg, Nancy claims, is not a true question but rather idle talk. The true problem, from which both Italian fascism and National Socialism stemmed, is our own modernity, by virtue of which *notre monde,* our world, is *immonde,* foul.[351] For Nancy, it does not matter that these totalitarian regimes can be explained historically in any other way, or that Heidegger was philosophically convinced of their destructive but positive role. Hence he prefers, after conceding a few aberrations, to rehabilitate the master's word by exploiting commonplaces, foremost among them Heideggerian idle talk[352] and political correctness.[353]

Sidonie Kellerer, responding to Nancy in *Le Monde,* made use for her part of suggestive conflation, tendentious translation, and decontexualized quotation. She conflates Heidegger, a member of the Commission for the Philosophy of Law in July 1942, with its president, Hans Frank, a lawyer for the Nazi Party and, as of 1939, governor general of Poland. The actual role of that commission is unknown: why, then, claim that Heidegger "never ceased to participate actively in the implementation of Nazi policy"?[354] Not only do we not know whether he was still contributing toward defining that policy, we know even less about whether he implemented it, like Hans Frank and his rival in the general government of Poland, Friedrich-Wilhelm Krüger, chief of police and head of the SS. Kellerer borrows her tendentious translation and decontextualized quotation from Faye's latest book, *Arendt and Heidegger: Nazi Extermination and the Destruction of Thought.*[355] In late 1941 Heidegger is said to have written in the black notebooks that " 'the highest act of politics' consists of forcing the enemy 'to proceed toward his own self-extermination.' "[356] When we look at the original text, however, we find that what is at issue is not "self-extermination" (*Selbstausrottung*) but the much vaguer term "self-annihilation" (*Selbstvernichtung*).[357] Above all, the immediate context of the pages into which this expression is inserted designates the enemy explicitly: "Americanism," not the Jews of Europe. In addition, the term used for "enemy" is not

Feind but *Gegner*, "opponent," or, in this case, "enemy" in the specifically military sense of an adversary on the battlefield. And in fact, following the Japanese attack on Pearl Harbor, Hitler declared war on the United States, on 11 December 1941, which Heidegger therefore understood as an act of grand strategy by which the Führer forced that "jewified" country to self-annihilate in a struggle against the Third Reich, which he judged essentially invincible. This was perfectly consistent with the passage from the summer semester of 1942 quoted above.[358]

Thirty years after the media storm launched by Victor Farías, it is high time to debate Heidegger's Nazism with more seriousness, without negationism or sensationalism. The respect of readers comes at that price. Nazism, inescapable in Heidegger's texts after 1933, cannot be concealed without risk of misrepresenting his thought; and the sources are now so abundant that there is no need to caricature him.

Conclusion

It's no common place where they were born
They pity the poor wretches with all their hearts
The feckless ones without the presence
The presence of mind to be born in the homeland
When the alarm bell sounds on their precarious good fortune
Against the foreigners, barbarians more or less
They come out of their holes to die at war
The happy imbeciles who were born somewhere
The happy imbeciles who were born somewhere.

Georges Brassens, "La ballade des gens qui sont nés quelque part" (1972)

Can songs contribute to the writing of history? That may seem like an odd or idle question here. But even when it is not considered a source, a song of high quality—like poetry—can express a phenomenon in concentrated form and compel us to ask questions. Such is the case for Georges Brassens's song, which raises the provocative and stimulating question of whether Heidegger, a patriot, a champion of rootedness, born and buried in Meßkirch after spending almost his entire life in Freiburg, was a "happy imbecile who was born somewhere." It is almost the opposite conclusion that seems unavoidable: Heidegger was an "unhappy intellectual who departed from somewhere." Although it is not possible to deduce logically the philosopher's life from what he received in Meßkirch, the importance of childhood cannot be underestimated. Even when we distance ourselves from what we were at the time, childhood is a starting point that defines in the first instance the course our life takes. The original foundations it lays may become stronger, more solid, or, having been undermined, they may partially collapse. Their ruins may remain intact; much more often, however, they become materials underlying a new construction.

Despite the great distance Heidegger subsequently took from his youth, the bedrock of his personality was established on the Meßkirch way in about 1900, in the countryside between Swabian Jura and Lake Constance gathered around Saint Martin's Church. The church overlooked the sexton's house on the square, a dense maze of medieval streets, modern suburbs, and fields. Visible from the bell tower was that rural and harsh land where the two branches of his family had their roots: the Heideggers around the sheepfold on the Danube, the Kempfs around the "farm in the hole" in Göggingen. These two familial "places of memory" had for centuries concentrated the sweat and toil, the hopes and fears, the pride and joy of his peasant race, which Heidegger's mother transmitted to him. Not far away stood the monastery of Beuron, where the monks maintained close ties with the parish of Meßkirch: they had helped the sexton and his wife relocate after they lost their house near the church. Little Martin often went by the monastery with his mother. Also not far from there were the woods he visited with his father, to look for the materials for making pails, vats, and barrels. There he may have become familiar with the indelible experience of opening up a clearing in the dark wood with an ax. The spectacle of his native land that he viewed from the top of the bell tower, something between play and reverie, was filled with the pronouncements of Time and God, marked by the rhythm of the bells that his father, his brother, and he himself rang, following the prescribed rule. The eldest son of loving parents, he also held a special place among the children of Meßkirch. To ascend to the very top of Saint Martin's, to look out over the town, to be able to activate the magic of the bronze sounds, were such intense pleasures for these children that, in exchange for the privilege he granted them, they recognized the superiority of the holder of the keys, the young lord of the bell tower of Meßkirch.

Martin Heidegger's life at fourteen may already have seemed a destiny: a brilliant student, a pious altar boy who celebrated mass with his little brother on their private altar in the sacristy, he was, in the eyes of adults, a priest in training, an extraordinary position to hold in a Catholic town. Obedience to the eternal order of things and beings; submission to the Church, its leader, and the tradition that had revealed his preeminence among the patriarchs and among men; respect for the rhythms of nature, for life, the nourishing earth, and the culture inherited from the people and from history: such were the values of that conservative Catholicism steeped in obedience that molded Heidegger. Camillo Brandhuber personified the model priest for him at the time. Brandhuber was a man of God who, far from confining his discourse to the private realm of faith and commending individuals to themselves and to the Lord, waged, against the age and its corrosive unbelief, a determined campaign in the political realm as well, where the Church's interests were under assault. In that respect, he was representative of the evolution of the branch of Zentrum in Baden, which gave clerics a leading role in the political and religious struggle. This intransigent Catholicism strongly opposed modern civilization, liberalism, the secular and even anti-Catholic state represented by Baden, Prussia, the Reich, and even the town itself, where notables, liberals for the most part, fought a fierce battle against the Roman Catholics. In that way, *Kulturkampf*, that vehemently anticlerical "battle for culture," favored the development of a combative Catholicism for which Rome's growing influence over its faithful had already prepared the way.

Meßkirch gradually acquired the characteristics of a "way" similar to those analyzed by the narrator of *In Search of Lost Time*. Heidegger's native and ancestral town had a unity in his mind that it lacked in reality. Initially the exclusive center of his childhood, with his departure for Gymnasium and the minor seminary it entered into competition with the big city, another "way" that first appeared to Heidegger in the guise of Konstanz. The polarity was both physical and psychological.

Trained at the Gymnasium, and ultimately at the university, in a bourgeois, secular, even Protestant milieu, he was confronted with a vast, unknown world. In leaving his hometown, he found an opening into that world, which surpassed anything he could have imagined and which led to a battle between two cultures: the clerical culture of the minor seminaries of Konstanz and Freiburg, then the seminary and the Faculty of Theology; and the secular, philosophical culture that he first came to know through his Catholic milieu, with the decisive figure of Conrad Gröber. Later, this philosophical culture was emancipated from its ecclesial meaning in Heidegger's mind and acquired a value of its own, both theoretical and practical. Heidegger's youth and adolescence, spent away from his native town, in Konstanz and then in Freiburg, made him a child of the big city, who gradually broke with his original environment and began to speak a pure German without a trace of dialect. Having left Meßkirch to become a priest, he eventually sought to pursue a career as an academic philosopher, against the wishes of his mother and the rest of the family. That career had the advantage of making him a scholar, which he had desired since he graduated from the Gymnasium, without condemning him to a mortification of the flesh that went against his nature. He did not abandon any part of his political, cultural, and religious heritage: it was imperative for him to pursue the Catholic *reconquista* of an impious world, using the weapons of philosophy.

The Great War was a second breach in his Catholic destiny. Largely untouched by combat because his heart problems kept him from being sent to the front lines, Heidegger spent more time at the university than in the army. In one of his first classes, he met Elfride Petri, a Protestant, who became his wife and, from the end of 1915 onward, exerted the greatest influence on him. Disappointed by the difficulty of a career as a Catholic philosopher, filled with bitterness at a university that engaged in idle talk and seemed moribund, he gradually took his distance from the faith into which he was born. His time in the army also contributed to that breach. The war conditions he faced, though mild compared to those that so many other young men of his time confronted, radicalized him, leading to a brutalization consistent with George Mosse's theory. Beginning with his training period, his experience of the army's arbitrariness and his sense that the state itself, in denying the person's authenticity, was an aspect of a modern, century-long decadent culture, convinced him that the regime had to be replaced. His assignment as a meteorologist, at a remove from the front lines but close enough to feel the presence of his own death, at least partly inspired his theory of the being-toward-death developed in *Being and Time*. It also favored radical choices in religion and politics. When the birth of his son Jörg required that he choose the religion in which the boy would be raised, he resolutely decided against his family, his upbringing, and, in short, the promise he had made upon his marriage to rear his children in the Roman faith. In the end, as the military collapse was announced by wild rumors and general discouragement, the philosopher approved of the defeat, because he believed it necessary for a spiritual revolution of the German people. Heidegger thus became a revolutionary in 1918, a prelude to the official break with Catholicism in early 1919. His destiny was no longer the priesthood; it was to rebuild the spiritual life of his people through his philosophical word. In 1920 he wrote to his student Karl Löwith that he was going through "a de facto revolution" and was unconcerned about the "ruin"[1] that could result from his research. The same year, he began to characterize philosophy as a battle, a notion he continued to embrace during the Third Reich.

This statement is congruent with the evolution of the German political field as Mosse described it. Other causes are also in line with that thesis: for

Heidegger, the "Myth of the War Experience" had found expression even before 1914, at school, within his family, even in the games he shared with his young companions, because militarism was the norm in Europe at the time. The myth gained in strength after he met Elfride, the daughter of a Saxon officer, who was very concerned about the "heroes" on the front line and sent them food. It was further fueled by the discovery of Karl Jaspers's *Psychology of Worldviews* (1919),[2] in which combat, like death, was seen as a "limit situation" by means of which existence attained its finitude and hence its full essence. Distance promotes the idealization of what often inspires horror close up. Hence the "Myth of the War Experience" was conveyed by two people dear to Heidegger, neither of whom had seen combat. And he himself, who had not been on the front lines, was inclined to heroize the storm troopers he saw going off to fight, driven by "quite unflagging strength."[3]

Unlike so many of his contemporaries, Heidegger was largely impervious to the idea of external threats. He had little interest in concrete policies, preferring to that political quagmire a politics viewed from the standpoint of his intellectual foundations. Domestically, he saw Marx and Hegel behind the KPD. In foreign affairs, he paid more attention to the great French thinkers such as Descartes and Bergson than to the details of diplomatic relations between Germany and France. That disdain was as much the result of his great ignorance on the subject as of the little value he granted to anything outside the university and philosophy, from the maintenance of the household to German politics, all matters he left to his wife. What the nationalist and anti-Semitic Elfride embraced resonated with her husband, often in an astonishingly abstract way. In his writings, the scandalous *Judenzählung* (Jewish Census), established to address the supposed cowardice of Germans of the Jewish faith, translated to the idea of a "horrifying" "jewification of our culture & our universities."[4] The campaign for the legislative elections of 1920, during which the right popularized the idea of a "stab in the back" by the Jews, appeared in greatly distorted form in one of his courses, through the evocation of Paul's fight against the "Jews" and "Jewish Christians."[5] Heidegger did not feel the "eschatological anxiety" about an annihilation of Germany that Christian Ingrao detected in a number of SS intellectuals. Conversely, whether as an effect of Nazi acculturation or of her innermost feeling, Elfride showed evidence of this anxiety in the early 1930s, in the way she viewed France and especially communism. Similarly, for Baeumler in 1932, communism roused fears of a subversion of the country, in the context of the rise of the KPD. That anxiety was transmitted to Heidegger, who had become Baeumler's friend. Heidegger approved Hitler's accession to the chancellery for precisely that reason: "Weimar—has failed completely against the danger of Bolshevism—which your average Joe of today [*heutige Spießer*] does not always see."[6]

Reinforced by the political instability after the First World War, that sense of being threatened was not a result of the conflict. On the contrary, it had contributed to triggering the latter. Before 1914 the Germans saw their country as surrounded, encircled, a notion that culminated in Hindenburg's evocation, in his announcement of the armistice in 1918, of a world of enemies.[7] This has led Gerd Krumeich[8] to understand the acceptance of war on the part of the German and Austrian authorities as a form of preemptive attack to better defend themselves against a world that placed them in grave peril.

Heidegger was more worried about the threats undermining his people. In 1932 he explained to his brother: "What is at issue is no longer some little partisan policy, but rather the salvation or collapse of Europe and Western culture."[9] As of 1916, he began to be anxious about cultural "jewification." In the late 1920s he raised the possibility that "German spiritual life" might have to be "definitively abandoned" to "growing jewification in the broad and the strict sense," if that pernicious tendency was not thwarted through preferential treatment for "authentically rooted forces and educators."[10] To what degree did that anxiety express an anti-Semitism? Heidegger shared the common prejudices against the Jews, who he imagined to be rootless and profiteering, and who supposedly enjoyed a disproportionate and growing place in German culture and German universities. That was "jewification" in the "strict sense." This unfavorable disposition was counterbalanced by his friendships with Edmund Husserl and many Jewish students, including his mistress Hannah Arendt. All these relationships tended to delegitimize his aversion and even to serve as an argument against narrow-minded colleagues. Heidegger also saw a Jewish spirit in persons who were not Jewish by faith or by background. The Catholic priest Georg Mönius's *Hölderlin* made him want to become a "spiritual anti-Semite."[11] Partly metaphorical, feeding on stereotypes, and combined with Jewish friendships and a deliberate lack of animosity toward peers, that type of anti-Semitism should hardly come as a surprise. In the late nineteenth century, for example, Jean Jaurès wrote that free trade "sacrificed the producers in favor of the exchangers, the transporters, the speculators, the cosmopolitan bank. It hands over the honey of French bees to the Jewish hornets."[12] Yet he stated three years later: "I have no prejudice against the Jews: I may even have prejudices in their favor, because for a long time I have counted excellent friends among them, who for me undoubtedly reflect favorably on

Israel as a whole. I do not like racial quarrels, and I hold to the idea of the French Revolution, however old-fashioned and pompous it may now seem, which is that there is only one race in the end: the human race."[13]

Apart from the fact that Heidegger was little inclined to celebrate the unity of humankind, he was distinguished from Jaurès by the central place that, in its scope, the question of "jewification" occupied in his mind. As the letter to Schwoerer shows, the Jewish spirit in "the broad sense" could cover anything that, in one way or another, was uprooted and not authentically German: communism but also and a fortiori neo-Kantianism, liberalism, Christianity in general, and Catholicism in particular. Although the instances in Heidegger's writings of anti-Semitism "in the strict sense" are few in number, those having to do with uprootedness are countless and converge toward a radical rejection of Weimar Germany. Heidegger, antibourgeois and anti-intellectualist because he rejected the conventions and cult of culture for its own sake, now wanted to eradicate not the culture of the Second Reich but that of the Republic, the party-system culture, the culture of liberalism permitted by Zentrum and the Catholic Church, the culture of general "jewification" that was becoming ever stronger.

In 1918 as in 1932, his wish to see the downfall of a modern German culture he judged decadent had its origin in the Youth Movement. Founded in 1901, the movement had an impressive success after the First World War, with more than 100,000 young "wayfarers" (*Wandervögel*)[14] rediscovering the German soul as well as their own persons while hiking on their native soil, far from the urban, bourgeois, and degenerate civilization that had nevertheless produced them. As of 1920, Heidegger too cultivated a taste for hiking, skiing, and canoeing, in what he experienced as an authentically German nature. And that taste, which at first glance seems to attest to the continuing influence of the Meßkirch way in his inner Germany, was in fact far from an expression of his origins. Rather, it was the effect of the culture he had received from his wife and which he appropriated by engaging in physical activities and by reading Dostoyevsky, Hamsun, and Hölderlin.

In 1923 a Todtnauberg way appeared, initially the creation of Elfride alone. Their cabin was built at a ski resort in imitation of the cabin erected in Silberberg, in the Black Forest, by the Hüttenzunft, a student organization to which she had belonged a few years earlier. The cabin was in fact only a secondary residence, like those that other German academics enjoyed. The philosopher saw that structure, utterly urban despite the appearances, as the ideal haven for his thought, the perfect backdrop against which to imagine himself a philosopher-peasant whose thinking was firmly rooted in the surrounding nature. The philosopher's patriotism was never so visible and evident as after the philosopher, dressed in a folk costume that was partly fanciful or reinvented, had left Meßkirch spiritually and psychologically. Todtnauberg and his "existential costume" were only the trappings of a city dweller who had cut himself off from his roots. High above the modern world, breaking with the superficiality of urban and academic life, Heidegger could dream of a destiny as a revolutionary of thought called upon to change the spirit of his people with his meditations, which flourished in the distress of his mountain solitude. Radically rejecting the institution of the Roman Church, he increasingly detached himself from the faith into which he was born, even coming to see it and its political party as the enemy par excellence to be destroyed, in order to make way for the revolution to which he aspired. Meßkirch, which had not long before taken precedence over Berlin, was now pushed completely to the background by the evenly matched battle between the capital and the little ski cabin of Todtnauberg.

The Youth Movement, as contemporary historiography increasingly sees it, helped spread an antidemocratic, ultranationalist (*völkisch*), and anti-Semitic culture,[15] whose rise was one of the factors accounting for the popularity of the "Myth of the War Experience," especially among the young. As Mosse points out, "in the aftermath of the First World War, the Myth of the War Experience had given the conflict a new dimension as a means of national and personal regeneration."[16] In the imaginary of the Youth Movement, soldiers found the courage to fight for their people, out of a sense of personal responsibility that was fully awakened in physical communion with the fatherland. The enhanced militarism that resulted tended to give even greater weight to heroism, already so important in European culture of the time. It kept alive the memory of the recent wars and was quick to celebrate in song dazzling chivalric exploits and to recall the austere bravery of ancient times.

Like others who had been receptive to that heritage before the war, Heidegger placed a high value on combat and combatants, in, for example, paragraph 74 of *Being and Time,* where he erected the heroes of the past as models. The people made their appearance as an armed troop that had to face death resolutely. This was one of the consequences of that excessive militarism: the army's aristocratic and authoritarian organization model increasingly took root among young people in a country where liberal democracy seemed to many a foreign import, in contrast to the Germanic custom of *Führer.* In the aftermath of the war, partly influenced by these ideas, Heidegger nurtured the hope that "authentically spiritual" leaders, *Führer,* would change the life course of the German people. He imagined that this revolution, both philosophical and political—which he identified with his own destiny as spiritual guide—would occur at the university, the place where real politics was played out. It would come, he believed, from an original synthesis combining Husserl's phenomenology and an ontology taken from the Catholic tradition, but revitalized by a return to the Greek origins, against a backdrop of particularly diverse influences, including Dilthey's philosophy of life, Schleiermacher's hermeneutics, Kierkegaard's existentialism, plus the Youth Movement's ideals of authenticity and responsibility.

In the late 1920s Heidegger came under the strong influence of, if not Nietzsche himself, then at least the ambient Nietzscheism so strong among intellectuals of the revolutionary right (Thomas Mann, Oswald Spengler, Ernst Jünger) and, more broadly, among educated youth. As a result, his criticism of modern culture took as its particular target what he saw as his era's rejection of distress, in favor of the pursuit of happiness and security. In his view, the evil from which Germany was suffering, its distress (*Not*), came precisely from the absence of distress (*Notlosigkeit*). This idea was one of the constants of his philosophy even before the Third Reich,[17] during which it flourished, in peacetime[18] and at war.[19] For Heidegger, distress was not a problem, but the essence of all finitude; it is what the German people had to find again. The combativeness necessary for authentic resoluteness in the face of existence could be rooted only in that soil. This was one of the main philosophical reasons for the philosopher's hostility toward Christianity, which he accused of softening the harshness of life on earth through the promise of salvation after death. Contrary to the Nazi intellectuals—they too anxious about the annihilation of Germany—whom Christian Ingrao and Johann Chapoutot have studied,[20] what motivated Heidegger's radicalism was not distress driven by extreme external circumstances but only a heroic, antibourgeois ideology hostile to the Enlightenment, anchored in a political culture that preexisted the war itself and which National Socialism had appropriated. Heidegger thereby confirms Mosse's theory of the "Myth of the War Experience," a militaristic state of mind quick to celebrate the heroism of soldiers, which could also be found in Nazism. But he was distinguished by his Nietzschean ontology and his rejection of social Darwinism, which placed biology and the struggle for survival at the foundation of everything.

The grave political crisis that shook Germany beginning in 1930, as well as Elfride's political evolution—for some years, she had already had Nazi sympathies—led Heidegger to make a place for an institutional and partisan revolution within the complete spiritual renewal that his people was to achieve. The revolutionary destiny as he conceived it, and as he assigned it to himself, was also becoming National Socialist. Berlin would no longer simply be conquered; it would play a fearsome role in countering the scourge of the age. Nazism would make a clean sweep of past culture and would favor the pugnacity of the German people in the face of the distress of existence. Without that existential courage, the German people would not have the strength to assume their destiny. It was up to that people, unique in history, to carry out the mission of reestablishing the connection with the greatness of the early days of Greek philosophy and becoming the vanguard of the West's spiritual rebirth. After Spengler and his highly successful *Decline of the West,* Heidegger now made the fate of Germany central to European civilization.

Nazism was not just an instrument, despite its cultural limitations, which Heidegger criticized on several occasions. The philosopher himself succumbed to the effects of a skillful and violent propaganda whose slogans suited his own polemology, further augmented by his wife's ardor for rejecting the Treaty of Versailles. Heidegger read and agreed with *Mein Kampf,* even gave a copy to his brother. He shared the secular religion at the root of Nazi ideology, as well as the cult of youth, the aristocratic cult of personality, and the *Führerprinzip* that resulted from it. For him, as for Adolf Hitler's party, their origins could be traced back to the Youth Movement. In the late 1920s, moreover, Heidegger's irreligion and anti-Catholicism brought him more in alignment with Baeumler and Rosenberg. In addition, though at first his anti-Semitism may have appeared largely metaphorical, the result of a displacement or broadening of its meaning, that changed in the early 1930s. The philosopher, like Rosenberg, saw Catholicism as a Judeo-Christianity, an actual Jewish religion and system of thought whose pernicious influence was jewifying the Roman faith.[21]

For a long time, Heidegger kept his distance from Nazism, in spite of his sympathies in its favor. The desire to become involved arose only after the elections of 5 March 1933 and the subsequent, often violent, seizure of power in most German institutions. Then, as a storm wind from Berlin was blowing across Germany, he arranged to spearhead that *Gleichschaltung* himself at the University of Freiburg. Heidegger adopted the *Führerprinzip* characteristic of the regime, describing his authority as a *Führung,* a leadership consisting of bonds of military loyalty between a *Führer* and a *Gefolgschaft,* a following, as the Nazis imagined it in reference to a Germanic past borrowed from Tacitus.

Somewhat naturally for an academic, he placed the emphasis on the intellectual dimension of *Führung*. He was obsessed with the Platonic idea that philosophers ought to be the guardians of their commonwealth. In his rector's address, he therefore assimilated professors and politicians. He declared great ambitions for the university, which would be responsible for molding the future *Führer* and guardians of the German people's destiny. Without necessarily being political leaders, they would lead the people, summoning one of the powers that shaped their "world": "nature, history, language; the people, morality, the state; poetry, thought, religion; illness, madness, death; law, economics, technology."[22] Heidegger was convinced that being a *Führer* did not necessarily entail being vested by the Party. Alongside the university, the youth camps also produced leaders, recognizable by the "firmness" of their features, the "hard clarity" of their gaze, the "resoluteness" of their handshake, and the "brutality"[23] of their discourse. The philosopher was ambivalent about the NSDAP: although he became a card-carrying member on 3 May (the card was antedated to 1 May), his apoliticism, his hostility toward all parties as such, which had contributed tremendously to his decision to vote for the Nazis, made him see no role for the movement. He reserved for the university the role of ideological oversight of the people; he could therefore say after the war that he did not prostitute the university to the Party.

The reservations Heidegger expressed about the NSDAP did not extend to its leaders. Bowing to the leadership of the *Gauleiter* of Baden, Robert Wagner, he collaborated closely with the Karlsruhe ministry and oversaw the drafting of a new university constitution, which established the *Führerprinzip* at universities in Baden. He worked with the authorities of the Land and of the Reich, and also with the German Student Union, to which he offered his revolutionary fervor and the existential uplift of his word. He felt an ideological proximity to the students, whom he recognized as the firebrands of revolution at the university, and who he hoped would acknowledge him as their spiritual *Führer*.[24] Fascinated by Hitler, on 11 November 1933 Heidegger took his place among the handful of academics who solemnly pledged their allegiance in Leipzig. A few months earlier, on 4 May of the same year, he had explained to his brother that, whatever the mediocrity of the NSDAP, it had to be considered in terms of the "great goals"[25] Hitler ascribed to it. The philosopher had nearly the same motivation as many other Nazis: to work "toward the Führer," in Ian Kershaw's expression.[26] Heidegger tried to disseminate that Hitler cult among the students of Freiburg, proclaiming the complete identity between German reality and Hitler[27] and arguing that "the leader state [*Führerstaat*]

[. . .] signifies the completion of historical development: the realization of the people in its leader."[28] This was the fascination of an ambitious philosopher: he would have liked to approach Hitler and influence him, perhaps even guide him, but he did not succeed.

Heidegger's Nazism surpassed mere idolatry of Hitler, but his philosophy was becoming radically Nazi, and convergences made way for strong influence. He adopted the racism and biologism of the NSDAP, its conviction of the importance of blood and soil, though he was more subtle than others. He conceived of them in Dilthey's terms, within a spiritual world and a human existence that had their own laws. Even Heidegger's notion of science as philosophy was influenced by Nazism. When he recognized, as characteristic of early Greek philosophy, the "creative weakness of knowledge,"[29] which required a combative courage in the face of the distress of existence, and when he understood theory as "*the* loftiest mode of man's 'being at work' (*ἐνέργεια, energeia*),"[30] he was in agreement with National Socialism. It valorized the ethos of both combat and work, which bound everyone together in the community of the people. That was the "socialism" of the new regime, which Heidegger emphasized after the war, in order to portray himself in a more acceptable light. And that "socialist" notion of science resulted from his longstanding rejection of culture for its own sake, an anti-intellectualism that partly explains his support as a philosopher for a regime that was itself anti-intellectualist.

Although radically Nazi, Heidegger remained an original thinker. Firmly convinced of the need for three services—defense, labor, and knowledge—to organize students' academic education, he believed, in opposition to the German Student Union, that these services had to be conceived within the spiritual unity of science and "German destiny."[31] His originality extended even to his notion of the *Führerprinzip:* in addition to claiming that *Führer* did not necessarily have to become civil servants to achieve their essence, he asserted the legitimacy of resistance by the *Gefolgschaft,* the followers, which alone founded the authenticity of the act of following. That originality was relative, marked by the degree of autonomy vis-à-vis the system that Heidegger recognized in agents. The Nazi *Führung* also required the consent of the *Gefolgschaft* over which the leadership extended its domination: the regime's ideologues theorized that system, and the enthusiastic plebiscites and many denunciations to the Gestapo put it into practice.[32] Even totalitarian leadership depended on the followers' willingness to follow. Étienne de la Boétie understood this in his *Discourse on Voluntary Servitude* (1549): the power of tyrants is nothing without the consent of the people who support or tolerate them. In the same way, Heidegger's notion of the German people's spiritual revolution was not unique. Right-wing forms of totalitarianism, such as the Third Reich and fascist Italy,[33] leaned toward a revolution of the mind or spirit by means of education. As he often did, the philosopher distinguished himself primarily by the ontological subtlety of his existentialist thought.

With qualifications and at times with reservations, Heidegger concurred with Nazi ideology, even when it was translated into acts. He approved of the policies conducted by the regime: the revanchism it directed at the Treaty of Versailles, its hygienics and forced sterilizations, the new student recruitment law and large-scale exclusion of non-Aryans from the universities, the fight against the "un-German" spirit, the burning of books. He personally called on the people to support Germany's departure from the League of Nations and to adopt a single slate of legislators for the Reichstag, all the while making even more stringent the conditions under which scholarships would be granted to Marxists and "non-Aryans."

The advent of the Third Reich served to legitimize anti-Semitism, while the emigration of his Jewish former students removed the powerful counterweight Heidegger had found in them. Declaring his "blood and soil" notions, which he had previously kept quiet and which had become stronger, Heidegger was driven by the same radicalism as the most brutal Nazis, the only difference being that he expressed them only through the word, the extended hand of his Nazi salute, and discriminatory administrative measures, not through book burnings or fists. Believing that his people were of the same blood, to the exclusion of "Jewish" blood, he worked to "Germanize" the Reich by promoting among his listeners the "true and common rootedness [*Verwurzelung*] in the essence of the German university,"[34] whose mission was to mold the future elites of the *German* nation. His discourse reached an unprecedented level of violence. In 1933, in "the spiritual battle" against the un-German spirit that the Deutsche Studentenschaft wanted to wage "to the point of complete annihilation"[35]—in particular, the burning of books—Heidegger aspired less to constrain the students than to serve as their guide, teaching them both the need for an enemy within and the difficulty of finding one before preparing "the long-term attack with the goal of complete annihilation."[36]

In keeping with the Nazism of the time, Heidegger's anti-Semitic policies had the primary aim of excluding the Jews from the nation, which would then be able to confront its destiny. He did not want to kill anyone, only to annihilate the "Jewish" spirit within national culture by barring from the universities the teachers and books that in his eyes had no place there. Just as before, his anti-Semitism remained discreet, for the most part passive, reactive, or mimetic, responding to external stimuli. Such was the case for his meditation on the "complete annihilation" of the enemy within. Such would also be the case when he adopted an anti-Jewish measure that further reduced the candidates eligible for academic scholarships. He did so in the footsteps of Eugen Fehrle, director of higher education in the Ministry of Religion, Education, and Justice in Baden. Heidegger simply made his directive harsher, in a "cumulative radicalization"[37] typical of the improvisation at work in Nazism.

Heidegger saw what was most at stake in the fight against spiritual uprootedness and the powers on which it rested: communism, liberalism, neo-Kantianism, pacifism, and a fortiori Catholicism, which, more than the supposed "non-Aryans," constituted the enemy within that ultimately had to be annihilated, by means of a war in which the university was the battlefield par excellence. Against the colleagues he judged uprooted, the philosopher's weapons were less blazing firebrands than incendiary reports, the effects of which could be just as devastating, if not more so, in the end. In his battle, he reckoned with his concern for Germany's self-interest. Thus "the Jew Fraenkel" could be retained because he was a brilliant classicist compatible with the new spiritual order; Hermann Staudinger, who was not a Jew but was a pacifist, had to go.

The philosopher submitted his resignation as rector on 14 April 1934. It was accepted on the 27th, after a suitable successor was found. Heidegger was appalled by the student unrest and the opposition he encountered among his colleagues, which gave him a sense of powerlessness too much in conflict with his legal powers as *Führer*-rector and with the very idea of his spiritual *Führung*. Having done everything he could in Baden, he believed that the task incumbent upon him henceforth was to place himself on a higher level, at the Prussian Academy of Professors. Ultimately unsuccessful in imposing his views and personality, facing the rivalry of colleagues such as Krieck and Jaensch, he gradually retreated to his teaching, but without breaking with the regime in any way.

Nazi violence was not directed only outward. It was also internal, bursting out in internecine conflicts, which were waged in the realms of ideology, culture, and the university. They involved confrontations between the rector, the SA, and the Deutsche Studentenschaft, as well as Heidegger's stance against Kolbenheyer and the covert struggle on the part of Jaensch and Krieck against the former rector. The problem Heidegger encountered with the students was one that Hitler himself faced with the SA before the Night of the Long Knives: lack of discipline. The criticisms directed at the philosopher and the criticisms he formulated were another transposition to the university of the Third Reich jungle. Heidegger objected not to Nazism but to Nazis; neither the Nazis nor the Party, whose weaknesses he revealed, led him to renounce his support for the principle he saw at work in history. What is evident in these criticisms, in his fits of temper, and in his decision to no longer give the Nazi salute is not a resistance but a *Resistenz*,[38] a relative immunity, an internal distance very remote from a will to combat the regime. In that he resembled Hans Grimm, the author of *People without Space,* whom Heidegger admired. Despite his reservations, Grimm did not reject the Third Reich even after 1945, because he considered it the only regime that had had the capacity to realize his ultranationalist and colonialist ideas.[39]

The philosopher's failure to gain recognition as the regime's ideologue and, on a higher level, to impose the university as the place where the new German elites would be molded, was a dual failure, which can be understood in terms both of Heidegger's esotericism and of the anti-intellectualism of the principal high-ranking members of the regime. He himself shared that anti-intellectualism, but, in his case, it was combined with a university education that Hitler and his most intimate loyal circle generally lacked. Heidegger was thus a philosopher on the margins of Nazism: geographically, in that Freiburg is a provincial city in the small Land of Baden, close to France and Switzerland and far from the central power and Bavaria, the historical birthplace of the movement; institutionally and culturally, because of the peripheral place occupied by universities and academics; chronologically, since his belated adherence hardly allowed him to hope that he would reach the inner circle around the Führer, where veterans from the earliest days were concentrated. Finally, he was marginal by virtue of the originality of his philosophy itself. That marginality does not make Heidegger insignificant within the history of Nazism. The heart, the center, has its value: it is not possible to understand Nazi ideas if the texts of Hitler and Rosenberg are omitted. But the margin defines; it separates the inside from the outside. It is the borderline itself, without which a phenomenon cannot be understood.

Heidegger's very existence was a sign that intellectual elevation was not unattainable for Nazism, an ideology less idiotic than we humanists and liberal democrats would like it to be. Nazism was not professed only by imbeciles. Rosenberg was already on a higher level than the unmethodical ideologue Hitler. With the advent of the regime, Schmitt also added a further level of intellectuality; and Heidegger, it seems to me, stood even higher. We would like to deny such intellectual sophistication to the regime, not only because it clashes with our notions but also because vulgar, everyday Nazism was often extremely crude, as attested by the *Völkischer Beobachter* and even more by *Der Stürmer.* Above all, perhaps, in relegating the regime to a cultural barbarism, we can also confine it to a moral barbarism. History does not necessarily correspond to our tastes or distastes. We must resign ourselves to acknowledging that, despite the forced emigration of so many prominent intellectuals, scholars, and artists, it was not only mediocre minds who rallied behind Nazism. In filmmaking, Leni Riefenstahl is evidence of that, having invented new ways to shoot a Party congress or a sporting event to glorify the regime. And Heidegger is further evidence, having ontologized, poeticized, and historicized that criminal and totalitarian ideology, on which he conferred the ultimate degree of sophistication.

Although Heidegger was a Nazi philosopher, I do not believe that Emmanuel Faye is right to speak of the "introduction of Nazism into philosophy." At issue, more prosaically perhaps, is the reverse, the introduction of philosophy into Nazism. When Heidegger took up the central themes of Nazism, he always, or almost always, remained a philosopher. The proclamation that, because he elaborated an explicitly Nazi mode of thought from 1933 on, his thinking was at odds with philosophy, which by its essence is necessarily humanistic, involves a bias whose foundations are difficult to see. Philosophy as such is neither right nor left, neither democratic nor aristocratic, neither liberal nor totalitarian. It is a mode of theoretical thought that privileges the questioning of the very essence of things. That questioning does not occur *ex nihilo* or *ex aeternitate,* but always in the present moment of a given culture. Heidegger's philosophizing stems, therefore, not only from a heritage and a topicality that are specifically philosophical but also from the culture of his time, in the guise of his parents' intransigent Catholicism, in the guise of Protestantism, the Youth Movement, then his wife's Nazism, and, more broadly, his exchanges with other intellectuals of all orientations: the art historian Jantzen, the Hellenist Stenzel, the theologian Bultmann, the philosopher and psychologist Jaspers, the jurist Schmitt, the writer and essayist Jünger.

Heidegger's marginality was a sign of the persistence of a certain degree of freedom within the Third Reich. Politically reliable, restricting himself to the university, useful because of his great prestige within Germany and outside it, he was a servant of value to the regime, whose establishment he had sought to facilitate. He had complete latitude to make obscure ontological speeches that few listeners could understand. A Nazi academic did not need to spout the regime's orthodoxy or to comment from the lectern on Hitler or Rosenberg. It was enough to be loyal, which Heidegger unfailingly was: his retreat after 1936 was entirely relative.

Having taken his distance from the apparatus of the Third Reich, the philosopher regarded from afar the Nazi destiny of the people, aspiring to be their prophet in stormy times. It was now less a question of revolution than of Nazism's participation in the history of being and of metaphysics, understood—in keeping with Nietzsche and with Ernst Jünger's *Worker*—as the technological struggle for universal domination tending toward the complete uprootedness of modern existence. Seeing Nazism as a destructive "barbaric principle"[40] translated into "a mode of organization determined by soldiers and engineers,"[41] the philosopher believed that the pursuit of power for its own sake, characteristic of the regime, was a necessary stage in history. The Nazi destiny as he now conceived it was that of an exhilarating catastrophe to come. The course of things could not be changed, only accelerated. It required an active nihilism, a *politique du pire,* that would show the nihility of pure will, pursuing to the bitter end the will to power's project of world domination.

After a trip to Rome in 1936, believing he recognized that active nihilism not only in Hitler but also in Mussolini, Heidegger wanted to see these dictators as disciples of Nietzsche, playing their role in the struggle against the nihilism of the time. To put an end to the nothingness of modernity, obsessed with the pursuit of power for its own sake, regimes had to move deliberately, radically, in that direction, to precipitate the end of the era. Such was the case for the Four-Year Plan of 1936, which resolutely rearmed Germany and prepared the country to sustain a long war by achieving autarky. The same was true for the Reich's eugenics policy: Heidegger believed it was good because it strengthened the people, which flattered his militaristic nationalism, and because it prepared the way for German domination of the entire planet. Such mass crimes as the forced sterilization of the ill and of the "Rhineland mongrels," the countless murders of the disabled, though inhumane and illegal, were in his eyes metaphysically beyond dispute.

Technical and military development, though bad in itself because it favored the forgetting of being, was good inasmuch as it precipitated ruin. Illustrating in his manner the tensions between tradition and modernity that pervaded Nazism, Heidegger believed that the pursuit of power for its own sake was the only way to reinvent a future that would return to the principles of the Greek past. Gradually, he even convinced himself that the historical role of the

Germans under the leadership of Nazism, a barbaric principle, surpassed the greatness of their elders from ancient times. And it was up to him, a philosopher leading the way toward the overcoming of metaphysics, to prepare his people spiritually for a rebirth through his meditation on Hölderlin and his confrontation with Nietzsche.

The spiritual death that lay in wait was the principal threat facing the West, an internal threat that did not rule out other, external dangers. National Socialism was based on an extremely violent vision: the world, humanity, and nature are the theater for permanent struggle, battles to the death—which are in fact desirable because, without combativeness, decadence and ruin assail the over-soft soul. Nazi foreign policy was at its root an all-out aggression, tempered only by questions of expediency. Similarly, it bore within itself a sense of universal threat, a form of paranoia in its relations with the outsider, to which Heidegger himself succumbed. In 1935, when Hitler, in violation of the Treaty of Versailles, decided to rebuild an army with the capacity to attack, the philosopher said that the German people was threatened because it was "the richest in neighbors."[42] He adopted the vision of an encircled country that had prevailed on the right since the beginning of the century, to which he added the "pincers"[43] constituted by the USSR and the United States. That theme took up the anti-Semitic commonplace of a global Jewish conspiracy at work within the country itself, a conspiracy the philosopher is said to have mentioned to Jaspers as early as 1933. Consistent with the Nazi worldview, Heidegger considered history the confrontation between powers tending toward global domination—except that this domination would be only a path toward renewal, made possible by the ordeal of that cosmic conflagration. The Second World War disappointed him. France, which he expected to be a military power equal to its metaphysical role as the nation of Descartes, was so inferior to the Wehrmacht that the German people did not adequately experience redemptive suffering. And, at the end of the conflict, facing the ruins for which the Germans were themselves responsible, the philosopher could only despair at their failure to react: their complete collapse ought to have led to a philosophical conversion, an overcoming of metaphysics that would have opened the future path of the West. With the approach of war and then its arrival, the murder of Jews was still not the path to greatness promised by Germany's history. Instead, this path lay in Germany's self-destruction through the conquest of the planet as a whole. Did Heidegger in fact know of the Holocaust? Although nothing permits us to think that he learned of the existence of the death camps while they were still in operation, a passage from a letter to his brother attests that he knew that the war in the East, a war of extermination, was striking for its brutality and was precipitating the final apocalypse. "*The war is only now beginning* [Heidegger's emphasis]. The brutality [*Brutalität*] of the fighting in the East is obviously of 'world-historical' 'dimensions' [*offenbar von 'welthistorischen' 'Ausmaßen'*]."[44] To what extent was he really aware that this brutality entailed large-scale massacres? It is difficult to say, though he was acquainted with young men, his sons and some of his students, who were fighting on that front.

The postwar period was a trial for Heidegger, who not only experienced the humiliation of denazification but also the dark depths of depression. Barred from teaching, he nonetheless rebuilt his career, thanks in particular to his French disciples, who provided him with a new audience. Similarly, he renewed his ties with some of his former students, Jewish by faith or background, and made the acquaintance of the poet Paul Celan. His anti-Semitism once again found a powerful counterweight, made all the heavier by the spirit of the new German republic, where that ideology no longer had the appearance of a commonplace acceptable to all. The same was not true of uprootedness, a notion linked to his anti-Semitism and thus given free rein until his death.

The war had prompted Heidegger to reestablish ties with the town of Meßkirch, where he could work in greater safety than in Freiburg, while having the joy and assistance provided by his brother, Fritz. He did not waver from his anti-Catholicism, of course; all the same, the ordeal of denazification forced him to throw himself at the feet of his former mentor Gröber, archbishop of Freiburg and fellow resident of Meßkirch. While Berlin had faded in importance with the fall of the Third Reich, and while the discomfort of Todtnauberg became more obvious as Heidegger grew older, Meßkirch served as the backdrop for the self-portrait as rooted thinker he liked to paint of himself in his various texts. He did so by evoking the geographical coincidences that united him to Hölderlin or by explaining his extraordinary destiny as a philosopher in terms of a soil that, precisely, was not extraordinary at all, a quality that had become rare in an age given over to continuous intoxication supplied by endless novelties. The rooted Heidegger conceived of his destiny in relation to ancient Greece, seeing himself as a remote descendant, a brilliant resurgence, of its people. The return of German prosperity favored mass tourism and allowed the philosopher to tread the ground of the ancients, while the fascination in France with his ontologico-prophetic word led him to see Provence as a new Greece and a new homeland.

Despite this happiness regained, Heidegger retained his radicalism. The chaos his country and a large part of the world had endured during the Second World War had been insufficient, because modernity remained under the spell of technology. In the midst of the Cold War, he therefore averred that hydrogen bombs were really only dangerous if they did *not* explode.[45] In the absence of divine intervention, only a nuclear holocaust could reveal the nihility of global technology and put an end to the disturbing transformation of modernity in the atomic age. Likewise, the fall of National Socialism left him with lasting regrets. Not that he was uncritical: again in 1966 he judged that its intellectual level fell short of its mission in the destiny of the German people. He had difficulty rejecting the metaphysical necessity of destiny he saw at the root of National Socialism. Thus, after he had further fueled the scandal of his Nazism by intimating the favor in which he still held the Third Reich, he had to resolve to disguise his thought, resign himself to making it more acceptable to a democratic, liberal, and humanistic age constructed in opposition to the regime he still supported. Like Stendhal writing freely for posterity, which would recognize him for the genius he was and appreciate him all the more for it,[46] Heidegger conceived of the publication of his works as the gradual revelation of his deep-seated convictions, stripped of the camouflage they at first needed to be transmitted through a hostile period.

His reception was a long but intermittent scandal, particularly intense because some philosophers in France, the country where it was most alive, combined a deep fascination with his oeuvre and a revulsion toward Nazism. Considered by some to be the greatest philosopher of the twentieth century, the master of Freiburg had no dearth of defenders, in France and in Germany, in Italy, and even in the United States. Having become public in 1934, the Heidegger affair had many startling twists; new ones continue to occur to this day. For historians, the novelty comes less from the themes, in that the main lines have not changed very much, than from the popularization of that polemic, which, having begun within the narrow circle of German-speaking academics, reached a broad international public by mobilizing increasingly popular media: the print press, radio, television, the internet.

The deafening thunderclap heard upon the recent discovery of the black notebooks may suggest that Heidegger's Nazi destiny is sealed, that the reception of his work will be enduringly affected by it, or even that Heideggerianism is in its death throes. Yet despite the shock it caused the radical Heideggerians, the publication of the notebooks did not provide any great revelations regarding Heidegger's hostility to "jewification," which is attested strongly by the letter to Viktor Schwoerer, somewhat by firsthand accounts, and above all by a whole range of writings, such as the letters to Elfride and those to Kurt Bauch, along with the recently published courses. Even his Holocaust negationism was known to some, though denied by a majority of specialists. The black notebooks have confirmed and clarified that anti-Semitism, placing it at the heart of his view of the history of metaphysics. This has led their editor, Peter Trawny, to speak of an "ontohistorical anti-Semitism" (*seinsgeschichtliche Antisemitismus*).[47] Trawny has pointed out that explicitly anti-Semitic statements are few in number in the black notebooks as a whole, as in the rest of Heidegger's oeuvre. In that regard, anti-Semitism was a secondary matter in the philosopher's thinking. A broader analysis, attentive to implicit statements on the theme of uprootedness (or rootlessness), shows that the number of passages where anti-Semitism surfaces in one way or another is much greater, especially in those written between the late 1920s and 1950. The various historical contexts require us to count as anti-Semitic the discussions of uprootedness, which make them a key element in Heidegger's understanding of the world at the time, but without the obsessive and vulgar characteristics of the Nazi press.

The novelty of the black notebooks comes less from their content itself than from the reading that a number of Heideggerians have given them. Heidegger is not only a name on the cover but a man caught up in history, who wrote philosophical texts that must also be understood in their historical context. And, with the omnipresence in our minds of the images of the death camps, the conclusion—albeit debatable—quickly takes root that the philosopher knew and approved of the full extent of the Holocaust and set out to minimize it after the war. Hence, undermined by what represents absolute evil in our time, one of the greatest philosophers of the twentieth century falls from his high pedestal overlooking beyng.

Finally, Heidegger's letters to his brother, Fritz, have revealed significant details: Heidegger's acknowledgment that he read *Mein Kampf* in 1931, the importance he granted to the communist danger, his knowledge of the war of extermination on the Russian front. But, having come after the cataclysm of the black notebooks, they did not cause a scandal commensurate with their interest, a sign that the affair has become common knowledge and a banality. Heidegger, a Nazi—again? Yes, and so what? This has been known for a very long time. There is nothing about it that can still shock the public and prompt it to buy a newspaper or magazine. His Nazi destiny seems to have definitively caught up with him after his death. Either multidisciplinary research will take advantage of the enormous quantity of sources that continue to accumulate, in order to understand the life and thought of one of the most important philosophers of the twentieth century, or scholars will turn away because of the strong smell of sulfur emanating from him, or even, no longer rousing passion, Heidegger will disappear beneath the ashen dust of oblivion.

A superb mind, predisposed by his education and culture and ignited by his egotism, may be inclined to think of his life as a destiny. The example of Martin Heidegger encourages greater circumspection, invites us to see the plurality of mutable possibilities and to grant to contingency the role he reserved for providence. No path was mapped out for Heidegger, only changing destinies. Social conditions should have dictated that this cooper's son would find work as a craftsman, or even as a clerk, like his brother, not attain the privileged position of a professor at a German university, even less the global aura of a philosopher recognized as one of the most important of his century. Contrary to what he liked to imagine, history was not waiting for him to revolutionize philosophy in the 1920s or to become the oracle of a Nazi Germany falling into the chaos of power and destruction. The destiny he imagined did not materialize. Modernity pursued its course in a century he judged superficial and decadent, though tributes were paid to him abroad, even as his homeland was heaping opprobrium on him. Contrary to his hope that, with the passing of time, "the inner truth and greatness"[48] of National Socialism would be recognized and his prescience acknowledged, Europe did not break with liberal democracy, did not rehabilitate the most criminal regime in history, did not rediscover a real taste for brownshirt philosophers.

By contrast, writing after the war that "what came in the beginning always remains yet to come,"[49] Heidegger sensed how indebted he was to the Catholicism of his childhood. The Catholic destiny that initially shaped him would provide the original orientation for the other two destinies—revolution and Nazism—that, one after the other, gave a new direction to his life. At the same time, Heidegger held onto his desire to oppose modernity with the weapons modernity itself could provide, in order to defend a past worthy of being preserved. To the end, he radically opposed liberalism, as did the Roman Church after Pius IX's *Syllabus of Errors*. What was peculiar to the Catholicism of Baden was that it was particularly open to that very modernity. Hence, even when the "Old Catholic" schism occurred after 1870, separating the proponents of a vigorous modernization from those more attached to the Roman heritage, the Old Catholics—Conrad Gröber, for example—still retained the desire to be of their time. Gröber was an admirer of Leo XIII, an audaciously conservative pope, and he was also Heidegger's mentor. In giving the young man Brentano's *Aristotle,* Gröber initiated him into a philosophy that was fully modern and at the same time Catholic. Heidegger's early writings demonstrate his interest in accepting modernity, the better to fight against it, or, rather, to fight against its irreligious, liberal, socialist, and atheistic aspects. He therefore imagined putting to good use Einstein's theory of special relativity. Similarly, the pugnacity he showed during the interwar period sprang from his Catholic childhood, forged in the Baden crucible of a combative Catholicism that had been grappling with a particularly aggressive form of liberalism since the 1860s. Thus molded, Heidegger quickly showed an intransigence similar to that of Joseph de Maistre, who saw divine providence behind the French Revolution, a providence working to purify the country of the Enlightenment, a country that had become only too irreligious. In 1915 the young German philosopher was delighted that the ordeal of the war had made his people graver, a necessary prelude to conversion to a true faith. And he had less fear of the tragedies that struck human destinies than of the possibility that the Germans would be defeated by a victory that came too soon. Although he gradually broke with Catholicism during the First World War, he retained that radical acceptance of the destruction and suffering endured by his fellow citizens, on the condition that these trials play a role in their conversion: in 1918, to the spiritual and philosophical revolution inspired by the Youth Movement; during the Second World War and then the Cold War, to an overcoming of metaphysics, which was assimilated to modern technology. That continuity was real, and it was accompanied by increased radicalization. When he was of mature years, Heidegger accepted every aspect of modernity, in the hope of being done with it once and for all. He fully embraced *la politique du pire.* His radicalism was also one of his motivations for supporting the Nazi regime, whose advent would subject German culture and the German universities to terrible treatment, from which they might never recover. This had no great importance for Heidegger, because they seemed so decadent to him. Heidegger's first, Catholic destiny remained decisive in his relationship with modernity, even where his anti-Semitism was concerned. Granted, it initially developed in spite of his original Catholicism and later in opposition to it. In Meßkirch, unlike in Vienna, the absolute enemy was the liberal, not the Jew. Nevertheless, what the philosopher denounced in speaking of "jewification" had to do in great part with the denunciation of modernity by the conservative Catholicism of his youth.

It is also ironic that Heidegger, though hostile to the system of Catholicism—which, like other Nazis, he saw as a check on the national revolution to which the movement aspired—developed a political theology in the manner of Hitler and Rosenberg. In doing so, he continued to embrace a fundamentally religious mode of thinking that referenced both his former Catholicism and his assiduous though temporary engagement with Protestantism. Transformed under the pressure of events into a philosophy of the great historical moment, a destiny or vocation to which one had to respond, that thinking had a theological foundation, which consisted of his reflection on truth as *aletheia* and, finally, as freedom, an openness to the manifestation or revelation of being. Like Goebbels, who placed the freedom of the people in opposition to that of the individual, in order to justify crushing individual freedom,[50] Heidegger's Nazism grounded the obedience of the *Gefolgschaft* in a freedom conceived in antiliberal terms, ontological in his case. One had to choose the freedom to answer the call of a common destiny, which commanded that one follow one's leaders. With the same certainty he had had in his battle as a seminarian against the irreligious thinking of the century, harboring no doubts about the veracity of his own thought because he saw it as consistent with the treasure of Catholic truth, Heidegger believed he detected in Nazism the path mapped out for the German people not by God but by history. The philosopher became an apostate, all the more vehement in that he erected against Christianity the intellectual foundations that had shaped him. He did so with an ardor hardly more chastened than the faith of his youth, when he defended the Church against the assaults of an impious century. Since that time, however, God had died. That blinding certainty of his own thought, however much it might change, explains his disdain for deliberation both public and private, which was only too liberal, an expression of the spirit of the Enlightenment. There was no need for a parliament, or for the League of Nations, or for temporizing; all that was needed was the resoluteness to bow to the vocation imparted by history. Similarly, when he imagined an academy of professors more likely than the (overly liberal) university to be up to the task of the age, an academy that would develop a "unitary worldview,"[51] he saw it as a kind of secularized monastery in the service of Nazism, a synthesis of sorts of the Meßkirch way and the Berlin way.

A former aspiring priest, Heidegger continued to feel he was guided by providence, or even that he was its envoy. This idea was similar to Hitler's own when he proclaimed before a large crowd in Munich, on 14 March 1936: "I advance with the assurance of a sleepwalker on the path that providence has called me to take."[52] The philosopher aspired to be not a sleepwalking chief of state but a seer and prophet, which after the rectorship took the form of a "prophetic exegesis"[53] of Hölderlin and Nietzsche and the search for a new discourse that would change the course of history. Well before the Third Reich, Heidegger managed to play for his disciples the role of priest and even guru, as well as master thinker. He imposed a "charismatic domination" (to use Max Weber's term) similar to what the Führer later exercised over the German people. That relationship required not only that the dominator feel touched by divine grace, allowing him to pose as an oracle or messiah, but also that he be recognized as such by a charismatic community, that is, that he be able to think of himself and live his life in religious terms. Hitler needed the grave political and economic crisis in order to be gradually perceived as a savior by the German people and to spark a fascination that affected even Heidegger: in 1932 he was awaiting "men who carry within themselves a distant readiness."[54] He had the same effect on his students in the 1920s, in many cases transforming them into followers. Relying on the authority that emanated from the lectern from which he was speaking, he cast his self-assured, acerbic gaze on philosophy as a whole, while employing a hermetic style to call for spiritual combat and revolution. Young people, easily influenced because of their youthful ignorance and their shared appetite for a modern and secularized theosophy, responded to the call, even despite their cultural differences: some, like Gadamer, were readers of Stefan George, while others, like Arendt, had their roots in Judaism.

Each in his own way, Hitler and Heidegger wanted to elevate themselves above the shared human condition. That pretention to be more than human is what the Greeks called *hubris* (ὕβρις). Hitler's hubris led Germany into totalitarianism, crime, and ruin. In Heidegger's case, even as it persuaded him to support Hitler's regime, that hubris sparked the grandiose hope of revolutionizing philosophy, of becoming the spiritual master of his age, of guiding Germany beyond metaphysics, even if that meant striding in sorrow across a planet in ashes. As it was for Hitler, who suffered from depression toward the end of 1942,[55] hubris was the cause of many of the philosopher's torments: the trauma of his rectorship's failure, then his depression about being implicated for his role in the Third Reich and seeing his grandiose dream to be Germany's spiritual guide crushed. Heidegger's hubris did not cause only his own unhappiness. His wife shed tears over the overly ardent homages he paid to so many women who came to worship him and whom he needed to accomplish his great Work.

Heidegger loved the Greek poets and thinkers. Perhaps he should have meditated more fully on Aeschylus, who gave him this warning in *The Persians:* "For hubris, when it springs, / Puts forth the blade of vengeance, and its fruit / Yields a ripe harvest of repentant tears."[56]

Notes

Preface

1. Martin Heidegger, *Gesamtausgabe,* 102 vols., Stuttgart: Klostermann, 1975–, vol. 97, p. 99. References to the authorized edition of Heidegger's works will henceforth be cited as GA, followed by the volume and page numbers. [If an English-language edition is used for quotations, the full reference is given at the first appearance in the note following the reference to GA.—Trans.]

2. "Humanas actiones non ridere, non lugere, neque detestari, sed intelligere" (Spinoza, *Political Treatise,* trans. R. H. M. Elwes, New York: Dover, 1951, chap. 1, §4, p. 288).

3. Translators' note: This refers to Diogenes' "refutation" of Zeno's paradox denying that movement exists (he just stood up and walked around).

Introduction

1. *Hegel's Philosophy of Mind,* translated from the *Encyclopaedia of the Philosophical Sciences,* with five introductory essays, by William Wallace, Oxford: Clarendon Press, 1894, §549, vol. 3, p. 151.

2. GA 40, 41.

3. GA 4, 30.

4. Speech given by Hitler in Potsdam on 21 March 1933, in Max Domarus (ed.), *Reden und Proklamationen. 1932–1945,* 2 vols., Neustadt an der Aisch: Schmidt, 1963, vol. 1, p. 226; hereafter cited as "ed. Domarus," followed by the volume and page number.

5. Marcel Proust, "Combray," in *Du côté de chez Swann,* Paris: Garnier Flammarion, 1987 [1913], p. 243; "Combray," in *Swann's Way,* trans. C. K. Scott Moncrieff and Terence Kilmartin, revised by D. J. Enright, New York: Modern Library, 1992, p. 189.

6. Proust, "Combray," p. 243; *Swann's Way,* p. 189.

7. Proust, "Combray," p. 255; *Swann's Way,* p. 205.

8. Proust, "Combray," p. 243; *Swann's Way*, p. 189.

9. Proust, "Combray," p. 243; *Swann's Way*, p. 189.

10. A major idea that Fédier developed notably in his edition of Heidegger's *Écrits politiques*, Paris: Gallimard, 1955, p. 17ff.

11. For example, the Greek philosopher Kostas Axelos wrote: "Heidegger was a National Socialist for a few months, published texts and gave speeches that were Nazi. That is a fact." ("Heidegger et le problème de la philosophie," in *Vers la pensée planétaire*, Paris: Minuit, 1964, p. 223.) Similarly, André Glucksmann asserted that "for a few months in 1933, Heidegger gave Nazi speeches [. . .]. Let us leave it to the learned who have had the good fortune to escape this wretchedness to demonstrate that it is solely a 'German wretchedness,' that Heidegger should be burned for his six months of sympathy with the National Socialists, and that we must skip over fifty years that others have spent saluting the (national) socialism of the country of the Gulag Archipelago." (André Glucksmann, *Les maîtres penseurs*, Paris: Grasset, 1977, p. 196.) More recently, Hadrien France-Lanord suggested that Heidegger was asked to resign after "ten months" ("Heidegger: Res loquitur ipse. À propos d'un raisonnement sophistiqué de monsieur Roger-Pol Droit," 25 March 2005, http://parolesdesjours.free.fr/scandale.htm). In the preface to his *Heidegger à plus forte raison* (Paris: Fayard, 2007), François Fédier referred to "a few months"; and Servanne Jollivet, despite her critical inclination, generally conformed to Heideggerian orthodoxy: "More than a mistake, it seems that we have to speak here of a genuine compromise of principles, a conscious and premeditated participation in National Socialism, at least during the first months of his involvement as rector of the University of Freiburg, while at the same time noting that he accepted this office only when called upon to do so by the former rector and was supported in this matter by his peers, encouraged by the hope that he would be able to guide and in a certain sense shape academic policy." (Servanne Jollivet, "Enjeux de la polémologie heideggerienne. Entre *Kriegsideologie* et refondation politique," *Astérion* 6 [April 2009], http://asterion.revues.org/document1504.html.)

12. Adolf Hitler, *Mein Kampf*, trans. Ralph Manheim, Boston: Houghton Mifflin, 1971 (henceforth cited as MK), 179.

13. MK, 477.

14. MK, 183.

15. MK, 267.

16. MK, 183, translation modified.

17. MK, 180–181.

18. Mosse started from the observation that following the First World War, German politics in the 1920s had become more brutal and opened the way to Nazi violence: in speeches, this increased brutality of politics was expressed as praise for war, fighting, death, and the reduction of the other to an enemy. In action, it was manifested by the 324 assassinations committed by the right wing and the 22 committed by the far left between 1919 and 1923 (George Lachmann Mosse, *Fallen Soldiers: Reshaping the Memory of the*

World Wars, Oxford: Oxford University Press, 1990, p. 169), or by the activities of the *Freikorps* and the partisan militias, especially on the right (p. 161). In general, Mosse explained this "ruthlessness" mainly as "an attitude of mind derived from the war and the acceptance of the war itself" (p. 159), an attitude of mind that proceeded in part from the physical or symbolic brutality undergone by soldiers at the front or simply in the army: "The strident tone of the officers, and the passivity of the men, as well as the rough-and-ready life in the squad, must have affected some soldiers" (p. 162). Undeniably, this experience of combat was not the sole reason given by Mosse, contrary to what some historians, such as Thomas Weber, seem to think: reducing the origin of brutalization to the experience at the front, Weber rejects Mosse's theory, basing his argument on the major role played by postwar violence among young people who had not fought in the war: "The generation that had been too young to fight in the First World War [. . .] were far more likely to join the Nazi Party than the veterans of the First World War. It was thus non-service in the war and a feeling of having been cheated from an opportunity to serve, rather than the experience of combat and an alleged brutalization during the First World War, which increased the likelihood of German men joining Private Hitler's party." (Thomas Weber, *Hitler's First War,* Oxford: Oxford University Press, 2010, pp. 262–263.) But Mosse himself pointed out that among the *Freikorps,* "they were officers and men who continued to fight between 1919 and 1921, though the war had ended, and many of them were not veterans but were recruited at school. They attempted to crush revolution at home, to drive the Bolsheviks from the Baltic states, and to defend Upper Silesia against the Poles. [. . .] They continued wartime traditions, opposed to the Germany which had accepted the humiliating treaty of peace" (p. 168). Noting the importance of the culture of war itself to explain the brutality of Nazism found even in men who were too young to fight, Mosse anticipated Christian Ingrao in *Croire et détruire* by emphasizing instead the moral and political value accorded to war as such. In the first sentence of his chapter on brutalization, Mosse clearly posited that, "in the aftermath of the First World War, the *Myth* [my emphasis] of the War Experience had given the conflict a new dimension as a means of national and personal regeneration" (p. 159). This "myth," which existed before the first worldwide conflict, was composed of militarism and the memory of German wars in the nineteenth century, and it continued to spread after 1918; this was particularly noticeable at the beginning and end of the Weimar Republic, and culminated in the Third Reich. For Mosse, the "brutalization" Germany underwent was an extreme case of the exaltation of the myth of war, whose roots lay in the French Revolution.

19. Christian Ingrao, *Croire et détruire. Les intellectuels dans la machine de guerre SS,* Paris: Fayard, 2010, p. 40.

20. Michael Wildt, *Generation des Unbedingten. Das Führungskorps des Reichssicherheitshauptamtes,* Hamburg: Hamburger Edition, 2002.

21. On the credibility that the October Revolution in Russia and the People's State of Bavaria tended to give to the far right's theses, see Weber, *Hitler's First War,* pp. 227–229.

22. "Sine ira et studio" (Tacitus, *Annals* 1, 1, 3).

23. This is precisely the meaning of Mosse's thesis regarding the brutalization of European societies.

24. I fully agree with Johann Chapoutot on this point (*La loi du sang. Penser et agir en nazi,* Paris: Gallimard, 2014, p. 13). The Third Reich was able to unite a considerable number of states and individuals around the idea of a "New Order" in Europe, in a battle with the Soviet Union or in more or less direct cooperation with the Nazis' efforts to exterminate Jews. Ideologically, we need only think of the influence on Nazism exerted by Frenchmen such as Gustave Lebon, Arthur de Gobineau, and Georges Vacher de Lapouge; Britons such as Charles Darwin, Francis Galton, the founder of eugenics, and especially Herbert Spencer. Houston Stewart Chamberlain, whose *Foundations of the Nineteenth Century* (1899) was a key reference for German far-right ideology, was a German-speaking Englishman; and, finally, *The Protocols of the Elders of Zion,* which was so important in the Nazis' anti-Semitic imagination, is a forgery written by the czar's secret police.

25. In this sense, despite the interest of his work, I cannot subscribe to Daniel Morat's claim that Heidegger's thought was "conservative," when, in fact, it was precisely at the end of the First World War that the project of a revolution was introduced into Heidegger's thinking (Daniel Morat, *Von der Tat zur Gelassenheit. Konservatives Denken bei Martin Heidegger, Ernst Jünger und Friedrich Georg Jünger. 1920–1960,* Göttingen: Wallstein, 2007).

26. Zeev Sternhell, *La droite révolutionnaire, 1885–1914. Les origines françaises du fascisme,* new enlarged edition, Paris: Fayard, 2000 [1st ed. 1978].

27. Jacques Digast, "Aspects d'une crise des cultures européennes au tournant du siècle (1890–1910)," in Barbara Koehn (ed.), *La crise de la modernité européenne,* Rennes: PUR, 2001.

28. A controversial term, the "Conservative Revolution" has inspired a significant body of historical literature, including: Stefan Breuer, *Anatomie der konservativen Revolution,* Darmstadt: Wissenschaftliche Buchgesellschaft, 1982; Louis Dupeux, "Révolution conservatrice et modernité," *Revue d'Allemagne* 14 (1982): 2–34; Louis Dupeux (ed.), *La "révolution conservatrice" allemande sous la république de Weimar,* Paris: Éd. Kimé, 1992; Barbara Koehn (ed.), *La révolution conservatrice et les élites intellectuelles en Europe,* Rennes: PUR, 2003; Armin Mohler, *Die Konservative Revolution in Deutschland:1918–1932* [1949], 6th revised and corrected edition, Graz: Ares, 2005. One of the shortcomings of this term is that it leads to a dissociation from Nazism of certain individuals who sympathized with the NSDAP; in addition, it tends to focus attention on the Germany of the 1920s.

29. Gilbert Merlio, "Die Idee einer Revolution von rechts am Ende der Weimarer Republik," in Koehn (ed.), *La crise de la modernité,* Rennes: PUR, 2001.

30. Jérôme Grondeux, *Georges Goyau. Un intellectuel catholique sous la IIIe République (1869–1939),* Rome: École française de Rome, 2007, p. 3.

31. Chapoutot, *La loi du sang*, pp. 519 and 522.

32. Bernd Martin (ed.), *Martin Heidegger und das "Dritte Reich." Ein Kompendium*, Darmstadt: Wissenschaftliche Buchgesellschaft, 1989; Bernd Martin & Gottfried Schramm (eds.), *Martin Heidegger. Ein Philosoph und die Politik*, Rombach: Freiburg, 2nd enlarged ed., 2000.

33. Domenico Losurdo, *La communità, la morte, l'Occidente. Heidegger e l'ideologia della guerra*, Turin: Bollati Boringhieri, 1991.

34. Hugo Ott, *Martin Heidegger: A Political Life*, trans. Allan Blunden, London: HarperCollins, 1993.

1. A Catholic Childhood in a Town in Southwestern Germany

1. GA 13, 87.

2. Armin Heim, *Meßkirch*, Erfurt: Sutton Verlag, "Die Reihe Archivbilder," 2005, p. 49.

3. *Oberbadischer Grenzbote*, 18 January 1899.

4. Fritz Heidegger, "Ein Geburtstagbrief des Bruders," in *Martin Heidegger zum 80. Geburtstag von seiner Heimatstadt Meßkirch*, Frankfurt: Klostermann, 1969, p. 62.

5. GA 16, 488–490.

6. Fritz Heidegger, "Ein Geburtstagbrief," pp. 59–60.

7. Letter to Elfride, 13 December 1915, in Martin Heidegger, *Letters to His Wife 1915–1970*, ed. Gertrud Heidegger, trans. R. D. V. Glasgow, Cambridge, U.K.: Polity Press, 2008, p. 5. Translation of *"Mein liebes Seelchen!" Briefe Martin Heideggers an seine Frau Elfride 1915–1970*, Munich: Deutsche Verlags-Anstalt, 2005.

8. Fritz Heidegger, "Ein Geburtstagbrief," p. 59.

9. GA 13, 88.

10. Fritz Heidegger, "Ein Geburtstagbrief," pp. 58–59.

11. Ibid., p. 58.

12. Ibid., pp. 58–59.

13. GA 13, 88.

14. Fritz Heidegger, "Ein Geburtstagbrief," pp. 60–61.

15. Adolphe Thiers, *De la propriété*, Paris: Paulin, Lheureux et Cie, 1848, p. 68.

16. Fritz Heidegger, "Vom Vorschussverein zur Volksbank 1864–1964," in *100 Jahre Volksbank e.G.m.b.H. 1864–1964*, Meßkirch, p. 22.

17. Ott, *Martin Heidegger*, p. 46.

18. Ibid., p. 44.

19. Ibid., p. 47.

20. Heim, *Meßkirch*, p. 75.

21. Fritz Heidegger, "Ein Geburtstagbrief," p. 59.

22. Letter to Elfride, 13 December 1915, p. 5.

23. Fritz Heidegger, "Ein Geburtstagbrief," p. 59.

24. Letter to Elfride, 17 March, 1918, p. 38.

25. Edwin Ernst Weber, "Bekannt durch seinen politisch wie religiös unsichern Charakter," in Weber (ed.), *Renitenz und Genie. Meßkirch und der badische Seekreis zwischen 1848/49 und dem Kulturkampf,* Konstanz: UVK, 2003, pp. 91–127, here p. 123.

26. On the family, see Elsbeth Büchin & Alfred Denker, *Martin Heidegger und seine Heimat,* Stuttgart: Klett-Cotta, 2005, Part 3: "Martin Heideggers Vorfahren," pp. 173–200, and Part 4: "Anhang," pp. 201–238, along with the family tree reproduced in the book.

27. Letter to Elfride, 13 December 1915, p. 5.

28. Quoted in Ott, *Martin Heidegger,* p. 45.

29. GA 16, 342.

30. GA 16, 341.

31. GA 16, 342.

32. Ibid.

33. Ibid.

34. GA 13, 65–66.

35. GA 13, 88.

36. Letter to Elfride, 27 September 1918, p. 116.

37. Letter to Elfride, 4 September 1918, p. 50.

38. Ibid.

39. Ibid.

40. Fritz Heidegger, "Ein Geburtstagbrief," p. 62.

41. Letter to Elfride, 13 December 1915, p. 5.

42. However, he did not receive this sacrament in Saint Martin's Church, but rather in the makeshift church that the Catholics used until 1895.

43. Büchin & Denker, *Martin Heidegger und seine Heimat,* p. 28.

44. GA 13, 113.

45. GA 16, 595.

46. Letter to Elfride, 13 December 1915, p. 5.

47. Ibid.

48. GA 13, 90.

49. GA 13, 113.

50. GA 13, 115–116.

51. "Allerseelenstimmungen," *Heuberger Volksblatt,* 5 November 1909, in Büchin & Denker, *Martin Heidegger und seine Heimat,* pp. 38–41, here p. 38.

52. GA 13, 6.

53. Letter from Fritz Heidegger, 26 October 1947, to Gröber, archbishop of Freiburg, in Büchin & Denker, *Martin Heidegger und seine Heimat,* p. 119.

54. Conrad Gröber, *Aus meinem römischen Tagebuch,* Freiburg: Herder, 1947, p. 180.

55. Ibid.

56. According to Karl Fischer's memories, as reported by Elsbeth Büchin in "Erinnerung des Altbürgermeister Karl Fischer aus Meßkirch an seine Begegnungen mit Martin Heidegger (hauptsächlich aus der Bubenzeit)," in Büchin & Denker, *Martin Heidegger und seine Heimat*, p. 242.

57. Letter to Elfride, 13 December 1915, p. 5.

58. *Mittlerer Katechismus der katholischen Religion für das Erzbistum Freiburg*, Freiburg: Herder, 1903, p. ix.

59. Ibid., p. 2.

60. Ibid., p. 6.

61. Ibid., p. 8.

62. Ibid., pp. 4–5.

63. Ibid., p. 21.

64. Ibid., p. 24.

65. Letter to Elfride, 3 May 1924, p. 97; letter to Elfride, 5 February 1927, pp. 107–108.

66. Letter to Ernst Jünger, 7 March 1969, p. 50.

67. R. P. Bailly, *La croix*, 6 November 1894.

68. Alfred Wahl, *Confession et comportement dans les campagnes d'Alsace et de Bade: 1871–1939. Catholiques, protestants et juifs, démographie, dynamisme économique et social, vie de relation et attitude politique*, 2 vols., Strasbourg: COPRUR, 1980, p. 1034.

69. *Mittlerer Katechismus*, p. 21.

70. *Heuberger Volksblatt*, 22 July 1914.

71. *Oberbadischer Grenzbote*, 18 January 1899. This musician must not be confused with Rodolphe Kreutzer (1766–1831), a French composer to whom Beethoven dedicated a sonata (Sonata No. 9 for violin and piano in A major, Op. 47). Perhaps the greatest musician from Baden, Conradin Kreutzer was known especially for his *Nachtlager in Granada*.

72. Julius Gischendorf, *Das deutsche Vaterland. Ein Beitrag zur nationalen Erdkunde*, vol. 2 of *Präparationen für den geographischen Unterricht an Volkschulen*, 5 vols., 22nd revised and improved edition, Leipzig: Ernst Wunderlich, pp. 3–4.

73. Jean-François Chanet, *L'école républicaine et les petites patries*, preface by Mona Ozouf, Paris: Aubier, "Histoires," 1996.

74. At the time, photography had made remarkable advances facilitating the reproduction of outdoor scenes, portraits of rural people, and landscapes of the *Heimat*, even though the cumbersomeness and weight of the equipment remained major handicaps.

75. *Heuberger Volksblatt*, Friday, 16 January 1903.

76. Valerian Kempf, "Gott, der Mensch und die Natur," December 1904, in Büchin & Denker, *Martin Heidegger und seine Heimat*, pp. 217–219.

77. GA 16, 37.

78. Letter to Elfride, 13 December 1915, p. 5.

79. According to Fritz Heidegger, "Ein Geburtstagbrief," p. 59 and Karl Fischer's memories, reported by Büchin, "Erinnerung des Altbürgermeister Karl Fischer," pp. 241–242.

80. Fritz Heidegger "Ein Geburtstagbrief," p. 59.

81. Letter to Elfride of 13 December 1915, p. 5.

82. Jean-Paul Bled, *Histoire de la Prusse,* Paris: Fayard, p. 120.

83. Friedrich Nietzsche, *The Gay Science,* Section 104, "The Sound of the German Language," trans. W. Kaufmann, New York: Random House/Vintage, 1974, p. 161.

84. Valerian Kempf, "Deutches Lied von 1870," in Büchin & Denker, *Martin Heidegger und seine Heimat,* p. 209, stanza b.

85. Valerian Kempf, "Erinnerung an die große Feldschlacht bei Hericourt und Montbeliard am 15., 16. und 17. Januar 1871," ibid., p. 213.

86. Valerian Kempf, "In Wendenheim. Zum Trost einer ängstlichen Familie," ibid., p. 208.

87. Weber, "Bekannt durch seinen politisch wie religiös unsichern Charakter," p. 118.

88. Fritz Heidegger, "Ein Geburtstagbrief," p. 58.

89. *Meßkirch gestern und heute. Heimatbuch zum 770-jährirgen Stadtjubiläum 1961,* Meßkirch: Stadt Meßkirch, p. 75.

90. Johann Gottlieb Fichte, *Reden an die deutsche Nation* (1807–1808).

91. Friedrich Ludwig Jahn, quoted by Horst Überhorst (ed.), *Geschichte der Leibesübungen* 3, 1. *Leibesübungen und Sport in Deutschland von den Anfängen bis zum Ersten Weltkrieg,* Berlin, Munich, Frankfurt: Bartels & Wernitz, p. 221.

92. Wolfgang Stump & Horst Überhorst, "Deutschland und Europa in der Epoche des Umbruchs. Vom Ancien Régime zur bürgerlichen Revolution und nationale Demokratie—Friedrich Ludwig Jahn in seiner Zeit," ibid., p. 222.

93. Nicolas Bancel & Jean-Marc Gayman, *Du guerrier à l'athlète. Éléments d'histoire des pratiques corporelles,* Paris: PUF, 2002, p. 146.

94. Ibid., p. 144.

95. Julius Gischendorf, *Das deutsche Vaterland. Ein Beitrag zur nationalen Erdkunde,* vol. 2 of *Präparationen für den geographischen Unterricht an Volkschulen,* 5 vols., 22nd revised and improved ed., Leipzig: Ernst Wunderlich, 1912, pp. 3–4.

96. Ernest Lavisse, *Questions d'enseignement national,* Paris: Colin, 1885, pp. 209–210.

97. Error 80 in the *Syllabus of Errors,* citing the allocution *Jamdudum cernimus,* given on 18 March 1861.

98. Valerian Kempf, "Der Wechsel der Zeit," in Büchin & Denker, *Martin Heidegger und seine Heimat,* pp. 219–220.

99. Antimodernism can refer to hostility to modernity in general; in the same way, during this period it designated the pope's reaction to new, more modern interpretations of the Bible, such as those of theologians like Alfred Loisy, which made use of new historical methods.

100. *Heuberger Volksblatt,* Friday, 16 January 1903.

101. Quoted by Michael Stürmer, *Das ruhelose Reich. Deutschland 1866–1918,* Berlin: 1983, p. 176.

102. The color black symbolized Roman Catholicism.

103. Conrad Gröber, "Der Altkatholizismus in Meßkirch. Die Geschichte seiner Entwicklung und Bekämpfung," *Freiburger Diözesanarchiv,* vol. 40, 1912, pp. 135–198, here p. 158.

104. Weber, "Bekannt durch seinen politisch wie religiös unsichern Charakter," p. 123.

105. Letter from Fritz Heidegger to Gröber, archbishop of Freiburg, dated 26 October 1947, in Büchin & Denker, *Martin Heidegger und seine Heimat,* p. 120.

106. Letter to Blochmann, 22 June 1932, p. 52.

107. Ott, *Martin Heidegger,* p. 48.

2. From the Future Priest to the Young Antimodern Philosopher

1. Letter to Elfride, 13 December 1915, p. 5.

2. All this information is taken from Ott, *Martin Heidegger,* p. 49.

3. *Oberbadischer Grenzbote,* 32nd year, no. 119, 7 August 1903, quoted in Büchin & Denker, *Martin Heidegger und seine Heimat,* p. 121.

4. The minor seminary had been given the name of the patron saint of Konstanz, Conrad.

5. All this information is taken from Ott, *Martin Heidegger,* p. 49.

6. Horstwalter Heitzer, *Der Volksverein für das katholische Deutschland im Kaiserreich 1890–1918,* Mainz: Matthias-Grünewald-Verlag, 1979.

7. Ott, *Martin Heidegger,* p. 64.

8. Hans Dieter Zimmerman, *Martin und Fritz Heidegger. Philosophie und Fastnacht,* Munich: C. H. Beck, 2005, p. 25.

9. Gert Zang (ed.), *Konstanz in der großherzoglichen Zeit,* vol. 2.: *Aufschwung im Kaiserreich,* Konstanz: Stadler Verlagsgesellschaft, 1993, pp. 192–193.

10. The Gymnasium was old and too small for the number of students, which had greatly increased, as had enrollment more or less everywhere in Europe, where secondary school studies were being democratized; a new building was under construction, but Heidegger never studied there.

11. Letter to Elfride, 21 July 1918, p. 45.

12. Günther Dehn, *Die alte Zeit. Die vorigen Jahre. Lebenserinnerungen,* Munich: Kaiser, 1962, pp. 33–34.

13. Ibid., p. 39.

14. Ott, *Martin Heidegger,* p. 64.

15. Letter to Matthäus Lang, 30 May 1928, quoted in Ott, *Martin Heidegger,* p. 52.

16. Alfred Denker, "Martin Heidegger und Konstanz" (Bausteine zur Biographie Martin Heideggers, Part 5), *Meßkircher Heimathefte* no. 13, 2005, pp. 129–137, here p. 136.

17. Letter to Paul Motz, 7 February 1947, quoted in Helmut Maurer, "Martin Heidegger als Mitschüler," in Ernst Ziegler (ed.), *Kunst und Kultur um den Bodensee,* Sigmaringen: Jan Thorbecke Verlag, 1986, p. 349.

18. Quoted in Ott, *Martin Heidegger,* p. 56.

19. Ibid., p. 54.

20. Sulpiz Boisserée, quoted by Wilhelm Kiefer, *Schwäbisches und alemannisches Land,* Weissenhorn: A. H. Konrad, 1975, p. 324.

21. Letter to Elfride, 21 July 1918, p. 45.

22. Heiko Haumann & Hans Schadek (eds.), *Geschichte der Stadt Freiburg,* vol. 3: *Von der badischen Herrschaft bis zur Gegenwart,* Stuttgart: Theiss, 1992, p. 180.

23. Letter to Elfride, 21 July 1918, p. 45.

24. Stefan Zweig, *Die Welt von Gestern,* Frankfurt: Fischer, 2007, p. 46.

25. GA 1, 55.

26. Christa Berg (ed.), *Handbuch der deutschen Bildungsgeschichte,* vol. 4: *1870–1918. Von der Reichsgründung bis zum Ende des Ersten Weltkriegs,* Munich: Beck, p. 278.

27. Protestants were therefore less overrepresented in the classical schools: 37 percent of the population and 43 percent of the students enrolled in the classical schools (*Gymnasien*), as opposed to 60 percent of the students enrolled in the modern schools (*Realgymnasien*).

28. Dehn, *Die alte Zeit,* p. 16.

29. Ibid. Starting in 1899: he was the last director that Dehn knew.

30. Ibid., p. 37.

31. GA 16, 37.

32. Marcel Proust, *À l'ombre des jeunes filles en fleurs,* part 2, Paris: Flammarion, 1987, p. 159; *Within a Budding Grove,* trans. C. K. Scott Moncrieff and Terence Kilmartin, revised by D. J. Enright, New York: Modern Library, 2003.

33. Proust, *À l'ombre des jeunes filles,* p. 117; *Within a Budding Grove.*

34. "Eröffnungsansprache zur Schulkonferenz 1890," in Gerhardt Giese (ed.), *Quellen zur deutschen Schulgeschichte seit 1800,* Göttingen: Musterschmidt-Verlag, 1961, p. 196.

35. Quoted in Christa Berg, *Die Okkupation der Schule,* Heidelberg: Quelle und Meyer, 1973, p. 103.

36. Nevertheless, Martens grants pre-1866 Austria as well as Prussia the right to rule Germany.

37. Quoted by Ott, *Martin Heidegger,* p. 56.

38. Maurer, "Martin Heidegger als Mietschüler," pp. 343–360.

39. Dehn, *Die alte Zeit,* p. 26.

40. Ibid., p. 39.

41. Letter to Elfride, 8 September 1920, p. 79.

42. GA 16, 37.

43. Ibid.

44. Martin Heidegger, "Was hat der 'junge unerfahrene Student' auf die oberflächen Ausführungen des römisch-katholischen Laien im Grenzboten zu sagen?" *Heuberger Volksblatt,* 1 May 1911, in Büchin & Denker, *Martin Heidegger und seine Heimat,* pp. 94–100, here p. 96.

45. GA 16, 37.

46. Herman Schell, *Der Katholicismus als Princip des Fortschritts,* Würzburg: Göbel, 1897.

47. Herman Schell, *Die neue Zeit und der alte Glaube. Eine culturgeschichtliche Studie,* Würzburg: Göbel, 1898.

48. Schell, *Der Katholicismus als Princip des Fortschritts;* Schell, *Die neue Zeit und der alte Glaube;* Schell, *Die göttliche Wahrheit des Christentums,* 2 vols., Paderborn: Schöningh, 1895–1896; Schell, *Katholische Dogmatik,* 3 vols., Paderborn: Schöningh, 1889–1893.

49. Herman Schell, *Haeckels Monismus und der christliche Glaube an Gott und Geist. Kleinere Schriften,* Paderborn: Schöningh, 1908, pp. 322–333.

50. Herman Schell, *Der Gottesglaube und die naturwissenschaftliche Welterkenntnis,* Bamberg: Schmidt, 1904.

51. Schell, *Haeckels Monismus,* p. 323.

52. Ibid.

53. Ibid., pp. 332–333.

54. GA 1, 56.

55. GA 16, 37.

56. GA 13, 187.

57. Gröber, *Aus meinem römischen Tagebuch,* pp. 97–98.

58. Conrad Gröber, *Religiöse Funkansprachen,* Freiburg: Herder, 1929.

59. Conrad Gröber, *Aus meinem römischen Tagebuch,* quoted in Erwin Keller, *Conrad Gröber, 1872–1948. Erzbischof in Schwerer Zeit,* 2nd ed., Freiburg, Basel, and Vienna: Herder, 1982, p. 20.

60. English translation online: https://reader.digitale-sammlungen.de/de/fs1/object/goToPage/bsb10234887.html?pageNo=5.

61. GA 1, 56.

62. GA 14, 93.

63. Ibid.

64. GA 1, 56.

65. GA 14, 18–82.

66. "An Heimatsinn und Vaterlandsliebe wollen wir Katholiken uns nicht übertreffen lassen." Preface to the Catholic almanac for the city of Konstanz, 1909: Conrad Gröber & Alfred Merk, *Katholisches Jahrbuch für die Stadt Konstanz 1909.*

67. Conrad Gröber, *Geschichte des Jesuitenkollegs und -Gymnasiums in Konstanz,* Konstanz: Streicher, 1904.

68. Conrad Gröber, *Das Konstanzer Münster. Seine Geschichte und Beschreibung,* Lindau: Stettner, 1914.

69. Conrad Gröber, *Reichenauer Kunst, Heimatblätter, "Vom Bodensee zum Main,"* Karlsruhe: Müller, vol. 1, 1922; vol. 2, 1924.

70. Conrad Gröber & Alfred Merk, *Katholisches Jarhbuch für die Stadt Konstanz 1913,* 3rd edition, Konstanz: A.-G. Preßverein, 1913.

71. "Rezension," *Volksblatt* 15, no. 43, 14 April 1913, p. 4, in Büchin & Denker, *Martin Heidegger und seine Heimat,* p. 108.

72. *Heuberger Volksblatt,* 1 September 1911, in Büchin & Denker, *Martin Heidegger und seine Heimat,* pp. 101–102, here p. 102.

73. *Heuberger Volksblatt* 11, no. 86, 21 July 1909, in Büchin & Denker, *Martin Heidegger und seine Heimat,* p. 121.

74. Letter to Elfride, 13 December 1915, p. 5.

75. Fritz Heidegger, "Ein Geburtstagbrief," p. 58.

76. GA 13, 87.

77. Letter to Elfride, 13 December 1915, p. 5.

78. Ibid., 8 September 1920, p. 80.

79. Quoted in Ott, *Martin Heidegger,* p. 56.

80. Letter to Elfride, 13 December 1915, p. 5.

81. Ott, *Martin Heidegger,* p. 55.

82. Bernd Martin, *550 Jahre Universität Freiburg (1457–2007). Ein historischer Überblick,* Freiburg: University of Freiburg, 2007, p. 7.

83. The "Faculty of Arts" is the medieval name for the Faculty of Philosophy in Germany and the Faculty of Letters in France.

84. Martin, *550 Jahre,* p. 24.

85. John 8:32.

86. Thomas Nipperdey, *Deutsche Geschichte (1866–1918),* vol. 1, Munich: Beck, 2nd ed., 1991, p. 578.

87. Ibid., p. 579.

88. Ott, *Martin Heidegger,* p. 64.

89. Each course was a semester long.

90. GA 14, 93.

91. GA 1, 57–58.

92. Carl Braig, *Vom Denken. Abriß der Logik,* Freiburg: Herder, 1896.

93. GA 16, 41.

94. GA 16, 37–38.

95. GA 1, 56.

96. GA 14, 93.

97. Bernhard Welte, *Meister Eckhart. Gedanken zu seinem Gedanken,* Freiburg: Herder, p. 5.

98. Translators' note: *Sein* and *Seiende:* This crucial distinction in Heidegger's thought is difficult to render into English. Both terms are substantive forms of the verb *sein,* "to be." *Das Sein (l'être* in French) is taken from the infinitive form: an abstract noun, it means "being" in the ontological sense. *Das Seiende (l'étant),* formed from the present participle (*seiend, étant*), refers to what is or, as a collective noun, to all the things that are (that have being). We will generally translate *das Sein/l'être* as "being" and *das Seiende/l'étant* as "beings" or "a being," with clarifications when necessary.

99. GA 13, 89.

100. Ibid.

101. GA 16, 37–38.

102. "Was hat der 'junge unerfahrene Student' [. . .] zu sagen?" p. 96.

103. Henry Duméry, "Blondel et la philosophie contemporaine (étude critique)," *Études blondéliennes* 2 (1952): 92.

104. GA 16, 37.

105. Ott, *Martin Heidegger,* p. 58.

106. Ibid., p. 65.

107. Letter to Ernst Laslowski, 22 September 1949, GA 16, 440–441.

108. *Heuberger Volksblatt,* 10 September 1909, in Büchin & Denker, *Martin Heidegger und seine Heimat,* pp. 122–124, here p. 122.

109. *Heuberger Volksblatt,* 10 February 1909.

110. Ibid., p. 122.

111. GA 13, 1.

112. Hans-Josef Olszewsky, "Richard von Kralik," *Biographisch-Bibliographisches Kirchenlexikon,* vol. 4, Nordhausen: Bautz, 1992, columns 598–601.

113. Winfried Becker, "Karl Muth," *Biographisch-Bibliographisches Kirchenlexikon,* vol. 6, Nordhausen: Bautz, 1993, columns 396–402.

114. Review in *Heuberger Volksblatt,* 10 September 1909, in Büchin & Denker, *Martin Heidegger und seine Heimat,* p. 123.

115. Richard (von) Kralik, "Das katholische Kulturprogramm," *Frankfurter Zeitgemässe Broschüren,* vol. 37 (1909): 33–63, here p. 47ff.

116. Ibid., p. 33.

117. Ibid., p. 35.

118. Ibid., p. 38.

119. Ibid., p. 39.

120. MK, 99–101.

121. GA 13, 2.

122. GA 13, 3.

123. "Allerseelenstimmungen," *Heuberger Volksblatt,* 5 November 1909, in Büchin & Denker, *Martin Heidegger und seine Heimat,* p. 38.

124. GA 16, 10.

125. GA 16, 9.

126. GA 16, 3.

127. GA 16, 15.

128. Encyclical *Aeterni Patris,* 4 August 1879, 7.

129. GA 16, 11.

130. GA 16, 7.

131. Encyclical *Aeterni Patris,* 14.

132. GA 16, 7.

133. GA 16, 11.

134. Ott, *Martin Heidegger,* p. 60.

135. GA 16, 7; "Two Articles for *The Academician,*" in *Becoming Heidegger: On the Trail of His Early Occasional Writings, 1910–1927,* Evanston, IL: Northwestern University Press, 2007, p. 13.

136. *Pascendi Dominici Gregis* (1909).

137. Ibid.

138. Carl Braig, "Was soll der Gebildete von dem Modernismus wissen?" *Frankfurter Zeitgemässe Broschüren,* vol. 28, Frankfurt: n.p., 1909, pp. 2–27.

139. Ibid., p. 3.

140. Ibid., p. 4.

141. Ibid., p. 6.

142. Ibid., p. 21.

143. Ibid., p. 24.

144. *Christusmythe:* a reference to *Die Christusmythe* (1909) by Arthur Drews (1865–1935). Heidegger's mentor Conrad Gröber subsequently published a critique of this work under the title *Christus lebt. Eine Kritik der "Christusmythe" Arthur Drews,* Konstanz: Oberbad Verlag anst., 1923.

145. GA 16, 8; "Two Articles for *The Academician,*" p. 13.

146. GA 16, 11–14.

147. However, according to Jacques Gadille, Germany was excused from this requirement. See Jean-Marie Mayeur and Jacques Gadille (eds.), *Histoire du christianisme dès origines à nos jours,* vol. 11, Paris: Desclée-Fayard, 1995, p. 461.

148. "Herr Odenwald führte weiter aus," *Oberbadischer Grenzbote,* 31 March 1911, in Büchin & Denker, *Martin Heidegger und seine Heimat,* p. 51.

149. "Ultramontanismus, Wissenschaft und Geistesfreiheit," *Oberbadischer Grenzbote,* 5 April 1911, in Büchin & Denker, *Martin Heidegger und seine Heimat,* pp. 60–61.

150. "Liberale Volksversammlung in Meßkirch," *Heuberger Volksblatt,* 27 March 1911, in Büchin & Denker, *Martin Heidegger und seine Heimat,* p. 45.

151. "Dem Grenzbot-Philosoph zur Antwort," *Heuberger Volksblatt,* 7 April 1911, in Büchin & Denker, *Martin Heidegger und seine Heimat,* pp. 63–64.

152. Ibid., pp. 67–68.

153. Ibid., p. 68.

154. *Heuberger Volksblatt,* 22 May 1911, in Büchin & Denker, *Martin Heidegger und seine Heimat,* pp. 90–91.

155. "Was hat der 'junge 'unerfahrene Student' [. . .] zu sagen?" p. 96.

156. *Heuberger Volksblatt,* 22 May 1911, in Büchin & Denker, *Martin Heidegger und seine Heimat,* p. 90.

157. *Heuberger Volksblatt,* 5 April 1911, in Büchin & Denker, *Martin Heidegger und seine Heimat,* p. 125.

158. GA 16, 41–45.

159. Ott, *Martin Heidegger,* p. 65.

160. Archiepiscopal archives of Freiburg B2–32/174. Report of 2 April 1911. Quoted in Ott, *Martin Heidegger,* pp. 70–71.

161. GA 16, 38.

162. Letter to Elfride, 13 December 1915, p. 5.

163. GA 16, 38.

164. Ibid.

165. GA 14, 94.

166. GA 16, 38.

167. Letter to Heinrich Rickert, 12 October 1913, p. 16.

168. GA 1, 56–57.

169. GA 1, 57–58.

170. Wilhelm Vöge, *Die Anfänge des monumentalen Stiles im Mittelalter. Eine Untersuchung über die erste Blütezeit französischer Plastik,* Paderborn: Heitz Universitätsbibliothek, 1894.

171. Letter to Rickert, 13 December 1913, p. 15.

172. Letter to Elfride, 13 December 1915, p. 5.

173. Ott, *Martin Heidegger,* p. 79.

174. Claus Arnold, *Katholizismus als Kulturmacht. Der Freiburger Theologe Joseph Sauer (1872–1949) und das Erbe des Franz Xaver Kraus,* Paderborn: Ferdinand Schöningh, 1999, pp. 137–168.

175. Letter to Josef Sauer, 12 March 1912, quoted in Ott, *Martin Heidegger,* pp. 70–71.

176. Quoted in Ott, *Martin Heidegger,* p. 73.

177. "Die Lehre vom Urteil im Psychologismus. Ein kritisch-positiver Beitrag zur Logik," doctoral thesis, published by Johann Ambrosius Bart, Leipzig, 1914; reprinted in GA 1, 59–188.

178. GA 16, 42.

179. GA 16, 39–40.

180. Zweig, *Die Welt von Gestern,* p. 45.

181. Gustave Flaubert, *L'Éducation sentimentale,* Paris: Gallimard, 1993, p. 271.

182. Letter to Elfride, 13 December 1915, p. 5.

183. Ibid.

184. Ibid.

185. *Heuberger Volksblatt,* 28 July 1913, in Büchin & Denker, *Martin Heidegger und seine Heimat,* p. 130.

186. *Heuberger Volksblatt,* 25 October 1912, in Büchin & Decker, *Martin Heidegger und seine Heimat,* p. 128.

187. *Heuberger Volksblatt,* 14 March 1913, in Büchin & Decker, *Martin Heidegger und seine Heimat,* p. 129.

188. *Heuberger Volksblatt,* 21 October 1912, in Büchin & Decker, *Martin Heidegger und seine Heimat,* pp. 127–128.

189. *Heuberger Volksblatt,* 14 April 1913, in Büchin & Decker, *Martin Heidegger und seine Heimat,* p. 129.

190. *Heuberger Volksblatt,* 25 October 1912, in Büchin & Decker, *Martin Heidegger und seine Heimat,* p. 128.

3. A Philosopher in the Great War

1. GA 1, 58.

2. GA 16, 43; GA 16, 247.

3. Letter to Rickert, 3 November 1914, p. 14.

4. "Erklärung der Hochschullehrer des Deutschen Reiches," in Klaus Böhme (ed.), *Aufrufe und Reden deutscher Professoren im Ersten Weltkrieg,* Stuttgart: Reclam, 1975, p. 49.

5. Letter no. 3694, archives of the University of Freiburg, B1/4358.

6. *"Kultur, Nationalbewußtsein und Krieg."*

7. *"Nationale Kultur und Einzelpersönlichkeit."*

8. Translators' note: This sounds like a joke or mistake ("Cousin"), but the Vetter family were in fact cousins of the Heideggers.

9. In Büchin & Denker, *Martin Heidegger und seine Heimat,* p. 110.

10. Ibid., p. 115.

11. Wilhelm Dilthey, *Die geistige Welt. Einleitung in die Philosophie des Lebens,* in two volumes of the complete works, which Heidegger read: vol 1. *Erste Hälfte: Abhandlung zur Grundlegung der Geisteswissenschaften;* vol. 2. *Abhandlung zur Poetik, Ethik und Pädagogik.*

12. In Büchin & Denker, *Martin Heidegger und seine Heimat,* p. 113.

13. GA 16, 39.

14. Ibid.

15. Quoted in Ott, *Martin Heidegger,* p. 78.

16. *Heuberger Volksblatt,* 9 August 1915, in Büchin & Denker, *Martin Heidegger und seine Heimat,* p. 132.

17. Letter to Elfride, 13 December 1915, p. 6.

18. Ibid.

19. Martin Heidegger, *Letters to His Wife, 1915–1970,* ed. Gertrud Heidegger, trans. R. D. V. Glasgow, Cambridge, U.K.: Polity Press, 2008, p. 130. Translation of *"Mein*

liebes Seelchen!" Briefe Martin Heideggers an seine Frau Elfride 1915–1970, Munich: Deutsche Verlags-Anstalt, 2005.

20. Ott, *Martin Heidegger,* p. 89.
21. Ibid.
22. Ibid., p. 83.
23. Letter to Rickert, 19 October 1915, p. 25.
24. Ott, *Martin Heidegger,* p. 83.
25. Letter to Engelbert Krebs, 19 July 1914, quoted ibid., p. 81.
26. Ott, *Martin Heidegger,* p. 80.
27. Ibid., pp. 87–88.
28. Ibid., p. 88.
29. Ibid., p. 91.
30. Ibid., p. 92.
31. Quoted ibid.
32. Ibid., p. 93.
33. Letter to Elfride, 11 October 1916, p. 27.
34. Ott, *Martin Heidegger,* p. 89.
35. *Letters to His Wife,* p. 32.
36. Ott, *Martin Heidegger,* p. 90.
37. Letter to Heinrich Rickert, 3 July 1914, p. 23.
38. Quoted in Ott, *Martin Heidegger,* p. 97.
39. Quoted in Ott, *Martin Heidegger,* p. 96.
40. GA 16, 43.
41. Ott, *Martin Heidegger,* p. 87.
42. *Letters to His Wife,* p. 7.
43. Ibid., p. 47.
44. Ibid., p. 3.
45. Agnes Günther, *Die Heilige und ihr Narr,* Stuttgart: J. F. Steinkopf, 1913.
46. Letter to Elfride, 22 January 1916, p. 14.
47. *Letters to His Wife,* pp. 6 and 318.
48. Ibid., p. 18.
49. Ibid., p. 9.
50. Houston Stewart Chamberlain, *Die Grundlagen des neunzehnten Jahrhunderts,* Munich: Verlagsanstalt F. Bruckmann A.-G., 10th ed., 1912 [1899], p. 450.
51. Letter to Elfride, 13 December 1915, p. 4.
52. See another letter to Elfride, 7 May 1918, pp. 39–40.
53. Letter to Elfride, 1 January 1916, p. 10.
54. Letter to Elfride, 22 January 1916, p. 14.
55. Letter to Elfride, 1 January 1916, p. 10.
56. Letter to Elfride, 1 January 1916, p. 11.
57. Letter to Elfride, 10 February 1916, pp. 15–16.

58. Letter to Elfride, 3 January 1916, p. 12.
59. Letter to Elfride, 5 March 1916, p. 17.
60. Letter to Elfride, 16 December 1915, pp. 8–9.
61. Letter to Elfride, 5 April 1916, p. 19.
62. Letter to Elfride, 1 February 1916, p. 14.
63. Letter to Elfride, 12 March 1917, p. 30.
64. Letter to Elfride, 27 September 1916, p. 26.
65. Letter to Elfride, 22 January 1916, p. 13.
66. Letter to Elfride, 30 December 1915, p. 9.
67. *Letters to His Wife*, p. 9.
68. Letter to Elfride, 3 April 1916, p. 18.
69. Letter from Ernst Laslowki to Martin Heidegger, 8 January 1917, quoted in Ott, *Martin Heidegger*, p. 99.
70. Letter to Elfride, 6 April 1916, p. 19.
71. *Letters to His Wife*, p. 18.
72. *Letters to His Wife*, p. 20.
73. Letter to Elfride, 27 September 1916, p. 25.
74. *Letters to His Wife*, p. 27.
75. Ibid., p. 28.
76. Ibid., p. 31.
77. Ott, *Martin Heidegger*, p. 100.
78. Quoted in Ott, *Martin Heidegger*, p. 101.
79. Ott, *Martin Heidegger*, p. 100.
80. *Letters to His Wife*, p. 31.
81. Ibid., p. 18.
82. Ibid., p. 31.
83. Letter to Elfride, 5 April 1916, p. 19.
84. *Letters to His Wife*, p. 32.
85. Ibid., p. 36.
86. Ibid., p. 32.
87. Letter to Elfride on Whit Sunday 1917, p. 34.
88. "Graecia capta ferum uictorem cepit et artes / intulit agresti Latio" (Horace, Epistle 2, 1, vv. 156–157); English translation by Charles E. Passage, in *The Complete Works of Horace*, New York: Ungar, 1983.
89. *Letters to His Wife*, p. 36.
90. *Letters to His Wife*, p. 7.
91. Letter to Elfride on Whit Sunday 1917, p. 34.
92. *Letters to His Wife*, p. 13.
93. *Heuberger Volksblatt*, 24 July 1914.
94. Letter to Elfride, 1 January 1916, p. 10.
95. Letter to Elfride, 3 January 1916, p. 13.

96. Letter to Elfride, 10 February 1916, p. 15.
97. *Letters to His Wife*, p. 29.
98. Letter to Elfride, 5 March 1916, p. 17.
99. *Letters to His Wife*, p. 18.
100. Letter to Elfride, 5 March 1916, p. 17.
101. *Letters to His Wife*, pp. 35–36.
102. GA 13, 7; *Letters to His Wife*, p. 24.
103. Letter to Elfride, 1 September 1919, p. 64.
104. *Letters to His Wife*, p. 23.
105. Ibid.
106. Ibid., p. 36.
107. Letter to Elfride, 8 September 1920, p. 80.
108. Letter to Elfride, 12 March 1917, pp. 30 and 32.
109. François-Georges Dreyfus, *L'Allemagne contemporaine, 1815–1990*, Paris: PUF, 1991, p. 273.
110. Letter to Elfride, 5 March 1916, p. 17.
111. *Letters to His Wife*, p. 28.
112. Ibid., p. 25.
113. Letter to Elfride, 18 October 1916, p. 28.
114. Letter to Elfride, 1 February 1916, p. 14.
115. Ibid.
116. Letter to Elfride, 3 January 1916, pp. 11–12.
117. Ott, *Martin Heidegger*, p. 100.
118. Letter to Elfride, 6 April 1916, p. 20.
119. Letter from Heinrich Ochnser, 2 August 1917, quoted in Ott, *Martin Heidegger*, pp. 101–102.
120. Letter to Elfride, 12 March 1917, p. 29.
121. Letter to Elfride, 1 July 1916, p. 22.
122. Ibid.
123. Ott, *Martin Heidegger*, p. 100.
124. Ibid., p. 103.
125. *Letters to His Wife*, p. 37.
126. Ott, *Martin Heidegger*, p. 193.
127. *Letters to His Wife*, p. 37.
128. Ott, *Martin Heidegger*, p. 104; GA 16, 247.
129. *Letters to His Wife*, pp. 37, 38, and 42.
130. Letter to Elfride, 17 March 1918, pp. 37–38.
131. *Letters to His Wife*, p. 37.
132. Letter to Elfride, 17 March 1918, pp. 37–38.
133. Letter to Elfride, 7 May 1918, p. 39.
134. Letter to Elfride, 12 May 1918, p. 41.

135. Ibid.

136. Heinrich Finke, *Über Friedrich Schlege. Schwierigkeiten seiner Beurteilung, die Arbeitsgebiete seiner zweiten Lebenshälfte,* Freiburg: Prorektoratsrede von Heinrich Finke.

137. Letter to Elfride, 12 May 1918, pp. 41–42.

138. Letter to Blochmann, 2 October 1918, pp. 8–9.

139. Letter to Blochmann, 15 June 1918, p. 7.

140. *Letters to His Wife,* p. 42.

141. Ott, *Martin Heidegger,* p. 105.

142. *Letters to His Wife,* p. 42.

143. Ibid.

144. Letter to Elfride, 8 July 1918, p. 43.

145. *Letters to His Wife,* p. 44.

146. Letter to Elfride, 8 July 1918, p. 43.

147. Letter to Elfride, 20 July 1918, p. 44.

148. Letter to Elfride, 8 July 1918, p. 43.

149. Letter to Elfride, 20 July 1918, p. 44.

150. Letter to Elfride, 8 July 1918, p. 43.

151. Letter to Elfride, 21 July 1918, p. 45.

152. Letter to Elfride, 8 July 1918, p. 43.

153. Letter to Elfride, 21 July 1918, p. 45.

154. Ibid.

155. Letter to Blochmann, 2 October 1918, p. 9.

156. *Letters to His Wife,* p. 46.

157. Letter to Elfride, 28 August 1918, p. 46.

158. Ott, *Martin Heidegger,* p. 105.

159. Letter to Elfride, 28 August 1918, p. 46.

160. Letter to Blochmann, 2 October 1918, p. 9.

161. Letter to Elfride, 28 August 1918, p. 46.

162. Letter to Elfride, 30 August 1918, pp. 47–48.

163. Letter to Elfride, 22 September 1918, pp. 52–53, translation modified.

164. Letter to Elfride, 28 August 1918, p. 48.

165. Letter to Elfride, 30 August 1918, p. 49.

166. Letter to Elfride, 28 August 1918, p. 48.

167. Letter to Elfride, 27 October 1918, p. 58.

168. Letter to Elfride, 28 August 1918, p. 48, translation modified.

169. Letter to Elfride, 30 August 1918, p. 49.

170. Letter to Elfride, 28 August 1918, p. 48.

171. Translators' note: This was an anesthetic and antispasmodic medicine.

172. Letter to Elfride, 30 August 1918, p. 49.

173. Letter to Elfride, 27 October 1918, p. 58.

174. *Letters to His Wife*, p. 53.
175. GA 16, 247.
176. Letter to Elfride, 28 August 1918, pp. 47–48.
177. Letter to Elfride, 30 August 1918, p. 49.
178. Letter to Elfride, 28 August 1918, p. 47.
179. Ernst Jünger, *Storm of Steel [Stahlgewittern]*, trans. Michael Hofmann, New York: Penguin, 2016.
180. Letter to Elfride, 28 August 1918, p. 48.
181. Letter to Elfride, 30 August 1918, p. 49.
182. Letter from Heinrich Ochsner, 20 October 1917, quoted in Curd Ochwadt & Erwin Tecklenborg (eds.), *Das Maß des Verborgenen. Heinrich Ochsner zum Gedächtnis*, Hanover: Charis, p. 93ff.
183. Letter to Heinrich Rickert, 27 January 1920, p. 49.
184. Letter from Husserl to Heidegger, 10 September 1918, p. 131.
185. Ott, *Martin Heidegger*, p. 171.
186. *Letters to His Wife*, pp. 54–55.
187. *Letters to His Wife*, p. 50.
188. Letter to Elfride, 13 September 1918, p. 51.
189. Letter to Elfride, 22 September 1918, p. 52.
190. Letter to Elfride, 13 September 1918, pp. 51–52.
191. Letter to Elfride, 27 October 1918, p. 56.
192. Letter to Elfride, 4 September 1918, pp. 49–50.
193. Letter to Elfride, 4 September 1918, pp. 50–51.
194. Letter to Elfride, 4 September 1918, p. 50.
195. Ibid.
196. Letter to Elfride, 7 May 1918, p. 39.
197. Letter to Elfride, 4 September 1918, p. 50.
198. Letter to Elfride, 4 September 1918, p. 51.
199. Letter to Blochmann, 2 October 1918, p. 9.
200. Letter to Blochmann, 6 November 1918, p. 10.
201. Letter to Elfride, 10 November 1918, p. 58.
202. Letter to Elfride, 17 October 1918, p. 55.
203. Letter to Elfride, 27 October 1918, p. 58.
204. Letter to Elfride, 5 October 1918, p. 53.
205. Letter to Elfride, 17 October 1918, p. 55.
206. Ibid.
207. Letter to Elfride, 27 October 1918, p. 128.
208. Letter to Blochmann, 7 November 1918, p. 12.
209. Letter to Elfride, 27 October 1918, pp. 57–58.
210. Letter to Blochmann, 7 November 1918, p. 12.
211. Ernst von Salomon, *Die Geächteten*, Gütersloh: C. Bertelsmann, 1930.

212. Arthur Moeller van den Bruck, *Das dritte Reich,* 3rd ed., Hamburg: Hanseatische Verlagsanstalt, 1933, p. 33.

213. Letter to Elfride, 17 October 1918, pp. 55–56.

214. Letter to Elfride, 10 November 1918, p. 58.

215. Letter to Elfride, 27 October 1918, p. 57.

216. Letter to Elfride, 17 October 1918, p. 55.

217. Letter to Elfride, 5 October 1918, p. 53.

218. Letter to Elfride, 10 November 1918, p. 59.

219. Letter to Elfride, 27 October 1918, p. 57.

220. Letter to Blochmann, 7 November 1918, p. 12.

221. Letter to Elfride, 10 November 1918, pp. 58–59.

222. Letter to Elfride, 5 October 1918, p. 53.

223. Ott, *Martin Heidegger,* p. 105.

224. Letter to Elfride, 10 November 1918, p. 59.

225. Moeller van den Bruck, *Das dritte Reich,* p. 230.

4. The Memory of Meßkirch Fades Away

1. Paul Valéry, "La crise de l'esprit," *Variété,* in *Oeuvres,* vol. 1, Paris: Gallimard, 1997, p. 988.

2. Ott, *Martin Heidegger,* p. 105.

3. Letter to Blochmann, 14 January 1919, p. 12.

4. Jean Solchany, *L'Allemagne au XXe siècle,* Paris: PUF, 2003, p. 34. The question of reparations was decided at the London Conference in January 1921. The payments were to be made annually in the amount of 2 billion gold marks, to which were added deliveries in kind (26 percent of Germany's annual exports) and an annual interest rate of 6 percent.

5. Solchany, *L'Allemagne au XXe siècle,* p. 27.

6. Letter to Elfride, 14 October 1923, p. 94.

7. Hans Jonas, *Memoirs,* trans. Krishna Winston, Boston: Brandeis University Press, 2008, p. 67.

8. Letter to Elfride, 1 July 1916, pp. 21–22.

9. Gerd Krumeich, " '*Stab-in-the-Back' Legend,*" https://referenceworks.brillonline.com/entries/brills-digital-library-of-world-war-i/stab-in-the-back-legend-dolchstosslegende-bewwi_en_0563

10. Saul Friedländer, "Die politischen Veränderungen der Kriegzeit und ihre Auswirkungen auf die Judenfrage," in Werner E. Mosse (ed.), *Deutsches Judentum in Krieg und Revolution, 1916–1923,* Tübingen: J. C. B. Mohr, 1971, pp. 27–66, here pp. 52–53. This thesis is also found in Hitler's *Mein Kampf,* which was written four years later.

11. GA 60, 36.

12. GA 60, 68.

13. Letter to Elfride, 20 August 1920, p. 77.

14. Letter to Elfride, 8 September 1920, p. 80.

15. Georg Mönius, "Hölderlin als Philosoph," Bamberg, 1920 (thesis in philosophy directed by Falckenberg and defended in Erlangen in 1919).

16. *Biographisch-Bibliographisches Kirchenlexikon,* vol. 6, 1993, columns 1–4.

17. Ott, *Martin Heidegger,* p. 116.

18. Letter to Elfride, 8 February 1920, p. 71.

19. Letter to Elfride, 2 August 1920, p. 74.

20. Letter to Elfride, 23 August 1920, p. 78.

21. Letter to Elfride, 2 August 1920, p. 74.

22. Letter to Elfride, 6 August 1920, p. 76.

23. Karl Löwith, *My Life in Germany before and after 1933,* trans. Elizabeth King, Urbana: University of Illinois Press, 1994, p. 27.

24. Letter to Elfride, 17 April 1919, p. 61.

25. Letter to Elfride, 30 August 1919, p. 62.

26. Quoted in Karl Löwith, "Les implications politiques de la philosophie de l'existence chez Heidegger," *Les temps modernes,* no. 14 (November 1946): 343–360, here p. 346.

27. Ibid.

28. Ibid.

29. GA 56–57, 110.

30. Letter to Elfride, 13 September 1919, p. 68.

31. Letter to Heinrich Rickert, 27 January 1920, pp. 50–51.

32. Actual, real, factual, not factitious.

33. GA 56/57, 63.

34. GA 56/57, 71–72.

35. Letter to Jaspers, 27 June 1922, p. 27.

36. Ibid.

37. Letter to Elfride, 10 November 1918, p. 59.

38. Letters to Elfride on Whit Sunday 1917, p. 34; and on 9 September 1919, p. 66.

39. Letter to Elfride, 22 October 1925, p. 104.

40. Carl Schmitt, *Political Theology,* trans. George Schwab, Chicago: University of Chicago Press, 2006, p. 5.

41. Ibid.

42. On combat (*Kampf*), see especially GA 9, 25.

43. Karl Jaspers, *Psychologie der Weltanschauungen,* 4th ed., Berlin: Springer, 1954 [1919], p. 229.

44. Letter to Jaspers, 14 July 1923, pp. 42–43.

45. Letter to Elfride, 8 July 1923, p. 92.

46. Letter to Elfride, 4 January 1920, p. 70.

47. Letter to Elfride, 30 August 1919, p. 63.

48. Letter to Elfride, 28 July 1920, p. 73.

49. Letter to Elfride, 8 September 1920, p. 79.

50. Letter to Rickert, 27 January 1920, p. 52.

51. Ibid.

52. *Letters to His Wife,* p. 86.

53. Karl Jaspers, *Philosophische Autobiographie,* expanded edition, Munich: Piper, 1977, p. 92.

54. Ibid.

55. Letter to Elfride, 12 May 1918, p. 41.

56. Jaspers, *Philosophische Autobiographie,* p. 92.

57. Ibid.

58. Ibid.

59. Ibid.

60. Letter to Jaspers, 21 April 1920, p. 15.

61. Letter from Jaspers, 1 August 1921, p. 23.

62. Letter to Jaspers, 27 June 1922, p. 26.

63. Ibid.

64. Letter to Elfride, 8 September 1920, p. 79.

65. Letter to Jaspers, 27 June 1922, p. 29.

66. Letter to Jaspers, 19 November 1922, p. 33.

67. Letter to Jaspers, 14 July 1923, p. 42.

68. George L. Mosse, *Fallen Soldiers,* part 3, chap. 8, "The Brutalization of German Politics."

69. Philipp Scheidemann (1865–1939), who had proclaimed the Republic from a window of the Reichstag, was the SPD chancellor on whom the victors imposed the Treaty of Versailles, which he refused to sign.

70. Mathias Erzberger (1875–1921), the centrist minister of finances, had signed the armistice at Rethondes.

71. Walther Rathenau (1867–1922) was the DDP (liberal) minister of foreign affairs.

72. GA 16, 759–760.

73. Letter to Jaspers, 27 June 1922, p. 29.

74. Letter to Jaspers, 19 November 1922, p. 33.

75. GA 56/57, 71–72.

76. Letter to Jaspers, 27 June 1922, p. 28.

77. Letter to Jaspers, 22 January 1921, pp. 18–19.

78. Letter to Elfride, 2 August 1920, p. 74.

79. Letter to Elfride, 26 January 1922, p. 85.

80. Letter to Elfride, 2 August 1920, p. 74.

81. Letter to Elfride, 8 February 1920, p. 71.

82. Löwith, *My Life in Germany,* p. 31, translation modified.

83. *Letters to His Wife*, p. 85.

84. Ibid., p. 93.

85. Hans-Georg Gadamer, *Philosophische Lehrjahre*, Frankfurt: Klostermann, 1977, p. 210.

86. Ibid., p. 212.

87. Ibid., p. 210.

88. Löwith, *My Life in Germany*, p. 28, translation modified.

89. Quoted in Löwith, *My Life in Germany*, p. 89, translation modified.

90. Jonas, *Memoirs*, p. 41.

91. Letter to Blochmann, 12 April 1933, p. 62.

92. Jonas, *Memoirs*, p. 42.

93. Letter to Elfride, 26 January 1922, p. 84.

94. Letter to Engelbert Krebs, 9 January 1919, in Ott, *Martin Heidegger*, pp. 106–107.

95. Letter to Heinrich Rickert, 27 January 1920.

96. Letter from Edmund Husserl to Roman Ingarden, 25 November 1921, quoted in Ott, *Martin Heidegger*, p. 118.

97. Letter to Engelbert Krebs, 9 January 1919, in Ott, *Martin Heidegger*, p. 106.

98. "You have a feeling about Schleiermacher that is fully justified—I am convinced that his personality can be grasped in a complete and immediate way only by a woman." Letter to Blochmann, 6 November 1918, p. 10.

99. GA 63.

100. Letter to Elfride, 9 September 1919, pp. 66–67.

101. Letter to Elfride, 20 August 1920, p. 77.

102. Letter to Engelbert Krebs, 9 January 1919, in Ott, *Martin Heidegger*, p. 107.

103. *Letters to His Wife*, p. 60.

104. Anne Roerkohl, *Hungerblockade und Heimatfront. Die kommunale Lebensmittelversorgung im Westfalen während des Ersten Weltkrieges*, Stuttgart: Steiner, 1991, p. 312; *Letters to His Wife*, p. 54. This epidemic was not limited to Germany: from 1918 to 1919, it infected a billion people throughout the world and killed 20 to 25 million; it took the life of Guillaume Apollinaire on 9 November, and it was particularly virulent in the Reich because its population was more weakened than others by the food shortages resulting from the Allied blockade. Olivier Lahaie, "L'Épidémie de grippe dite 'espagnole' et sa perception par l'armée française (1918–1919)," *Revue historique des armées* 262 (2011), posted online 16 March 2011, http://rha.revues.org/7163, consulted 26 October 2014.

105. *Letters to His Wife*, p. 62.

106. Letter to Elfride, 22 January 1919, p. 60.

107. *Letters to His Wife*, p. 69.

108. Letter to Elfride, 13 September 1919, p. 67.

109. Letter to Elfride, 28 July 1920, p. 72.

110. Letter to Elfride, 23 August 1920, p. 77.

111. Letter to Elfride, 28 July 1920, p. 72.
112. Letter to Elfride, 6 August 1920, p. 75.
113. Letter to Elfride, 28 July 1920, pp. 72–73.
114. Letter to Elfride, 2 August 1920, p. 74.
115. Letter to Elfride, 28 July 1920, p. 72.
116. Letter to Elfride, 6 August 1920, p. 75.
117. Letter to Elfride, 8 September 1920, pp. 79–80.
118. Letter to Elfride, 28 July 1920, pp. 72–73.
119. Letter to Elfride, 6 August 1920, p. 75, translation modified.
120. Reinhard Piper, *Vormittag. Erinnerungen eines Verlegers,* Munich: Piper, 1947, p. 411.
121. *Letters to His Wife,* p. 74.
122. Letter to Elfride, 6 August 1920, p. 75.
123. Letter to Elfride, 12 August 1920, p. 76.
124. Letter to Elfride, 6 August 1920, p. 76.
125. Letter to Elfride, 12 August 1920, p. 76.
126. *Letters to His Wife,* p. 78.
127. Ibid.
128. Letter to Elfride, 8 September 1920, p. 80.
129. Letter to Elfride, 26 January 1922, p. 85.
130. *Letters to His Wife,* p. 80.
131. Letter to Elfride, 28 July 1920, p. 72.
132. Letter to Elfride, 8 September 1920, p. 79, translation modified.
133. Letters to Elfride, 4 September 1918, pp. 50–51; 27 September 1928, p. 116.
134. *Letters to His Wife,* p. 82.
135. Letter to Jaspers, 19 November 1922, pp. 33–34.
136. Letter to Elfride, 27 September 1922, p. 87.
137. Letter to Rickert, 27 January 1920.
138. Letter to Elfride, 28 July 1920, pp. 72–73.
139. Letter to Elfride, 13 September 1919, p. 69.
140. Letter to Elfride, 17 April 1919, p. 62.
141. Letter to Elfride, 12 August 1920, p. 75.
142. Letter to Elfride, 13 September 1919, p. 68.
143. Letter to Elfride, 17 April 1919, p. 62.
144. Letter to Elfride, 13 September 1919, p. 68.
145. Letter to Elfride, 6 August 1920, p. 76.
146. Letters to Elfride, 4 January 1920, p. 70; 23 August 1920, p. 77.
147. Letter to Elfride, 7 May 1918, p. 39.
148. Letter to Elfride, 1 September 1919, p. 64.
149. Letter to Elfride, 8 February 1920, p. 71.
150. *Letters to His Wife,* p. 77.

151. Letter to Elfride, Whit Sunday, 1917, p. 34; letter to Elfride, 9 September 1919, pp. 65–66.

152. Letter to Elfride, 23 August 1920, p. 77, translation modified.

5. Rootedness on the Mountain Heights of Todtnauberg?

1. Letter to Rickert, 27 January 1917, p. 42.

2. Heidegger came in second after Max Wundt, who was older than he (Ernst Troeltsch's letter to Heidegger, 4 February 1918, *Heidegger Jahrbuch* 1 [2004]: p. 75).

3. Ott, *Martin Heidegger*, p. 98.

4. Letter to Jaspers, 14 July 1923, p. 40.

5. Letter to Elfride, 17 March 1918, p. 38.

6. Letter to Jaspers, 5 August 1921, p. 25 .

7. Among them, Hans-Georg Gadamer.

8. Letter to Elfride, 27 September 1922, p. 87.

9. Letter to Jaspers, 19 November 1922, p. 34.

10. Letter to Jaspers, 19 November 1922, p. 34.

11. Letter from Paul Natorp to Husserl, late October 1922, quoted by Ott, *Martin Heidegger*, p. 124.

12. Ott, *Martin Heidegger*, p. 124.

13. Letter to Elfride, 27 March 1923, p. 90.

14. Letter to Elfride, Easter 1923, p. 91.

15. Letter to Jaspers, 19 June 1923, p. 37.

16. Letter to Jaspers, 14 July 1923, pp. 41.

17. Letter to Jaspers, 19 June 1923, p. 38.

18. *Letters to His Wife*, p. 93.

19. *Letters to His Wife*, p. 94.

20. Letter to Elfride, 14 October 1923, p. 93.

21. Letter to Elfride, 27 October 1923, p. 95.

22. *Letters to His Wife*, p. 93.

23. Letter to Elfride, 14 October 1923, pp. 93–94.

24. Letter to Jaspers, 18 June 1924, p. 49.

25. Letter to Jaspers, 4 October 1926, p. 68.

26. Letter to Jaspers, 24 July 1925, p. 54.

27. Letter to Jaspers, 31 July 1926, p. 66.

28. Letter to Jaspers, 4 October 1926, p. 68.

29. Letter to Jaspers, 2 December 1926, p. 69.

30. *Letters to His Wife*, p. 105.

31. Letter to Jaspers, 4 October 1926, p. 68.

32. Letter to Blochmann, 10 November 1926, p. 18.

33. Cf. his letters to Jaspers, 18 June 1924, p. 49; and 2 December 1926, p. 69.

34. Letter to Jaspers, 13 May 1928, p. 96.

35. *Letters to His Wife*, p. 92.

36. Letter to Jaspers, 18 June 1924, p. 48.

37. Letter to Elfride, 2 August 1924, p. 99.

38. Letter to Jaspers, 18 June 1924, p. 49.

39. Letter to Elfride, 23 August 1924, p. 100.

40. GA 19, 4–5; "*In memoriam* Paul Natorp," in *Plato's Sophist*, trans. Roger Rojcewicz and André Schuwer, Bloomington: Indiana University Press, 1992, pp. 3–4.

41. Letter to Hannah Arendt, 23 August 1925, p. 32.

42. Letter to Elfride, 10 August 1924, p. 99.

43. Letter to Jaspers, 2 December 1926, p. 69.

44. Letter from Rudolf Bultmann to Hans von Soden, 23 December 1923, quoted by Antje Bultmann Lemke, "Der unveröffentlichte Nachlass von Rudolf Bultmann," in Bernd Jaspert (ed.), *Rudolf Bultmanns Werk und Wirkung*, Darmstadt: Wissenschaftliche Buchgesellschaft, 1984, p. 202.

45. Letter to Elfride, 22 October 1925, p. 104.

46. Letter to Elfride, 30 June 1925, p. 102.

47. Letter to Jaspers, 24 May 1926, p. 64.

48. Letter to Bultmann, 23 October 1928.

49. Letter to Jaspers, 17 April 1924, p. 46.

50. Letter to Elfride, 2 August 1924, p. 99.

51. Letter to Elfride, 21 January 1928, p. 113.

52. Letter to Jaspers, 14 July 1923, p. 41.

53. Jonas, *Memoirs*, p. 59.

54. Stern, the future author and essayist, and Hannah Arendt's first husband, is better known under his pseudonym, Günther Anders ("Gunther Otherwise").

55. Letter to Elfride, 9 February 1928, p. 115.

56. Jonas, *Memoirs*, p. 66.

57. Ibid., pp. 66–67.

58. Löwith, *My Life in Germany*, p. 46, translation modified.

59. Ibid.

60. Jonas, *Memoirs*, p. 59.

61. Ibid., p. 60.

62. See the recent biography by Thomas Karlauf, *Stefan George. Die Entdeckung des Charisma*, Munich: Karl Blessing Verlag, 2007.

63. Ian Kershaw, *Hitler*, vol. 1: *1889–1936: Hubris*, New York: W. W. Norton, 1991.

64. Max Weber calls this "charisma," the "extraordinary quality of a person who is, so to speak, endowed with powers or supernatural or superhuman characteristics, or at least outside everyday life, inaccessible to ordinary mortals; or again who is considered as sent by God or as an example, and consequently considered as a 'leader' (or guide, *Führer*). Of course, conceptually it is a matter of complete indifference whether the

quality must be judged correctly on the 'objective' level, from an ethical, aesthetic, or other point of view; what matters is only how this quality is actually seen by those who are dominated charismatically, the followers [*Anhänger*]." *Economy and Society,* trans. Keith Tribe, Cambridge, MA: Harvard University Press, 2019.

65. Löwith, *My Life in Germany,* p. 44.
66. Ibid., translation modified.
67. Jonas, *Memoirs,* p. 60.
68. Letter to Arendt, 21 March 1925, p. 9.
69. Ibid.
70. Letter to Arendt, 7 December 1927, p. 46.
71. Arendt, quoted by Jonas, *Memoirs,* p. 63.
72. Letter to Arendt, 21 March 1925, p. 9.
73. Letter to Arendt, 8 May 1925, p. 19.
74. Letter to Jaspers, 2 December 1926, p. 69.
75. Letter to Arendt, 21 February 1925, pp. 5–6.
76. Letter from Arendt to Heidegger, 22 April 1928, p. 50.
77. Letter from Arendt to Heidegger, dated only "1929," p. 50.
78. Ibid., p. 51.
79. Letter to Elfride, 8 July 1923, p. 92.
80. Ott, *Martin Heidegger,* pp. 114–115.
81. Letter to Elfride, 10 August 1924, p. 100.
82. Löwith, *My Life in Germany,* p. 27.
83. Letter to Blochmann, 21 October 1927, p. 21.
84. Letter to Elfride, 21 October 1927, p. 109.
85. Letter to Elfride, 9 February 1928, p. 114.
86. Letter from Husserl to Heidegger, 21 January 1928, p. 151.
87. Letter from Husserl to Heidegger, 7 February 1928, p. 152.
88. Letter to Elfride, 9 February 1928, p. 114.
89. Letter to Jaspers, 25 February 1928, p. 90.
90. Letter to Jaspers, 6 March 1928, pp. 90–91.
91. Letter from Jaspers to Heidegger, 23 March 1928, p. 92.
92. Letter to Jaspers, 25 March 1928, p. 92.
93. Letter to Bultmann, 2 April 1928, p. 56.
94. Letter to Jaspers, 25 March 1928, p. 92.
95. GA 2, 12–13; *Being and Time,* 29.
96. GA 2, 4; *Being and Time,* 22.
97. This can be done, for example, with the concept of man. Man can be linked to the class of animals and distinguished from all the other animals through the statement that he is endowed with speech and reason.
98. GA 2, 10; *Being and Time,* 27. [Macquarrie and Robinson translate *Sein* as "Being" (always capitalized) and *Seiende(n)* as "entity"/"entities." We have retained the

capitalization of "Being" in the passages quoted from *Being and Time,* but, in the interest of consistency, have modified "entity" to "a being" and "entities" to "beings."—Trans.]

99. GA 2, 10; *Being and Time,* 27.

100. GA 2, 16; *Being and Time,* 32.

101. GA 2, 52; *Being and Time,* 63.

102. Saint Augustine, *Confessions,* 11, 20, 26.

103. Heidegger cited this passage from Pascal in his book (GA 2, 5; *Being and Time,* 49): "We cannot set out to define being without falling into absurdity, for we cannot define a word without starting with this one, 'it is,' whether expressed or implicit. Thus, to define being, we would have to say 'it is' and thus use in its definition the word to be defined." Blaise Pascal, *Pensées et opuscules,* Brunschvicg: Paris, 1912, p. 169.

104. Löwith, "Les implications politiques de la philosophie de l'existence chez Heidegger," p. 347.

105. Translators' note: The German term *man* is an indefinite third-person pronoun (the equivalent of "one" in English); *das Man,* which Macquarrie and Robinson translate as "the 'they,' " is its substantive form.

106. GA 2, 170–171; *Being and Time,* 165.

107. GA 2, 507; *Being and Time,* 435.

108. In 1918 Heidegger still embraced "the most painstaking discharge of duties" and felt a "sense of responsibility," which led him back to what really mattered to him, what was "dearest & most beloved," and made him realize for the first time what "home" [*Heimat*] meant (letter to Elfride, 4 September 1918, p. 51).

109. D. A. F. de Sade, "L'Instituteur philosophe," in *Historiettes, contes et fabliaux,* Paris: Norbert Crochet, 2008, pp. 41–42.

110. GA 2, 170; *Being and Time,* 165.

111. For the reception of Heidegger, I have relied heavily on the bibliography composed by the University of Freiburg and available online (2009 version): https://www.freidok.uni-freiburg.de/data/6593, downloaded 11 July 2015.

112. Bronislaus Wladislaus Switalski, "Die Kategorien und Bedeutungslehre des Duns Scotus / Martin Heidegger, 1916," *Kant-Studien* 30 (1925): 520–521.

113. "Die Kategorien und Bedeutungslehre des Duns Scotus / Martin Heidegger, Tübingen, 1916," *Archivum Franciscanum historicum* 14 (1925): 371.

114. "Heidegger, Martin," in *Enciclopedia universal ilustrada europeo-americana,* vol. 27, Madrid: Espasa-Calpe, 1925, p. 926.

115. On Miki specifically, see Susan C. Townsend, *Miki Kiyoshi 1897–1945: Japan's Itinerant Philosopher,* Leiden: Brill, 2009.

116. Bernard Stevens, "L'attrait de la phénoménologie auprès des philosophes de l'école de Kyoto," *Philosophie* 79 (2003): 3–42.

117. Gadamer, *Philosophische Lehrjahre,* p. 210.

118. Gilbert Ryle, "Sein und Zeit," *Mind* 38 (1929): 355–370.

119. David Dilworth, "Watsuji Tetsurō (1889–1960): Cultural Phenomenologist and Ethician," *Philosophy East and West* 24, no. 1 (January 1947): 11–12.

120. Dominique Janicaud, *Heidegger en France,* vol. 1, Paris: Albin Michel, 2001, p. 31.

121. Emmanuel Levinas, "Martin Heidegger et l'ontologie," *Revue philosophique* (May–June 1932): 395–431, here p. 395.

122. Preface to the Japanese translation of "What Is Metaphysics?" GA 16, 66.

123. Löwith, *My Life in Germany,* p. 29, translation modified (German ed., Stuttgart, Metzler, 1986, p. 44).

124. Heinrich Barth, "Kant und die moderne Metaphysik," *Zwischen den Zeiten,* no. 6 (1928): 406–428.

125. Erich Przywara, "Drei Richtungen der Phänomenologie?" *Stimmen der Zeit* 115 (1928): 252–264, here p. 261; quoted by Emilio Brito, "La réception de la pensée de Heidegger dans la théologie catholique," *Nouvelle revue théologique* 49 (1997): 352–374, here p. 352.

126. Heidegger obviously would have objected to this assertion: for him, what was at issue was not man as subject but *Dasein* as a way of studying the meaning of being. The historian, who is necessarily critical in his approach, is not obliged to adopt word for word the way the actors whose history he is writing describe themselves or their projects.

127. Herbert Marcuse, "Über konkrete Philosophie," *Archiv für Sozialwissenschaft und Sozialpolitik* 62 (1929): 111–128. The Frenchman Jean Wahl would also be receptive to that aspect: "Vers le concret," *Recherches philosophiques* 1 (1921): 1–16.

128. Herbert Marcuse, "Enttäuschung," in Günter Neske (ed.), *Erinnerung an Martin Heidegger,* Pfullingen: Neske, 1977, p. 162.

129. Martin Heidegger, *El ser y el tiempo,* trans. José Gaos, Mexico City: Editorial Fondo de Cultura Económico, 1951.

130. Martin Heidegger, *Essere et tiempo,* Milan: Fratelli Bocca, 1953.

131. It was followed by a second translation in 1996, by Joan Stambaugh.

132. Martin Heidegger, *Être et temps,* trans. François Vezin, based on the work of Rudolf Boehm and Alphonse de Waelhens (for part 1) and of Jean Lauxerois and Claude Roëls (for part 2), Paris: Gallimard, 1986.

133. Martin Heidegger, *Être et temps,* new and unabridged translation of the text of the 2nd edition by Emmanuel Martineau, J. Lechaux, and É. Ledru, Paris: Authentica, 1985.

134. Martin Heidegger, *L'Être et le temps,* translated with annotations of §§1–44 by Rudolf Boehm and Alphonse de Waelhens, Paris: Gallimard, 1964.

135. Martin Heidegger, *Qu'est-ce que la métaphysique? suivi d'extraits sur "L'être et le temps" et d'une conférence sur Hölderlin,* translated with a foreword and notes by Henry Corbin, Paris: Gallimard, 1938.

136. Janicaud, *Heidegger en France,* vol. 1, pp. 47–48.

137. Letter to Husserl, 22 October 1927, p. 144.

138. Letter from Husserl to Alexandre Pfänder, 6 January 1931, in Herbert Spiegelberg and Eberhard Avé-Lallemant (eds.), *Pfänder Studien,* The Hague: M. Nijhoff, 1982, p. 348.
139. Jaspers, *Philosophische Autobiographie,* p. 97.
140. Letter to Husserl, 22 October 1927, p. 144.
141. Letter from Husserl to Alexandre Pfänder, 6 January 1931, pp. 348–349.
142. Ibid., p. 349.
143. Letter to Jaspers, 13 April 1928, p. 93.
144. Letter to Elfride, 27 September 1928, p. 116.
145. *Letters to His Wife,* pp. 115–116.
146. Letter to Jaspers, 10 November 1928, p. 110.
147. Ibid.
148. Ibid.
149. Letter to Rickert, 25 July 1929, pp. 65–66.
150. Letter to Jaspers, 10 November 1928, p. 110.
151. Letter to Elfride, 27 September 1928, p. 117.
152. Ott, *Martin Heidegger,* p. 120.
153. *Letters to His Wife,* p. 70.
154. Ibid.
155. Ibid., p. 71.
156. Letter to Elfride, 4 January 1920, p. 70.
157. Letter to Elfride, 2 March 1921, p. 82.
158. *Letters to His Wife,* p. 83.
159. Ibid., p. 85.
160. Ibid., p. 86.
161. GA 13, 9; "Why Do I Stay in the Provinces?" in Manfred Strasser (ed.), *Philosophical and Political Writings,* trans. Thomas J. Sheehan, New York: Continuum, 2003, p. 16.
162. *Letters to His Wife,* p. 86.
163. Ibid., p. 105.
164. Letter to Blochmann, 22 December 1926, pp. 18–19.
165. *Letters to His Wife,* p. 137.
166. Letter to Elfride, 27 September 1928, p. 117.
167. Letter to Blochmann, 21 October 1927, p. 21.
168. Letter to Blochmann, 12 September 1929, p. 33.
169. Letter to Elfride, 27 September 1928, pp. 116–117.
170. Letter to Blochmann, 29 March 1927, p. 19.
171. Letter to Jaspers, 24 July 1925, p. 54.
172. Letter to Blochmann, 10 November 1926, p. 18.
173. Letter to Blochmann, 12 April 1929, p. 29.
174. Letter to Viktor Schwoerer, 2 October 1929.

175. Letter to Blochmann, 19 January 1933, p. 57.
176. GA 13, 9; "Why Do I Stay in the Provinces?" 16.
177. Letter to Blochmann, 17 October 1928, p. 28.
178. Letter to Elfride, 6 October 1932, p. 138.
179. Letter to Jaspers, 20 December 1931, p. 145.
180. Letter to Elfride, 14 September 1932, pp. 138–139.
181. Letter to Elfride, 15 October 1932, pp. 139–140.
182. Letter to Jaspers, 24 April 1926, p. 63.
183. Letter to Elfride, 6 October 1932, p. 139.
184. Letter to Arendt, 23 August 1925, p. 33.
185. Friedrich Hölderlin, *Hyperion,* trans. Ross Benjamin, New York: Archipelago, 2008 [1797 and 1799], p. 12.
186. Letter to Arendt, 23 August 1925, p. 32.
187. Letter to Arendt, 21 March 1925, p. 9.
188. Letter to Elfride, 9 February 1928, p. 115.
189. Letter to Blochmann, 17 October 1928, p. 27.
190. Ibid.
191. Letter to Jaspers, 27 September 1927, pp. 79–80.
192. Letter to Arendt, 19 February 1928, p. 47.
193. Letter to Elfride, 21 January 1928, p. 113.
194. Gadamer, *Philosophische Lehrjahre,* p. 215.
195. Letter to Elfride, 27 March 1923, p. 91.
196. Letter to Blochmann, 16 September 1926, p. 16.
197. Letter to Jaspers, 4 October 1926, p. 67.
198. Letter to Blochmann, 20 September 1930, p. 38.
199. Letter to Blochmann, 29 March 1927, p. 19.
200. Letter to Jaspers, 23 September 1925, p. 54.
201. Letter to Elfride, 6 October 1932, p. 139.
202. Letter to Elfride, 27 September 1928, p. 117.
203. Letter to Elfride, 15 October 1932, p. 140.
204. Letter to Blochmann, 20 September 1930, p. 38.
205. Günther Anders, "Wenn ich verzweifelt bin, was geht's mich an," interview with Mathias Greffrath, in Mathias Greffrath (ed.), *Die Zerstörung einer Zukunft. Gespräche mit emigrierten Sozialwissenschaftlern,* Frankfurt: Campus Verlag, 1989.
206. Müller, "Ein Gespräch mit Max Müller," p. 81.
207. Letter to Blochmann, 10 December 1927, p. 23.
208. *Letters to His Wife,* p. 7.
209. Letter to Blochmann, 21 October 1927, p. 21.
210. *Letter to His Wife,* p. 116.
211. Friedrich Nietzsche, *Ecce Homo,* Preface, §3, trans. Walter Kaufmann, New York: Random House, 1967, rpt. 1969, p. 218.

212. Letter from Husserl to Heidegger, 10 December 1916, p. 128.

213. Letter from Husserl to Heidegger, 30 January 1918, p. 129.

214. GA 13, 9; "Why Do I Stay in the Provinces?" p. 17.

215. *Plato's Sophist*, 116.

216. The notion of *Umwelt* is already found in Husserl (in *Ideen I* of 1913), among others. In everyday German, *Umwelt* has environmental connotations. Hence the German term for "environmentally friendly" is *umweltfreundlich*.

217. Letter to Elfride, 6 April 1930, p. 123.

218. Letter from Paul Yorck von Wartenburg to Dilthey, 18 February 1884, in Wilhelm Dilthey & Paul Yorck von Wartenburg, *Briefwechsel (1877–1897)*, Halle: Niemeyer, 1923, p. 254.

219. Letter to Arendt, 18 October 1925, p. 36.

220. " '*In*' is derived from *innan-*, 'to reside,' *habitare*, 'to dwell.' '*An*' signifies: 'I am accustomed,' 'I am familiar with,' 'I look after something.' It has the signification of *colo* in the senses of *habito* and *diligo*. The being (*Seiende*) to which Being-in in this signification belongs is one which we have characterized as that being which in each case I myself am [*bin*]. The expression '*bin*' is connected with '*bei*,' and so '*ich bin*' ['I am'] means in its turn 'I reside' or 'dwell alongside' the world, as that which is familiar to me in such and such a way." GA 2, 73; *Being and Time*, 80.

221. Letter to Arendt, 14 September 1925, p. 35.

222. Hölderlin, *Hyperion*, p. 69.

223. Letter to Arendt, 23 August 1925, p. 32, translation modified.

224. GA 2, 27; *Being and Time*, 41.

225. GA 2, 27; *Being and Time*, 41–42, translation slightly modified.

226. GA 1, 56.

227. *Vom Sein: Abriß der Ontologie*; see GA 14, 93.

228. GA 2, 510; *Being and Time*, 435–437.

229. GA 56/57, 91.

230. GA 56/57, 89.

231. Letter to Matthäus Lang of 30 May 1928, in Ott, *Martin Heidegger*, p. 52, translation modified.

232. Letter to Elfride, 5 February 1927, p. 108.

233. See esp. GA 16, 52–54, here p. 53; and letter to Elfride, 23 March 1929, p. 108.

234. Letter to Elfride, 6 August 1920, p. 75.

235. GA 2, 94; *Being and Time*, 100.

236. GA 2, 157; *Being and Time*, 153–154.

237. Proust, "Combray," p. 242; *Swann's Way*, p. 206.

238. GA 2, 163; *Being and Time*, 167.

239. Letter to Elfride, 5 February 1927, pp. 107–108.

240. GA 2, 218–219; *Being and Time*, 208.

241. Letter to Elfride, 13 December 1915, p. 5.

242. Letter to Bultmann, 14 March 1927, p. 20.
243. *Letters to His Wife,* p. 91.
244. Letter to Elfride, 1 October 1923, p. 92.
245. Letter to Elfride, 3 May 1924, p. 97.
246. Letter to Jaspers, 2 May 1924, p. 47.
247. Letter to Elfride, 3 May 1924, p. 97.
248. *Letters to His Wife,* p. 103.
249. GA 16, 53.
250. Postcard to Bultmann, 15 October 1925, p. 3.
251. GA 2, 29; *Being and Time,* 43.
252. Ibid.
253. Martin Heidegger, "Wilhelm Dilthey's Research and the Current Struggle for a Historical Worldview," in Kisiel and Sheehan (eds.), *Becoming Heidegger,* 271.
254. GA 2, 29; *Being and Time,* 43.
255. Letter to Elfride, 5 February 1927, p. 108.
256. Letter to Jaspers, 1 March 1927, p. 73.
257. Letter to Elfride, 5 February 1927, p. 108.
258. Letter to Elfride, 21 April 1927, p. 108.
259. Letter to Jaspers, 27 September 1927, p. 79.
260. Letter to Elfride, 21 October 1927, p. 109.
261. Letter to Blochmann, 12 September 1929, p. 33.
262. Letter to Blochmann, 20 September 1930, pp. 37–38.
263. *Letters to His Wife,* p. 125.
264. *Letters to His Wife,* p. 130.
265. Letter to Blochmann, 19 September 1931, p. 43.
266. Letter to Elfride, 20 June 1932, p. 137.
267. Rüdiger Safranski, *Martin Heidegger: Between Good and Evil,* trans. Ewald Osers, Cambridge, MA: Harvard University Press, 1998, p. 4.
268. Letter to Blochmann, 11 October 1931, p. 43.
269. Letter to Elfride, 19 October 1930, p. 126.
270. Letter to Blochmann, 11 October 1931, p. 43.
271. Letter to Elfride, 19 October 1931, pp. 125–126.
272. Letter to Blochmann, 11 October 1931, p. 43.
273. Letter to Elfride, 19 October 1930, p. 125.
274. Ibid.
275. Buchin & Denker, *Martin Heidegger und seine Heimat,* p. 30.
276. Letter to Elfride, 19 October 1930, pp. 125–126.
277. Letter to Blochmann, 11 October 1931, p. 43.
278. Letter to Blochmann, 19 October 1931, p. 45.
279. Letter to Blochmann, 8 April 1931, pp. 39–40.
280. Letter to Blochmann, 12 September 1929, p. 32.

281. GA 29/30, 243; *The Fundamental Concepts of Metaphysics,* trans. William McNeill & Nicholas Walker, Bloomington: Indiana University Press, 1995, pp. 162–163, translation modified.

282. Ibid., p. 163, translation modified.

283. GA 29/30, 245; *Fundamental Concepts,* 164.

284. Thomas Mann, *Politische Schriften und Reden,* vol. 1: *Betrachtungen eines Unpolitischen,* Frankfurt am Main, Fischer Bücherei, 1968, p. 242.

285. Ernst Jünger, *Der Arbeiter. Herrschaft und Gestalt,* Hamburg: Hanseatische Verlagsanstalt, 1932, p. 49.

286. Oswald Spengler, *Jahre der Entscheidung. Deutschland und die weltgeschichtliche Entwicklung,* Munich: Beck, 1933, p. 10.

287. Notably in *Thus Spake Zarathustra,* where the chapter "The Cry of Distress" is devoted to this theme.

288. Nietzsche, *The Gay Science,* trans. Walter Kaufmann, New York: Vintage, 1974, p. 118.

289. Plato, *Republic,* 7, 514c; in Plato: *Collected Dialogues,* ed. Edith Hamilton and Huntington Cairns, p. 747.

290. Ibid., 515c, p. 748.

291. GA 28, 354.

292. GA 28, 353.

293. "What Is Metaphysics?" in *Basic Writings,* ed. David Farrell Krell, New York: Harper & Row, 1977, pp. 109–110.

294. John 8:32.

295. "On the Essence of Truth," in *Basic Writings,* p. 125.

296. "On the Essence of Truth," p. 119, translation modified.

297. "On the Essence of Truth," p. 120.

298. "On the Essence of Truth," pp. 120–121, translation modified.

299. Part A of Bultmann's research on the Gospel According to John ("Untersuchungen zum Johannesevangelium," *Zeitschrift für neutestamentliche Wissenschaft* 27 (1928): 113–163. The full text was published in Rudolf Bultmann, *Exegetica. Aufsätze zur Erforschung des Neuen Testaments, ausgewählt, eingeleitet und hg. von Erich Dinkler,* Tübingen: J. C. B. Mohr, 1967, pp. 124–197.

300. Letter to Bultmann, 23 October 1928, p. 68.

301. "On the Essence of Truth," p. 127, translation modified.

302. "On the Essence of Truth," p. 125.

303. "On the Essence of Truth," p. 134, translation modified.

304. "On the Essence of Truth," p. 135.

305. "On the Essence of Truth," pp. 136–137, translation modified.

306. "On the Essence of Truth," pp. 137–139.

307. Letter to Engelbert Krebs, 9 January 1919, quoted in Ott, *Martin Heidegger,* p. 107.

308. Letter to Elfride, 21 October 1927, p. 109.

309. Letter to Matthäus Lang, 30 May 1928, in Ott, *Martin Heidegger,* p. 52.

310. Alfred Denker, "Martin Heidegger und die Erzabtei Beuron," *Meßkircher Heimathefte* 9 (2002): 47.

311. Letter to Blochmann, 18 September 1932, p. 53.

312. GA 29/30, 7; *Fundamental Concepts,* p. 5.

313. GA 29/30, 12; *Fundamental Concepts,* pp. 8–9.

314. Letter to Elfride, 23 March 1929, p. 120.

315. GA 29/30, 31; *Fundamental Concepts,* p. 21.

316. GA 29/30, 11; *Fundamental Concepts,* p. 8.

317. Nietzsche conceived of this courage as what allowed one to resist morals and observe man freely beyond good and evil.

318. Friedrich Nietzsche, *Ecce Homo,* in *On the Genealogy of Morals* and *Ecce Homo,* trans. Walter Kaufmann, New York: Vintage, 1969, preface §3, p. 218.

319. Letter to Elfride, 5 February 1927, p. 108.

6. The Wind Blowing from Berlin

1. GA 2, 169; *Being and Time,* 164.

2. Ibid.

3. Notably, in the letters to Elfride, 8 July 1918, pp. 42–44, and 27 October 1918, pp. 57–58.

4. Pierre Drieu La Rochelle, *Le jeune européen,* Paris: Gallimard, 1978 [1927], p. 70.

5. Ibid.

6. Letter to Elfride, 8 September 1920, p. 79, translation modified.

7. GA 2, 238; *Being and Time,* 223.

8. GA 2, 237; *Being and Time,* 223.

9. GA 2, 224; *Being and Time,* 212.

10. GA 2, 225; *Being and Time,* 214.

11. Ibid.

12. Letter to Elfride, 17 October 1918, pp. 55–56.

13. Oswald Spengler, *Decline of the West: Form and Actuality,* trans. Charles Francis Atkinson, New York: Alfred A. Knopf, 1927, p. 32.

14. Translators' note: Translation modified. Macquarrie and Robinson translate *Geschehen* as "historizing."

15. GA 2, 507; *Being and Time,* 435.

16. GA 2, 508; *Being and Time,* 436.

17. G. W. F. Hegel, *Elements of the Philosophy of Right,* ed. Allen W. Wood, trans. H. B. Nisbet, Cambridge, U.K.: Cambridge University Press, §324, p. 361, translation modified.

18. GA 2, 508; *Being and Time,* 436.

19. Ibid., translation modified.

20. GA 2, 511; *Being and Time,* 438.

21. GA 2, 510; *Being and Time,* 438.

22. Moeller van den Bruck, *Das Dritte Reich,* pp. 230–232.

23. Giovanni Gentile, "Manifesto of the Fascist Intellectuals to the Intellectuals of Other Nations" (1925), reproduced at https://en.wikipedia.org/wiki/Manifesto_of_the_Fascist_Intellectuals.

24. GA 2, 509; *Being and Time,* 437, translation slightly modified.

25. As Thomas Sheehan has pointed out in *Making Sense of Heidegger,* London: Rowman & Littlefield International, 2015, p. 181, n. 90.

26. "Ein jeglicher muß seinen Helden wählen, / Dem er die Wege zum Olymp hinauf / Sich nacharbeiten" (Johann Wolfgang von Goethe, *Iphigenia in Tauris,* act 2, scene 1).

27. Moses Finley, *The World of Odysseus,* New York: New York Review Books, 2002 [1954], p. 20.

28. Louis Dupeux, *Histoire culturelle de l'Allemagne, 1919–1960,* Paris: PUF, "Questions," 1989, p. 50.

29. Spengler, *Decline of the West,* p. 35.

30. Ibid., p. 156.

31. Letter to Arendt, 8 May 1925, pp. 19–20.

32. GA 20, 37; *History of the Concept of Time: Prolegomena,* trans. Theodore Kiesel, Bloomington: Indiana University Press, 1992, translation modified.

33. Ibid., translation modified.

34. GA 16, 759.

35. Letter to Elfride, 21 January 1928, p. 113, translation modified.

36. Schmitt, *Political Theology,* p. 59.

37. Mann, *Betrachtungen eines Unpolitischen,* p. 41.

38. Ibid., p. 50.

39. Ibid., p. 38.

40. Letter to Elfride, 11 October 1931, p. 130.

41. Mann, *Betrachtungen eines Unpolitischen,* p. 39.

42. Moeller van den Bruck, *Das Dritte Reich,* p. 214.

43. Letter to Blochmann, 20 December 1931, p. 46.

44. Ibid.

45. Ibid.

46. Letter to Blochmann, 19 January 1933, p. 58.

47. Letter to Blochmann, 22 June 1932, p. 52.

48. Nietzsche, *Ecce Homo,* "The Case of Wagner," §4, pp. 322–323.

49. Ibid., p. 323.

50. Nietzsche, *Ecce Homo,* "Why I Am So Clever," p. 240.

51. G. W. F. Hegel, *Lectures on the History of Philosophy,* trans. E. S. Haldane, London: Routledge and Kegan Paul, 1955, vol. 1, p. 149.

52. Mann, *Betrachtungen eines Unpolitischen,* p. 38.

53. "Now I am lecturing for the first time on Fichte, Hegel, Schelling—and a world has opened up for me again, the old experience that others cannot read for you." Letter to Jaspers, 25 June 1929, p. 123.

54. "German Idealism (Fichte, Schelling, Hegel) and the Philosophical Problems of the Present," a course given in the summer semester of 1929; GA 28.

55. Johann Gottlieb Fichte, *Reden an die deutsche Nation,* Hamburg, Severus Verlag, 2013, p. 74.

56. Ibid., p. 132.

57. Ibid., p. 74.

58. Ibid., p. 91.

59. Spengler, *Decline of the West,* p. 16.

60. GA 29/30, 103–104.

61. GA 29/30, 116.

62. GA 29/30, 244.

63. GA 2, 502; *Being and Time,* 436.

64. Letter from Jaspers to Arendt, 3 January 1933.

65. Barbara Koehn (ed.), *La révolution conservatrice et les élites intellectuelles en Europe,* Rennes: Presses universitaires de Rennes, 2003, pp. 43–44.

66. Drieu la Rochelle, *Le jeune européen,* p. 115.

67. Ibid., p. 95.

68. Letter to Blochmann, 11 January 1928, p. 23.

69. Letter to Elfride, 10 January 1928, p. 112.

70. Letter to Blochmann, 11 January 1928, p. 23.

71. Letter to Blochmann, 18 December 1929, p. 34.

72. Letter from Jaspers to Heidegger, 12 November 1928, p. 111.

73. Letter from Jaspers to Heidegger, 1 December 1928, pp. 111–112.

74. *Letters to His Wife,* p. 119.

75. Letter to Elfride, 21 March 1929, p. 120.

76. Letter to Blochmann, 12 September 1929, p. 33.

77. Letter to Jaspers, 29 March 1930, p. 130.

78. Manfred Geier, *Martin Heidegger,* Reinbek: Rowohlt Taschenbuch Verlag, 2005, p. 80.

79. Letter from Jaspers to Heidegger, 29 March 1930, p. 130.

80. Letter to Jaspers, 29 March 1930, p. 130.

81. Letter to Elfride, 6 April 1930, p. 122.

82. Ibid., p. 123.

83. Ibid.

84. Horst Möller, "Gottfried Reinhold Treviranus. Ein Konservativer zwischen den Zeiten," in Horst Möller & Andreas Wirsching, *Aufklärung und Demokratie. Historische Studien zur politischen Vernunft,* Munich: Oldenburg Wissenschaftsverlag, pp. 226–245.

85. Letter to Elfride, 6 April 1930, p. 123.

86. Walther G. Oschilewski, "Grimme, Adolf," *Neue Deutsche Biographie,* vol. 7, Berlin: Duncker & Humblot, 1966, p. 88.

87. Letter to Elfride, 6 April 1930, p. 123.

88. Letter to Elfride, 21 July 1918, p. 45.

89. Letter to Elfride, 6 April 1930, p. 123.

90. Letter to Julius Stenzel, 17 August 1930, *Heidegger Studies* 16 (2000): 21.

91. Letter to Elfride, 2 October 1930, p. 124.

92. Letter to Elfride, 6 April 1930, p. 123.

93. Ibid.

94. Letter to Blochmann, 10 December 1927, p. 22.

95. Ibid.

96. Ibid.

97. Jünger, *The Worker,* trans. Laurence Paul Hemming, Evanston, IL: Northwestern University Press, 2017, p. 104.

98. Letter to the minister for science, art, and popular education, Adolf Grimme, 10 May 1930, GA 16, 61.

99. Letter to Blochmann, 8 April 1931, p. 39.

100. Ibid.

101. Letter to Jaspers, 20 December 1931, p. 144.

102. Ibid.

103. Letter to Blochmann, 10 May 1930, p. 35.

104. Letter to Jaspers, 3 December 1928, p. 114.

105. Letter to Matthäus Lang, 30 May 1928, quoted in Ott, *Martin Heidegger,* p. 52.

106. Letter to Blochmann, 17 October 1928, p. 27.

107. Letter to Jaspers, 24 September 1928, p. 103.

108. *Letters to His Wife,* p. 119.

109. Ibid., pp. 124–125.

110. Letter to Elfride, 21 March 1929, p. 119.

111. Ibid.

112. Letter to Blochmann, 22 December 1928, p. 28.

113. Letter to Elfride, 21 March 1929, p. 120.

114. François Jaran, *Heidegger inédit (1929–1930). L'inachevable Être et temps,* Paris: Vrin, 2012, p. 42.

115. In this capacity, he represented the minister at the university.

116. *Letters to His Wife,* p. 119.

117. Letter to Elfride, 21 March 1929, p. 119.

118. Ibid.

119. Letter to Blochmann, 12 April 1929, p. 30.

120. Letter to Elfride, 21 March 1929, p. 119.

121. Letter to Elfride, 23 March 1929, p. 120.

122. Ernst Cassirer, *The Philosophy of Symbolic Forms*, vol. 2: *Mythical Thought*, trans. Ralph Manheim, New Haven, CT: Yale University Press, 1965.

123. GA 2, 69; *Being and Time*, 490, n. xi.

124. Ernst Cassirer, lecture in Davos, 26 March 1929.

125. Letter to Blochmann, 12 April 1929, p. 29.

126. Martin Heidegger, "Kant's *Critique of Pure Reason* and the Task of a Laying of the Ground for Metaphysics," Appendix 3 of *Kant and the Problem of Metaphysics*, trans. Richard Taft, Bloomington: Indiana University Press, 1997, p. 192.

127. "Davos Disputation between Ernst Cassirer and Martin Heidegger," Appendix 4 of *Kant and the Problem of Metaphysics*, p. 201.

128. Ibid., p. 204.

129. Letter to Elfride, 26 March 1929, p. 120.

130. Otto Friedrich Bollnow, "Gespräche in Davos," in Günther Neske (ed.), *Erinnerung an Martin Heidegger*, Pfullingen: Neske, 1977, p. 28.

131. Letter to Blochmann, 12 April 1929, p. 30.

132. Letter to Elfride, 23 March 1929, p. 120.

133. Ibid.

134. Recounted by Maurice de Gandillac, based on his manuscript, quoted by Dominique Janicaud in *Heidegger en France*, vol. 1, Paris: Albin Michel, 2001, p. 30.

135. Georges Gurvitch, *Les tendances actuelles de la philosophie allemande*, Paris: Vrin, 1930, p. 207.

136. *Letters to His Wife*, p. 121.

137. Letter to Blochmann, 7 July 1931, p. 41.

138. Letter to Elfride, 17 August 1931, p. 128.

139. Ibid., translation modified. [The English-language translation reads: "This time Holland in general made a much better & more agreeable impression on me." The German is ambiguous: "Holland im Ganzen machte mir diesmal einen noch viel satteren u. bequemeren Eindruck."—Trans.]

140. Ibid.

141. Letter to Jaspers, 21 April 1920, p. 15.

142. Letter to Jaspers, 18 June 1924, p. 48.

143. Letter to Elfride, 21 March 1929, p. 119.

144. Letter to Elfride, 27 September 1922, p. 87.

145. "Er war ein lieber Vater," interview with Hermann Heidegger, with the participation of his wife, conducted by Iris Radisch, *Die Zeit*, no. 11, 6 March 2014.

146. "Martin Heidegger, el hombre," interview with Hermann Heidegger conducted by Ángel X. Yáñez, *El semanal. La jornada*, 27 May 2007, no. 638.

147. Letter to Elfride, 14 February 1950, p. 213.

148. "Er war ein lieber Vater."

149. Letter to Arendt, 29 July 1926, p. 44.

150. Letter to Blochmann, 11 January 1928, p. 23.

151. Letter to Arendt, 7 December 1927, p. 44.

152. Letter to Jaspers, 19 May 1931, p. 140; letter to Blochmann, 7 July 1931, p. 41; *Letters to His Wife*, p. 127; letter to Jaspers, 20 December 1931, p. 145.

153. *Badische Zeitung*, 5 September 1996.

154. "Er war ein lieber Vater," *Die Zeit* n°11/2014, 6 March 2014.

155. René Schickelé, "Tagebücher," *Werke in drei Bänden*, Köln and Berlin: Kiepenheuer und Witsch, 1959, p. 1040.

156. Letter to Arendt, winter 1932–1933, p. 52.

157. Letter from Husserl to Ludwig Landgrebe, 28 May 1932, *Husserliana—Dokumente*, vol. 4, Dordrecht: Kluwer Academic Publishers, 1994, p. 288.

158. Letter to Bultmann, 16 December 1932, p. 191.

159. Schickelé, "Tagebücher," p. 1040.

160. Ott, *Martin Heidegger*, p. 194.

161. Gertrud Fischer testifies to this in Benno Müller-Hill, *Tödliche Wissenschaft. Die Aussonderung von Juden, Zigeunern und Geisteskranken (1933–1945)*, Berlin: Volk und Gesundheit, 1989, p. 120.

162. Alfred Baeumler, *Nietzsche, der Philosoph und Politiker*, Leipzig: Reclam, 1931.

163. Alfred Baeumler, *Nietzsche in seinen Briefe und Berichten der Genosse. Die Lebensgeschichte in Dokumenten*, Leipzig: Kröner, 1932.

164. Letter to Blochmann, 25 May 1932, p. 50.

165. Johann Jakob Bachofen, *Selbstbiographie und Antrittsrede über das Naturrecht*, edited with an introduction by Alfred Baeumler, Halle/Saale: M. Niemeyer, "Philosophie und Geisteswissenschaften" 5, 1927.

166. "Wohl dagegen stehe ich *sehr positiv* zu Vielem [. . .]." Letter to Bultmann, 16 December 1932, p. 191.

167. "Entretien de Hans-Georg Gadamer avec Philippe Forget et Jacques Le Rider du 18 avril 1981," *Entretiens avec* Le Monde, vol. 1: *Philosophies*, Paris: La Découverte, 1984, p. 237.

168. Letter to Elfride, 2 October 1930, p. 124.

169. Letter to Elfride, 19 October 1930, pp. 125–126.

170. Letter to Fritz, 13 January 1932, p. 25.

171. Letter to Elfride, 2 October 1930, p. 124.

172. *Völkischer Beobachter*, 25 September 1930, *Reich* edition.

173. Kershaw, *Hitler*, vol. 1: *1889–1936: Hubris*, p. 318.

174. Ibid., p. 319.

175. Letter to Elfride, 2 October 1930, p. 124, translation modified.

176. Kershaw, *Hitler*, vol. 1, p. 338.

177. Steven Bach, *Leni Riefenstahl. Une ambition allemande,* Arles: Jacqueline Chambon, 2007, p. 135.

178. Letter to Elfride, 2 October 1930, p. 124.

179. Jaspers, *Philosophical Autobiography,* Munich: Piper, enlarged edition, 1977, p. 101.

180. Quoted by Kershaw, *Hitler,* vol. 2: *Nemesis,* New York: W. W. Norton, 2000, p. 303.

181. Helmut Weisshaupt, "Die Entwicklung der NSDAP in Meßkirch bis 1934," *Meßkircher Heimathefte* 5 (1999): 57–80.

182. Letter to Fritz, 18 December 1931, p. 21.

183. Ibid., p. 22.

184. Ibid., p. 21.

185. Ibid.

186. Letter to Blochmann, 24 March 1932, p. 47.

187. Excerpt from Hermann Mörchen's diary, published by Otto Pöggeler in "Praktische Philosophie als Antwort an Heidegger," in Bernd Martin (ed.), *Martin Heidegger und das "Dritte Reich." Ein Kompendium,* Darmstadt: Wissenschaftliche Buchgesellschaft, 1989, p. 84.

188. Ibid.

189. Letter to Elfride, 1 July 1916, p. 22.

190. Letter to Elfride, 20 June 1932, p. 136.

191. Anders, "Wenn ich verzweifelt bin, was geht's mich an."

192. Letter from Elfride Heidegger to Elfriede Lieber, dated 12 January 1932, Alfred Denker & Holger Zaborowski (eds.), *Heidegger-Jahrbuch* 4: *Heidegger und der Nationalsozialismus,* vol. 1: *Dokumente.* Freiburg: Karl Alber, 2009, p. 269. Henceforth abbreviated as HJB4, followed by the page number.

193. Ibid.

194. Ibid.

195. Like her husband, Elfride attributed a rare prescience to Hitler (to his brother, Heidegger spoke of the Führer's "sure and extraordinary political instinct," adding that "he already had it when we were all still lost in the fog" [letter to Fritz, 18 December 1931, p. 22]).

196. Letter from Elfride Heidegger to Elfriede Lieber, 12 January 1932, HJB4, pp. 268–269.

197. Ibid.

198. Mörchen, quoted by Martin (ed.), *Martin Heidegger und das "Dritte Reich,"* p. 84.

199. MK, 352.

200. MK, 320.

201. MK, 688.

202. Letter to Blochmann, 14 January 1919, p. 12.

203. Letter to Blochmann, 17 October 1928, p. 27.

204. Letter to Elfride, 9 June 1932, p. 134.

205. Ibid., p. 133.

206. Ibid., p. 134.

207. Viktor Cathrein, *Der Sozialismus. Eine Untersuchung seiner Grundlagen und seiner Durchführbarkeit,* 16th ed., Freiburg: Herder, 1923 [1890].

208. Waldemar Gurian, *Der Bolschewismus. Einführung in Geschichte und Lehre,* 2nd ed., Freiburg: Herder, 1932 [1931].

209. Letter to Elfride, 9 June 1932, p. 134.

210. Letter to Elfride, 18 October 1916, p. 28.

211. Letter to Elfride, 9 June 1932, p. 133.

212. Letter from Elfride Heidegger to Elfriede Lieber, 12 January 1932, HJB4, 269.

213. Alfred Rosenberg, *Der Mythus des 20. Jahrhunderts.* 189th–194th ed. Munich: Hoheneichen-Verlag, 1942 [1930], p. 17. For the translation, we've used *The Myth of the Twentieth Century: An Evaluation of the Spiritual-Intellectual Confrontation of Our Age,* convenient but without mention of pages (http://www.nommeraadio.ee/meedia/pdf/RRS/Alfred%20Rosenberg%20-%20The%20Myth%20of%20the%2020th%20Century.pdf). We give the page numbers of the German edition.

214. Letter to Elfride, 9 June 1932, p. 133.

215. Jaspers, *Philosophische Autobiographie,* p. 101.

216. Letter from Elfride Heidegger to Elfriede Lieber, 12 January 1932, HJB4, 269.

217. Mörchen, quoted by Martin (ed.), *Martin Heidegger und das "Dritte Reich,"* p. 84.

218. Thilo Vogelsang, *Reichswehr, Staat und NSDAP. Beiträge zur deutschen Geschichte, 1930–1932,* Stuttgart: Deutsche Verlags-Anstalt, 1962, p. 145.

219. Ernst Kantorowicz, *Kaiser Friedrich der Zweite,* Stuttgart: Klett-Cotta, 1927.

220. Drieu La Rochelle, *Le jeune européen,* pp. 95–96.

221. Letter to Elfride, 2 October 1930, p. 124.

222. Letter to Blochmann, 22 June 1932, p. 52.

223. Letter to Fritz, 27 July 1932, p. 29.

224. This was the final stage of an excruciating crisis that his cabinet underwent as a result of the economic and social crisis; although Brüning still had a majority in the Reichstag, President Hindenburg had made this decision to please the Junkers, who were unhappy about the plans for redistributing bankrupt agricultural lands and were complaining about "agrarian Bolshevism."

225. Letter to Blochmann, 22 June 1932, p. 52.

226. Letter to Elfride, 10 November 1932, p. 134.

227. MK, 454.

228. MK, 406.

229. Letter to Elfride, 10 November 1918, p. 59.

230. Letter to Blochmann, 30 March 1933, p. 61.

231. Letter to Blochmann, 22 June 1932, p. 52.

232. "The Program of the NSDAP," https://sourcebooks.fordham.edu/mod/25points.asp, quoted in German by Walter Hofer, *Der Nationalsozialismus. Dokumente, 1933–1945*, 50th ed., Frankfurt: Fischer, 2011 [1957], pp. 28–31. [The preamble, with its reference to the "masses' dissatisfaction," does not appear in the English translation.—Trans.]

233. Kershaw, *Hitler*, vol. 1, pp. 474–475 and 532.

234. *Völkischer Beobachter*, Bavarian edition, 18 September 1930, p. 2.

235. Letter to Blochmann, 22 June 1932, p. 52.

236. Letter to Arendt, 9 July 1925, p. 28.

237. Letter to Arendt, 23 August 1925, p. 32.

238. Letter to Arendt, 17 August 1925, p. 29.

239. Thomas Mann, *Ein Appell an die Vernunft. Rede, gehalten am 17. Oktober im Beethovensaal zu Berlin*, Berlin: Fischer, 1930, p. 9.

240. Ibid., p. 16.

241. Ibid., p. 17.

242. Ibid., p. 19.

243. Letter to Bultmann, 16 December 1932, p. 191.

244. Letter from Rudolf Bultmann to Heidegger, 14 December 1932, pp. 186–187.

245. Letter to Fritz, 28 October 1932, p. 30.

246. Ibid.

247. Ibid.

248. Letter to Bultmann, 16 December 1932, p. 191.

249. Letter to Elfride, 20 June 1932, p. 137.

250. Letter to Elfride, 9 June 1932, p. 134.

251. Ibid., p. 133.

252. Ibid.

253. Letter to Elfride, 17 August 1931, p. 129.

254. Letter to Elfride, 9 June 1932, p. 133.

255. Letter to Elfride, 18 June 1932, p. 136.

256. Letter to Elfride, 9 June 1932, p. 133.

257. Anne Christine Nagle, *Die Philipps-Universität Marburg im Nationalsozialismus. Dokumente zu ihrer Geschichte*, Stuttgart: F. Steiner Verlag, p. 149.

258. Hans Zehrer, "Worum geht es?" *Die Tat* 24 (October 1932): 529–536, here p. 529.

259. Letter to Elfride, 15 October 1932, p. 140.

260. Zehrer, "*Worum geht* es?" pp. 532–533.

261. Letter to Blochmann, 19 December 1932, p. 55.

262. Letter to Elfride, 20 June 1932, p. 137.

263. Ibid., p. 136, translation modified.

264. Ibid.

265. Ibid., p. 137.

266. Mörchen, quoted by Martin (ed.), *Martin Heidegger und das "Dritte Reich,"* p. 84.

267. Letter to Fritz, 28 October 1932, p. 30.

268. Letter to Elfride, 18 June 1932, pp. 135–136.

269. "Er war ein lieber Vater."

270. Letter from Fritz to Heidegger, 30 January 1933, p. 31.

271. Letter from Heidegger to Fritz, 4 February 1933, p. 32.

272. Ibid.

273. *Verordnung des Reichspräsidents zum Schutz von Volk und Staat, Reichsgesetzblatt,* 1933, 1, p. 83 (henceforth abbreviated RGBl, followed by year, volume number, and page).

274. Ott, *Martin Heidegger,* p. 150.

275. Martin Harry Sommerfeldt, *Hermann Göring. Ein Lebensbild,* 3rd ed., Berlin: E. S. Mittler, 1933.

276. Letter to Elfride, 19 March 1933, p. 141.

277. Letter to Blochmann, 22 March 1933, p. 59.

278. Letter to Elfride, 19 March 1933, p. 141.

279. Ibid.

280. Ibid.

281. Ibid., pp. 141–142.

282. Ibid., p. 142.

283. Ibid.

284. Ibid.

285. *Gesetz zur Behebung der Not von Volk und Reich,* RGBl 1933, 1, p. 141.

286. Letter to Blochmann, 30 March 1933, p. 60.

287. Ibid.

288. Ibid.

289. Ibid.

290. Ibid.

291. Ibid.

292. Ibid.

293. Letter to Jaspers, 8 December 1932, p. 149.

294. His friend had just published *The Spiritual Situation of the Time* (*Die geistige Situation der Zeit,* 1931), in which he denounced, in terms very close to Heidegger's, the utilitarian and excessively specialized development of the universities, which were now corrupted by the masses: "The existence of the masses [*massendasein*] in higher education has a tendency to destroy science *qua* science. The latter has to adapt to the crowds, which pursue only its practical goal, an investigation and the legitimacy connected with it; research must be conducted only so long as it corresponds to results that have practical value. Science is consequently reduced to the intellectual objectivity of what can be learned. Instead of higher education, which science experiences with the spiritual

uneasiness of *sapere aude*, all that emerges is mere training." Karl Jaspers, *Die geistige Situation der Zeit*, Berlin: De Gruyter, 1953 [1931], based on the 5th ed. of 1932, p. 137.

295. Letter to Blochmann, 30 March 1933, p. 61.

296. Ibid.

297. Letter to Jaspers, 3 April 1933, p. 151.

298. Recall that among Heidegger's professors, Sauer was the one who protected him as a young Catholic with a bright future.

299. Ott, *Martin Heidegger*, p. 142.

300. Letter to Blochmann, 12 April 1933, p. 62.

301. Quoted in Martin (ed.), *Martin Heidegger und das "Dritte Reich,"* p. 232.

302. Martin, "Die Universität Freiburg im Breisgau im Jahre 1933, eine Nachlese zu Heideggers Rektorat," *Zeitschrift für die Geschichte des Oberrheins* 136 (1988): 445–477, here p. 452.

303. Stuttgart Hauptstaatsarchiv, Ministry of Higher Education, EA III/1 University of Freiburg, Heidegger, Martin, quoted by Ott, *Martin Heidegger*, p. 144.

304. *Der Alemanne*, 20 April 1933, quoted by Ott, *Martin Heidegger*, p. 145.

305. Diary of Josef Sauer, 6 March 1933, p. 36; HJB4, 228.

306. Ott, *Martin Heidegger*, p. 146.

307. HJB4, 245.

308. Martin Broszat and Norbert Frei (eds.), *Das Dritte Reich im Überblick. Chronik, Ereignisse, Zusammenhänge*, Munich: Piper, 1989, p. 195, 212; Michael H. Kater, *The Nazi Party: A Social Profile of Members and Leaders, 1945*, Oxford: Basil Blackwell, 1983, p. 262 (figure 1).

309. Ott, *Martin Heidegger*, p. 136.

310. Letter from Vossler to Croce, 25 August 1933, *Carteggio Croce-Vossler, 1899–1949*, Naples: Bibliopolis, p. 359: "Il Heidegger, e accanto a lui quel Carl Schmitt, autore di libri di diritto publico e politico, discepolo, fino a un certo punto, di Georges Sorel, si van rivelando come i due desastri intellettuali della nuova Germania."

311. Letter to Fritz, 4 May 1933, p. 36.

312. Ibid.

7. The Rector's Address, or a Self-Portrait of the Philosopher as *Führer*

1. Diary of Josef Sauer, 28 May 1933, p. 63; HJB4, 231.

2. "Ein sonderbares Gemisch war die Aula mit den mittelalterl. Talaren, dem Wichs und den Fahnen der Korporationen und daneben das Grau und Schwarz der SA und SS.-Leute. Der kleine M. im roten Samt war in seiner Blässe fast etwas rührend." Letter from Blochmann to Hermann Nohl, 29 May 1933, quoted by Eva D. Becker, " 'Armes Deutschland'—'Glückliches England.' Elisabeth Blochmann in Oxford 1934 bis 1952," *Exil* 2 (2003): 69–83, here p. 71.

3. Diary of Josef Sauer, 28 May 1933, p. 63; HJB4, 231.

4. Letter from Blochmann to Hermann Nohl, 29 May 1933, p. 71.

5. Hermann later said he was present (in "Er war ein lieber Vater"); it would be surprising if his mother or brother had not attended.

6. Letter from Wolfgang Aly to Heidegger, 26 May 1933, UAF II/1 32, quoted by Bernd Martin, "Die Universität Freiburg im Breisgau im Jahre 1933. Eine Nachlese zu Heideggers Rektorat," *Zeitschrift für die Geschichte des Oberrheins* 136 (1988): 445–477, here p. 454.

7. Letter from Konrad Guenther to the rector's office, 19 February 1933, UAF II/1 32, quoted by Martin, "Die Universität Freiburg," p. 454.

8. *Academic Festival Overture* in C minor, Op. 80.

9. Letter to Franz Kerber, 19 May 1933, UAF II/1 32, quoted by Martin, "Die Universität Freiburg," p. 455.

10. Translators' note: In German, *Führer* is both singular and plural; here it would be translated as "leaders."

11. GA 16, 107.

12. GA 19, 337.

13. GA 19, 319.

14. GA 19, 337.

15. On this question, see especially Christian Sommer, "Métapolitique de l'université. Le programme platonicien de Heidegger," *Les études philosophiques* 2 (2010): 255–275.

16. GA 36/37, 158.

17. GA 16, 107.

18. Alfred Baeumler, *Nietzsche. Der Philosoph und Politiker,* Leipzig: Reclam, 1931, pp. 15, 93, and 179.

19. Ernst Krieck, *Heil und Kraft,* Leipzig: Armanen, 1934, pp. 3–4 and 82.

20. Ernst Horneffer, *Nietzsche als Vorbote der Gegenwart,* Düsseldorf: Bagel, 1934, p. 43.

21. GA 16, 116.

22. Ibid.

23. Plato, *Republic,* 497d 9.

24. GA 16, 117; "All great things are precarious." Plato, *Republic,* trans. Paul Shorey, 2 vols., Cambridge, MA: Loeb Classical Library, 1953 [1930].

25. Friedrich Nietzsche, *The Gay Science,* trans. Walter Kaufmann, New York: Vintage, 1974, 1, 19, p. 91.

26. Ernst Jünger, *Sturm,* Stuttgart: Klett-Cota, 1979.

27. See particularly Johann Chapoutot, *La loi du sang. Penser et agir en nazi,* Paris: Gallimard, 2014.

28. Johann Chapoutot, "Régénération et dégénérescence. La philosophie grecque reçue et relue par les nazis (Platon et la Stoa)," *Anabases* 7 (2008): 141–161.

29. Rosenberg, *Der Mythus des 20. Jahrhunderts*, p. 2.
30. GA 16, 95.
31. Carl Schmitt, *Staat, Bewegung, Volk. Die Dreigliederung des politischen Einheit*, Hamburg: Hanseat. Verl. Anst, 1933, p. 42.
32. MK, 345.
33. Ibid.
34. Letter to Elfride, 17 October 1918, p. 55.
35. MK, 304.
36. MK, 345.
37. Ibid.
38. Letter to Elfride, 17 October 1918, p. 55.
39. MK, 345.
40. GA 2, 509; *Being and Time*, 437.
41. GA 16, 111.
42. MK, 382.
43. GA 16, 97.
44. GA 16, 108.
45. Plato, *Republic*, 474b–c.
46. GA 16, 114.
47. GA 16, 111.
48. GA 16, 204.
49. GA 16, 112.
50. GA 16, 114.
51. GA 16, 192.
52. Ibid.
53. Diary of Josef Sauer, 13 May 1933, p. 61; HJB4, 230.
54. GA 16, 112.
55. Olivier Jouanjan, "*Gefolgschaft et Studentenrecht*. Deux gloses en marge du Discours de rectorat," *Les études philosophiques* 2 (2010): 211–233, here p. 216.
56. "The Program of the NSDAP," quoted in German by Hofer, *Der Nationalsozialismus*, p. 29.
57. For another perspective on this question under the Third Reich, see esp. Chapoutot, *La loi du sang*, p. 121ff.
58. Victor Klemperer, *LTI: The Language of the Third Reich*, trans. Martin Brady, London and New Brunswick, NJ: Bloomsbury, 2000, p. 244.
59. Ibid.
60. GA 16, 107.
61. Ibid.
62. GA 16, 112.
63. GA 16, 116.
64. Ernst Forsthoff, *Der totale Staat*, Hamburg: Hanseat Verl. Anst., 1933.

65. Otto Koellreutter, *Der deutsche Führerstaat,* Tübingen: Mohr, 1934, p. 13.

66. Ibid., p. 16.

67. Schmitt, *Staat, Bewegung, Volk,* p. 42.

68. Eugen Fischer, "Vorspruch," in Nationalsozialistischen Lehrerbund Deutschland-Sachsen (ed.), *Bekenntnis der Professoren an den Universitäten und Hochschulen zu Adolf Hitler und dem nationalsozialistischen Staat,* Dresden: Wilhelm Limpert, 1934, pp. 9–10, here p. 9.

69. GA 16, 107.

70. Chapoutot, *La loi du sang,* p. 38.

71. GA 16, 108, my emphasis.

72. Ibid.

73. Having remained almost anonymous, unlike the first two, Seinosuke Yuasa translated the 1930 lecture "What Is Metaphysics?" (GA 16, 66ff.) into Japanese.

74. GA 2, 508; *Being and Time,* 436.

75. Gesetz über die Bildung von Studentenschaften an den wissenschaftlichen Hochschulen, RGBl 1933, 1, p. 215.

76. Gesetz gegen die Überfüllung deutscher Schulen und Hochschulen, RGBl 1933 1, p. 225.

77. RGBl 1933, 1, p. 226.

78. RGBl 1933, 1, p. 195.

79. GA 16, 113.

80. GA 16, 107.

81. GA 16, 108.

82. GA 2, 508; *Being and Time,* 436.

83. GA 36–37, 158.

84. Forsthoff, *Der totale Staat,* p. 46.

85. Koellreutter, *Der deutsche Führerstaat,* pp. 15–16.

86. GA 16, 98.

87. MK, 410–411.

88. MK, 286.

89. MK, 688.

90. Rosenberg, *Der Mythus des 20. Jahrhunderts,* p. 2.

91. Ibid., p. 625.

92. Ibid., p. 12. [This passage does not appear in the English-language edition cited.—Trans.]

93. Fischer, "Vorspruch," p. 9.

94. MK, 106.

95. MK, 107.

96. GA 16, 112.

97. GA 16, 108.

98. MK, 408, translation modified.

99. Rosenberg, *Der Mythus des 20. Jahrhunderts*, p. 624.
100. GA 16, 108.
101. GA 16, 113.
102. GA 16, 83.
103. RGB1 1933, 1, p. 215.
104. Harald Lönnecker, "Vorbild ... für das kommende Reich. Die Deutsche Studentenschaft (Dst) 1918–1933," *GDS-Archiv für Hochschul- und Studentengeschichte*, vol. 7, Köln: SH-Verlag, 2004, pp. 37–53, here p. 45.
105. Arnold Köttgen, "Hochschulrechtliche Reformen," *Deutsche Juristen-Zeitung*, 1933, columns 1523ff. Quoted by Jouanjan, "Gefolgschaft und Studentenrecht," p. 224.
106. GA 16, 96.
107. GA 16, 113.
108. RGBl 1933, 1, p. 215.
109. Jouanjan, "Gefolgschaft und Studentenrecht," p. 225.
110. Martin, "Die Universität Freiburg im Breisgau im Jahre 1933," pp. 455–456.
111. MK, 408.
112. Jouanjan, "Gefolgschaft und Studentenrecht," p. 229.
113. Verfügung des Reichskommissars für den Arbeitsdienst Hierl zur Aufstellung von Stammabteilungen vor Einführung der Arbeitsdienstpflicht, Federal Archives R 77/77.
114. Reichsarbeitsdienstgesetz, RGBl 1935, 1, p. 769.
115. Anordnung über die zahlenmäßige Begrenzung des Zugangs zu den Hochschulen, 28 December 1933, *Reichsministerialblatt* 62, 12 January 1934, p. 17.
116. Claudia Huerkamp, *Bildungsbürgerinnen. Frauen im Studien und in akademischen Berufen, 1900–1945*, Göttingen: Vandenhoeck & Ruprecht, 1996, p. 80.
117. Quoted by Jouanjan, "Gefolgschaft und Studentenrecht," p. 226.
118. Köttgen, "Hochschulrechtliche Reformen."
119. GA 16, 97.
120. GA 16, 113.
121. Ibid.
122. Ibid.
123. GA 38, 156.
124. GA 16, 113.
125. GA 16, 112.
126. GA 16, 111.
127. GA 16, 96.
128. GA 16, 108.
129. GA 16, 204.
130. "Er war ein lieber Vater."
131. GA 16, 114.

132. GA 16, 108.
133. GA 16, 200–201.
134. GA 16, 108.
135. GA 16, 114.
136. GA 16, 109.
137. GA 16, 114.
138. GA 16, 109.
139. GA 16, 110.
140. GA 16, 109.
141. GA 16, 111–112.
142. Wilhelm Dilthey, *Einleitung in den Geisteswissenschaften,* vol. 1 of *Gesammelte Schriften,* Stuttgart: B. G. Teubner, p. 6.
143. Ibid.
144. GA 16, 113.
145. Letter from Konrad Guenther to the rector's office, 19 February 1933, UAF II/1 32, quoted by Martin (ed.), *Martin Heidegger,* p. 454.
146. GA 16, 111.
147. GA 16, 112.
148. GA 16, 97.
149. GA 13, 9–10; "Why Do I Stay in the Provinces?" 16.
150. GA 16, 97.
151. GA 13, 9; "Why Do I Stay in the Provinces?" 16.
152. GA 16, 759.
153. GA 2, 73; *Being and Time,* 80.
154. Gröber, *Aus meinem römischen Tagebuch,* p. 181.
155. GA 16, 97.
156. GA 13, 10–11; "Why Do I Stay in the Provinces?" 17.
157. GA 16, 759.
158. GA 16, 207.
159. GA 2, 509; *Being and Time,* 437.
160. Johann Chapoutot, *Le nazisme et l'antiquité,* Paris: PUF, 2012 [2008], p. 29.
161. Hans F. K. Günther, *Rassenkunde des deutschen Volkes,* Munich: Lehmann, 1922, p. 3.
162. MK, 389.
163. MK, 398.
164. MK, 405, translation modified.
165. Rosenberg, *Der Mythus des 20. Jahrhunderts,* p. 17.
166. Ibid., pp. 24–25, translation modified.
167. Ibid., p. 25.
168. Ibid., p. 2.
169. Ibid., p. 22, translation modified.

170. Ibid., p. 2.
171. GA 16, 112.
172. Erwin Guido Kolbenheyer, "Lebenswert und Lebenswirkung der Dichtkunst in einem Volke," in *Werke,* vol. 8, Munich: Langen/Müller, 1941, pp. 63–86.
173. GA 36/37, 209.
174. GA 36/37, 178.
175. "Verschafft Adel auf dem Boden zum Austrag, wo er zu tragen vermag." GA 36/37, 263.
176. GA 38, 153.
177. GA 38, 153.
178. GA 38, 153.
179. Plato, *Theaetetus,* 159d–e.
180. GA 38, 153.
181. GA 16, 114.
182. GA 36/37, 6.
183. Rosenberg, *Der Mythus des 20. Jahrhunderts,* p. 28.
184. GA 16, 112.
185. GA 16, 111.
186. Friedrich Nietzsche, *The Gay Science,* bk. 5, §343.
187. GA 16, 111.
188. GA 28, 354.
189. Letter from Blochmann to Hermann Nohl, 29 May 1933, p. 71.
190. Diary of Josef Sauer, 28 May 1933, p. 63; HJB4, 231.
191. Letter to Blochmann, 12 April 1933, p. 62.
192. Denker, "Martin Heidegger und die Erzabtei Beuron," *Meßkircher Heimathefte* 9 (2002): 47.
193. GA 16, 95.
194. GA 36/37, 3; see also p. 5ff.
195. "Und das bedeutet: sie lebt aus dem Willen, diejenige Zucht und diejenige Erziehung zu finden, die sie reif und stark macht zu der geistig-politischen Führerschaft, die ihr künftig aus dem Volk für das Volk aufgetragen werden soll" (GA 16, 95).
196. GA 16, 108.
197. GA 16, 96.
198. GA 16, 113.
199. GA 12, 91.
200. GA 16, 111.
201. Erich Rothacker, "Geschichtsphilosophie," in Alfred Baeumler & Manfred Schröter (eds.), *Handbuch der Philosophie,* vol. 4: *Staat und Geschichte,* Munich and Berlin: R. Oldenbourg, p. 145.
202. Rosenberg, *Der Mythus des 20. Jahrhunderts,* pp. 1–2.
203. Ibid., p. 85.

204. MK, 345, translation modified, my emphasis.

205. MK, 3, translation modified.

206. MK, 645–646, my emphasis. [In the Manheim translation of *Mein Kampf,* this entire passage is in italics. We have removed the italics to highlight the emphasis given by the author.—Trans.]

207. MK, 632–633.

208. MK, 395.

209. MK, 402, my emphasis. [Once again, the entire passage is in italics in the Manheim translation.—Trans.]

210. MK, 402, my emphasis. [Italics in the original deleted.—Trans.]

211. HJB4, 77.

212. GA 16, 116.

213. Diary of Josef Sauer, 28 May 1933, p. 63; HJB4, 231.

214. Letter from Blochmann to Hermann Nohl, 29 May 1933, p. 71.

215. Hugo Ott, *Martin Heidegger,* p. 200.

216. Ibid., p. 189.

217. Letter to Jaspers, 14 July 1923, p. 41.

218. Löwith, *My Life in Germany,* p. 34, translation modified.

219. Letter from Jaspers to Heidegger, 23 August 1933, p. 155.

220. Letter from Bultmann to Heidegger, 18 June 1933, pp. 193–194.

221. Friedrich Nietzsche, *The Dawn of Day,* trans. John McFarland Kennedy, Create Space, 2018, p. 150.

8. An Albatross Tries Out the Goose Step

1. GA 16, 196.
2. GA 16, 150–153.
3. GA 16, 230–231.
4. GA 16, 104.
5. GA 16, 131.
6. GA 16, 232–237.
7. Letter to Elfride, 18 June 1932, pp. 135–136.
8. Ott, *Martin Heidegger,* p. 193.
9. GA 16, 172.
10. GA 16, 106.
11. GA 36/37.
12. GA 16, 761.
13. GA 16, 115.
14. On this camp, see Ott, *Martin Heidegger,* pp. 224–234.
15. GA 16, 170.
16. Ott, *Martin Heidegger,* p. 229.

17. GA 16, 170.

18. GA 2, 509; *Being and Time,* 436.

19. GA 16, 760.

20. GA 16, 190.

21. GA 2, 509; *Being and Time,* 437.

22. GA 2, 508; *Being and Time,* 436–437.

23. *Akten der Reichskanzlei Reg. Hitler,* vol. 2, pt. 2, p. 939, no. 1.

24. GA 38, 154.

25. GA 38, 165.

26. RGBl 1933, 1, pp. 529–531.

27. Gisela Bock, *Zwangssterilisation im Nationalsozialismus. Studien zur Rassenpolitik und Frauenpolitik,* Opladen: Westdeutscher Verlag, 1986, p. 233.

28. GA 16, 150.

29. GA 16, 151.

30. GA 16, 763.

31. GA 38, 153.

32. GA 38, 61.

33. GA 16, 269.

34. GA 16, 99.

35. This was a speech at the Reichstag (often called the "first peace speech," the second being that of 21 May 1935), in which Hitler subscribed to the idea of disarmament, provided that equal treatment was granted to Germany. At the same time, he brandished the threat of leaving the League of Nations (Hitler, *Reden und Proklamationen,* ed. Domarus, vol. 1, p. 270ff.).

36. GA 16, 104.

37. Letter to Fritz, 13 April 1933, pp. 34–35.

38. Letter to Fritz, 13 April 1933, p. 35.

39. Ibid.

40. Letter from Heidegger to Fritz, 4 May 1933, p. 36.

41. Letter to Blochmann, 19 September 1933, p. 74.

42. Letter from Fritz Heidegger to his brother, 3 April 1933, p. 33.

43. GA 16, 184.

44. HJB4, 88.

45. Quoted in Martin (ed.), *Martin Heidegger und das "Dritte Reich,"* p. 232.

46. GA 16, 105.

47. Diary of Josef Sauer, 22 May 1933, p. 62; HJB4, 230–231.

48. Martin, "Die Universität Freiburg im Breisgau im Jahre 1933," p. 455.

49. Ibid.

50. Diary of Josef Sauer, 13 May 1933, p. 61; HJB4, 230.

51. Diary of Josef Sauer, 22 May 1933, p. 62; HJB4, 230.

52. Ott, *Martin Heidegger,* p. 198.

53. GA 94, 151; *Ponderings II–VI: Black Notebooks, 1931–1938,* trans. Richard Rojcewicz, Bloomington: Indiana University Press, 2016, 111, translation modified. Hereafter cited as *Black Notebooks,* 1.

54. Letter to Carl Schmitt, 22 August 1933, GA 16, 156.

55. Ibid.

56. Diary of Josef Sauer, 22 August 1933, p. 79; HJB4, 232–233. Quoted in Ott, *Martin Heidegger,* p. 199, translation modified.

57. Letter from Jaspers to Heidegger, 23 August 1933, p. 149.

58. Ibid.

59. Ibid.

60. Ibid., p. 150.

61. Ott, *Martin Heidegger,* p. 230.

62. Martin, "Die Universität Freiburg im Breisgau im Jahre 1933," p. 465.

63. GA 16, 137.

64. GA 16, 100.

65. GA 16, 119.

66. GA 16, 103.

67. Ott, *Martin Heidegger,* pp. 151–152.

68. RGBl 1933, 1, p. 215.

69. Jouanjan, "*Gefolgschaft et Studentenrecht,*" p. 228.

70. GA 16, 256–257.

71. GA 16, 113.

72. Ott, *Martin Heidegger,* p. 176.

73. RGBl 1933, 1, p. 175.

74. Ott, *Martin Heidegger,* p. 177; see also GA 16, 84–85; GA 16, 91–92.

75. Ott, *Martin Heidegger,* pp. 380–381. The text published in the second German edition of Ott's book (1992, pp. 353–354) includes this expression, which had been crossed out and which Hermann Heidegger did not reprint in his edition of GA 16 (pp. 87–88): "Es ist ja nur im Sinne dieses neuen harten, vom deutschen Standpunkt vernünftigen Gesetzes." It is possible to think, with Ott, that the strikethrough was made in 1945 when these terms were no longer appropriate, or, with H. Heidegger, that it was made back in 1933. That hardly changes the fact that Elfride Heidegger thought them. Conversely, the strikethrough did allow her son to relegate the line to a note at the end of the volume (GA 16, 787), an act of a nature to appease his filial piety.

76. Letter from Jaspers to Oelkers, 22 December 1945, quoted in Ott, *Martin Heidegger,* p. 338.

77. "Ein Gespräch mit Max Müller," in Martin (ed.), *Martin Heidegger und das "Dritte Reich,"* p. 96.

78. Löwith, *My Life in Germany,* p. 42.

79. Jonas, *Memoirs,* p. 68.

80. "Es geht um nichts Geringeres als um die unaufschiebbare Besinnung darauf, dass wir vor der Wahl stehen, unserem deutschen Geistesleben wieder echte bodenständige Kräfte und Erzieher zuzuführen oder es der wachsenden Verjudung im weiteren u. engeren Sinne endgültig auszuliefern. Wir werden den Weg nur zurückfinden, wenn wir imstande sind, ohne Hetze und unfruchtbare Auseinandersetzung, frischen Kräften zur Entfaltung zu verhelfen." Letter of 2 October 1929 to Viktor Schwoerer, published by Ulrich Sieg, "Die Verjudung des deutschen Geistes," *Die Zeit*, no. 52, 22 December 1989.

81. Letter to Elfride, 8 September 1920, p. 80.

82. MK, 382.

83. Rosenberg, *Der Mythus des 20. Jahrhunderts*, p. 5.

84. Ibid, p. 252.

85. GA 35, 1.

86. Ibid.

87. Ibid.

88. Ibid.

89. GA 9, 104.

90. GA 2, 29; *Being and Time*, 43.

91. Cassirer, *The Philosophy of Symbolic Forms*, vol. 2: *Mythical Thought*.

92. GA 2, 68; *Being and Time*, 76.

93. Ibid.

94. Ibid.

95. GA 2, 229; *Being and Time*, 217.

96. Letter to Arendt, winter 1932–1933, p. 53.

97. Letter to Elfride, 23 March 1929, p. 120.

98. Siegfried Marck, *Die Dialektik in der Philosophie der Gegenwart*, Tübingen: J. C. B. Mohr, 1929.

99. Fritz Heinemann, *Neue Wege der Philosophie. Geist, Leben, Existenz, eine Einführung in die Philosophie der Gegenwart*, Leipzig: Quelle & Meyer, 1929.

100. Quoted by Norbert Kapferer, *Die Nazifizierung der Philosophie an der Universität Breslau 1933–1945*, Münster: Lit Verlag, 2001, pp. 28–30, here p. 29.

101. Quoted ibid., p. 30.

102. Emmanuel Faye, *Heidegger: The Introduction of Nazism into Philosophy in Light of the Unpublished Seminars of 1933–1935*, trans. Michael B. Smith, New Haven, CT: Yale University Press, 2009, pp. 35–36.

103. Especially *Imperialismus und Pazifismus als Weltanschauungen*, Tübingen: Mohr, 1918; *Das Jahrhundert der Aufklärung*, Leipzig: B. G. Teubner, 1923; *Marxische Staatsbejahung*, Breslau: Volkswacht-Buchh., 1925; and *Reformismus und Radikalismus in der deutschen Sozialdemokratie*, Berlin: E. Laub, 1927.

104. Letter to Elfride, 9 February 1928, pp. 114–115.

105. Anders, "Wenn ich verzweifelt bin, was geht's mich an."

106. Jonas, *Memoirs,* pp. 68–69.

107. HJB4, 82.

108. MK, 168.

109. MK, 57–58.

110. Letter from Paul Yorck von Wartenburg to Dilthey, 18 February 1884, in Wilhelm Dilthey & Paul Yorck von Wartenburg, *Briefwechsel (1877–1897),* Halle: Niemeyer, 1923, p. 254.

111. Kershaw, *Hitler,* vol. 1, p. 320.

112. "The Program of the NSDAP," https://sourcebooks.fordham.edu/mod/25points.asp, quoted in German in Hofer, *Der Nationalsozialismus. Dokumente,* pp. 28–31.

113. Letter to Rickert, 7 February 1932.

114. Eduard Baumgarten, *Nationalismus und Sozialdemokratie,* Freiburg and Leipzig: F. P. Lorenz, "Schriften der sozialistische Studentengruppe der Universität Freiburg in Baden," 1919.

115. Franz Josef Brecht, *Platon und der Georg-Kreis,* Leipzig: Dieterich'sche Verlh., "Des Erbe der Alten," 1929.

116. Letter to Arendt, winter 1932–1933, pp. 52–53.

117. Löwith, *My Life in Germany,* p. 65.

118. Letter to Elfride, 9 June 1932, p. 134.

119. Jonas, *Memoirs,* p. 68.

120. "Um den Nationalsozialismus. Und was geschiet met den Juden?" *Jüdische Rundschau,* 3 June 1932, p. 209.

121. Patrick McGilligan, *Fritz Lang: The Nature of the Beast,* New York: St. Martin's Press, 1997, p. 176.

122. Quoted by Brigitte Hamann, *Hitlers Edeljude. Das Leben des Armenarztes Eduard Bloch,* Munich: Piper, 2008, p. 261.

123. Suzanne Mauss, *Nicht zugelassen. Die jüdischen Rechtsanwälte im Oberlandesgerichtsbezirk Düsseldorf 1933–1945,* Essen: Klartext Verlag, 2013; "Hitler's Jewish Commander and Victim," 4 July 2012, http://jewish-voice-from-germany.de/cms/hitlers-jewish-commander-and-victim/, consulted 25 January 2014.

124. "Himmler Speech in Posen," https://www.facinghistory.org/holocaust-human-behavior/himmler-speech-posen-1943.

125. Ott, *Martin Heidegger,* p. 188.

126. HJB4, 13.

127. "Gewährung von Vergünstigungen an Studierende der basischen Hochschulen," *Freiburger Studentenzeitung,* 3 November 1933, p. 6, quoted in Guido Schneeberger (ed.), *Nachlese zu Heidegger. Dokumente zu seinem Leben und Denken,* Bern: Buchdruckerei AG, Suhr, 1962, p. 137.

128. Ibid.

129. Hans Mommsen, *From Weimar to Auschwitz,* trans. Philip O'Connor, Princeton, NJ: Princeton University Press, 1991, p. 159 and passim.

130. GA 16, 217.

131. RGBl 1933, 1, p. 51.

132. GA 16, 142–143.

133. Ott, *Martin Heidegger,* p. 207.

134. GA 16, 144–146.

135. GA 16, 774.

136. Ott, *Martin Heidegger,* p. 223.

137. Quoted ibid., pp. 210–211.

138. GA 16, 248–249.

139. Quoted in Ott, *Martin Heidegger,* p. 217.

140. GA 16, 123.

141. GA 16, 261.

142. Ott, *Martin Heidegger,* p. 220.

143. GA 16, 111–112.

144. GA 16, 112.

145. GA 36/37, 94.

146. Letter from Elfride Heidegger to Elfriede Lieber, 12 January 1932, HJB4, 268–269.

147. GA 16, 134.

148. GA 16, 132.

149. Ott, *Martin Heidegger,* p. 188.

150. *Breisgauer Zeitung,* 8 May 1933, in Schneeberger (ed.), *Nachlese zu Heidegger,* pp. 29–30.

151. Alfred Baeumler, "Antrittsvorslesung in Berlin," *Männerbund und Wissenschaft,* Berlin: Junker & Dünnhaupt, 1934, pp. 123–138, here p. 137.

152. Ernesto Grassi, *Die Macht des Bilder. Ohnmacht der rationalen Sprache. Zur Rettung des Rhetorischen,* Munich: Wilhelm Fink Verlag, 1979, p. 11.

153. MK, 453.

154. "The Program of the NSDAP," https://sourcebooks.fordham.edu/mod/25points.asp.

155. Ott, *Martin Heidegger,* p. 224.

156. A few days earlier, Hitler Youth had held another book burning on Cathedral Square, which rain had twice thwarted, on 17 June and again on 21 June (*Der Alemanne,* 20 June 1933, p. 12, quoted in Schneeberger [ed.], *Nachlese zu Heidegger,* p. 66).

157. GA 16, 131.

158. Chapoutot, *Le nazisme et l'antiquité,* p. 39.

159. MK, 290.

160. GA 16, 109.

161. GA 16, 131.

162. GA 16, 112.

163. Hans L. Gottschalk, "Heideggers Rectoratszeit" (1978), in Neske (ed.), *Erinnerung an Martin Heidegger,* p. 187.

164. GA 16, 131.

165. GA 36/37, 90.

166. GA 36/37, 91.

167. Ibid.

168. Ibid.

169. Speech of 15 July 1932, https://archive.org/stream/HitlerAppealToTheNationSpeech15July1932/1932_07_15Hitlerappealtothenationae_djvu.txt, ed. Domarus, vol. 1, p. 116.

170. Speech of 1 February 1933, http://www.hitler.org/speeches/02-01-33.html, ed. Domarus, vol. 1, p. 192, translation modified.

171. Speech of 10 March 1933, ed. Domarus, vol. 1, p. 219.

172. Hans Buchheim, Martin Broszat, & Hans-Adolf Jacobsen, *Anatomie des SS-Staates,* 2 vols., Olten/Freiburg im Brisgau: Deutscher Taschenbuch Verlag, 1965, vol. 2, p. 20.

173. Martin Broszat, Elke Fröhlich, & Falk Wiesemann (eds.), *Bayern in der NS-Zeit,* vol. 1, Munich: R. Oldenbourg, 1977, p. 209, n. 30, and pp. 240–241.

174. Hermann Göring used the expression the next day to ban the SPD in Prussia. "Betätigungsverbot gegen die Sozialdemokratische Partei Deutschlands," *Ministerialblatt für die preußische inner Verwaltung,* part 1, 94th year, Berlin, 1933, p. 750, quoted by Werner Müller, "Der doppelte Untergang. Die SPD 1933 im Deutschen Reich und 1946 in der Sowjetischen Besatzungszone Deutschlands," in Andreas Kötzing, Francesca Weil, Mike Schmeitzner, & Jan Erik Schulte (eds.), *Vergleich als Herausforderung. Festschrift zum 65. Geburtstag von Günther Heydemann,* Göttingen: Vandenhoeck & Ruprecht, 2015, pp. 59–72, here p. 59.

175. RGBl 1933, 1, p. 479.

176. Carl Schmitt, "Die deutsche Rechtswissenschaft im Kampf gegen den jüdischen Geist," *Deutsche Juristen-Zeitung* 41, no. 20, 15 October 1936, p. 1193.

177. GA 16, 132.

178. GA 16, 170.

179. Heinrich Buhr & Erika Reichle, "Der weltliche Theolog. Vor der Gemeinde als vor dem lieben Gott," in Neske (ed.), *Erinnerung an Martin Heidegger,* pp. 53–63, here p. 53.

180. GA 16, 108.

181. GA 16, 224.

182. Rosenberg, *Der Mythus des 20. Jahrhunderts,* p. 624.

183. GA 36/37, 90–91.

184. Letter to Blochmann, 22 June 1932, p. 52.

185. Ott, *Martin Heidegger,* p. 209.

186. GA 16, 246.

187. Martin (ed.), *Ein Gespräch mit Max Müller,* p. 99.

188. Löwith, *My Life in Germany,* p. 59.

189. See also GA 16, 35.

190. See the clearly supportive letter of recommendation sent to his colleague in Basel, Paul Häberlin, on 30 April 1933 (GA 16, 89).

191. Jonas, *Memoirs,* p. 68.

192. Letter from Husserl to Ludwig Landgrebe, 28 May 1932, in *Husserliana—Dokumente,* vol. 4, p. 289.

193. Letter from Jaspers to Heidegger, 25 July 1931, pp. 137–138.

194. Letter to Jaspers, 20 December 1931, p. 145.

195. Letter from Jaspers to Heidegger, 24 December 1931, p. 147.

196. Letter from Jaspers to Friedrich Oehlkers, 22 December 1945, reproduced in Ott, *Martin Heidegger,* p. 338.

197. GA 16, 84–85; GA 16, 91–92.

198. GA 16, 154.

199. Letter to Blochmann, 30 August 1933, p. 70.

200. Letter from Jaspers to Oehlkers, 22 December 1945, reproduced in Ott, *Martin Heidegger,* p. 338.

201. Wolfgang Klafki & Helmut-Gerhard Müller, *Elisabeth Blochmann (1892–1972),* Marburg: Universitätsbibliothek, 1992.

202. "Gedenke daß du ein Teuscher bist."

203. Letter from Blochman to Elfride, 18 April 1933, p. 64.

204. Blochmann to Heidegger, 10 May 1933, p. 67.

205. Card to Blochmann, 10 June 1933, p. 67.

206. Ott, *Martin Heidegger,* p. 188.

207. Letter to Arendt, winter 1932–1933, p. 52.

208. GA 16, 787.

209. Letter to Elfride, 19 March 1933, p. 141.

210. Letter from Jaspers to Heidegger, 23 June 1933, p. 154.

211. Karl Jaspers, *Philosophische Autobiographie,* augmented edition, Munich: Piper, 1977, p. 101.

212. Letter from Jaspers to Heidegger, 23 August 1933, pp. 155–156.

213. Letter from Jaspers to Heidegger, 6 February 1949, pp. 168–169.

214. Unsent letter from Jaspers to Heidegger, 1 March 1948, pp. 166–167; letter of 6 February 1949, p. 169.

215. GA 16, 774.

216. Letter to Jaspers, 8 December 1932, p. 148.

217. Letter from Jaspers to Heidegger, 10 March 1933, p. 150.

218. Letter from Jaspers to Heidegger, 10 July 1949, p. 176.

9. An Oracle Facing the Storm

1. Letter to Blochmann, 5 September 1933, p. 71.

2. GA 13, 9–14.

3. Letter to Blochmann, 19 September 1933, pp. 73–74.
4. GA 94, 157, §105; *Black Notebooks*, 1, 115.
5. Ibid., translation modified.
6. Ibid.
7. Ott, *Martin Heidegger*, p. 249.
8. Ibid., p. 248.
9. Quoted ibid., p. 247.
10. GA 16, 256–257.
11. GA 16, 272.
12. GA 16, 273.
13. GA 16, 274.
14. Ott, *Martin Heidegger*, p. 139.
15. GA 94, 162, §113; *Black Notebooks*, 1, 119.
16. Quoted in Ott, *Martin Heidegger*, p. 251.
17. GA 94, 160, §112; *Black Notebooks*, 1, 117.
18. GA 94, 161, §112; *Black Notebooks*, 1, 118, translation modified.
19. Diary of Josef Sauer, 29 May 1934, p. 127; HJB4, 233.
20. Even in 1942, Heidegger was again reinterpreting his error; GA 97, 98.
21. GA 94, 162, §114; *Black Notebooks*, 1, 119.
22. GA 94, 198–199, §219; *Black Notebooks*, 1, 145–146.
23. Letter to Jaspers, 1 July 1935, p. 157.
24. Löwith, *My Life in Germany*, pp. 59–60.
25. Herbert Marcuse, "Der Kampf gegen den Liberalismus in der totalitären Staatsauffassung," *Zeitschrift für Sozialforschung* 3, no. 2 (1934): 161–195.
26. GA 16, 184.
27. Hans Barth, "Vom Ursprung des Kunstwerks. Über einen Vortrag von Martin Heidegger," *Neue Zürcher Zeitung*, 20 January 1936.
28. Emil Staiger, "Noch einmal Heidegger," *Neue Zürcher Zeitung*, 23 January 1936.
29. Löwith, *My Life in Germany*, p. 60.
30. Ibid.
31. GA 16, 204.
32. Löwith, *My Life in Germany*, p. 60.
33. GA 16, 390; 16, 414.
34. GA 16, 283.
35. GA 16, 111–112.
36. GA 16, 283.
37. Moeller van den Bruck, *Das Dritte Reich*, p. 33.
38. GA 16, 284.
39. GA 16, 281.
40. GA 42, 3; *Schelling's Treatise on the Essence of Human Freedom*, trans. Joan Stambaugh, Athens: Ohio University Press, 1985, p. 2.

41. GA 16, 302.
42. GA 38, 83.
43. GA 16, 315.
44. On this matter, see Farías, *Heidegger and Nazism,* pp. 205–207.
45. Letter to Bauch, 7 February 1935, p. 18.
46. Published by Sieg, "Die Verjudung des deutschen Geistes."
47. Letter to Bauch, 15 June 1936, p. 32.
48. Letter to Rothacker, 11 August 1934, *Dilthey-Jahrbuch,* no. 8, 1993, p. 223.
49. GA 16, 272.
50. For more details on this project, see Farías, *Heidegger and Nazism,* pp. 193–194.
51. GA 16, 508.
52. GA 16, 509.
53. Letter to Jaspers, 2 December 1926, p. 69.
54. Quoted by Ott, *Martin Heidegger,* pp. 255–257.
55. Reichsminister für Volksaufklärung und Propaganda.
56. In 1921 Goebbels had defended a thesis in literature in Heidelberg titled "Wilhelm von Schütz as Playwright."
57. GA 40, 8; *Introduction to Metaphysics,* trans. Gregory Fried & Richard Polt, New Haven, CT: Yale University Press, 2000, pp. 10–11.
58. Letter from Bauch, 23 December 1935, p. 26.
59. *Letters to His Wife,* p. 143.
60. Letter to Elfride, 26 January 1939, p. 159.
61. *Letters to His Wife,* p. 153.
62. Letter to Elfride, 2 July 1937, p. 152.
63. Letter to Elfride, 26 January 1939, p. 160.
64. *Letters to His Wife,* p. 320.
65. Ibid., p. 162.
66. Ibid., p. 150.
67. Letter to Elfride, 11 August 1936, pp. 148–149.
68. Letter to Elfride, 24 September 1938, p. 154.
69. *Letters to His Wife,* p. 144.
70. Letter to Elfride, 20 June 1932, p. 136.
71. Letter to Elfride, 20 June 1932, p. 137.
72. *Letters to His Wife,* p. 146.
73. Letter to Elfride, 25 February 1937, p. 151.
74. *Letters to His Wife,* p. 152.
75. Ibid., p. 161.
76. Letter to Elfride, 11 August 1936, p. 150.
77. *Letters to His Wife,* p. 150.
78. Ibid., p. 144.
79. Hermann Heidegger, "Martin Heidegger, el hombre."

80. Hermann Heidegger, "Mio padre, un genio normal," *La repubblica,* 12 April 1996.

81. "Er war ein lieber Vater."

82. Letter to Elfride, 3 October 1935, p. 147.

83. *Letters to His Wife,* p. 317.

84. Letter to Elfride, 2 March 1936, p. 148.

85. Letter to Elfride, 19 January 1939, p. 157.

86. *Letters to His Wife,* p. 146.

87. Letter to Elfride, 19 January 1939, p. 157.

88. *Letters to His Wife,* p. 156.

89. Letter to Elfride, 19 January 1939, p. 157.

90. Letter to Bauch, 7 February 1935, p. 17.

91. Letter to Jaspers, 16 May 1936, p. 161.

92. Letter to Blochmann, 12 April 1938, p. 91.

93. Letter to Elfride, 11 August 1936, p. 149.

94. Letter to Elfride, 11 October 1934, p. 144, translation modified.

95. Quoted by Ott, *Martin Heidegger,* p. 56.

96. Letter to Elfride, 10 January 1945, p. 182.

97. GA 97, 27.

98. I borrow this expression from the doctoral thesis in history by Sumi Shimahara, published after revisions under the title *Haymon d'Auxerre, exégète carolingien,* Turnhout: Brepols, "Haut Moyen Âge," 2013.

99. GA 43, 4–5.

100. Nietzsche, *Twilight of the Idols,* 8, 78, quoted in GA 40, 39; *Introduction to Metaphysics,* 38.

101. GA 43, 4–5.

102. Letter from Jaspers to Heidegger, 16 May 1936, p. 162.

103. Letter to Jaspers, 16 May 1936, p. 160.

104. GA 43, 26.

105. GA 39, 214 and 220; *Hölderlin's Hymns "Germania" and "The Rhine,"* trans. William McNeill & Julia Ireland, Bloomington: Indiana University Press, 2014, pp. 195 and 201.

106. Letter to Elfride, 11 October 1934, p. 144.

107. GA 39, 214; *Hölderlin's Hymns "Germania" and "The Rhine,"* 195, translation modified.

108. Letter to Elfride, 11 October 1934, pp. 144–145.

109. GA 39, 210; *Hölderlin's Hymns "Germania" and "The Rhine,"* 192, translation modified.

110. GA 39, 174 (and, similarly, GA 39, 283); *Hölderlin's Hymns "Germania" and "The Rhine,"* 159 and 257.

111. GA 39, 121; *Hölderlin's Hymns "Germania" and "The Rhine,"* 109.

112. Letter to Elfride, 30 August 1918, p. 49.

113. Letter to Arendt, 23 August 1925, p. 33.

114. Letter to Jaspers, 16 May 1936, p. 160.

115. GA 43, 13.

116. GA 94, 194; *Black Notebooks,* 1, 142.

117. Alfred Rosenberg, *Der Mythus des 20. Jahrhunderts,* p. 5. [This passage does not appear in the English-language edition cited above.—Trans.]

118. GA 39, 19; *Hölderlin's Hymns "Germania" and "The Rhine,"* 21.

119. "I am a man and nothing human is alien to me." Terence, *Heautontimorumenos, "The Self-Tormentor,"* act 1, line 77.

120. Quoted in GA 39, 18; *Hölderlin's Hymns "Germania" and "The Rhine,"* 20.

121. On this subject, see Michael E. Zimmerman, "Die Entwicklung von Heideggers Nietzsche-Interpretation," in Alfred Denker et al. (eds.), *Heidegger und Nietzsche, Heidegger-Jahrbuch* 2, Freiburg i. Br.: Karl Alber, 2005, pp. 97–116. Hereafter cited as HJB2.

122. GA 40, 41; *Introduction to Metaphysics,* 40.

123. Letters to Elfride, 20 August 1920, p. 77 and 10 August 1924, p. 99.

124. GA 95, 97; *Ponderings VII–XI: Black Notebooks, 1938–1939,* trans. Richard Rojcewicz, Bloomington: Indiana University Press, 2017, 76. Hereafter cited as *Black Notebooks,* 2.

125. GA 96, 46–47; *Ponderings XII–XV: Black Notebooks, 1939–1941,* trans. Richard Rojcewicz, Bloomington: Indiana University Press, 2017, 37. Hereafter cited as *Black Notebooks,* 3.

126. GA 40, 40–41; *Introduction to Metaphysics,* 40, translation modified.

127. GA 16, 284.

128. GA 40, 40; *Introduction to Metaphysics,* 40.

129. Martin Heidegger, *Introduction à la métaphysique,* trans. Gilbert Kahn, Paris: Gallimard, 1994, p. 48. [Fried and Polt's English translation of 2000, though it accurately translates *großen Zange* as "great pincers," also obscures the issue, by rendering "stabbing itself in the back" (*sich selbst zu erdolchen*) as "cutting its own throat."—Trans.]

130. GA 40, 50; *Introduction to Metaphysics,* 49.

131. An idea found, for example, in Hilter's *Mein Kampf,* which refers to the "gigantic American colossus of states" (*dem gigantischen amerikanischen Staatenkoloß*), MK, 638.

132. Jaspers, *Philosophische Autobiographie,* p. 101.

133. MK, 638.

134. MK, 639.

135. GA 40, 41; *Introduction to Metaphysics,* 40.

136. GA 65, 61–62; *Contributions to Philosophy,* trans. Richard Rojcewicz & Daniela Vallega-Neu, Bloomington: Indiana University Press, p. 49.

137. GA 42, 40–41. [Not in *Schelling's Treatise on the Essence of Freedom.*—Trans.]

138. GA 16, 333.

139. GA 39, 134; *Hölderlin's Hymns "Germania" and "The Rhine,"* 118.

140. GA 39, 173; *Hölderlin's Hymns "Germania" and "The Rhine,"* 158.

141. MK, 639.

142. Rosenberg, *Der Mythus des 20. Jahrhunderts,* p. 33, translation modified.

143. Löwith, *My Life in Germany,* p. 60.

144. Letter from Jaspers to Oehlkers, 22 December 1945, quoted by Ott, *Martin Heidegger,* p. 338.

145. GA 94, 179; *Black Notebooks,* 1, 131.

146. GA 65, 163; *Contributions to Philosophy,* 127, translation modified.

147. GA 65, 319; *Contributions to Philosophy,* 252.

148. Letter to Bauch, 7 June 1936, pp. 29–30.

149. GA 94, 194; *Black Notebooks,* 1, 142.

150. GA 43, 193.

151. GA 40, 41; *Introduction to Metaphysics,* 41.

152. On this matter, see esp. Jean-François Courtine, "Un peuple métaphysique," *Revue de métaphysique et de morale,* no. 3, *Philosophies nationales? Controverses franco-allemandes* (July–September 2001): 39–61.

153. GA 40, 41; *Introduction to Metaphysics,* 41.

154. GA 40, 42 and 211; *Introduction to Metaphysics,* 41 and 217.

155. MK, 135.

156. GA 40, 41; *Introduction to Metaphysics,* 41.

157. Löwith, *My Life in Germany,* p. 60.

158. Otmar Jung, *Plebiszit und Diktatur. Die Volksabstimmungern der Nationalsozialisten. Die Fälle "Austritt aus dem Völkerbund" (1933), "Staatsoberhaupt" (1934) und "Anschluss Österreichs" (1938),* Tübingen: Mohr, 1995, p. 119ff.

159. Letter to Elfride, 27 September 1938, p. 155.

160. GA 50, 28ff.

161. Letter to Elfride, 26 January 1939, p. 159.

162. Letter to Elfride, 22 May 1940, p. 168.

163. Letter to Bauch, 10 August 1941, p. 70.

164. GA 53, 106; *Hölderlin's Hymn "The Ister,"* trans. William McNeill & Julia Davis, Bloomington: Indiana University Press, 1996, p. 86.

165. *Letters to His Wife,* p. 161.

166. Letter to Elfride, 6 November 1939, p. 162.

167. Letter to Elfride, 26 November 1939, p. 164.

168. *Letters to His Wife,* p. 161.

169. Ibid., p. 165.

170. Ibid., p. 162.

171. Ibid., p. 175.

172. GA 16, 341ff.

173. Letter to Elfride, 6 November 1939, p. 161.

174. Letter to Elfride, 6 November 1939, p. 161.

175. Letter to Elfride, 6 November 1939, p. 162.

176. Letter to Elfride, 6 November 1939, p. 161; *Letters to His Wife,* p. 161.

177. Letter to Elfride, 6 November 1939, p. 161.

178. Letter to Elfride, 6 November 1939, p. 161.

179. Letter to Elfride, 6 November 1939, pp. 161–162.

180. "*Koinon.* Aus der Geschichte des Seyns."

181. GA 69, 208.

182. Letter to Elfride, 6 November 1939, p. 162.

183. GA 96, 235; *Black Notebooks,* 3, 185.

184. GA 69, 208–209.

185. Letter to Elfride, 22 November 1939, p. 162.

186. *Letters to His Wife,* p. 166.

187. Ibid., p. 162.

188. Letter to Elfride, 26 November 1939, p. 165.

189. GA 48, 94–95.

190. Letter to Elfride, 18 May 1940, pp. 166–167.

191. GA 48, 333.

192. GA 48, 205.

193. Ibid.

194. GA 48, 264–265.

195. GA 48, 265.

196. Letter to Elfride, 18 May 1940, p. 166, translation modified.

197. Letter to Elfride, 18 May 1940, p. 167.

198. GA 7, 98.

199. GA 69, 70.

200. GA 69, 223.

201. GA 50, 56–57.

202. Niels C. Lösch, *Rasse als Konstrukt. Leben und Werk Eugen Fischers,* Frankfurt: Peter Lang, 1997, pp. 344ff.

203. Ernst Klee, *"Euthanasie" im NS-Staat. Die "Vernichtung lebensunwerten Lebens,"* Frankfurt: Fischer, 1983, pp. 340–341; Henry Friedlander, *The Origins of Nazi Genocide,* Chapel Hill: University of North Carolina Press, 1995, p. 110.

204. GA 96, 242; *Black Notebooks,* 3, 208.

205. Adolf Hitler, proclamation to the German people, 22 June 1941, quoted in GA 96, 242; *Black Notebooks,* 3, 190.

206. GA 96, 242; *Black Notebooks,* 3, 190.

207. GA 96, 243; *Black Notebooks,* 3, 191.

208. GA 69, 209.

209. Rosenberg, *Der Mythus des 20. Jahrhunderts,* p. 55.

210. Willi Dressen, "Intelligenzaktion," in Wolfgang Benz, Hermann Graml, & Hermann Weiss (eds.), *Enzyklopädie des Nationalsozialismus,* 3rd ed., Stuttgart: Klett-Cotta, 1998, p. 524; Ernst Klee & Willi Dressen (eds.), *"Gott mit uns." Der deutsche Vernichtungskrieg im Osten (1939–1945),* Frankfurt: S. Fischer, 1989, p. 7; Peter Longerich, *Holocaust: The Nazi Persecution and Murder of the Jews,* Oxford: Oxford University Press, 2010, pp. 143–145.

211. Militärgeschichtlichen Forschungsamt (ed.), *Das Deutsche Reich und der Zweite Weltkrieg,* vol. 4: *Der Angriff auf die Sowjetunion,* Stuttgart: Deutsche Verlags-anstalt, 1983, p. 441.

212. Ortwin Buchbender & Reinhold Stertz (eds.), *Das andere Gesicht des Krieges,* Munich: C. H. Beck, 1982, pp. 172–173, letter 353.

213. Omer Bartov, "Barbarossa et les origines de la Solution finale," in Stéphane Audoin-Rouzeau, Annette Becker, Christian Ingrao, & Henry Rousso (eds.), *La violence de guerre (1914–1945). Approches comparées des deux conflits mondiaux,* Paris: Éditions Complexe, "Histoire du temps présent," 2002, pp. 193–217, here p. 196.

214. *Letters to His Wife,* p. 169.

215. Letter to Bultmann, 21 May 1941, p. 204.

216. Letter to Bauch, 10 August 1941, p. 67.

217. Letter to Elfride, 25 September 1941, p. 169.

218. Wolfgang Benz & Brigitte Mihok (eds.), *Holocaust an der Peripherie. Judenpolitik und Judenmord in Rumänien und Transnistrien, 1940–1944,* Berlin: Metropol, 2009.

219. "Er war ein lieber Vater."

220. E-mail from Arnulf Heidegger, 26 July 2012.

221. Letter to Fritz Heidegger, 20 July 1941, p. 72.

222. On this subject, see esp. Nicholas Stargardt, *The German War: A Nation under Arms (1939–1945),* New York: Basic Books, 2015. Stargardt, however, tends to minimize the level of ignorance among the Germans, which can be attributed to the inaccuracy of the information that was able to reach them. The camps themselves remained largely unknown to the German people, and the details about the persecution of the Jews were enveloped in fog: "For the entire period between 1933 and 1945, it may be observed that the illegal anti-Semitic actions and the use of physical violence against the Jews were only rarely, or even absolutely not, mentioned in the propaganda. Hence the acts of violence during the boycott of 1933 were left unreported, the anti-Semitic brutality of 1935 was portrayed as a trifling matter, and the true dimensions of *Kristallnacht* were concealed. The deportations from Germany had no place in the propaganda, and the systematic massacres were described with such concepts as 'annihilation' or 'eradication,' but without the details of the program of genocide being revealed." (Peter Longerich, *"Davon haben wir nichts gewusst." Deutschen und die Judenverfolgung 1933–1945,* Munich: Pantheon, 2007, p. 412.)

223. GA 50, 70.

224. GA 69, 48.

225. GA 69, 94.
226. Letter to Bauch, 10 August 1941, p. 68.
227. GA 69, 208–209.
228. GA 96, 243; *Black Notebooks,* 3, 191.
229. Letter to Kurt Bauch, 10 August 1941, p. 67.
230. GA 96, 261; *Black Notebooks,* 3, 207.
231. GA 96, 262; *Black Notebooks,* 3, 208.
232. *Letters to His Wife,* p. 169.
233. Letter to Elfride, 21 July 1918, p. 45.
234. Letter from Bauch to Heidegger (quoting Heidegger's letter to him), 13 July 1943, p. 91.
235. GA 97, 5.
236. GA 53, 68; *Hölderlin's Hymn "The Ister,"* 54.
237. GA 53, 86; *Hölderlin's Hymn "The Ister,"* 70.
238. GA 97, 20.
239. Ibid.
240. Ibid.
241. Letter to Fritz, 29 January 1943, p. 87.
242. Letter to Fritz, 29 January 1943, p. 86.
243. GA 97, 20.
244. GA 97, 21.
245. GA 97, 20.
246. GA 54, 67–68; *Parmenides,* trans. André Schuwer & Richard Rojcewicz, Bloomington: Indiana University Press, 1992, p. 46, translation modified.
247. GA 54, 68; *Parmenides,* 46.
248. GA 54, 75; *Parmenides,* 50.
249. GA 54, 78; *Parmenides,* 53.
250. GA 97, 144.
251. *Letters to His Wife,* p. 171.
252. Ibid.
253. GA 16, 362–363.
254. GA 4, 30.
255. This theme in itself was not new; hence "the one who seeks comfort minimizes and misunderstands the sacrifice" (GA 94, 301; *Black Notebooks,* 1, 220).
256. GA 97, 38.
257. *Letters to His Wife,* p. 173.
258. Ibid., p. 172.
259. Ibid., p. 176.
260. Ott, *Martin Heidegger,* p. 288.
261. GA 7, 92; "Overcoming Metaphysics," in Richard Wolin (ed.), *The Heidegger Controversy: A Critical Reader,* Cambridge, MA: MIT Press, 1993, p. 85, translation modified.

262. Ibid., translation modified. [The French is significantly different from the English translation.—Trans.]

263. GA 4, 30.

264. GA 50, 151.

265. Hitler's speech in Potsdam, 21 March 1933, ed. Domarus, vol. 1, p. 226.

266. GA 96, 177; *Black Notebooks*, 3, 139.

267. Letter to Elfride, 18 May 1940, p. 168.

268. GA 50, 150–151.

269. *Letters to His Wife*, p. 184.

270. Letter to Fritz, 18 January 1945, p. 118.

271. *Letters to His Wife*, p. 182.

272. Ott, *Martin Heidegger*, pp. 297–298.

273. Letter to Elfride, 25 November 1944, p. 179.

274. *Letters to His Wife*, p. 179.

275. Ibid.

276. Ibid., p. 186.

277. Letter to Elfride, 15 April 1945, p. 188.

278. GA 53.

279. "Ister" in Latin, a name adopted by Hölderlin for the title of his poem on the Danube.

280. Quoted by Otto Pöggeler, "Heideggers politisches Selbstverständnis," in Anne-Marie Gethmann-Siefert & Otto Pöggeler (eds.), *Heidegger und die praktische Philosophie*, Frankfurt: Suhrkamp, 1988, p. 41.

281. GA 97, 54.

282. Letter to Elfride, 2 February 1945, p. 185.

283. Letter to Elfride, 17 February 1945, p. 186.

284. Ibid., p. 186.

285. Ibid., p. 186.

10. In Distress over Germany in Ruins

1. Ott, *Martin Heidegger*, p. 313.
2. Quoted ibid., p. 314.
3. Quoted ibid., p. 315, translation modified.
4. *Letters to His Wife*, p. 181.
5. Ibid., p. 191.
6. Ibid., p. 203.
7. GA 16, 806.
8. Letter to Fritz, 23 July 1945, p. 126.
9. Ott, *Martin Heidegger*, p. 248.
10. Ibid., p. 320.

11. Ibid., pp. 248–249.

12. Ibid., p. 318.

13. Letter to Fritz, 23 July 1945, p. 127.

14. Ibid.

15. Ibid.

16. Quoted by Ott, *Martin Heidegger,* pp. 324–327, translation modified.

17. GA 16, 395.

18. Ott, *Martin Heidegger,* p. 328.

19. GA 16, 414.

20. Ott, *Martin Heidegger,* pp. 323–324.

21. GA 16, 414.

22. GA 16, 112.

23. GA 16, 151.

24. GA 16, 414–415.

25. *Letters to His Wife,* p. 171.

26. Ibid., p. 191.

27. GA 97, 57.

28. Erwin Keller, *Conrad Gröber (1872–1948). Erzbischof in schwerer Zeit,* Freiburg: Herder, 1981, p. 129.

29. Ibid., p. 150.

30. Beginning on 1 August 1940, for example, Gröber was among the first members of the clergy to denounce the mass murder of the mentally ill or mentally impaired, committed in the name of euthanasia (Ernest Klee, *Euthanasie im NS-Staat,* Frankfurt: Fischer, 1983, p. 220).

31. Ott, *Martin Heidegger,* p. 343.

32. Ibid., p. 347.

33. Quoted ibid., p. 344.

34. Ibid., p. 318.

35. Postscript to Oehlkers, 24 December 1945, in the appendix to the Heidegger-Jaspers correspondence, p. 212.

36. Letter from Jaspers to Friedrich Oehlkers, 22 December 1945, quoted by Ott, *Martin Heidegger,* p. 337.

37. Ibid., pp. 337–338.

38. Ibid., p. 338.

39. Ibid., p. 339.

40. Ibid., p. 340.

41. Ibid.

42. Karl Jaspers, *Notizen zu Heidegger,* Munich: Piper, 1978, p. 236.

43. Letter from Jaspers to Oehlkers, 22 December 1945, quoted by Ott, *Martin Heidegger,* pp. 340–341.

44. Safranski, *Martin Heidegger,* p. 476.

45. Quoted by Ott, *Martin Heidegger,* p. 345.
46. Ibid., p. 347.
47. Ibid., pp. 347–348.
48. Ibid., p. 350.
49. Ibid., p. 349.
50. Ibid., pp. 362–363.
51. GA 16, 445.
52. Ott, *Martin Heidegger,* p. 364.
53. *Letters to His Wife,* p. 206.
54. Letter to Fritz, 29 April 1949, p. 142.
55. Letter to Elfride, 12 December 1949, p. 210, translation modified.
56. Letter to Elfride, 2 March 1948, p. 204.
57. Ott, *Martin Heidegger,* p. 346.
58. Letter to Elfride, 17 February 1946, pp. 192–193.
59. GA 97, 131.
60. GA 97, 112.
61. GA 97, 82.
62. GA 97, 88.
63. GA 97, 83.
64. GA 97, 84–85.
65. GA 97, 84.
66. GA 97, 99.
67. Hence, for example, GA 97, 98, 130, 143, 147, and 148.
68. GA 97, 70.
69. Letter to Elfride, 15 March 1946, p. 195.
70. Ibid.
71. Ibid.
72. Hans Dieter Zimmermann, *Martin und Fritz Heidegger. Philosophie und Fastnacht,* Munich: C. H. Beck, 2005, p. 23.
73. Letter to Elfride, 15 March 1946, p. 195.
74. Ibid.
75. Letter to Elfride, 2 June 1949, p. 207.
76. Letter to Elfride, 14 June 1945, p. 190.
77. Ott, *Martin Heidegger,* p. 351.
78. Letter to Jaspers, 12 August 1949, p. 181.
79. GA 42, 1; *Schelling's Treatise on Human Freedom,* 1.
80. GA 13, 15–21.
81. Maurice de Gandillac & Frédéric de Towarnicki, "Deux documents sur Heidegger," *Les temps modernes* 4 (1945): 713–724.
82. Maurice de Gandillac, "Entretien avec Martin Heidegger," *Les temps modernes* 4 (1945): 716.

83. Ibid., p. 713.

84. Ibid.

85. Ibid., p. 714.

86. Cited by Janicaud, *Heidegger en France,* vol. 1, p. 83, n. 7.

87. Gandillac, "Entretiens avec Martin Heidegger," p. 715.

88. Ibid., p. 716.

89. Ibid.

90. Frédéric de Towarnicki, "Visite à Martin Heidegger," *Les temps modernes* 4 (1945): 724.

91. Letter to Beaufret, 23 November 1945, in *Questions III et IV,* trans. Jean Beaufret et al., Paris: Gallimard, 1996, pp. 129–130.

92. Letter to Elfride, 4 March 1946, p. 193.

93. *Letters to His Wife,* p. 199.

94. The first example seems to be the letter to Elfride, 24 October 1946, pp. 199–200.

95. Letter to Blochmann, 3 March 1947, p. 92.

96. Jean-Paul Sartre, *L'existentialisme est un humanisme* (1945), Paris: Nagel, 1970, pp. 84–85.

97. Heidegger's cryptic explanation: "Written in 1940 to be read before a limited audience, the text that follows was printed in 1942. [. . .] This study was presented in the first place in a set of two public lectures, during the winter semesters of 1930–1931 and 1933–1934." *Questions I et II,* trans. Kostas Axelos et al., Paris: Gallimard, "Tel," 1990, p. 425.

98. Translators' note: The English translator renders *Mensch* as "human being" or "human beings," to achieve gender-neutral language. It should be kept in mind that the word "being" in "human being" does not occur in the German.

99. GA 9, 203–238; "Plato's Doctrine of Truth," trans. Thomas Sheehan, in *Pathmarks,* ed. William McNeill, Cambridge, U.K.: Cambridge University Press, 1998, pp. 151–182, here p. 181.

100. GA 9, 238; "Plato's Doctrine of Truth," 181.

101. GA 9, 321–322; "Letter on 'Humanism,' " trans. Frank A. Capuzzi, in *Pathmarks,* p. 145, translation modified.

102. Roger Munier, *Stèle pour Heidegger,* Paris: Arfuyen, 1992, p. 11.

103. Alexandre Koyré, "L'évolution philosophique de Heidegger," *Critique* 1 (1946): 73–82 and *Critique* 2 (1946): 161–183.

104. Gandillac & Towarnicki, "Deux documents sur Heidegger," pp. 713–724.

105. Löwith, "Les implications politiques de la philosophie de l'existence," pp. 343–360; Alphonse de Waelhens, "La philosophie de Heidegger et le nazisme," *Les temps modernes* 22 (July 1947): 115–127; Karl Löwith, "Réponse à M. de Waelhens," *Les temps modernes* 35 (August 148): 370–373; Alphonse de Waelhens, "Réponse à cette réponse," *Les temps modernes* 35 (August 1948): 374–377.

106. Weil seemed unfamiliar with the idea of destiny as the authentic repetition of a possibility that *Dasein* has inherited but also chosen, as Heidegger had developed it in *Being and Time,* and which for a people amounted to the freedom to say resolutely "yes" inasmuch as "our fates have already been guided in advance, in our Being with one another in the same world and in our resoluteness for definite possibilities" (GA 2, 508; *Being and Time,* 438). As we have seen, that was the philosophical bedrock of the text in honor of Schlageter, for example.

107. Éric Weil, "Le cas Heidegger," *Les temps modernes* 22 (July 1947): 128–138.

108. Ernst Jünger, *Rivarol et autres essais,* trans. Jeanne Naujac and Louis Eze, Paris: Grasset, 1974, pp. 130ff.

109. Letter to Ernst Jünger, 23 June 1949, pp. 6–7, emphasis mine, translation modified.

110. The letter was sent to their publisher, Ernst Klett, on 11 June 1949; Jünger sent a copy of it to Heidegger.

111. Quoted in Jünger-Heidegger correspondence, p. 5, n. 4, translation modified.

112. *Letters to His Wife,* p. 125.

113. GA 79, 27.

114. Because Holocaust denial is a complex phenomenon, the definitions given by the specialists are so as well, though they agree on one essential point. At issue here is a negation of the Holocaust's importance, not of its existence, though denying the former tends, whether intentionally or not, to lead to the negation of the latter. In the collection edited by Richard S. Wistrich (*Holocaust Denial: The Politics of Perfidy,* Berlin: W. de Gruyter, 2012), "Holocaust denial" is defined as "the minimization, banalization, and relativization of the relevant facts and events, so as to cast doubt on the uniqueness or authenticity of what happened during the Shoah" (p. 1). The question of uniqueness is problematic, however. Understood in radical terms, the claim that the Holocaust was unique tends to stand in the way of one of the most fruitful approaches of contemporary historiography, the study of genocides in the plural (Armenian, Polish, Rwandan). Similar in spirit though without that stumbling block, Richard G. Hovannisian's characterization of Holocaust denial as a "four-headed hydra" ("negationism," "rationalization," "relativization," and "banalization") has the shortcoming of not being a definition and of not illuminating its object perfectly (Richard G. Hovannisian, "L'hydre à quatre têtes du négationnisme. Négation, rationalisation, relativisation, banalisation," *Actualité du génocide des Arméniens,* proceedings of the colloquium organized by the Defense Committee for the Armenian Cause at the Université de Paris-Sorbonne on 16, 17, and 18 April 1998, Paris: Edipol, 1999, pp. 143–177). Working on the French case, Valérie Igounet has shown how the denial of the extermination of the Jews leads to the exoneration of Germany and the indictment of the Jews themselves for creating that "lie": "The discourse of Holocaust denial denies the Nazi extermination policy against the Jews of Europe. It is a double negation: on one hand, the negation of the Third Reich's will to exterminate [. . .]; on the other, the negation of the systematic, massive,

and industrial annihilation of the Jewish community. [. . .] Exonerating Germany, [. . .] the rhetoric of Holocaust denial accuses the Jews of being the principal instigators of the biggest 'lie of the twentieth century' " (Valérie Igounet, *Histoire du négationnisme en France,* Paris: Seuil, 2000, p. 14).

115. GA 97, 230.

116. GA 79, 56.

117. GA 29/30, 388; *Fundamental Concepts of Metaphysics,* 267, translation modified.

118. Martin Broszat, "Vorbemerkung der Schriftleitung," *Vierteljahrshefte für Zeitgeschichte* 24 (1976): 105–112, here p. 112.

119. GA 16, 431.

120. Carl Schmitt, *Glossarium,* 23 August 1949, Berlin: Duncker & Humblot, 1991, p. 267.

121. Letter from Gottfried Benn to Max Niedermayer, 6 April 1949, in *Briefe an den Limes-Verlag 1948–1956,* Stuttgart: Klett-Cotta-Verlag, 2006, p. 26.

122. "Du baroque au nazisme: Une histoire religieuse de la politique. Entretien avec George Mosse," *Revue européenne d'histoire* 1, no. 2 (1994): 247–252, here p. 251.

123. *Letters to His Wife,* p. 201.

124. Letter to Elfride, 12 December 1949, p. 211.

125. Letter to Elfride, 20 March 1946, pp. 196–197, translation modified.

126. GA 54, 124; *Parmenides,* 85.

127. GA 16, 431.

128. See esp. R. M. Douglas, *Orderly and Humane: The Expulsion of the Germans after the Second World War,* New Haven, CT: Yale University Press, 2013.

129. Unsent letter from Jaspers to Heidegger, 1 March 1948, pp. 158–160.

130. Letter from Jaspers to Heidegger, 6 February 1949, pp. 160–162.

131. Letter to Jaspers, 22 June 1949, pp. 171–172.

132. Letter to Jaspers, 5 July 1949, pp. 173–174.

133. Letter to Jaspers, 7 March 1950, p. 196.

134. Letter from Jaspers to Heidegger, 19 March 1950, p. 198.

135. Letter to Jaspers, 8 April 1950, p. 202.

136. GA 16, 453.

137. GA 16, 525.

138. Letter to Jaspers, 10 December 1949, p. 193.

139. Letter to Jaspers, 8 April 1950, p. 203.

140. Karl Jaspers, *The Question of German Guilt* (1946), trans. E. B. Ashton, New York: Fordham University Press, 2000.

141. Ibid., p. 66.

142. Letter from Jaspers to Heidegger, 24 July 1952, p. 208.

143. GA 16, 659.

144. Letter to Blochmann, 3 March 1947, p. 92.

11. End Paths

1. *Letters to His Wife*, p. 206.
2. Ibid., p. 220.
3. Ibid., p. 329.
4. Ibid., p. 209.
5. Letter to Elfride, 12 December 1949, p. 210.
6. *Letters to His Wife*, p. 214.
7. Ibid., p. 228.
8. Ibid., p. 234.
9. The thesis was directed by Gerhard Ritter, defended at the University of Freiburg in 1953, and published three years later under the title *Die deutsche Sozialdemokratie und der nationale Staat, 1870–1920. Unter besonderer Berücksichtigung der Kriegs- und Revolutionsjahre*, Göttingen: Musterschmidt, 1956.
10. *Letters to His Wife*, p. 241.
11. Ibid., p. 248.
12. Ibid., p. 241.
13. Letter to Elfride, 18 August 1954, p. 244.
14. *Letters to His Wife*, p. 190.
15. Ibid., p. 328.
16. Ibid., p. 246.
17. Ibid., p. 258.
18. Letter to Elfride, 27 October 1954, p. 246, translation modified.
19. Letter to Elfride, 21 May 1955, p. 247.
20. Letter to Elfride, 20 November 1949, p. 210.
21. Letter to Elfride, 12 December 1949, p. 211.
22. *Letters to His Wife*, p. 289.
23. GA 13, 87–90.
24. Letter to Elfride, 8 September 1920, p. 80.
25. GA 16, 560.
26. GA 16, 526–527; "Releasement," in *Discourse on Thinking*, trans. John M. Anderson and E. Hans Freund, New York: Harper & Row, 1966, p. 54.
27. Quoted by Ott, *Martin Heidegger*, p. 46.
28. Büchin & Denker, *Martin Heidegger und seine Heimat*, pp. 30–32.
29. Letter to Elfride, 9 September 1919, pp. 66–67.
30. Letter to Elfride, 25 October 1951, p. 219, translation modified.
31. GA 7, 36; *The Question Concerning Technology*, 35.
32. Letter to Elfride, 21 October 1954, p. 245.
33. Letter to Elfride, 4 May 1950, p. 215.
34. Letter to Elfride, 10 April 1949, p. 206.
35. Martin Heidegger & Ludwig von Ficker, *Briefwechsel, 1952–1967*, ed. Mattias Flatscher, Stuttgart: Klett-Cotta, 2004, p. 7.

36. Letter to Blochmann, 19 December 1953, p. 102.
37. *Letters to His Wife*, p. 327.
38. Ibid., p. 218.
39. Ibid., p. 321.
40. Ibid., p. 262.
41. GA 16, 828.
42. *Letters to His Wife*, p. 262.
43. Letter to Elfride, 6 July 1966, p. 295.
44. *Letters to His Wife*, p. 315.
45. Jean Beaufret, "En France," in Neske (ed.), *Erinnerung an Martin Heidegger*, pp. 9–13, here p. 9.
46. *Letters to His Wife*, p. 258.
47. Beaufret, "En France," p. 11.
48. Letter to Elfride, 5 September 1966, pp. 296–297.
49. Letter to Elfride, 5 September 1966, p. 297.
50. François Fédier, *Soixante-deux photographies de Martin Heidegger*, Paris: Gallimard, 1999.
51. Letter to Elfride, 5 September 1966, p. 297.
52. Letter to Elfride, 5 September 1966, p. 297.
53. Letter to Elfride, 1 September 1968, p. 308.
54. Letter to Elfride, 5 September 1966, p. 297.
55. Letter to Elfride, 1 September 1968, p. 308.
56. GA 16, 551.
57. *Letters to His Wife*, p. 286.
58. Ibid., p. 295.
59. Ibid., p. 327.
60. Letter to Blochmann, 12 December 1968, p. 117.
61. Letter from Arendt to Jaspers, 29 September 1949, p. 142.
62. Jonas, *Memoirs*, p. 63.
63. Letter from Arendt to Heidegger, dated 1929 without further specifications, p. 51.
64. Letter from Arendt to Heidegger, 7 February 1950, p. 57.
65. Letter from Arendt, 9 February 1950, p. 60.
66. Letter to Elfride, 14 February 1950, pp. 212–213.
67. Letter to Arendt, 19 March 1950, p. 71, translation modified.
68. Letter to Arendt, 12 April 1950, p. 74.
69. Letter from Arendt to Kurt Blumenfeld, 16 December 1957, in Iris Pilling (ed.), *". . . In keinem Besitz verwurzelt." Die Korrespondenz*, Hamburg: Rotbuch, 1995, p. 197.
70. Letter from Arendt to Heidegger, 9 February 1950, p. 60.
71. Hannah Arendt, *The Origins of Totalitarianism*, New York: Harcourt, Brace and Co., 1951, p. 419.

72. Ibid., pp. 423–424.

73. Letter from Arendt to Kurt Blumenfeld, 16 December 1957, p. 197.

74. Letter from Arendt to Heidegger, 28 October 1960, p. 124.

75. Letter from Arendt to Jaspers, 1 November 1961, p. 457.

76. Letter from Hannah Arendt to Heinrich Blücher, 24 May 1952, in Lotte Köhler (ed.), *Briefe 1936–1968,* Munich: Piper, 1996.

77. *Letters to His Wife,* p. 251.

78. Ibid. p. 262.

79. Ibid., p. 265.

80. Ibid.

81. Letter to Elfride, 28 April 1958, p. 267.

82. *Letters to His Wife,* p. 221; letters to Elfride of June and 8 August 1952, pp. 221–222.

83. *Letters to His Wife,* p. 321.

84. Ibid., p. 292.

85. Letter to Elfride, 1 February 1960, p. 277, translation modified.

86. *Letters to His Wife,* p. 267; and letter to Elfride, 28 April 1958, p. 267.

87. Letter from Elfride to Heidegger, 28 June 1956, in *Letters to His Wife,* p. 255.

88. Barbara Cassin, "Nous savions tous qu'il avait été nazi," *Le nouvel observateur,* 11 September 2017, p. 14.

89. Frédéric de Towarnicki, *À la rencontre de Heidegger. Souvenirs d'un messager de la Forêt-Noire,* Paris: Gallimard Arcades, 1993, p. 125.

90. Interview with François Fédier, *Le nouvel observateur,* 27 October 1987, p. 84.

91. Heinrich Wiegand Petzet, *Auf einen Stern zugehen. Begegnungen und Gespräche mit Martin Heidegger 1929–1976,* Frankfurt: Societäts-Verlag, 1983, p. 43.

92. GA 94, 198–199; *Black Notebooks,* 1, 145.

93. GA 7, 92; "Overcoming Metaphysics," 85.

94. Hartmut Buchner, "Fragmentarisches," in Neske (ed.), *Erinnerung an Martin Heidegger,* pp. 47–51, here p. 49.

95. Walter Bröcker attended the class and, as he remembered it, Heidegger spoke not "of National Socialism" (or even "of this movement") but "of the movement." "That is the reason Heidegger's 'the' remained unforgettable to me." Quoted by Otto Pöggeler, "Heideggers politisches Selbstverständnis," in Annemarie Gethmann-Siefert & Otto Pöggeler (eds.), *Heidegger und die praktische Philosophie,* 2nd ed., Frankfurt: Suhrkamp, 1989, p. 59, no. 11.

96. GA 40, 152. [Not in *Introduction to Metaphysics.*—Trans.]

97. Jürgen Habermas, "Mit Heidegger gegen Heidegger denken. Veröffentlichung von Vorlesungen aus dem Jahre 1935," *Frankfurter Allgemeine Zeitung* 170, 25 July 1953.

98. Ibid.

99. Ibid.

100. Letter to Elfride, 7 August 1953, p. 234.

101. Letter to Elfride, 7 August 1953, p. 235.

102. Christian E. Lewalter, "Wie liest man 1953 Sätze von 1935?" *Die Zeit*, 13 August 1953.

103. Ibid.

104. Letter to Christian E. Lewalter, 15 September 1953, published under the title "Heidegger über Heidegger," *Die Zeit*, 24 September 1953.

105. GA 16, 668.

106. Jean Wahl, *Vers la fin de l'ontologie. Étude sur l'introduction dans la métaphysique par Heidegger*, Paris: Société d'édition d'enseignement supérieur, 1956, p. 5.

107. Letter to Stefan Zemach, 18 March 1968, GA 40, 233.

108. Petra Jaeger, "Nachwort der Herausgeberin," GA 40, 231 and esp. GA 40, 234.

109. Translators' note: The English-language edition of *Nietzsche* was first published in two volumes, vol. 1 in 1979 and vol. 2 in 1984, New York: Harper & Row.

110. GA 6.1, p. 10; "Author's Foreword to All Volumes," in *Nietzsche*, 1, xl.

111. On the differences, see Katrin Meyer, "Denkweg ohne Abschweifungen. Heideggers Nietzsche-Vorlesungen und das Nietzsche-Buch von 1961 im Vergleich," HJB2, pp. 132–156. The book in its 1961 German version is now published as GA 6.1 and GA 6.2, while the courses in their original version appear as six smaller volumes: GA 43, GA 44, GA 46, GA 47, GA 48, and GA 50.

112. GA 43, 13.

113. GA 43, 105.

114. GA 48, 205.

115. GA 42, 40–41.

116. Friedrich Hölderlin, *Sämtliche Werke. Historisch-kritische Ausgabe, begonnen durch Norbert v. Hellingrath, fortgeführt durch Friedrich Seebass und Ludwig v. Pigenot*, 2nd ed., Berlin: Propylaen, 1923.

117. GA 39, 9; *Hölderlin's Hymns "Germania" and "The Rhine,"* 9.

118. GA 39, 6–7; *Hölderlin's Hymns "Germania" and "The Rhine,"* 5–6.

119. GA 43, 10–11; GA 43, 14–15; letter to Jaspers, 16 May 1936, pp. 160–161.

120. GA 42, 1–14; *Schelling's Treatise on the Essence of Human Freedom*, 1–8.

121. GA 42, 5.

122. Michel Haar, "La biographie reléguée," in *Martin Heidegger. Cahier de l'Herne*, Paris: Le Livre de Poche, 1983, p. 22.

123. "Bei der Persönlichkeit eines Philosophen hat nur das Interesse: er war dann und dann geboren, er arbeitete und starb"; GA 18, 5.

124. GA 1, 438.

125. Letter to Elfride, 10 May 1950, pp. 215–216.

126. Hadrien France-Lanord, *Paul Celan et Martin Heidegger. Le sens d'un dialogue*, Paris: Fayard, 2004, p. 68.

127. Letter to Gerhart Baumann, quoted by Baumann in *Erinnerungen an Paul Celan*, Frankfurt: Suhrkamp, 1992, p. 60.

128. Quoted by Otto Pöggeler, *Spur des Wortes. Zur Lyrik Paul Celans,* Freiburg: K. Albers, 1986, p. 259.

129. Karl Löwith, *Heidegger. Denker in dürftiger Zeit,* Frankfurt a.M.: Fischer, 1953.

130. Paul Hühnerfeld, *In Sachen Heidegger. Versuch einer Entmythologisierung Martin Heideggers,* Hamburg: Hoffmann & Campe Verlag, 1959.

131. Schneeberger, *Nachlese zu Heidegger.*

132. Dagobert D. Runes, *Martin Heidegger: German Existentialism,* New York: Philosophical Library, 1965.

133. Theodor Adorno, *The Jargon of Authenticity* (1964), trans. Knut Tarnowski & Frederic Will, Evanston, IL: Northwestern University Press, 1973.

134. Alexander Schwan, *Politische Philosophie im Denken Heideggers,* Opladen & Cologne: Westdeutscher Verlag, 1965.

135. Günter Grass, *Dog Years,* trans. Ralph Manheim, Boston: Houghton Mifflin, 1989 [1963], p. 392.

136. Jean-Pierre Faye, "Discours et proclamations," *Méditations* 3 (1961): 139–150.

137. François Fédier, "Trois attaques contre Heidegger," *Critique* 234 (November 1966): 883–904; "À propos de Heidegger: Une lecture dénoncée," *Critique* 242 (July 1967): 672–686.

138. Robert Minder, "Hebel et Heidegger: Lumières et obscurantisme," in Pierre Francastel (ed.), *Utopies et institutions au XVIIIe siècle, le pragmatisme des lumières,* Paris: Mouton et Cie, 1963; Minder, "Heidegger und Hebel oder Die Sprache von Meßkirch," in his *Dichter in der Gesellschaft,* Frankfurt: Insel Verlag, 1966; Minder, "Martin Heidegger ou le conservatisme agraire," *Allemagne d'aujourd'hui* 6 (January–February 1967): 34–49.

139. Jean-Michel Palmier, *Les écrits politiques de Heidegger,* Paris: L'Herne, 1968.

140. Ludwig Marcuse, "Das heikelste Thema der gegenwärtigen Philosophie," *Die Zeit,* 1 May 1959.

141. Adorno, *Jargon of Authenticity,* p. 47.

142. Letter to Elfride, 14 June 1964, p. 290.

143. Letter to Jünger, 27 August 1966, p. 37.

144. "Mitternacht einer Weltnacht," *Der Spiegel,* 7 February 1966.

145. Letter from Jaspers to Arendt, 9 March 1966, p. 630, translation modified.

146. Letter from Arendt to Jaspers, 18 April 1966, p. 634.

147. Letter from Kästner to Heidegger, 4 March 1966, pp. 79–80.

148. HJB4, 122. No trace of it is found in the correspondence with Arendt, however.

149. GA 16, 639.

150. Palmier, *Les écrits politiques de Heidegger,* p. 278.

151. Letter to Jünger, 20 November 1968, p. 45, translation modified.

152. Letter to Jean-Michel Palmier, 10 January 1969, GA 16, 698.

153. Letter to Kästner, 11 March 1966, p. 82.

154. Letter to Hugo Friedrich, 14 April 1966, HJB4, 122.

155. GA 16, 816.
156. GA 16, 652.
157. GA 16, 658.
158. GA 16, 668.
159. GA 16, 677.
160. GA 16, 679.
161. GA 16, 679–680.
162. GA 16, 671.
163. GA 16, 670.
164. GA 16, 525; "Releasement," 52.
165. Letter to Elfride, 11 November 1966, p. 299.
166. Letter to Elfride, 4 July 1961, p. 280.
167. Letter to Blochmann, 12 October 1968, p. 116.
168. Letter to Blochmann, 5 December 1969, p. 119.
169. *Letters to His Wife,* p. 321.
170. "La philosophie est-elle soluble dans le nazisme?" interview with Jacques Taminiaux by Martin Legros, *Philosophie Magazine* 13, special issue (February–March 2012): 74–77, here p. 76.
171. Letter from Blochmann, 23 March 1969, p. 117.
172. Karl Löwith, "The Nature of Man and the World of Nature for Heidegger's Eightieth Birthday," in Edward G. Ballard & Charles E. Scott (eds.), *Martin Heidegger: In Europe and America,* Dordrecht: Springer Netherlands, 1974, p. 37.
173. Letter to Elfride, 17 July 1969, p. 310.
174. Letter from Arendt to Heidegger, 8 August 1969, p. 148.
175. Letter to Elfride, 17 July 1969, pp. 310–311.
176. "Du baroque au nazisme," pp. 247–252, here p. 249.
177. Quoted in Arendt-Heidegger correspondence, pp. 161–162.
178. Arendt-Heidegger correspondence, p. 148.
179. Letter from Arendt to Mary McCarthy, 22 August 1975, in Carol Brightman (ed.), *Between Friends: The Correspondence of Hannah Arendt and Mary McCarthy,* New York: Harcourt Brace, 1995, p. 385.
180. Jaspers, *Notizen zu Martin Heidegger,* p. 264.
181. Bernhard Welte, "Erinnerung an ein spätes Gespräch," in Neske (ed.), *Erinnerung an Martin Heidegger,* pp. 249–252.
182. "Er war ein lieber Vater."
183. GA 13, 243.

12. The Heidegger Affair after Heidegger

1. Ott, *Martin Heidegger.*
2. Faye, *The Introduction of Nazism into Philosophy.*

3. Japan should probably be added, but one would need to read Japanese to study this question.

4. Victor Farías, *Heidegger et le nazisme,* trans. from the Spanish and German by Myriam Benarroch and Jean-Baptiste Grasset, preface by Christian Jambet, Paris: Verdier, 1987.

5. Josef Jurt, "L'itinéraire de Heidegger," *Actes de la recherche en sciences sociales* 80 (November 1989): 76–80, here p. 76.

6. Victor Farías, *Heidegger und der Nationalsozialismus,* translated from the Spanish and French by Klaus Laermann, with a preface by Jürgen Habermas, Frankfurt: Fischer, 1989.

7. Jean-Pierre Faye, *Le piège. La philosophie heideggerienne et le national-socialisme,* Paris: Balland, 1994. Faye, *The Introduction of Nazism into Philosophy.*

8. The *khâgne* and the year before it, called *hypokhâgne,* are two or three years of typically French undergraduate study in humanities and social sciences, taking place in a few élite high schools and preparing students for the national competitive examinations of the *écoles normales supérieures.* These are again typically French graduate schools, the most famous of them being the one located at rue d'Ulm in Paris (many prominent thinkers of the French theory, like Jean-Paul Sartre, were students there).

9. The subject, central to the reception of Heidegger, occupies a large place in Dominique Janicaud's book, which deals with it from a philosophical and French point of view (*Heidegger en France,* 2 vols., Paris: Albin Michel, "Idées," 2011). France being the most important pole in the Heidegger affair, Janicaud studies a substantial part of it. Conversely, the wealth of recent events has limited the importance of Janicaud's book, since, for good reason, it was unable to deal with the last two episodes: the publication of Faye's *Introduction of Nazism into Philosophy* in 2005 and of the black notebooks in 2014.

10. Schneeberger, *Nachlese zu Heidegger.*

11. These articles include Hugo Ott, "Martin Heidegger als Rektor der Universität Freiburg i. Br. 1933–1934, I. Die Übernahme des Rektorats von Martin Heidegger (23. April 1933 bis 23. April 1934," *Zeitschrift des Breisgau-Geschichtsvereins ("Schau-ins-Land")* 102 (1983): 102–36; "Martin Heidegger als Rektor der Universität Freiburg i. Br. 1933–1934, II. Die Zeit des Rektorats von Martin Heidegger (23. April bis 23. April 1934)," *Zeitschrift des Breisgau-Geschichtsvereins ("Schau-ins-Land")* 103 (1984): 107–130; "Martin Heidegger als Rektor der Universität Freiburg i. Br. 1933-1934," *Zeitschrift für die Geschichte des Oberrheins* 132 (1984): 343–358; "Der junge Martin Heidegger. Gymnasial-Konviktstzeit und Studium," *Freiburger Diözesan-Archiv* 104 (1984): 315–325; "Der Philosoph im politischen Zwielicht. Martin Heidegger und der Nationalsozialismus," *Neue Zürcher Zeitung,* 3–4 November 1984; "Martin Heidegger und die Universität Freiburg nach 1945. Ein Beispiel für die Auseinandersetzung mit der politischen Vergangenheit," *Historisches Jahrbuch* 105 (1985): 95–128; "Der Habilitand Martin Hei-

degger und das von Schäzlersche Stipendium. Ein Beitrag zur Wissenschaftsförderung der katholischen Kirche," *Freiburger Diözesan-Archiv* 106 (1986): 141–160.

12. Roger-Pol Droit, "Heidegger était-il nazi?" *Le monde,* 14 October 1987.

13. "Nuove accuse contro Heidegger: 'Era un nazista,' " *La repubblica,* 18–19 October 1987.

14. Gianni Vattimo, "Il pensiero di Heidegger più forte di chi lo accusa," *La stampa,* "Tuttolibri" supplement of 21 November 1987.

15. Quoted by Michael Haller, "Die Philosophen-Streit," *Die Zeit,* 29 January 1988.

16. Jürgen Busche, "Also gut. Heidegger war ein Nazi!" *Pflasterstrand,* nos. 279–280, 23 January 1988.

17. Hans-Georg Gadamer, "Oberflächlichkeit und Unkenntnis. Zur Veröffentlichung von Victor Farias," in Günther Neske (ed.), Antwort, *Martin Heidegger im Gespräch,* Pfullingen: Neske, 1988, pp. 153–154, translated by John McCumber as "Back from Syracuse?" *Critical Inquiry* 15, no. 2 (1989): 427.

18. Interview of Jacques Derrida, *Le nouvel observateur,* 6 November 1987.

19. Philippe Lacoue-Labarthe, "Heidegger. Les textes en appel," *Le journal littéraire* 2 (January 1988): 115–117.

20. *Le débat* 48 (January–February 1988).

21. Gadamer, "Back from Syracuse?" p. 427.

22. François Fédier, *Heidegger. Anatomie d'un scandale,* Paris: R. Laffont, 1988, p. 137.

23. Martin Heidegger, *Écrits politiques (1933–1966),* edited, translated, and annotated by François Fédier, Paris: Gallimard, 1995, p. 10.

24. Hugo Ott, "Heidegger et le nazisme. Chemins et fourvoiements," *Le débat* 49 (March–April 1988): 185–189.

25. Hugo Ott, "Wege und Abwege. Zu Victor Farias' kritischer Heidegger-Studie," *Neue Zürcher Zeitung,* 27 November 1987.

26. Hugo Ott, "Der Philosoph und die Diktatur. Zur deutschen Übersetzung von Victor Farias' Buch 'Heidegger und der Nationalsozialismus,' " *Neue Zürcher Zeitung,* 24 February 1989, Fernasugabe 45, and *Neue Zürcher Zeitung* 47, 25/26 February 1989.

27. Ott, "Wege und Abwege."

28. Luc Ferry & Alain Renaut, *Heidegger et les modernes,* Paris: Grasset, 1988.

29. Fédier, *Anatomie d'un scandale.*

30. He published a book ten years after the broadcast: Philippe Capelle, *Philosophie et théologie dans la pensée de Martin Heidegger,* Paris: Éd. du Cerf, revised and augmented edition, 2001 [1998].

31. More than his 1970 book (Jean-Luc Marion, *Avec ou sans Dieu,* Paris: Beauchesne), let us note his collection of essays, whose title is both Catholic and Heideggerian in its inspiration: *Dieu sans l'être. Hors-texte,* Paris: Fayard, "Communio," 1982.

32. Janicaud, *Heidegger en France,* 1, p. 153ff.

33. Ibid., p. 145.

34. Ibid., p. 154.

35. Claire Bretécher, *Agrippine,* Paris: C. Bretécher, 1988.

36. This was a focus of attack in Fédier's contribution to the January–February 1988 issue of *Le débat* (pp. 176–192).

37. For example, as Thomas Sheehan indicates in his review, the works attributed to Karl Oehling were actually written by Karl Moehling (Thomas Sheehan, "Heidegger and the Nazis," *New York Review of Books* 35, no. 10 [16 June 1988]: n. 4). The rest of the note gives other details along the same lines.

38. Victor Farías, *Heidegger et le nazisme,* translated from the Spanish and German by Myriam Benarroch & Jean-Baptiste Grasset, preface by Christian Jambet, 2nd ed., Paris: Le Livre de Poche, 1989.

39. Ott, "Wege und Abwege."

40. Roger-Pol Droit, "Heidegger était-il nazi?" *Le monde,* 14 October 1987.

41. Roger-Pol Droit, "De nouveau Heidegger, les Grecs et le Reich," *Le monde,* 5 February 1988.

42. Bernard Pivot, "Doit-on les condamner?" *Apostrophes,* 20 May 1988.

43. " 'Océaniques' à Beaubourg," *Le monde,* 14 November 1989.

44. Pierre Bourdieu, *L'ontologie politique de Martin Heidegger,* Paris: Éd. de Minuit, "Le Sens commun," 1988 [1975].

45. Theodor Adorno, *Jargon der Eigentlichkeit. Zur deutschen Ideologie* (1964), translated into French as *Jargon de l'authenticité: De l'idéologie allemande,* with a preface by Eliane Escoubas and an afterword by Guy Petitdemange, Paris: Payot, "Critique de la politique Payot," 1989.

46. Karl Löwith, *Ma vie en Allemagne avant et après 1933,* trans. Monique Lebedel, Paris: Hachette, 1988.

47. Ferry & Renaut, *Heidegger et les modernes.*

48. Dominique Janicaud, *L'ombre de cette pensée,* Paris: Jérôme Millon, 1990.

49. Philippe Lacoue-Labarthe, *La fiction du politique. Heidegger, l'art et la politique,* Paris: Bourgois, 1988.

50. Jean-François Lyotard, *Heidegger et "les juifs,"* Paris: Éd. Galilée, 1988.

51. Henri Meschonnic, *Le langage Heidegger,* Paris: PUF, 1990.

52. Jürgen Habermas, *Martin Heidegger: L'oeuvre et l'engagement,* Paris: Cerf, 1988.

53. He received an appointment at Stanford in 1999.

54. Sheehan, "Heidegger and the Nazis."

55. Ibid.

56. Ibid.

57. Ibid.

58. Ibid.

59. Ibid.

60. Michael Zimmerman, "L'affaire Heidegger," *Times Literary Supplement*, 7–13 October 1988.

61. Alain Milchman and Alan Rosenberg (eds.), *Martin Heidegger and the Holocaust*, Atlantic Highlands, NJ: Humanities Press, 1996.

62. Tom Rockmore, *On Heidegger's Nazism and Philosophy*, London, Toronto, Sydney, Tokyo, and Singapore: Harvester Wheatsheaf, 1992.

63. Richard Wolin, *The Politics of Being*, New York: Columbia University Press, 1990.

64. Richard Wolin (ed.), *The Heidegger Controversy: A Critical Reader*, Cambridge, MA, and London: MIT Press, 1993.

65. H. L. Dreyfus, *Being-in-the-World: A Commentary on Heidegger's* Being and Time *Division 1*, Cambridge, MA: MIT Press, 1991; H. L. Dreyfus & H. Hall, *Heidegger: A Critical Reader*, Oxford: Blackwell, 1992; C. Guignon, *The Cambridge Companion to Heidegger*, Cambridge, U.K.: Cambridge University Press, 1993; M. E. Zimmerman, *Heidegger's Confrontation with Modernity*, Bloomington: Indiana University Press, 1990.

66. Julian Young, *Heidegger, Philosophy, Nazism*, Cambridge, U.K.: Cambridge University Press, 1997.

67. Victor Farías, *Heidegger and Nazism*, ed. Joseph Margolis & Tom Rockmore, trans. Paul Burrell, Dominic Di Bernardi, & Gabriel R. Ricci, Philadelphia: Temple University Press, 1991.

68. Thelma Z. Lavine, "Thinking Like a Nazi," *Washington Post*, 25 March 1990.

69. Allen Lacy, "Comfortable with Hitler," *New York Times*, 17 December 1989.

70. "Le dossier d'un nazi ordinaire," *Le monde*, 14 October 1988.

71. Jacques Le Rider, "Le dossier Heidegger des Archives du Ministère des Affaires Étrangères," *Allemagne d'aujourd'hui* 107 (January–March 1989): 97–109.

72. Ernst Nolte, *Martin Heidegger. Politik und Geschichte im Leben und Denken*, Berlin and Frankfurt: Propyläen Verlag, 1992.

73. Domenico Losurdo, *La communità, la morte: l'Occidente. Heidegger e l'ideologia della guerra*, Turin: Bollati Boringhieri; translated into French by Jean-Michel Buée as *Heidegger et l'idéologie de la guerre*, Paris: PUF, 1998.

74. Hugo Ott, *Martin Heidegger: Éléments pour une biographie*, trans. Jean-Michel Beloeil, Paris: Payot, 1990; and *Martin Heidegger: Sentieri biografici*, trans. Flavio Cassinari, preface by Carlo Sini, Milan: SugarCo, 1988.

75. Ott, *Martin Heidegger*.

76. Hugo Ott, *Martin Heidegger. En camino hacia su biografia*, trans. Helena Cortés Gabaudan, Madrid: Alianza, 1993.

77. Hugo Ott, *Martin Heidegger. W drodze ku biografii*, trans. Janusz Sidorek, Warsaw: Oficyna Wydawnicza Volumen, 1997.

78. Hugo Ott, *Martin Heidegger. Unterwegs zu seiner Biographie*, Japanese edition by arrangement of the Orion Literary Agency, Tokyo, 1995.

79. Figures reproduced on Hugo Ott's curriculum vitae on his web page for the Alemannisches Institut at the University of Freiburg: http://www.alemannisches-institut.de/cms/website.php?id=wir/ottcv.htm, consulted 6 August 2015. I found two other Italian reviews in addition to the one indicated. The richness of the Italian case would require in-depth research.

80. Hugo Ott, "Das Land Baden im Dritten Reich," in Landeszentrale für Politische Bildung Baden-Württemberg (ed.), *Badische Geschichte. Vom Großherzogtum bis zur Gegenwart*, Stuttgart: Theiss, 1979, pp. 184–208.

81. Giuliano Ferrara, "Heil Heidegger!" *L'espresso*, 26 August 1984.

82. Sheehan, "Heidegger and the Nazis."

83. Nicolas Tertulian, *La quinzaine littéraire*, 16–28 February 1989.

84. Luc Rosenzweig, "Heidegger et la tempête: Le débat en Allemagne fédérale sur l'engagement du philosophe," *Le monde*, 9 March 1988.

85. Josef Jurt, "L'itinéraire de Heidegger," *Actes de la recherche en sciences sociales* 80 (November 1989): 76–80.

86. Bernd Grün, Hans-Georg Hofer, & Karl-Heinz Leven (eds.), *Medizin und Nationalsozialismus. Die Freiburger Medizinische Fakultät und das Klinikum in der Weimarer Republik un im "Dritten Reich,"* Frankfurt: Peter Lang, 2002; Bernd Grün, *Der Rektor als Führer? Die Universität Freiburg i. Br. von 1933 bis 1945*, Freiburg: Karl Alber, 2010.

87. Josef Jurt, "Heidegger et les historiens allemands," *Le monde*, 11 October 1989.

88. Jean-Michel Palmier, "Heidegger face à l'histoire," afterword to Ott, *Martin Heidegger. Éléments pour une biographie*, pp. 379–413, here p. 412.

89. Michel Trebitsch, "Ott Hugo, Martin Heidegger: Éléments pour une biographie," *Vingtième siècle, revue d'histoire* 31 (July–September 1991): 100.

90. Ibid., pp. 100–101.

91. Ibid., p. 101.

92. Ibid.

93. Thomas Ferenczi, "Douze ans dans la vie de Heidegger," *Le monde*, 16 November 1990.

94. Ibid.

95. François Fédier, Preface to *Martin Heidegger, Écrits politiques*, p. 9.

96. Ibid., p. 10.

97. Ibid.

98. Hermann Heidegger, "Die Wirtschaftshistoriker und die Warhheit: Notwendige Bemerkungen zu den Veröffentlichungen Hugo Otts über Martin Heidegger," *Études heideggeriennes* 13 (1997): 177–192.

99. H. Heidegger, "Die Wirtschaftshistoriker und die Wahrheit," p. 179.

100. Chair of social history and economics.

101. H. Heidegger, "Die Wirtschaftshistoriker und die Wahrheit," p. 177.

102. Ibid.

103. Ibid., pp. 179–180.

104. Ibid., p. 184.

105. Letter of 2 October 1929 to Victor Schwoerer.

106. *Schellings Abhandlung über das Wesen der menschlichen Freiheit* (1809), Tübingen: Niemeyer, 1971.

107. Karl Ulmer, *Der Spiegel* 19, 2 May 1977, p. 10.

108. "Edition und Übersetzung, Unterwegs von Tatsachen zu Gedanken, von Werken zu Wegen," in Dietrich Papenfuss & Otto Pöggeler (eds.), *Zur philosophischen Aktualität Heideggers*, vol. 3, Frankfurt: Klostermann, 1992, pp. 89–107; Friedrich-Wilhelm von Herrmann, "Wirkungen der Martin-Heidegger-Gesamtausgabe," in Markus Happel (ed.), *Heidegger—neu gelesen*, Würzburg: Königshausen & Neumann, 1997, pp. 87–96; Theodore Kisiel, "Heidegger's Gesamtausgabe: An International Scandal of Scholarship," *Philosophy Today* 39 (1995): 3–15; Reinhard Mehring, "Die Stiftung der Gesamtausgabe," in *Heideggers Überlieferungsgeschick. Eine dionysische Inszenierung*, Würzburg: Königshausen & Neumann, 1992, pp. 136–164.

109. *Die Selbstbehauptung der deutschen Universität. Das Rektorat 1933–34—Tatsachen und Gedanken*, Frankfurt: Klostermann, 1983, translated into French by François Fédier in *Le débat* 27 (November 1983).

110. Letter to Elfride, 18 October 1916, p. 28.

111. *Letters to His Wife*, p. 317.

112. Hermann Heidegger, "Ergänzung einiger Tatsachen zu Martin Heidegger," letter to the editor published in *Frankfurter Allgemeine Zeitung* 266, 15 November 2005, p. 37.

113. Arno Münster, *Heidegger, la "science allemande" et le national-socialisme: Suite d'un polémique*, Paris: Kimé, 2002.

114. GA 16, 269.

115. Ludger Lütkehaus, "Der Staat am Sterbebett. Noch ein Sündenfall: Martin Heidegger über 'Krankheit' und Gesundheit, über Erbbiologie und die Grenzen der Therapie," *Die Zeit*, 23 May 2001.

116. Arno Münster, "Une adhésion sans réserve à l'idéologie du 'sang et du sol,' " *Libération*, 9 June 2001.

117. GA 16, 151.

118. Münster, "Une adhésion sans réserve."

119. Christian Sommer, "Heidegger, une histoire allemande," *Libération*, 15 August 2001.

120. Ibid.

121. Pierre Aubenque, "Heidegger, Löwith et l'antisémitisme," *Le monde*, 17 June 1988.

122. François Fédier, "L'irréprochable," *L'infini* 95, special issue, *Heidegger: Le danger en l'Être* (Summer 2006): 140–153, here p. 148. A similar version of this text had appeared in the Romanian review *Studia phaenomenologica* 3 (2003): 119–130.

123. GA 16, 571.

124. GA 16, 382.

125. Heidegger, *Écrits politiques*, p. 77.

126. Fédier, "L'irréprochable," p. 148.

127. Marcel Conche, *Heidegger résistant*, Treffort: Éd. de Mégare, 1996, p. 8.

128. That, for example, is what Fédier does in *Écrits politiques*, p. 32.

129. Barash noted that Heidegger called into question the notion of universal validity (*Allgemeingültigkeit*) in science: "In no science are the 'universal validity' of standards and the claims to 'universality' [. . .] less possible as criteria of 'truth' than in authentic historiology." [This passage appears in GA 2, 522; *Being and Time*, 447.—Trans.] According to Barash, this was linked to the fact that, for Heidegger, "the representation of the past depends on the capacity for comprehension by the theorist anchored in the mode of being (*Seinsweise*) on the basis of which the past is thematized, in accordance with the presupposition of Sein und Zeit." Barash thinks that, from that standpoint, "there is a risk that the arbitrariness of partial judgment will directly insinuate itself wherever the requirement of universal validity is set aside."

130. Barash began an earlier article, "The Perspective of Being," with a quotation from Heidegger from the course of summer semester 1942, a few months after the United States entered the war following the Japanese attack on Pearl Harbor: "We know today that the Anglo-Saxon world of Americanism has resolved to annihilate Europe, that is, the homeland [*Heimat*], and that means: the commencement of the Western world [*Anfang des Abendländischen*]. Whatever has the character of commencement is indestructible. America's entry into this planetary war is not its entry into history; rather, it is already the ultimate American act of American ahistoricality [*Geschichtslosigkeit*] and self-devastation [*Selbstverwüstung*]" (GA 53, 68; Hölderlin's hymn "The Ister," 54–55). And he commented with a suggestive understatement: "In the context of Heidegger's writings, such sentences, reprinted in the Gesamtausgabe without the slightest commentary, seem to me particularly disconcerting." Jeffrey Barash, "La perspective de l'être," in Philippe Soulez (ed.), *La guerre et les philosophes, de la fin des années 1920 aux années 1950*, Paris: Presses universitaires de Vincennes, 1992, pp. 33–43, here p. 33.

131. Jeffrey Barash, *Heidegger et son siècle: Temps de l'être, temps de l'histoire*, Paris: PUF, "Pratiques théoriques,"1995.

132. GA 69, 163, 223; *History of Beyng*, 34–35, 188.

133. Jeffrey Barash, "Heidegger et la question de la race," *Les temps modernes* 63, no. 650 (July–October 2008): 290–305, here p. 303.

134. Jean Blain, "Heidegger et son temps," *L'express*, 1 October 1996.

135. Ray Monk, "Nasty Moments," *Times Literary Supplement*, 27 November 1998.

136. Richard Rorty, "A Master from Germany," *New York Review of Books*, 3 May 1998.

137. Ibid.

138. Dietrich Orlow, "Great Mind, Dim Idea," *Boston Globe*, 3 May 1998.

139. Elisabeth Young-Bruehl, *Hannah Arendt: For Love of the World*, New Haven, CT: Yale University Press, 1982.

140. Elzbieta Ettinger, *Hannah Arendt, Martin Heidegger,* New Haven, CT: Yale University Press, 1995.

141. Judith Shulevitz, "Arendt and Heidegger—An Affair to Forget?" *New York Times,* 1 October 1995; Alan Ryan, "Dangerous Liaison," *New York Review of Books,* 11 January 1996.

142. Mark Lilla, "Ménage à Trois," *New York Review of Books,* 18 November 1999.

143. Quoted by Alex Steiner, "The Case of Martin Heidegger, Philosopher and Nazi," part 1, World Socialist Website, 3 April 2000, https://www.wsws.org/en/articles/2000/04/heid-a03.html, consulted 29 August 2017.

144. https://en.wikipedia.org/wiki/Human,_All_Too_Human_(TV_series), consulted 29 August 2017.

145. https://www.youtube.com/watch?v=onxDro6THUg, consulted 29 August 2017.

146. Sophie-Jan Arrien, "Vie et logos: La phénoménologie de la vie du jeune Heidegger (1919–1923)," doctoral thesis in philosophy (Paris IV), 2004; Jean-François Courtine & Jean-François Marquet, *Heidegger 1919–1929. De l'herméneutique de la facticité à la métaphysique du Dasein,* Paris: Vrin, 1996; Dominque Janicaud, *Heidegger en France,* 2 vols., Paris: Albin Michel, "Idées," 2001; Servanne Jollivet & Claude Romano (eds.), *Heidegger en dialogue (1912–1930). Rencontres, affinités, confrontations,* Paris: Vrin, 2009; Christian Sommer (ed.), *Les études philosophiques* 2 (2010).

147. Theodore Kisiel, *The Genesis of Heidegger's* Being and Time, Berkeley: University of California Press, 1993.

148. HJB1; HJB4; Büchin & Denker, *Martin Heidegger und seine Heimat;* Daniel Morat, *Von der Tat zur Gelassenheit. Konservatives Denken bei Martin Heidegger, Ernst Jünger und Friedrich Georg Jünger, 1920–1960,* Göttingen: Wallstein, 2007. Note, finally, that Alfred Denker has published a few biographical articles in the local history review *Meßkircher Heimathefte.*

149. Faye, *The Introduction of Nazism into Philosophy,* p. 1.

150. Ibid., p. xxiii.

151. Ibid., p. xxv.

152. GA 36/37, 90–91, quoted in Faye, *The Introduction of Nazism into Philosophy,* p. 168.

153. Faye, *The Introduction of Nazism into Philosophy,* p. 170.

154. Ibid., pp. 54–55.

155. Ibid., p. 172.

156. Emmanuel Faye, *Heidegger. L'introduction du nazisme dans la philosophie,* preface to the second edition, Paris: Le Livre de Poche, "Biblio essais," 2007, p. 16.

157. Wolfgang Benz, "Gedanken töten, um den Feind zu vernichten, Die Bücherverbrennung 1933 als aktuelles Ereignis," *Zeitschrift für Geschichtswissenschaft,* notebook 5, May 2013, pp. 389–397.

158. Faye, *The Introduction of Nazism into Philosophy,* pp. 148–149.

159. Ibid., p. 171.

160. Figures based on the list of book reviews drawn up by Faye: http://eriac.net/author/emmanuel-faye/, consulted 9 March 2014.

161. Roger-Pol Droit, "Les crimes d'idées de Schmitt et de Heidegger," *Le monde des livres*, 25 March 2005.

162. Xavier Lacavalerie, "Le philosophe au menu de l'agrégation. Heidegger est déterré," *Télérama* 2891, 8 June 2005.

163. Frediano Sessi, "Quando Heidegger scriveva discorsi per il Führer," *Corriere della sera*, 3 June 2005, p. 24.

164. Thomas Meyer, "Denker für Hitler?" *Die Zeit*, 21 July 2005.

165. Joseph Hanimann, "Grundsatzdebatte auf schmaler Basis," *Frankfurter Allgemeine Zeitung*, 20 June 2005.

166. Éric Loret, "Heidegger lasse," Libération, "Livres," 8 February 2007. [The passage quoted from Faye is from the second edition of the French version. It does not appear in the English-language translation.—Trans.].

167. "Pour la jeune garde heideggérienne, l'oeuvre est indemne de toute imprégnation nazie," *Le monde*, 25 March 2005.

168. The *agrégation* is the more prestigious national competitive examination by which the French state recruits high school teachers (the other is called the "CAPES").

169. Emmanuel Faye, "Pour l'ouverture des archives Heidegger," *Le monde*, 4 January 2006.

170. Faye, *The Introduction of Nazism into Philosophy*, p. 319.

171. *Letters to His Wife*.

172. François Fédier, "Faux procès," in Massimo Amato, François Fédier, et al., *Heidegger à plus forte raison*, Paris: Fayard, 2007, p. 28.

173. Televised debate "Bibliothèque Médicis," 23 February 2007, hosted by Jean-Pierre Elkabach, with guests Emmanuel Faye, François Fédier, Pascal David, Édouard Husson, and Monique Canto-Sperber: http://www.publicsenat.fr/emissions/bibliotheque-medicis/edouard-husson,pascal-david,emmanuel-faye,francoisfedier,emmanuel-kessler/54395; http://www.dailymotion.com/video/x1asyb_heidegger-1-4_news.

174. Letter to Elfride, 18 October 1916, p. 28.

175. Televised debate "Bibliothèque Médicis," 23 February 2007.

176. See the Translators' note, p. 9, in Hannah Arendt and Martin Heidegger's correspondence, *Lettres et autres documents (1925–1975)*, trans. Pascal David, Paris: Gallimard, "Bibliothèque de philosophie," 2001.

177. "Ein Volk, ein Sein, ein Denker? Le nouveau débat sur le fascisme de Heidegger," *Cahiers philosophiques* 3, no. 111 (2007): 127–144, here p. 128.

178. "Heidegger, le nazisme et la philosophie," *L'humanité*, 1 September 2005.

179. http://www.jeuxvideo.com/forums/1-51-4569910-1-0-1-0-l-affaire-heidegger.htm, consulted 20 November 2013.

180. http://passouline.blog.lemonde.fr/2005/05/19/2005_05_les_gardiens_du/, article published 19 May 2005, last comment on 19 July 2007, consulted 20 November 2013.

181. http://passouline.blog.lemonde.fr/2005/06/23/2005_06_laffaire_heideg/, article published 23 June 2005, last comment on 30 June 2010, consulted 20 November 2013.

182. http://passouline.blog.lemonde.fr/2006/02/22/2006_02_rififi_dans_les/, article published 22 February 2006, last comment on 7 March 2006, consulted 20 November 2013.

183. http://passouline.blog.lemonde.fr/2005/06/23/2005_06_laffaire_heideg/#comment-311639, consulted 20 November 2013.

184. http://paris4philo.over-blog.org/.

185. http://skildy.blog.lemonde.fr/.

186. Consulted 12 March 2014.

187. E-mail from Ritoyenne to the author, 18 November 2013.

188. http://atelier-philo.over-blog.com/article-13561467.html and http://atelier-philo.over-blog.com/article-13561467.html, consulted 12 March 2014.

189. Joseph Plichart (ed.), *L'imaginaire. Cours de François Fédier professé dans la classe de première supérieure, tronc commun, du lycée Pasteur année 1998–1999, à partir des notes de Émilie Chevrillon, François Fédier, Hadrien France-Lanord et al.*, Mayet: Grand-Est, 2009.

190. http://de.wikipedia.org/w/index.php?title=Martin_Heidegger_und_der_Nationalsozialismus&action=info, consulted 12 March 2014.

191. http://en.wikipedia.org/w/index.php?title=Martin_Heidegger_and_Nazism&action=info, consulted 12 March 2014.

192. http://fr.wikipedia.org/w/index.php?title=Heidegger_et_le_nazisme&action=info, consulted 12 March 2014.

193. http://it.wikipedia.org/w/index.php?title=Heidegger_e_il_Nazionalsocialismo&action=info, consulted 12 March 2014.

194. http://de.wikipedia.org/wiki/Spezial:Statistik; http://en.wikipedia.org/wiki/Special:Statistics; http://fr.wikipedia.org/wiki/Sp%C3%A9cial:Statistiques; http://it.wikipedia.org/wiki/Speciale:Statistiche, consulted 12 March 2014.

195. http://it.wikipedia.org/wiki/Heidegger_e_il_Nazionalsocialismo, consulted 12 March 2014.

196. http://de.wikipedia.org/wiki/Martin_Heidegger_und_der_Nationalsozialismus, consulted 12 March 2014, translation modified.

197. http://toolserver.org/~daniel/WikiSense/Contributors.php?wikilang=de&wikifam=.wikipedia.org&grouped=on&page=Martin_Heidegger_und_der_Nationalsozialismus, consulted 12 March 2014.

198. http://toolserver.org/~daniel/WikiSense/Contributors.php?wikilang=en&wikifam=.wikipedia.org&grouped=on&page=Martin_Heidegger_and_Nazism, consulted 12 March 2014.

199. http://toolserver.org/~daniel/WikiSense/Contributors.php?wikilang=fr&wikifam=.wikipedia.org&page=Heidegger_et_le_nazisme&grouped=on&order=-edit_count&max=100&format=html, consulted 12 March 2014.

200. http://fr.wikipedia.org/w/index.php?title=Utilisateur:Filinthe, consulted 12 March 2014.

201. http://de.wikipedia.org/wiki/Benutzer:Filinthe, consulted 12 March 2014.

202. http://en.wikipedia.org/w/index.php?title=User:Filinthe, consulted 12 March 2014.

203. http://parolesdesjours.free.fr/scandale.htm, consulted 12 March 2014.

204. Philippe Arjakovsky, François Fédier, & Hadrien France-Lanord (eds.), *Dictionnaire Martin Heidegger*, Paris: Éd. du Cerf, 2013.

205. Letter to Claude Caseran, Agence France Presse, 19 May 2005, http://parolesdesjours.free.fr/afp.pdf, consulted 4 August 2015.

206. http://eriac.univ-rouen.fr/author/eemmanuel-faye/, consulted 27 July 2017.

207. Yale University Press: Faye, *The Introduction of Nazism into Philosophy*.

208. Carlin Romano, "Heil Heidegger!" *Chronicle of Higher Education*, http://www.chronicle.com/article/Heil-Heidegger-/48806/, consulted 30 July 2017.

209. Ibid.

210. Ibid.

211. Patricia Cohen, "An Ethical Question: Does a Nazi Deserve a Place among Philosophers?" *New York Times*, 8 November 2009, consulted 30 July 2017. Romano's article is now closed to readers' comments.

212. https://www.amazon.com/Heidegger-Introduction-Philosophy-Unpublished-1933-1935/dp/0300120869/ref=sr_1_1?ie=UTF8&qid=1501409567&sr=8-1&keywords=faye+heidegger, consulted online 30 July 2017.

213. Peter N. Nevraumont, "Heidegger the Nazi," 7 January 2010, https://www.amazon.com/gp/customer-reviews/R3EWH3V6NKNINI/ref=cm_cr_arp_d_rvw_ttl?ie=UTF8&ASIN=0300120869, consulted 30 July 2017.

214. Terence Kuch, "Thorough Scholarship with a Fatal Flaw," 1 September 2013, https://www.amazon.com/gp/customer-reviews/R2WQG85LNTNXP6/ref=cm_cr_arp_d_rvw_ttl?ie=UTF8&ASIN=0300120869, consulted 30 July 2017.

215. Gregory Fried, "A Letter to Emmanuel Faye," *Philosophy Today* 55, no. 3 (Autumn 2011): 219–252, here p. 248, n. 3.

216. Comment no. 69 to Romano, "Heil Heidegger," quoted in Fried, "A Letter to Emmanuel Faye," p. 219.

217. Fried, "Heil Heidegger!" p. 231.

218. Ibid.

219. Ibid., p. 243.

220. Ibid., p. 247.

221. Peter E. Gordon, review of Faye, *The Introduction of Nazism into Philosophy*, https://ndpr.nd.edu/news/heidegger-the-introduction-of-nazism-into-philosophy-in-light-of-the-unpublished-seminars-of-1933-1935/, consulted 30 July 2017.

222. Ibid.

223. Ibid.

224. See Tom Rockmore, *On Heidegger's Nazism and Philosophy*, Berkeley: University of California Press, 1997.

225. Tom Rockmore, Foreword, in Faye, *The Introduction of Nazism into Philosophy*, p. xiv.

226. Ibid., p. xv.

227. Thomas Sheehan, "Emmanuel Faye: The Introduction of Fraud into Philosophy?" *Philosophy Today* 59, no. 3 (Summer 2015): 367–400, here p. 388.

228. Ibid., pp. 376–377.

229. Letter to Kurt Bauch of 1 August 1943, p. 91.

230. Sheehan, "Emmanuel Faye," p. 389.

231. GA 39, 121; *Hölderlin's Hymns "Germania" and "The Rhine,"* 109.

232. Emmanuel Faye, "Être, histoire, technique et extermination dans l'oeuvre de Heidegger," lecture at the Brazilian Academy of Philosophy in April 2011, quoted by Sheehan, "Emmanuel Faye," p. 390.

233. Sheehan, "Emmanuel Faye," p. 390.

234. Emmanuel Faye (ed.), *Heidegger. Le sol, la communauté, la race*, Paris: Beauchesne, 2014.

235. Sidonie Kellerer, "Quand Heidegger réécrit son histoire," *Philosophie Magazine* 13, special issue, *Les philosophes face au nazisme* (February–March 2012): 78–81; "Heideggers Maske. Die Zeit des Weltbildes—Metamorphose eines Textes," *Zeitschrift für Ideengeschichte*, notebook V/2 (Summer 2011): 109–120.

236. François Rastier, *Naufrage d'un prophète. Heidegger aujourd'hui*, Paris: PUF, 2015, p. 10.

237. Sheehan, "Emmanuel Faye," p. 390, n. 74; p. 395, n. 88; p. 396, n. 91.

238. Johannes Fritsche, "Absence of Soil, Historicity, and Goethe in Heidegger's *Being and Time*: Sheehan on Faye," *Philosophy Today* 60, no. 2 (Spring 2016): 429–445; Gaëtan Pégny, "The Right of Reply to Professor Sheehan," ibid., pp. 447–479. The debate continued with an article by Sheehan ("L'affaire Faye. Faut-il brûler Heidegger? A Reply to Frische, Pégny, and Rastier," ibid., pp. 481–535) and a response by Fritsche published online (Johannes Fritsche, "The Affaire Sheehan / Birmingham: Fritsche's Rülpser on Heidegger's *Being and Time*," 5 October 2016, https://yadi.sk/i/uP-HIioy-wc42s, consulted 31 July 2017).

239. François Rastier et al., "An Open Letter to *Philosophy Today*," *Philosophy Today* 59, no. 4 (Autumn 2015): 713–717, here p. 713.

240. Allow me to cite his critique, not only of Farías (Thomas Sheehan, "Heidegger and the Nazis," *New York Review of Books* 5, no. 10, 16 June 1988), but also of Ernest Nolte's book ("A Normal Nazi," *New York Review of Books* 40, nos. 1 and 2, 14 January 1993, pp. 30–35).

241. On the black notebooks, see the following section.

242. Sheehan, "Emmanuel Faye," p. 370.

243. Rastier et al., "An Open Letter to *Philosophy Today*," p. 713.

244. Ibid., p. 714.

245. Note that Johannes Fritsche had published a book in English, following the general tendency of German academics, at the turn of the 2000s, to shift to that language (Johannes Fritsche, *Historical Destiny and National Socialism in Heidegger's* Being and Time, Berkeley: University of California Press, 1999).

246. In descending order: Martin Heidegger Facebook Society, with 9,858 members; Heidegger Research Group, with 5,642 members; Being Beyond Heidegger, with 2,896 members; Martin Heidegger, with 813 members. The French audience is smaller, consisting of a single group, Heidegger, les cahiers noirs, with 1,474 members (figures on 1 August 2017).

247. Regarding anglicization, some may object that Facebook offers the possibility of translation into many other languages.

248. Alain Badiou & Barbara Cassin, *Heidegger. Le nazisme, les femmes, la philosophie*, Paris: Fayard, "Ouvertures," 2010; Jean-Marie Brohm, Roger Dadoun, & Fabien Ollier, *Heidegger, Le berger du Néant. Critique d'une pensée politique*, Paris: Homnisphères, "Horizon critique," 2007; Henri Meschonnic, *Heidegger ou le national-essentialisme*, Paris: Éd. L. Teper, 2007.

249. Bernhard Taureck (ed.), *Politische Unschuld? In Sachen Martin Heidegger*, Munich: Wilhelm Fink, 2008. The volume includes a contribution by Emmanuel Faye: "Heidegger, der Nationalsozialismus und die Zerstörung der Philosophie," pp. 45–77.

250. Julio Quesada, *Heidegger de camino al Holocausto*, Madrid: Biblioteca Nueva, 2008.

251. Holger Zaborowski, *Eine Frage von Irre und Schuld?* Frankfurt: Fischer, 2009.

252. Alfred Denker, *Unterwegs in Sein und Zeit. Einführung in das Leben und Denken Martin Heideggers*, Stuttgart: Klett-Cotta, 2011.

253. Philippe Arjakovsky, François Fédier, & Hadrien France-Lanord (eds.), *Le dictionnaire Martin Heidegger*, Paris: Cerf, 2013.

254. Richard Wolin, *Heidegger's Children*, Princeton, NJ: Princeton University Press, 2001, p. 6.

255. Hadrien France-Lanord, "Antisémitisme," in Arjakovsky, Fédier, & France-Lanord (eds.), *Le dictionnaire Martin Heidegger*, pp. 85–90, here p. 85.

256. Ibid.

257. Ibid.

258. On the broadcast "Bibliothèque Médicis," 23 February 2007.

259. Now published in GA 94, 104; *Black Notebooks*, 1, 142.

260. "Gli 'Schwarze Hefte' di Heidegger: Un gossip filosofico," http://www.alteracultura.org/?p=4259, consulted 9 October 2014.

261. http://laphilosophie.blog.lemonde.fr/2013/12/05/heidegger-la-preuve-du-nazisme-par-le-cahier-noir/#xtor=RSS-32280322, consulted 10 October 2014.

262. Jonathan Derbyshire, "Heidegger in France: Nazism and Philosophy," *Prospect* 13 December 2013, https://www.prospectmagazine.co.uk/blogs/jonathan-derbyshire/heidegger-in-france-nazism-and-philosophy, consulted 31 July 2017.

263. http://contrapunto2002.blogspot.fr/2013/12/heidegger-la-preuve-du-nazisme-par-le.html, consulted 10 October 2014.

264. Éric Aeschimann, " 'Cahiers noirs.' Vers une nouvelle affaire Heidegger," *Le nouvel observateur,* 6 December 2013.

265. Ibid.

266. Ibid.

267. Stefano G. Azzarà, "I taccuini inediti di Heidegger. Nazismo o 'antisemitismo' eterno?" http://materialismostorico.blogspot.fr/2013/12/i-taccuini-inediti-di-heidegger-nazismo.html, consulted 9 October 2014.

268. "Sobre la próxima publicación de los 'Cuadernos negros' de Heidegger," *Alea,* 18 December 2013, http://alea-blog.blogspot.fr/2013/12/sobre-la-proxima-publicacion-de-los.html, consulted 10 October 2014.

269. Gianluca Veneziani, "Guerra Francia-Germania per il filosofo antisemita," *Libero,* 12 December 2013.

270. Azzarà, "I taccuini inediti di Heidegger."

271. Emmanuel Faye, "Die Krönung der Gesamtausgabe," *Die Zeit* 1 (2014).

272. Jürg Altwegg, "Ein Debakel für Frankreichs Philosophie," *Frankfurter Allgemeine Zeitung,* 13 December 2013.

273. Interview of Günter Figal with Liane von Billerbeck on Deutschlandradio Kultur, 18 December 2013, transcribed on the radio station's website under the title "Überlegungen zum Judentum, die eindeutig antisemitisch sind," http://www.deutschlandradiokultur.de/umstrittender-philosoph-ueberlegungen-zum-judentum-die.954.de.html?dram:article_id=272402, consulted 9 October 2014.

274. Günter Figal, "Disgustose e terribili quelle frasi del mio Heidegger," *La stampa,* 18 March 2014.

275. "Martin Heidegger. Un migliaio di pagine," *La repubblica,* 13 December 2013.

276. Peter Trawny, "Ein neue Dimension," *Die Zeit* 1 (2014).

277. "Nachwort des Herausgebers," GA 94, 529; "Editor's Afterword," *Black Notebooks,* 1, 383.

278. "Nachwort des Herausgebers," GA 94, 531; "Editor's Afterword," *Black Notebooks,* 1, 384.

279. Alexander Cammann & Adam Soboczynski, "Es ist wieder da," *Die Zeit* 5, 30 January 2014.

280. "Nachwort des Herausgebers," GA 94, 531; "Editor's Afterword," *Black Notebooks,* 1, 384.

281. GA 97, 325.

282. Michel de Montaigne, "To the Reader" (1580), in *The Complete Essays of Montaigne,* trans. Donald Frame (Stanford, CA: Stanford University Press, 1957), p. 2.

283. The title selected for the French edition a few months later is different: Peter Trawny, *Heidegger et l'antisémitisme. Sur les "Cahiers noirs"* (Heidegger and Anti-Semitism: On the "Black Notebooks"), Paris: Seuil, 2014, translation of *Heidegger und der Mythos der jüdischen Weltverschwörung*, Frankfurt: Klostermann, 2014. English: *Heidegger and the Myth of a Jewish World Conspiracy*, trans. Andrew J. Mitchell, Chicago: University of Chicago Press, 2016.

284. Trawny, Preface to *Heidegger et l'antisémitisme*, p. 19.

285. Ibid., p. 18.

286. Trawny, *Heidegger and the Myth of a Jewish World Conspiracy*, p. 97.

287. "Literaturclub" broadcast, 19 March 2014, 3sat, http://www.3sat.de/mediathek/?mode=play&obj=42478, consulted 10 October 2014.

288. Deutschlandradio Kultur, 12 March 2014, http://www.deutschlandradiokultur.de/debatte-als-harten-antisemiten-wuerde-ich-ihn-nicht.954.de.html?dram:article_id=279889, consulted 10 October 2014.

289. Jürgen Kaube, "Martin Heideggers Schwarze Hefte beweisen den Antisemitismus des Philosophen," *Frankfurter Allgemeine Zeitung*, 12 March 2014.

290. Philip Oltermann, "Heidegger's 'Black Notebooks' Reveal Antisemitism at Core of His Philosophy," *Guardian*, 13 March 2014.

291. HJB4.

292. Martin Heidegger, *Nature, History, State: 1933–1934*, edited and translated by Gregory Fried & Richard Polt, with original essays, London: Bloomsbury Academic, 2013.

293. Faye, *The Introduction of Nazism into Philosophy*, p. 144.

294. That is what his book, published the following year, attempts to do. Thomas Sheehan, *Making Sense of Heidegger*, London: Rowman & Littlefield International, 2014.

295. Jennifer Schuessler, "Heidegger's Notebooks Renew Focus on Anti-Semitism," *New York Times*, 30 March 2014.

296. Peter E. Gordon, "Heidegger in Black," *New York Review of Books*, 9 October 2014, http://www.nybooks.com/articles/2014/10/09/heidegger-in-black/#fnr-3, consulted 2 August 2017.

297. Ibid.

298. Schuessler, "Heidegger's Notebooks Renew Focus."

299. At a presentation at the Deutsche Nationalbibliothek (German National Library) on 12 March 2014, https://www.youtube.com/watch?v=Wnqk6cYbzFU, consulted 10 October 2014.

300. Debate in Meßkirch, 22 May 2014: https://www.youtube.com/watch?v=BE6hc3_txvk, consulted 10 October 2014.

301. International colloquium at the University of Siegen, "Philosophie und Politik, Untersuchungen zu Martin Heideggers 'Schwarzen Heften,' " 22–25 April 2015.

302. "Private" one-day workshop at the École Normale Supérieure, 3 May 2014; roundtable on "Heidegger, Race, and Community," 27 May 2014, at the Maison

Heinrich Heine in Paris, France, http://www.youtube.com/watch?v=j81LJdW3eJ4, consulted 10 October 2014; and a high-profile conference at the Bibliothèque Nationale de France, "Heidegger et 'les juifs,' " 22–25 January 2015.

303. University of Pisa, 1 July 2014.

304. 8 April 2014 at the Goethe Institute in New York, http://vimeo.com/93670604 http://vimeo.com/93782805, consulted 10 October 2014; at the Graduate Center of the City University of New York, 12 September 2014.

305. Seminar organized by the Faculty of Philosophy at the University City of Bogotá, 11 October to 6 December 2014.

306. Donatella Di Cesare, *Heidegger e gli ebrei*, Turin: Bollati Boringhieri, 2014.

307. Donatella Di Cesare, "Heidegger—'Jews Self-Destructed,' " *Corriere della sera / English*, http://www.corriere.it/english/15_febbraio_09/heidegger-jews-self-destructed-47cd3930-b03b-11e4-8615-d0fd07eabd28.shtml, consulted 9 January 2020.

308. Ibid.

309. Ibid.

310. Ibid.

311. Ibid.

312. See esp. Longerich, "Davon haben wir nichts gewusst."

313. Emmanuel Alloa, "Affaire Heidegger. Nouveau scandale en vue," *Le monde*, 3 March 2015.

314. Donatella Di Cesare, "Selbstvernichtung der Juden," *Hohe Luft*, 10 February 2015.

315. Emmanuel Faye, "Heidegger profeta del IV Reich," *Corriere della sera*, 23 February 2015.

316. Daniel Goldhagen, *Hitler's Willing Executioners: Ordinary Germans and the Holocaust*, New York: Random House, 1997.

317. Richard Wolin, "Heidegger hielt 'Endlösung' für notwendig," interview granted to *Hohe Luft*, 27 March 2015.

318. https://rdl.de/beitrag/so-denkt-man-nicht-wenn-man-philosophie-betreibt consulted 24 March 2015.

319. Figal, "Disgustose e terribili quelle frasi."

320. "Crisi al vertice della 'Heidegger,' " *Corriere della sera*, 23 January 2015.

321. " 'Das Ende des Heideggerianertums,' " *Badische Zeitung*, 23 January 2015.

322. Rainer Marten, "Gralshüter mit letzter Treuebereitschaft," *Die Zeit* 11, 22 March 2015.

323. Adam Soboczynski, "Antisemitismus. Was heißt 'N. soz.'?" *Die Zeit* 13, 26 March 2015.

324. "Worin die eigentümliche Vorbestimmung der Judenschaft für das planetarische Verbrechertum begründet ist," in Eggert Blum, "Die Marke Heidegger," *Die Zeit* 47, 29 November 2014.

325. Jürgen Kaube, "Streit um Heidegger-Lehrstuhl. Martin? Edmund!" *Frankfurter Allgemeine Zeitung*, 27 February 2015; Kaube, "Ein Rektor versteht nicht," *Frankfurter*

Allgemeine Zeitung, 18 March 2015; Hannah Lühmann, "Deutsche Angst vor dem Geist der Schwarzen Hefte," *Die Welt*, 26 March 2015.

326. https://www.openpetition.de/petition/online/save-phenomenology-and-hermeneutics-in-freiburg?language=en_GB.utf8, consulted 25 August 2015.

327. "Antisemit und Ehrenbürger, Streit um Martin Heidegger in Meßkirch," Südwestrundfunk, 16 February 2015, http://www.swr.de/landesschau-aktuell/bw/bodensee/streit-um-martin-heidegger-in-messkirch-antisemit-und-ehrenbuerger/-/id=1542/did=15091290/nid=1542/asz8xm/index.html, consulted 9 August 2015; "Heidegger und Meßkirch: Die Stadt hält sich zurück," 4 March 2015, http://www.schwaebische.de/region_artikel,-Heidegger-und-Messkirch-Die-Stadt-haelt-sich-zurueck-_arid,10187537_toid,494.html, consulted 31 July 2017.

328. Walter Homolka & Arnulf Heidegger (eds.), *Heidegger und der Antisemitismus. Positionen im Widerstreit. Mit Briefen von Martin und Fritz Heidegger*, Freiburg: Herder, 2016.

329. Adam Soboczynski & Alexander Cammann, "Martin Heidegger. Ein moralisches Desaster," *Die Zeit*, 12 October 2016; long excerpts from the letters were published sometime later (Martin Heidegger & Fritz Heidegger, " 'Ich schicke Dir die neue Hitlerrede,' " *Die Zeit*, 27 October 2017).

330. Letter to Fritz, 18 December 1931, p. 22.

331. Letter to Fritz, 28 October 1932, p. 30.

332. Letter to Fritz, 27 July 1932, p. 29.

333. Donatella Di Cesare, "Il nazismo secondo Heidegger. 'Hitler risveglia il nostro popolo,' " *Corriere della sera*, 12 October 2016.

334. Nicolas Weill, "Heidegger en grand frère nazi," *Le monde*, 13 October 2016.

335. Adam Soboczynski, "Heidegger, nazi jusque dans les lettres à son frère," 13 October 2016, http://bibliobs.nouvelobs.com/idees/20161012.OBS9743/heidegger-nazi-jusque-dans-les-lettres-a-son-frere.html, consulted 15 October 2016.

336. http://www.juif.org/antisemitisme-juif/214886,heidegger-nazi-jusque-dans-les-lettres-a-son-frere.php, consulted 2 August 2017.

337. http://nuagesneuf.blogspot.fr/2016/10/heidegger-nazi-jusque-dans-les-lettres.html, consulted 2 August 2017.

338. Luisa Zielinski, "In His Own Words," *Paris Review*, 18 October 2016, https://www.theparisreview.org/blog/2016/10/18/in-his-own-words/, consulted 2 August 2017. Living in Berlin, Zielinski read both the article from *Die Zeit* and the one from *Le monde*.

339. Steven Hayward, "Yes, He Was a Nazi," 19 October 2016, http://www.powerlineblog.com/archives/2016/10/yes-he-was-a-nazi.php, consulted 2 August 2017.

340. Bettina Schulte, "Martin und Fritz Heideggers Briefwechsels: Mitläufer des Seyns," *Badische Zeitung*, 25 October 2016, http://www.badische-zeitung.de/literatur-und-vortraege/martin-und-fritz-heideggers-briefwechsel-mitlaeufer-des-seyns—128993733.html, consulted 2 August 2017.

341. Joaquin Rábago, “Nazi hasta el tuétano,” *La opinión de Málaga*, 18 December 2016, http://www.laopiniondemalaga.es/opinion/2016/10/18/nazi-tuetano/883455.html, consulted 2 August 2017.

342. “Nuevas cartas confirman sin lugar a dudas el nazismo de Martin Heidegger,” 24 October 2016, http://pijamasurf.com/2016/10/nuevas_cartas_confirman_sin_lugar_a_dudas_el_nazismo_de_martin_heidegger/, consulted 2 August 2017.

343. Carmen Valero, “Heidegger. Cartas de furia nazi,” *El mundo*, 4 January 2017, http://www.elmundo.es/cultura/2017/01/04/586a982e46163f91758b45d1.html, consulted 2 August 2017.

344. David Hernández de la Fuente, “Heidegger, el Filósofo-Führer,” *La razón*, 15 January 2017.

345. “Nuevo libro sobre Heidegger reproduce correspondencia mostrando su adhesión por el Tercer Reich,” *Despiertainfo*, 5 January 2017, http://www.despiertainfo.com/2017/01/05/nuevo-libro-sobre-heidegger-reproduce-correspondencia-mostrando-su-adhesion-por-el-tercer-reich/, consulted 2 August 2017; Juan Ángel Juristo, “Cuando Heidegger se fascinó por las manos de Hitler,” *Cuartopoder*, 9 January 2017, https://www.cuartopoder.es/cultura/2017/01/09/cuando-heidegger-se-fascino-por-las-manos-de-hitler/, consulted 2 August 2017.

346. Adam Soboczynski & Alexander Cammann, “Heidegger and Anti-Semitism Yet Again: The Correspondence between the Philosopher and His Brother Fritz Heidegger Exposed,” *Los Angeles Review of Books*, 25 December 2016, https://lareviewofbooks.org/article/heidegger-anti-semitism-yet-correspondence-philosopher-brother-fritz-heidegger-exposed/, consulted 2 August 2017.

347. Mick Hartley, “A Scholarly and Moral Disaster,” 1 January 2017, http://mickhartley.typepad.com/blog/2017/01/a-scholarly-and-moral-disaster.html; Logical Meme, “Martin & Fritz,” 1 January 2017, http://logicalmeme.com/?p=9351; Jake Romm, “Philosopher Martin Heidegger Spent Years Trying to Convince His Brother to Become a Nazi,” *Forward*, 3 January 2017, http://forward.com/culture/358715/philosopher-martin-heidegger-spent-years-trying-to-convince-his-brother-to/, consulted 2 August 2017.

348. Michael Marder, “A Fight for the Right to Read Heidegger,” http://opinionator.blogs.nytimes.com/2014/07/20/a-fight-for-the-right-to-read-heidegger/?_php=true&_type=blogs&_php=true&_type=blogs&_r=1&, consulted 31 July 2017.

349. Alfred Denker & Holger Zaborowski, *Heidegger-Jahrbuch* 11: *Zur Hermeneutik der “Schwarzen Hefte,”* Freiburg: Karl Alber, 2017; Ingo Farin & Jeff Malpas (eds.), *Reading Heidegger’s Black Notebooks 1931–1941*, Cambridge, MA: MIT Press, 2016; Emmanuel Faye, *Arendt et Heidegger. Extermination nazie et destruction de la pensée*, Paris: Albin Michel, 2016; Marion Heinz and Sidonie Kellerer (eds.), *Martin Heideggers “Schwarze Hefte.” Eine philosophisch-politische Debatte*, Berlin: Suhrkamp Verlag, 2016; Walter Homolka & A. Heidegger (eds.), *Heidegger und der Antisemitismus*; Jean-Luc Nancy, *Banalité de Heidegger*, Paris: Éditions Galilée, 2016; Alfred J. Noll, *Der rechte Werkmeister.*

Martin Heidegger nach den "Schwarzen Heften," Cologne: Papyrossa Verlag, 2015; Guillaume Payen, *Martin Heidegger. Catholicisme, révolution, nazisme,* Paris: Perrin, 2016; François Rastier, *Naufrage d'un prophète. Heidegger aujourd'hui,* Paris: PUF, 2015; Peter Trawny & Andrew J. Mitchell (eds.), *Heidegger, die Juden, noch einmal,* Frankfurt: Klostermann, 2015; Hans-Helmuth Gander & Magnus Striet (eds.), *Heideggers Weg in die Moderne. Eine Verortung der "Schwarzen Hefte,"* Frankfurt: Klostermann, 2017; Friedrich-Willhelm von Hermann & Francesco Alfieri, *Martin Heidegger. La verità sui Quaderni neri,* Brescia: Morcelliana, 2016.

350. Jean-Luc Nancy, "Heidegger incorrect," *Libération,* 12 October 2017; Stéphane Domeracki, "L'antisémitisme génocidaire de Heidegger, banqueroute de la philosophie?" *Agoravox,* 20 October 2017, https://www.agoravox.fr/tribune-libre/article/l-antisemitisme-genocidaire-de-197928, consulted 17 November 2017; Sidonie Kellerer, "Heidegger n'a jamais cessé de participer à la mise en oeuvre de la politique nazie," *Le monde,* 26 October 2017; François Rastier, "Heidegger, théoricien et acteur de l'extermination des juifs?" *Conversation* 1 November 2017, https://theconversation.com/heidegger-theoricien-et-acteur-de-lextermination-des-juifs-86334, consulted 2 November 2017; François Rastier, "Un antisémitisme exterminateur," *Libération,* 5 November 2017; Jean-Luc Nancy, "Heidegger et l'échec de l'Occident," *Libération,* 5 November 2017; Emmanuel Faye, "Heidegger ou le national-socialisme essentialisé," *Libération,* 8 November 2017.

351. Nancy, "Heidegger incorrect."

352. "One wishes to exorcise [. . .]—an event too significant for the arguing idle talkers [my emphasis]: namely, that in all the fascist eruptions [. . .], it is well and truly our whole society, our whole civilization even, our culture, our humanism, and our idealo-materialism that are on the line." Ibid.

353. "We cannot nestle in the politically correct, which behaves as if *notre monde,* our world, were not *immonde,* foul." Ibid.

354. Kellerer, "Heidegger n'a jamais cessé."

355. Faye, *Arendt and Heidegger,* p. 261.

356. Kellerer, "Heidegger n'a jamais cessé."

357. GA 96, 260; *Black Notebooks,* 3, 206.

358. GA 53, 68; Hölderlin's hymn "The Ister," 54.

Conclusion

1. Quoted by Löwith, "Les implications politiques de la philosophie de l'existence," p. 346.

2. GA 9, 25.

3. Letter to Elfride, 13 September 1918, p. 51.

4. Letter to Elfride, 18 October 1916, p. 28.

5. GA 60, 68.

6. Letter to Fritz, 4 February 1933, p. 32.

7. Hindenburg's address to the army, 12 November 1918, quoted by Krumeich, " 'Stab-in-the-Back' Legend."

8. See Gerd Krumeich, *Juli 1914. Eine Bilanz,* Paderborn: Schöningh, 2014.

9. Letter to Fritz, 18 December 1931, p. 22.

10. Letter to Victor Schwoerer, 2 October 1929.

11. Letter to Elfride, 8 September 1920, p. 80.

12. Jean Jaurès, "Programme économique," *La dépêche,* 1 September 1889.

13. Jean Jaurès, "La question juive," *La dépêche de Toulouse,* 2 June 1892.

14. George Mosse, *The Crisis of German Ideology: Intellectual Origins of the Third Reich,* New York: Grosset & Dunlap, 1964, p. 6.

15. After George Mosse, the role of the Youth Movement as a breeding ground for Nazis has been further reassessed by Christian Niemeyer (*Die dunklen Seiten der Jugendbewegung. Vom Wandervogel zur Hitlerjugend,* Tübingen: A. Francke Verlag, 2013).

16. Mosse does not explicitly make the connection here with the Youth Movement, though the formulation he chooses is clear: "national and personal regeneration" (Mosse, *Fallen Soldiers,* p. 159).

17. GA 29/30, 243ff.

18. It is very important in *Contributions to Philosophy* (1936). The *Not der Notlosigkeit* runs through the entire book, often with several references per page (GA 65, 11, 24, 107, 113, 114, 119, 125, 130, 137, 234, 235, 237, 429, and 484; *Contributions to Philosophy,* 11, 21, 85, 89–90, 94, 97, 102, 103, 108, 185, 339, and 380). [Rojcewicz and Vallega-Neu translate *Not* as "plight" and *Notlosigkeit* as "the lack of a sense of plight."—Trans.]

19. GA 97, 5.

20. Chapoutot, *La loi du sang,* pp. 228–233.

21. GA 35, 1.

22. GA 16, 111.

23. GA 16, 204.

24. GA 16, 112.

25. GA 16, 93.

26. The expression was coined by Werner Willikens, state secretary in the Prussian agriculture ministry. It is the focus of chap. 13 in Kershaw, *Hitler,* vol. 1.

27. GA 16, 184.

28. HBJ4, 88.

29. GA 16, 109.

30. GA 16, 110.

31. GA 16, 108.

32. On this subject, see Robert Gellately, *The Gestapo and German Society: Enforcing Racial Policy (1933–1945),* Oxford: Clarendon Press, 1990; Robert Gellately, *Backing Hitler: Consent and Coercion in Nazi Germany,* Oxford: Clarendon Press, 2001; and Eric

A. Johnson, *Nazi Terror: The Gestapo, Jews, and Ordinary Germans,* New York: Basic Books, 1999.

33. Gabriele Turi, *Lo stato educatore politica e intelletuali nell'Italia fascista,* Rome: Editori Laterza, "Storia e società," 2002.

34. GA 16, 107.

35. *Breisgauer Zeitung,* 8 May 1933, in Schneeberger (ed.), *Nachlese zu Heidegger,* pp. 29–30.

36. GA 36/37, 90–91.

37. Mommsen, *From Weimar to Auschwitz,* p. 159 and passim.

38. This is Martin Broszat's expression. See esp. Martin Broszat, Elke Fröhlich, & Falk Wiesemann (eds.), *Bayern in der NS-Zeit,* Munich: R. Oldenbourg, vol. 1 (1977), p. 11 and vol. 4 (1981), p. 697.

39. On Hans Grimm and Nazism, see Manfred Franke, *Grimm ohne Glocken. Ambivalenzen im politischen Denken und Handeln des Schriftstellers Hans Grimm,* Cologne: SH-Verlag, 2009; and Hans Sarkowicz, "Zwischen Sympathie und Apologie. Der Schriftsteller Hans Grimm und sein Verhältnis zum Nationalsozialismus," in Karl Corino (ed.), *Intellektuelle im Bann des Nationalsozialismus,* Hamburg: Hoffmann und Campe, 1980.

40. GA 94, 194; *Black Notebooks,* 1, 142.

41. GA 94, 157, §105; *Black Notebooks,* 1, 115.

42. GA 40, 41; *Introduction to Metaphysics,* 40.

43. Ibid.

44. Letter to Fritz, 20 July 1941, p. 72.

45. GA 16, 525; "Releasement," 52.

46. Stendhal, *Vie de Henry Brulard,* in *Oeuvres intimes,* ed. V. del Litto, vol. 2, Paris: Gallimard, "Bibliothèque de la Pléiade," 1982, p. 536.

47. Trawny, *Heidegger et l'antisémitisme,* pp. 31–56 and passim.

48. GA 40, 208.

49. "Herkunft aber bleibt stets Zukunft" (GA 12, 91).

50. "Whereas liberalism began with the individual and placed him at the center of everything, we have substituted the people and the community for the individual. The freedom of the individual naturally had to be reduced, inasmuch as it clashed with or stood in contradiction to the nation's freedom. That is not a limitation of the notion of freedom per se: to increase it in the individual is to undercut the people's freedom and to place it in grave peril. The boundaries of individual freedom are therefore those of the people's freedom." Joseph Goebbels, *Rede des Reichsministers Dr. Goebbels bei der Eröffnung der Reichskulturkammer am 15. November 1933,* Frankfurt: Brönner's Druckerei, 1933, p. 12.

51. GA 16, 508.

52. "Ich gehe mit traumwandlerischer Sicherheit den Weg, den mich die Vorsehung gehen heißt." Hitler's speech in Munich, 14 March 1936, ed. Domarus, vol. 1, p. 606.

53. I borrow this expression from Sumi Shimahara's *Haymon d'Auxerre.*

54. Letter to Jaspers, 8 December 1932, p. 143.

55. Ian Kershaw, *Hitler: Profiles in Power,* London: Routledge, 2013, p. 163.

56. Aeschylus, *The Persians,* trans. Robert Potter, lines 821–822, http://classics.mit.edu/Aeschylus/persians.html, translation modified.

Bibliography

An exhaustive bibliography of the books and articles on Martin Heidegger's life and thought would fill a thick volume, and a list of all the writings dealing with his relationship to politics would cover dozens of pages. I have provided here only a few studies on the philosopher's life and on his Nazism. Many other references are given in the notes in the chapter devoted to the Heidegger affair.

Principal Sources

Citations of Heidegger's works usually refer to the German edition of the complete works (Gesamtausgabe, 102 vols., Stuttgart: Klostermann, 1975–), abbreviated in the notes as GA, followed by the volume and page number.

Büchin, Elsbeth, & Alfred Denker. *Martin Heidegger und seine Heimat.* Stuttgart: Klett-Cotta, 2005.

Denker, Alfred, Hans-Helmuth Gander, & Holger Zaborowski (eds.). *Heidegger-Jahrbuch* 1: *Heidegger und die Anfänge seines Denkens.* Freiburg: Karl Alber, 2004.

Denker, Alfred, & Holger Zaborowski (eds.). *Heidegger-Jahrbuch* 4: *Heidegger und der Nationalsozialismus.* Vol. 1: *Dokumente.* Freiburg: Karl Alber, 2009.

Schneeberger, Guido. *Nachlese zu Heidegger. Dokumente zu seinem Leben und Denken.* Bern: Buchdruckerei AG, Suhr, 1962.

Principal Letters and Correspondence Used

Arendt, Hannah, & Martin Heidegger. *Letters, 1925–1975.* Edited by Ursula Ludz. Translated by Andrew Shields. Orlando, FL: Harcourt, Inc., 2004.

Arendt, Hannah, & Karl Jaspers. *Briefwechsel (1926–1969).* Munich: Piper, 1985.

Bauch, Kurt, & Martin Heidegger. *Briefwechsel (1932–1975).* Freiburg: Karl Alber, 2010.

Bultmann, Rudolf, & Martin Heidegger. *Briefwechsel, 1925 bis 1975*. Edited by Andreas Großmann & Christof Landmesser. Frankfurt: Klostermann, 2009.

Heidegger, Fritz, & Martin Heidegger. "Briefen." In *Heidegger und der Antisemitismus: Positionen im Widerstreit*. Edited by Walter Homolka & Arnulf Heidegger. Freiburg: Herder, 2016.

Heidegger, Martin. Letter of 2 October 1929 to Viktor Schwoerer, published by Ulrich Sieg in "Die Verjudung des deutschen Geistes." *Die Zeit* 52, 22 December 1989.

———. "Briefe Martin Heideggers an Julius Stenzel." *Études heideggeriennes* 16 (2000): 11–33.

———. *Letters to His Wife, 1915–1970*. Edited by Gertrud Heidegger. Translated by R. D. V. Glasgow. Cambridge, U.K.: Polity Press, 2008. Translation of *"Mein liebes Seelchen!" Briefe Martin Heideggers an seine Frau Elfride, 1915–1970*. Munich: Deutsche Verlags-Anstalt, 2005.

Heidegger, Martin, & Elisabeth Blochmann. *Briefwechsel, 1918–1969*. Edited by Joachim W. Storck. Marbach am Neckar: Deutsche Schillergesellschaft, 1990.

Heidegger, Martin, & Edmund Husserl. *Briefwechsel (1916–1933), Husserliana Dokumente*. Vol. 3, pt. 4. Dordrecht: Kluwer, 1994.

Heidegger, Martin, & Karl Jaspers. *Briefwechsel, 1920–1963*. Edited by Walter Biemel and Hans Saner. München; Frankfurt am Main : Piper : Klostermann, 1992.

Heidegger, Martin, & Ernst Jünger. *Correspondence, 1945–1975*. Translated by Timothy Sean Quinn. London: Rowman & Littlefield International, 2016.

Heidegger, Martin, & Erhart Kästner. *Briefwechsel (1953–1974)*. Frankfurt: Insel-Verlag, 1986.

Heidegger, Martin, & Heinrich Rickert. *Briefe 1912–1933 und andere Dokumente*. Frankfurt: Klostermann, 2002.

Memoirs and Other First-Person Accounts

Anders, Günther. "Wenn ich verzweifelt bin, was geht's mich an." Interview with Mathias Greffrath. In Mathias Greffrath (ed.), *Die Zerstörung einer Zukunft. Gespräche mit emigrierten Sozialwissenschaftlern*. Frankfurt: Campus Verlag, 1989.

Gadamer, Hans-Georg. *Philosophische Lehrjahre*. Frankfurt: Klostermann, 1977.

Heidegger, Fritz. "Vom Vorschussverein zur Volksbank, 1864–1964." *100 Jahre Volksbank e.G.m.b.H. 1864–1964*. Meßkirch, 1964.

———. "Ein Geburtstagbrief des Bruders." *Martin Heidegger zum 80. Geburtstag von seiner Heimatstadt Meßkirch*. Frankfurt: Klostermann, 1969.

Jaspers, Karl. *Philosophische Autobiographie*. Augmented edition. Munich: Piper, 1977.

———. *Notizen zu Martin Heidegger*. Edited by Hans Saner. 3rd revised and corrected edition. Munich: Piper, 1989.

Jonas, Hans. *Memoirs*. Edited by Christian Wiese. Translated by Krishna Winston. Hanover, NH: University Press of New England, 2008.

Löwith, Karl. *My Life in Germany before and after 1933: A Report*. Translated by Elizabeth King. Urbana: University of Illinois Press, 1994.

Müller, Max. "Ein Gespräch mit Max Müller." In his *Martin Heidegger. Ein Philosoph und die Politik*. Edited by Gottfried Schramm & Bernd Martin. Freiburg: Rombach, 2001 [1985].

Neske, Günther (ed). *Erinnerung an Martin Heidegger*. Pfullingen: G. Neske, 1977.

Petzet, Heinrich. *Auf einen Stern zugehen*. Frankfurt: Societäts Verlag, 1983.

On Nazism and the Third Reich

Hitler, Adolf. *Mein Kampf*. Translated by Ralph Manheim. Boston: Houghton Mifflin, 1971.

———. *Reden und Proklamationen, 1932–1945*. Edited by Max Domarus. 2 vols. 1: *Triumph, 1932–1938*; 2: *Untergang, 1939–1945*, Neustadt an der Aisch: Schmidt, 1963.

Reichsgesetzblatt.

Rosenberg, Alfred. *Der Mythus des 20. Jahrhunderts*. 189th–194th ed. Munich: Hoheneichen-Verlag, 1942 [1930]. English edition: Alfred Rosenberg, *The Myth of the Twentieth Century: An Evaluation of the Spiritual-Intellectual Confrontations*. Translated from the 3rd German edition, http://www.nommeraadio.ee/meedia/pdf/RRS/Alfred%20Rosenberg%20-%20The%20Myth%20of%20the%2020th%20Century.pdf.

Biographies and Other Studies

Amato, Massimo, François Fédier, et al. *Heidegger à plus forte raison*. Paris: Fayard, 2007.

Biemel, Walter. *Martin Heidegger, mit Selbstzeugnissen und Bilddokumenten*. 12th ed. Reinbek: Rowohlt, 1993 [1973].

Denker, Alfred. *Unterwegs in Sein und Zeit. Einführung in das Leben und Denken Martin Heideggers*. Stuttgart: Klett-Cotta, 2011.

Denker, Alfred, & Holger Zaborowski (eds.). *Heidegger-Jahrbuch 5: Heidegger und der Nationalsozialismus*. Vol. 2: *Interpretationen*. Freiburg: Karl Alber Verlag, 2009.

Farías, Víctor. *Heidegger and Nazism*. Edited by Joseph Margolis & Tom Rockmore. Translated by Paul Burrell, Dominic Di Bernardi, & Gabriel R. Ricci. Philadelphia: Temple University Press, 1991 [1987].

Faye, Emmanuel. *Heidegger: The Introduction of Nazism into Philosophy in Light of the Unpublished Seminars of 1933–1935*. Translated by Michael B. Smith. New Haven, CT: Yale University Press, 2009 [2005].

———. *Heidegger, l'introduction du nazisme dans la philosophie*. Paris: Albin Michel. 2nd ed. Paris: Gallimard, "Livre de poche," 2007, with an original preface.

Fédier, François. *Heidegger. Anatomie d'un scandale*. Paris: R. Laffont, 1988.

Fischer, Anton M. *Martin Heidegger. Der gottlose Priester. Psychogramm eines Denkers*. Zurich: Rüffer & Rub, 2008.

Grün, Bernd. *Der Rektor als Führer? Die Universität Freiburg i. Br. von 1933 bis 1945*. Freiburg: Karl Alber, 2010.

Janicaud, Dominique. *Heidegger en France*. 2 vols. Paris: Albin Michel, "Idées," 2001.

Losurdo, Domenico. *La communità, la morte, l'Occidente. Heidegger e l'ideologia della guerra*. Turin: Bollati Boringhieri, 1991.

Martin, Bernd (ed.). *Martin Heidegger und das "Dritte Reich." Ein Kompendium*. Darmstadt: Wissenschaftliche Buchgesellschaft, 1989.

Martin, Bernd, & Gottfried Schramm (eds.). *Martin Heidegger. Ein Philosoph und die Politik*. 2nd augmented edition. Freiburg: Rombach, 2000.

Morat, Daniel. *Von der Tat zur Gelassenheit. Konservatives Denken bei Martin Heidegger, Ernst Jünger und Friedrich Georg Jünger, 1920–1960*. Göttingen: Wallstein, 2007.

Ott, Hugo. *Martin Heidegger: A Political Life*. Translated by Allan Blunden. London: Harper Collins, 1993 [1988].

Safranski, Rüdiger. *Martin Heidegger: Between Good and Evil*. Translated by Ewald Osers. Cambridge, MA: Harvard University Press, 1998 [1994].

Schramm, Gottfried, & Bernd Martin. *Martin Heidegger. Ein Philosoph und die Politik*. 2nd augmented edition. Freiburg: Rombach Verlag, 2001 [1986].

Sommer, Christian (ed.). *Autour de Heidegger, discours de rectorat. Contextes, problèmes, débats*. Paris: PUF, "Les études philosophiques 2," 2010.

Vetter, Helmuth. *Grundriss Heidegger. Ein Handbuch zu Leben und Werk*. Hamburg: Meiner, 2014.

Zaborowski, Holger. *Eine Frage von Irre und Schuld? Martin Heidegger und der Nationalsozialismus*. Frankfurt: Fischer Taschenbuch Verlag, 2010.

Zimmermann, Hans Dieter. *Martin und Fritz Heidegger. Philosophie und Fastnacht*. Munich: C. H. Beck, 2005.

Index

Martin Heidegger is indicated by "MH" in index subentries.